Lab Manual for
CompTIA A+ Guide to
IT Technical Support
NINTH EDITION

Jean Andrews, Ph.D.

Joy Dark

Jill West

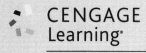

CENGAGE
Learning·

Australia • Canada • Mexico • Singapore • Spain • United Kingdom • United States

CENGAGE
Learning®

Lab Manual for CompTIA A+ Guide to IT Technical Support, Ninth Edition

Jean Andrews, Joy Dark, Jill West

SVP, GM Skills & Global Product Management: Dawn Gerrain

Product Director: Kathleen McMahon

Product Team Manager: Kristin McNary

Senior Director, Development: Marah Bellegarde

Product Development Manager: Leigh Hefferon

Senior Content Developer: Michelle Ruelos Cannistraci

Product Assistant: Abigail Pufpaff

Vice President, Marketing Services: Jennifer Ann Baker

Marketing Director: Michele McTighe

Senior Production Director: Wendy Troeger

Production Director: Patty Stephan

Senior Content Project Manager: Brooke Greenhouse

Managing Art Director: Jack Pendleton

Cover images:

©iStockphoto/saicle

©iStockphoto/traffic_analyzer

©iStockphoto/simon2579

©iStockphoto/Kotkoa

> For product information and technology assistance, contact us at
> **Cengage Learning Customer & Sales Support, 1-800-354-9706**
>
> For permission to use material from this text or product,
> submit all requests online at **www.cengage.com/permissions**
> Further permissions questions can be e-mailed to
> **permissionrequest@cengage.com**

Library of Congress Control Number: 2015957525

ISBN: 978-1-305-26654-4

Cengage Learning
20 Channel Center Street
Boston, MA 02210
USA

Cengage Learning is a leading provider of customized learning solutions with employees residing in nearly 40 different countries and sales in more than 125 countries around the world. Find your local representative at **www.cengage.com.**

Cengage Learning products are represented in Canada by Nelson Education, Ltd.

To learn more about Cengage Learning, visit **www.cengage.com**

Purchase any of our products at your local college store or at our preferred online store **www.cengagebrain.com**

Printed in the United States of America
Print Number: 01   Print Year: 2015

Table of Contents

CHAPTER 20

Virtualization, Linux, and Mac OS X 529

Preface

This lab manual is designed to be the best tool on the market to help you get hands-on practical experience troubleshooting and repairing personal computers and operating systems. The manual contains more than 130 labs, each of which targets a practical problem you're likely to face when troubleshooting systems in the real world. Every attempt has been made to write labs that allow you to use generic hardware devices. A specific hardware configuration isn't necessary to complete the labs. In learning to install, support, and troubleshoot hardware devices and operating systems, the focus is on Windows 8 and Windows 7, with minor coverage of Windows Vista. Each chapter contains labs designed to provide the structure novices need, as well as labs that challenge experienced and inquisitive students.

This book helps prepare you for the new CompTIA A+ 900 series Certification exams offered through the Computer Technology Industry Association (CompTIA): A+ 220-901 and A+ 220-902. The A+ 220-901 exam includes selecting, installing, maintaining, and troubleshooting the hardware components of computers, networks, printers, and mobile devices, and the A+ 220-902 exam focuses on operating systems, security, troubleshooting skills, and operational procedures.

Because this certification credential is quickly growing in popularity among employers, becoming certified increases your ability to gain employment, improve your salary, and enhance your career. To find more information about A+ Certification and its sponsoring organization, CompTIA, go to the CompTIA website at *comptia.org*.

Whether your goal is to become an A+ certified technician or a computer support technician, the *Lab Manual for CompTIA A+ Guide to IT Technical Support*, Ninth Edition, along with Jean Andrews's textbooks, will take you there!

FEATURES

To ensure a successful experience for both instructors and students, this book includes the following pedagogical features:

- *Objectives*. Every lab opens with learning objectives that set the stage for students to absorb the lab's lessons.
- *Materials Required*. This feature outlines all the materials students need to successfully complete the lab.
- *Lab Preparation*. This feature alerts instructors and lab assistants to items to check or set up before the lab begins.
- *Activity Background*. A brief discussion at the beginning of each lab provides important background information.
- *Estimated Completion Time*. To help students plan their work, each lab includes an estimate of the total amount of time required to complete it.
- *Activity*. Detailed, numbered steps walk students through the lab. These steps are divided into manageable sections, with explanatory material between each section. Questions within each activity help students think through exactly what they are doing as they follow the steps.
- *Figures*. Where appropriate, photographs of hardware or screen shots of software are provided to increase student mastery of the lab topic.
- *Review Questions*. Questions at the end of each lab help students test their understanding of the lab material.
- *Website*. For updates to this book and information about other A+ and IT products, go to *login.cengage.com*.

WHAT'S NEW IN THE NINTH EDITION

- Steps are updated to focus on Microsoft Windows 8 and Windows 7. New projects cover Android and iOS.
- New projects are added to cover new technology and higher-level thinking skills, which reflect updates to CompTIA's A+ 220-901 and 220-902 exams.
- Enhanced coverage on supporting UEFI firmware is now included.
- Projects provide additional coverage of laptop parts.
- Enhanced coverage on supporting mobile devices is covered in the chapter, "Supporting Mobile Operating Systems."

ACKNOWLEDGMENTS

The authors would first like to thank Mary Pat Shaffer, the Developmental Editor, for keeping us on track and providing the occasional comic relief. Mary Pat, your meticulous work and encouraging attitude made the process more fun and made a significantly positive impact on the quality of the final product. Thank you to Michelle Ruelos Cannistraci, Kristin McNary, Amy Savino, Brooke Greenhouse, Danielle Shaw, and all the Cengage Learning staff for their instrumental roles in developing this lab manual. Michelle, Brooke, and Amy, we so appreciate all your hard work and impressive dedication to excellence. Many thanks to all the instructors who offered great suggestions for new labs and encouraged us to make other changes to the previous editions. Keep those suggestions coming!

This manual was written with the extraordinary help of awesome collaborators. We did it together, and we're grateful for your help:

Bill Jaber, Lee University, Cleveland, TN

Ronald E. Koci, Madison Area Technical College, Madison, WI

Isaias Leiva, San Francisco City College, San Francisco, CA

Terry Moberley, Unisys Corporation, Culpepper, VA

Robert Ray, Digital Communications & Display, LLC, Raleigh, NC

CLASSROOM SETUP

Lab activities have been designed to explore many different Windows and hardware setups and troubleshooting problems, while attempting to keep the requirements for specific hardware to a minimum. Most labs can be done alone, although a few ask you to work with a partner. If you prefer to work alone, simply do all the steps yourself. Lab activities that use an operating system have been designed to work in Windows 8 or Windows 7, although you can use Windows Vista for some labs. In some cases, Windows 8/7 Professional will be required.

Typical labs take 30 to 45 minutes; a few might take a little longer. For several of the labs, your classroom should be networked and provide access to the Internet. When access to Windows setup files is required, these files can be provided on the Windows installation DVD, a network drive made available to the computer, or some other type of removable storage media.

These are the minimum hardware requirements for Windows 8:

- 1 GHz or better Pentium-compatible computer
- 1 GB of RAM for 32-bit Windows 8 or 2 GB of RAM for 64-bit Windows 8
- 16 GB free hard drive space for 32-bit Windows 8 or 20 GB for 64-bit Windows 8
- DirectX 9 or higher video device
- A user account with administrator privileges

A few labs focus on special hardware. One lab requires a wireless card and router. Another lab requires the use of a multimeter, and some labs require software that can be freely downloaded from the Internet. Labs in the chapter titled "Supporting Printers and Customizing a System" require a local or network printer.

LAB SETUP INSTRUCTIONS

CONFIGURATION TYPE AND OPERATING SYSTEMS

Each lab begins with a list of required materials. Before beginning a lab activity, each student workgroup or individual should verify access to these materials. Then, students should ensure the correct operating system is installed and in good health. Note that in some cases, installing an operating system isn't necessary. In some labs, device drivers are needed. Students can work more efficiently if these drivers are available before beginning the lab.

PROTECT DATA

In several labs, data on the hard drive might get lost or corrupted. For this reason, it's important that valuable data stored on the hard drive is backed up to another medium.

ACCESS TO THE INTERNET

Several labs require access to the Internet. If necessary, students can use one computer to search the Internet and download software or documentation and another computer for performing the lab procedures. If the lab doesn't have Internet access, students can download the required software or documentation before the lab and bring the files to the lab on some sort of storage medium or network share.

UTILITIES TO DOWNLOAD FROM THE WEB

The following table includes a list of software that can be downloaded free from the web. As new releases of software appear, the steps in the lab that use the software might need adjusting. It is suggested that instructors test each of these labs to make sure the software still works before students do the lab.

Lab	Software and URL
Lab 1.2: Gather and Record System Information	Belarc Advisor at *belarc.com/free_download.html*
Lab 3.1: Use the HWiNFO Hardware Information Utility	HWiNFO at *hwinfo.com*
Lab 3.2: Examine and Adjust BIOS Settings	Speccy at *piriform.com/speccy*

(Continues)

Lab	Software and URL
Lab 3.5: Remove and Replace a Motherboard	CPU-Z at *cpuid.com/softwares/cpu-z.html*
Lab 3.8: Manage Power on a Laptop	BIOSAgentPlus at *biosagentplus.com*
Lab 4.2: Burn-In Test and Benchmark a CPU	Burn-In Test at *passmark.com/download/bit_download.htm*
Lab 4.5: Benchmark RAM and Plan an Upgrade	NovaBench at *novabench.com*
Lab 5.4: Measure Temperature and Adjust Fan Speed	SpeedFan at *filehippo.com/download_speedfan*
Lab 5.6: Troubleshoot Memory Problems	Memtest86 at *memtest86.com*
Lab 6.1: Test Hard Drive Performance Using HD Tune	HD Tune at *hdtune.com*
Lab 6.2: Examine Your Hard Drive Using Four Methods	Speccy at *piriform.com/speccy*
Lab 6.4: Use Hard Drive Utilities	SeaTools at *seagate.com/support/downloads/seatools* Data Lifeguard Diagnostic at *support.wdc.com*
Lab 8.1: Use the Windows 8 Upgrade Assistant	Windows 8 Upgrade Assistant at *windows.microsoft.com/ en-us/windows-8/upgrade-assistant-download-online-faq*
Lab 8.6: Use Windows Virtual PC to Install Windows 7 in a Virtual Machine (VM)	Windows Virtual PC at *microsoft.com/en-us/download/details. aspx?id=3702*
Lab 9.2: Use Diagnostics Software to Test I/O Devices	MonitorTest at *passmark.com/products/monitortest.htm* SoundCheck at *passmark.com/products/soundcheck.htm* KeyboardTest at *passmark.com/products/keytest.htm*
Lab 11.7: Critical Thinking: Use Windows Utilities to Speed Up a System	Autoruns at *technet.microsoft.com/en-us/sysinternals/ bb963902*
Lab 12.8: Find a Driver for an Unknown Device	Hiren's BootCD at *hirensbootcd.org/download* Grub4Dos at *hirensbootcd.org/files/grub4dos.zip*
Lab 12.9: Research Data Recovery Software	Recuva at *piriform.com/recuva*
Lab 13.3: Create and Use a Custom Refresh Image	Chrome at *google.com/chrome* Firefox at *mozilla.org/firefox*
Lab 15.5: Set Up Advanced IP Scanner and Wake-on-LAN	Advanced IP Scanner at *advanced-ip-scanner.com*
Lab 16.2: Research Android Apps and Use Dropbox	Dropbox at *dropbox.com*
Lab 16.3: Explore How Android Apps Are Developed and Tested	Java Platform (JDK) at *java.oracle.com* Android Studio for Windows at *developer.android.com*
Lab 18.4: Deal with a Rootkit	AVG Rescue CD (for USB stick) at *avg.com/us-en/download* EICAR virus test file at *eicar.org/85-0-download.html*
Lab 18.7: Download and Use Microsoft Security Essentials in Windows 7	Microsoft Security Essentials at *windows.microsoft.com/mse*
Lab 20.1: Use Oracle VirtualBox to Install and Explore Virtual Machines (VMs)	Oracle VirtualBox at *virtualbox.org*
Lab 20.3: Investigate Linux and Create a Bootable Ubuntu Flash Drive	Ubuntu at *ubuntu.com* Universal USB Installer at *pendrivelinux.com*
Lab 20.5: Use TeamViewer to Remotely Access Another Computer	TeamViewer at *teamviewer.com*
Lab 20.6: Set Up a VPN	Hotspot Shield at *hotspotshield.com*

ONLINE RESOURCES AND STUDY TOOLS

A few labs require students to download documents and optional content to use during the lab. For example, several labs use the Computer Inventory and Maintenance form made available online. To access the form, please go to *login.cengage.com*. After signing in or creating a new account, search for the ISBN of the title (from the back cover of the main textbook) using the search box at the top of the page to get to the product page where these free resources can be found.

THE TECHNICIAN'S WORK AREA

When opening a computer case, it's important to have the right tools and to be properly grounded to ensure that you don't cause more damage than you repair. Take a look at the items that should be part of any technician's work area:

- Grounding mat or bench (with grounding wire properly grounded)
- Grounding wrist strap, also known as an ESD (electrostatic discharge) strap, attached to the grounding mat
- Noncarpet flooring
- A clean work area (no clutter)
- A set of screwdrivers
- 1/4-inch Torx bit screwdriver
- 1/8-inch Torx bit screwdriver
- Needle-nose pliers
- Pen light (flashlight)
- Several new antistatic bags (for transporting and storing hardware)

At minimum, you must have at least two key items. The first is an ESD strap. If a grounding mat isn't available, you can attach the ESD strap to the computer's chassis and, in most cases, provide sufficient grounding for handling hardware components inside the computer case. The second key item is, of course, a screwdriver. You won't be able to open most cases without some type of screwdriver.

PROTECT YOURSELF, YOUR HARDWARE, AND YOUR SOFTWARE

When you work on a computer, harming both the computer and yourself is possible. The most common accident when attempting to fix a computer problem is erasing software or data. Experimenting without knowing what you're doing can cause damage. To prevent these sorts of accidents as well as physically dangerous ones, take a few safety precautions. The following sections describe potential sources of damage to computers and explain how to protect against them.

POWER TO THE COMPUTER

To protect yourself and the equipment when working inside a computer, turn off the power, unplug the computer, press the power button to drain power, and always use an ESD strap. Consider the monitor and the power supply to be "black boxes." Never remove the cover or put your hands inside this equipment unless you know the hazards of charged capacitors. Both the power supply and the monitor can hold a dangerous level of electricity even after they're turned off and disconnected from a power source.

STATIC ELECTRICITY OR ESD

Electrostatic discharge (ESD), commonly known as static electricity, is an electrical charge at rest. A static charge can build up on the surface of a nongrounded conductor and on non-conductive surfaces, such as clothing or plastic. When two objects with dissimilar electrical charges touch, static electricity passes between them until the dissimilar charges are made equal. To see how this works, turn off the lights in a room, scuff your feet on the carpet, and touch another person. Occasionally, you see and feel the charge in your fingers. If you can feel the charge, you discharged at least 3000 volts of static electricity. If you hear the discharge, you released at least 6000 volts. If you see the discharge, you released at least 8000 volts of ESD. A charge of less than 3000 volts can damage most electronic components. That means you can touch a chip on an expansion card or system board and damage the chip with ESD and never feel, hear, or see the discharge.

ESD can cause two types of damage in an electronic component: catastrophic failures and upset failures. A catastrophic failure destroys the component beyond use. An upset failure damages the component so that it doesn't perform well, even though it might still function to some degree. Upset failures are the most difficult to detect because they aren't easily observed.

PROTECT AGAINST ESD

To protect the computer against ESD, always ground yourself before touching electronic components, including the hard drive, system board, expansion cards, processors, and memory modules, by using one or more of the following static control devices or methods:

- *ESD strap.* An ESD strap is a bracelet you wear around your wrist. The other end is attached to a grounded conductor, such as the computer case or a ground mat, or it can be plugged into a wall outlet. (Only the ground prong makes a connection!)
- *Grounding mats.* Grounding mats can come equipped with a cord to plug into a wall outlet to provide a grounded surface on which to work. Remember, if you lift the component off the mat, it's no longer grounded and is susceptible to ESD.
- *Static shielding bags.* New components come shipped in static shielding bags. Save the bags to store other devices that aren't currently installed in a PC.

The best way to protect against ESD is to use an ESD strap with a grounding mat. You should consider an ESD strap essential equipment when working on a computer. However, if you're in a situation where you must work without one, touch the computer case before you touch a component. When passing a component to another person, ground yourself. Leave components inside their protective bags until you're ready to use them. Work on hard floors, not carpet, or use antistatic spray on carpets.

There's an exception to the ground-yourself rule. Inside a monitor case, the electricity stored in capacitors poses a substantial danger. When working inside a monitor, you don't want to be grounded because you would provide a conduit for the voltage to discharge through your body. In this situation, be careful not to ground yourself.

When handling system boards and expansion cards, don't touch the chips on the boards. Don't stack boards on top of each other; doing so could accidentally dislodge a chip. Hold cards by the edges, but don't touch the edge connections on the card.

After you unpack a new device or software that has been wrapped in cellophane, remove the cellophane from the work area quickly. Don't allow anyone who's not properly grounded to touch components. Don't store expansion cards within one foot of a CRT monitor because the monitor can discharge as much as 29,000 volts of ESD from the screen.

Hold an expansion card by the edges. Don't touch any of the soldered components on a card. If you need to put an electronic device down, place it on a grounding mat or a static shielding bag. Keep components away from your hair and clothing.

PROTECT HARD DRIVES AND DISKS

Always turn off a computer before moving it. Doing so protects the hard drive, which might be spinning when the computer is turned on. Never jar a computer while the hard disk is running. Avoid placing a computer on the floor, where users could accidentally kick it.

Follow the usual precautions to protect CDs and DVDs. Protect the bottom of optical discs from scratches and keep them away from heat and direct sunlight. Treat discs with care, and they'll usually last for years.

First Look at Computer Parts and Tools

Labs included in this chapter:

- **Lab 1.1:** Record Your Work and Make Deliverables
- **Lab 1.2:** Gather and Record System Information
- **Lab 1.3:** Identify Computer Parts
- **Lab 1.4:** Identify Form Factors
- **Lab 1.5:** Find Documentation on the Internet About Power Ratings
- **Lab 1.6:** Use Laptop Display Options

LAB 1.1 RECORD YOUR WORK AND MAKE DELIVERABLES

OBJECTIVES

The goal of this lab is to use different methods to create a submission file for your instructor and to familiarize yourself with your version of the operating system. After completing this lab, you will be able to:

⊿ Determine what type and version of operating system your computer is running

⊿ Use the Snipping Tool to take a snapshot of your screen

⊿ Create a submission file for your instructor in one of four formats

MATERIALS REQUIRED

This lab requires the following:

⊿ Windows 8 or Windows 7 operating system

LAB PREPARATION

Before the lab begins, the instructor or lab assistant needs to do the following:

⊿ Verify Windows starts with no errors

ACTIVITY BACKGROUND

The pages of this lab manual are perforated to allow students to tear off the pages and submit them to instructors for grading. However, your instructor might prefer you to submit your work using email or an online interface such as Moodle, Blackboard, or WebCT. This lab prepares you to submit your work using an electronic method.

ESTIMATED COMPLETION TIME: 20 MINUTES

Activity

The Windows Snipping Tool lets you take screen shots or snips of the entire Windows desktop, a window, or any region of the desktop. Follow these steps to explore the Control Panel and System windows and take snips of your work on the desktop:

1. To open Control Panel, right-click **Start** and click **Control Panel**. (In Windows 7, click **Start**, type **Control Panel** in the Search programs and files box, and press **Enter**.)

2. Drill down into the links, icons, and options in the Control Panel window and familiarize yourself with all the icons and options in both Icons view (called Classic view in Vista and on the A+ exam) and in Category view. Figure 1-1 shows Control Panel in Large icons view in Windows 8. Explain in your own words the difference between Large icons view and Category view:

Category View groups all the icons under eight different groups whiles Large icon view shows all icons under Computer Settings.

Figure 1-1 Windows 8 Large icons view

3. In Large icons view, click the **System** icon.

4. Examine the System window. What is the operating system and system type running on your computer? What processor is installed and how much installed memory (RAM) do you have on your computer?

Windows 8.1 Pro |Intel(R) Core (TM) i7-3537U CPU @ 2.00GHz 2.50 GHz | 7.88GB RAM|

5. If you're using a Windows 7 computer, what is the Windows Experience Index rating for your computer?

N/A

6. Leave the System window open as your active window. Press **Win+S**, type **Snipping Tool** in the Search box, and then click **Snipping Tool**. (In Windows 7, click **Start**, and in the Search programs and files box, type **Snipping Tool**, and then press **Enter**.)

7. In the Snipping Tool dialog box, click the **New** drop-down arrow. What are the four types of snips you can take using the Snipping Tool?

Free-form Snip

Rectangular Snip

Window Snip

Full-screen Snip

8. Select **Free-form Snip** from the drop-down list. Click and hold the mouse button, drag your cursor around the edges of the System window, and then release the mouse button. The Snipping Tool window opens showing your snip.

9. On the menu bar, click **File, Save As**.

10. Save the file on your desktop using naming and file compression standards (usually in .jpg or .png format) as directed by your instructor.

11. Email the file to your instructor, or upload it to your online interface.

12. Close all windows.

REVIEW QUESTIONS

1. What are the eight categories in the Category view in Control Panel?

System and Security / Network and Internet User Accounts and Family Safety / Appearance and Personalization Hardware and Sound / Clock, language and Region / Programs / Ease of Access

2. What are the four file types that can be used to save a snip using the Windows Snipping Tool?

PNG / GIF / JPEG and MHT

3. The Windows Experience Index rates a computer's performance on a scale of 1.0 to 7.9. If you're using a Windows 7 system, what can you conclude about its performance based on the rating of your computer?

N/A

4. Search the web for information about the price of Windows 8. How much would it cost to buy your current edition (such as Home, Professional, etc.) of the Windows 8 operating system as an upgrade from Windows 7?

$ 79.98

LAB 1.2 GATHER AND RECORD SYSTEM INFORMATION

OBJECTIVES

The goal of this lab is to document a system configuration. In this lab, you use a system's physical characteristics and operating system to determine how the system is configured. After completing this lab, you will be able to:

◢ Gather system information by observing a system

◢ Use available Windows tools to access specific system information

MATERIALS REQUIRED

This lab requires the following:

◢ Windows 8 or Windows 7 operating system with administrator access

◢ A copy of the Computer Inventory and Maintenance form, either provided by your instructor or downloaded from *www.cengagebrain.com*; for more information, see the Preface

LAB PREPARATION

Before the lab begins, the instructor or lab assistant needs to do the following:

◢ Verify Windows starts with no errors

◢ Either verify Internet access is available so students can download the Computer Inventory and Maintenance form or provide the form in print or digitally

Notes The Computer Inventory and Maintenance form is used in several labs in this lab manual.

ACTIVITY BACKGROUND

When you first become responsible for a computer, you need to document its current configuration. Put this documentation in a notebook or other secure location and then use it whenever you do maintenance, upgrades, or repairs on the system. When you are responsible for several computers, it is difficult to remember the administrative passwords to each computer. In this lab, you collect system password information in your documentation. Therefore, the documentation needs to be kept confidential and secured.

In the four parts of this lab, you identify installed components and the Windows configuration by observing the system and by using Windows tools. In Part 1, you explore the physical system and Windows settings. In Part 2, you explore the network settings. In Part 3, you gather information about applications installed. In Part 4, you gather information about hardware installed.

Save a copy of the Computer Inventory and Maintenance form because you will need it for labs in later chapters.

ESTIMATED COMPLETION TIME: 45 MINUTES

 Activity

PART 1: EXPLORE THE PHYSICAL SYSTEM AND WINDOWS SETTINGS

Observe the physical characteristics of your system, and answer the following questions:

1. Does the outside of the case have any identification on it indicating manufacturer, model, or component information? If so, list this information here:

   Lenovo IdeaPad Yoga 13 / Model = 20175
   Manufacturer = Lenovo PC HK limited

2. How many CD or DVD drives does your system have?

   0

3. Describe the shape or type of the connection your mouse uses:

   USB

4. How many USB ports are in the back of your system? How many are in the front?

   2

Most versions of Windows allow users to customize the display of information to suit their tastes. Complete the following steps to restore Windows defaults to your system:

1. Boot your system and log on, if necessary. Right-click **Start**, and then click **Control Panel** to open the Control Panel window. (In Windows 7, click **Start**, and then click **Control Panel**.)

2. If Large icons or Small icons view has been enabled, click the **View by** drop-down menu and select **Category**. Figure 1-2 shows Control Panel in Category view for Windows 8.

Figure 1-2 Windows 8 Control Panel in Category view

3. With Category view enabled, click the **Appearance and Personalization** category. The Appearance and Personalization window opens.

4. In the Appearance and Personalization window, click **Folder Options** to open the Folder Options dialog box.

5. On the General tab of the Folder Options dialog box, click the **Restore Defaults** button (see Figure 1-3), and then click **Apply**.

Figure 1-3 Use the Folder Options dialog box to restore Windows defaults to all folders

6. Click the **View** tab in the Folder Options dialog box (see Figure 1-4). Click the **Restore Defaults** button, and then click **OK** to apply the settings and close the dialog box.

Figure 1-4 The View tab of the Folder Options dialog box

7. In the Appearance and Personalization window, click the **Taskbar and Navigation** icon (called **Taskbar and Start Menu** in Windows 7). The Taskbar and Navigation properties dialog box opens.

8. On the Taskbar tab, verify the **Lock the taskbar** check box is selected. Also verify the **Auto-hide the taskbar** and **Use small taskbar buttons** check boxes (or in Windows 7, the **Use small icons** check box) are not selected, as shown in Figure 1-5. Click **Apply** if any changes were made.

9. Click the **Jump Lists** tab in the Taskbar and Navigation properties dialog box. (In Windows 7, click the **Start Menu** tab in the Taskbar and Start Menu Properties dialog box.) Verify both check boxes under Privacy are selected, as shown in Figure 1-6. Click **OK** to apply the settings and close the dialog box. Close the Appearance and Personalization window.

Figure 1-5   Use the Taskbar and Navigation properties dialog box to control how the taskbar appears and functions

Figure 1-6   The left side shows the Jump Lists tab in Windows 8, and the right side shows the Start Menu tab in Windows 7

When you are responsible for several computers—or when several people share that responsibility—a base inventory and running record of each system's characteristics and maintenance are fundamental for quick reference. Do the following to document your system's configuration:

1. If your instructor hasn't already provided the Computer Inventory and Maintenance form, download and print it from **www.cengagebrain.com**. For detailed instructions on how to use the website, see the Preface.

2. *Computer identification:* Fill in the first page of the Inventory form using information about your computer. Also fill in the administrator account name and password under the Windows and Windows Settings heading. (Because this information is confidential, you must be careful to protect this form from unauthorized viewing.)

3. *System:* Open **Control Panel** and click the **System and Security** category. The System and Security window opens. In the System and Security window, click the **System** icon to view the System window. Using the information shown in Figure 1-7 for Windows 8 and in Figure 1-8 for Windows 7, fill in the System subsection under the Windows

Figure 1-7 The Windows 8 System applet provides basic system information

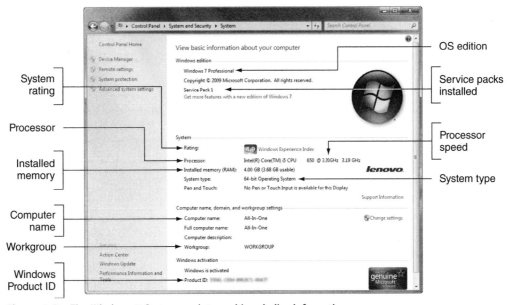

Figure 1-8 The Windows 7 System applet provides similar information

and Windows Settings heading of your Inventory form. Note that in Windows 7, this window also links to the Windows Experience Index, which rates your system's performance on a scale from 1.0 to 7.9.

4. *Windows Update:* Click the **Back** button in the upper-left corner of Control Panel to go back to the System and Security window. Click the **Windows Update** category, and then click **Change settings** from the menu in the left pane. The Change settings window shows the schedule for updates to Windows. Record this information in your Inventory form. Click **Cancel** to return to the Windows Update window, and then click the **Back** button again to return to the System and Security window.

5. *File History (Backup and Restore in Windows 7):* Click **File History** (**Backup and Restore** in Windows 7). If your computer is set to back up automatically, record the information requested in your Inventory form in the File History/Backup and Restore subsection.

6. Notice at the top of the Control Panel window that you'll always see a path in the address bar for whatever window is active. You can click on various parts of this path to go to those levels of Control Panel. The Inventory form lists the corresponding path for each section's information. To return to the main Control Panel window, click **Control Panel** at the beginning of the path.

7. *User accounts:* To complete the Windows and Windows Settings section of the Inventory form, click the **User Accounts and Family Safety** category. Click **User Accounts**, and then click **Manage another account** (in Windows 7, click **Add or remove user accounts**). The Manage Accounts window shows all local user accounts in the system. Record this information on your Inventory form.

PART 2: EXPLORE NETWORK SETTINGS

Follow these steps to gather information about network settings:

1. To access the Network Settings information of your computer, click **Control Panel** in the address bar path at the top of the window, and then click the **Network and Internet** category.

> **Notes** If you can't see the beginning of the path in the address bar, click the double left arrows on the left of the address bar to display the entire path in a drop-down list.

2. Click the **Network and Sharing Center** link to open the Network and Sharing Center window. Click **Change adapter settings** in the left pane to access the Network Connections window.

3. *Network TCP/IP settings:* Right-click the active network connection, whether it's an Ethernet connection or a Wi-Fi connection, and then click **Properties** from the shortcut menu to open the connection's Properties dialog box. Select **Internet Protocol Version 4 (TCP/IPv4)**, and then click the **Properties** button to view the Internet Protocol Version 4 (TCP/IPv4) Properties dialog box, shown in Figure 1-9. If the radio button for Obtain an IP address automatically is selected, then the connection has a dynamic configuration, meaning Windows will request an IP address from a server each time it connects to the network. If the radio button for Use the following IP address is selected, an administrator has assigned a static IP address that the computer will always use when connecting to this network. Add the appropriate information in this subsection of your Inventory form, and then click **Cancel** twice to return to the Network Connections window. Repeat this step for any other available network connection.

Figure 1-9 TCP/IP is a group of protocols that controls various aspects of communication between two devices on a network

4. *Wireless security settings:* Complete the following if your computer is currently connected to a wireless network; if not, skip to Step 5. To return to the Network and Sharing Center, click **Network and Internet** in the address bar path, and then click the **Network and Sharing Center** category. Under View your active networks, click the wireless connection and then click **Wireless Properties**.

> **Notes** If the connection is not secured, the Wireless Properties button will not be available.

Click the **Security** tab to find the security information for this network to fill in the Wireless Network Connection subsection of your Inventory form. You can select the **Show characters** check box to see the Network security key, as shown in Figure 1-10. Click **Cancel** and then click **Close** to return to the Network and Sharing Center.

5. *Homegroup settings:* Click the **Back** button in the Control Panel window to return to the Network and Internet window. Click **HomeGroup** to view the HomeGroup window and determine whether your computer belongs to a homegroup. If it does, click **View or print the homegroup password** and record this information on your Inventory form. Click **Cancel** to close the View and print your homegroup password window.

Figure 1-10 Secure all wireless networks to protect data and equipment

6. *Internet Options:* Click **Network and Internet** in the address bar to return to the Network and Internet window. Click **Internet Options** to open the Internet Properties dialog box. Using the information on the General tab, record the home page or pages on your Inventory form. Click **Cancel** to close the Internet Properties dialog box.

PART 3: EXPLORE APPLICATIONS INSTALLED

Follow these steps to gather information about installed applications:

1. *Applications installed:* Control Panel provides access to a list of all programs installed on the system. Click **Control Panel** in the address bar, then click **Programs** and then **Programs and Features**. Scroll down to find the version of Microsoft Office installed on your computer and enter this information on your Inventory form. Search the list for anti-malware software, such as McAfee, Norton, or Microsoft Security Essentials (Windows 7). Also look for web browsers, such as Mozilla Firefox and Google Chrome. Then list any other productivity applications (like Dropbox or a graphic design program) installed on the computer, along with their publishers. When you are finished, close the Programs and Features window.

> **Notes** Your inventory of installed applications should include any productivity software or anti-malware software installed. However, it is not necessary to record every item listed in the Programs and Features window.

2. *Anti-malware software:* If applicable, open an anti-malware program you found on the list of programs and determine whether the program updates automatically and, if so, when scans are scheduled to occur. Often, this information will be on the program's home page or in the Settings menu. Record this information on your Inventory form. Close the program when you are finished.

PART 4: EXPLORE HARDWARE INSTALLED

The System Information Utility provides additional information about hardware components and configuration of your system. Do the following to gather this information:

1. *System manufacturer and model:* To open the System Information Utility, press **Win+S**, type **msinfo32.exe**, and then click **msinfo32** (in Windows 7, click **Start**, type **msinfo32. exe** in the Search programs and files box, and press **Enter**). The System Information window opens. On the System Summary page, find your system's manufacturer and model number and record this information on your Inventory form.

2. *Drives:* Click the **+** sign next to the Components node on the navigation tree in the left pane. Click the **+** sign next to the Storage node, and then click **Drives**, as shown in Figure 1-11. Add the information requested on your Inventory form for this subsection.

3. *Disks:* Click **Disks** in the navigation tree and add the remaining information requested for the System Information Utility section. Close the System Information window.

Figure 1-11   Each computer may have several drives

The next two sections of the Inventory form will be completed in future labs. Record today's date and your name in the Routine Maintenance section beginning on page 5 next to "Initial inventory taken." Make a habit of documenting all maintenance and troubleshooting activities for any computer you work on.

ESTIMATED COMPLETION TIME: 15 MINUTES

CHALLENGE ACTIVITY

Programs are available to collect most, if not all, of the configuration information about a computer for you. One of the more popular programs is Belarc Advisor, which compiles information on system components, including manufacturer names, license numbers, and product keys. The program also analyzes your system for weaknesses and may suggest improvements or maintenance. To download and use Belarc Advisor, do the following:

1. Go to **www.belarc.com/free_download.html** and click the free download icon.

2. When the file has completed downloading, use File Explorer (Windows Explorer in Windows 7) to find the .exe file that you just downloaded. At the time of this writing, the file name was **advisorinstaller.exe**. What is the exact path and name of the downloaded file?

3. Double-click the file to install the program. If a UAC box appears, click **Yes**.

4. When the License Agreement window appears, click **I Agree**. Click **Install**.

5. If the program asks to check for new definitions, click **Yes**. When it reports that it is up to date, click **OK**.

6. The program creates a profile for your system and proceeds with the analysis. The process might take a few minutes. Once the analysis is presented in your browser, print your analysis and file it with your other documentation for this computer. See Figure 1-12 for a sample report.

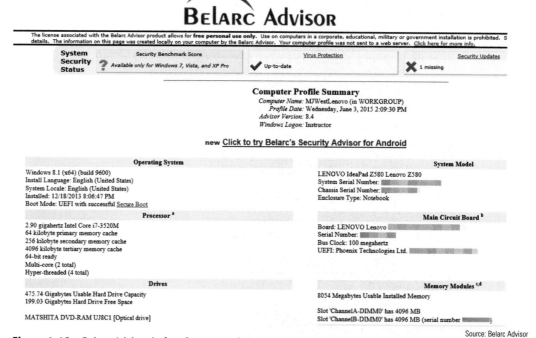

Figure 1-12 Belarc Advisor is free for personal use only

Source: Belarc Advisor

> **Notes** When using Belarc Advisor, your information remains on your local computer and is not transmitted over the Internet. The program simply uses your computer's browser to display the data.

REVIEW QUESTIONS

1. List two categories available in Control Panel that were not mentioned in the lab:

_____

_____

2. (Windows 7 only) Based on the Windows Experience Index, what component of your computer would you upgrade first? Why?

_____

_____

3. Based on what you found while taking inventory of your computer's system, what maintenance does this computer currently need?

_____

_____

4. Besides the Computer Inventory and Maintenance form, what other documentation should you keep on each computer? How might you store that information?

_____

_____

_____

5. What differences, if any, are there between a list of components derived from a physical inspection and a list of components derived from Control Panel and System Properties?

_____

_____

LAB 1.3 IDENTIFY COMPUTER PARTS

OBJECTIVES

The goal of this lab is to examine your computer to identify the parts inside and outside the case. After completing this lab, you will be able to:

⊿ Identify computer components outside the case

⊿ Identify computer components inside the case

MATERIALS REQUIRED

This lab requires the following:

⊿ A computer that can be disassembled

⊿ A Phillips-head screwdriver

⊿ An ESD strap

⊿ Measuring tape or ruler

⊿ Workgroup of two to four students

⊿ A display of six or more computer parts to be identified by students

⊿ Internet access on a separate computer (if needed to look up more information)

LAB PREPARATION

Before the lab begins, the instructor or lab assistant needs to do the following for each workgroup:

⊿ Gather six or more computer parts for display on a table in the lab area

⊿ Put a number on each computer part accordingly from one to six

⊿ Provide a computer that can have the cover removed

⊿ Verify Internet access is available

ACTIVITY BACKGROUND

When working with a computer system, you must be able to identify the hardware components, both inside and outside the case. Components are not always labeled adequately, especially those inside the case. This lab helps you learn to recognize these components.

ESTIMATED COMPLETION TIME: 30 MINUTES

Activity

Using the assorted computer parts your instructor has prepared and displayed, fill in the following chart:

Identify the Part	Describe the Computer Component and its Use
1.	
2.	
3.	
4.	
5.	
6.	

Next, observe the external physical characteristics of your computer system and answer the following questions:

1. What size monitor do you have? Use your measuring tape or ruler to measure from the upper-left corner to the lower-right corner (the diagonal) on the monitor screen. Is the measurement what you expected based on the size of the monitor?

   _____

2. What other external components does your computer have (speakers, printer, and so forth)? Describe each component with as much detail as you can.

   _____

   _____

3. Look at the back of your computer and locate all the cables and cords connected to ports and other connections. Fill in the following chart:

Describe the Port or Connector to Which the Cable or Cord is Connected	Purpose of the Cable or Cord
1.	
2.	
3.	
4.	
5.	
6.	

4. What other ports on the computer are not being used? List them:

_____

_____

Next, you'll open the computer case and examine the components inside. As you work, make sure you do not touch anything inside the case unless you're wearing an ESD strap that's clipped to the case so that any electrical difference between you and the case is dissipated.

To remove the cover from a computer with screws, follow these steps:

1. Power down the computer and unplug it. Next, unplug the monitor, the printer, and any other device that has its own external power supply. After all power sources are unplugged, press the power button on the computer for three seconds to drain any remaining power.

2. The method required to open a computer case varies depending on the manufacturer. Many newer cases require that you remove the faceplate on the front of the case first. Other cases require removing a side panel first, and very old cases require removing the sides and top as a single unit first. Study your case for the correct approach.

> **Notes** In the steps that follow, you will find general guidelines for disassembling a computer. If any of these steps do not seem to apply to your system, you'll need to consult the user manual or download a PDF of the manual from the manufacturer's website for more detailed instructions.

3. For a desktop or tower case, locate and remove the screws on the back of the case on the opposite side from the ports. Be careful not to unscrew any screws besides the ones attaching the cover. The other screws are probably holding the power supply in place.

4. After you remove the cover screws, slide the cover back to remove it from the case, as shown in Figure 1-13.

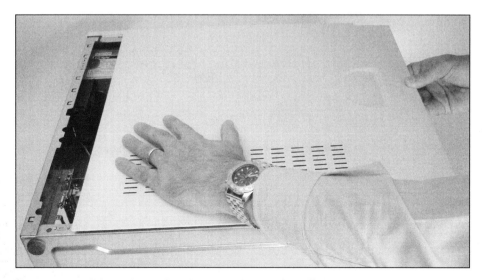

Figure 1-13 Slide a side panel to the rear and then lift it off the case

To remove the cover from a tower computer with no visible case screws, follow these steps:

1. Power down the computer and unplug it from its power outlet. Next, unplug the monitor and any other device with an external power source from the power outlet. After all power sources are unplugged, press the power button on the computer for three seconds to drain any remaining power.

2. On some cases, you must pop the front panel off the case before removing the side panels. Look for a lever on the bottom of the panel and hinges at the top. Squeeze the lever to release the front panel and lift it off the case (see Figure 1-14). Then remove any screws holding the side panel in place, as shown in Figure 1-15, and slide the side panel to the front and then off the case.

Figure 1-14 Some cases require removing the front panel before removing the side panels

Figure 1-15 Screws hold the side panel in place

> **Notes** Some case panels don't use screws at all; these side panels usually have buttons or tabs to release the cover.

With the cover removed, you're ready to look for some components. As you complete the following, you might want to refer to drawings and photos on the Internet for additional information on the specific components in your system:

1. Put on your ESD strap, and connect the clip to the side of the computer case.

2. Identify and describe the following major components. List any other components you find inside the case. Fill in the following chart. For any drives you find installed, describe the type of interface used (for example, IDE or SATA):

Component	Description—Include the Manufacturer And Model Name (If Listed) as Well as its Distinguishing Characteristics
Power supply	
Motherboard	
Hard drive(s)	
CD/DVD-ROM drive(s)	
RAM	
System fan (not inside the power supply)	
Video card (if not integrated)	
Network card (if not integrated)	
Sound card (if not integrated)	

REVIEW QUESTIONS

1. How did you decide which expansion card was the video card?

_____

2. How did you identify the type of CPU you have?

_____

3. Does your system have much room for adding new components? What types of expansion bus slots are available for adding new cards?

_____

4. Is there space for upgrading the RAM? If there isn't, what could you do instead to upgrade?

_____

5. Where (specifically) would you go on the Internet to download a PDF of the motherboard or system manual? What information would be required?

_____

LAB 1.4 IDENTIFY FORM FACTORS

OBJECTIVES

The goal of this lab is to gain experience in identifying form factors. After completing this lab, you will be able to:

▲ Identify the form factor of the case, motherboard, and power supply

▲ Select appropriate components to match an existing form factor

MATERIALS REQUIRED

This lab requires the following:

▲ A computer designated for this lab

▲ A computer toolkit with ESD strap

▲ Internet access

LAB PREPARATION

Before the lab begins, the instructor or lab assistant needs to do the following:

▲ Verify Windows starts with no errors

▲ Verify Internet access is available

ACTIVITY BACKGROUND

The form factor is a set of specifications for the size, shape, and configuration of the components that make up a computer system. Sharing a common standard allows components such as the case, motherboard, and power supply to fit together and function properly. Some common form factors are ATX, microATX, FlexATX, and Mini-ITX. Each comes in several variations that determine characteristics such as size and shape. In this lab, you identify your system's form factor and research some identifying characteristics of common form factors.

ESTIMATED COMPLETION TIME: 30 MINUTES

Activity

1. Open your browser and go to your favorite search engine, such as *google.com*.
2. Use the Internet to research the main differences between ATX and FlexATX and list them here:

_____

_____

_____

3. Now explain the main differences between ATX and Mini-ITX (also known as ITX):

_____

_____

_____

4. Each form factor comes in several sizes. How could you tell whether a system was Regular ATX, microATX, or Mini-ITX?

_____

_____

_____

5. Form factors are also available in various shapes. What slimline form factor is similar to but not compatible with ATX?

_____

6. Now turn the computer off and unplug the power cord.

7. Disconnect all peripherals and remove the case cover.

8. Examine the case, motherboard, and power supply.

9. What is the form factor of this system?

_____

10. Close the case, reattach the peripherals, and test the system to make sure it boots without errors.

REVIEW QUESTIONS

1. Why is it important that your case and motherboard share a compatible form factor?

_____

2. When might you want to use a slimline form factor?

_____

3. What advantages does ATX have over microATX?

_____

4. Which operating systems can be installed on Mini-ITX motherboards?

_____

5. Is it possible to determine the form factor without opening the case?

_____

LAB 1.5 FIND DOCUMENTATION ON THE INTERNET ABOUT POWER RATINGS

OBJECTIVES

The goal of this lab is to learn how to locate documentation on the Internet so that you can determine how much power a component uses. After completing this lab, you will be able to:

◢ Find the manufacturer and model of a component

◢ Locate a product's documentation or manual

◢ Download and view a product manual

MATERIALS REQUIRED

This lab requires the following:

◢ A computer designated for disassembly

◢ Internet access

◢ Adobe Acrobat Reader or a browser plug-in to view PDFs

◢ A computer toolkit with ESD strap

◢ A workgroup of 2 or 3 students or individual students

◢ Access to a printer

LAB PREPARATION

Before the lab begins, the instructor or lab assistant needs to do the following:

◢ Verify a computer designated for disassembly is available for each student or workgroup

◢ Verify Internet access is available

ACTIVITY BACKGROUND

Often the power specifications for a component aren't labeled on the component itself but are included in the documentation. When working with computers, it's common to encounter a component for which you have no documentation on hand. In this lab, you learn how to find a component's make and model and, if possible, find online documentation for it.

ESTIMATED COMPLETION TIME: 30 MINUTES

 Activity

1. Open the computer's case and locate the component your instructor assigned to you (or select a component randomly). If you're in a workgroup, each person should be assigned a different component.

> **Notes** The manufacturer and model aren't marked clearly on every component. If you're having trouble finding this information on a component, such as a video card, try researching based on the component's chipset. The information identifying the chip is usually stenciled on the chip. For communication devices, such as a modem or network card, look for an FCC number printed on the card and use it for your search. If you need to find out how much power an unlabeled component uses, sometimes it's helpful to consult the documentation for similar components.

2. Examine the component until you find a sticker or stenciled label identifying its manufacturer and model number. Write down the identifiers.

3. Take your notes to a computer that has Internet access.

4. If you already know the manufacturer's URL, go to that site and try to find documentation in these locations:

   ◢ The Support section of the site

   ◢ The Download section, as shown in Figure 1-16

   ◢ The Customer Service section

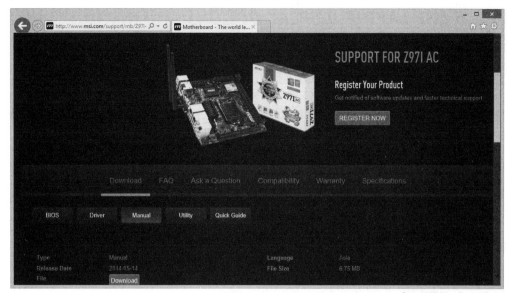

Source: 2015 Micro-Star Int'l Co.,Ltd

Figure 1-16 Manuals are available for download from the Download section of a manufacturer's website

If you're not sure of the manufacturer's URL, try searching for the manufacturer or model number using an Internet search engine. In fact, searching by model number often locates the information in the fewest steps. For example, if Z97I AC is imprinted on your motherboard, searching for "Z97I AC" can take you right to the documentation you need. Keep in mind that most documentation is in PDF format, which means you will need Adobe Acrobat Reader or a browser plug-in to view the documentation.

5. Print or save the documentation, and file it as a reference for when you need information about that component.

6. Now determine what CPU your system uses, and list that CPU here:

_____

7. Go to the manufacturer's website, and find and print the webpage showing the power consumption of your CPU expressed in watts.

REVIEW QUESTIONS

1. How is a computer component, such as a network card, commonly marked for identification?

_____

2. In what sections of a website are manuals commonly found?

_____

3. In what format are manuals usually provided?

_____

4. What is the URL where you can download the product guide for an Intel DQ87PG motherboard?

_____

5. Why would a computer repair technician need to know the power consumption of a peripheral component?

_____

LAB 1.6 USE LAPTOP DISPLAY OPTIONS

OBJECTIVES

The goal of this lab is to learn how to support laptop displays. IT technicians are often called on to support a variety of computers and peripherals; therefore, it's important to learn how to use more than one type of laptop. If possible, perform this lab using more than one type of laptop and with more than one operating system. After completing this lab, you will be able to:

◢ Change the display settings

◢ Use an external monitor or video projector

MATERIALS REQUIRED

This lab requires the following:

◢ Laptop computer running Windows

◢ Second laptop computer (optional)

◢ External monitor or projector

LAB PREPARATION

Before the lab begins, the instructor or lab assistant needs to do the following:

◢ Verify the laptop computers start without errors

◢ Verify the external video device is available and working

ACTIVITY BACKGROUND

IT support technicians often find themselves needing to respond to emergencies created by the lack of preparation by others. As you respond to these types of technical challenges, experience helps! Good communication skills and professional behavior are also needed to help calm nervous users in desperate situations.

ESTIMATED COMPLETION TIME: 45 MINUTES

 Activity

Sharon has worked for two weeks to put together a PowerPoint presentation to support her important speech to her company's top executives. The presentation is scheduled for 9:00 this Friday morning. On Monday, she requests that a projector be set up in the conference room by Thursday afternoon, so that she'll have plenty of time to make sure all is working before people start to arrive around 8:45 on Friday morning. Late Thursday evening, she puts the finishing touches on the presentation and prints 25 copies, more than enough for the expected 20 attendees. She arrives at work at 8:00 AM the next day and heads for the conference room to hook up her laptop to the video projector. So far, so good. But when she arrives in the conference room with printouts, laptop, and coffee in hand, she finds no projector! She calls technical support (that's you) to fix the problem.

You find a projector and bring it to the conference room. Sharon has powered up her Windows laptop and opened the PowerPoint presentation. Listed below are the steps to connect the projector and set up the display so that the PowerPoint presentation is displayed on Sharon's laptop and also on the projector. (In a lab environment where you don't have a projector, use an external monitor to practice these steps.) Follow these steps:

1. Physically attach the second display to the laptop. What kind of connector does it use?

   _____

2. On your particular laptop, what key do you use along with the Fn key to toggle the display between video devices?

   _____

> **Notes** A projector must support the screen resolution used by the laptop it is connected to. If the projector shows a blank screen, try a different screen resolution setting on the laptop. Make certain that the entire window displays on the projected screen.

3. If Sharon pauses too long during the presentation, the screen saver might activate and cause the screen to go blank or the system might go into sleep mode. How do you set the power options and display settings on a laptop so that these potential interruptions to the presentation won't happen?

   _____

   _____

4. Sharon decides she needs her Windows desktop available on the laptop's screen at the same time the PowerPoint presentation is displayed on the projector, but she has no clue how to do this. List the steps to make this adjustment:

   _____

   _____

   _____

   _____

   _____

5. When the projector displays the presentation, you find that it's difficult to see the images clearly from the back of the room. What are the steps to increase the brightness of the laptop's display?

   _____

   _____

   _____

   _____

REVIEW QUESTIONS

1. What display options are available on your laptop to help conserve battery power?

   _____

   _____

2. Laptops vary in the key combination used to toggle video. Without having a user manual available, describe how you would figure out which key combination to use on a laptop:

   _____

   _____

3. List three types of ports a laptop might provide for an external monitor:

   _____

   _____

   _____

4. When using an external monitor with Windows, what is the name of the window accessed through Control Panel that is used to switch between a duplicate desktop and an extended desktop?

   _____

5. When troubleshooting an LCD panel monitor that is malfunctioning or is blank, how can using an external monitor help you?

   _____

   _____

CHAPTER 2

Working Inside Desktop Computers and Laptops

Labs included in this chapter:

- **Lab 2.1:** Take a Computer Apart and Put It Back Together
- **Lab 2.2:** Examine Laptop Documentation
- **Lab 2.3:** Compare Laptops and Desktops
- **Lab 2.4:** Use Laptop Diagnostic Software
- **Lab 2.5:** Investigate Computer Teardown Procedures

LAB 2.1 TAKE A COMPUTER APART AND PUT IT BACK TOGETHER

OBJECTIVES

The goal of this lab is to get comfortable working inside a computer case. After completing this lab, you will be able to:

◢ Take a computer apart

◢ Recognize components

◢ Reassemble the computer

MATERIALS REQUIRED

This lab requires the following:

◢ A computer designated for disassembly

◢ A computer toolkit with an ESD strap and mat

◢ A marker and masking tape

◢ Small containers, such as paper cups, to hold screws as you work

◢ A workgroup of two to four students; an individual student can work this lab as well

LAB PREPARATION

Before the lab begins, the instructor or lab assistant needs to do the following:

◢ Verify a computer designated for disassembly is available to each student or workgroup

ACTIVITY BACKGROUND

If you follow directions and take your time, there's no reason to be intimidated by working inside a computer case. This lab takes you step-by-step through the process of disassembling and reassembling a computer. Follow your computer lab's posted safety procedures when disassembling and reassembling a computer, and remember to always wear your ESD strap. Also, never force a component to fit into its slot. Doing so might damage the card or the motherboard.

You begin this lab by removing the cover of your computer and then removing the components inside. Next, you reassemble the components and replace the cover. This lab includes steps for working with a desktop computer and a tower computer. Follow the steps that apply to your computer.

In this lab, you're instructed to disassemble your computer in this order: case cover, interior cables and cords, expansion cards, motherboard, drives, power supply, and case fans. Because some systems require a different disassembly order, your instructor might change the order. For example, you might not be able to get to the power supply to remove it until drives or the motherboard are out of the way. Be sure to follow any specific directions from your instructor.

> **Notes** In a lab environment, the instructor might consider giving a demonstration of tearing down a computer and putting it back together before students begin this lab.

As you work, when you remove a screw, place it in a paper cup or on a piece of paper so that you can keep different size screws separated. Later, when you reassemble your computer, having the screws organized in this way makes it easier to match the right screw to the hole.

Activity

Follow the procedure outlined in the following steps to remove the case cover and expansion cards. (If you're working with a tower case, lay it on its side so that the motherboard is on the bottom.)

1. Remove the cover from your computer, and attach your ESD strap to the side of the case.

2. To make reassembly easier, take notes or make a sketch (or take a picture) of the current placement of boards and cables and identify each board and cable. You can mark the location of a cable on an expansion card or the motherboard with a marker, if you like. Note the orientation of the cable. Each cable for an ATA hard drive, a CD/DVD-ROM drive, or a floppy drive has a colored marking on one side of the cable called the "edge color." This color marks pin 1 of the cable. On the board, pin 1 is marked with the number 1 or 2 beside the pin or with a square soldering pad on the back side of the board, as shown in Figure 2-1. You might not be able to see this soldering pad now.

Pin 1 is shown by a stencil on the circuit board.

Pin 1 is shown by square solder pads on the reverse side of the circuit board.

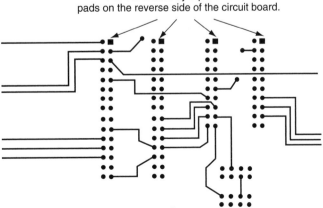

Figure 2-1 How to find pin 1 on an expansion card

> **Notes** Unless your system is really old, it most likely does not have a floppy drive.

3. Remove any cables from the expansion cards. There's no need to remove the other end of the cable from its component (hard drive, CD/DVD-ROM drive, or floppy disk drive). Lay the cable over the top of the component or case.

4. Remove the screw holding the card to the back of the case.

5. Grasp the card with both hands and remove it by lifting straight up and rocking the card from end to end (not side to side). Rocking the card from side to side might spread the slot opening and weaken the connection. When you remove the card, be sure you don't touch the edge connectors on the card. (Oil from fingers can tarnish or corrode these connectors.)

6. If the card had a cable attached, examine the card connector for the cable. Can you identify pin 1? Lay the card aside on a flat surface. Don't stack cards.

7. Remove any other expansion cards the same way.

8. In some proprietary systems, a riser card assembly attaches to the motherboard, with each card attached to the assembly. If your system has this arrangement, remove it now. It's probably held in place by screws or clips and may or may not have a rail guide you can use to locate the assembly in the case.

9. Unplug any case fans.

In some systems, it's easier to remove the drives first and then the motherboard. In other systems, it's easier to remove the motherboard first. In these instructions, to make sure you don't risk dropping a drive on the motherboard when removing the drive, you're directed to remove the motherboard first and then the drives. Your instructor, however, might prefer that you remove the drives first and then the motherboard.

1. Begin removing the motherboard by removing any remaining wires or cables such as power cables, audio wires, or wires from the front of the case. Be sure to make notes or label the cables so that you can reinstall them correctly.

2. Finish removing the motherboard by removing the screws holding the board to the spacers or standoffs. Usually six to nine screws attach the motherboard to the case. Be careful not to gouge the board or damage components with the screwdriver. Because the screws on the motherboard are often located between components, they can be hard to reach. Be very careful not to damage the motherboard. See Figure 2-2.

3. The motherboard should now be free and you can carefully remove it from the case. See Figure 2-3.

4. To remove drives, remove the data cable if it's still attached. Many cases have a removable drive bay. The drives are attached to this bay, and the bay can be removed with all the drives attached. This arrangement gives you easier access to drive-mounting screws than from inside the case. If your case has a removable drive bay, this removal method is preferred. Otherwise, remove each drive separately. Be careful not to jar the drive as you remove it from the case.

5. If your system has a removable drive bay, the floppy drive (if there is one) likely came out with the removable bay. If the floppy drive is still in the system, remove the screws holding the drive in place, and slide the drive out of the case.

6. Remove any CD-ROM, DVD, or tape drives from the case. These drives are usually in the 5-inch drive bays and are normally held in place by four screws. After the screws are removed, the drive slides out the front of the case.

Figure 2-2 Remove the screws that hold the motherboard to the case

Figure 2-3 Carefully remove the motherboard from the case

7. Support the power supply with one hand, and remove the screws attaching it to the case. You can then remove the power supply from the case.

8. Remove any other components, such as a case fan.

Now that you have removed all the components, you're ready to reassemble the computer. Replace each component carefully. Take care to install each component firmly without overtightening the screws. Don't force components to fit. If a component won't fit easily the way it should, look for some obstruction preventing it from falling into place. Look carefully for the reason the component won't fit correctly, and make any small adjustments as necessary. The following steps outline the assembly procedure, which is essentially the reverse of the disassembly procedure:

1. Install the case fan.

2. Install the power supply, and replace the screws holding it in position.

3. Install the drives in their bays and then install the motherboard, unless your instructor prefers that you install the motherboard first.

4. Connect wires from the front of the case to the motherboard.

5. Connect the power cables from the power supply to the drives and the motherboard. Double-check to make sure all the power supply connectors to the motherboard are connected correctly.

6. Place each card in its slot (it doesn't have to be the same slot, just the same bus), and replace the screw. Don't place a PCI video card near the power supply; otherwise, electromagnetic interference (EMI) from the power supply might affect the video picture.

7. Replace any cables to expansion cards, being sure to align the colored edge with pin 1. (In some cases, it might work better to connect the cable to the card before you put the card in the expansion slot.)

8. Check to make sure no cables are interfering with any fan's ability to turn. A common cause of an overheated system is a fan that can't move air because a cable is preventing it from spinning.

9. When all components are installed, you should have refitted all the screws you removed earlier. If some screws are missing, it's important to turn the case upside down and gently shake the case to dislodge any wayward screws. Any screw left lying on a board has the potential to short out that board when power is applied. Don't use a magnet to try to find missing screws in the case because you might damage data on hard drives or—on older computers—on floppy disks left in the floppy disk drives.

10. Plug in the keyboard, monitor, and mouse.

11. In a classroom environment, have the instructor check your work before you power up.

12. Plug in the power cord to the computer and to the power outlet or surge protector. Verify any power switches on the rear of the case are set correctly. Some cases have a power switch to close the AC voltage, and others have an on/off switch.

13. Using the power button on the front of the case, turn on the power and check that the computer is working properly before you replace the cover. Don't touch the inside of the case while the power is on.

14. If all is well, turn off the computer and replace the cover and its screws. If the computer doesn't work, don't panic. Turn off the power, and then go back and check each cable connection and each expansion card. You probably haven't seated a card solidly in the slot. After you have double-checked everything, try again.

REVIEW QUESTIONS

1. When removing the cover, why should you take care to remove only the screws that hold the cover on?

_____

_____

_____

2. How should you rock a card to remove it from its slot? Why is it important to know how to rock a card correctly?

_____

3. What should you do to help you remember which components connect to which cables?

_____

4. What marking on a ribbon cable identifies pin 1?

_____

5. What component(s) defines the system's form factor?

_____

_____

6. What form factor does your computer use?

_____

7. Why would an IT technician ever have to change out a computer's motherboard?

_____

_____

_____

_____

LAB 2.2 EXAMINE LAPTOP DOCUMENTATION

OBJECTIVES

The goal of this lab is to find documentation for a laptop on a manufacturer's website and become familiar with it. After completing this lab, you will be able to:

◢ Locate documentation for two specific laptop computer models (one running Windows and one running Apple's OS X)

◢ Download the documentation

◢ Use the documentation to find critical information

MATERIALS REQUIRED

This lab requires the following:

◢ Internet access

LAB PREPARATION

Before the lab begins, the instructor or lab assistant needs to do the following:

◢ Verify Internet access is available

ACTIVITY BACKGROUND

Laptops are designed for portability, compactness, and energy conservation, and their designs are often highly proprietary. Therefore, establishing general procedures for supporting laptops is more difficult than for desktop computers. Often, consulting the documentation for a particular model is necessary to get information on technical specifications and support procedures. In this lab, you locate and download documentation for two different laptop computers, and then use that documentation to answer questions about each model.

> **ESTIMATED COMPLETION TIME: 30 MINUTES**

Activity

Some major manufacturers of laptop computers are listed in Table 2-1. Of these, Lenovo, Dell, and HP have a reputation in the industry for providing more extensive technical documentation than other manufacturers. To draw your own conclusions, follow these steps:

1. Choose Lenovo, Dell, or HP to research. Then go to the Lenovo, Dell, or HP website and select a laptop model to research. Which manufacturer and model of laptop did you select?

   _____

2. Other than these three manufacturers, select another manufacturer from Table 2-1. Go to that company's website and select one model to research. Which manufacturer and model did you select?

   _____

Manufacturer	Websites
Acer	us.acer.com
	support.acer.com
Apple Computer	apple.com
	apple.com/support
ASUS	usa.asus.com
	service.asus.com
Dell Computer	dell.com
	support.dell.com
Fujitsu/Fuji	fujitsu.com
	fujitsu.com/support
Gateway	gateway.com
	support.gateway.com
Hewlett Packard (HP)	hp.com
	www8.hp.com/us/en/support-drivers.html
Lenovo (formerly IBM ThinkPads)	lenovo.com
	support.lenovo.com

Table 2-1 Laptop manufacturers (*continues*)

Manufacturer	Websites
Samsung	*samsung.com*
	samsung.com/support
Sony (VAIO)	*store.sony.com*
	esupport.sony.com
Toshiba America	*toshiba.com*
	toshiba.com/tai/support.jsp

Table 2-1 Laptop manufacturers (*continued*)

3. For each of the two models, go to the Support section of the manufacturer's website, search for documentation on the model, and follow the directions to download the documentation. Search for a user manual and a service manual. Also search for other types of technical support the sites might offer for this particular model. List the types of documentation you were able to find for each model. For each model, indicate if you were able to download or save the documentation locally, or if you could only view it on the company's website.

   ◢ Documentation for a Lenovo, Dell, or HP laptop:

   _____

   _____

   _____

   _____

   ◢ Documentation for the second laptop you selected:

   _____

   _____

   _____

   _____

4. Using the documentation you found, answer questions *a* through *e* for each model in Table 2-2. If you can't answer a question because the information isn't included in the documentation, write "information unavailable."

   a. What type of processor does the laptop use?

   b. How much and what type of RAM is installed?

   c. What edition and type of operating system is currently installed on the laptop?

   d. What type of optical storage (CD, CD-RW, DVD, and so forth) does the laptop offer, if any?

   e. What type of wired or wireless networking (for example, NIC, Infrared, Wi-Fi, and Bluetooth) comes built in?

	Model 1	Model 2
a.		
b.		
c.		
d.		
e.		

Table 2-2 Compare general documentation for two laptops

5. For each model, record your answers to the following questions in Table 2-3 about the information the two websites provide about servicing the laptop:

   a. Are instructions available for exchanging the hard drive?

   b. Are instructions available for upgrading RAM?

   c. Can you obtain recovery media for the laptop in the event the hard drive needs replacing?

   d. Are instructions available for replacing the optical drive, if one is included?

   e. Are instructions available for replacing the processor?

   f. Are UEFI/BIOS updates available for the laptop? Are instructions available to perform a UEFI/BIOS update?

   g. Is a recovery partition available on the laptop? If so, how do you access the recovery tools and partition?

	Model 1	Model 2
a.		
b.		
c.		
d.		
e.		
f.		
g.		

Table 2-3 Compare documentation needed to service a laptop

6. Answer the following questions about what you learned regarding manufacturer documentation:

   ◢ Of the two manufacturers you researched, which one provided the better documentation? Explain your answer.

   _____

   ◢ Which manufacturer's website was easier to use? Why?

   _____

◢ What type of documentation did you find missing that would be helpful when supporting a laptop?

_____

REVIEW QUESTIONS

1. Other than documentation, what resources are available on a manufacturer's website to help you support a laptop?

_____

_____

2. Which manufacturer's site did you think was the most user friendly and, in general, offered the best support?

_____

3. Besides the questions you researched in the lab, what other type of information is available in the manuals you reviewed?

_____

_____

4. Of the laptops you researched, which one would you purchase? Explain your answer, listing the features that you liked best.

_____

_____

LAB 2.3 COMPARE LAPTOPS AND DESKTOPS

OBJECTIVES

The goal of this lab is to compare the specifications and costs for laptop and desktop computers. After completing this lab, you will be able to:

◢ Compile a list of specifications for a computer according to its purpose

◢ Locate a desktop computer and a laptop computer with similar specifications

◢ Compare the price of a desktop computer to a similar laptop computer and decide which you would purchase

MATERIALS REQUIRED

This lab requires the following:

◢ Internet access

◢ Access to a printer (optional)

LAB PREPARATION

Before the lab begins, the instructor or lab assistant needs to do the following:

◢ Verify Internet access is available

ACTIVITY BACKGROUND

When you shop for a computer, your purchasing decisions are generally driven by questions such as the following: For what will the computer be used? What features are required to accomplish your goals? What features would be nice to have but aren't essential? On what features are you willing to compromise to gain others? What future needs do you anticipate? If you understand your needs before you start shopping, you're less likely to regret your purchase.

One of the most basic decisions is whether to choose a laptop computer or a desktop computer. Unlike desktops, laptops are portable; however, to make laptops portable, manufacturers often sacrifice performance, storage space, or other features. In addition, you usually pay more for a laptop than for a desktop computer with comparable features. In this lab, you compile a list of requirements for a computer, locate a laptop computer and a desktop computer with those features, and compare the two systems.

ESTIMATED COMPLETION TIME: 30 MINUTES

 Activity

Pretend you are about to buy a computer. The two most important criteria to determine which computer to buy are usually how the computer will be used and the price. Do the following to determine your requirements for your new computer:

1. You first need to decide how the computer will be used. Answer the following questions:

    ◢ For what will the computer be used? (Possible uses include office applications, video playback, high-end gaming, and software development.)

    _____

    _____

    _____

    ◢ What features are required to make the computer usable for its intended purpose? Include in your list the amount of memory and hard drive space you want. (Some features you might consider include wireless [Wi-Fi, Bluetooth, or cellular] support, display or screen type, software packages supported, and I/O ports.)

    _____

    _____

    _____

    _____

    ◢ List any additional features you would like to have but don't require:

    _____

    _____

    _____

    _____

◢ Which operating system do you want to use with your computer?

2. Use computer manufacturers' websites (such as the ones listed in Table 2-1) or comparison websites (such as *cnet.com* or *pricewatch.com*) to find one laptop and one desktop computer that fulfill as many of your requirements as possible and are as similar to each other as possible. Summarize your findings in Table 2-4. Save or print the webpages supporting your gathered information.

Features	Desktop Computer	Laptop Computer
Manufacturer and model		
Processor type and frequency		
Memory installed		
Hard drive space		
Operating system		
Video card		
Optical drive		
Display size		
External ports		
Preinstalled applications		
Price		

Table 2-4 Desktop and laptop computer specifications

3. Online reviews of a computer can help you find out what others think of the computer, how it performs, and what problems to expect. Find two or three reviews for each of the two computers you researched in Step 2, and summarize the best review you found for each computer:

◢ For the desktop computer, what is the URL of the review?

◢ List the major points in the review about the desktop computer:

◢ How does this review affect your opinion of this desktop computer, its warranty, online support of the desktop, or the computer's manufacturer?

_____

_____

◢ For the laptop computer, what is the URL of the review?

_____

◢ List the major points in the review about the laptop:

_____

_____

_____

_____

◢ How does this review affect your opinion of this laptop, its warranty, online support of the laptop, or the computer's manufacturer?

_____

_____

4. If the desktop computer package does not include the monitor, keyboard, and mouse, you need to include the price of these peripherals so that you can make a fair comparison between the cost of a desktop and the cost of a laptop. Answer the following:

◢ Are the monitor, keyboard, and mouse included in the desktop computer package?

_____

◢ If not, what is the total price of these three peripherals? Provide webpages to support your answer.

_____

5. Based on your requirements and the research you recorded in Table 2-4, would you buy the desktop computer or the laptop? Explain your answer.

_____

_____

_____

6. How did the reviews of the desktop and laptop affect your decision? Explain your answer.

_____

_____

_____

7. For an operating system, you might want to consider using Windows by Microsoft or Mac OS X by Apple. Compare two laptop computers that are similar in features except that one uses Windows and the other uses OS X. Fill in Table 2-5 with the results of your research. You may use the laptop from Table 2-4.

Installed Features	Windows	Mac OS X
Website (URL)		
Brand and model		
Operating system		
Processor type		
Processor speed		
RAM		
Hard drive type/speed		
Optical drive type		
Networking		
I/O ports		
Warranty		
Other features		
Installed software		
Price		

Table 2-5 Windows and Mac OS X laptop computer comparison

8. Based on the research you recorded in Table 2-5, which is the better buy, a Windows laptop or Mac OS X laptop? Explain your answer.

_____

_____

_____

REVIEW QUESTIONS

1. What are the two most important criteria when deciding which computer to buy?

_____

_____

2. Why do laptop computers cost more than desktop computers?

_____

_____

3. List three reasons why it is easier to upgrade a desktop computer than a laptop computer:

_____

_____

4. Other than price, what factors might someone consider when deciding whether to buy a Windows laptop or a Mac OS X laptop?

_____

_____

_____

5. In this lab, was it easier comparing a desktop computer with a laptop, or comparing a Windows laptop with a Mac OS X laptop? Explain your answer.

_____

_____

_____

LAB 2.4 USE LAPTOP DIAGNOSTIC SOFTWARE

OBJECTIVES

The goal of this lab is to learn to research and use diagnostic software to troubleshoot problems with laptop computers. After completing this lab, you will be able to:

◢ Research and use diagnostic software on a laptop computer

◢ Research replacing a part on a laptop

MATERIALS REQUIRED

This lab requires the following:

◢ A working laptop computer

◢ Internet access on this or another computer

LAB PREPARATION

Before the lab begins, the instructor or lab assistant needs to do the following:

◢ Verify a working laptop is available for each student or workgroup

◢ Verify Internet access is available

ACTIVITY BACKGROUND

Servicing laptops is different from servicing desktop systems in many respects. One difference is that because laptops are more proprietary in design, you are more dependent on tools and manuals provided by the laptop manufacturer than you are when working with desktops. Some manufacturers provide excellent service manuals that you can download from their websites. On video-hosting sites such as *youtube.com*, you can also find good step-by-step tutorials.

Many laptop manufacturers store diagnostic software on the laptop's hard drive, where it can be accessed at startup. This software can be used to test key hardware components and can be useful when troubleshooting a laptop. In this lab, you learn about service manuals, diagnostic software, and other tools that are available and how to access and use them.

ESTIMATED COMPLETION TIME: 60 MINUTES

 Activity

You run a small computer repair shop, and Janice comes in with a laptop computer that has been dropped. The laptop is an HP Pavilion x360 (model number 11-n010dx) that is not under warranty. Janice tells you that she thinks the entire computer is useless because it appeared "dead" when she turned it on. She's especially upset over data on the hard drive that she believes has been lost. Do the following:

1. After you fill out the customer intake form, you are ready to tackle the problem. List the first three things you should do to try to save the data and troubleshoot the problem:

   _____

   _____

   _____

   _____

   _____

2. After you plug in the AC adapter and turn on the laptop, you discover the lights on the computer are lit and you hear the fan running, but the LED touch screen is blank. When you connect an external monitor, you see the Windows 8 logon screen. Janice breathes a sigh of relief. What do you do now?

   _____

   _____

You suspect that the LED touch screen is broken, but you decide it would be a good idea to run hardware diagnostic software to check for other hardware problems. Diagnostic software is written specifically for a particular brand of laptop and is often stored in a hidden utility partition on the hard drive or on the recovery disc that comes with the laptop. The software is accessed by pressing a key at startup or by booting from a recovery disc. For some laptops, the diagnostic software in the hidden partition is disabled by default and must be enabled in UEFI/BIOS setup before you can use it.

Do the following to find out about diagnostic software and how to use it:

1. Go to the HP website at **hp.com** and download the service manual for this laptop. What is the name of the downloaded PDF file?

   _____

2. Are there any recall alerts for this laptop? If so, which parts are included?

   _____

3. What key do you press at startup to access the diagnostic software stored on this laptop?

_____

4. What types of tests can you run using the HP PC Hardware Diagnostics (UEFI) software?

_____

_____

5. If the hard drive is broken, what other method can you use to run the HP PC Hardware Diagnostics (UEFI) software?

_____

_____

6. Based on the information in the service manual, what is the part number of the LED touch screen?

_____

7. The laptop is fairly old, so HP might not still offer parts for sale. Are you able to buy the part from the HP website? What is the price of the LED touch screen if you buy it from the HP website?

_____

8. Do you think the laptop is worth the cost of the repair, including parts and labor?

_____

9. Research the service manual, and list the high-level steps to replace the display assembly:

_____

_____

_____

_____

_____

10. Before you commit to replacing an internal laptop component, you need to be confident that you have enough information and directions to open the laptop, access the part, and reassemble the laptop. Do you think you have enough information to do the repair? Why or why not?

_____

_____

11. If you don't think you have enough information, what is your next step?

_____

HP offers excellent diagnostic software, but not all laptop manufacturers do. Also, HP makes its laptop service manuals available on the web, but many laptop manufacturers release their service manuals only to authorized service centers. For these manufacturers, you can sometimes search the web to find alternative tutorials and advice. Using your lab laptop, available documentation for the laptop, and the web, answer these questions:

1. What is the brand and model of your laptop? What is the website of your laptop manufacturer?

   _____

   _____

2. Can you obtain the service manual for your laptop? If so, from where?

   _____

   _____

3. Does your laptop have diagnostic software? If so, how is it accessed? List all the methods:

   _____

   _____

   _____

   _____

4. If you have diagnostic software, how does this software compare with the HP PC Hardware Diagnostics (UEFI) software?

   _____

   _____

5. If you have diagnostic software, run it using the most thorough test that the software offers. List the results of the test:

   _____

   _____

REVIEW QUESTIONS

1. What kinds of information can be found in a technical service manual?

   _____

   _____

2. Why would you want to run diagnostic software after you have repaired a laptop and verified that the repaired component works?

   _____

   _____

3. Before you purchase an internal laptop part to replace a broken one, what should you verify?

_____

4. List three troubleshooting situations in which diagnostic software might be useful:

_____

_____

_____

LAB 2.5 INVESTIGATE COMPUTER TEARDOWN PROCEDURES

OBJECTIVES

The goal of this lab is to increase your familiarity with the process of taking apart a computer and reassembling it. After completing this lab, you will be able to:

◢ Identify multiple factors that affect the teardown process

◢ Distinguish between best practices and potentially problematic shortcuts

◢ Anticipate additional considerations for disassembling a laptop as compared to a desktop computer

MATERIALS REQUIRED

This lab requires the following:

◢ Internet access

LAB PREPARATION

Before the lab begins, the instructor or lab assistant needs to do the following:

◢ Verify Internet access is available

ACTIVITY BACKGROUND

With such a variety of computer cases and parts options available, it helps to become familiar with as many different systems as possible before working in the field. Familiarity, however, can breed its own challenges. Some technicians, as they become more comfortable working inside a computer case, start to take shortcuts that can damage equipment or cause injury.

In this lab, you find and review an online video showing the teardown of a desktop or tower computer and then evaluate the technician's teardown process. Watch for errors the technician makes, such as not using an ESD strap or having screws left over after reassembly. Refer to the textbook as needed to help you remember the various guidelines and safety precautions. Finally, you select an online video of a laptop teardown, and identify significant differences in this process as compared to taking apart a desktop computer.

> **Notes** This lab should be completed after you've completed Lab 2.1 so that you can identify what is different about the system in your selected video compared to the system you worked on.

ESTIMATED COMPLETION TIME: 30 MINUTES

Activity

Complete the following steps to investigate different procedures for taking apart a computer and putting it back together:

1. Review the portions of the chapter that discuss the proper procedures for taking apart and reassembling a computer. Pay particular attention to the safety precautions, and take notes as needed.

2. Search the web to find a video that shows the entire process of taking apart a desktop or tower computer and putting it back together. Some videos can be found on *youtube.com*. Try to find a video that is done well, with good camera angles and useful discussion about the parts shown in the video. What is the URL for the video you selected?

   _____

3. Describe at least four mistakes made by the technician in the teardown or reassembly process. Sometimes the technician will notice a mistake himself, such as missing screws that should have been loosened before attempting to remove the motherboard. Sometimes the technician doesn't seem to be aware—or chooses to ignore—that he is risking damage to expensive parts or taking unnecessary safety risks.

   _____

   _____

   _____

   _____

4. Identify the possible consequences of each mistake along with ways to prevent those mistakes in the future:

   _____

   _____

   _____

   _____

   _____

   _____

5. Identify at least two significant differences between the system you worked on for Lab 2.1 and the system shown in the video. Are there different drives in the case, such as multiple hard disk drives or a floppy drive? Was there a graphics card or a riser card? Was a different order of steps needed because of component placement inside the case?

_____

_____

_____

6. Select a video showing the disassembly and reassembly of a laptop computer. What is the URL for the video you selected?

_____

7. What are three significant differences you notice about the parts or their arrangement inside a laptop compared to the desktop computer you worked with in Lab 2.1? What is one significant difference about the process of taking apart a laptop compared to taking apart a desktop?

_____

_____

_____

_____

_____

REVIEW QUESTIONS

1. What are three notable characteristics of the system shown in the first video you selected? For example, was this an older or newer system? How can you tell? Who is the manufacturer of the system, the case, and/or the components? What drives or other optional components were included in the system?

_____

_____

_____

2. What tools did the technician use in each video? What additional tools would you recommend having on hand to take apart and reassemble a computer?

_____

_____

_____

3. Which two components of a computer should be treated as "black boxes" and not opened without specialized training?

   _____

   _____

4. What are two methods for keeping track of screws during disassembly so that reassembly goes more smoothly?

   _____

   _____

All About Motherboards

Labs included in this chapter:

LAB 3.1 USE THE HWiNFO HARDWARE INFORMATION UTILITY

OBJECTIVES

The goal of this lab is to learn how to use a hardware information utility. After completing this lab, you will be able to:

- Download and install the HWiNFO utility
- Use the HWiNFO utility to examine your system

MATERIALS REQUIRED

This lab requires the following:

- A computer designated for this lab
- Windows 8 or Windows 7 operating system
- Internet access for file downloading only

LAB PREPARATION

Before the lab begins, the instructor or lab assistant needs to do the following:

- Verify Windows starts with no errors
- Verify Internet access is available
- For labs that don't have Internet access, download the following file to a file server or other storage media available to students in the lab: latest version of HWiNFO downloaded from *hwinfo.com*. At the time this lab was tested, the latest version was Version 4.64 and the file name was hw32_502.exe or hw64_502.exe, depending on your version of Windows (either the 32-bit version or the 64-bit version). Be sure to download the latest version of the file.

ACTIVITY BACKGROUND

A hardware information utility can be useful when you want to identify a hardware component in a system without having to open the computer case. Also, a hardware information utility can help you identify features of a motherboard, video card, or processor installed in a system and establish benchmarks for these components. In this lab, you learn to use HWiNFO, written by Martin Malík from Slovak Republic. The utility comes in a Windows version and a DOS version. You can use the Windows version on Windows Vista, 7, 8, or 8.1 computers, and you can install the portable version on a USB flash drive or CD so that the utility is available on any computer you're troubleshooting.

In this lab, you download a shareware Windows version of HWiNFO from the web and then learn how to use it. Websites sometimes change, so as you follow the instructions in this lab, you might have to adjust for changes to the *hwinfo.com* site. If your lab doesn't have Internet access, ask your instructor for the location of the file downloaded previously for your use. Write the path to that file here:

ESTIMATED COMPLETION TIME: 30 MINUTES

Activity

Follow these steps to download and run the Windows HWiNFO utility:

1. Go to the HWiNFO website at **hwinfo.com.** Be careful not to click links to ads or to other downloads. Click the **Free Download** button. Then, depending on which version of Windows your computer uses, select **HWiNFO32** or **HWiNFO64,** by clicking the correct **DOWNLOAD INSTALLER** button at the bottom of the page. Select a download source. Students in the United States can select **Local (U.S.).** Those in other locations should select one of the other options. Save the file to your hard drive. What is the path and name of the downloaded file?

2. When the download is complete, close your browser. Open File Explorer (Windows Explorer in Windows 7), and then double-click the application file to install HWiNFO for Windows. If the UAC dialog box opens, click **Run** or **Yes** to start setup. Follow the directions on the screen to install the software. Retain all the default settings. You can launch the application upon completion of installation by making sure the **Launch** check box is checked before clicking **Finish.** In the Welcome dialog box, click **Run.**

3. When the utility runs, it examines your system, and then the HWiNFO window shown in Figure 3-1 opens.

Often, you are not given step-by-step directions when using utility software but must learn how to use it by exploring menus and using the software's help functions. The following steps give you practice in doing that.

1. Use the HWiNFO utility to find the following information about your system:

   ◢ Motherboard model and manufacturer:

Source: www.hwinfo.com

Figure 3-1 HWiNFO for Windows hardware information's initial display

◢ Motherboard chipset:

_____

◢ Motherboard slots:

_____

◢ BIOS manufacturer:

_____

◢ BIOS version:

_____

◢ BIOS (release) date:

_____

◢ CPU brand name:

_____

◢ Processor socket (platform):

_____

◢ Original processor frequency:

_____

◢ Number of CPU cores:

_____

◢ Amount of L1 cache:

_____

◢ Amount of L2 cache:

_____

◢ Amount of L3 cache:

_____

◢ Slot type of the video bus, as reported by the video card:

_____

◢ Video chipset:

_____

◢ Amount of video memory (RAM):

_____

2. To identify your motherboard's serial number, expand **Motherboard, SMBIOS DMI,** and then click **Mainboard.** What is your motherboard's serial number?

_____

3. Exit the program.

REVIEW QUESTIONS

1. List the steps to display information about memory using HWiNFO:

_____

_____

_____

2. List three reasons you might use HWiNFO when troubleshooting or upgrading a computer:

_____

_____

_____

3. What is one advantage of using the portable version instead of the Windows version of the HWiNFO utility?

_____

_____

LAB 3.2 EXAMINE AND ADJUST BIOS SETTINGS

OBJECTIVES

The goal of this lab is to explore and modify BIOS settings. After completing this lab, you will be able to:

⊿ Enter the BIOS setup utility

⊿ Navigate the BIOS setup utility

⊿ Examine some setup options

⊿ Save changes to setup options

MATERIALS REQUIRED

This lab requires the following:

⊿ A Windows 7 computer designated for this lab

⊿ Any necessary BIOS passwords (may need to be obtained from your instructor)

⊿ A copy of the Computer Inventory and Maintenance form used in Lab 1.2

LAB PREPARATION

Before the lab begins, the instructor or lab assistant needs to do the following:

◢ Verify Windows starts with no errors

◢ Verify Internet access is available

◢ Provide the Computer Inventory and Maintenance form in print or digital format, or verify that students can download the form online

ACTIVITY BACKGROUND

When a system is powered up, the startup process is managed by a set of instructions called the basic input/output system (BIOS). BIOS, in turn, relies on a set of configuration information stored in CMOS (complementary metal-oxide semiconductor), which is recharged continuously by battery power when the system is off. You can access and modify CMOS setup information via the CMOS setup utility in BIOS. In this lab, you examine the BIOS setup utility, make some changes, and observe the effects of your changes.

> **Notes** Although BIOS is being replaced by UEFI on newer motherboards, older BIOS motherboards are still in use. Also, many UEFI motherboards provide a legacy BIOS option for compatibility with certain operating systems.
> This lab is designed to be performed on a Windows 7 machine with legacy BIOS. A later lab will explore UEFI on a Windows 8.1 machine.

Setup utilities vary slightly in appearance and function, depending on the manufacturer and version. The steps in this lab are based on the BIOS setup program for Award BIOS, which is a common BIOS. You might have to perform different steps to access and use the BIOS utility on your computer.

Changes in BIOS are often performed by computer technicians. One reason to change BIOS settings is if you're attempting to overclock a system, which is done by changing the default frequencies of the processor and/or motherboard. Overclocking isn't a recommended best practice, however, because of potential problems with overheating and possibly causing the system to become unstable. Overclocking usually voids any manufacturer warranty on the system.

ESTIMATED COMPLETION TIME: 30 MINUTES

 Activity

Before you access the BIOS on your computer, you need to record the exact date and time indicated by your computer's internal clock. (You use this information later to confirm that you have indeed changed some BIOS settings.) Do the following:

1. Start your computer. On the Windows 7 taskbar, move your mouse over the clock, and record the time and date:

   _____

2. Use a system analyzer such as Speccy (*piriform.com/speccy*) to obtain information about the motherboard and installed BIOS on your computer. In Speccy, you'll find Manufacturer, BIOS, and Revision data under the Motherboard section. Record the following information:

◢ BIOS brand:

_____

◢ BIOS version:

_____

◢ Revision date:

_____

◢ System temperature:

_____

◢ Slots in use:

_____

Now that you know which BIOS your computer runs, you can determine how to enter the setup utility. In general, to start the setup utility, you need to press a key or key combination as the computer is booting. Some BIOS utilities are password protected with a supervisor password and a user password (also called a power-on password). A supervisor password allows full access to BIOS setup, whereas a user password only allows you to view BIOS setup screens. In most cases, you can't change any settings with a user password, although in some instances you are allowed to change certain settings. (In addition, if the user password is also set to be a power-on password and you don't know this password, you won't be able to boot the system.) When you attempt to access BIOS setup, if password protection has been enabled, you must enter a valid password to continue.

> **Notes** BIOS setup supervisor, user, and power-on passwords are different from the Windows password required to log on to Windows. Also, if you're responsible for a computer and have forgotten the supervisor password, you can move a jumper on the motherboard to return all BIOS settings to their default values, which erases any BIOS passwords. Lab 3.5 covers how to find this jumper.
> Another way to cause CMOS setup to return to default settings and erase passwords is to remove the CMOS battery.

To learn more about entering the setup utility on your computer, follow these steps:

1. Using the information you recorded in the previous exercise, consult Table 3-1 to find out how to enter your system's setup utility. (Alternatively, when you first turn on your computer, look for a message on your screen, such as "Press F2 to access setup" or "Press Del to change BIOS settings.")

Now you're ready to enter the CMOS setup utility included in your BIOS. As you examine the BIOS settings, you will also record information in the UEFI/BIOS Settings and Data section of the Computer Inventory and Maintenance form that you used in Lab 1.2. Follow these steps to enter the BIOS utility:

1. Restart the computer.

2. When the system restarts, enter the setup utility using the correct method for your computer. If you weren't fast enough and the computer boots to the operating system, return to Step 1.

Notice that the BIOS utility groups settings by function. For example, all the power-management features are grouped together in a Power Management section.

BIOS Brand	Method for Entering CMOS Setup Utility
Intel BIOS	Boot the computer, and then press the F2 key.
AMI BIOS	Boot the computer, and then press the Delete key.
Award BIOS	Boot the computer, and then press the Delete key.
Newer Phoenix BIOS	Boot the computer, and then press the F2 or F1 key.
Older Phoenix BIOS	Boot the computer, and then press the Ctrl+Alt+Esc or Ctrl+Alt+S key combination.
Dell Computers with Phoenix BIOS	Boot the computer, and then press the Ctrl+Alt+Enter key combination.
Some Compaq computers, such as Prolinea, Deskpro, Deskpro XL, Deskpro LE, or Presario	Boot the computer, wait for two beeps, and when the cursor is in the upper-right corner of the screen, press the F10 key.
Some older Compaq computers, such as Deskpro 286 or 386	Place the diagnostics disk in the drive, reboot the system, and choose Computer Setup from the menu.
All other older computers	Use the setup program on the floppy disk that came with the computer. If the floppy disk is lost, contact the motherboard manufacturer to get a replacement.

Table 3-1   Methods for entering CMOS setup utilities by BIOS

The main screen usually has a Help section that describes how to make selections and exit the utility. Typically, you can use the arrow keys or Tab key to highlight options. After you have highlighted your selection, usually you need to press Enter, Page Down, or the Spacebar. The main screen might display a short summary of the highlighted category. Look for and select a category called something like Standard BIOS Features. Follow these steps to gather and record BIOS information:

1. In the Standard BIOS Setup screen, you should see some or all of the following settings. If the information is available in your BIOS utility, record the current setting for each of the following:

   ◢ Date: _____

   ◢ Time: _____

   ◢ For SATA hard drives, write down the drive size and mode of operation. Is your SATA drive set to RAID?

   _____

   _____

   ◢ Installed drives:

   _____

   ◢ Virtualization support:

   _____

   ◢ Halt on error setup (the type of error that halts the boot process):

   _____

   ◢ Memory summary (summary of system memory divisions):

   _____

◢ Boot sequence (drives that BIOS searches for an OS):

_____

◢ Temperature and fan speed:

_____

◢ Intrusion detection:

_____

2. Return to the main screen. Select a section called something like Advanced Chipset Features. This section may be split into North Bridge and South Bridge sections. Record settings for the following as well as any other settings in this section:

◢ Setup options for memory or RAM:

_____

_____

◢ Setup options for expansion buses such as PCIe or AGP:

_____

_____

◢ CPU-specific setup options:

_____

_____

◢ Settings for I/O ports such as USB:

_____

_____

◢ Provisions for enabling and disabling onboard drive controllers and other embedded devices:

_____

_____

_____

_____

3. Return to the main screen. Explore the menus and submenus of the BIOS setup utility, and answer the following questions. Note that most of the BIOS settings never need changing, so understanding every setting isn't necessary.

◢ Does BIOS setup offer the option to set a supervisor password? If so, what's the name of the screen where the password is set?

_____

_____

◢ Does BIOS setup offer the option to set a user password? Is so, what options can affect the way users are able to access and use BIOS setup?

_____

_____

_____

4. Fill in all the information required in the "UEFI/BIOS Settings and Data" section of the Computer Inventory and Maintenance form that you used in Lab 1.2.

5. Return to the main screen. You might see options for loading BIOS defaults (which restore factory settings and can be helpful in troubleshooting) as well as options for exiting with or without saving changes. Exit BIOS without saving any changes to prevent saving any accidental changes made while you were exploring the BIOS setup utility.

Now that you're familiar with the way the BIOS setup utility works, you can change the date and time settings. Follow these steps to change the date and time settings:

1. Reboot the computer, and go to the Standard BIOS Setup screen.

2. Highlight the time field(s), and set the time ahead one hour.

3. Move to the date field(s), and set the date ahead one year.

4. Return to the main BIOS setup screen, and select an option named something like **Save Settings and Exit**. If prompted, verify you want to save the settings.

5. Wait while the system reboots, and then log on to Windows.

6. At the desktop, check the time and date. Are your BIOS setup changes reflected in Windows?

_____

> **Notes** If a computer is connected to a network that is managed by a domain controller, such as Windows Server 2012 R2, the server might automatically push a new date and time to the computer, which can cause your changes to be overwritten.

7. Manually update the time on the computer via the Windows Internet Time feature. To do this, right-click the **time** on the taskbar, and select **Adjust date/time** from the shortcut menu to open the Date and Time dialog box. Click the **Internet Time** tab. Click **Change settings**. Click **Update now**. Click **OK** to close both open windows.

8. Reboot the computer and return to BIOS setup. Note the time in BIOS.

_____

9. Exit BIOS and log on to the computer. Verify again that the changes are reflected in Windows.

CRITICAL THINKING (ADDITIONAL 30 MINUTES)

Form workgroups of two to four people, and do the following to practice troubleshooting problems with BIOS:

1. Propose a change you could make to BIOS setup that would prevent a computer from booting successfully. What change did you propose?

_____

2. Have your instructor approve the change because some changes might cause information written to the hard drive to be lost, making it difficult to recover from the problem without reloading the hard drive. Did your instructor approve the change?

_____

3. Now go to another team's computer and make the change to BIOS setup while the other team makes a change to your system.

4. Return to your computer and troubleshoot the problem. Describe the problem as a user would:

_____

_____

5. What steps did you go through to discover the source of the problem and fix it?

_____

_____

6. If you were to encounter this same problem in the future, what might you do differently to troubleshoot it?

_____

_____

REVIEW QUESTIONS

1. Do all systems use the same method to enter BIOS setup? On a Windows 7 computer, can you enter BIOS setup after the system has booted?

_____

2. How are settings usually grouped in the BIOS setup utility?

_____

3. In what section of the BIOS setup utility do you usually find time and date setup?

_____

_____

4. What types of options are shown on the BIOS setup main screen?

_____

5. What happens automatically after you exit BIOS setup?

_____

6. Is it possible for a virus to infect the BIOS of a computer system?

_____

_____

7. Why does a computer need BIOS?

_____

_____

8. When troubleshooting a computer, why might you have to enter BIOS setup? List at least three reasons:

_____

_____

_____

LAB 3.3 IDENTIFY MOTHERBOARD COMPONENTS

OBJECTIVES

The goal of this lab is to learn to identify motherboard form factors and components. After completing this lab, you will be able to:

⊿ Identify a motherboard's CPU type

⊿ Identify connectors

⊿ Identify the form factor based on component type and placement

MATERIALS REQUIRED

Instructors are encouraged to supply a variety of motherboards, some common and others not as common. At the very least, this lab requires the following:

⊿ Three different motherboards

> **Notes** If three motherboards aren't available, refer to the websites of three motherboard manufacturers.

LAB PREPARATION

Before the lab begins, the instructor or lab assistant needs to do the following:

⊿ Gather an assortment of motherboards, with as many form factors as possible, and label the motherboards as Motherboard 1, Motherboard 2, and Motherboard 3

ACTIVITY BACKGROUND

As an IT technician, you should be able to look at a motherboard and determine what type of CPU, RAM, and form factor you're working with. You should also be able to recognize any unusual components the board might have. In this lab, you examine different motherboards and note some important information about them.

ESTIMATED COMPLETION TIME: 30 MINUTES

 Activity

Fill in the following chart for your assigned motherboards. If you have more than three motherboards, use additional paper. When the entry in the Item column is a question (such as "SCSI Controller?"), write a yes or no answer.

Item	Motherboard 1	Motherboard 2	Motherboard 3
Manufacturer/model			
UEFI/BIOS manufacturer			
CPU socket			
Chipset			
RAM slot type			
How many RAM slots?			
How many RAM channels?			
How many PCI slots?			
How many PCIe ×1 slots?			
How many PCIe ×16 slots?			
How many AGP slots?			
Parallel ATA (IDE) connectors?			
Serial ATA (SATA) connectors?			
SCSI controller?			
Embedded audio, video, and so on			
How many power connectors?			
Form factor			
Describe any unusual components			

REVIEW QUESTIONS

1. What are the two main differences between an ATX and a microATX board?

_____

_____

2. How can you determine the chipset if it's not written on the board?

_____

_____

3. Of the motherboards you examined, which do you think is the oldest? Why?

_____

_____

_____

4. Which motherboard best supports old and new technology? Why?

_____

_____

_____

5. Which motherboard seems to provide the best possibility for expansion? Why?

_____

_____

_____

6. Which motherboard is most likely the easiest to configure? Why?

_____

7. Which motherboard do you think is the most expensive? Why?

_____

8. What are some considerations a motherboard manufacturer has to contend with when designing a motherboard? (For example, consider room for large CPUs and cooling fans, where the power supply is located in relationship to the power connector, new technologies, and so forth.)

_____

_____

LAB 3.4 IDENTIFY A MOTHERBOARD AND FIND DOCUMENTATION AND DRIVERS ON THE INTERNET

OBJECTIVES

The goal of this lab is to learn to identify a motherboard and find online documentation for it. After completing this lab, you will be able to:

◢ Identify a motherboard by examining it physically

◢ Determine a motherboard's manufacturer and model

◢ Search the Internet for motherboard documentation

MATERIALS REQUIRED

This lab requires the following:

◢ A computer designated for disassembly

◢ Internet access

◢ Adobe Acrobat Reader

◢ A computer toolkit with ESD strap

◢ Ability to print (optional)

LAB PREPARATION

Before the lab begins, the instructor or lab assistant needs to do the following:

◢ Verify Windows starts with no errors

◢ Verify Internet access is available

◢ Verify Adobe Acrobat Reader is installed

ACTIVITY BACKGROUND

Often, an IT technician is asked to repair a computer for which the documentation is lost or not available. Fortunately, you can usually find documentation for a device online, as long as you have the device's manufacturer name and model number. In this lab, you learn how to find the manufacturer's name and model number on a motherboard, and then locate documentation for that device on the Internet.

ESTIMATED COMPLETION TIME: 30 MINUTES

 Activity

Follow these steps to gather information about your motherboard and processor:

1. Windows can identify a system's installed processor and might be able to identify the motherboard installed. Boot your computer to the Windows desktop. Press **Win+S** (in Windows 7, click **Start**), enter **msinfo32.exe** in the Search box, and then press **Enter**. The System Information window opens. Write down the following information:

   ◢ Processor installed:

   _____

   ◢ System manufacturer (likely to be the motherboard manufacturer):

   _____

   ◢ System model (likely to be the motherboard model):

   _____

   ◢ BIOS version/date (might help identify the motherboard):

   _____

2. Shut down the system, unplug the power cord, and then press the power button for three seconds to drain residual power.

3. Following safety precautions, including using an ESD strap, remove the computer's case cover, and then remove any components obscuring your view of the motherboard. In some cases, you might have to remove the motherboard itself, but this step usually isn't necessary. If you think it is necessary to remove the motherboard, ask your instructor for guidance.

4. Look for a stenciled or silkscreened label printed on the circuit board that indicates the manufacturer and model. Note that other components sometimes have labels printed on a sticker affixed to the component. On a motherboard, the label is usually printed directly on the circuit board. Common motherboard manufacturers include AOPEN, ASUS, and Intel.

> **Notes** Note that the manufacturer name is usually printed in much larger type than the model number. Model numbers often include both letters and numbers, and many indicate a version number as well. Figure 3-2 shows an example of a motherboard label.

5. Record the information on the motherboard label:

   _____

6. Take your information to a computer with Internet access, and open a web browser.

Figure 3-2 Label printed directly on a motherboard

7. If you know the manufacturer's URL, go directly to the manufacturer's website. (Table 3-2 lists the URLs for some motherboard manufacturers.) If you don't know the manufacturer's URL, search using the manufacturer or model with your favorite search engine, as shown in Figure 3-3. In the search results, click a link associated with the manufacturer. If this link doesn't take you directly to the documentation, it usually gets you within two or three links. Continue until you find the manufacturer's website.

> **Notes** For a listing of websites about motherboards, including motherboard manufacturers, diagnostics, and product comparisons and reviews, see *motherboards.org*.

Manufacturer	URL
AOPEN	*aopen.com*
ASUS	*asus.com*
ASRock	*asrock.com*
Biostar	*biostar-usa.com*
Dell	*dell.com*
EliteGroup	*ecsusa.com*
EVGA	*evga.com*
Foxconn	*foxconnchannel.com*
Gateway	*gateway.com*
GIGABYTE	*gigabyte.us*
IBM	*ibm.com*
Intel Corporation	*intel.com*
MSI	*us.msi.com*
Supermicro Computer, Inc.	*supermicro.com*
Tyan Computer Corporation	*tyan.com*

Table 3-2 URLs for major motherboard manufacturers

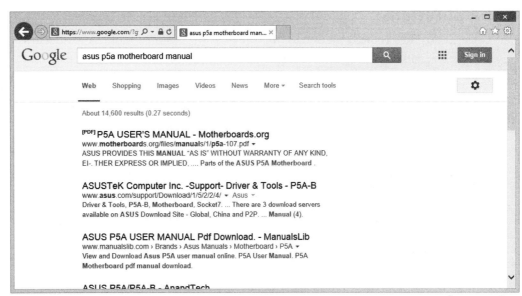

Source: www.google.com

Figure 3-3 Search results using manufacturer name and model number

8. When you have found the site of your motherboard's manufacturer, look for a link for service or support. Click this link, and, if necessary, select a product category and model number. Sometimes knowing the type of processor the board supports can be useful in finding the right motherboard.

9. Continue working your way through the site until you find the motherboard documentation. The documentation might include a variety of documents covering technical specifications and installation instructions. Often the documentation includes a basic manual, which is usually a combination of technical and installation specifications.

10. When you find the documentation, you might also find a link to updated drivers. If you see this link, click it and note the release date of the drivers. If they are newer than your system's current drivers, it's often advisable to update the drivers as well. If available, record the release dates for updated drivers:

---

11. Return to the main documentation page, and, if available, select the manual. If it's not available, select the installation instructions.

12. The manual is probably in PDF format, so you need to have Adobe Acrobat Reader installed. If you have the Adobe browser plug-in, you can open the document from the source location; if not, you can download the manual to your computer and then open it. Using your preferred method, open the document. Either save or print the document because you will need it in Lab 3.5.

REVIEW QUESTIONS

1. How is the label usually applied to or written on a motherboard? How is it most often applied to other components?

2. How can you differentiate between the manufacturer and the model number on the labels of most motherboards and other components?

3. What type of link on a manufacturer's website usually leads you to manuals and other documentation?

4. What other information about your motherboard might you want to examine on the manufacturer's website?

5. In what format is documentation most often available for download?

6. What information besides motherboard documentation, such as UEFI/BIOS updates and drivers, can be found on the manufacturer's website?

LAB 3.5 REMOVE AND REPLACE A MOTHERBOARD

OBJECTIVES

The goal of this lab is to familiarize yourself with the process of replacing an old or faulty motherboard. After completing this lab, you will be able to:

◢ Use CPU-Z to determine the motherboard's specifications

◢ Remove a motherboard

◢ Install a replacement motherboard

◢ Configure a new motherboard according to its documentation

MATERIALS REQUIRED

This lab requires the following:

◢ A computer designated for this lab

◢ Motherboard manual (see manufacturer's website or use documentation from Lab 3.4)

◢ A workgroup of two to four students

◢ A computer toolkit with ESD strap

◢ Internet access to download CPU-Z

LAB PREPARATION

Before the lab begins, the instructor or lab assistant needs to do the following:

◢ Verify Windows starts with no errors

◢ Verify Internet access is available or provide the downloaded CPU-Z installation file from *cpuid.com/softwares/cpu-z.html*

ACTIVITY BACKGROUND

In this lab, you exchange a motherboard with another team to simulate the process of replacing a faulty motherboard. When you install the new motherboard, you must configure it for your system by adjusting jumper and CMOS settings as needed, according to the documentation you found on the manufacturer's website or saved in Lab 3.4. Then you install the replacement motherboard.

ESTIMATED COMPLETION TIME: 60 MINUTES

 Activity

In this lab, you download and install CPU-Z, and then remove and install the motherboard. While removing the motherboard, follow the safety precautions discussed in earlier chapters as well as those outlined in the motherboard's documentation. Be sure to use an ESD strap to protect the motherboard, as well as other devices, from ESD. Follow these steps to gather information about your motherboard:

1. Using your favorite web browser, go to **cpuid.com/softwares/cpu-z.html.**

2. Be careful not to click an advertisement that has a download link. Locate the download section on the page, and click the **ZIP - ENGLISH** link. On the next screen, click **DOWNLOAD NOW!** to start the download. At the time of this revision, the latest version was 1.72.1 and the file name was cpu-z_1.72.1-en.zip. This file contains both the 32-bit and 64-bit versions. Click **Save**, then save the file to your computer in the Downloads folder. Navigate to the file using File Explorer (Windows Explorer in Windows 7), extract all of the files, and run the correct version of the application for your computer. If necessary, click **Yes** in the UAC dialog box. CPU-Z displays as shown in Figure 3-4.

Source: CPU-Z by CPUID

Figure 3-4 CPU-Z initially displays CPU information

3. Click the Mainboard tab in CPU-Z, and record information about the motherboard:

- Manufacturer: _____

- Model: _____

4. If this is a different motherboard than you used in Lab 3.4, use the motherboard information to search for the documentation on the manufacturer's website. Save or print the documentation.

Follow these steps to remove your motherboard from your computer:

1. Power down the system, unplug all cords and cables connected to the computer, press the power button for three seconds to drain any remaining power, and remove the case cover. Take all necessary precautions (including using an ESD strap), and make a sketch of cabling and component placement. Then remove the cabling and expansion cards from the motherboard.

2. Six to nine screws usually attach the motherboard to the case via spacers or standoffs. The spacers prevent the printed circuitry from shorting out on the metal case and provide space for air circulation. Also, it's important that the motherboard be securely attached to the case with enough spacers and screws so that the motherboard won't crack when expansion cards are being inserted. Remove the screws attaching the motherboard to the case, and set them aside in a cup, bag, or bowl so that you don't lose any of them.

> **💡 Tip**   In this lab, it's not necessary to remove the spacers from the holes in the computer case. However, sometimes you might have to move a spacer from one hole to another, such as when you're replacing a motherboard and the new board lines up over different holes in the computer case. To remove a plastic spacer held in place with barbs, use needle-nose pliers to pinch the spacer and slide it out of the hole. To install it in a new hole, push the spacer into the hole until it pops into place. For metal spacers, carefully squeeze the spacer with pliers and remove it from the bracket holding it to the computer case.

3. Carefully lift the motherboard out of the case. You might have to tilt the board to clear the drive bays and power supply. In some cases, you might have to remove the drives to get the motherboard out.

4. Exchange the motherboard and motherboard documentation with that of another team. You might also exchange the CPU and memory, depending on whether your current CPU and memory modules are compatible with the new motherboard. Follow directions from your instructor on what to exchange. Be sure you have the new motherboard's documentation, which you should have previously found on the Internet.

Your instructor might ask you to remove jumpers on your motherboard before passing it to the other team. These modifications will make the other team's configuration more challenging. As an alternative, your instructor might have a display motherboard somewhere in the lab that uses jumpers for part of its configuration. Follow these steps to install the new motherboard:

1. With the new motherboard in front of you, consult its documentation, and find any jumpers that must be configured to match the system. Older motherboards use jumpers to adjust clock multipliers and memory speeds, and to clear CMOS settings. Unless otherwise instructed, do not remove the jumper to clear CMOS settings. Note that newer boards are often "jumperless," with all configuration settings made in CMOS setup. The only jumper these boards have is the one to clear CMOS settings. Remove and replace the jumpers in the configuration specified to match your processor information.

2. Install the motherboard, cabling, memory, expansion cards, and any other components you removed.

3. Have your instructor check your work before you attach the case cover and turn on the power.

4. Boot the system and enter the UEFI/BIOS setup utility. For jumperless motherboards, make any adjustments specified in the motherboard's documentation.

5. Save your settings and exit UEFI/BIOS setup.

6. Reboot the system and verify the system is functioning correctly. Describe any error messages:

_____

_____

7. If an error appears, what steps do you plan to take to troubleshoot this error?

_____

_____

_____

CRITICAL THINKING (ADDITIONAL 30 MINUTES)

To learn more about motherboards, do the following:

1. After the computer is working, ask your instructor to configure a power-on password on your computer.

2. Without knowing the password, boot the computer.

3. List the steps required to boot the computer without the power-on password:

_____

_____

_____

REVIEW QUESTIONS

1. How many screws usually attach the motherboard to the computer case?

_____

2. What is the purpose of spacers?

_____

3. Even a jumperless motherboard is likely to have one jumper. Which jumper is it?

_____

4. Where can you access configuration settings for a jumperless motherboard?

_____

LAB 3.6 FLASH BIOS

OBJECTIVES

The goal of this lab is to examine the process of flashing BIOS. After completing this lab, you will be able to:

▲ Gather motherboard information

▲ Gather BIOS string information

- Research correct BIOS update information
- Record current BIOS settings
- Flash your BIOS, if permitted by your instructor

MATERIALS REQUIRED

This lab requires the following:

- Windows 7 operating system
- Motherboard documentation or Speccy by Piriform (installed in Lab 3.2)
- A copy of the Computer Inventory and Maintenance form used in the chapter, "First Look at Computer Parts and Tools"

Internet access

- Some BIOS may require a bootable USB or CD drive
- Printer access (optional)

LAB PREPARATION

Before the lab begins, the instructor or lab assistant needs to do the following:

- Verify Windows starts with no errors
- Verify Internet access is available
- Determine if the flash program will require any external media

ACTIVITY BACKGROUND

The BIOS on a motherboard controls many of the system's basic input/output (I/O) functions. You can update the BIOS programming by downloading the latest update from the BIOS or motherboard manufacturer's website and then following specific procedures to update (or "flash") the BIOS. Flashing a computer's BIOS is necessary when troubleshooting an unstable motherboard. You might also need to flash a computer's BIOS to provide support for new hardware (such as a processor, hard drive, or DVD-ROM drive) or an operating system you're about to install. For example, before upgrading your operating system to Windows 7 x64 edition, you might need to update your computer's BIOS to support 64-bit drivers. Because flashing BIOS sometimes causes problems of its own, don't flash the BIOS unless you have a good reason to do so. Do not update BIOS on computers that do not need it.

In this lab, you gather information about your system, including what BIOS your computer is using and how to flash it. If your instructor permits, you also flash your BIOS.

ESTIMATED COMPLETION TIME: 30 MINUTES

 Activity

Before making hardware, software, or BIOS changes to a system, it's important to know your starting point so that if problems occur, you know if the problems already existed or if you created them by any changes you made to the system. Complete the following steps to verify if your computer is functioning:

1. Verify your computer can boot successfully to a Windows desktop with no errors.
2. How long does it take your computer to boot?

When flashing BIOS, using the correct BIOS update is critical. Using the wrong BIOS update can render your system inoperable. Follow these steps to gather information on the motherboard chipset and BIOS:

1. Use motherboard documentation or Speccy to find and record the following:

◢ Motherboard manufacturer:

_____

◢ Motherboard model number and version/revision:

_____

◢ Chipset manufacturer:

_____

◢ Chipset model number and version/revision:

_____

Next, you need to record the BIOS manufacturer and version as BIOS reports it. Follow these steps:

1. Reboot the system and enter BIOS setup.
2. Look on the main screen of BIOS setup. What is the BIOS identifying information?

_____

For older computers, you might need to record the BIOS string and manufacturer information displayed during the boot process. Follow these steps:

1. To make it possible to record this information, for an older computer, turn off the computer, unplug your keyboard, and then turn on the computer. In most cases, the first screen contains video BIOS information from the video card and is identified by "VGA BIOS" or "Video BIOS." Ignore this screen and wait for the next screen, which indicates the start of POST (power-on self test). At this point, because you unplugged the keyboard, POST stops and reports the error about a missing keyboard. This freezes the screen so that you can read the BIOS information. For a newer computer, turn off the computer and then turn it on again while pressing the Pause/Break key, which causes POST to halt.

2. Usually, you can find the BIOS manufacturer and version at the upper left of the POST screen. You might also see a release date, which is useful in determining whether newer versions of BIOS are available. The motherboard identification string is usually located at the lower left and often contains dozens of characters. Make sure you verify this string is correct so that you get the correct BIOS update. Record your information here:

◢ BIOS manufacturer and version:

_____

◢ BIOS release date:

_____

◢ Motherboard identification string:

_____

Using the information you gathered, you can search the web to determine what files you need to update your BIOS:

1. The motherboard manual gives detailed directions as to how to flash BIOS. If you have the manual saved from Lab 3.4, use it to answer the following questions.

If you don't have the manual or the manual does not give the information you need, search the Support sections of the motherboard manufacturer's website and then the BIOS manufacturer's website for information on updating your BIOS. Alternatively, search by motherboard model number or BIOS version number. Answer the following questions:

◢ Which manufacturer provides BIOS for this system: the BIOS manufacturer or the motherboard manufacturer?

_____

◢ What is the latest BIOS version released? What is the release date of the latest version?

_____

◢ Is the latest BIOS version a later version than the one you have installed?

_____

◢ Do you think your system would benefit from flashing BIOS? Explain your answer.

_____

_____

2. Download the files to update your BIOS or, if your computer is running the latest BIOS version, download the files to refresh your existing BIOS.

◢ Were the files you downloaded to update or refresh your BIOS? What is the name of the file you downloaded?

_____

3. Search the motherboard manual or the manufacturer's website for the steps to flash your BIOS. Print this procedure so that you can use it during the upgrade. Download any additional BIOS utility or flash utility the procedure requires as documented in the manual or on the website.

4. If you are having problems finding the directions to flash your BIOS, research flash utilities on *wimsbios.com*. Wim's BIOS is an excellent website for researching BIOS information in general. List the names and descriptions of three BIOS utilities available on this site:

_____

_____

_____

5. The next step is to record any changes you have made previously to BIOS settings. Generally, when BIOS is updated, settings are returned to their default state, so you probably need to return the settings to their present state after you have flashed BIOS. In addition, you might need to manually input settings for all hard drives (or allow these settings to be detected automatically). Use the UEFI/BIOS Settings and Data section of the Computer Inventory and Maintenance form from Lab 1.2 to record any settings you know you changed, any hard drive settings that might have to be reconfigured

after you update BIOS, and any additional settings specified by your instructor. Record the following information:

⊿ Hard drive information:

_____

⊿ Settings you have changed:

_____

_____

⊿ Settings specified by your instructor:

_____

_____

6. At this point, if your update procedure requires using external media, verify the boot order allows you to boot from it before the local hard drive.

7. Sometimes you need to recover from a failed BIOS update, which can be tricky. What directions, if any, does the documentation give about recovering from a failed BIOS update?

_____

_____

8. Before you flash BIOS, find out if the manufacturer offers a way to save the current BIOS code. If so, list these steps to save BIOS before you flash it:

_____

_____

_____

⊿ On what storage media does the manufacturer recommend you save the BIOS code?

_____

9. Why would you want to save the current BIOS before you update it?

_____

10. Prepare to update your BIOS. Uncompress any files, double-check the necessary procedures, read any readme.txt files included in the upgrade files (which often contain last-minute adjustments to the procedure), and create the upgrade boot disk, if necessary.

11. If your instructor permits, follow the BIOS update procedure to flash your BIOS. During the procedure, if you're given the opportunity to save your old BIOS, do so. This information makes it possible to return to the previous BIOS version if you encounter problems with the new BIOS.

12. Reboot, verify BIOS settings, and verify the computer boots to a Windows desktop successfully.

REVIEW QUESTIONS

1. At what point in the boot process is BIOS information displayed?

   _____

2. For an older computer, how can you freeze the screen during POST so that you can read
   the BIOS information?

   _____

3. Why is it so important to record BIOS and motherboard information correctly?

   _____

4. What file might contain last-minute adjustments to the upgrade procedures?

   _____

5. In what state are BIOS settings usually placed after an update?

   _____

6. Why should you not update BIOS unless a computer needs it?

   _____

7. When flashing BIOS, why is it always important to save the old version of the BIOS code?

   _____

LAB 3.7 EXAMINE UEFI SETTINGS AND RESEARCH UEFI UPDATES

OBJECTIVES

The goal of this lab is to explore and modify UEFI settings. After completing this lab, you
will be able to:

◢ Enter the UEFI setup utility

◢ Navigate the UEFI setup utility

◢ Examine some setup options

◢ Research UEFI update information

MATERIALS REQUIRED

This lab requires the following:

◢ A Windows 8 computer designated for this lab

◢ Any necessary UEFI passwords (may need to be obtained from your instructor)

◢ A copy of the Computer Inventory and Maintenance form used in Lab 1.2

◢ Motherboard documentation or Speccy by Piriform (installed in Lab 3.2)

◢ Internet access

LAB PREPARATION

Before the lab begins, the instructor or lab assistant needs to do the following:

◢ Verify Windows starts with no errors

◢ Verify Internet access is available

◢ Provide the Computer Inventory and Maintenance form in print or digital format, or verify students can download the form online

ACTIVITY BACKGROUND

UEFI provides a more user-friendly interface than does BIOS, and it also includes a somewhat different set of features and options. Additionally, the UEFI setup utility interface can be activated through Windows after the computer has booted. While you can still use the traditional function keys during the boot process to activate the UEFI interface, the option to activate it through Windows can save you time spent on research and trial-and-error attempts to determine the correct function key to use.

In this lab, you examine the UEFI setup utility and research updates to the UEFI firmware and drivers.

ESTIMATED COMPLETION TIME: 30 MINUTES

 Activity

Complete the following steps to enter and explore the UEFI setup utility:

1. Press **Win+C** to open the charms bar, and click **Settings**. Click **Change PC settings**. In the left pane, click **Update and recovery**, and then click **Recovery**. Under Advanced start-up, click **Restart now**.

> **Notes** Alternatively, from the power menu (Win+C, Settings, Power), you can press and hold the **Shift** key while clicking **Restart** to perform an advanced startup.

2. When the system restarts, click **Troubleshoot**. On the Troubleshoot page, click **Advanced options**. On the Advanced options page, examine the various options available. Click **UEFI Firmware Settings**, and then click **Restart** on the UEFI Firmware Settings page. The system will restart again and boot to the UEFI user interface.

3. Examine the information and options available on the first screen. Each manufacturer's UEFI interface has its own variations, but much of the elemental information is common to all UEFI utilities. Some manufacturers, such as ASRock, include a UEFI tutorial within the UEFI itself. If your version provides this feature, explore it now and take notes of significant options and menus.

4. Look for some or all of the following information. Be aware that some UEFI utilities offer an advanced mode that provides additional information. However, some UEFI interfaces provide only limited information. If necessary, use a system analyzer such as Speccy (installed in Lab 3.2) to fill in the gaps below as much as possible.

◢ Date: _____

◢ Time: _____

◢ UEFI/BIOS brand: _____

◢ UEFI/BIOS version: _____

◢ Revision date: _____

◢ CPU temperature: _____

◢ CPU voltage: _____

◢ Motherboard temperature: _____

◢ SATA information: _____

_____

◢ Memory summary: _____

_____

◢ Boot sequence: _____

◢ Fast boot setting: _____

◢ CSM setting: _____

◢ Secure boot setting: _____

◢ Temperature and fan speed (for all fans listed): _____

◢ System performance settings (energy saving, performance, etc.): _____

◢ What password options are available? _____

_____

5. Fill in all the information required in the "UEFI/BIOS Settings and Data" section of the Computer Inventory and Maintenance form that you used in Lab 1.2.

6. Exit UEFI without saving any changes to prevent saving any accidental changes made while you were exploring the UEFI setup utility.

BIOSAgentPlus is a free tool that scans a computer to determine if BIOS updates are available for that system. The scanner also identifies updates needed for UEFI systems as well as for other drivers in the system. To determine whether an update is available for your computer, complete the following steps:

1. Using your favorite web browser, go to the website at **biosagentplus.com,** and download the free BIOSAgentPlus program.

2. Using File Explorer, locate the executable file on your computer, and install the application. At the time of this writing, the file name was biosagentplus.exe. The scan will run automatically, and results will be presented in your browser. Is a UEFI/BIOS update available for your system? How many device drivers are out of date?

_____

_____

3. The UEFI/BIOS update files available online at the manufacturer's website are most likely to be free of adware, which is safer than using links from other websites or scanning tools. If a UEFI/BIOS update is available for your system, explore the computer or motherboard manufacturer's website, and attempt to locate the update files. If a readme.txt file is available or if other update instructions are available, read through these instructions. It is not necessary to download the update files for this lab. However, if you were to proceed with the download, what is the name of the file(s) you would need to locate and open after downloading in order to install the update? What warnings are included in the instructions to help ensure the update goes smoothly?

_____

_____

_____

_____

_____

REVIEW QUESTIONS

1. What are the steps to enter the UEFI setup utility after the system has booted to Windows?

_____

_____

_____

2. What other startup options are available in the advanced options menu?

_____

_____

_____

3. Where should you go online to get UEFI/BIOS update files?

_____

4. What precautions should you take during the update process to help reduce the chance of problems occurring during the update?

_____

_____

LAB 3.8 MANAGE POWER ON A LAPTOP

OBJECTIVES

The goal of this lab is to demonstrate the effect that power-management features have on the running time of a laptop battery. After completing this lab, you will be able to:

- Manage laptop power-saving features
- Select a replacement laptop battery

MATERIALS REQUIRED

This lab requires the following:

- A Windows 8 or Windows 7 laptop computer
- Internet access

LAB PREPARATION

Before the lab begins, the instructor or lab assistant needs to do the following:

◢ Verify Windows starts with no errors

◢ Verify Internet access is available

ACTIVITY BACKGROUND

Many factors affect the running time or battery life of a laptop computer. A typical lithium ion laptop battery might last from one to five hours of normal use. As you might expect, however, "normal use" is a subjective term. The way you use your laptop can significantly affect battery life. For instance, editing text in a word processor doesn't require much power compared with playing a DVD. The word processor uses only a little processor time and occasionally reads or writes to the hard drive. Playing a DVD is processor-intensive and requires powering the optical drive, thus requiring more power than the word processor.

What the laptop does when you stop using it for a period of time also affects battery life. For instance, if you don't use the laptop for 10 minutes, it might go into hibernation mode automatically to conserve power. Laptops also have a few additional power-management features to extend battery life during inactivity and to protect data when the battery charge becomes low. Some of these features depend on the laptop being able to accurately judge how much life is left in the battery. In this lab, you explore how power management and battery life are related.

ESTIMATED COMPLETION TIME: 30–90 MINUTES

 Activity

Windows on a laptop allows you to set power-saving features that include a screen saver, sleep mode, and hibernation. Do the following to learn more:

1. Use Control Panel in Windows to find answers to the following questions about the current power-saving settings:

    ◢ When the laptop is plugged in, how many minutes of inactivity must pass before the screen is turned off? Before the computer goes to sleep? Before the computer goes into hibernation?

    _____

    _____

    _____

> **Notes** Hibernation might be disabled on a Windows 8 or 8.1 computer. It can be enabled in Control Panel by clicking **System and Security**, and then **Power Options**. In the left pane of the Power Options window, click **Choose what the power buttons do**. Click **Change settings that are currently unavailable**. Scroll down, and check **Hibernate**. Hibernate will now appear as an option in the Power menu. Click **Save changes**, and close the Power Options window.

◢ When the laptop is on battery power, how many minutes of inactivity must pass before the screen is turned off? Before the computer goes to sleep? Before the computer goes into hibernation?

_____

_____

_____

◢ What effect does closing the lid have on your laptop?

_____

◢ What happens when you press the power button of your laptop?

_____

2. A hibernation state uses less power than a sleep state. Using your favorite search engine, research the differences between sleep and hibernation modes. Answer the follow questions:

◢ In your own words, give a short description of the essential differences between sleep and hibernation modes in a laptop:

_____

_____

_____

◢ What is hybrid sleep mode? What type of computer uses this option?

_____

_____

3. Shut down the computer, and identify the location of your laptop computer battery. Describe how to change the battery in your laptop computer:

_____

_____

_____

4. Remove and examine the battery, identify the size and model of your battery, and list it here:

_____

_____

5. Research the website of the laptop manufacturer.

◢ What is the brand and model of your laptop?

_____

◢ What is the cost of replacing the battery?

_____

◢ Can a larger battery be installed? What would be the advantage of installing a larger battery?

_____

_____

_____

◢ What is a sheet battery (also called a battery slice)? Is your laptop designed to accept a sheet battery?

_____

_____

◢ What DC voltage does the AC adapter provide to the laptop? (This value might be 16 V, 20 V, or another value.)

_____

REVIEW QUESTIONS

1. What types of activity might decrease the battery life of a fully charged battery more quickly than reading a document or spreadsheet stored on the hard drive? Give three examples:

_____

_____

_____

2. Suppose you're packing your laptop in a case to carry with you on a three-hour flight, followed by a one-hour drive. When powering down your computer, which option would be better to select: sleep, hibernate, or shut down? Explain your reasoning.

_____

_____

_____

3. The BIOS of older computers offered many power-management features also offered by Windows. Why do you think the trend for newer computers is for power-saving features to be in Windows, but not in BIOS?

_____

_____

4. If you configure Windows on a laptop to hibernate after 30 minutes of inactivity, but the laptop remains functioning after that period of time, what might be the source of the problem?

_____

_____

5. What type of electrical current does a laptop require? What device provides this current?

_____

Supporting Processors and Upgrading Memory

Labs included in this chapter:

- **Lab 4.1:** Remove and Replace a CPU
- **Lab 4.2:** Burn-in Test and Benchmark a CPU
- **Lab 4.3:** Explore How CPUs Work
- **Lab 4.4:** Research a RAM Upgrade on the Web
- **Lab 4.5:** Benchmark RAM and Plan an Upgrade

LAB 4.1 REMOVE AND REPLACE A CPU

OBJECTIVES

The goal of this lab is to learn the correct procedure for removing and reinstalling a CPU. After completing this lab, you will be able to:

⊿ Remove the CPU from your system

⊿ Install a CPU into your system

MATERIALS REQUIRED

This lab requires the following:

⊿ A computer designated for disassembly in this lab

⊿ Flathead screwdriver

⊿ ESD strap

⊿ Masking tape and marker, or another method of labeling parts

⊿ Another computer, which has Internet access

⊿ Alcohol wipe to remove thermal compound from the CPU

⊿ Additional thermal compound (if necessary)

LAB PREPARATION

Before the lab begins, the instructor or lab assistant needs to do the following:

⊿ Verify Windows starts with no errors

⊿ Verify Internet access is available

ACTIVITY BACKGROUND

Removing and installing a CPU isn't difficult after you have done it a time or two. In today's systems, it's fairly rare for the CPU to malfunction and need to be replaced. Instead, a CPU replacement is usually done to increase the system's operating speed. In this lab, you remove the CPU and cooling unit (heat sink and fan, or HSF), and then replace both. When you're considering upgrading the CPU in a system, be aware that if you upgrade the CPU, you might not experience the new processor's full potential if other components remain outdated.

Often, when disassembling or assembling parts in a system, you won't have step-by-step directions for completing a particular task. Removing the heat sink and fan for the CPU is one of these tasks. Because of the overwhelming number of models on the market, you might need to refer to the manufacturer's documentation for exact details on how to remove the cooling unit.

> **⚡ Caution** **An important note on electrostatic discharge (ESD):** The CPU is an intricate and complicated array of wires and transistors. When you feel a static shock, you're feeling somewhere in the neighborhood of 3000 volts or more. The CPU can be damaged by a shock of 10 to 1000 volts, which is a discharge you would never feel. It's important to wear your ESD strap while handling the CPU and memory. Without it, you could easily damage components by ESD and never know that you have done so.

Activity

Because the CPU is a delicate component and is easily damaged, watch your instructor demonstrate how to remove and replace one before you attempt to do so. Then, answer the following questions about the demonstration:

1. What CPU did the instructor remove and replace?

   _____

2. What type of heat sink or cooler was attached to the CPU?

   _____

3. How was the heat sink or cooler attached to the motherboard?

   _____

4. What precautions did the instructor take to protect the CPU against ESD?

   _____

   _____

5. How did the instructor protect the CPU while it was out of its socket?

   _____

   _____

Do the following to remove the CPU from your system:

1. Power down the computer.

2. Unplug any cords or cables connected to it.

3. Press the power button for three seconds to drain any remaining power.

4. Remove the case cover.

5. Examine the inside of the case, and decide what you need to remove so that you have easy access to the CPU. Next, remove and carefully label any wires or other parts that need to be removed to expose the CPU. Later, these labels can help you remember how to reconnect or reinstall any wires or parts you remove. With some system cases, the power supply needs to be removed before you can proceed. (Removing a power supply is covered in the chapter, "Working Inside Desktop Computers and Laptops.")

6. Disconnect the power cord from the cooler to the motherboard.

7. The steps required to remove and install a cooler vary by CPU. Some units can be removed simply by opening the levers that attach them to the socket. Other units require you to use the eraser end of a pencil to carefully dislodge the unit from the retaining mechanism hooks. Typically, the cooler is latched on two sides or uses pins on all four corners. Those with latches on two sides unlatch easily after the pressure is removed from the main latch. Rather than use a screwdriver or other metal object to unlatch a stubborn latch, the preferred method is to use the eraser end of a pencil. Be careful because if you slip while releasing the latch mechanism, the motherboard might be damaged beyond repair. Also, some heat sinks are permanently glued to the processor and aren't intended to be removed. In this case, leave the heat sink attached. Decide how to proceed, and, if appropriate, carefully remove the heat sink and fan unit.

4

8. After you have removed the cooler, you can proceed to removing the CPU. Handling the CPU must be done using your full attention. Some CPUs have tiny pins on the bottom of the chip that can be bent easily and need to be handled with care. Typically, CPUs and motherboards are shipped with antistatic foam, which is an ideal surface to set CPU pins into for protection. If you don't have this shipping container, when you remove the CPU, lay it bottom-side up so that the pins aren't sitting on your work surface. Before removing the CPU, find the CPU shipping container or plan for another way to store the CPU safely.

9. You'll see a metal bar right next to the socket of the base of the CPU. This metal bar is the lever for the zero insertion force (ZIF) socket. Pull the lever out slightly and then up 90° to release the CPU. In Figure 4-1, you can see the lever about to be released from an empty LGA775 socket.

Figure 4-1   Open the socket lever

10. Carefully grasp the sides of the CPU and gently pull straight up to remove it from the socket.

11. Using an alcohol wipe, carefully remove any thermal compound (also called thermal grease) that's smeared on the top of the CPU. Wipe in a direction from the outside toward the center so thermal compound doesn't accidentally spread over the edge. You can now safely store the CPU.

12. In the same way, carefully remove any thermal compound that's smeared on the bottom of the cooler.

Now you're ready to install the new CPU or, for this lab, replace the CPU. If you're actually upgrading to a new CPU, you need to make several checks before installing the new CPU into a motherboard. You need to verify the socket type, clock speed, and multiplier match the new CPU.

In this lab, you're replacing the existing CPU; however, go through the following steps to practice as though you were installing a new, upgraded CPU:

1. Remember that the CPU is a delicate piece of equipment. If there are pins on the processor, they can be bent easily, and if the cooler isn't connected properly, you run the risk of the CPU overheating. Inspect the new CPU to verify it has no bent pins (some CPUs will have landing pads instead, in which case you will need to check the pins on the

socket for signs of damage). If you suspect the CPU has been damaged, or if the pins are bent, you might need to replace the CPU.

2. Visually inspect the socket on the motherboard for any indication as to what type of socket it is. Usually, the socket type is clearly marked. Double-check that the new CPU was manufactured for the type of socket on the motherboard. What CPU socket is this motherboard using?

_____

3. Using the manual for the CPU, determine the correct system bus speed, clock multiplier (also called the bus/core ratio), and voltage for the CPU. (Older CPUs and motherboards called the system bus the Front Side Bus [FSB], and newer Intel CPUs and motherboards refer to the system bus as the QuickPath Interconnect [QPI] in documentation.) If you don't have the manual, visit the manufacturer's website. Although some motherboards configure this information automatically, as a technician you need to be able to determine that it was done correctly. Your CPU is most likely manufactured by Intel (*ark.intel.com*) or AMD (*amd.com*). Go to the CPU's documentation or the manufacturer's website, and write down the following information:

   ◢ System bus speed:

   _____

   ◢ Multiplier or bus/core ratio:

   _____

   ◢ Voltage:

   _____

4. You might need to set the system bus speed, multiplier, and voltage in UEFI/BIOS. (For really old motherboards, these settings are changed with jumpers on the board.) Again, read the motherboard manufacturer's documentation for guidance. If you don't have the documentation, visit the manufacturer's website and download it. Most newer motherboards detect the CPU and configure everything for you automatically. How does this motherboard recognize and configure the CPU?

   _____

   _____

5. Before you install the CPU in the socket, practice raising and lowering the socket lever so that you can feel how much force is necessary to close the lever.

6. Now you're ready to install the CPU. Verify the power cable has been removed from the machine. Unlatch the ZIF lever and bring it to the open position. For AMD processors, a small, gold triangle on one corner of the processor lines up with a triangle on one corner of the socket. For Intel CPUs, the CPU and motherboard usually have notches to clearly align the CPU to the socket. Align the CPU with the socket (see Figure 4-2), and allow it to fall gently into place.

7. Carefully replace the socket lever so that force is applied to the top of the CPU and the CPU is installed securely in the socket. You need to place a little more pressure on the lever than you did when no CPU was present, but don't force it! If you have to force it, the CPU is probably not oriented in the socket correctly.

8. Now you're ready to install the cooler. First, examine the underside of the cooler for any foreign matter. New coolers often come with a thermal pad that's covered by a protective film of plastic. Always remember to remove this protective film, because if it isn't

Figure 4-2 Align the CPU over the socket

removed, you run the risk of damaging your CPU. If there's no thermal pad, gently apply a small amount of thermal compound—about the size of a grain of rice—to the center of the cooler that will come into contact with the CPU. It is not necessary to spread the compound, and it's important not to use too much. Be careful that you don't apply so much that the thermal compound later squeezes out the sides and comes in contact with the edges of the processor or the socket. You don't want grease to get down into the CPU socket. Figure 4-3 shows just about the right amount of thermal grease applied.

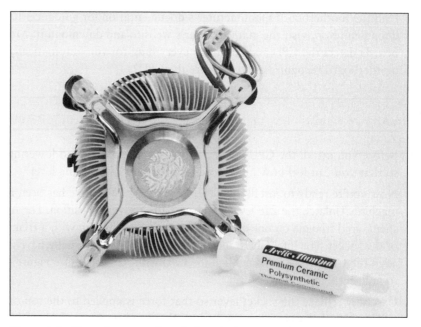

Figure 4-3 Thermal compound applied to the bottom of the heat sink assembly

> **Notes** It's important thpat no thermal compound gets down into the socket or on the bottom of the CPU. If this happens, let the paste dry for a few days and then blow it out with compressed air.

9. Carefully align the bottom of the cooler with the socket, and attach the cooler. Plug the cooler fan's power cord into the motherboard.

10. Have your instructor inspect your work to make sure the cooler is attached correctly. Booting up a system with an incorrectly attached cooler can cause damage to the processor because it will overheat

11. It's always a good idea to test the CPU operating temperature after replacing the cooler. Most UEFI/BIOS programs will display the current temperature of the CPU. Boot your machine to the UEFI/BIOS setup screen and make sure the CPU is not overheating. The CPU temperature should not exceed 43° C or 110° F

REVIEW QUESTIONS

1. Why shouldn't you use a screwdriver to remove a heat sink?

   _____

2. What is the minimum voltage of an electrostatic discharge (ESD) that you can feel?

   _____

3. What is the voltage range in which ESD can affect components?

   _____

4. What was the operating temperature of the CPU?

   _____

5. Why is it important to double-check the bottom of the heat sink before attaching it to the CPU socket?

   _____

LAB 4.2 BURN-IN TEST AND BENCHMARK A CPU

OBJECTIVES

The goal of this lab is to make sure the CPU is stable, to learn how to compare your CPU's performance in relation to other processors, and to ensure that the heat sink and fan are working correctly. After completing this lab, you will be able to:

◢ Burn-in test a CPU

◢ Benchmark a CPU

MATERIALS REQUIRED

This lab requires the following:

◢ A computer running Windows 8 or Windows 7

◢ Internet access

◢ A blank optical data disc

LAB PREPARATION

Before the lab begins, the instructor or lab assistant needs to do the following:

◢ Verify Windows starts with no errors

◢ Verify Internet access is available

ACTIVITY BACKGROUND

Today's CPUs are very reliable. In spite of this reliability, after completing a system build or installing a new CPU, you should test the CPU for stability before sending it out to the end user. This testing is known as burn-in testing or stress testing.

An unstable system might boot without any errors; however, it might show problems when a load is placed on the system. Before running a burn-in test, you should back up any important data on the computer in case the computer experiences irrecoverable problems during the test. Older systems required that you carefully monitor the temperature during a stress test so that you didn't damage the CPU if a problem caused the processor to overheat. Newer computers automatically shut down when the CPU overheats.

ESTIMATED COMPLETION TIME: 45 MINUTES

 Activity

For this lab, you download BurnInTest Professional edition trial version and run a burn-in test. After the burn-in is complete, you compare the performance of your CPU with the performance of similar CPUs. This process is called benchmarking the CPU. Follow these steps:

1. Using your favorite web browser, go to **passmark.com/download/bit_download.htm**.

2. In the BurnInTest Software Download section, click **Download BurnInTest Professional edition**. At the time this lab was written, the file name was bitpro.exe, and the version was version 8. A newer version might be available.

3. Download the file to your computer, and open it to launch the installation wizard. Respond to the UAC dialog box if necessary.

4. The Welcome to the BurnInTest Setup Wizard appears. Click **Next**.

5. Accept the License Agreement, and click **Next**.

6. Leave the default destination for the installation of the application, and click **Next**.

7. Leave the default destination for the Start Menu Folder, and click **Next**.

8. In the Ready to Install dialog box, click **Install**. After installation, remove the checkmark to view the Readme text file, and leave the checkmark to launch BurnInTest. Click **Finish**.

9. When the BurnInTest launches, you will be using the trial version, which is valid for 30 days. Click **Continue** to display BurnInTest information, as displayed in Figure 4-4.

A burn-in test allows you to simultaneously stress test all major subsystems of a computer for endurance, reliability, and stability. Follow these steps to run BurnInTest:

1. On the menu bar, click **Test,** and then click **Start Test Run**. The Getting ready to run Burn in tests warning box appears warning you that proper backups should have been performed before starting this test. Insert an optical data disc in the disc drive, and then click **OK** to start the test. The test will bring up several smaller boxes displaying the test on each of the subsystems, as shown in Figure 4-5. The test will take approximately 15 minutes.

2. After your test has completed, answer the following questions using the results from your test:

   ◢ Did your system pass or fail the burn-in test? If your system failed, use the report to outline the reasons why it failed the burn-in test:

   _____

   _____

   _____

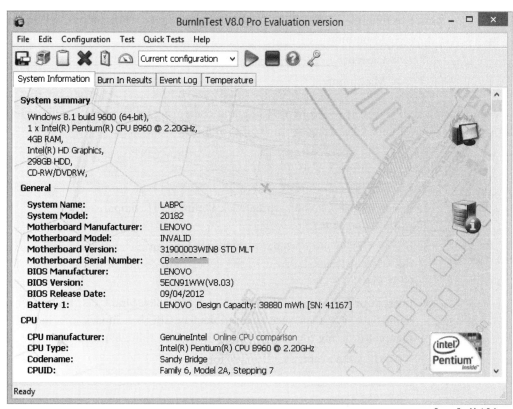

Source: PassMark Software

Figure 4-4 BurnInTest gathers system information before running the test

Source: PassMark Software

Figure 4-5 While BurnInTest runs, there is a stop button available to cancel the test

⊿ Using the Temperature tab, record the average temperatures during the burn-in test:

⊿ Minimum: _____

⊿ Current: _____

⊿ Maximum: _____

Benchmarking a CPU is the process of assessing and comparing its performance characteristics to other CPUs. To benchmark your CPU using BurnInTest Pro, follow these steps:

1. Using the System Information tab, record the CPU type:

   _____

2. Beside the CPU manufacturer, click **Online CPU comparison** to open *cpubenchmark.net*.

3. If your CPU is not automatically highlighted on the *cpubenchmark.net* website, click the **Select A Page** list arrow in the upper-right corner of the page, and choose **Searchable CPU List**.

4. Enter your CPU type in the Search box, and click **Find CPU**. Click on your CPU name once, and then once again to display CPU benchmark information, as shown in Figure 4-6. Using this information, answer the following questions:

⊿ What is the average CPU mark for your CPU?

   _____

⊿ What is the overall rank of your CPU?

   _____

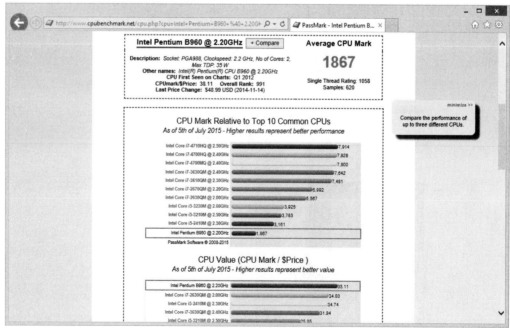

Source: PassMark Software

Figure 4-6   The CPUBenchmark.net website offers benchmarks for CPUs

REVIEW QUESTIONS

1. Why do you place a system under a load when you are testing for errors?

   _____

   _____

2. Why shouldn't a technician simply put the lowest-price CPU into a machine to save costs?

   _____

   _____

3. What is the purpose of benchmarking a CPU?

   _____

   _____

4. It seems that for the best performance, you could simply choose the fastest model in each category. Why isn't this method a good way to choose a CPU?

   _____

   _____

5. Why is it important to back up data on a computer before you burn-in test the CPU?

   _____

   _____

LAB 4.3 EXPLORE HOW CPUs WORK

OBJECTIVES

The goal of this lab is to explore the structure and design of CPUs and the way they interact with RAM on a motherboard. After completing this lab, you will be able to:

◢ Describe the relationship between processors and memory

◢ Explain the functions of primary components within a CPU

MATERIALS REQUIRED

This lab requires the following:

◢ Internet access

LAB PREPARATION

Before the lab begins, the instructor or lab assistant needs to do the following:

◢ Verify Internet access is available

ACTIVITY BACKGROUND

The CPU is often described as the brain of the computer—it performs the actual computations that give a computer its name. Similar to a human brain, the CPU is sometimes regarded as a "black box" of sorts, which is never opened and is not well understood. You put something in, and in return you get something out.

In this lab, you explore the inner workings of a computer processor and how it communicates with RAM and other components of the computer system.

ESTIMATED COMPLETION TIME: 30 MINUTES

 Activity

Complete the following steps to explore the internal structure of a CPU:

1. Use your favorite search engine to locate three articles and/or videos explaining how a CPU works and how it relates to RAM. Make sure the sources provide a detailed explanation of the various components, especially the control unit, ALUs, registers, and the various bus lines. List the URLs for each article or video here:

   _____

   _____

   _____

2. Read the articles and watch the videos, taking notes along the way. Identify the function of each primary component within the CPU:

   Control unit: _____

   _____

   Arithmetic logic unit (ALU): _____

   _____

   Registers: _____

   _____

   Bus lines: _____

   _____

3. Draw a diagram of the internal components of a CPU, and label the parts. Add arrows and notes to show the flow of information, the types of information exchanged, and the results of the computations performed.

4. Using the information you learned, answer the following questions. If necessary, check with additional sources to help you answer the questions.

   a. What two primary types of bus lines on the motherboard run between the CPU and the RAM sockets?

   _____

   b. Where do the control unit's instructions come from?

   _____

   c. What type of component inside the CPU acts like internal RAM?

   _____

   d. What component inside the CPU transfers numbers between the other components?

   _____

e. How many numbers can a bus line contain at any given time?

_____

f. Why must data be copied from the hard drive to RAM in order for it to be used in processing operations?

_____

_____

g. Why is data in RAM lost when power to the computer is turned off?

_____

_____

_____

h. List at least three different types of registers included in the CPU:

_____

_____

5. Partner with one or two other students, and compare notes. As a team, create an analogy that describes the primary CPU components and their functions. For example, an analogy might compare the control unit to a train engineer who is responsible for coordinating the operation of the train. In this analogy, the ALUs would be like the train engines, which do the actual work; the registers might be train cars, which hold data until that information is needed; and the bus lines in the CPU might be analogous to the train tracks. Now that you've seen an example, you can develop your own with the help of your team. Describe your analogy below:

_____

_____

_____

_____

REVIEW QUESTIONS

1. What are the primary components found within a CPU?

_____

_____

2. Which component of the CPU performs the actual calculations?

_____

3. Which device inside the computer case stores information after power is turned off?

_____

4. Which component inside the CPU directs the processor's activities?

_____

LAB 4.4 RESEARCH A RAM UPGRADE ON THE WEB

OBJECTIVES

The goal of this lab is to learn how to find important information about RAM that you need when upgrading memory. After completing this lab, you will be able to:

⬧ Find documentation on your system's motherboard

⬧ Read documentation for your system's RAM specifications

⬧ Search the web for RAM prices and availability

MATERIALS REQUIRED

This lab requires the following:

⬧ A computer running Windows 8 or Windows 7, with CPU-Z installed (CPU-Z was installed in the chapter, "All About Motherboards")

⬧ Internet access

LAB PREPARATION

Before the lab begins, the instructor or lab assistant needs to do the following:

⬧ Verify Windows starts with no errors

⬧ Verify CPU-Z is installed

⬧ Verify Internet access is available

ACTIVITY BACKGROUND

As an IT technician, you will find that a computer's performance can often be improved by installing more RAM. Upgrading the system RAM is probably one of the easiest and most cost-effective upgrades that you can perform on a workstation. To install RAM, you need to know not only the maximum amount of memory you can install, but also which memory technology will match the motherboard. Ignoring the demands of the motherboard or compatibility with existing memory modules may jeopardize the goal of increased performance. In this lab, you determine the characteristics of the memory that is currently installed and the maximum memory the motherboard can support. Then you research the web to find the memory you need for the upgrade and the price of the upgrade.

> **ESTIMATED COMPLETION TIME: 30 MINUTES**

 Activity

Follow these steps to find information about the installed RAM and motherboard in your system:

1. Open the CPU-Z software installed on your computer to determine the attributes of the RAM currently installed. Using information on the Memory tab, record the following attributes of RAM here:

    ⬧ RAM type: _____

    ⬧ RAM size: _____

    ⬧ RAM channels #: _____

◢ DRAM frequency: _____

◢ CAS# latency (CL) rating: _____

◢ RAS# to CAS# delay rating: _____

2. Open the SPD tab, and complete the following table for each memory slot. If a slot is empty, write "empty" across that row in the table.

Slot #	Memory Type	Module Size	Max Bandwidth	Speed	Manufacturer
1					
2					
3					
4					

> **Notes** CPU-Z clocks the detected speed of each module and reports that information in the same cell as the Max bandwidth. The actual speed of a DDR, DDR2, or DDR3 module, however, will be twice the number reported by the software because these modules transfer data on both the upside and the downside of the clock signal.

3. Using skills you learned in previous lab activities, determine your motherboard's manufacturer and model number, and record that information here. (If you don't have the motherboard documentation available, search for it on the web.)

◢ Manufacturer: _____

◢ Model #: _____

Use the documentation for your motherboard or research your motherboard on the web to answer these questions:

1. Does your motherboard support dual, triple, or quad channels? Explain how this affects the memory modules you need to install:

_____

_____

2. What type (or types) of memory does your motherboard support? Be sure to include details such as physical type (for example, DDR3 or DDR4), speed, ECC or non-ECC, un-buffered, or registered:

_____

_____

_____

_____

_____

3. What is the maximum amount of memory your motherboard supports?

_____

4. To install the maximum amount of memory the board supports, it might be necessary to replace a smaller-size module with a larger-size module. Can you use the existing memory modules to upgrade to the maximum amount of supported memory? Explain your answer:

   _____

   _____

5. What size and how many memory modules would be needed to upgrade your system to the maximum amount of supported memory and make use of the dual, triple, or quad channels that the board might support?

   _____

Now that you have the necessary information about your system's memory, go to *pricewatch.com*, *newegg.com*, or a similar website, and answer the following questions:

1. Suppose you need to replace all the modules on the board. What size and how many modules should you purchase? What is the total price of the upgrade? Be sure to take advantage of dual, triple, or quad channels the board might support.

   _____

2. Suppose you want to install the maximum amount of memory the board supports and, if possible, use the old modules already installed. What size and how many modules should you purchase? What is the total price of the upgrade?

   _____

3. If there are empty memory slots on your motherboard, you might want to buy additional memory to fill these empty slots. Search for matching modules of the same style, speed, and latency ratings that are currently installed in your system. List the details and price of one memory module that matches a module already installed in your system:

   _____

Explore other types of memory on *pricewatch.com*, *newegg.com*, *crucial.com*, or another similar website, and answer the following questions:

1. On average, what is the least expensive type of memory per MB you can find? What is its price?

   _____

2. On average, what is the most expensive type of memory per MB you can find? What is its price?

   _____

3. Pick one of the DIMMs that you selected for purchase in this lab. Search for a SO-DIMM for a laptop computer that is of the same size (in MB or GB), speed, and type (DDR2, DDR3, or DDR4) as the DIMM. Do you find that SO-DIMM for a laptop is more or less expensive than an equivalent DIMM for a desktop computer? List the DIMM and SO-DIMM you are comparing, and give their prices:

   _____

   _____

REVIEW QUESTIONS

1. Why might you want to upgrade RAM on a system?

   _____

   _____

2. Why is it important to match the latencies of the older modules to the newer modules?

   _____

   _____

3. What must be true before a motherboard can take advantage of the triple memory channels on the board?

   _____

4. Explain the following description of a memory module: DDR3 PC10600 1333MHz:

   _____

   _____

5. Explain the differences between ECC memory and non-ECC memory:

   _____

   _____

   _____

LAB 4.5 BENCHMARK RAM AND PLAN AN UPGRADE

OBJECTIVES

The goal of this lab is to observe the effects of a memory upgrade (or downgrade) on the speed of your system, and to plan and price a memory upgrade. After completing this lab, you will be able to:

◢ Install and remove RAM modules and record the effects

◢ Determine how much and what kind of memory is needed for an upgrade

MATERIALS REQUIRED

This lab requires the following:

◢ Windows 8 or Windows 7 operating system

◢ An account with administrator privileges

◢ Internet access

◢ A computer designated for disassembly

◢ A computer toolkit and ESD strap

◢ A clock with a second hand or a smartphone stopwatch app to be used to measure the computer boot time

◢ One of the following:

- Additional memory module compatible with your system
- A system with two memory modules already installed
- Access to a partner's system that has a memory module compatible with yours

LAB PREPARATION

Before the lab begins, the instructor or lab assistant needs to do the following:

◢ Verify a computer designated for disassembly is available

◢ Verify each student has access to a user account with administrator privileges

◢ Verify the student has available two compatible memory modules. This can be done in one of three ways:

- The instructor provides an additional compatible memory module for each student
- The student system already has two or more memory modules installed
- The student works with a partner having a system with a compatible memory module

◢ Verify each student has a clock or watch with a second hand or a smartphone stopwatch app to measure the system boot time

◢ Verify Internet access is available

ACTIVITY BACKGROUND

In Part 1 of this lab, you time how long it takes your system to boot up. Then you download, install, and run NovaBench to benchmark the speed of your system. In Part 2, you add or remove RAM from your system, restart it, and time how long it takes your system to boot after the memory change. In Part 3, you run NovaBench again, and compare the results. In Part 4, you research the documentation for your system to gather information on its memory subsystem and determine the maximum amount of RAM it will accept. Finally, you shop online to determine the cost of the upgrade.

ESTIMATED COMPLETION TIME: 45 MINUTES

 Activity

PART 1: USE NOVABENCH TO BENCHMARK THE SYSTEM

In this part of the lab, you time how long it takes your system to boot up:

1. Power off your computer if it is not already powered off.
2. Prepare your stopwatch so that you will be ready to start timing as soon as you press the power button on your computer.
3. Start your computer, and immediately start your stopwatch. Time how long it takes for the Windows sign-in screen (or desktop, if set to automatic logon) to appear, and record the time:

_____

Follow these steps to download, install, and run NovaBench on your computer:

1. Sign in to your computer with a user account that has administrator privileges.
2. Use your web browser to go to **novabench.com**.

3. Click **Download Now**. What is the version and size (MB) of the available download for Windows?

_____

4. To download NovaBench, click the Windows **Download Now** button (make sure it's the button with the Windows icon, not an ad near the download button). Download the file to your computer. What is the name of the file?

_____

5. To install the application, double-click the application file for NovaBench in the Downloads folder. If necessary, respond to the UAC dialog box.

6. In the License Agreement dialog box, select **I accept the agreement**, and then click **Next**.

7. For both the Destination Location and Start Menu Folder, keep the default locations, and click **Next**.

8. When the Ready to Install dialog box comes up, click **Install** to continue the installation.

9. When the installation is complete, keep the check box to launch NovaBench selected, and click **Finish**. NovaBench will open on your desktop (see Figure 4-7).

10. Take a minute to explore the various testing options under the Tests menu. What two tests are available under Hardware Tests?

_____

_____

Source: Novawave Inc.

Figure 4-7   The Start Page of NovaBench displays system information

Now you are ready to begin the testing. Follow these steps to run the NovaBench tests and record the results:

1. Click **Start Benchmark Tests**.

2. NovaBench will check to see if you have any programs running that could interfere with the testing, and will prompt you to close them. After closing the recommended programs (if any), click **Proceed** to continue. You will see the progress bars appear as NovaBench tests various components of your system.

3. When complete, the NovaBench Score results screen will appear (see Figure 4-8). Using this data, record the following information:

◢ List the four main categories that were tested, and record their scores:

_____

_____

_____

_____

◢ Record the RAM speed in MB/s:

_____

◢ Record the drive write speed in MB/s:

_____

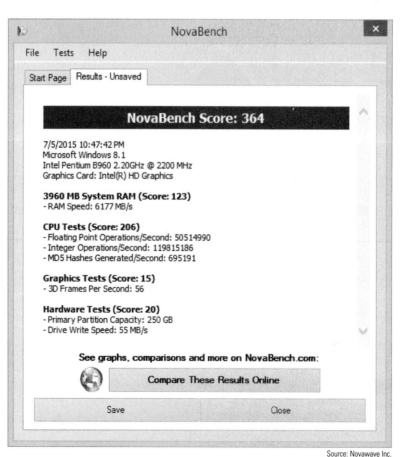

Figure 4-8 NovaBench offers scores of four components of your system and an overall score of your system

PART 2: ADD OR REMOVE RAM FROM YOUR COMPUTER

If your computer started with two or more RAM modules, you now remove the extra module(s), leaving one in your system. If your computer started with one RAM module, you now install a second module. You upgrade (or downgrade) the memory by following these steps:

1. Shut down your system and remove all exterior cabling. Press and hold the power button for three seconds to drain any remaining power.

2. Be sure you're wearing your ESD strap. Open the system case, and locate the slots for memory modules.

3. Remove any data cabling and other devices preventing you from accessing the slots. Answer the following questions:

   ◢ How many modules are currently installed?

   _____

   ◢ Are there any empty slots to install an additional module?

   _____

4. Notice that the slots have a retaining mechanism at each end to secure each module in the slot. Typically, these mechanisms are plastic levers that you spread outward to unseat and remove the module. Modules are inserted and removed straight up and down. Spread the plastic levers apart before inserting or removing the memory modules.

5. Examine an empty slot and note the raised ridges that line up with notches on the memory module's pin edge. Because modules are designed to be inserted in only one orientation, these ridges prevent them from being inserted incorrectly.

6. If you are inserting a module, verify the module is oriented correctly to the slot. Insert the module, and gently but firmly push it in. If you are removing a module, carefully spread the levers apart, and remove the module.

7. Reassemble your system. Have your instructor inspect your work before putting the case back together.

PART 3: COMPARE BENCHMARK RESULTS

In this part of the lab, you again time how long it takes for your computer to boot. Then, you run NovaBench, and compare the results to those from before the memory change. Follow these steps:

1. Prepare your stopwatch so that you will be ready to start timing as soon as you press the power button on your computer.

2. Start your computer and immediately start your stopwatch. Time how long it takes for the Windows sign-in screen (or desktop) to appear, and record the time here:

   _____

   ◢ How much faster did your computer boot with more memory, or how much slower did it boot with less memory?

   _____

3. Start NovaBench from the Start Menu, and click **Start Benchmark Tests**. After closing the recommended programs (if any), click **Proceed** to continue.

4. When complete, the NovaBench Score results screen will appear. Using this data, record the following information:

◢ Record the score for each of the four categories and the difference from the first information :

_____

_____

_____

_____

◢ Record the RAM speed in MB/s and the difference from the first test:

_____

◢ Record the drive write speed in MB/s and the difference from the first test:

_____

5. Repeat Part 2 to restore your computer to its original condition when you started this lab.

PART 4: PLAN AND PRICE A MAXIMUM MEMORY UPGRADE

In this part of the lab, you use your web browser to research the documentation for your system to gather information on its memory subsystem and to determine the maximum amount of RAM it will accept.

The best way to do this is to go to the manufacturer's website and look for the support page. In most cases, it is best to search using the serial number or service tag number of your system, then look for any links referring to upgrades or system configuration. After you have found the information on upgrading your memory, answer the following questions:

1. What is the type and maximum speed of RAM your hardware supports, for example DDR3 1600 (PC3 12800)?

_____

2. How many total memory slots are on your motherboard?

_____

3. What is the maximum amount of RAM (GB) each slot supports?

_____

4. What is the maximum amount of RAM (GB) your system supports?

_____

5. Will you need to remove any existing RAM to upgrade to the system maximum?

_____

6. What is the maximum amount of RAM your OS supports?

_____

7. Taking into account the above information, what type of memory modules and how many of each will you need to buy to upgrade your system to maximum RAM at maximum speed?

_____

You are now ready to shop online for the best price for your RAM upgrade. Using quality, name-brand RAM for your upgrade will help avoid potential problems. Record the total price of the RAM upgrade if you were to purchase it from the following vendors:

◢ Your system manufacturer's website: _____

◢ *kingston.com*: _____

◢ *memory4less.com*: _____

REVIEW QUESTIONS

1. What feature is used on memory slots and modules to prevent modules from being inserted incorrectly?

_____

_____

2. Why was the drive write speed affected by the RAM?

_____

_____

_____

3. Why does the amount of RAM installed affect boot time?

_____

_____

4. Which website gave you the best buy for the memory upgrade? Which website would you use to make the purchase? Why?

_____

_____

CHAPTER 5

Supporting the Power System and Troubleshooting Computers

Labs included in this chapter:

- **Lab 5.1:** Measure the Output of Your Power Supply
- **Lab 5.2:** Choose the Right Power Supply
- **Lab 5.3:** Replace a Power Supply
- **Lab 5.4:** Measure Temperature and Adjust Fan Speed
- **Lab 5.5:** Choose a CPU Cooling Solution
- **Lab 5.6:** Troubleshoot Memory Problems
- **Lab 5.7:** Evaluate Troubleshooting Processes
- **Lab 5.8:** Diagnose Simple Hardware Boot Problems
- **Lab 5.9:** Troubleshoot General Computer Problems

LAB 5.1 MEASURE THE OUTPUT OF YOUR POWER SUPPLY

OBJECTIVES

The goal of this lab is to use a multimeter to measure the voltages provided by a power supply. After completing this lab, you will be able to:

▲ Use a multimeter

▲ Measure voltage provided by a power supply

MATERIALS REQUIRED

This lab requires the following:

▲ A computer designated for this lab

▲ A computer toolkit with ESD strap

▲ A multimeter

▲ Access to the online content "Electricity and Multimeters," downloaded from the companion website at *cengagebrain.com*. For more information, see the Preface.

▲ A workgroup of two to four students

LAB PREPARATION

Before the lab begins, the instructor or lab assistant needs to do the following:

▲ Announce to students that before they come to lab, they should read the online content "Electricity and Multimeters." It is also suggested that students bring this content to class in printed form.

ACTIVITY BACKGROUND

In most situations, if you suspect a problem with a power supply, you simply exchange it for a known good one. In a few instances, however, you might want to measure your power supply's output by using a multimeter.

A multimeter is an electrical tool that performs several tests. It can typically measure continuity, resistance, and voltage. It might have a digital or an analog meter that displays output. It also has two leads used to contact the component you're testing. The various models of multimeters each work slightly differently. Follow the correct procedure for your specific multimeter. In this lab, you measure the electrical voltage supplied to the motherboard and hard drives. Follow your computer lab's posted safety procedures when completing this lab.

ESTIMATED COMPLETION TIME: 30 MINUTES

 Activity

Using your multimeter, measure the power output to your system's motherboard and to a disc drive, and then fill in the following charts that apply to your system. Note that the column headings "Red Lead" and "Black Lead" refer to the color of the probes.

> ⚡ **Caution** Be sure you have your multimeter set to measure voltage, not resistance (ohms) or current (amps). If the multimeter is set to measure current, you might damage the power supply, the motherboard, or both.

Again, detailed directions for using a multimeter can be found in the online content "Electricity and Multimeters." Be very careful as you work inside the computer case with the power on. Don't touch any components other than those described in the steps.

The following steps outline the basic procedure for using a multimeter:

1. Remove the cover from the computer case.

2. Set the multimeter to measure voltage of approximately 20 V, and set the AC/DC switch to DC. Insert the black probe into the meter's 2 jack and the red probe into the meter's 1 jack.

3. Turn on the multimeter, and then turn on the computer.

4. Measure each circuit by placing a red probe on the lead and a black probe on ground (see Figure 5-1).

Figure 5-1 A multimeter measuring voltage on an ATX motherboard

5. If you're using an older ATX power supply with a 20-pin P1 connector, compare your connector with the 20-pin P1 power connector on an ATX motherboard shown in Figure 5-2. Refer to Table 5-1 for the purpose of each pin.

Figure 5-2   P1 20-pin power connection on an ATX motherboard

Unnotched Side			Notched Side		
Lead or Pin	Description	Acceptable Range (Volts = V)	Lead or Pin	Description	Acceptable Range (Volts = V)
1	+3.3 V	+3.1 to +3.5 V	11	+3.3 V	+3.1 to +3.5 V
2	+3.3 V	+3.1 to +3.5 V	12	−12 V	−10.8 to −13.2 V
3	Black ground		13	Black ground	
4	+5 V	+4.5 to +5.5 V	14	Power supply on	
5	Black ground		15	Black ground	
6	+5 V	+4.5 to +5.5 V	16	Black ground	
7	Black ground		17	Black ground	
8	Power good		18	−5 V	−4.5 to −5.5 V
9	+5 V standby	+4.5 to +5.5 V	19	+5 V	+4.5 to +5.5 V
10	+12 V	+10.8 to +13.2 V	20	+5 V	+4.5 to +5.5 V

Table 5-1   20 leads to the ATX motherboard from the ATX power supply

6. If you are working with a 20-pin P1 connector on an ATX motherboard, complete the following chart:

Red Lead (Positive)	Black Lead (Ground)	Voltage Measure
10	7	
10	5	
10	3	
10	17	

Red Lead (Positive)	Black Lead (Ground)	Voltage Measure
10	16	
10	15	
10	13	
9	Ground	
6	Ground	
4	Ground	
2	Ground	
1	Ground	
20	Ground	
19	Ground	
18	Ground	
12	Ground	
11	Ground	

7. A newer ATX Version 2.2 motherboard and power supply use a 24-pin P1 connector. This connector is designed so that the power supply monitors the range of voltages provided to the motherboard and halts the motherboard if voltages are inadequate. Therefore, measuring voltage for a 24-pin P1 connector isn't usually necessary. However, if you have access only to a 24-pin P1 system, you can still complete this lab, using the chart in Step 8. Figure 5-3 shows the 24-pin P1 power connector for an ATX motherboard, and the purposes of the pins are listed in Table 5-2. The colors listed are the colors of the wires on the P1 power connector to the power supply, which are shown in Figure 5-4.

Figure 5-3 ATX 24-pin P1 power connector on the motherboard

Lead or Pin	Description and Signal	Acceptable Range (Volts = V)
1	Orange, +3.3 V	3.2 to 3.5 V
2	Orange, +3.3 V	3.2 to 3.5 V
3	Black, COM	
4	Red, +5 V	4.75 to 5.25 V
5	Black, COM	
6	Red, +5 V	4.75 to 5.25 V

Table 5-2 ATX 24-pin P1 power connector pinouts (continues)

Lead or Pin	Description and Signal	Acceptable Range (Volts = V)
7	Black, COM	
8	Gray, Power OK	Voltages are in acceptable range
9	Purple, +5 V	Standby voltage always on
10	Yellow, +12 V	11.4 to 12.6 V
11	Yellow, +12 V	11.4 to 12.6 V
12	Orange, +3.3 V	3.2 to 3.5 V
13	Orange/Brown, +3.3 V	3.2 to 3.5 V
14	Blue, −12 V	−10.8 to −13.2 V
15	Black, COM	
16	Green, Signal	
17	Black, COM	
18	Black, COM	
19	Black, COM	
20	White, NC	
21	Red, +5 V	4.75 to 5.25 V
22	Red, +5 V	4.75 to 5.25 V
23	Red, +5 V	4.75 to 5.25 V
24	Black, COM	

Table 5-2   ATX 24-pin P1 power connector pinouts (continued)

1   13

Orange — +3.3V   +3.3V — Orange/Brown
Orange — +3.3V   −12V — Blue
Black — COM   COM — Black
Red — +5V   PS_ON# — Green
Black — COM   COM — Black
Red — +5V   COM — Black
Black — COM   COM — Black
Gray — PWR_ON   NC — White
Purple — +5VSB   +5V — Red
Yellow — +12V1   +5V — Red
Yellow — +12V1   +5V — Red
Orange — +3.3V   COM — Black

Figure 5-4   P1 24-pin power connection follows ATX Version 2.2 and higher standards

8. If you are working with a 24-pin P1 ATX motherboard, complete the following chart:

Red Lead (Positive)	Black Lead (Ground)	Voltage Measure
1	Ground	
2	Ground	
4	Ground	
6	Ground	
9	Ground	
10	Ground	
11	Ground	
12	Ground	
13	Ground	
14	Ground	
21	Ground	
22	Ground	
23	Ground	

9. A 4-pin Molex power connector is used to provide power to some older hard drives or other devices. Table 5-3 shows the pinouts for this type connector.

Lead or Pin	Description and Signal	Acceptable Ranges (Volts=V)
1	Yellow, +12 V	11.4 to 12.6 V
2	Black, ground	
3	Black, ground	
4	Red, +5 V	4.75 to 5.25 V

Table 5-3 Pinouts for a 4-pin Molex power connector

10. Using a 4-pin Molex power connector, complete the following chart:

Red Lead	Black Lead	Voltage Measure
1	3	
4	2	

11. Turn off the computer and replace the cover.

CRITICAL THINKING (ADDITIONAL 15 MINUTES)

If a laptop battery doesn't charge correctly, the problem might be the battery, the motherboard, or the AC adapter. The voltage output of an AC adapter can be tested using a multimeter. Do the following to learn more:

1. Unplug the AC adapter from the laptop. Plug the AC adapter into a wall outlet.

2. Using a multimeter, set the meter to measure voltage in the range of 1 to 20 V DC range.

3. Place the red probe of the multimeter in the center of the DC connector of the AC adapter. Place the black probe on the outside cylinder of the DC connector.

   ◢ What is the DC voltage measurement?

   _____

   ◢ Is the value within 5 percent of the expected voltage according to the laptop documentation?

   _____

REVIEW QUESTIONS

1. What is the electrical voltage from a house outlet to a computer's power supply?

   _____

2. What voltages are supplied by the power supply on your system?

   _____

3. What model of multimeter are you using?

   _____

4. List the steps to set your multimeter to measure resistance:

   _____

   _____

   _____

5. Besides voltage and resistance, what else can your multimeter measure?

   _____

LAB 5.2 CHOOSE THE RIGHT POWER SUPPLY

OBJECTIVES

The goal of this lab is to locate documentation on the Internet so that you can determine how much power a system as a whole uses. You can use this information to decide the wattage rating of the power supply you need to purchase for a new or upgraded system. After completing this lab, you will be able to:

◢ Calculate the total wattage requirements for a system

◢ Choose the correct type and rating of a power supply

MATERIALS REQUIRED

This lab requires the following:

◢ A computer designated for disassembly

◢ A computer toolkit with ESD strap

◢ A workgroup of two or three students or individual students

⊿ Access to a printer

⊿ Optional: Internet access

LAB PREPARATION

Before the lab begins, the instructor or lab assistant needs to do the following:

⊿ Verify a computer designated for disassembly is available for each student or workgroup

⊿ Optional: Verify Internet access is available

ACTIVITY BACKGROUND

When selecting a power supply for a computer system, you must take many factors into account. It's important to look at the system's components as a whole and to consider how the system will be used. You might be tempted to simply purchase a power supply that has a very high wattage rating, but this choice isn't always the most economical. The typical efficiency rating of a power supply is 60 percent to 70 percent. Usually, this rating means 30 percent to 40 percent of the power is blowing out of the case as wasted heat. You want to keep waste to a minimum. On the other hand, if you intend to upgrade your system, buying an overrated power supply might be wise.

Running a system with an inadequate power supply can cause the power supply to wear out faster than normal. Also, an inadequate power supply can cause a system to reboot at odd times and experience other types of intermittent errors. It pays to install a correctly rated power supply for a system.

5

ESTIMATED COMPLETION TIME: 45 MINUTES

 Activity

1. The following chart shows the estimated power requirements for components inside a computer case. These estimates come from the website FirePower Technology, Inc., at *firepower-technology.com*. Open your computer's case, and locate each component listed in the following chart. Record how many components are present. Note that some entries will be zero.

Component	Wattage Requirement	Number Present	Total Wattage
AGP video card	30 W–50 W		
PCI Express video card	50 W–100 W (one power connector)		
	150 W–300 W (two power connectors)		
Average PCI card	5 W–10 W		
DVD or CD drive	20 W–30 W		
Hard drive	15 W–30 W		
Case fan or CPU fan	3 W (each)		
Motherboard (without CPU or RAM)	50 W–150 W		
RAM module	15 W per stick of RAM		
Processor	80 W–140 W		
		Total Wattage	

2. To fill in the Total Wattage column, first check the manufacturer's website for each component to find the exact wattage amounts. If this information isn't available, use the estimate provided or the median of the estimate. Add the wattage for all components to come up with the total wattage. Record the system's total wattage in the last row of the chart.

3. Multiply the total wattage by 1.5 to reflect a 50 percent increase. This multiplier takes into account the overhead of the system, today's technology demands, and the goal of running a system at about 30 percent to 70 percent of its maximum capacity. What is your calculated total wattage, taking into account the required overhead?

4. Now look at the power supply, and make sure it has the number and type of connectors needed for your system. Figure 5-5 can help you identify connectors.

Figure 5-5   ATX power supply with connectors

5. Fill in the following chart to show the quantity of currently available power connectors as well as how many are needed for your system:

Connector	Current Quantity	Quantity Needed
EIDE drive connectors (Molex)		
Floppy drive connectors (Berg)		
SATA connectors		
ATX connector (20 or 24 pins)		
Auxiliary power (4, 6, or 8 pins)		
PCIe connector		

6. Look on the power supply label for the peak load rating in watts. What is this value?

7. Based on what you have learned in this lab, is the power supply adequate for the system? Why or why not?

CRITICAL THINKING (ADDITIONAL 30 MINUTES)

1. Many power supply manufacturers offer a PSU wattage calculator on their websites that can save you time when deciding on the wattage requirements. Go to **extreme.outervision .com/psucalculator.jsp** and use the wattage calculator to determine the wattage requirements for your system. What is the minimum and recommended PSU wattage given by the calculator? How do these values compare with your own manual calculations?

2. Suppose your power supply stops working, and you must buy a replacement. Search the Internet for a comparable power supply. The cost of power supplies varies widely. For example, a 400 W power supply can cost from $15 to $115. The difference in quality can be judged partly by the weight of the power supply because, in general, the heavier it is, the more transistors it has and the more heavy-duty the transistors are, which makes for a better power supply. Another factor to consider is noise level; quiet power supplies can be more expensive than noisy ones. Print two webpages showing a high-end and a low-end power supply that would meet your system's needs. Which power supply would you recommend purchasing for your system, and why?

REVIEW QUESTIONS

1. The estimated wattages for individual components were provided in the lab. How can you find the actual wattage for each component?

2. What is the typical efficiency rating for a power supply?

3. Are there any connectors your system needs that the power supply doesn't have? If so, what are they?

4. Are there any connectors provided by the power supply that your system isn't using? If so, what are they?

5. Why is it important to buy a power supply that's close to the requirements for your system instead of buying a higher-wattage power supply? Under what circumstances might it be better to buy a higher-wattage power supply?

_____

_____

6. Why would you need to be concerned with your power supply having the capability of providing power directly to the PCIe card(s)?

_____

_____

_____

LAB 5.3 REPLACE A POWER SUPPLY

OBJECTIVES

The goal of this lab is to replace a power supply. After completing this lab, you will be able to:

◢ Identify the power supply

◢ Remove the power supply from the case

◢ Install a new power supply and new cabling

MATERIALS REQUIRED

This lab requires the following:

◢ A computer designated for this lab

◢ A computer toolkit with ESD strap

◢ A workgroup of two to four students

LAB PREPARATION

Before the lab begins, the instructor or lab assistant needs to do the following:

◢ Verify a computer designated for disassembly is available for each workgroup

ACTIVITY BACKGROUND

This lab tests your ability to remove and replace a power supply. Power supplies, as a rule, are considered field replaceable units (FRUs). To save time and avoid the danger of working inside power supplies, IT technicians don't repair power supplies; they replace them. If you find that a power supply is faulty, replace it with a compatible power supply, and then send the original off to be reconditioned or recycled.

ESTIMATED COMPLETION TIME: 30 MINUTES

 Activity

Follow these steps to examine and replace a power supply:

1. Turn the computer off, and unplug the power cord. Press the power button for three seconds to drain any remaining power.

2. Disconnect all peripherals, and remove the case cover.

3. Examine the label on the power supply. Answer the following questions:

   ◢ What is the peak load rating of the power supply? A system requiring more power than the power supply provides can contribute to an early failure of the power supply.

   _____

   ◢ How many and what type of power connectors does the power supply provide? (For example, six SATA connectors.)

   _____

   _____

   _____

   ◢ How many and what type of power connectors is the system currently using?

   _____

   _____

   ◢ What is the form factor of the power supply?

   _____

4. Remove the cabling and the power supply. Usually the power supply is held in place by four screws in the back of the case and perhaps a tab under the power supply. Some systems might use other methods of securing the power supply.

5. Examine the new power supply provided by your instructor, or swap your power supply with another workgroup. Answer the following questions:

   ◢ What is the form factor of this new power supply?

   _____

   ◢ What is the power rating of this new power supply?

   _____

   ◢ Does the power supply provide all the power connectors the system needs?

   _____

   ◢ Will this new power supply satisfy the needs of your system?

   _____

6. Install the new power supply. Ask your instructor to check your work before you close the case. This check is crucial because some older power supplies must be connected correctly to ensure that they aren't damaged when they're turned on.

7. Close the case, reattach the peripherals, and test the system.

REVIEW QUESTIONS

1. How many connectors linked your original power supply to the motherboard?

   _____

2. How many watts of peak power could the original power supply provide?

   _____

3. Why is it important to be able to calculate the peak power required for all components?

   _____

4. What are two reasons that IT technicians don't usually repair a power supply?

   _____

5. What term is used to refer to components that are commonly replaced but not repaired?

   _____

6. What is the most efficient way to determine whether your power supply is bad?

   _____

LAB 5.4 MEASURE TEMPERATURE AND ADJUST FAN SPEED

OBJECTIVES

This goal of this lab is to become familiar with thermal issues in your computer and how to adjust the system to compensate for them. After completing this lab, you will be able to:

◢ Access a system's temperature data

◢ Adjust the speed of the cooling fans

MATERIALS REQUIRED

This lab requires the following:

◢ A computer running Windows 8 or Windows 7

◢ Internet access

◢ SpeedFan software downloaded from *filehippo.com/download_speedfan*

LAB PREPARATION

Before the lab begins, the instructor or lab assistant needs to do the following:

◢ Verify Windows starts with no errors

◢ Verify Internet access is available

ACTIVITY BACKGROUND

In the course of your career as a computer technician you will become familiar with the problems that heat causes in a computer system. A computer's CPU is particularly susceptible to damage from excessive heat, but hard drives, RAM chips, video cards, and just about any other component you can think of are all susceptible to damage. If you suspect a computer is having a problem with overheating, you can install diagnostic software to monitor the temperatures from the Windows desktop. If the feature is enabled in UEFI/ BIOS setup, you can also use this software to monitor and control the computer's fans.

In this lab, you use diagnostic software to look at the readouts from the computer's built-in temperature sensors and then adjust the temperature thresholds, which can be used to alter the behavior of the computer's fans in order to improve their efficiency.

Activity

Follow these steps to install SpeedFan:

1. Go to **filehippo.com/download_speedfan**. At the time this lab was written, the latest version of SpeedFan is Version 4.51.

2. Click **Download Latest Version (2.12 MB)** to start the download. Note that several other ad-supported download buttons are displayed on this webpage, and if clicked, they will download other files to your computer that are unrelated to this lab. Be careful to click the correct Download button for the SpeedFan freeware. At the time of this writing, the SpeedFan Download button includes the file size (2.12 MB). Save the file to your Downloads folder.

3. Double-click the **instspeedfan451.exe** file in the Downloads folder. (The .exe file might be named slightly differently if there is a newer version available.) Respond to the UAC dialog box, if necessary. Leave the default settings for SpeedFan, but remove any unnecessary software that attempts to install with SpeedFan, such as Google Chrome toolbar. When the installation is complete, click **Close**.

After installing the SpeedFan utility, follow these steps to record information about the cooling system on your computer:

1. Open the SpeedFan software by double-clicking the SpeedFan icon on the desktop. Respond to the UAC dialog box, if necessary. Click **Close** to close the Hint dialog box.

2. Figure 5-6 shows the Readings tab of SpeedFan. Using this tab, record the current fan speeds and temperatures for your computer:

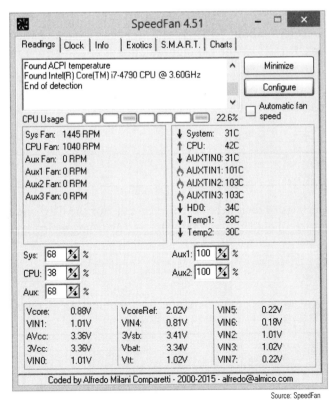

Source: SpeedFan

Figure 5-6 The Readings tab of SpeedFan displays current fan speeds and temperatures

_____

_____

_____

3. Take a screen shot of the SpeedFan window displaying the Readings tab. Save this to your desktop to compare readings after changing settings.

Use the SpeedFan program to adjust the settings for the fans in your computer. You can raise the desired temperature to make a fan quieter, or lower the desired temperature if your computer is overheating.

1. Click the **Configure** button to open the Configure dialog box.

2. Click the **Fan Control** tab and place a checkmark to select the **Advanced fan control** option.

3. To create a new fan controller, click **Add**. Enter the name **Test** and click **OK**. In this lab, you will not activate the fan controller. Some computers require alterations be made in UEFI/BIOS in order for this feature to work. Also, it's easy to damage your computer equipment if the settings aren't carefully configured and monitored for a while. However, you can walk through the steps for creating a Test fan controller to see how it's done.

4. Click **Test** to view settings options for this fan controller.

5. Select **SUM of speeds** as your method. To add temperature sensors into your configuration, click **Add** under the Temperatures box.

6. Create a setting using the temperature of the processor. For multicore processors, there will be a temperature for each core. To do this, select the CPU from the list of available temperature sensors, and click **OK** to add it to this fan controller. Repeat this step for each of the cores of your processor.

7. Return to the **Temperatures** tab, and click the CPU to view the settings options. Turn down the **Desired** temperature to about **20°C (68°F)**, and turn down the **Warning** temperature to about 25°C (77°F). Repeat for each of the cores of your processor. Click **OK** to close the Configure dialog box and return to the SpeedFan main display.

8. On the Readings tab, how do the readings compare with the initial readings when you first opened SpeedFan? View the screen shot you took earlier in the lab to make the comparison.

_____

_____

9. Return the fan settings to their default temperatures. For the CPU and each core, Desired temperatures should be 40°C (104°F), and Warning temperatures should be 50°C (122°F).

REVIEW QUESTIONS

1. Where does SpeedFan get the information it uses to monitor the computer?

_____

_____

2. Why would you use a utility such as SpeedFan?

_____

_____

_____

_____

3. In what situations would you want to adjust the speed of a fan on your computer?

_____

_____

4. Is it possible to damage a computer with a utility like SpeedFan? How?

_____

_____

LAB 5.5 CHOOSE A CPU COOLING SOLUTION

OBJECTIVES

Matching a CPU to an appropriate fan or other cooling system is a critical part of the process for replacing a CPU. The goal of this lab is to practice researching cooling options for a specific CPU. After completing this lab, you will be able to:

◢ Choose a heat sink and fan appropriate for your CPU

MATERIALS REQUIRED

This lab requires the following:

◢ A computer running Windows 8 or Windows 7

◢ Internet access

LAB PREPARATION

Before the lab begins, the instructor or lab assistant needs to do the following:

◢ Verify Windows starts with no errors

◢ Verify Internet access is available

ACTIVITY BACKGROUND

A CPU handles a lot of information in its internal circuitry. Data processed in a CPU is represented by bits, which are 0s and 1s. Each transistor in a CPU can hold 1 bit, and today's CPUs contain several trillion transistors. Transistors can produce a large amount of heat, which needs to be dissipated in some way in order to keep the CPU operating temperature at an acceptable level. Most commonly, a heat sink and fan are used to reduce heat in a CPU. The heat sink is a metal unit that conducts heat away from the CPU and dissipates that heat into the air. A fan forces the hot air over the top or the side of the heat sink. Some fans are variable-speed fans that adjust their speeds according to the CPU's temperature.

The fan and heat sink are called a cooler or HSF (heat sink and fan). The most important factors to look for when choosing a cooling system for your CPU is that the cooler unit must fit the CPU and socket you are using. In addition, the cooler must provide adequate cooling at an acceptable noise level. Finally, the preferred unit should be easy to mount. Gaming enthusiasts might overclock the CPU. Overclocking your CPU also means that more heat will be produced; in this case, upgrading your cooling system to a more efficient one might be necessary to protect your overclocked CPU.

ESTIMATED COMPLETION TIME: 45 MINUTES

 Activity

It's essential to choose a heat sink and fan made specifically for the processor you're using. Not only should the cooler fit, but it should cool the CPU sufficiently. Follow these steps to investigate coolers:

1. Using your favorite web browser, go to **frozencpu.com**.

2. On the left of the screen, under Shop by Category, click **CPU Heatsinks**. The CPU Heatsinks Categories screen is displayed.

3. Under CPU Heatsinks – Socket, click **Socket LGA 115x**.

4. Choose a heat sink and fan with a high star rating, and write down the following information:

   ◢ Brand and model: _____

   ◢ Price: _____

5. Read the product description, features information, and reviews, and then skim through the purchase options. List three features of this cooler:

   _____

   _____

   _____

6. Click the **Specifications** tab, and use the information provided there to fill in the table below. If the product specifications do not provide all of this information, find a different heat sink and fan with more complete information.

Feature	Specification
Socket type/compatibility	
Heat sink material	
Fan weight	
Fan speed	
Fan noise level	
Fan life expectancy	
Connector	

Complete the following steps to match a cooler to a processor used for gaming:

1. AMD makes processors popular in gaming computers. Go to the AMD website at **amd.com**. Explore the product menus, select a processor for gaming, and then answer these questions:

   ◢ Which processor did you select?

   _____

   ◢ Describe the processor specifications:

   _____

   _____

   ◢ Why did you select this processor?

   _____

   _____

2. Using other websites that sell or manufacture coolers, select the best cooler for the AMD processor that you selected in Step 1. Answer these questions:

   ◢ What is the cooler manufacturer and model?

   _____

   _____

   ◢ Why did you select this cooler?

   _____

   _____

   _____

Follow these steps to match a cooler for the socket and CPU installed in your system:

1. Using the skills you have learned so far in this course, determine the socket and processor installed in your lab computer.

   ◢ What processor is installed?

   _____

   ◢ What processor socket does the motherboard use?

   _____

2. Suppose the cooler on your processor has gone bad. Search the web for a cooler assembly that will work for the socket and processor your system uses.

   ◢ What is the cooler manufacturer and model?

   _____

   ◢ What is the price of the cooler?

   _____

REVIEW QUESTIONS

1. List three factors mentioned in this lab that you should consider when selecting a cooler:

   _____

   _____

   _____

2. What is the measurement unit for noise level when rating coolers? If you were in an office building and needed a very quiet system, what would be an acceptable noise level?

   _____

   _____

3. Suppose you have a CPU that gets very hot and will be used in a noisy industrial building. How would those factors affect your choice of coolers?

   _____

   _____

4. Why is it important to know the weight of a cooler when comparing coolers?

   _____

   _____

5. Why is it important to upgrade the CPU cooling system when overclocking the CPU?

   _____

   _____

LAB 5.6 TROUBLESHOOT MEMORY PROBLEMS

OBJECTIVES

The goal of this lab is to get hands-on experience in troubleshooting memory problems. After completing this lab, you will be able to:

◢ Identify some symptoms that indicate memory problems

◢ Identify a faulty module

◢ Use Memtest86 to test installed RAM

◢ Use Windows Memory Diagnostics to test installed RAM

MATERIALS REQUIRED

This lab requires the following:

◢ Internet access

◢ Windows 8 or Windows 7 operating system

◢ A bootable USB flash drive and a felt-tip pen to label the flash drive

⊿ A computer designated for disassembly

⊿ A computer toolkit and ESD strap

LAB PREPARATION

Before the lab begins, the instructor or lab assistant needs to do the following:

⊿ Verify a computer designated for disassembly is available to each student or workgroup.

⊿ Verify Internet access is available. For labs that don't have Internet access, download the latest image of Memtest86 from *memtest86.com* to a file server or other storage media available to students in the lab.

ACTIVITY BACKGROUND

The symptoms of faulty RAM are many and varied. Faulty memory can cause a complete failure to boot, fatal exception errors while working with an application, or catastrophic data loss. However, sometimes faulty memory is noticeable only as annoying interruptions while you're working. RAM that's outright dead is fairly easy to identify. If the dead module is the only module installed, the system won't boot. If it's one of several modules, you'll notice that the system reports less memory than you expected.

A module might fail absolutely. More often, however, a module develops intermittent problems that cause data corruption, applications hanging at unexpected times, the system rebooting, or Windows hanging and displaying a stop error, also called the blue screen of death (which is an error message displayed on a blue background). In this lab, you learn how to detect and isolate faulty memory modules to prevent these problems.

ESTIMATED COMPLETION TIME: 60 MINUTES

 Activity

Reliable memory function is essential to system operation. Therefore, when the system is booted, if memory isn't detected or if it has major problems, the startup UEFI/BIOS emits a beep code to define a general or particular memory problem. The memory testing on a computer is quite extensive. After POST startup does an initial test, the UEFI/BIOS does a more thorough test of physical memory, which is usually repeated three times before the system summary is displayed and booting continues. Then while Windows is loading, Windows tests memory again.

These tests are all completed at startup, but often partially corrupted modules don't show a problem until they're running at certain temperatures. When problems do show up at certain temperatures, these problems are referred to as thermal intermittents. Although thermal intermittents are difficult to nail down and document, they are actually fairly easy to remedy if the fault is on the memory module instead of on the motherboard.

Memtest86 is a utility that allows you to test the memory from a bootable CD or flash drive. This kind of test is particularly useful in discovering a thermal intermittent fault.

In the following steps, you use Memtest86 to test installed RAM. First, you create a bootable flash drive with the Memtest86 software on it; you then use the USB flash drive to boot a computer and test memory on that computer. Follow these steps:

1. Open your browser, and go to **memtest86.com**. Click the **Download now!** link. Scroll down, and click the link to download the latest version of Memtest86 for a bootable USB drive for Windows. At the time of this writing, you click **Image for creating bootable USB Drive** under the Windows Downloads section. The current version might be different.

2. Save the zipped file to your Downloads folder. What is the name of the down-loaded file?

_____

3. Extract the contents of the downloaded Zip file. The extracted folder contains the files that will be copied to your blank flash drive. One file has an .img file extension. What is the name of the IMG file in your Downloads folder? Close any open windows.

_____

4. Next, you'll install the memtest86 application on the flash drive using the imaging tool. Insert your USB flash drive, then double-click the **imageUSB.exe** file in the extracted folder. Respond to the UAC dialog box, then select the correct USB flash drive in the box for Step 1. Leave the default settings for Steps 2 and 3, then click **Write to USB** in Step 4 to begin imaging the flash drive. All previous data on the flash drive will be erased. In the imageUSB Confirmation/Verification dialog box, click **Yes**. When the imageUSB-FINAL Warning dialog box appears, check one last time to ensure you have selected the correct USB flash drive, and then click **Yes**. The imaging process begins.

5. After the imaging process is complete, in the imageUSB-Imaging complete dialog box, click **OK**. Then click **Exit**.

6. Label the flash drive **Memtest86** using the felt-tip pen. Include the version number and date on the flash drive.

7. The flash drive is now ready to be used on any computer. Reinsert the flash drive, and boot the system to the flash drive. If necessary, go into UEFI/BIOS setup and change the boot device priority order to boot to the USB drive first.

8. The system boots into the Memtest86 utility. From the configuration menu, if necessary, select the option appropriate to your computer hardware. The utility displays the progress of the tests as it runs; see Figure 5-7.

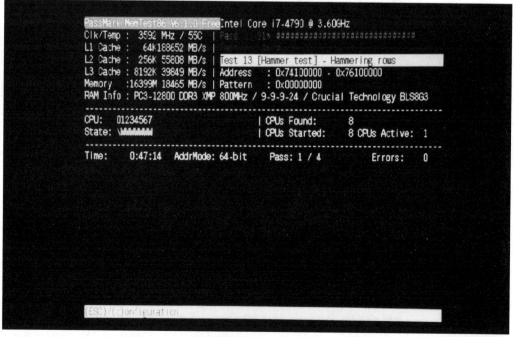

Source: Brady Tech, Inc.

Figure 5-7 Memtest86 utility tests installed RAM

9. Allow the test to finish one pass and then press **Esc** to exit and reboot to Windows. Did the test detect any errors?

10. Return to the **Memtest86.com** website, select **Technical Info**, and answer the following questions:

   ◢ What two options does Memtest86 have for reporting errors?

   ◢ Besides memory, what other component(s) does Memtest86 test?

   ◢ What is the first test (Test 0) that is performed by Memtest86?

   ◢ Why does Memtest86 not require operating system support to run?

Windows 7 and 8 offer the Memory Diagnostics utility, which you can use to test memory. Follow these steps to launch the utility:

1. In the Search box (in Windows 8, press **Win+S**; in Windows 7, click **Start**), type **mdsched.exe**, then press **Enter**. Click **Restart now and check for problems (recommended)**. The computer reboots, and the Windows Memory Diagnostics Tool screen appears (see Figure 5-8). The memory test begins. How many times does the utility test memory?

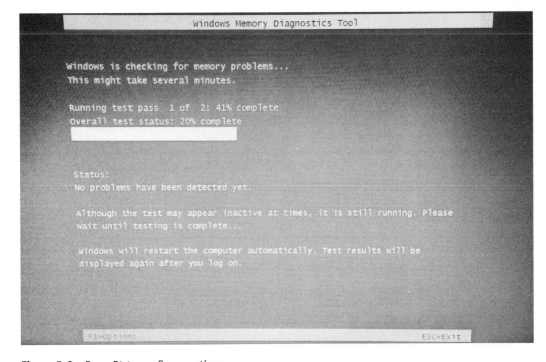

Figure 5-8 Press F1 to configure options

2. Wait until the test completes. Did the test discover any memory problems?

_____

Follow these steps to observe the effects of a faulty memory module and interpret beep codes:

1. Using skills you have learned in previous labs, determine the UEFI/BIOS manufacturer for your system, and record it here:

_____

2. Search documentation or the web for a list of beep codes for that manufacturer.

3. Shut down the system, and remove all external cabling. Press the power button for three seconds to drain residual power.

4. Put on your ESD strap, open the case, remove all memory modules, and set them aside in an antistatic bag.

5. Reassemble the system, leaving out the memory.

6. Power up the system, and describe the outcome, including any beep codes:

_____

7. If you heard beep codes, interpret their meaning using the information you found in Step 2:

_____

8. Shut down the system, disassemble it, install the RAM, and reassemble.

9. Boot the system to verify the system is functional.

REVIEW QUESTIONS

1. What are some common symptoms of a thermal intermittent?

_____

_____

_____

2. How many times does POST usually test memory?

_____

3. Why must the Memtest86 software run from bootable media?

_____

_____

4. Describe the symptoms caused by a dead memory module:

_____

_____

5. Why would a continuous test be ideal for diagnosing a thermal intermittent?

_____

_____

LAB 5.7 EVALUATE TROUBLESHOOTING PROCESSES

OBJECTIVES

The goal of this lab is to learn how to solve hardware-related computer problems by evaluating the troubleshooting processes used by others. After completing this lab, you will be able to:

◢ Troubleshoot boot problems caused by hardware

MATERIALS REQUIRED

This lab requires the following:

◢ A computer designated for this lab

◢ Windows 8 or Windows 7 operating system

◢ Internet access

LAB PREPARATION

Before the lab begins, the instructor or lab assistant needs to do the following:

◢ Verify Windows starts with no errors

◢ Verify Internet access is available

ACTIVITY BACKGROUND

When a computer does not boot or boots with errors, the problem might be software or hardware related. After you have observed the problem, the next step is to make your best educated guess: Is the problem caused by hardware or software? Then begin troubleshooting from there. Sometimes as you work, you can accidentally create a new problem, so you need to always be aware that the problem might have more than one source. This lab takes you through some real-life troubleshooting situations to help build your troubleshooting skills.

ESTIMATED COMPLETION TIME: 60 MINUTES

Activity

Matt is in the habit of leaving his computer turned on when he leaves the office in the evening. Each morning, pressing a key returns the computer to activity from standby mode and he's good to go. However, one morning he sits down at his desk to discover a window with this information on the screen:

P4P800 Asus Motherboard

Press DEL to run Setup

Matt calls over his business partner, Katie, for help. She recognizes that the system is stuck at the very beginning of a restart, and the information on the screen is from startup BIOS. Follow along as Katie troubleshoots the problem:

1. First, Katie presses the Delete key, but nothing happens. She tries other keys, but still no action. She tries pressing the power button on the front of the computer case, but that doesn't work either.

2. Katie unplugs the power cord to the system, waits several seconds, plugs it back in, and presses the power button. The system powers up and hangs with the text shown on screen in Figure 5-9.

Source: American Megatrends Inc.

Figure 5-9 Matt's system hangs early in the boot and displays this screen

3. Katie knows that Matt has not overclocked his system, and she does not want to use BIOS default settings unless she has no other option. She presses F1, and the system enters BIOS setup.

4. In BIOS setup, she notices the date and time are correct, and exits without saving changes. The Windows 7 desktop loads normally. In the lower-right corner of the screen, she sees the bubble shown in Figure 5-10.

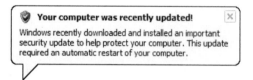

Figure 5-10 This bubble appeared on the Windows desktop

5. Katie is not satisfied that all is well, so she reboots the system. As the startup BIOS performs POST, she hears a single beep followed by two beeps, and the Windows desktop again loads normally.

6. Katie looks up the beep codes in the AMI documentation and finds that one, two, and three beeps are all memory-related errors.

7. She powers down the system, and reseats the two memory modules. As a preventive measure, she uses a can of compressed air to blow dust out of the case. And, because she suspects she might later need to replace the DIMMs, she records this information printed on each DIMM:

   Elixir 256 MB DDR-400 MHz CL3 PC3200

8. She replaces the front panel and side panel of the computer case, and powers up the system. When she does, the monitor screen is totally blank and she hears no beeps. She does hear the fans spinning.

9. She powers down the system again, reseats the DIMMs again, replaces the front panel, and powers up the system. The system boots to the Windows desktop.

10. Katie decides to perform a memory test using third-party memory-testing software. Memory failed the first test, but when she tried it a second time, memory passed with no errors.

TROUBLESHOOTING

Answer the following questions about what Katie did, the source of the problem(s), and what to do next:

◢ Why did Matt's computer reboot during the night?

_____

_____

◢ How can you be certain that the problem is hardware related rather than software related?

_____

_____

◢ What do you think is the source of the original problem?

_____

◢ In Step 4, Katie discovers the date and time are correct. What does this indicate?

_____

◢ In Step 8, why do you think the monitor was blank?

_____

◢ What are four things you would suggest that Katie do next? List the four things in the order Katie should do them:

_____

_____

_____

_____

The motherboard documentation does not normally contain the beep codes needed for troubleshooting, but you should be able to find the documentation for Matt's system online.

◢ What is the URL of the website you found that explains the beep codes for Matt's motherboard?

_____

◢ What information do you need about your own system in order to locate the documentation on the web that contains an explanation of the beep codes used on your system?

_____

_____

◢ List the information from your system that you need to find an explanation of beep codes:

_____

_____

◢ Locate the documentation about the beep codes used by your system on the web. What is the URL of the website where you found them?

_____

REVIEW QUESTIONS

1. In troubleshooting a boot problem, what is the advantage of restoring all UEFI/BIOS settings to their default values?

_____

2. In troubleshooting a boot problem, what is the disadvantage of restoring all UEFI/BIOS settings to their default values?

_____

3. In troubleshooting a boot problem, what would be the point of disabling the quick boot feature in UEFI/BIOS setup?

_____

4. Search online for an example of a third-party memory-testing program. What is the name and URL for the software you found?

_____

5. What made Katie suspect she might be dealing with a memory problem?

_____

LAB 5.8 DIAGNOSE SIMPLE HARDWARE BOOT PROBLEMS

OBJECTIVES

The goal of this lab is to practice diagnosing and repairing simple hardware problems. After completing this lab, you will be able to:

◢ Gather information useful in troubleshooting

◢ Diagnose a problem caused by someone else

◢ Record the troubleshooting process

MATERIALS REQUIRED

This lab requires the following:

◢ Computer designated for this lab

◢ Windows 8 or Windows 7 operating system

◢ A computer toolkit, including screwdrivers and an ESD strap

◢ A pen and paper for taking notes

◢ The Computer Inventory and Maintenance form you first used in the chapter, "First Look at Computer Parts and Tools." You can download the form from *cengagebrain.com*. For more information, see the Preface.

◢ A workgroup of two students

LAB PREPARATION

Before the lab begins, the instructor or lab assistant needs to do the following:

⊿ Verify Windows starts with no errors

ACTIVITY BACKGROUND

If you have worked in a computer repair shop dealing with the general public, you know that about half the problems you see are the result of an inexperienced person making a slight mistake when configuring a system and lacking the knowledge to diagnose and remedy the problem. Unless you're very skilled and lucky, you'll make similar mistakes from time to time. Your advantage is that you'll have the experience to narrow down and identify the problem, and then fix it. This lab gives you experience troubleshooting and repairing simple problems. You also learn how good documentation can help you when troubleshooting a computer problem.

Before you begin, team up with another workgroup in your class. Your team works with this other group throughout the lab.

ESTIMATED COMPLETION TIME: 60–90 MINUTES

 Activity

Do the following to gather useful information about a system, and then troubleshoot a problem with that system that was created by another team:

1. Verify your team's system is working correctly. Skim over the Computer Inventory and Maintenance form, examine the system, and record any information on the form about your system that you think would be useful when troubleshooting a problem with this computer (for example, the user account name and password for an administrator account and the brand and model of the motherboard).

   ⊿ What type of information did you decide was important to record?

   _____

   _____

   _____

2. Switch places with the other team. Make one of the following changes to the other team's system:

   ⊿ Remove the power cable from the hard drive on which Windows is installed.

   ⊿ Disconnect the P1 power cable from the motherboard.

   ⊿ Remove the RAM and place it safely inside the case so that the other team can't see it.

   ⊿ Disable SATA controllers in UEFI/BIOS setup.

   ⊿ Remove the power-on wire from the motherboard header to the front of the computer case.

   ⊿ Partially remove the data cable from the hard drive.

3. If you removed the case cover, replace the cover. Record the change you made to your team's system:

   _____

   _____

4. Again switch places with the other team. Diagnose and remedy the problem on your system. Record the troubleshooting process in Section 7, Troubleshooting, on your Computer Inventory and Maintenance form. Make sure you answer the following questions here and on the form:

▲ Date, technician (your name), and symptoms. The symptoms are a description of the problem as a user would describe it to you if you were working at a help desk.

_____

_____

▲ What is your first guess as to the source of the problem?

_____

_____

▲ What did you do that solved the problem and returned the system to good working order? Describe the actions taken and outcome below and on the Computer Inventory and Maintenance form:

_____

_____

_____

_____

_____

▲ What information that you recorded earlier in the lab helped with the troubleshooting process?

_____

_____

▲ What information that you did not record would have been useful?

_____

5. Repeat Steps 2 through 4, choosing items at random from the list in Step 2. Continue until your team has made all the changes listed in Step 2 that are possible for your system.

CRITICAL THINKING (ADDITIONAL 30 MINUTES)

If time permits, try introducing two changes at a time. This approach can prove much more difficult.

REVIEW QUESTIONS

1. What problems resulted in a "No boot device available" error?

_____

2. Typically, what's the first indication that RAM has been removed?

_____

3. What was the first indication of a problem with drive assignments?

_____

_____

4. When a user calls to say his system is dead and nothing shows on screen, what is one good suggestion you can offer for troubleshooting the problem?

_____

5. When a user calls to say he sees a strange error message on the screen when he first turns on his computer, what should be your first question?

_____

LAB 5.9 TROUBLESHOOT GENERAL COMPUTER PROBLEMS

OBJECTIVES

The goal of this lab is to troubleshoot and remedy general computer problems. After completing this lab, you will be able to:

◢ Diagnose and solve problems with various hardware devices

◢ Document the troubleshooting process

MATERIALS REQUIRED

This lab requires the following:

◢ A computer designated for this lab

◢ Windows 8 or Windows 7 operating system

◢ Windows installation DVD or flash drive, or installation files

◢ Drivers for all devices

◢ A pen and paper for taking notes

◢ A computer toolkit with ESD strap

◢ A workgroup partner

LAB PREPARATION

Before the lab begins, the instructor or lab assistant needs to do the following:

◢ Verify Windows starts with no errors

◢ Provide access to the Windows installation files

ACTIVITY BACKGROUND

In previous labs, you have learned to troubleshoot specific problems. This lab takes a comprehensive approach to troubleshooting an entire system, so the problem might relate to any subsystem. Troubleshooting a general problem is no different from troubleshooting a specific subsystem. You simply apply your troubleshooting techniques to a wider range of possibilities.

ESTIMATED COMPLETION TIME: 60–90 MINUTES

 Activity

Do the following to create a problem on your system, and then troubleshoot the problem your partner created on his or her system:

1. Verify your computer and your partner's computer are working by checking that the systems both run smoothly and all drives are accessible. Browse the network and connect to a website.

2. Randomly pick one of the following hardware or software problems and introduce it on your computer:

   ⊿ Change the boot sequence to boot from a nonexistent device.

   ⊿ If both the mouse and the keyboard have PS/2 connectors, switch the connectors at the case.

   ⊿ Using Control Panel, install a nonexistent device.

   ⊿ Remove the data cable from the primary master hard drive.

   ⊿ Change the display settings to two colors that are hard to read.

   ⊿ Remove the RAM from the system. (Be sure to store all memory modules in an antistatic bag while they're outside the case.)

   ⊿ Unplug the monitor from the video adapter.

   ⊿ Use Control Panel to switch the primary and secondary buttons on the mouse.

   ⊿ Unplug the network cable from the wall or switch.

   ⊿ Use Control Panel to disable your current network connection.

3. If you removed the case cover, replace it. What problem did you introduce to your computer?

   _____

4. Switch computers with your partner. Troubleshoot your partner's computer while your partner troubleshoots your computer. Verify you can accomplish all the tasks you could before the computer was sabotaged.

5. On a separate sheet of paper, answer these questions:

   ⊿ What is the initial symptom of the problem as a user would describe it?

   _____

   _____

   ⊿ How did you discover the source of the problem?

   _____

   _____

   ⊿ How did you solve the problem?

   _____

   _____

   _____

◢ If you were working at a help desk and someone called with this problem, could the problem have been solved over the phone, or would it have required a visit from a technician? Explain your answer:

_____

_____

6. Return to your computer and repeat Steps 2 through 5. Continue until you have solved all the problems listed in Step 2. For each problem, make sure to answer the questions in Step 5.

7. Which problem was the most difficult to repair? Why?

_____

_____

_____

8. Of those problems that allowed the computer to boot, which problem was easiest to detect? Why?

_____

_____

_____

9. Of those problems that prevented the computer from booting, which problem was easiest to detect? Why?

_____

REVIEW QUESTIONS

1. Which problems caused the computer to halt during the boot process?

_____

_____

2. Was the solution to the problem usually obvious once you had discovered its source? Explain your answer:

_____

_____

_____

3. What did you usually check first when you were troubleshooting? Why?

_____

_____

_____

4. Now that you have been through this troubleshooting experience, what would you do differently the next time the same symptoms are exhibited?

_____

5. What operating system utilities did you use or could you have used to solve a problem in this lab?

_____

6. Is there any third-party software that might have been useful in solving the problems?

_____

7. Which problem was the most difficult to solve? Why? In a real-life situation, what might happen that would cause this problem to occur?

_____

_____

_____

CHAPTER 6

Supporting Hard Drives and Other Storage Devices

Labs included in this chapter:

- **Lab 6.1:** Test Hard Drive Performance Using HD Tune
- **Lab 6.2:** Examine Your Hard Drive Using Four Methods
- **Lab 6.3:** Install a Second Hard Drive for Data Recovery
- **Lab 6.4:** Use Hard Drive Utilities
- **Lab 6.5:** Sabotage and Repair a System
- **Lab 6.6:** Replace a Laptop Hard Drive

LAB 6.1 TEST HARD DRIVE PERFORMANCE USING HD TUNE

OBJECTIVES

The goal of this lab is to use HD Tune to evaluate the performance of your system's hard drives against similar hard drives. After completing this lab, you will be able to:

▴ Use HD Tune to test the performance of your hard drives

▴ Use the HD Tune website to compare your system's drives with similar drives

MATERIALS REQUIRED

This lab requires the following:

▴ Windows 8 or Windows 7 operating system

▴ An account with administrator privileges

▴ Internet access

LAB PREPARATION

Before the lab begins, the instructor or lab assistant needs to do the following:

▴ Verify Windows starts with no errors

▴ Verify each student has access to a user account with administrator privileges

▴ Verify Internet access is available

ACTIVITY BACKGROUND

You can use HD Tune to run routine tests on your drive. You can also use the HD Tune website to report your results and compare your drive to a selection of comparable drives. This lab gives you an indication of how your drive is performing and whether another product is available that better meets your performance needs. Some tasks, such as video editing, make heavy demands on the drive where files are stored; a faster drive can increase productivity. When making an upgrade decision, it's helpful to compare results reported by HD Tune to information on other hard drives. In this lab, you use HD Tune to test your drive.

ESTIMATED COMPLETION TIME: 30 MINUTES

 Activity

Follow these steps to download and install HD Tune on your computer:

1. Log on to Windows using an account with administrator privileges.

2. Using your browser, navigate to **hdtune.com**.

3. Click the **Download** tab. Scroll down to the HD Tune section, shown in Figure 6-1, and click the file name to download. At the time of this writing, the file name was **hdtune_255.exe**.

Source: 2013 by EFD Software

Figure 6-1 HD Tune is the free version of HD Tune Pro

4. Save the file to your hard drive. When the download is complete, open the folder where the file is saved. Do not close your web browser yet.

▲ What is the path and file name (including file extension) of the downloaded file? What is the size of the file?

5. To execute the downloaded file, double-click the file you just downloaded. If a UAC dialog box appears, click **Yes**.

6. In the Setup – HD Tune dialog box, click **Next** to proceed with the installation. Select the **I accept the agreement** option button, and click **Next**.

7. Click **Next** to select the default destination location. Click **Next** again to select the default Start Menu folder. Click **Next** again, and then click **Install** and **Finish**. The HD Tune Hard Disk Utility window appears.

Now that you have installed HD Tune, follow these steps to obtain benchmarks on your system's performance:

1. Make sure the drive you want to scan is selected from the drop-down list. In Figure 6-2, there is only one drive listed. How is your drive displayed in the drop-down menu?

Source: 2013 by EFD Software

Figure 6-2 In this example, the drive is listed by manufacturer, model number, and capacity

2. Record the following information for your drive. If the information is not included in the drop-down list, search the web using the information that appears in the drop-down list to find the missing information for the table.

Manufacturer	Model Number	Capacity

▲ What temperature is reported for your drive?

_____

> **Notes** Some drives don't monitor temperature and so they won't be able to report that information to HD Tune.

3. While running the scan, do not move your mouse or do anything on your computer until the scan is complete because this input will affect performance readings. Click the **Start** button to initiate the scan. After the scan is finished, a graph and summary are displayed. Use the summary to complete the following table:

Average Transfer Rate	Access Time

4. Click the **Info** tab.

▲ What are the drive's serial number and standard?

_____

_____

▲ How many partitions are on the drive?

_____

5. Click the **Health** tab, and check the reported status for each attribute ID.

▲ Are there any attributes that are not OK? If so, list them here:

_____

_____

▲ What is the overall health status of the system?

_____

▲ The power-on time shows how many hours the computer has been on since it was first booted. What is the power-on time for this system?

_____

To compare your drive results with other test results on the HD Tune website, do the following:

1. Return to your browser window and look at the HD Tune website. Click the **Test results** tab.

2. Using the information you collected earlier, search for your drive's manufacturer and model number in the results list. If your drive is not available, find one that is similar in manufacturer, model number, and/or capacity. Select four reference drives that are closest in size to your drive, and note their performance results.

   ◢ List two drives with performance results similar to your drive's results:

   _____

   _____

> **Notes** You can sort the results list by Brand/Model, Capacity, Maximum Speed, or Access Time by clicking on the respective column title.

HD Tune continues to monitor the system's operating temperature and reports this information in the taskbar while the program is open. You can view this data in the taskbar. (You might need to click the Show hidden icons arrow in the taskbar to see the temperature.) The temperature is displayed along with the hidden icons. By default, the temperature is shown in Celsius, but the unit can be changed to Fahrenheit in HD Tune's Options menu. Normal temperatures are shown in black font, and critical temperatures are shown in red font. The critical threshold can also be set in the Options menu. The default critical threshold is 55°C.

   ◢ What is the current operating temperature?

   _____

3. Exit HD Tune, and close all open windows.

REVIEW QUESTIONS

1. Why might you want to test your drive with HD Tune?

   _____

   _____

2. Why is it important to monitor a drive's temperature?

   _____

3. Based on the drive ratings information you got from the HD Tune website, does a higher-capacity drive generally perform faster or slower than a lower-capacity drive?

   _____

4. Why shouldn't you use the system when HD Tune is testing a drive?

   _____

   _____

5. If the HD Tune results were to indicate an obvious problem with a drive, such as a slow transfer rate, what is another feature of HD Tune you might use to give you additional information about the drive?

LAB 6.2 EXAMINE YOUR HARD DRIVE USING FOUR METHODS

OBJECTIVES

The purpose of this lab is to examine your hard drive and computer to find information about your hard drive. After completing this lab, you will be able to:

◢ Identify the manufacturer and model of your hard drive

◢ Determine the capacity of your hard drive

◢ Gather other information about your hard drive

MATERIALS REQUIRED

This lab requires the following:

◢ A computer running Windows 8 or Windows 7

◢ Tools to open the computer case and examine the hard drive

◢ Internet access

LAB PREPARATION

Before the lab begins, the instructor or lab assistant needs to do the following:

◢ Verify the Windows computer starts with no errors

◢ Verify students have access to tools needed to open the computer case

◢ Verify Internet access is available

ACTIVITY BACKGROUND

In the course of your career, you will frequently find yourself dealing with hard drives. It is necessary to be able to determine the vital statistics of a hard drive in order to resolve problems and upgrade a system. Information about a hard drive can be found in multiple locations. In this lab, you find this information using four different methods: physically inspecting the hard drive, looking in the UEFI/BIOS setup, using a third-party utility, and referring to the manufacturer's documentation.

ESTIMATED COMPLETION TIME: 30 MINUTES

 Activity

PART 1: GET INFORMATION BY PHYSICALLY INSPECTING THE DRIVE

Follow these steps to physically inspect your hard drive:

1. Open the computer's case, and locate the hard drive seated in a bay.

> **Notes** Because computer cases come in many different configurations, you might need to consult the manual for your specific computer hand your experience may differ slightly from the instructions here.

2. If you can read the label on the hard drive, you may skip this step. If you cannot read the label on the hard drive, remove the cables (data and power), release the drive from its bay, and remove it for inspection.

3. Not all labels provide the same information. Using the label on the hard drive, write down the following information if available:

   ◢ Manufacturer:

   _____

   ◢ Model:

   _____

   ◢ Serial number:

   _____

   ◢ Part number:

   _____

   ◢ Capacity:

   _____

   ◢ SSD drive (yes or no):

   _____

4. Inspect the physical connection from the hard drive to the motherboard. What is the interface type?

   _____

5. Return the hard drive to its bay, plug it back in, and reassemble the computer.

PART 2: GET INFORMATION USING THE SYSTEM UEFI/BIOS

The UEFI/BIOS setup offers information about the hard drive(s) installed on a computer. Follow these steps to gather information about your computer using the system UEFI/BIOS:

1. Turn on your computer and enter the UEFI/BIOS setup.

2. Navigate to the drives section of UEFI/BIOS.

3. UEFI/BIOS uses a string of information to identify the hard drive. Write down this string exactly as it appears in UEFI/BIOS:

   _____

4. Use the information in this string to determine as much of the following information as possible:

   ◢ Manufacturer:

   _____

   ◢ Model:

   _____

   ◢ Capacity:

   _____

◢ Speed:

_____

5. Using the speed of your hard drive, which version of SATA or PATA is your hard drive (SATA I, SATA II, SATA III or ATA 2, ATA 3, ATA 4, ATA 5, ATA 6, ATA 7)?

_____

6. Is S.M.A.R.T. enabled on your system? What does S.M.A.R.T. stand for?

_____

_____

7. Exit the UEFI/BIOS setup without saving any changes made, and allow the computer to boot normally.

PART 3: GET INFORMATION USING THIRD-PARTY SOFTWARE

Using third-party software is another method to gather information about the hard drive(s) installed on a computer. Follow these steps to use Speccy to gather information about the hard drive installed on your computer:

1. Speccy might already be installed from a previous lab. If Speccy is not installed, download the Speccy utility by Piriform at **piriform.com/speccy**.

2. Open Speccy, and go to the Storage section.

3. Using the information in the Storage section, write down the following information:

◢ Manufacturer:

_____

◢ Device type:

_____

◢ Interface:

_____

◢ SATA type (including speed):

_____

◢ ATA standard:

_____

◢ Speed (expressed in revolutions per minute, or RPM):

_____

◢ Transfer mode:

_____

◢ Capacity:

_____

◢ Form factor:

_____

◢ S.M.A.R.T. temperature:

_____

◢ S.M.A.R.T. status:

_____

4. Based on the SATA type and the transfer mode, what speed is your hard drive actually operating at in your system?

_____

PART 4: GET INFORMATION FROM THE MANUFACTURER'S WEBSITE

The documentation for a hard drive offers any and all information about the hard drive that you might need. If you do not already have the printed documentation for your hard drive, research the web to find the documentation from the manufacturer's website. Complete the following steps:

1. Download the documentation, and write down the file name of the documentation:

_____

2. Search through the documentation and determine the technology type of your hard drive. Is the hard drive a magnetic hard drive or an SSD drive?

_____

REVIEW QUESTIONS

1. What important information can you consistently find on a hard drive's label?

_____

_____

2. What information about the hard drive can you _not_ find on a hard drive's label?

_____

_____

3. What four methods do you have at your disposal to learn about a hard drive?

_____

_____

4. In this lab, you used a third-party utility to gather information about your hard drive. List two Windows utilities that can give you information about your hard drive. Describe the steps you take to access these utilities:

_____

_____

_____

_____

5. What is the advantage of an SSD over a regular magnetic hard drive? What is the advantage of a magnetic hard drive over an SSD?

_____

_____

_____

LAB 6.3 INSTALL A SECOND HARD DRIVE FOR DATA RECOVERY

OBJECTIVES

The goal of this lab is to install a second internal hard drive to recover data files. After completing this lab, you will be able to:

◢ Physically install a second hard drive

◢ Configure hard drive jumpers for proper operation

◢ Configure a hard drive in the UEFI/BIOS setup

◢ Use File Explorer/Windows Explorer to move files

MATERIALS REQUIRED

This lab requires the following:

◢ Two computers that can be disassembled

◢ Cables necessary to attach the drive swapped between the computers

◢ A computer toolkit with ESD strap

◢ A workgroup of two to four students

LAB PREPARATION

Before the lab begins, the instructor or lab assistant needs to do the following:

◢ Verify Windows starts with no errors on both computers

◢ Verify both computers use compatible hard drives

ACTIVITY BACKGROUND

The precious thing about hard drives is the data they contain. Sometimes a hard drive may not boot properly, which could cause problems with access to the data stored on the drive or even prevent an operating system from booting properly. In this lab, we assume that your drive has failed to boot and you need to install the drive in another workstation so that you can recover the data files.

ESTIMATED COMPLETION TIME: 30 MINUTES

 Activity

With your lab partner, decide which workstation has a drive that does not boot properly, and refer to this one as Workstation 1. The other workstation will be the data recovery workstation, Workstation 2.

On Workstation 1, follow these steps to create a folder with a couple of files that you will recover:

1. Boot Workstation 1. Open File Explorer in Windows 8 or Windows Explorer in Windows 7. Open the Documents library, and create a folder named **Recovery**.

2. Copy/paste a couple of other library document files into the Recovery folder. If no documents are available to copy, create two new document files.

3. Shut down Workstation 1.

Next, remove the hard drive from Workstation 1, and gather the information that you need to install the drive into Workstation 2. Follow these steps:

1. Using safety precautions and the ESD strap, remove the cover from Workstation 1, and then remove its hard drive. Be careful about disconnecting the cables from the hard drive so you don't bend or break connectors.

2. Examine the hard drive, and record the following information:

   ◢ Manufacturer:

   _____

   ◢ Model:

   _____

   ◢ Capacity:

   _____

   ◢ Interface (PATA or SATA):

   _____

If your hard drive's interface is PATA, answer the following questions and review the information to make sure you are able to properly install the hard drive into Workstation 2:

1. If the drive is a PATA drive, jumpers on the drive have been set for the PATA configuration in Workstation 1. These jumpers might need to be changed before you can install the drive in Workstation 2. Does the drive share a data cable with an existing drive or is it the only drive installed on its data cable? Record the drive cable configuration here:

   _____

2. If the drive is a PATA drive, view the jumper settings on the drive. How are the jumpers set? Are they CS (cable select), device 0, or device 1? Record the jumper settings here:

   _____

If the PATA drive is sharing a data cable, the jumpers on both drives may need to be configured so that both drives are set to cable select (CS), or one drive is manually set as device 0 and the other is manually set as device 1. The original drive should be configured as device 0, and the second drive configured as device 1. If the jumpers are not set properly, BIOS might not be able to detect the new drive. If you're unsure about how to set the jumpers, you can either consult the hard drive's documentation or ask your instructor. Most PATA drives are labeled with a diagram showing the proper jumper settings.

Complete the following steps to install and configure the hard drive from Workstation 1 into Workstation 2:

1. Go to Workstation 2. Remove the case cover, and examine the hard drive configuration.

   ◢ Can you locate an unused power connector for the second drive? What type power connector are you using?

   _____

2. If you are installing a PATA drive in a system that already has PATA drives installed, you must decide how the two PATA drives will be configured. Answer the following:

   ◢ Are you installing a PATA drive in a system that already has PATA drives installed? If so, describe how you will configure the PATA system:

   _____

   _____

   ◢ When installing a PATA drive, what jumper settings, if any, need to be changed on the PATA drive to be installed and/or on the PATA drives already installed? Be specific.

   _____

3. If your hard drive's interface is SATA, review the information to make sure you are able to properly install the hard drive into Workstation 2. If the drive is a SATA drive, it will not be sharing a data cable. The SATA system uses one drive per controller/port on the motherboard. Your additional drive will need an additional SATA cable to attach to the motherboard port. Depending on your motherboard, you may need to attach the cable to the next available port, such as SATA 1, while your original drive is attached at SATA 0. Answer the following:

   ◢ Is there an extra SATA port for the drive? Which SATA port on the motherboard should you use? Verify the port with your instructor.

   _____

4. Install the hard drive from Workstation 1 in a free bay, and attach both the data and power cables. Be careful to align the connectors correctly on the back of the drive. The connectors are keyed so that they will insert in only one direction. The same goes for attaching cables to the port on the motherboard. Have your instructor verify your connections.

5. Boot the computer into the UEFI/BIOS setup screen, and ensure that UEFI/BIOS automatically detects the new hard drive in the storage section of the UEFI/BIOS information. Record the information that UEFI/BIOS gives about the hard drives:

   ◢ If there are PATA drives:

   • IDE Primary:

   _____

   • IDE Secondary:

   _____

   ◢ If there are SATA drives:

   • SATA 0:

   _____

   • SATA 1:

   _____

6. Boot the computer into Windows, and use File Explorer/Windows Explorer to examine the files on the new drive.

   ◿ What is the drive letter designation for the added drive?

   _____

7. On the added drive, locate the Recovery folder you made earlier.

8. Copy the Recovery folder from the added drive to the Documents library of the C: drive, which will put it on the Workstation 2 original drive.

9. Open the Recovery folder on the C: drive. Are the files you saved into that folder from Workstation 1 there?

   _____

You have now recovered data files from a "damaged" system that you installed in another workstation. Complete the following steps to restore your computers to their original configurations:

1. Shut down Workstation 2, remove the drive you installed, and reinstall it in Workstation 1 in its original location. Be sure to use proper safety precautions including using an ESD strap. Be mindful to restore the proper jumper and cable attachment configurations.

2. After physical reinstallation, have your instructor verify your work. Reboot and enter the UEFI/BIOS setup of the workstation to verify the drive is properly configured. Boot Workstation 1 to the Windows desktop, and verify all is well.

3. Replace the cover on Workstation 2, and boot it up. Verify you can boot it to the Windows desktop with no errors.

REVIEW QUESTIONS

1. If a hard drive fails to boot, why is it possible to recover data files by installing that drive in another system?

   _____

   _____

2. What is one way to determine how to set the jumpers on a hard drive?

   _____

   _____

3. Was it necessary to install the second drive in Workstation 2 in order to recover the data? What are two reasons why you might *not* want to install the drive during recovery?

   _____

   _____

4. If you had been unable to locate an available power connector in Workstation 2 for the recovered hard drive, what could you have done to power the hard drive?

   _____

   _____

5. If you installed a second hard drive in a workstation and UEFI/BIOS does not report it being on the system, what is a possible cause?

_____

_____

_____

LAB 6.4 USE HARD DRIVE UTILITIES

OBJECTIVES

The goal of this lab is to work with utilities from hard drive manufacturers that examine and diagnose hard drive problems. After completing this lab, you will be able to:

◢ Identify your hard drive manufacturer

◢ Evaluate utilities that hard drive manufacturers provide for their drives

◢ Test for hard drive problems

MATERIALS REQUIRED

This lab requires the following:

◢ Windows 8 or Windows 7 operating system

◢ Internet access

LAB PREPARATION

Before the lab begins, the instructor or lab assistant needs to do the following:

◢ Verify Windows starts with no errors

◢ Verify Internet access is available

ACTIVITY BACKGROUND

Hard drive problems can manifest themselves in different ways. The drive might exhibit immediate and total failure so that it doesn't operate at all. If the failure is caused by a problem with the platters in the area where system files are stored, your computer might not be able to boot. If system files aren't affected, you might be able to boot and work normally, but you might have some file corruption or loss. Then again, you might not realize you have a hard drive problem if your hard drive has bad sectors in a physical area of the disk where data has not yet been saved. More often, however, when a disk begins to fail, Event Viewer in Windows reports errors. One tool you can use to diagnose hard drive problems is diagnostic software that your hard drive manufacturer supplies. In this lab, you identify your drive manufacturer and use its software to examine your drive.

Activity

In order to use a hard drive diagnostic utility, you must first identify your hard drive's manufacturer and model number.

> **Notes** Hard drive manufacturers often abbreviate their names when providing information about their drives. Western Digital Corporation, for example, may be abbreviated as WDC, followed by a model number, or you might see ST for Seagate Technology, followed by a series of numbers and letters that provide further information.

1. Use the skills you've practiced in this chapter to find information about the hard drive you want to test. Record the following information:

   ◢ Hard drive manufacturer:

   _____

   ◢ Hard drive model:

   _____

Next, you find out about hard drive utilities supplied by two hard drive manufacturers, Seagate and Western Digital.

> **Notes** Websites change often. You might need to adjust the steps in this lab to account for changes to the websites used.

Follow these steps to find out about the Windows version of this software, called SeaTools for Windows, which works with Seagate and Maxtor hard drives as well as other brands of hard drives:

1. In your web browser, go to **seagate.com/support/downloads/seatools**. In the Downloads section, click **Sea Tools for Windows**.

2. Click **I ACCEPT** to accept the End-User License Agreement (EULA). Then under Instructions, click the **DOWNLOAD** link. Save the file to your hard drive.

3. Locate the file on your hard drive and double-click it. At the time of this writing, the name of the application file was SeaToolsforWindowsSetup.exe. Click **Yes** to respond to the UAC dialog box. Follow the SeaTools for Windows Setup Wizard to install the software, accepting default settings. (You might be required to download and install .NET Framework software from Microsoft to complete the installation of SeaTools.)

4. SeaTools for Windows automatically places a shortcut icon on your desktop. Double-click the icon to open the application. Click Yes to respond to the UAC dialog box. The first time you run the software, the EULA may appear. If the EULA appears, click **I Accept**. The SeaTools for Windows window is displayed, as shown in Figure 6-3.

6

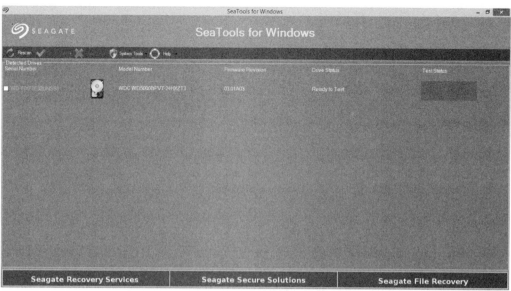

Figure 6-3 SeaTools for Windows is a useful diagnostic utility for hard drives

5. Select the drive on which you would like to run a test. On the toolbar, select **Basic Tests**. In the Basic Tests submenu, click **S.M.A.R.T Check**.

◢ What are the results of the S.M.A.R.T. test?

6. Select the drive again. In the Basic Test submenu, click **Drive Information,** and record the following information:

◢ Serial number:

◢ Drive temperature:

◢ Power-on hours:

7. Using the Help feature on the SeaTools for Windows window, answer the following question:

◢ What is the difference between a fast and long test?

Another very popular tool that Western Digital provides is the Data Lifeguard Diagnostic. Do the following to find out more about this software:

1. In your web browser, go to **support.wdc.com**, and click the **Downloads** link. In the list of products, click **SATA & SAS**. Choose a hard drive that lists Data Lifeguard Diagnostic for Windows as available.

◢ Write down the drive model you selected:

◢ List the types of Data Lifeguard software available for this drive:

_____

_____

_____

◢ What might be the advantage of having the utility stored on a bootable CD or flash drive?

_____

_____

2. Click the **Data Lifeguard Diagnostic for Windows** link in the Downloads section on the product's webpage. Scroll down, and click to download the **Release Notes** in PDF format. Examine the information, and then answer these questions:

◢ What are the four basic functions of this software?

_____

_____

_____

_____

◢ Which kind of test offers the option to correct errors on the hard drive? What step in running the program is particularly important when using this test?

_____

_____

3. On the product's webpage, click **Download** to download the utility, and save it to a folder on your hard drive. What is the file name and path to the file?

_____

4. Install the Data Lifeguard program by double-clicking the **setup.exe** file in the downloaded Zip file, responding to the UAC dialog box, and accepting the default settings during installation. Then, launch the program, and accept the License Agreement. The Western Digital Data LifeGuard Diagnostics window is shown in Figure 6-4. Double-click the hard drive listed, and answer the following questions:

◢ What type of test does the Quick Test perform?

_____

◢ What type of test does the Extended Test perform? How long does the Extended Test take?

_____

_____

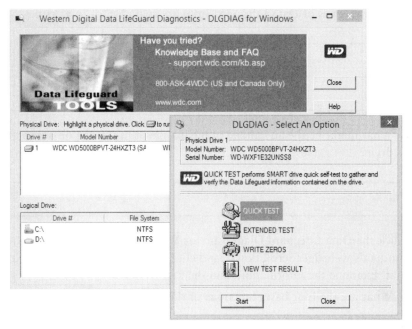

Figure 6-4   Data LifeGuard Diagnostics software reports information about a drive

◢ Describe what the Write Zeros option does. What is one purpose of this option?

_____

_____

_____

Next, follow these steps to explore a manufacturer's utility to test your drive:

1. If your hard drive isn't made by Seagate, Maxtor, or Western Digital, go to your manufacturer's website and search for diagnostic software. If your hard drive manufacturer is Seagate, Maxtor, or Western Digital, do a quick search online to identify a different hard drive manufacturer, then check their website for diagnostic software. What software did you find?

_____

2. Why do you think it's important to test a hard drive with software provided by the manufacturer of the drive rather than that of another manufacturer?

_____

_____

REVIEW QUESTIONS

1. What are some symptoms of hard drive problems listed on the hard drive manufacturers' websites? List three in order of seriousness:

_____

_____

_____

2. Which hard drive manufacturer's website was the most informative and easiest to use? Why?

_____

_____

_____

3. Which utility from a hard drive manufacturer seemed to be the most powerful? Why?

_____

_____

_____

4. What were the most common two methods used to run the utilities?

_____

5. Why is it useful to run the utility from bootable media rather than from Windows?

_____

6. How do you determine that your system is set to boot from a CD or flash drive?

_____

LAB 6.5 SABOTAGE AND REPAIR A SYSTEM

OBJECTIVES

Having a seemingly unlimited number of possible causes for a computer's problems makes troubleshooting a bit more challenging. The goal of this lab is to learn to troubleshoot a system by recovering from a sabotaged system. After completing this lab, you will be able to:

◢ Apply effective troubleshooting skills to identify and repair a computer problem

◢ Use appropriate tools to resolve computer problems

MATERIALS REQUIRED

This lab requires the following:

◢ A computer (containing no important data) that has been designated for sabotage

◢ The Computer Inventory and Maintenance form you first used in the chapter, "First Look at Computer Parts and Tools." You can download the form from *cengagebrain. com*. For more information, see the Preface.

◢ Windows installation DVD or installation files

◢ A computer toolkit with ESD strap

◢ A workgroup of two to four students

LAB PREPARATION

Before the lab begins, the instructor or lab assistant needs to do the following:

◢ Verify Windows starts with no errors

◢ Provide access to the Windows installation files

◢ Verify students' computers contain no important data and can be sabotaged

ACTIVITY BACKGROUND

You have learned about several tools and methods you can use to troubleshoot and repair a failed system or failed hardware devices. This lab gives you the opportunity to use these skills in a simulated troubleshooting situation. Your group will work with another group to sabotage a system and then repair another failed system. This lab is more advanced than previous labs in this chapter because other than not doing physical damage to the system, you are not limited in what you do to sabotage a computer.

Please don't introduce a problem on a computer in this lab that will cause permanent damage to a component!

ESTIMATED COMPLETION TIME: 60-90 MINUTES

 Activity

This lab works best and is more fun if you are troubleshooting a system that you have not worked on in previous labs. Do the following to gather information about the system, sabotage another team's computer, and then troubleshoot your system:

1. If possible, use a computer that you are not yet familiar with and have not used in previous labs. Examine the system. If the hard drive contains important data, back it up to another medium. Using your Computer Inventory and Maintenance form, record any information that you think might be useful when troubleshooting the system. Take note of anything else about the system you think might be useful and record it here:

   _____

2. Trade systems with another group, and sabotage the other group's system while that group sabotages your system. Do something that will cause the system to fail to work or give errors after booting.

   You can use any of the problems included in this lab manual, such as those used in the chapter, "Supporting the Power System and Troubleshooting Computers." You can search the web or use your imagination to introduce a new nondestructive problem, such as turning down the brightness on the monitor or removing the CPU. Be creative and have fun. What did you do to sabotage the other team's system?

   _____

   _____

3. Return to your system and troubleshoot it. Record the symptoms and the troubleshooting process in Section 7 of your Computer Inventory and Maintenance form.

   ◢ Describe the problem as a user would describe it to you if you were working at a help desk:

   _____

   _____

◢ What was your first guess as to the source of the problem?

_____

◢ List the steps you took in the troubleshooting process:

_____

_____

_____

_____

_____

_____

◢ What did you do that finally solved the problem and returned the system to good working order?

_____

_____

4. Repeat Steps 2 and 3 so that each member of your group has an opportunity to create and solve several problems.

CHALLENGE ACTIVITY

Perform this lab again, but this time introduce two problems into the system at the same time.

1. What two problems did you introduce into the other team's computer?

_____

_____

2. How much more difficult was it to troubleshoot your computer with two problems compared with having only one problem to solve?

_____

_____

3. Describe the troubleshooting process, and explain how you were able to distinguish between the two problems you needed to solve:

_____

_____

_____

_____

REVIEW QUESTIONS

1. Think back on this troubleshooting experience to the problem that caused you the most difficulty. What would you do differently the next time you encounter the same symptoms?

   _____

   _____

2. Did you use any third-party software utilities or hardware devices to solve any of your problems? If so, what were they?

   _____

3. Think of a computer problem you've experienced in the past. How did you handle the problem?

   _____

   _____

   _____

4. Is there anything you could have done differently to diagnose the solution earlier or avoid the problem altogether?

   _____

LAB 6.6 REPLACE A LAPTOP HARD DRIVE

OBJECTIVES

The goal of this lab is to practice replacing a hard drive in a laptop computer. After completing this lab, you will be able to:

◢ Locate the hard drive in a laptop computer

◢ Remove the hard drive from a laptop computer

◢ Replace the hard drive in a laptop computer

MATERIALS REQUIRED

This lab requires the following:

◢ A laptop computer or Internet access

◢ A computer toolkit with ESD strap

◢ Additional smaller screwdrivers, if necessary

LAB PREPARATION

Before the lab begins, the instructor or lab assistant needs to do the following:

◢ Verify Internet access is available

ACTIVITY BACKGROUND

Hard disk drives are delicate devices. Dropping one, even a few inches, can cause permanent damage to the read/write heads, platter surfaces, or both. laptop systems are, of course, often moved and commonly subjected to forces that most other hard drives never encounter. Although drives intended for laptop systems are designed to be resistant to movement and shock, they are still more likely to fail than any other laptop component. In this lab, you remove a hard drive from a laptop computer, and then reinstall the same hard drive. If you don't have access to a laptop, skip to the alternate activity at the end of this lab.

Hard drives designed for laptop computers tend to be 50 percent to 75 percent more expensive than the standard 3.5-inch drives of comparable capacity for desktop computers. Also, although the majority of newer laptops support most 2.5-inch drives designed for laptops, some laptop computers require a proprietary hard drive. For these reasons, researching your replacement options before you purchase a new drive is important. Read the documentation that came with your laptop to determine what drives it supports. If this information isn't available in the documentation, search the manufacturer's website. In this lab, you remove the existing drive, and then reinstall the same drive. The steps for your laptop might be slightly different from the procedures in this lab, so make sure you study the documentation before you begin.

ESTIMATED COMPLETION TIME: 30 MINUTES

 Activity

Follow these steps to gather information about the laptop you are using in this lab:

1. What are the manufacturer and model of your laptop computer?

   _____

2. Using one or more of the methods you learned earlier in this chapter, gather the following information about your hard drive:
   ◢ Manufacturer: _____
   ◢ Model: _____
   ◢ Capacity: _____
   ◢ Speed: _____

3. Based on the laptop's documentation or information on the manufacturer's website, what type of hard drive can be used to replace the existing hard drive? Be as specific as you can:

   _____

   _____

4. Look for specific directions (in the documentation or on the website) for removing and replacing your laptop's hard drive. If you find any, summarize those directions here. (If you're using the website as your source of information, save or print any relevant webpages.)

   _____

   _____

   _____

Follow these general steps to remove the hard drive from a laptop computer. Note that these directions might not list every step necessary for your model. Refer to specific directions in the documentation or on the manufacturer's website, as needed.

1. Remove the main battery or batteries, and, if necessary, unplug the computer from the AC adapter. Close the lid, and turn the computer so that the bottom is facing up.

2. Locate and remove the access panel or component enclosing the drive bay. For older laptops, the hard drive is typically located beneath a floppy drive or other removable device. For newer laptops, the hard drive might be located beneath the battery, or behind a dedicated cover, as shown in Figure 6-5.

Figure 6-5   Remove a cover on the bottom of the laptop to exchange the hard drive, which is attached to a proprietary bracket

3. After you have accessed the drive, determine how it's secured in the system. It's commonly attached to a frame or "cradle" with small screws, and the cradle is often attached directly to the system chassis. This cradle helps locate and support the drive inside the drive bay. Remove the screws securing the cradle. In some systems, the hard drive is held in place by only a single screw. For these systems, remove the screw, then turn the laptop on its side and push the drive out of its bay.

4. In most laptops, data cables don't connect the hard drive to the motherboard, as is the case with desktop computers. Instead, a hard drive connects to the laptop's motherboard by way of an edge connector, similar to those on expansion cards in desktop computers. This type of direct connection has two advantages. First, it improves reliability because it reduces the total number of connection points; fewer connection points mean fewer connections that could shake loose as the laptop is moved around during daily use. The second advantage is that the lack of data cables reduces the laptop's overall size and weight. To remove the drive-cradle assembly, slide the cradle away from the connector. Slide the assembly back until all pins are clear of the connector. When the pins are clear, lift the assembly straight up out of the drive bay.

5. Note the orientation of the drive in the cradle so that when you reinstall the drive, you can mount it in the same direction. Remove the screws securing the drive in the cradle, and then remove the drive.

6. Examine the drive connections.

◢ Is the drive using a SATA interface or a PATA interface? How do you know?

_____

_____

◢ Is the drive a magnetic drive or an SSD drive? How do you know?

_____

_____

7. Using the information you have gathered about the drive, including its capacity, type (SSD or magnetic), speed (if a magnetic drive), brand, model, and interface, find a comparable hard drive on the web. Print or save the webpage showing the drive and its price. What is the drive brand, model, and price?

_____

Follow these general steps to reinstall the hard drive. Note that these directions might not list every step necessary for your model. Refer to specific directions in the documentation or on the manufacturer's website, as needed.

1. For a PATA drive, examine the jumper settings. What setting is currently used for the drive?

_____

2. Place the drive in the cradle so that the pins are oriented correctly, and then secure it with screws.

3. Set the drive-cradle assembly straight down into the drive bay. Gently slide the assembly to the connector, and verify the pins are aligned correctly with the connector. Slide the assembly until the drive is fully seated in the connector. The cradle should now align with the holes in the chassis. If the holes don't align, you should remove the assembly, loosen the drive-retaining screws, and adjust the drive's position in the cradle. Repeat this process until the drive is fully seated so that there's no room for it to move after the cradle is secured. When the assembly is seated, secure it with screws.

4. Replace any components or access covers you removed to get at the hard drive.

5. Reinstall any batteries and reconnect to AC power, if necessary. As with any other hard drive, a new laptop drive must be correctly recognized by UEFI/BIOS, and then partitioned and formatted before it can be used. This process isn't necessary in this lab because you haven't installed a new hard drive.

ALTERNATE ACTIVITY

If you don't have access to a laptop computer, follow these steps:

1. Using the documentation for one of the laptops you selected in the chapter titled, "Working Inside Desktops and Laptops and First Look at Mobile Devices" as your source, record the specific requirements for a replacement hard drive. Be as detailed as possible:

_____

_____

_____

2. Search the web for information on replacement hard drives, and print the webpage showing the correct specifications for a replacement hard drive. What is the cost of the drive? How much capacity does the drive have?

_____

3. Locate the steps for replacing the hard drive. To find this information, use the manuals you downloaded in the chapter titled, "Working Inside Desktops and Laptops and First Look at Mobile Devices", the manufacturers' websites, and other Internet resources (such as websites for manufacturers of replacement laptop hard drives). How do the steps you found differ from the steps in this lab? Note the differences here:

_____

_____

_____

_____

_____

_____

_____

_____

_____

REVIEW QUESTIONS

1. Why should you research hard drives thoroughly when replacing one in a laptop computer?

_____

_____

2. What criteria should you consider when selecting a comparable hard drive to replace a hard drive in a laptop?

_____

_____

3. Why is hard drive cabling commonly not included in laptop systems?

_____

_____

4. How did the installation procedure for your laptop differ from the directions given in this lab?

_____

_____

_____

5. Suppose you need to install a hard drive in a laptop that doesn't include an access panel for the hard drive. Where should you look for the hard drive inside the laptop?

_____

_____

CHAPTER 7

Survey of Windows Features and Support Tools

Labs included in this chapter:

- **Lab 7.1:** Install a Windows 8 App and Manage the Start Screen
- **Lab 7.2:** Use a Microsoft Account and OneDrive
- **Lab 7.3:** Use the Mail and People Apps
- **Lab 7.4:** Use Windows Keyboard Shortcuts
- **Lab 7.5:** Gather and Record System Information
- **Lab 7.6:** Manage Windows 7 Libraries

LAB 7.1 INSTALL A WINDOWS 8 APP AND MANAGE THE START SCREEN

OBJECTIVES

The goal of this lab is to become familiar with Windows 8. After completing this lab, you will be able to:

◢ Use the Windows 8 Start screen

◢ Find apps and settings

◢ Shut down Windows 8

MATERIALS REQUIRED

This lab requires the following:

◢ Windows 8 operating system

◢ Internet access

LAB PREPARATION

Before the lab begins, the instructor or lab assistant needs to do the following:

◢ Verify Windows starts with no errors

◢ Verify Internet access is available

ACTIVITY BACKGROUND

Windows 8 has a very different user interface than previous editions of Windows. It can feel a little awkward or clumsy at first, but with time and practice, you will become comfortable using the new user interface.

> **Notes** Windows 8 hides shortcuts and menus. You can access them by placing your pointer in the corners of the screen.

ESTIMATED COMPLETION TIME: 45 MINUTES

 Activity

Follow these steps to become familiar with the Start screen:

1. On the Start screen, find your user name in the upper-right corner of the screen. Click your **user name** icon.

2. Click **Lock** to password protect your screen. Click the **screen** to access the sign-in screen. Sign in to your account.

3. The Start screen has tiles used to open commonly used programs. Click the **Desktop** tile to access the Windows desktop. In Windows 8, the desktop is itself considered an app. To toggle between the Start screen and the desktop, use one of two methods:

    ◢ Click the **Start** (Windows logo) button in the taskbar. This button is hidden in this same corner when you're on the Start screen.

    ◢ Press the ⊞ **Windows logo** key on your keyboard.

4. After you open the desktop, you can return to it from the Start screen using one of three methods:

   ◿ Click the **Desktop** tile on the Start screen.

   ◿ Move your mouse to the upper-left corner of the screen, and click the **desktop** thumbnail.

   ◿ Move your mouse to the lower-left corner of the screen, and click the ▦ Windows logo button that appears.

> **Notes** If more than one app is open, you can quickly view one of these apps by moving your mouse to the upper-left corner of the screen and then moving your mouse down the left side of the screen. Thumbnails of the open apps appear for you to choose the app you want to view.

5. The desktop is itself an app, and you close it as you would any app. To close an app, drag the top edge of the page to the bottom edge of the screen. Close the desktop, and return to the Start screen.

6. On the Start screen, move an app tile. To move a tile, click and drag the tile to a different location on the screen.

7. Not all the tiles are the same size. To change the size of a tile, right-click the tile, which opens the shortcut menu for the tile.

> **Notes** You can change the settings of multiple tiles at the same time if you hold down the Ctrl key while you right-click the tiles.

8. In the shortcut menu, click **Resize**. Choose a different size. Notice the size of the tile changes.

9. To open a program that does not have a tile on the Start screen, simply start typing the name of the program. To open the Paint program, on the Start screen, type **Paint**. The Search pane opens with a list of search results. Select the **Paint** program in the search results. The Paint program opens on the desktop.

10. Close the Paint program. Return to the **Start** screen.

11. You're looking for a cooking and recipes app, and a friend recommended Allrecipes. To search for and download a new app, click the **Store** tile. The Store app opens. In the Search box, type **Allrecipes**. In the results, click the **Allrecipes** icon.

12. Click **Install**, as shown in Figure 7-1. When Windows is done installing the Allrecipes app, a notification will appear on screen. Close the Store app by dragging the top edge of the page down to the bottom of the screen.

13. If you do not see the Allrecipes tile on the Start screen when you scroll to the right and left, type **Allrecipes**. In the search results, right-click the **Allrecipes** tile, and select **Pin to Start**. Click the **Start** screen to close the search results pane.

14. Scroll to the right until you see the Allrecipes tile. Open the **Allrecipes** app. Close the Allrecipes app.

15. To uninstall the Allrecipes app, right-click the **Allrecipes** tile. Click **Uninstall** in the status bar that appears at the bottom of the screen. Click **Uninstall** again.

16. Access the **charms** bar by moving your mouse to the upper-right or lower-right corner of the screen. You can access the charms bar from anywhere in Windows, but the items on the charms bar might change, depending on the situation. What are the items in the charms bar you see on the screen?

7

Figure 7-1 The Store is used to install the Allrecipes app
Source: Allrecipes.com

17. On the charms bar, click the **Settings** charm (gear icon), and then click **Personalize**. Change the Start screen background picture or colors. Click the **Start** screen to close the Personalize pane.

18. On the Start screen, click the **down arrow** near the lower-left corner of the screen. The Apps screen appears, listing all apps installed on the computer. Click the **up arrow** to return to the Start screen.

19. There are two ways to shut down the system:

   ◢ Open the **charms** bar, and click the **Settings** charm. Click the **Power** button, and select **Shut down** to turn off your computer.

   ◢ Press ⊞ **Windows logo + X**, select **Shut down or sign out**, and then click **Shut down**.

REVIEW QUESTIONS

1. How do you open the Windows desktop? How do you close the desktop?

_____

_____

2. How do you install an app that uses the Windows 8 interface? How do you uninstall a Windows 8 app?

_____

_____

3. How do you access the Apps screen?

_____

_____

4. How do you add a tile to the Start screen?

_____

_____

5. How do you sign out from the computer? How do you shut down the computer?

_____

_____

LAB 7.2 USE A MICROSOFT ACCOUNT AND ONEDRIVE

OBJECTIVES

The goal of this lab is to set up and use a Microsoft account. After completing this lab, you will be able to:

- Use a local account, a Microsoft account, and OneDrive
- Switch between a Microsoft account and a local account

MATERIALS REQUIRED

This lab requires the following:

- Windows 8 operating system
- Internet access

LAB PREPARATION

Before the lab begins, the instructor or lab assistant needs to do the following:

- Verify Windows starts with no errors
- Verify Internet access is available

ACTIVITY BACKGROUND

Windows 8 gives the user the option to log in with a Microsoft account. Using that account, the user can access his or her OneDrive without entering a password. In this lab, you learn how all this works.

ESTIMATED COMPLETION TIME: 45–60 MINUTES

 Activity

1. What is the local account user name for your computer?

_____

2. Do you have an existing Microsoft account using an Outlook.com, Hotmail.com, Live.com, or another email address? If so, what is the email address associated with your Microsoft account?

_____

Windows requires that you sign in with a Microsoft account before you can use the OneDrive app. If you don't already have a Microsoft account, you'll have the opportunity to create one when you first attempt to open the app.

PART 1: USE A LOCAL ACCOUNT, A MICROSOFT ACCOUNT, AND ONEDRIVE

1. Sign in with a local account.

2. On the Start screen, click the **OneDrive** app. The OneDrive app opens, but because you are signed in using a local account, OneDrive cannot access your Microsoft account. Click **Go to PC settings**.

3. Click **Connect to a Microsoft account**. The "Switch to a Microsoft account on this PC" screen appears. Enter your local account password. Click **Next**.

4. If you already have a Microsoft account, enter your sign-in information now. If you do not have a Microsoft account, click **Create a new account**.

> **Notes** If you already have a Microsoft account, sign in to OneDrive. When the OneDrive app opens, skip to Step 6.

5. A Microsoft account is associated with an email address. You can use an existing email address or create a new one. Windows 8 apps work best if your Microsoft account uses an Outlook.com, Hotmail.com, or Live.com email address. When you set up your Microsoft account, you can create an email address that has an Outlook.com or a Hotmail.com ending. What is your new Microsoft account email address? (You might also want to write down your password in a safe place so you won't forget it.)

_____

6. Complete the steps to set up your new Microsoft account, including creating the email address and password, entering the security information, and finalizing the account.

7. You can skip the step to use the security code for now.

8. OneDrive is introduced. Click **Next**.

9. Click **Switch**. Your local account has now been switched to a Microsoft account on the computer. Now, when you sign in to your computer, you will use your Microsoft account information and *not* the local account sign-in information.

10. Close the OneDrive app, and reopen it to verify you are signed in.

To add a document to the OneDrive folder, you will first create one on the desktop. Follow these steps to upload a file to OneDrive:

1. Open the **desktop**.

2. Right-click the **desktop**, and select **New, Text Document**. Rename the document **OneDriveTest**.

3. Open the document, and type **This is my test document for OneDrive in Windows 8**. Save the file, and close Notepad. Return to the **OneDrive** app.

4. Right-click anywhere on the screen. Click the **Add items** icon in the status pane. A browsing screen opens.

5. With "This PC" showing, click the **Desktop** tile. (If "This PC" isn't showing, click the down arrow next to the title of the screen, and select "This PC".) Select the **OneDriveTest** file, and then click the **Copy to OneDrive** button. The file is added to your OneDrive account.

6. View your document from your OneDrive. Then return to the **Start** screen.

PART 2: SWITCH BETWEEN A MICROSOFT ACCOUNT AND A LOCAL ACCOUNT

Next, you'll disconnect the Microsoft account, and then reconnect it. Follow these steps to disconnect your Microsoft account from your local account:

1. From the Start screen, go to the **charms** bar, and click **Settings**. Click **Change PC settings**, and then click **Accounts** in the left pane.

2. On the Accounts screen, click **Disconnect** under your account name and email address, as shown in Figure 7-2. Confirm your current Microsoft password, and click **Next**.

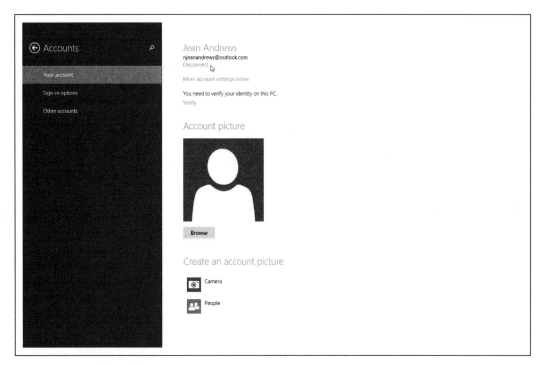

Figure 7-2   The Accounts page is used to connect or disconnect a Microsoft account to a local account

3. You cannot reuse your same local account user name; however, the user folders remain the same. Enter an alternate local account user name. Create the password and password hint. (You can reuse the local account password you used in the beginning of this lab.) Click **Next**.

4. You need to sign out, and then sign back in to complete the process. Click **Sign out and finish**.

5. Sign in to your new local account. Do you think you can now use the OneDrive app without entering your password again?

6. Return to the **PC settings** screen, and reconnect to your Microsoft account.

7. Sign out, and then sign back in using your Microsoft account. Verify you can use the OneDrive app.

REVIEW QUESTIONS

1. Why can you not use the OneDrive app while signed in using a local account?

2. What are the two domain name endings offered when creating a new Microsoft account?

_____

3. How do you access the menu to add a new document to your OneDrive?

_____

4. Why might you want to save files to OneDrive instead of just saving to your local hard drive?

_____

5. List the steps to disconnect your Windows 8 local account from a Microsoft user account:

_____

_____

LAB 7.3 USE THE MAIL AND PEOPLE APPS

OBJECTIVES

The goal of this lab is to use your Microsoft account to learn about the Mail and People apps. After completing this lab, you will be able to:

◢ Use the Mail app

◢ Use the People app to connect to other social accounts

MATERIALS REQUIRED

This lab requires the following:

◢ Windows 8 operating system

◢ Internet access

LAB PREPARATION

Before the lab begins, the instructor or lab assistant needs to do the following:

◢ Verify Windows starts with no errors

◢ Verify Internet access is available

ACTIVITY BACKGROUND

After you have set up your Microsoft account, you can send and receive mail through the Mail app, and connect to other contacts—such as those in your Facebook and Twitter accounts—using the People app. In this lab, you learn how all this works.

ESTIMATED COMPLETION TIME: 45–60 MINUTES

 Activity

This activity is divided into two parts. In Part 1, you learn to use the Mail app. In Part 2, you learn to use the People app.

PART 1: USE THE MAIL APP

Follow these steps to check if your Mail app is syncing with your Microsoft account:

1. Sign in using the Microsoft account you set up in the previous lab.

2. Click the **Mail** tile. You don't need to add another account at this time.

3. Open the **charms** bar, and click **Settings**. In the Settings pane (see Figure 7-3), click **Accounts**. In the Account pane, verify the email address is correct. If no email address is listed or the address is wrong, click **Add an account,** and follow the on-screen instructions to set up your email using your Microsoft email. To close the Accounts pane, click somewhere else on the screen.

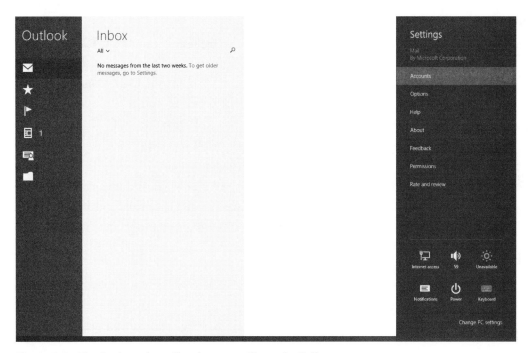

Figure 7-3 The Settings charm lists items specific to the Mail app

4. By default, the Inbox for your email account is selected in the left pane. The list of emails in your Inbox appears in the middle pane. When you click an email, its contents appear in the right pane.

5. Send an email to yourself (or exchange emails with a classmate) to test the Mail app. To send the test email, click the **New** button in the upper-right corner of the screen, and type a short message to yourself. Add a subject line, and click the **Send** button. The message quickly appears in your Inbox.

> **Notes** If you don't see the message, you might have typed the wrong email address. You can also try refreshing the sync with the mail server. Right-click somewhere in the Mail app. In the status bar, click **More**, then **Sync**.

6. There are a few ways to display the status bar, which includes options for handling your mail:

   ◢ Right-click in the Mail app.

   ◢ Place a check mark by the email to select it.

   ◢ Click the three dots in the lower-right corner of the screen.

7

In the status bar that appears at the bottom of the screen, you can select an option to print the message or mark it as Junk mail, among other things.

7. By default, mail is downloaded as it arrives. To see other options, open the **Settings** charm, and click **Accounts**. Then click your **email** address in the Accounts pane. What are the options for how often email is downloaded?

_____

_____

8. Close the Mail app.

PART 2: USE THE PEOPLE APP

The People app is used to maintain all of your contacts, including those from Facebook, Outlook Mail, Google, and Twitter.

1. Return to the **Start** screen, and click the **People** app. Click **Connected to** in the lower-right corner to access the Accounts menu.

2. Click **Add an account**.

3. Choose **Facebook** from the list. Click **What else happens when I connect?**

4. Click **Connect**. A Facebook login screen appears.

5. Enter your Facebook email account and password, and then click **Log In**.

6. Microsoft asks to share your information, and then asks you a few other questions. Click **OK** for each question to complete the connection of the People app to Facebook.

REVIEW QUESTIONS

1. What are the steps to add a second email account to the Mail app?

_____

_____

_____

_____

2. By default, only email received in the last two weeks is downloaded to the Mail app. List the steps to have the Mail app download email from the last month:

_____

_____

_____

3. What are the steps to add an account in the People app?

_____

_____

_____

_____

_____

4. Using the People app, what can you do when connected to your Twitter account?

_____

_____

LAB 7.4 USE WINDOWS KEYBOARD SHORTCUTS

OBJECTIVES

The goal of this lab is to learn some keyboard shortcuts. After completing this lab, you will be able to use the keyboard to:

◢ Display the Start menu

◢ Launch Help and Support

◢ Switch between open applications

◢ Launch utilities with the Windows logo key

MATERIALS REQUIRED

This lab requires the following:

◢ Windows 8 or Windows 7 operating system

◢ A keyboard with the Windows logo key

LAB PREPARATION

Before the lab begins, the instructor or lab assistant needs to do the following:

◢ Verify Windows starts with no errors

ACTIVITY BACKGROUND

You can use certain keys or key combinations (called keyboard shortcuts) to perform repetitive tasks more efficiently. These shortcuts are also useful if your mouse is not working. In this lab, you learn to use some common keyboard shortcuts. You can find a full list of keyboard shortcuts by searching for "keyboard shortcuts" in the Windows Help and Support Center.

ESTIMATED COMPLETION TIME: 30 MINUTES

 Activity

The F1 key is the universal keyboard shortcut for launching Help. To learn more, follow these steps:

1. Click the desktop, and then press **F1**. Windows Help and Support opens.

2. Close Windows Help and Support.

3. Open File Explorer in Windows 8 or Windows Explorer in Windows 7.

4. With the File Explorer/Windows Explorer window as the active window, press **F1**.

5. Explore the Help options available for File Explorer/Windows Explorer.

6. Open Notepad.

7. With the Notepad window as the active window, press **F1**.

8. Explore the Help options available for Notepad.

◢ How are the Windows Help and Support options different when you press F1 when the desktop is active as opposed to when the File Explorer/Windows Explorer window or Notepad window is active?

_____

_____

_____

9. Use Windows Help and Support to find a list of general keyboard shortcuts. What key can you press to activate the menu in an application window? Close all windows.

_____

10. You can activate many shortcuts by pressing the Windows logo key in combination with other keys. An enhanced keyboard has two Windows logo keys, usually located between the Ctrl and Alt keys on either side of the Spacebar. Try the combinations listed in Table 7-1, and record the result of each key combination in the Result column. (Close each window you open before proceeding to the next key combination.)

Key or Key Combination	Result
⊞ Windows logo	
⊞ Windows logo + E	
⊞ Windows logo + F	
⊞ Windows logo + R	
⊞ Windows logo + Pause	
⊞ Windows logo + M	

Table 7-1 Key combinations using the Windows logo key

To become more efficient and productive with your work by using shortcut keystrokes, follow these steps:

1. Press the Windows logo on your keyboard; the Start screen or menu opens. In Windows 8, type **notepad** and press **Enter**. In Windows 7, in the Search programs and files box, type **notepad** and press **Enter**. The Notepad opens.

2. Press the Windows logo on your keyboard; the Start screen or menu opens. In Windows 8, type **paint** and press **Enter**. In Windows 7, in the Search programs and files box, type **mspaint** and press **Enter**. Microsoft Paint opens.

3. Press the Windows logo on your keyboard; the Start screen or menu opens. In Windows 8, type **calc** and **press** Enter. In Windows 7, in the Search programs and files box, type **calc** and press **Enter**. The Calculator opens.

4. With all those applications open, try the following key combinations:

   a. Press the **Alt + Tab** keys.

   b. Continue to hold down the **Alt** key, and repeatedly tap the **Tab** key.

   ◢ How can these key combinations assist you in being more efficient with your work?

   _____

   _____

CRITICAL THINKING (ADDITIONAL 15 MINUTES)

Using the keyboard skills you have learned in this lab, complete the following steps without using the mouse, and answer the respective questions:

1. Where online can you find a more complete list of keyboard shortcuts for Windows operating systems? Record the URL for this list:

   _____

   _____

2. Using the Windows Help and Support utility, what key combination can be used for printing a document?

   _____

3. Using the Windows Help and Support utility, what key combination can be used to save your work in a document in progress?

   _____

4. What key combination can you use with Internet Explorer that may help you when browsing?

   _____

REVIEW QUESTIONS

1. What key is universally used to launch help?

   _____

2. How many Windows logo keys are usually included on an enhanced keyboard?

   _____

3. What keyboard shortcut combinations can be used to copy and paste a block of text?

   _____

4. Which key can you press to open the Start menu?

   _____

7

5. What is the result of pressing the ▦ Windows logo + P key combination? Describe a situation in which a user might find this menu helpful:

_____

_____

LAB 7.5 GATHER AND RECORD SYSTEM INFORMATION

OBJECTIVES

The goal of this lab is to document a system configuration. In this lab, you use the operating system to determine how the system is configured. You also observe the condition of the system using a health report. After completing this lab, you will be able to:

▵ Gather system information using Windows tools

▵ Use available Windows tools to evaluate the condition of a system

MATERIALS REQUIRED

This lab requires the following:

▵ Windows 8 operating system

▵ Network connection

LAB PREPARATION

Before the lab begins, the instructor or lab assistant needs to do the following:

▵ Verify Windows starts with no errors

▵ Verify each computer is connected to the network

ACTIVITY BACKGROUND

This lab is completed in two parts. In Part 1, you identify the Windows configuration by using Windows tools. In Part 2, you learn an interesting shortcut to help you find several different ways to customize settings in Windows 8.

 Activity

PART 1: EXPLORE THE SYSTEM USING WINDOWS TOOLS

The System Information window provides information about your system. Follow these steps to gather information about your system using the System Information window:

1. Open the Windows desktop. Right-click the **Start** button in the taskbar, and select **System**, or simply press the ▦ **Windows logo** + **Pause** keys. The System window opens.

2. If necessary, expand this window so you can see all the information, and then record the following information:

   ▵ OS edition: _____

   ▵ Processor: _____

� Processor speed: _____

� Installed memory (RAM): _____

� System type: _____

� Computer name: _____

� Workgroup: _____

3. Close the System window.

The System Information utility provides additional information about hardware components and configuration of your system. Do the following to gather this information:

1. *System manufacturer and model:* To open the System Information utility, right-click the **Start** button, click **Run**, type **msinfo32.exe** in the Run box, and then press **Enter**. The System Information window opens. On the System Summary page, find your system's manufacturer and model number and record them here:

System manufacturer: _____

System model: _____

2. *Drives:* Click the **+** sign next to the Components node on the navigation tree in the left pane. Next, click the **+** sign next to the Storage node, and then click **Drives**. Record the following information:

Drive #1		Drive #2		Drive #3	
#1 Drive letter		#2 Drive letter		#3 Drive letter	
#1 Description		#2 Description		#3 Description	
#1 Size		#2 Size		#3 Size	
#1 Vol. name		#2 Vol. name		#3 Vol. name	
#1 Serial no.		#2 Serial no.		#3 Serial no.	

3. *Disks:* Click **Disks** in the navigation tree, and record the following information:

Disk #1		Disk #2	
#1 Manufacturer		#2 Manufacturer	
#1 Model		#2 Model	
#1 Partitions		#2 Partitions	
#1 Size		#2 Size	

4. Close the System Information window.

The Network screen offers information about your network connections. Follow these steps to gather information about your network connection:

1. On the charms bar, click the **Settings** charm, and then click **Change PC settings**.

2. Click **Network** in the left pane. Click to open your network connection. Record the following information:

IP address: _____

Physical address: _____

3. Close the Network Properties page.

7

PART 2: TRY A COOL SHORTCUT FOR WINDOWS 8

Windows 8 offers all kinds of settings to customize the Windows experience. The problem is that these settings can sometimes be hard to find. Follow these steps to create a shortcut to many settings, all to one easy-to-locate icon.

1. On the desktop, create a new folder.

2. Rename this folder using this text (no spaces):
   Settings.{ED7BA470-8E54-465E-825C-99712043E01C}

3. The icon changes appearance and is now named Settings. Double-click the new icon on your desktop, and explore the settings that are included in this new Settings window. The first category of settings is the Action Center, which has 17 items (see Figure 7-4). How many categories of settings do you see in your Settings window?

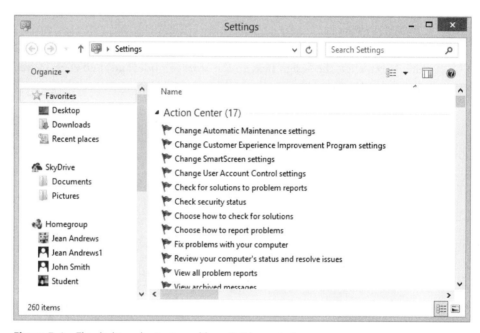

Figure 7-4 The desktop shortcut provides a Settings window

REVIEW QUESTIONS

1. What are two ways to access the System window?

2. Using the charms bar, what are the steps to set the network security so that your computer does not automatically connect to devices, such as on a public network?

3. Based on the system information you gathered, what component of your computer would you upgrade first? Why?

4. Why is it beneficial to keep a written record of your system's configuration?

_____

_____

LAB 7.6 MANAGE WINDOWS 7 LIBRARIES

OBJECTIVES

The goal of this lab is to learn to use Windows 7 libraries to help manage user folders. After completing this lab, you will be able to:

◢ Understand the structure of the Documents library

◢ Create a library and add three folders to it

MATERIALS REQUIRED

This lab requires the following:

◢ Windows 7 operating system, any edition

LAB PREPARATION

Before the lab begins, the instructor or the lab assistant needs to do the following:

◢ Verify Windows starts with no errors

ACTIVITY BACKGROUND

A Windows 7 library works like a folder that can contain files and other folders. These files and other folders can be located in any storage media on the local computer or on the network. Users might keep their data files in many locations on the local computer or on the network. A library is a good way to collect all these folders in a central, easy-to-access location. One good reason to set up a library is to make it easier for a technician to back up data. When a technician uses the Windows Backup and Restore utility to schedule a backup of a library, all the individual folders in that library are backed up. In this lab, you learn to examine the structure of a library, set up a library, and add folders to it.

ESTIMATED COMPLETION TIME: 30 MINUTES

 Activity

Windows 7 creates four libraries by default (Documents, Music, Pictures, and Videos), and you can create additional libraries. Three libraries (Documents, Pictures, and Music) are pinned to the right side of the Start menu by default (see Figure 7-5), and you can access these pinned libraries by clicking them.

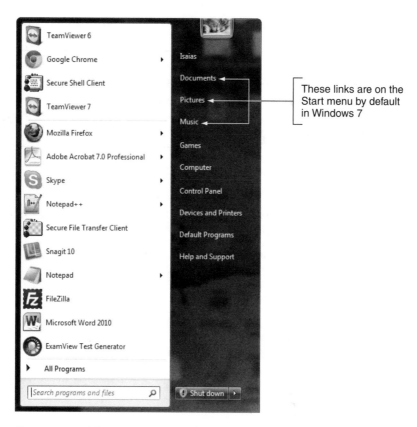

Figure 7-5   Windows 7 creates four libraries by default, three of which have links on the Start menu

You can use Windows Explorer to manage libraries. Follow these steps to see how the default Documents library is constructed:

1. To open the Documents library, click **Start,** and then click **Documents**. The Documents library opens in Windows Explorer. See Figure 7-6.

Figure 7-6   Contents of the Documents library

2. In Windows Explorer, above the Documents library, click **2 locations**. The Documents Library Locations dialog box appears (see Figure 7-7). Close the dialog box.

Figure 7-7 The Documents library gathers files from two locations by default

To learn more about the Documents library, follow these steps:

1. In the left pane of Windows Explorer, right-click the **Documents** library, and select **Properties** from the shortcut menu. The Documents Properties dialog box opens. Notice the check mark beside the My Documents folder.

2. Select the **Public Documents** folder, and then click **Set save location**. Notice the check mark is now beside the Public Documents folder. Files placed in the Documents library will now be stored in the Public Documents folder.

3. Select the **My Documents** folder, and click **Set save location**. Files placed in the Documents library will now be stored in the My Documents folder.

4. Click **OK** to close the Documents Properties window.

To create a library with three folders, follow these steps:

1. You can use Windows Explorer to create a folder in the root directory of drive C: To do so, click **Local Disk(C:)** to select it. The contents of drive C: appear in the right pane of Windows Explorer.

> **Notes** If drive C: has been assigned a volume name on your computer, you might see the volume name beside C: in Windows Explorer rather than Local Disk.

2. In the menu bar of Windows Explorer, click **New folder**.

3. To name the folder, type **Project One** in the highlighted area, and then press **Enter**.

4. Repeat Steps 2 and 3 to create two more folders in the root directory of drive C: Name the folders **Project Two** and **Project Three**.

You should see the three folders listed together in Windows Explorer as subfolders of Local Disk (C:). To create a new library, follow these steps:

1. Click **Libraries** in the left pane of Windows Explorer to select it. The libraries appear in the right pane of Windows Explorer.

2. In the menu bar of Windows Explorer, click **New library**. A new library is created and its name is highlighted.

3. In the highlighted area, type **Work Projects**, and then press **Enter**. The new library is created, as shown in Figure 7-8.

Figure 7-8 List of Libraries on this computer

To add folders to the newly created Work Projects library, follow these steps:

1. Double-click **Work Projects** in the right pane of Windows Explorer. The Work Projects library should be empty.

2. Click **Include a folder**.

3. Browse to the Project One folder you just created, and add that folder to the library.

4. If necessary, click **Work Projects** in the left pane of Windows Explorer. The contents of the Work Projects appear in the right pane.

5. At the top of the right pane, click **1 location**. The Work Projects Library Locations dialog box opens (see Figure 7-9).

6. To add additional folders to the library, click **Add**. In the Include Folder in Work Projects dialog box, navigate to the Project Two folder, and click **Include folder**.

Figure 7-9 New folders can be added to a newly created library

7. Repeat Step 6 to add the Project Three folder to the Work Projects library. The library now has three folders.

8. Click **OK** to close the Work Projects Library Locations dialog box.

9. Close all windows.

REVIEW QUESTIONS

1. What four libraries does Windows 7 create by default?

_____

_____

2. What two folders are included in the Documents library by default?

_____

3. What dialog box is used to change the save location of a library?

_____

4. What are the steps to create a new library?

_____

_____

_____

5. Research online, and decide if and how libraries can be used in Windows 8:

_____

_____

Installing Windows

Labs included in this chapter:

- **Lab 8.1:** Use the Windows 8 Upgrade Assistant
- **Lab 8.2:** Perform a Clean Installation of Windows 8.1
- **Lab 8.3:** Upgrade to Windows 8
- **Lab 8.4:** Update to Windows 8.1 Using Windows Store
- **Lab 8.5:** Use Client Hyper-V to Manage a Virtual Machine (VM)
- **Lab 8.6:** Use Windows Virtual PC to Install Windows 7 in a Virtual Machine (VM)

Notes The instructions in these labs assume that you are using a mouse and a keyboard. If you're using a touch screen, simply tap instead of click, press and hold instead of right-click, double-tap instead of double-click, and swipe to scroll the screen to the right or left.

LAB 8.1 USE THE WINDOWS 8 UPGRADE ASSISTANT

OBJECTIVES

The goal of this lab is to decide if you should upgrade your computer to Windows 8. After completing this lab, you will be able to:

◢ Verify the compatibility of your computer, apps, and connected devices with Windows 8

MATERIALS REQUIRED

This lab requires the following:

◢ Windows 7 operating system

◢ Internet access

LAB PREPARATION

Before the lab begins, the instructor or lab assistant needs to do the following:

◢ Verify Windows starts with no errors

◢ Verify Internet access is available

ACTIVITY BACKGROUND

There are many reasons to upgrade your computer from Windows 7 to Windows 8. Maybe Windows 8 is a requirement for your job, or maybe you just want to see what all the fuss is about. No matter the reason, you need to make sure your computer is compatible with the new OS before you perform the upgrade. Microsoft offers the Windows 8 Upgrade Assistant to scan your hardware, apps, and connected devices for compatibility for an upgrade. Before installing Windows 8, run the Upgrade Assistant from the Microsoft website.

ESTIMATED COMPLETION TIME: 30 MINUTES

 Activity

To download and run the Windows 8 Upgrade Assistant, follow these steps:

1. Open **Internet Explorer**, and browse to **windows.microsoft.com/en-us/windows-8/ upgrade-assistant-download-online-faq**. Review the information given about the Windows 8 Upgrade Assistant.

> **Notes** Websites change often. If you can't find the Upgrade Assistant at the link provided, try this search string using Google.com: **Windows 8 Upgrade Assistant site:microsoft.com.**

2. Click **Download Windows 8 Upgrade Assistant**.

3. Internet Explorer pops up a notification asking if you want to run or save the file Windows8-UpgradeAssistant.exe. Select **Save**, and Internet Explorer automatically saves the file to the Downloads folder for the current user. When the download is complete, click **View downloads**.

4. In the View Downloads window, click **Downloads** beside the file name you just downloaded. What is the path and file name (including file extension) of the downloaded file? What is the size of the file?

5. Close Internet Explorer and the View Downloads window.

6. To use the Upgrade Assistant, double-click the file you just downloaded to your Downloads folder. In the warning dialog box, click **Run**.

7. When the scan is complete, click **See compatibility details** to review the items scanned. Write down all the items you need to review and all actions you take to resolve the compatibility issues:

_____

_____

_____

_____

_____

_____

_____

_____

_____

_____

8. To save the report, click **Save**. What is the path and file name (including file extension) of the downloaded file? What is the size of the file?

_____

9. Email the file to your instructor, or upload it to your online interface.

10. In the Windows 8 Upgrade Assistant, click **Next**.

11. With Windows settings, personal files, and apps selected, click **Next**.

12. The Windows 8 Upgrade Assistant displays the Windows 8 options for your computer. Which version or versions of Windows 8 can you upgrade to?

_____

13. Click **Close**.

REVIEW QUESTIONS

1. Why is it a good idea to run the Windows 8 Upgrade Assistant before upgrading to Windows 8?

_____

2. What is the URL for the Windows 8 Upgrade Assistant?

_____

3. When preparing for an upgrade, is it more important to make sure you have Windows 8 drivers for your network adapter or your sound card? Explain your answer:

_____

_____

4. Describe the difficulty level of preparing your computer for an upgrade to Windows 8 and the problems you might encounter as you work:

_____

_____

_____

LAB 8.2 PERFORM A CLEAN INSTALLATION OF WINDOWS 8.1

OBJECTIVES

The goal of this lab is to install Windows 8.1 without already having an OS installed on your computer. After completing this lab, you will be able to:

◢ Perform a clean installation of Windows 8.1

MATERIALS REQUIRED

This lab requires the following:

◢ Windows 8.1 setup DVD or installation files on another medium, such as a USB flash drive; any edition of Windows 8 will work in this lab.

◢ Product key from Windows 8.1 package or downloaded from the web

> **Notes** This lab gives steps for performing a clean installation of Windows 8.1. If you are using Windows 8, your steps might differ slightly.

LAB PREPARATION

Before the lab begins, the instructor or lab assistant needs to do the following:

◢ Verify the computer powers up properly

◢ Provide each student with access to the Windows 8.1 installation files and product key

◢ Verify any necessary Windows 8.1 drivers are available

ACTIVITY BACKGROUND

When deciding whether to do a clean installation or an upgrade to Windows 8.1, you need to consider the condition of your current system. If the Windows 7 system is giving trouble, performing a clean installation is a good idea so that current problems don't follow you into the new installation. Also, you might do a clean installation if your computer does not already have an OS installed, such as on a new virtual machine.

ESTIMATED COMPLETION TIME: 60 MINUTES

 Activity

Follow these steps to perform a clean installation using a Windows 8.1 installation DVD:

1. Start up your computer, and access UEFI/BIOS setup. Change the boot sequence so the DVD-ROM is the first boot device.

> **Notes** If the installation files are on a USB flash drive, change UEFI/BIOS to first boot to USB.

2. Insert the Windows 8.1 DVD into the optical drive.
3. Shut down your computer, and start it up again.
4. You might be asked to press any key on your keyboard to boot from the DVD. The computer should boot the DVD and begin the installation process.
5. A Windows Setup dialog box appears asking you to select your language, time and currency format, and keyboard input method. Make the appropriate selections. Click **Next**.
6. In the next Windows Setup dialog box, click **Install now**.
7. A Windows Setup dialog box asks for the product key that is used to activate Windows. Enter the product key for Windows 8.1, and click **Next**.
8. The License terms dialog box appears. Check **I accept the license terms**, and click **Next**.
9. When prompted for the type of installation, select **Custom: Install Windows only (advanced)**.
10. In the next dialog box, select a drive and volume, and then click **Next**. (If you need clarification at this point in the installation, ask your instructor for assistance.) The installation process, which can take several minutes, begins. What is the size of the partition that will hold Windows 8.1?

_____

11. The computer might restart by itself several times as part of the installation process. If prompted to press any key to boot the DVD, *ignore the message* because pressing any key will start the installation again from scratch.
12. The Personalize screen asks you to choose a screen color and type the PC name. Enter the PC name as assigned by your instructor. Click **Next**.
13. In the Settings window, click **Use express settings**.
14. You will set up a local account to sign in to Windows. In the "Sign in to your Microsoft account" window, click **Create a new account** from the options at the bottom of the screen, as shown in Figure 8-1. Click **Sign in without a Microsoft account** to create a local account. Type the user name, the password (in both boxes), and the password hint. Click **Finish**. So you do not forget your password, write your user name and password here:

_____

15. The computer takes a few minutes while Windows 8.1 finalizes settings, and then the Start screen appears. You are finished performing a clean installation of Windows 8.1.
16. Open **File Explorer** or the **Computer** window. How much space on the hard drive did the Windows 8.1 installation use?

_____

8

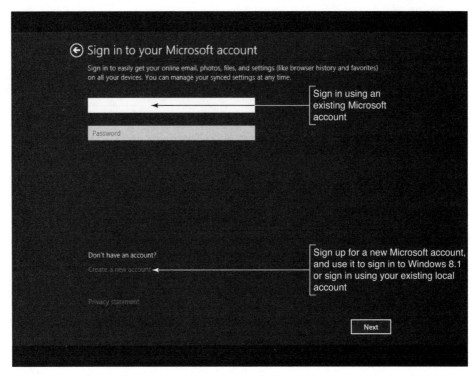

Figure 8-1 Decide which account you will use to sign in to Windows 8.1

REVIEW QUESTIONS

1. Was the Windows 8.1 installation a success? If so, what did you find most challenging about the installation process?

   _____

   _____

2. When is a clean installation preferred over an upgrade to Windows 8.1?

   _____

   _____

   _____

   _____

3. In this lab, you created a local account to sign in to Windows. Was it necessary to be connected to the Internet to create the account? If you had created a Microsoft account to sign in to Windows, would it be necessary to be connected to the Internet to create the account?

   _____

4. Why do you need to access UEFI/BIOS setup before the installation process?

   _____

   _____

5. Did Windows automatically activate during the installation? How can you find out if Windows is activated?

_____

_____

LAB 8.3 UPGRADE TO WINDOWS 8

OBJECTIVES

The goal of this lab is to upgrade to Windows 8. After completing this lab, you will be able to:

◢ Upgrade to Windows 8

MATERIALS REQUIRED

This lab requires the following:

◢ Windows 7 operating system

◢ Windows 8 setup DVD or installation files on another medium, such as a USB flash drive; the Windows 7 edition must qualify for the upgrade license for the Windows 8 edition. Windows 7 Starter, Home Basic, and Home Premium can upgrade to Windows 8 or Windows 8 Pro. Windows 7 Professional and Ultimate can upgrade to Windows 8 Pro.

◢ Product key from Windows 8 package or available on the web

> **Notes** If you are performing an upgrade to Windows 8.1, your steps might differ slightly.

LAB PREPARATION

Before the lab begins, the instructor or lab assistant needs to do the following:

◢ Verify Windows starts with no errors

◢ Provide each student with access to the Windows 8 installation files and product key

◢ Verify any necessary Windows 8 drivers are available

ACTIVITY BACKGROUND

Performing an upgrade to Windows 8 takes less time than performing a clean installation of Windows 8. It also has the advantages that user preferences and settings are not lost and applications are left in working condition. If there isn't a reason for a clean install, an upgrade is recommended.

> **ESTIMATED COMPLETION TIME: 45 MINUTES**

 Activity

The following steps are representative of a typical upgrade. Don't be alarmed if your experience differs slightly. Use your knowledge to solve any problems on your own, and ask your instructor for help if you get stuck. You might want to record any differences between these steps and your own experience. Also, record any decisions you make and any information you enter during the installation process.

8

Follow these steps to perform an in-place upgrade to Windows 8 when you're working with a Windows 8 setup DVD:

1. As with any upgrade installation, before you start the upgrade, do the following:

    a. Scan the system for malware using an updated version of anti-malware software. When you're done, be sure to close the anti-malware application so it's not running in the background.

    > **Notes** If you need help running anti-malware software, refer to the lab "Protect Against Malware in Windows 8" in the chapter, "Security Strategies."

    b. Uninstall any applications or device drivers you don't intend to use in the new installation.

    c. Make sure your backups of important data are up to date, and then close any backup software running in the background.

2. Insert the Windows 8 setup DVD. If the setup program doesn't start automatically, open Windows Explorer, and double-click the setup program in the root of the DVD. (If you're not using a DVD to perform the upgrade, launch the setup program from wherever it is stored.)

3. Respond to any UAC dialog boxes.

4. The setup program loads files, examines the system, and reports any problems it finds. If it finds the system meets minimum hardware requirements, setup asks permission to go online for updates. Make your selection, and click **Next**.

5. The next window requests the product key. Enter the product key, and click **Next**.

6. The product key is verified, and then the License terms window appears. Check **I accept the license terms**, and click **Accept**.

7. On the "Choose what to keep" screen, with **Keep Windows settings, personal files, and apps** selected, click **Next**.

8. On the next screen, verify the choices listed, and click **Install** to begin the installation.

9. During the installation, setup might restart the system several times. If prompted to press any key to boot into the DVD, *ignore the message* because pressing any key will start the installation again from scratch.

10. The Personalize window asks you to choose a screen color. Click **Next**.

11. On the Settings window, click **Use express settings**.

12. On the next screen, enter the password for your local user account.

13. On the next screen, you are given the opportunity to enter a Microsoft account. To skip this step, click **Skip**. You can set up a Microsoft account later. The computer takes a few minutes while Windows 8 finalizes settings, then the Start screen appears. You are finished performing an upgrade installation of Windows 8.

REVIEW QUESTIONS

1. Was the Windows 8 installation a success? If so, what did you find most challenging about the upgrade process?

_____

_____

2. Using File Explorer, find out how much free space is on drive C: Also, how large is the Windows folder?

_____

_____

3. What is the size of the Windows.old folder? What is the purpose of this folder?

_____

_____

4. When performing a clean install of Windows, setup gives you the opportunity to create a user account and password during the installation process. Why do you think setup skipped this step in an upgrade installation?

_____

_____

LAB 8.4 UPDATE TO WINDOWS 8.1 USING WINDOWS STORE

OBJECTIVES

The goal of this lab is to update to Windows 8.1. After completing this lab, you will be able to:

◢ Update to Windows 8.1 using the Windows Store

MATERIALS REQUIRED

This lab requires the following:

◢ Windows 8 operating system that does not have the Windows 8.1 update

◢ Internet access

LAB PREPARATION

Before the lab begins, the instructor or lab assistant needs to do the following:

◢ Verify Windows starts with no errors

◢ Verify Internet access is available

◢ Verify any necessary Windows 8.1 drivers are available

ACTIVITY BACKGROUND

Windows 8.1 is offered as a free upgrade if you already have Windows 8 installed on your computer. The Windows 8.1 release works for any edition of Windows 8. To make sure you have the latest features of Windows 8, always install new releases of Windows 8 as they become available.

ESTIMATED COMPLETION TIME: 30 MINUTES

 Activity

Follow these steps to update to Windows 8.1:

1. As with any update, before you start the update, do the following:

    a. In Windows 8, use the **System** window to check for updates and verify all important updates are installed. If the KB2871389 updated is not installed, the Windows 8.1 update will not appear in the Windows Store.

    b. Scan the system for malware using an updated version of anti-malware software. When you're done, be sure to close the anti-malware application so it's not running in the background.

> **Notes** If you need help running anti-malware software, refer to the lab "Protect Against Malware in Windows 8" in the chapter, "Security Strategies."

    c. Uninstall any applications or device drivers you don't intend to use after the update.

    d. Make sure your backups of important data are up to date, and then close any backup software running in the background.

2. To view which release of Windows is installed, press **Win+X**, and click **System**. The System window reports the release. Which release is installed? Is the installation a 32-bit or 64-bit installation?

3. Go to the **Start** screen, and open the **Store** app. Find and download the Windows 8.1 release. The process of installing Windows 8.1 is similar to installing Windows as an upgrade.

4. You must restart Windows, accept the license agreement, decide how settings are handled, and set up a user account or use an existing account. Sign in using a local account. To use a local account, when asked to sign in to your Microsoft account, click **Create a new account**. Then click **Sign in without a Microsoft account**.

REVIEW QUESTIONS

1. Was the Windows 8.1 update a success? If so, what did you find most challenging about the update process?

2. Why is it a good idea to scan your system for malware before performing an update?

3. Why do you not need the Windows 8 setup DVD or installation files to update to Windows 8.1?

4. Where do you find the Windows 8.1 update?

LAB 8.5 USE CLIENT HYPER-V TO MANAGE A VIRTUAL MACHINE (VM)

OBJECTIVES

The goal of this lab is to install and use virtual machines with Client Hyper-V in Windows 8 Pro. After completing this lab, you will be able to:

◢ Turn on Hyper-V in Windows 8 Pro

◢ Set up Hyper-V to allow a VM to connect to the network

◢ Create a VM using Hyper-V

◢ Use the VM in Hyper-V

MATERIALS REQUIRED

This lab requires the following:

◢ Windows 8 Professional 64-bit operating system

◢ Windows 8 setup DVD or installation files on another medium, such as a flash drive

> **Notes** The steps in this lab use Windows 8.1 Professional. If you are using a different edition of Windows 8, your screens and steps may differ slightly from those presented here.

LAB PREPARATION

Before the lab begins, the instructor or lab assistant needs to do the following:

◢ Verify Windows starts with no errors

◢ Provide each student with access to the Windows 8 installation files and product key

ACTIVITY BACKGROUND

If you need quick and easy access to more than one operating system or to different configurations of the same operating system, a virtual machine is a handy tool to have. The virtual machine creates a computer within a computer, almost as if you are remotely controlling a computer in a different location from a window on your desktop. Virtual machines are heavily used by IT support to replicate and resolve issues, test software, and learn about new operating systems.

8

> **Notes** Hyper-V will not work in Windows 8 Pro that is installed in a virtual machine. In other words, you can't use Hyper-V to create a VM within a VM. You must have the 64-bit version of Windows 8 Pro installed to use Hyper-V. Also, Hyper-V does not play well with other virtual machine management software, so be mindful if you try to install another virtual machine management software when you are already using Hyper-V.

ESTIMATED COMPLETION TIME: 45 MINUTES

 Activity

The steps to set up a VM using Windows 8 Pro are presented in three parts in this lab. In Part 1, you prepare Hyper-V to create a VM, and then you create the VM in Part 2. In Part 3, you manage and use the VM.

PART 1: PREPARE HYPER-V USING WINDOWS 8 PRO

To configure Hyper-V in Windows 8 Pro, follow these steps:

1. For Hyper-V to work, hardware-assisted virtualization (HAV) must be enabled in UEFI/BIOS setup. If you are not sure it is enabled, power down your computer, turn it back on, go into UEFI/BIOS setup, and make sure hardware-assisted virtualization is enabled. Also make sure that all subcategory items under HAV are enabled. Save your changes, exit UEFI/BIOS setup, and allow the system to restart to Windows 8.

> **Notes** HAV might have a different name in the UEFI/BIOS setup screens for your motherboard. Intel UEFI/BIOS calls HAV Intel Virtualization Technology. AMD calls it AMD-V.

2. Open the **System** window. Which edition and version of Windows 8 is installed? If 64-bit Windows 8 Pro is not installed, don't continue with this lab.

3. Hyper-V is disabled in Windows 8 Pro by default. To turn it on, press **Win+X**. In the Quick Launch menu that appears, click **Programs and Features**.

4. Click **Turn Windows features on or off**. Place a check mark next to Hyper-V, as shown in Figure 8-2, and click **OK**.

Figure 8-2 Turn on or off a Windows feature

5. Windows applies the changes. Click **Restart now**, and sign in to the computer after it has restarted a couple of times.

6. To launch the Hyper-V Manager, go to the Start screen, start typing **Hyper-V**, and then click the **Hyper-V Manager** tile. The Hyper-V Manager window appears on the desktop.

7. In the left pane of the Hyper-V Manager, select the host computer.

8. To make sure your VMs have access to the network or the Internet, you need to first install a virtual switch in Hyper-V. To create a virtual switch, in the Actions pane on the right, click **Virtual Switch Manager**.

9. The Virtual Switch Manager dialog box appears. In the left pane, make sure **New virtual network switch** is selected. To bind the virtual switch to the physical network adapter so the VMs can access the physical network, select **External** in the left pane, and click **Create Virtual Switch**.

10. In the Virtual Switch Properties pane that appears, make sure **Allow management operating system to share this network adapter** is checked, and then click **Apply**. Click **Yes**, and the virtual switch is created. Click **OK** to close the Virtual Switch Manager.

PART 2: CREATE A VM USING HYPER-V

To create a VM, follow these steps:

1. In the Actions pane of the Hyper-V Manager window, click **New**, and then click **Virtual Machine**. The New Virtual Machine Wizard launches. Click **Next**.

2. In the next dialog box, assign a name to the VM. Click **Next**. What is the name you assigned the VM?

   _____

3. In the Specify Generation dialog box, Generation 1 is selected. Click **Next**.

4. In the next dialog box, set the amount of RAM for the VM at **4096 MB**. Check **Use Dynamic Memory for this virtual machine**. Click **Next** to continue.

5. In the Configure Networking dialog box, in the drop-down options, select the new virtual switch you created earlier, and click **Next**.

6. In the Connect Virtual Hard Disk dialog box, with **Create a virtual hard disk** selected, leave the default settings. Click **Next**.

7. Your instructor will provide access to operating system installation files. In the Installation Options dialog box, decide how you will install an OS in the VM, and click **Next**. How are you planning to install an OS in the VM?

   _____

8. The last dialog box shows a summary of your selections. Click **Finish** to create the VM. The new VM is listed in the Virtual Machines pane in the Hyper-V Manager window.

PART 3: MANAGE AND USE THE VM

Follow these steps to configure and use the VM:

1. To manage the VM's virtual hardware, select the VM, and click **Settings** near the bottom of the Actions pane. The Settings dialog box for the VM appears.

2. Explore the hardware listed in the left pane, and apply your settings in the right pane. Using the right pane, you can mount a physical CD or DVD to the drive or you can mount an ISO file.

3. To install an OS in the VM, you can boot the VM to the DVD drive, which is mounted either to a physical setup DVD or to a bootable ISO file. To boot to the DVD drive, use the Settings dialog box to verify UEFI/BIOS for the VM has the correct boot priority order. To view and change this setting, click **BIOS** in the left pane.

4. Click **OK** to close the Settings dialog box. To start the VM, select it, and click **Start** in the Actions pane. The VM boots up, and you can then install an OS. Which OS are you installing?

   _____

5. A thumbnail of the VM appears in the bottom-middle pane of the Hyper-V Manager window. To see the VM in its own window, double-click the thumbnail, as shown in Figure 8-3.

Figure 8-3   Windows 8 setup is running in the VM

6. Install the OS, and start the operating system in the VM.

7. In the VM, open **Internet Explorer** to confirm the VM has a good Internet connection.

8. Hyper-V allows you to close the application without shutting down virtual machines that are running in it. Close the VM window. Notice the state of the VM is listed as Running. How much memory is currently assigned to the VM?

_____

9. Close the Hyper-V Manager window and any other open Windows. Restart **Windows 8**.

10. After Windows restarts, sign in to Windows. On the Start screen, launch the **Hyper-V Manager**. What is the state of the VM you created? How much memory is currently assigned to the VM?

_____

11. Open the VM window, and use the VM to surf the web. Finally, using the toolbar in the Virtual Machine Connection window, under "Action," select **Shut Down**. Confirm your action by clicking **Shut Down** again. Now what is the state of the VM?

_____

12. Close all open windows.

REVIEW QUESTIONS

1. Were you able to successfully install the virtual machine using Hyper-V? If so, what did you find most challenging about the process?

_____

_____

2. Which edition and version of Windows 8 did you use during this lab, and why?

_____

3. Why did you create a virtual switch?

_____

_____

_____

_____

4. Why would you use dynamic memory with a virtual machine?

_____

5. When you close the Hyper-V application and have VMs running in it, what happens to the states of the VMs? What happens to the VM states when you open Hyper-V?

_____

_____

LAB 8.6 USE WINDOWS VIRTUAL PC TO INSTALL WINDOWS 7 IN A VIRTUAL MACHINE (VM)

OBJECTIVES

The goal of this lab is to install Windows 7 in a virtual machine. After completing this lab, you will be able to:

◢ Install Windows Virtual PC and use it to set up a new VM

◢ Install Windows 7 in the VM

> **Notes** You will use Virtual PC and the VM with Windows 7 installed in it in future labs in this lab manual.

8

MATERIALS REQUIRED

This lab requires the following:

◢ A computer running Windows 7, any edition and any version (32-bit or 64-bit)

◢ A minimum of 2.0-GHz CPU power is advised

◢ A minimum of 4 GB of RAM is advised

◢ A minimum of 20 GB of available hard disk drive space

◢ Internet access

> **Notes** Virtual machine software and virtual machines tend to require heavy system resources. Don't forget that whatever memory you assign to a VM will not be available to the host operating system while the VM is open.

LAB PREPARATION

Before the lab begins, the instructor or lab assistant needs to do the following:

▲ Verify Windows 7 starts with no errors

▲ Verify Internet access is available

▲ Create or download an ISO file of a Windows 7 operating system, and make this file available to students. The OS can be any edition of Windows 7, but needs to be a 32-bit version.

ACTIVITY BACKGROUND

Virtual machines borrow hardware power from the host operating system to run operating systems in a virtual or simulated computer environment. In this lab, you install Virtual PC and use it to install Windows 7 in a virtual machine.

Your instructor has created an ISO image file that you will use to install Windows 7 in the virtual machine. Ask your instructor for the following information:

▲ What is the name and path to this ISO file?

_____

▲ What is the edition of Windows 7 in the ISO image?

_____

▲ What is the product key for the Windows installation?

_____

ESTIMATED COMPLETION TIME: 60-120 MINUTES

 Activity

PART 1: INSTALL WINDOWS VIRTUAL PC

Follow these steps to download and install Windows Virtual PC:

1. Click **Start**, right-click **Computer**, and then select **Properties**. The System window opens.

   ▲ What edition of Windows 7 are you using?

   _____

   ▲ Are you using a 32-bit version or 64-bit version of the OS?

   _____

2. Go to the Windows Virtual PC home page at **microsoft.com/en-us/download/details.aspx?id=3702**.

3. In the drop-down list of languages, select **English**.

4. Click **Download**. Choose the file you want to download, depending on whether you are using a 32-bit OS or a 64-bit OS. Click **Next**.

> **Notes** The x86 file is for 32-bit operating systems. The x64 file is for 64-bit operating systems.

5. Follow the on-screen directions to **Save** (not Run) the program file.

   ◢ What folder was used to receive the download?

   _____

   ◢ What is the name of the downloaded file?

   _____

6. Double-click the downloaded file. A dialog box appears asking if you want to install a Windows update. Click **Yes**. (Virtual PC is part of this update.)

7. A License terms box opens. Click **I Accept**. When you are asked permission to restart the computer, click **Restart Now**. After the restart, log back on to Windows. Virtual PC is now installed on your system.

PART 2: CREATE A NEW VM AND INSTALL WINDOWS 7 IN IT

Follow these steps to create a new VM and install Windows 7:

1. Click **Start, All Programs,** and then **Windows Virtual PC**. Click **Windows Virtual PC** again. The Virtual Machines folder opens in Windows Explorer. In the menu bar, click **Create virtual machine**.

2. The "Create a virtual machine" dialog box opens (see Figure 8-4). Enter the name of the virtual machine. A good practice is to name the VM by the OS you plan to install, such as **Windows 7 Home Premium** or **Windows 7 Professional**. By default, the VM is stored in a folder in your user profile. What name did you assign to your VM?

   _____

Figure 8-4   Virtual PC steps you through the process of creating a new virtual machine

3. If you want to change the location of the virtual machine file, click **Browse**, navigate to a new location, and click **OK**. What is the drive and folder where your VM will be stored?

4. Click **Next**. In the "Specify memory and networking options" box, enter **2024** for the amount of RAM. Verify **Use computer network connections** is checked. Click **Next**.

5. In the "Add a virtual hard disk" dialog box, leave the selection at **Create a dynamically expanding virtual hard disk**. Click **Create**. The VM is created.

You are now ready to mount the ISO file that holds the Windows 7 installation files to the virtual DVD drive. Follow these steps:

1. In Windows Explorer, in the Virtual Machines folder, click your VM to select it. Click **Settings** in the menu bar. The Settings dialog box opens.

2. In the left pane of the Settings dialog box, click **DVD Drive**. In the right pane of the Settings dialog box, select **Open an ISO image**. See Figure 8-5.

Figure 8-5 Mount the ISO image file to the DVD drive in the VM

3. Click **Browse**, and navigate to the location of the ISO file provided by your instructor. If necessary, double-click the ISO file to select it. Click **OK** to close the Settings dialog box for your VM.

4. When you boot up your VM, it will find the Windows 7 virtual DVD and launch Windows 7 setup. To start the VM, double-click it. The VM boots, Windows loads setup files, and the Windows installation begins.

5. Complete the installation of Windows 7.

   ◢ What is the user account you created during the Windows 7 installation?

   _____

   ◢ What is the password to this user account?

   _____

6. After you click inside the VM window, your keyboard and mouse are captured by the VM until you release them. To release the keyboard and mouse to your host Windows desktop, press the **Alt + Tab** keys. To return to the VM, click inside the VM window.

7. After Windows is installed in the VM, shut down the VM using the **Start** menu on the VM Windows desktop.

You will use this virtual machine installation of Windows 7 in future labs in this lab manual.

REVIEW QUESTIONS

1. How much memory or RAM does Virtual PC allot to a VM by default?

   _____

2. By default, where does Virtual PC store the files for a virtual machine?

   _____

3. After you installed Windows 7 in the VM, what is the size of the Virtual Machine Hard Drive Image file?

   _____

4. How would you configure your virtual machine if you wanted to install Windows 7 from a DVD rather than an ISO image?

   _____

5. What keystroke combination can you use to release your keyboard and mouse from a VM window in Virtual PC?

   _____

   _____

8

Supporting I/O Devices

Labs included in this chapter:

- **Lab 9.1:** Use Device Manager
- **Lab 9.2:** Use Diagnostics Software to Test I/O Devices
- **Lab 9.3:** Install a Sound Card
- **Lab 9.4:** Install Dual Displays in Windows
- **Lab 9.5:** Research High-End Video Cards
- **Lab 9.6:** Repair a Laptop LCD Panel

LAB 9.1 USE DEVICE MANAGER

OBJECTIVES

The goal of this lab is to use Device Manager to compile information on your system's devices and drivers, and to uninstall and reinstall a device. After completing this lab, you will be able to:

- Use Device Manager to investigate your system specifications
- Compile additional information for your Computer Inventory and Maintenance form
- Uninstall and reinstall a device

MATERIALS REQUIRED

This lab requires the following:

- Windows 8 or Windows 7 operating system
- Computer Inventory and Maintenance form you first used in the chapter, "First Look at Computer Parts and Tools"

LAB PREPARATION

Before the lab begins, the instructor or lab assistant needs to do the following:

- Verify Windows starts with no errors

ACTIVITY BACKGROUND

Device Manager is an excellent tool for finding information about hardware specifications. As you continue to work with different kinds of computers, you'll find it extremely useful to maintain a report listing the components installed on each computer. This report is especially important if you're responsible for many computers.

When a device is malfunctioning, one thing you can do is to uninstall and reinstall the device. Suppose, for example, you cannot connect a computer to the network. After verifying network physical connections, confirming Windows network settings, and checking Device Manager for reported errors, you consider that the network adapter drivers might be corrupted. You can eliminate the drivers as the source of the problem by uninstalling and reinstalling the device. When you first install a device, Windows stores a backup copy of the device drivers in a driver store. Later, if you uninstall and reinstall the device, it uses the drivers in the driver store rather than requesting that you provide the drivers again. This can be a convenience, but can also present a problem if the driver store is corrupted. To thoroughly eliminate the drivers as the source of a problem, take time to delete the driver store when you uninstall the drivers. Then you must provide a fresh copy of the device drivers when you reinstall the device.

In this lab, you use Device Manager to manage device drivers and to gather additional information for the Computer Inventory and Maintenance form that you started in the chapter, "First Look at Computer Parts and Tools."

Activity

In earlier labs, you completed Sections 1 through 3, Section 5, and part of Section 4 on the Computer Inventory and Maintenance form. This lab continues under Section 4: Hardware Installed, in the Device Manager subsection.

1. To open Device Manager, right-click **Start,** and then click **Device Manager.** (In Windows 7, first open **Control Panel,** and then click **Device Manager.**) The Device Manager console opens, as shown in Figure 9-1.

Figure 9-1 Device Manager in Windows 8

2. Expand **Display adapters,** and record the name of the adapter(s) here and on the Computer Inventory and Maintenance form:

_____

3. Right-click the adapter name, and then click **Properties** to open the adapter's Properties dialog box. (If you have more than one display adapter, use the first adapter listed.)

4. Click the **Driver** tab, and record the driver version below and on the Computer Inventory and Maintenance form:

_____

5. On the Driver tab, click **Driver Details** to view the driver file names and the paths to those files. Record that information for up to three files below and on the Computer Inventory and Maintenance form:

_____

_____

_____

6. Repeat the same procedure to collect similar information on your computer's wired and wireless network adapters and its sound controller. Record that information on the Computer Inventory and Maintenance form.

7. In Section 6 ("Routine Maintenance") of the Computer Inventory and Maintenance form, add an activity titled "Additional inventory taken" along with your name and today's date.

When you first install a device and its drivers, Windows installs the drivers and also keeps the driver package in a driver store. This driver store is available if you later uninstall and reinstall the device.

> **Notes** For a more thorough explanation of how Windows uses a driver store, see *technet.microsoft.com/en-us/library/cc731478.*

When you want to permanently remove a device from your system, you should uninstall it in Device Manager before you physically remove the device. If you don't, and you later install a similar device, you will end up with both devices installed under Device Manager, which can cause the new device not to work. When you uninstall a device, Windows gives you the option to also delete the driver store, which Windows calls the driver software. Follow these steps to learn more:

1. In Device Manager, open the Properties dialog box for a sound controller, and then click the **Driver** tab. What is the exact name of the adapter shown near the top of the Driver tab? What is the driver version?

_____

_____

2. Click **Driver Details**. Record the path and file name(s) of up to three driver files. Click **OK** to close the Driver File Details dialog box.

_____

_____

3. Click **Uninstall**. The Confirm Device Uninstall dialog box appears (see Figure 9-2).

Figure 9-2 Decide whether you want to delete driver files when you uninstall a device

4. Notice that in the dialog box you can choose to delete the driver software, which deletes all driver files that are being used by this device (and that are *not* being used by other devices). This option also deletes the driver package in the driver store. Click **Cancel** to close the dialog box without uninstalling the network adapter.

Now let's uninstall and reinstall the optical drive. Before you uninstall a device, be sure to record information about the device and its drivers in case you need that information later. Follow these steps to uninstall and reinstall the optical drive in Device Manager:

1. In Device Manager, open the Properties box for your optical drive (for example, the DVD/CD-ROM drive), and then click the **Driver** tab. What is the exact name of the optical drive shown near the top of the Driver tab? What is the driver version? Write that information below and on the Computer Inventory and Maintenance form:

   _____

   _____

2. Click **Driver Details**. Record the path and file name(s) of up to three driver files below and on the Computer Inventory and Maintenance form. Click **OK** to close the Driver File Details dialog box.

   _____

   _____

3. Click **Uninstall**. The Confirm Device Uninstall box appears. Why do you think the option to delete the driver software for this device is missing?

   _____

   _____

4. Click **OK** to uninstall the device. Is the device removed from the Device Manager listing?

   _____

5. Close Device Manager, and restart the computer.
6. Return to Device Manager. Did the optical drive you just uninstalled reappear? Why?

   _____

   _____

REVIEW QUESTIONS

1. Why is it important for IT technicians to keep documentation on computers for which they are responsible?

   _____

   _____

2. What can happen if you don't uninstall a device before removing it from your system?

   _____

   _____

9

3. Why does Windows keep a driver package in the driver store?

_____

_____

4. What are two reasons why you might want to delete the drivers and driver package when you uninstall a device?

_____

_____

5. List the steps to uninstall a device and delete the device driver files and the driver package in the driver store:

_____

_____

6. When Windows deletes the driver package and driver files, in what situation might it not delete driver files used by the device that is being uninstalled?

_____

_____

LAB 9.2 USE DIAGNOSTICS SOFTWARE TO TEST I/O DEVICES

OBJECTIVES

The goal of this lab is to experiment with different diagnostic and performance tools to test and evaluate I/O devices. After completing this lab, you will be able to:

◢ Investigate the quality and performance of your monitor or LCD display using MonitorTest

◢ Understand how to test your sound card features using SoundCheck

◢ Use Keyboard Test to check that all your keyboard keys are working properly

MATERIALS REQUIRED

This lab requires the following:

◢ Windows 8 or Windows 7 operating system

◢ Internet access

LAB PREPARATION

Before the lab begins, the instructor or lab assistant needs to do the following:

◢ Verify Windows starts with no errors

◢ Verify Internet access is available

ACTIVITY BACKGROUND

Intel has compiled a list of links to Intel and other third-party applications that can be used to test and diagnose computer systems. This list can be found at *intel.com/support/ motherboards/desktop/sb/CS-032037.htm*. Many of these utilities will help you test the performance and functionality of I/O devices by stressing their features. In this lab, you explore some of these utilities. In Part 1, you test your monitor using MonitorTest. In Part 2, you assess your system's audio components using SoundCheck. In Part 3, you check your keyboard for stuck or broken keys with Keyboard Test.

> **ESTIMATED COMPLETION TIME: 30 MINUTES**

 Activity

PART 1: USE MONITORTEST

MonitorTest is a utility that allows you to test the performance and quality of your monitor or LCD display. To learn more, follow these steps:

1. Using your favorite browser, go to **passmark.com/products/monitortest.htm**.

2. Download MonitorTest, and install it on your computer. Answer the following questions:

   ◢ What is the name of the downloaded file?

   _____

   ◢ How many days does the evaluation version last?

   _____

   ◢ What is the price after the evaluation period?

   _____

3. Run the test. Describe what happened during the test:

   _____

   _____

4. Use the help feature to answer the following questions:

   ◢ What is a solid color test screen?

   _____

   _____

   ◢ What is the contrast test screen?

   _____

   _____

   ◢ What is the LCD Persistence test screen?

   _____

   _____

   _____

9

PART 2: USE SOUNDCHECK

Before you rule out a sound card as defective, you might want to test it. SoundCheck is a Windows-based application that allows you to test your sound card, speakers, and microphone. To learn more, follow these steps:

1. Using your favorite browser, go to **passmark.com/products/soundcheck.htm**.

2. Download SoundCheck, and install it on your computer. Answer the following questions:

   ◢ What is the name of the downloaded file?

   _____

   ◢ What is the cost of this utility?

   _____

3. Run the test. List the steps you took to run the test:

   _____

   _____

   _____

   _____

   _____

> **Notes** You need a microphone attached to your system to run this test. If you do not have a microphone available, try using TrueRTA (*trueaudio.com*) instead.

4. Use the help feature to answer the following questions:

   ◢ What is 3D Audio Testing?

   _____

   _____

   ◢ What is Loopback Testing, and what special precautions should you take when performing this test?

   _____

   _____

   ◢ What are three of the parameters of Audio FX Testing?

   _____

   _____

PART 3: USE KEYBOARDTEST

Before you replace a suspected defective keyboard, you might want to run KeyboardTest to determine which key(s) is causing the problem. Follow these steps to learn more:

1. Open your browser and go to **passmark.com/products/keytest.htm**.

2. Download KeyboardTest, and install it on your computer.

   ◢ What is the name of the downloaded file?

   _____

   ◢ How many days does the evaluation version last?

   _____

   ◢ What is the price after the evaluation period?

   _____

3. Run the test. Describe what happened during the test:

   _____

   _____

4. Using the help feature, answer the following questions:

   ◢ What is batch testing?

   _____

   _____

   ◢ Which keys can't be tested?

   _____

   ◢ What are four command-line parameters available in KeyboardTest?

   _____

   _____

   _____

   _____

REVIEW QUESTIONS

1. In the list of utilities compiled by Intel, what other utilities (besides the ones used in this lab) test only I/O devices?

   _____

2. In the list of utilities compiled by Intel, what are three utilities that can be used to evaluate or display information about I/O devices in addition to other components?

   _____

   _____

3. For what purposes might you use KeyboardTest?

_____

_____

_____

4. When using MonitorTest, what is the purpose of running the Fonts Test?

_____

LAB 9.3 INSTALL A SOUND CARD

OBJECTIVES

The goal of this lab is to learn how to install a sound card. After completing this lab, you will be able to:

◢ Physically install a sound card

◢ Install device drivers

◢ Test the card and adjust the volume

MATERIALS REQUIRED

This lab requires the following:

◢ Windows 8 or Windows 7 operating system

◢ An account with administrator privileges

◢ An empty expansion slot

◢ A compatible sound card with speakers or headphones

◢ Sound card device drivers

◢ Motherboard documentation, if your system uses embedded audio

◢ A computer toolkit with ESD strap

LAB PREPARATION

Before the lab begins, the instructor or lab assistant needs to do the following:

◢ Verify Windows starts with no errors

◢ Verify each student has access to a user account with administrator privileges

◢ Verify availability of motherboard and sound card documentation

ACTIVITY BACKGROUND

Two of the most popular multimedia devices are the sound card and the embedded audio device. A sound card enables a computer to receive sound input, as when recording an interview, and to output sound, as when playing music. Many systems have audio embedded on the motherboard. As a computer technician, you need to know how to install a sound card, whether you're putting together a computer from scratch, repairing a failed device, or upgrading components on an existing system. In this lab, you disable, install, configure, and test a sound card.

Activity

First, you need to find out whether your system has a sound card, an embedded audio device, or perhaps both or neither. Use the skills you have learned to discover and describe your system's audio configuration, and then work through the steps to complete the lab in the following general order:

- Disable any existing audio devices in Windows.
- Remove or disable the hardware device(s).
- Verify the audio is disabled.
- Physically install a sound card.
- Install the drivers in Windows.
- Verify the function of audio features.
- Return the system to its original state (optional, per your instructor's directions).

Follow these steps to uninstall a sound card or embedded audio device in Windows:

1. After you have signed in as an administrator, open **Device Manager**.
2. Expand **Sound, video and game controllers,** and then select your audio device.
3. Right-click your device, and then click **Uninstall**.
4. If necessary, check the **Delete the driver software for this device** box, as shown in Figure 9-3, and click **OK**.

Figure 9-3 Confirm that this device should be uninstalled

5. Close any open windows, sign out, and shut down your computer.

Next, you either physically remove the sound card from your system or disable an audio device that's embedded in the motherboard.

Follow these steps to remove a sound card:

1. Disconnect all external cables and cords from the case. Press and hold the power button for three seconds to drain any remaining power in your computer.

2. Using all safety precautions, including an ESD strap, remove the case cover, and locate the sound card. Describe any cables connected to the sound card and the ports they are connected to:

_____

_____

_____

3. Disconnect any cables from the sound card. Remove the sound card, and place it in a safe place.

4. Reassemble the computer without the sound card, and boot to Windows to verify the audio isn't functioning.

Your system's motherboard might have onboard (embedded) audio ports or headers. If so, you should disable these audio devices. For most computers, this is done using the UEFI/BIOS setup utility. Older computers used jumpers on the motherboard to enable or disable onboard audio. Follow these steps to disable the embedded audio device:

1. Examine the motherboard ports. Does the motherboard have onboard audio ports?

_____

2. Consult the motherboard documentation to learn how to disable any embedded audio devices. How is onboard audio enabled and disabled?

_____

3. If your motherboard has onboard audio that is disabled using UEFI/BIOS setup, enter UEFI/BIOS setup and disable the embedded audio device. Describe the steps you took:

_____

_____

_____

4. If your motherboard has onboard audio that is disabled using jumpers, follow these steps:

- Disconnect all external cables. Press and hold the power button for three seconds to drain any remaining power.

- Using all safety precautions, including an ESD strap, remove the case cover and locate the way to disable the embedded audio (if applicable). Write down the steps you took to disable the embedded audio:

_____

_____

- Remove any internal audio cables.

- Reassemble the system and boot to Windows to verify the audio isn't functioning.

Now you are ready to physically install a new sound card. Follow these steps:

1. Shut down the computer, and disconnect all external cables from the case. Press and hold the power button for three seconds to drain any remaining power.

2. Using all safety precautions, including an ESD strap, remove the case cover.

3. Locate an empty expansion slot that you can use for the sound card. On some systems, expansion cards are attached to a riser card, which you might have to remove at this time. If necessary, remove the expansion slot faceplate on the case so that the sound card fits into the expansion slot. Some systems use a screw to hold a slot faceplate in place, while others use a clip or passive restraint system to hold the faceplate in place.

4. Insert the sound card into the expansion slot on the motherboard (or insert the sound card into the riser card and the riser card into the motherboard). Line up the sound card on the slot, and press it straight down, making sure the tab on the backplate (the metal plate on the rear of the card where sound ports are located) fits into the slot on the case. Normally, seating the card requires a little effort, but don't force it. If you can't insert the card with just a little effort, something is preventing it from seating. Check for obstructions and try again, removing components that are in the way, if needed. After you have inserted the sound card, verify the gold "fingers" on the sound card are even across the length of the slot or that no gold is showing.

5. After the card is installed, secure it to the case with a screw or the passive restraint flange. The screw goes through a hole in the card's backplate, securing the backplate to the case.

6. Attach all cables required to carry an audio signal from other multimedia devices, such as an optical drive.

7. Replace any components you removed while installing the sound card, and replace and secure the cover on the case.

8. Reattach all cables from external devices to the correct ports. Attach speakers or headphones. (Some speakers receive power from the computer, and others have to be plugged into an external power source, such as a wall outlet.)

Next, you configure the drivers and other software for your sound card. If you have the documentation for your sound card, follow those instructions. Otherwise, follow these general steps to install software for most sound cards, keeping in mind that your sound card might require a slightly different procedure:

1. Start the computer, and sign in as an administrator. If an "Installing device driver software" balloon pops up, wait for the drivers to install.

   ◢ If the installing device driver balloon has popped up, what does the system recognize this device as?

   _____

   ◢ Is this the full name of the sound card you are installing? If not, why?

   _____

   _____

2. If the drivers do not automatically install, insert the disc containing the drivers. When the AutoPlay window appears, click **Run setup.exe**.

3. Typically, the next window that appears asks about install options, including installing drivers and installing additional software for supporting the sound card's functionality. In this lab, you are just installing the device drivers. Select that option.

4. Follow the on-screen prompts to complete the install. At the end of the process, the software might ask to reboot the system.

Follow these steps to test the sound card and adjust the volume in Windows:

1. Open **Control Panel**, and then click **Sound**. The Sound dialog box opens, as shown in Figure 9-4.

Figure 9-4   Check the settings on the Sounds tab

2. Click the **Sounds** tab. Scroll down, and select **System Notification** in the Program Events section. Click the **Test** button, and you should hear the system notification sound from your speakers/headphones. Click **OK** to close the dialog box, and then close Control Panel.

3. On the right side of the taskbar, the speaker volume setting—represented by a speaker icon—is displayed. Click the speaker icon. A pop-up tool opens with a mute button and a slider for adjusting speaker volume.

4. Drag the volume slider all the way to the top, and then click somewhere on the desktop to close the pop-up tool.

5. Right-click the speaker icon, and then click **Open Volume Mixer**. The Volume Mixer window gives you more control than the pop-up tool you used in Step 4. On the following lines, list the volume controls that appear in the Volume Mixer window from left to right, and identify any settings (other than volume) that can be changed:

_____

_____

_____

_____

6. Set the Speakers volume slider to half volume, and then close the Volume Mixer window.

7. Next, to do a further test of your sound card, open Internet Explorer, find a video on **youtube.com** or a similar website, and play the video. Did you hear the video play?

_____

Follow your instructor's directions to return the system to its previous state if necessary.

REVIEW QUESTIONS

1. Was Windows able to find and install the drivers for your new device automatically? If not, what steps did you follow to install the drivers?

_____

_____

_____

2. What other devices embedded on the sound card might Windows detect after the sound card installation is finished?

_____

_____

_____

3. Why might you want to mute the Windows Sounds but not mute the speakers?

_____

_____

4. Why might someone need to remove and then reinstall the drivers for his or her sound card?

_____

_____

5. Why might someone choose to disable an embedded sound device and then add a sound card instead?

_____

_____

LAB 9.4 INSTALL DUAL DISPLAYS IN WINDOWS

OBJECTIVES

The goal of this lab is to set up a second monitor on a system. After completing this lab, you will be able to:

- Install a second video card and its drivers
- Attach a second monitor or LCD projector
- Configure the system to use both monitors at the same time

MATERIALS REQUIRED

This lab requires the following:

- Windows 8 or Windows 7 operating system
- An account with administrator privileges
- A computer toolkit with ESD strap

◢ A second video card with drivers (if needed, borrow one from another computer and work with a partner)

◢ Optional dual-ported video card installed

◢ Appropriate cables and adapters

◢ A second monitor or LCD projector

◢ Internet access (optional)

LAB PREPARATION

Before the lab begins, the instructor or lab assistant needs to do the following:

◢ Verify Windows starts with no errors

◢ Verify each student has access to a user account with administrator privileges

◢ Verify all equipment is functioning

◢ Verify Internet access is available

ACTIVITY BACKGROUND

Having two displays on a system is often quite handy. For instance, two monitors give you more desktop space and make it easier to work with multiple applications simultaneously. You might keep tabs on your email on one screen, while surfing the Internet on the other. Alternatively, your second display could be something else, like an LCD display for presentations or a television for watching movies. In this lab, you install and configure a second display on a computer.

ESTIMATED COMPLETION TIME: 45 MINUTES

 Activity

It's important to verify the original hardware is working correctly before you try to add a second monitor and video card (also called a display adapter or video adapter). That way, if a problem comes up after you install new hardware, you can be fairly sure something is wrong with the newly added components rather than the original equipment. Also, you should make sure the new hardware is on the Windows Hardware Compatibility List (HCL) or, at the very least, that the device manufacturer offers drivers and specific instructions for use with your version of Windows.

In this lab, you explore two options to attach a second monitor. In Part 1 of this lab, you install a second video card. In Part 2, you install a second monitor using a dual-ported video adapter card. Finally, in Part 3, you activate and use a second monitor.

PART 1: INSTALL A SECOND VIDEO CARD

Follow these steps to physically install the second video card:

> **Notes** You can borrow a video card from another computer in the lab and work with a partner, if needed.

1. Check to see if the original video card uses a PCI or PCIe standard, and decide whether it will be the primary or secondary display.

   ◢ What is the standard of the original video card?

⊿ Will the monitor attached to the original video card be the primary or secondary display?

_____

2. Determine which standard the new video card follows (PCI or PCIe), and install the second video card in the closest available slot to the original video card.

⊿ What is the standard of the new video card?

_____

> **Notes** If you need additional guidance on installing an I/O card, use a process similar to the one you used to install the sound card in the previous lab.

3. Attach the second display to the port on the back of the video card.

4. Boot your computer, and enter UEFI/BIOS setup. If your setup has display settings for dual monitors, adjust them so that the card you've chosen as your primary video card is initialized first. If you don't see this setting, your UEFI/BIOS doesn't support this option, and your system will make the adjustment automatically. In that case, exit UEFI/BIOS setup, and wait for your system to finish booting.

Follow these steps to install device drivers and adjust Windows display settings:

1. When the system boots, sign in as an administrator. Windows recognizes the new video card and displays a Driver Software Installation icon in the taskbar's notification area. Above the icon, a balloon tip appears with a notification about the driver installation.

2. At this point, Windows might install the drivers automatically for you (if the drivers were available when your version of Windows was published), or if the card is so new that Windows needs to locate the correct drivers, it will launch the Found New Hardware Wizard. Complete the steps in the wizard to install the card. When the installation is complete, shut down the system.

3. Plug the second monitor into the video port on the second video card.

PART 2: USE A DUAL-PORTED VIDEO CARD

Follow these steps to install a second monitor on a dual-ported video card:

1. Locate the port(s) on the video card. You will be able to attach either a monitor cable to each port or a splitter adapter for two monitors. Attach the appropriate cable. Be aware of the appropriate port interfaces, and have the correct adapter.

2. Plug each monitor into the video card, and then turn the monitors on.

PART 3: USE A SECOND MONITOR

Before you use a second display, you must activate it. To do so, follow these steps:

1. Boot your computer. Both screens will initially show a loading Windows display before one of the monitors goes black.

2. If necessary, sign in as an administrator. Upon reaching the desktop, the second monitor may activate. If it doesn't, you need to change a Control Panel setting.

3. Open **Control Panel**, and click **Display**. Click **Adjust resolution** to open the Screen Resolution window.

4. The area at the top of the Screen Resolution window displays two monitors. Click the **Identify** button to determine how the system is labeling your new monitor. Click the image of the monitor that is your new monitor.

5. Adjust the resolution to your preference by clicking the down arrow on the **Resolution** drop-down box.

6. Click the down arrow on the **Multiple displays** drop-down box, and then click the **Extend these displays.**

7. Click **Apply** to apply the settings. The second monitor displays the desktop.

8. There is a shortcut to get to this Screen Resolution window. Write down the steps to access the Screen Resolution window more quickly:

_____

_____

Follow these steps to test your dual-display configuration:

1. Open Paint, and then drag the Paint program window to the second display. Does your desktop extend to the second display as expected?

_____

2. Open File Explorer or Windows Explorer on the original display.

   ◢ Can you see your mouse move as expected from one display to the next?

_____

   ◢ Does the mouse interact with applications on each display?

_____

3. Close Paint and then reopen it. Which screen did the program open up on? What does this tell you?

_____

_____

4. Return to the Screen Resolution window.

5. You can change the position of Screen #1 and Screen #2. Click and hold Screen #1, move the graphic to the other side of Screen #2, and release the mouse button. Click **Apply**. Move your mouse across the screens. What happens to the monitor display? How would you use this feature?

_____

_____

6. With the Screen Resolution window open, click the down arrow for the **Multiple displays** drop-down box.

7. Select **Show desktop only on X** (X being the number of your added monitor, 1 or 2). Click **Apply**, and then click **Keep changes**. What changed as a result of this setting change?

_____

_____

8. Return to the Screen Resolution window, click the down arrow for **Multiple displays**, and then select **Duplicate these displays**. Click **Apply**, and then click **Keep changes**. What changed as a result of this selection?

_____

_____

9. How does adjusting the settings of one display affect the settings of the other?

_____

Follow these steps to remove the second adapter and return to a single-monitor configuration:

1. Open Device Manager, find the second display adapter, and click it to select it. (Make sure you're choosing the second adapter, not the first.)

2. Right-click the display adapter, and then click **Uninstall**. If prompted, confirm that you want to remove the device. When asked if you want to restart the computer, click **No**.

3. Shut down the computer. Don't restart the computer at this time.

4. Remove the second display and video card. If necessary, reverse any UEFI/BIOS changes you made that affect the display initialization sequence, and then reboot the system to verify the system no longer recognizes the video card.

Follow these steps if you are using a dual-ported video card:

1. Shut down your computer system.

2. Remove the second video cable to return the video card to single-monitor setup.

CRITICAL THINKING (ADDITIONAL 20 MINUTES)

Use the Internet to compare the costs of two sample systems: one with dual 17-inch LCD displays and one with a single 24-inch LCD display. Don't forget about the video card.

1. Which is less expensive?

_____

2. Which is a better value? Why?

_____

_____

9

REVIEW QUESTIONS

1. What might be some advantages to using two video cards instead of one video card with two ports?

_____

_____

2. Why do you think it is necessary to set the sequence in which the system initializes video cards so that the primary display is initialized first?

_____

_____

3. In a multiple-monitor setup, why would it be better to open frequently used applications on one monitor rather than the other?

_____

4. Why would the positioning of the primary (#1) and secondary (#2) monitors be important to a user?

_____

5. Why might you want to install multiple monitors on a system?

_____

_____

LAB 9.5 RESEARCH HIGH-END VIDEO CARDS

OBJECTIVES

The goal of this lab is to gather information about new video cards. After completing this lab, you will be able to:

◢ Research video cards on the manufacturer's website

◢ Choose a video card to meet your needs

MATERIALS REQUIRED

This lab requires the following:

◢ Windows 8 or Windows 7 operating system

◢ Internet access

◢ Adobe Acrobat Reader

LAB PREPARATION

Before the lab begins, the instructor or lab assistant needs to do the following:

◢ Verify Windows starts with no errors

◢ Verify Internet access is available

◢ Verify Adobe Acrobat Reader works with no errors

ACTIVITY BACKGROUND

Your choice of video card can have a profound effect on your computer's performance, especially with applications that use 3D effects, such as computer-aided design (CAD) software and games. To meet the ever-increasing requirements of new programs and operating systems, many people choose to upgrade their video card. In this lab, you research several new video cards on the web.

The two largest manufacturers of video cards are AMD (*amd.com*) and NVIDIA (*nvidia. com*). Each produces several video cards and graphics processor units (GPUs), and the GPU was actually invented by NVIDIA. GPUs from both manufacturers are also used by other video card manufacturers. You also need to know that in 2006, AMD purchased ATI to acquire the ATI line of video cards and GPUs. In ads, therefore, you might see an AMD video card or GPU listed with the name ATI in it.

As you customize computers, you'll learn about the different lines of video cards and GPUs. For example, the NVIDIA Quadro line of video cards is designed for workstation needs, such as CAD software, while the NVIDIA GeForce cards are more suitable for gaming. Within each line, some cards are better than others. For example, the GeForce GTX 950 is better than the GeForce GTX 750. To find the best card for your situation, you need to compare features and read reviews.

ESTIMATED COMPLETION TIME: 30 MINUTES

Activity

In this scenario, you are building a high-end gaming system. Your system has an available PCIe x16, version 3, slot and a surplus of 500 watts of power that can be used for a video card. You are working within a limited budget. Limit your search to the two largest manufacturers of video cards: AMD (*amd.com*) and NVIDIA (*nvidia.com*). Follow these steps to research the video cards:

1. Go to **amd.com**. Under the **Products** drop-down menu, click **Desktop Graphics**. At the time of this writing, there is a link on this page titled **Compare GPUs**, which redirects to the URL *products.amd.com/en-us/search/desktop-graphics*. If you don't see this link, look for another way to compare AMD's GPU products on their website.

2. Use the check boxes to select five products that are compatible with your new gaming system (keeping in mind the PCIe version and wattage needs) to compare, and then click **Compare**. Use this information to fill in the following table.

Model	Maximum Engine Clock	Memory Bandwidth and Speed

◢ Of the cards listed in the table, which card(s) offers an HDMI connection?

_____

_____

◢ Of the five cards listed, which would you choose for a gaming machine? What criteria influenced your choice?

_____

_____

_____

3. AMD sells its GPUs to other manufacturers that use them in their own video cards. Find a video card produced by a video card manufacturer other than AMD that uses a GPU listed in the table on the AMD website. What is the manufacturer and card?

_____

_____

9

4. Now go to **nvidia.com**, and click **USA/Canada** under the North America heading on the home page (or select your geographic location if different). Under the **Products** drop-down menu, point to **Processors**, and then click **GeForce**. In the Compare & Buy section on the GeForce page, click **Desktop GPUs & Gaming PCs**, which redirects to the URL *geforce.com/hardware/compare-buy-gpus*. If you don't see this link, look for another way to compare NVIDIA's GeForce GPU products on their website.

5. Click **Show Specs** on five different GPUs that are compatible with the new gaming system to examine information on each product. Use this information to answer the following questions:

   ◢ Which card offers the best base clock and boost clock performances?

   _____

   ◢ Which card offers the highest bandwidth?

   _____

   ◢ Which card(s) is scalable link interface (SLI) ready?

   _____

   _____

   ◢ Which of these video cards would you choose for a gaming machine? What criteria influenced your choice?

   _____

   _____

   _____

Now use these same two websites to find the best new video card based on each of the following criteria. Be sure to include the model number and price.

   1. A Windows 8-certified video card for under $100:

   _____

   2. A card that supports DirectX 12 and uses less than 300 W for less than $200:

   _____

   3. A card that incorporates a TV tuner and DVI outputs for less than $250:

   _____

   4. A pair of SLI (NVIDIA) or CrossFire (AMD) cards for less than $800 total:

   _____

   ◢ What extra power connectors do these cards require?

   _____

   5. A 2 GB or better high-end gaming card by NVIDIA for less than $300:

   _____

   6. Find a video card made by a manufacturer other than NVIDIA that is comparable to the card you selected in Step 5.

◢ Which manufacturer and card did you select?

_____

◢ How does the price of this card compare with the price of the NVIDIA card?

_____

Now use a third-party review website to compare the best video cards from AMD and NVIDIA. For example, you can use _videocardbenchmark.net_, _gpureview.com_, or another website recommended by your instructor. Follow these steps:

1. Go to a third-party review website, and find the reviews of two video cards from each manufacturer that you think are best for a high-end gaming system. Answer the following questions:

   ◢ What information were you able to find on the third-party website that was not available on the manufacturers' websites?

   _____

   _____

   _____

   ◢ What information was not available on the third-party website that was available on the manufacturers' websites?

   _____

   _____

   _____

   ◢ Based on the opinion of the reviewers on the third-party website, which of the two video cards is the best? Why?

   _____

   _____

   _____

REVIEW QUESTIONS

1. Why might you choose to upgrade your video card?

   _____

2. Which manufacturer had the largest and most useful selection of video cards?

   _____

3. Which website did you find most informative? Why?

   _____

   _____

4. When upgrading a video card, why might you also have to upgrade your power supply?

_____

_____

5. Suppose a video card requires a 6-pin PCIe power connector, but your motherboard does not have this connector. What can you do to solve this problem without replacing the motherboard?

_____

_____

LAB 9.6 REPAIR A LAPTOP LCD PANEL

OBJECTIVES

The goal of this lab is to troubleshoot hardware problems with a laptop's LCD panel. After completing this lab, you will be able to:

◢ Identify hardware problems with the LCD panel

◢ Replace LCD panel components

MATERIALS REQUIRED

This lab requires the following:

◢ An older laptop computer with an LCD monitor that uses fluorescent backlighting (rather than LED backlighting) that can be disassembled

◢ The laptop's service manual that contains instructions for disassembly

◢ Internet access

LAB PREPARATION

Before the lab begins, the instructor or lab assistant needs to do the following:

◢ Provide each student or workgroup with a laptop computer that has an LCD monitor and can be disassembled

◢ Provide a service manual that matches the laptop computer being disassembled

◢ Verify Internet access is available

ACTIVITY BACKGROUND

The A+ exams require that you know about replacing internal laptop components that are field replaceable units (FRUs). The internal FRUs for a laptop computer differ for each laptop and might include the hard drive, RAM, optical drive, LCD or LED panel assembly, Mini PCIe card, CPU, keyboard, speaker, and system board (motherboard). Depending on the laptop, the LCD panel assembly FRU might be the entire LCD assembly or the individual parts, which are the screen, the inverter, and the video card (if one is present).

Laptop computers vary drastically in the way they are assembled and disassembled. As an IT support technician, you are not required to know how to disassemble every brand and model of laptop. However, if you have a hardware service manual that includes the steps to disassemble a laptop to replace a component, you should be able to do the job. This lab gives you that information and experience. The instructions in this lab refer to an older IBM ThinkPad X20. However, you will most likely use a different laptop, which will have its own reference manual.

ESTIMATED COMPLETION TIME: 3 HOURS

 Activity

Joseph brings you his laptop computer complaining that it is "dead," and asks you to repair it. Before you service any laptop, always ask these questions:

- Does it hold important data not backed up?
- Is the laptop under warranty?
- What recently happened to the computer before the problem appeared (such as installing new programs, loaning the computer to a friend, or losing power during a thunderstorm)?
- What do I need to do to reproduce the problem?

In asking these four questions, you find out the laptop does hold important data and that it is not under warranty. You also find out that Joseph allowed a coworker to carry his laptop from one building to another along with a bunch of other computers and components. Joseph suspects the coworker was not careful when handling the laptop. The first time Joseph turned on the laptop after this move, he found it "dead."

You're now ready to investigate the problem. You plug in the laptop, turn it on, and make these observations: The LCD panel appears blank, but the laptop is running. The keyboard lights are lit, and you hear the sound of the fan when you first turn on the computer. You look very carefully at the LCD panel and notice a faint display that you cannot read. You next try to use the keys to increase the LCD panel brightness. Even when you have increased the brightness as far as possible, you still can't read what's on the screen. Next, you plug in an external monitor and use the appropriate keys to direct video output to this device. You can now read the display on the external monitor. What is the next (very important) thing you should do?

_____

_____

_____

You're now ready to discuss the repair options with Joseph. The laptop does not use a video card, so the two FRUs that apply to video in this case are the LCD panel and the inverter (recall that an LCD panel using LED backlighting, however, does not use an inverter). A damaged inverter can cause the display to be dim. The price of the inverter is minimal compared with the value of the laptop or the cost of replacing the entire LCD panel. However, you make sure that Joseph understands that the entire LCD panel might need to be replaced. Because the laptop is several years old, you suspect that replacing the LCD panel would cost more than the laptop is worth.

Research and answer these questions about the laptop you are using in this lab:

1. What is the brand and model of the laptop?

_____

2. Search the service manual for information about the video inverter, if applicable, and the LCD panel. What are the part numbers for the inverter and the LCD panel?

_____

_____

9

3. Search the manufacturer's website or other online sources to find information about the cost of replacing the inverter and the LCD panel on your laptop.

◢ What is the price of the video inverter? Save or print webpages supporting your answer.

_____

◢ What is the price of the LCD panel? Save or print the webpages supporting your answer.

_____

◢ What is the value of this laptop? Determining the value of a laptop can be a little difficult and is usually a best guess. Try searching auction sites such as eBay.com for a match or near match.

_____

◢ What sources of information did you use to determine the value of the laptop?

_____

_____

After Joseph and you discuss the prices of the components and go over his options, Joseph decides to have you try replacing the inverter. If that doesn't solve the problem, then he plans to buy a new laptop. After purchasing the inverter, you're ready to replace this component. Listed below are the steps to replace the inverter in the ThinkPad X20. The steps for your laptop will vary.

1. Power down the laptop, unplug it, and remove the battery.

2. The next step is to remove the keyboard following the directions in the service manual. Remove four screws on the bottom of the laptop. These four screws are marked by two triangles imprinted beside each screw. Be sure to keep the removed screws well organized and labeled so you will be able to put the right screws in the right holes when you reassemble the laptop.

3. Push up on the keyboard from the bottom, and carefully lift the keyboard out of the cavity, as shown in Figure 9-5.

> **Notes** Be careful as you work. Many laptop parts are plastic and are fragile. If you force them, they might break.

Figure 9-5 Push up on the keyboard to remove it

4. Remove the keyboard ribbon cable from the laptop so you can lift the keyboard out and place it out of your way while you work. See Figure 9-6. Don't stack components as you remove them.

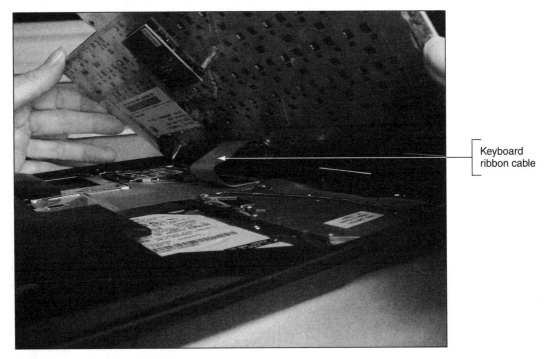

Figure 9-6 Disconnect the keyboard cable and then remove the keyboard

5. You're now ready to remove the LCD assembly. Begin by removing the two screws on the back of the laptop near the LCD panel hinges. Next, remove the hinge covers. You can then remove the two screws holding the LCD panel to the laptop. As shown in Figure 9-7, disconnect the video ribbon cable from the base of the laptop, and then remove the LCD panel.

Figure 9-7 Disconnect the video cable and then remove the LCD panel

9

6. By removing the screws along the sides and bottom of the LCD panel assembly, you can carefully lift the LCD panel out of its enclosure to expose the inverter, as shown in Figure 9-8. Also shown in the figure is the new inverter. Before proceeding, make sure your new component fits the space and that the connectors match. The new inverter shown in Figure 9-8 is not an exact match, but it does fit.

Figure 9-8 The inverter is exposed and is compared with the new one

7. Disconnect the old inverter, and install the new one. When disconnecting the ribbon cable from the old inverter, notice you must first lift up on the lock holding the ZIF connector in place, as shown in Figure 9-9.

Figure 9-9 Lift up on the ZIF connector locking mechanism before removing the ribbon cable

8. Install the new inverter. (For the purposes of this lab, reinstall the same inverter.)

9. Reassemble the LCD panel assembly. Make sure the assembly is put together with a tight fit so that all screws line up well.

10. Reattach the LCD panel assembly to the laptop base.

11. Replace the keyboard, and then replace the four screws on the bottom of the laptop holding the keyboard in place.

12. Replace the battery.

13. Plug in the AC adapter, and then power up the laptop.

REVIEW QUESTIONS

1. What are the three FRUs of the video subsystem for an LCD display using fluorescent backlighting?

_____

_____

_____

2. Of the three video FRUs, which one is optional?

_____

3. Which of these three video FRUs is not present in an LED display?

_____

4. To protect the user's investments in time and money, before disassembling a laptop, what two very important questions should a technician always ask the user?

_____

_____

5. Generally, if a laptop display has a broken inverter but everything else is meeting the user's needs, is it worth replacing the inverter?

_____

_____

9

CHAPTER 10

Maintaining Windows

LAB 10.1 PERFORM HARD DRIVE ROUTINE MAINTENANCE

OBJECTIVES

The goal of this lab is to perform routine maintenance on a hard drive. After completing this lab, you will be able to:

◢ Delete unneeded files on a hard drive

◢ Verify defragment settings on a hard drive

◢ Scan a hard drive for errors

MATERIALS REQUIRED

This lab requires the following:

◢ Windows 8 operating system

LAB PREPARATION

Before the lab begins, the instructor or lab assistant needs to do the following:

◢ Verify Windows starts with no errors

ACTIVITY BACKGROUND

To ensure that your hard drive operates in peak condition, you should perform some routine maintenance tasks regularly. For starters, you need to ensure that your hard drive has enough unused space (which it requires to operate efficiently). In other words, you should remove unnecessary files from the drive.

In addition, files on a hard drive sometimes become fragmented over time; defragmenting the drive can improve performance because files can be read sequentially without jumping around on the drive. Other routine maintenance tasks include scanning the hard drive for errors and repairing those errors. In this lab, you learn about three tools you can use for important disk maintenance tasks. You should use these tools on a scheduled basis to keep your hard drive error free and performing well.

ESTIMATED COMPLETION TIME: 30–45 MINUTES

 Activity

PART 1: USE THE DISK CLEANUP TOOL

Follow these steps to delete unnecessary files on your hard drive:

1. Close all open applications.

2. Open **Control Panel**. Open Administrative Tools, and then open **Disk Cleanup**.

3. If the Disk Cleanup Drive Selection dialog box opens, select the drive you want to clean up in the drop-down list, and click **OK** to close the Disk Cleanup Drive Selection dialog box.

4. The Disk Cleanup dialog box opens, listing the various types of files you can clean up. To include more items in the list, click **Clean up system files**. If a UAC dialog box appears, respond to it. If the Disk Cleanup Drive Selection dialog box appears, select the drive you want to clean up, and click **OK** to close the dialog box.

5. You need to select the types of files you want Disk Cleanup to delete. Select all the file types in the list you want to delete. Depending on your system, these options might include Downloaded Program Files, Recycle Bin, Temporary files, and Temporary Internet Files.

◢ How much disk space does each group of files take up?

_____

_____

_____

_____

◢ Click on the name of a file group you might want to delete to read a description of the files included in that group. Based on information in the Disk Cleanup dialog box, what is the purpose of each group of files listed in the Disk Cleanup dialog box? Record that information here:

Downloaded Program Files	
Temporary Internet Files	
Offline Webpages	
Game Statistics Files	
Recycle Bin	
Setup Log Files	
Temporary Files	
Thumbnails	
Per User Archived Windows Error Reporting	
System Archived Windows Error Reporting	

◢ What is the total amount of disk space you would gain by deleting all of these files?

_____

◢ What types of files might you not want to delete during Disk Cleanup? Why?

_____

_____

6. Click **OK** to delete the selected groups of files.

7. When asked to confirm the deletion, click **Delete Files**. The Disk Cleanup dialog box closes, and a progress indicator appears while the cleanup is under way. The progress indicator closes when the cleanup is finished, returning you to the desktop.

10

PART 2: USE THE CHKDSK TOOL

The next step in routine maintenance is to use Windows Chkdsk to examine the hard drive and repair errors. Follow these steps:

1. Close any open applications so they aren't trying to write to the hard drive while it's being repaired.

2. On the Start screen, type **cmd** in the Start Search box. Right-click **Command Prompt** in the Search pane, and click **Run as administrator**. Respond to the UAC dialog box. The command prompt window opens.

3. Several switches (options) are associated with the Chkdsk utility. To show all available switches, type **chkdsk /?** at the command prompt, and press **Enter**. Answer the following:

   ◢ What are two switches used to fix errors that Chkdsk finds?

   _____

   ◢ Why do the /I and /C switches in Chkdsk reduce the amount of time needed to run the scan?

   _____

4. To use the Chkdsk utility to scan the C: hard drive for errors and repair them, type **chkdsk C: /R** and press **Enter**. (Note: You may have to substitute a different drive letter depending on your computer's configuration.) A message appears saying that Chkdsk cannot run because the volume is in use by another process. Type **Y** and then press **Enter** to run Chkdsk the next time the system is restarted. Close the command prompt window, and restart your computer.

5. After Chkdsk runs, log back on to Windows.

PART 3: USE THE DEFRAGMENT AND OPTIMIZE DRIVES TOOL

The last step in routine hard drive maintenance is to use the Optimize Drives tool to locate fragmented files and rewrite them to the hard drive in contiguous segments. You should do the defragmentation last because other actions, such as cleaning up files, can further fragment the files on the disk. Follow these steps:

1. Close all open applications.

2. From the desktop, right-click the Windows logo, and select **Control Panel**. Open Administrative Tools, and then open **Defragment and Optimize Drives**.

3. Confirm that your primary hard drive is included in the system's list of drives to be optimized. Why would a solid-state drive not appear in the list of drives in the Optimize Drives window?

   _____

   _____

4. Confirm that scheduled optimization is turned on. If it's not on, or if you want to adjust the schedule, click **Change settings**. Figure 10-1 shows the schedule box for Optimize Drives.

5. To analyze the drive's degree of fragmentation before defragmenting, highlight the primary hard drive and click **Analyze**. If the disk is less than 10% fragmented, there's no need to defragment now.

Figure 10-1 Confirm that optimization is scheduled

6. If the disk is at least 10% fragmented, click **Optimize**. If prompted, select the drive you want to defragment. The Optimize Drives tool begins defragmenting the drive.

> **Notes** Fully defragmenting your hard drive can take a few hours, depending on how fragmented it is. If you don't have time to wait, you can stop the process by clicking **Stop**.

7. When defragmentation is completed, close the Optimize Drives window.

REVIEW QUESTIONS

1. Why should you run Disk Cleanup before running the Optimize Drives tool?

_____

_____

2. How does defragmentation improve performance?

_____

_____

3. When you ran the Chkdsk command in this lab, it had to run during the startup process. Why was this necessary? What form of the Chkdsk command can you use in a command prompt window that does not require a restart to run?

_____

_____

4. Based on what you learned in this lab along with your other experiences with Disk Cleanup, which type of files removed by Disk Cleanup took up the most space?

_____

_____

10

LAB 10.2 BACK UP AND RESTORE FILES IN WINDOWS 7

OBJECTIVES

The goal of this lab is to use Windows Backup and Restore to back up and recover lost files. After completing this lab, you will be able to:

◢ Set up a Windows backup, and back up files

◢ Restore deleted or modified files

MATERIALS REQUIRED

This lab requires the following:

◢ Windows 7 operating system

◢ An account with administrator privileges

LAB PREPARATION

Before the lab begins, the instructor or lab assistant needs to do the following:

◢ Verify Windows starts with no errors

◢ Verify each student has access to a user account with administrator privileges

◢ Decide which backup media will be used, for example, an external hard drive, a CD/DVD/BRD drive, or a USB flash drive

ACTIVITY BACKGROUND

Windows provides the File History tool in Windows 8 and the Backup and Restore tool in Windows 7 to help you safeguard data and Windows system files. Using this tool, you can back up one or more folders, or even an entire drive. You should back up your files to a different storage device than your hard drive, such as a CD, DVD, or Blu-ray disc; an external hard drive; or a USB flash drive. Windows 8 and Windows 7 Professional and Ultimate also allow you to back up files to a network server. In this lab, you back up and restore your Documents library using Windows Backup and Restore.

ESTIMATED COMPLETION TIME: 45 MINUTES

 Activity

Follow these steps to create some files in the Documents library and then back up the Documents library:

1. Start Windows and log on using an administrator account. Connect or plug in your backup media (USB flash drive or other storage device) to the computer.

2. To make sure your storage device is large enough to hold all the files and folders in your Documents library, open the Computer window or Windows Explorer, and use it to answer these questions:

    ◢ What backup storage device are you using? (For example, are you using a USB flash drive or an external hard drive?) What is the drive letter assigned to this device?

    _____

    ◢ What is the storage capacity of your backup storage device? How much free space is on the device?

    _____

◿ What is the size of your Documents library?

_____

◿ Does your storage device have enough free space to hold the backup of the Documents library?

_____

3. Using Notepad, create a text file in your Documents library named **File1.txt**. Enter into the text file your name and address and the name of your favorite movie. Close the file.

4. Using Notepad, create a second text file in your Documents library named **File2.txt**. Enter into this file your email address. Close the file.

5. Open **Control Panel,** and click **Back up your computer** in the System and Security group. The Backup and Restore window opens. What options are shown at the top of the left pane of the Backup and Restore window?

_____

_____

_____

6. If a backup schedule has never been configured on this system, the _Set up backup_ link appears in the upper-right area of the window. If a backup schedule has previously been configured, you will see the backup schedule information and the link _Change settings_.

◿ Does your computer already have a backup schedule in place?

_____

7. If you are creating the first backup schedule for this system, click **Set up backup.** If a backup schedule is already in place, click **Change settings.** Follow the steps in the Backup Wizard to decide where to save the backup. What is the drive letter and name of the device that will receive your backup?

_____

8. When asked "What do you want to back up?", click **Let me choose,** and then click **Next.** Uncheck all items designated for backup. Be sure you uncheck **Include a system image of drives: System Reserved, (C:).** In this lab, you are not backing up the system image.

9. Drill down to the **Documents Library** and check it. In this backup, the only item that will be backed up is the Documents library. The backup will include all files and folders in the library.

10. Follow the wizard to review your backup information, and verify you are only backing up the Documents library. What is the day and time the backup is scheduled to run? Save your changes, and run the backup now.

_____

11. The Backup and Restore window shows the progress of the backup. After the backup completes, close the **Backup and Restore** window.

12. Now you will make some changes to the files you backed up. Open the **Documents** library, delete **File1.txt,** and then empty the Recycle Bin. Open **File2.txt,** and add another email address. Save and close the document. What steps did you use to empty the Recycle Bin?

_____

10

Follow these steps to restore the deleted file from backup:

1. Open the Backup and Restore window, and click **Restore my files**. The Restore Files dialog box appears.

2. Click **Browse for files**, and drill down to the **File1** text file. What is the path to the file?

_____

3. Click on the file to select it, and then click **Add files**. File1 is listed in the Restore Files box. Click **Next**.

4. In the next box, decide where you want to restore the file. The default setting is the original location, but you can also change that to a new location. For this lab, restore the file to the original location. Click **Restore**. Click **Finish**. (If the file already existed at this location, you would have had to choose whether to Copy and Replace, Don't Copy, or Copy, but keep both files.)

5. Open the Documents library, and verify File1 is restored. Open File1. Are the file contents as you created them?

_____

Sometimes a file gets corrupted or you make changes to a file that you wish you could undo. If your file is backed up, you can restore it to that previous version. Follow these steps to find out how:

1. Open the Backup and Restore window to run a backup. In the window, click **Back up now**.

2. Open **File2** in your Documents library, and add a third email address. Close the file.

3. Use the Backup and Restore window to run the backup. You should now have three backups of File2.

4. To see the different backups of File2 from which you can choose, open Windows Explorer and locate File2. Right-click **File2** and click **Properties**. The Properties dialog box for the file appears. Click the **Previous Versions** tab. See Figure 10-2.

Figure 10-2 Use the Previous Versions tab to restore a file from backup

5. To restore a file, first select it, and then click **Restore**. A box appears giving you the options to Copy and Replace, Don't Copy, or Copy, but keep both files. Choose the last option, **Copy, but keep both files,** and then click **Finish**.

6. Keep restoring previous versions of File2 until you have one copy of File2 that has one email address in it, another copy of File2 with two email addresses in it, and a third copy of File2 with three email addresses in it.

   ◢ What is the name of the file that contains one email address? Two email addresses? Three email addresses?

   _____

   _____

   ◢ The Previous Versions tab indicates that some backups of File2 are stored at the backup location and others are stored in a restore point. Where does Windows store a restore point? Why would a backup of a file in a restore point not be available if the hard drive crashes?

   _____

CRITICAL THINKING (ADDITIONAL 10 MINUTES)

Windows 8 offers the File History utility to replace the Windows 7 Backup and Restore Center for backing up personal data files and folders, and for creating system images. List two methods for accessing the File History utility:

_____

_____

_____

_____

REVIEW QUESTIONS

1. Is it more important to back up Windows system files or data files? Why?

   _____

   _____

2. By default, how often does Windows back up?

   _____

3. In the lab, you saw two ways to restore files: use the Backup and Restore window or use the Previous Versions tab. Which method is best to use when you want to restore a corrupted file? Three deleted folders? When you want to recover a folder from a backup made over three weeks ago?

   _____

4. What is a system image, and how do you create one?

   _____

10

5. If you decide to restore a corrupted file from a restore point, what should you do first so you don't overwrite the corrupted file? Why?

_____

6. In the lab, File2 appears in the Documents library. What is the actual folder that File2 is stored in?

_____

7. Based on the information you see in Figure 10-2, what action triggers Windows to create a restore point?

_____

LAB 10.3 SET UP A VIRTUAL HARD DRIVE IN WINDOWS

OBJECTIVES

The goal of this lab is to learn how to create a virtual hard drive in your Windows system. After completing this lab, you will be able to:

◢ Create a virtual hard drive (VHD)

◢ Use File Explorer or Windows Explorer to explore the VHD

MATERIALS REQUIRED

This lab requires the following:

◢ Windows 8 or Windows 7 operating system

◢ A USB flash drive or other storage media; if the device is not already formatted using the NTFS file system, all data on the device will be lost.

LAB PREPARATION

Before the lab begins, the instructor or lab assistant needs to do the following:

◢ Verify Windows starts with no errors

ACTIVITY BACKGROUND

A virtual hard drive (VHD) is a file that acts like a hard drive. You can create a VHD and access it through File Explorer in Windows 8 or Windows Explorer in Windows 7. You can also attach an existing VHD to your Windows installation. In Windows 8 and Windows 7, a system image is stored in a VHD. A VHD is sometimes used to hold a deployment image when that image is deployed to computers over the network. Using Windows 8 or Windows 7, it is possible to boot a computer to Windows installed on a VHD. A VHD is used as a hard drive in a virtual machine. In this lab, you create a VHD in your regular Windows installation, and then explore the VHD using File Explorer or Windows Explorer.

ESTIMATED COMPLETION TIME: 30 MINUTES

Activity

Follow these steps to create a new VHD:

1. Plug in your USB flash drive. In Windows 8, right-click the **Windows logo**, and select **Disk Management**. In Windows 7, click **Start**, type **diskmgmt.msc** in the Search box, and then press **Enter**. How many disks are installed in your system? List the Disk number and size of each disk:

   _____

   _____

2. For best results, a VHD should be installed on a device using the NTFS file system. What file system is used for the USB flash drive? If the file system is not NTFS, format it for NTFS. To format for NTFS, right-click the drive, click **Format**, select **NTFS** for the File system, and click **OK**. A warning message displays. Click **OK** again. The drive is formatted, and all data on the drive is lost.

3. To create the VHD, on the menu bar, click **Action**, and then click **Create VHD**. In the Create and Attach Virtual Hard Disk window, click **Browse**, and then browse to the location where you want to store the VHD. In the Browse Virtual Disk files box, navigate to your USB flash drive or other storage device. Enter the name of your VHD as **VHD001**. Click **Save**.

4. Enter 5000 for the virtual hard disk size in MB. Under Virtual hard disk format, select **Dynamically expanding**. Click **OK** to create the VHD.

   ◢ What is the number assigned to the disk by Disk Management? What is the status of your VHD in the Disk Management window?

   _____

   ◢ What is the reported size of the disk?

   _____

5. To initialize the disk, right-click in the Disk area, and select **Initialize Disk** in the shortcut menu. In the Initialize Disk box, if necessary, select the **GPT partitioning system**, and then click **OK**.

6. The next step to prepare the disk for use is to create and format a volume on the disk. To start the process, right-click in unallocated space on the disk, and select **New Simple Volume** in the shortcut menu. The New Simple Volume Wizard starts. Step through the wizard to assign all unallocated space to the volume and format the volume using the NTFS file system. What drive letter did Windows assign to the volume?

   _____

7. Close Disk Management and open File Explorer/Windows Explorer. What capacity does it report for the new volume? How much free space is available?

   _____

10

8. Drill down into your USB flash drive and locate the VHD001 file.

⊿ What is the file size? What is the file name, including the file extension?

_____

⊿ What happens when you double-click or otherwise attempt to open the VHD001 file?

_____

REVIEW QUESTIONS

1. How does Windows 8/7 use a VHD when creating a backup of the Windows volume?

_____

2. How is a VHD sometimes used when deploying Windows 8/7 in an enterprise?

_____

3. Why can you not use an array of VHDs to create a striped volume in a Windows system?

_____

4. List the steps you would take to attach (or install) the VHD001 virtual disk on another computer:

_____

_____

_____

LAB 10.4 MANAGE HARD DRIVE PARTITIONS USING A VIRTUAL MACHINE (VM)

OBJECTIVES

The goal of this lab is to explore the different features of the Disk Management utility using a virtual machine. After completing this lab, you will be able to:

⊿ Create a virtual hard disk drive in a virtual machine

⊿ Format a partition using the Disk Management utility

⊿ Assign a drive letter to a partition using the Disk Management utility

⊿ Split a partition using the Disk Management utility

MATERIALS REQUIRED

This lab requires the following:

⊿ Oracle VirtualBox or Windows Virtual PC installed on a Windows 8 or Windows 7 system

⊿ Installation of Windows 7 in a virtual machine

LAB PREPARATION

Before the lab begins, the instructor or lab assistant needs to do the following:

⊿ Verify Windows starts with no errors

⊿ Verify Windows 7 is installed in a virtual machine in your local host machine

⊿ Verify Windows 7 starts in the virtual machine (VM) with no errors

ACTIVITY BACKGROUND

Disk Management is a Windows utility that can be used to perform disk-related tasks, such as creating and formatting partitions and volumes, and assigning drive letters. Additionally, Disk Management can be used to extend, shrink, or split partitions, and to manage unallocated space. In most cases, you can perform Disk Management tasks without having to restart the system or interrupt users. Most configuration changes take effect immediately.

A virtual machine (VM) is a great tool to use when learning to use Disk Management, because you can install a new hard drive in a virtual machine without having to physically install a hard drive in a computer case. In this lab, you use a VM with Windows 7 installed in it. You can use Windows 7 installed in either Oracle VirtualBox or in Windows Virtual PC.

ESTIMATED COMPLETION TIME: 30 MINUTES

 Activity

In the field, you might be required by your client to install a second hard drive—either physically or virtually—to increase the storage capacity of a system. In this lab, you'll gain some experience installing a second hard drive in a VM and preparing it for first use.

PART 1: EXAMINE THE DRIVES IN YOUR VM

In addition to the powerful features of Disk Management, in its most basic form the utility displays installed disks' configurations, which can be useful if you need to document current information before making a decision on disk-related tasks. To learn more, first start your virtual machine that has Windows 7 installed in it.

If you are using Oracle VirtualBox, follow these steps:

1. Start Oracle VirtualBox Manager. The Oracle VM VirtualBox Manager window opens (see Figure 10-3). The left pane lists the VMs installed in VirtualBox.

Figure 10-3 Oracle VM VirtualBox Manager displaying available virtual machines

2. In the list of virtual machines in the left pane, click the Windows 7 virtual machine. The name of your VM might be different than the one shown in Figure 10-3.

3. In the toolbar, click **Start**. The Windows 7 virtual machine starts. Close any information or warning boxes that appear in the VM. Log on to Windows, and wait for the Windows 7 desktop to display.

If you are using Windows Virtual PC, follow these steps:

1. Start Windows Virtual PC, and view the Virtual Machines folder in File Explorer/Windows Explorer.

2. To start the Window 7 VM, double-click it. The VM opens. Log on to Windows, and wait for the Windows 7 desktop to display.

To examine the drives in your VM, do the following:

1. To open the Computer Management console in the VM, click **Start**, right-click **Computer**, and select **Manage** in the shortcut menu. The Computer Management console opens.

2. In the left pane of the console, under the heading Storage, click the subheading **Disk Management**. Use the current disk configuration to answer the following questions:

◢ How many hard drives does your VM currently have? What is the size of each drive?

_____

◢ How many volumes are currently configured on the system?

_____

◢ What drive letter is assigned to each volume?

_____

◢ What is the size of the primary partition for drive C:?

_____

3. Close the Computer Management console, and shut down Windows 7 in the virtual machine. The virtual machine window closes.

If you are using Oracle VirtualBox, continue to Part 2 to install a second hard drive in the VM. If you are using Windows Virtual PC, proceed to Part 3 to install a second hard drive in the VM.

PART 2: USE ORACLE VIRTUALBOX TO INSTALL A SECOND HARD DRIVE IN A VM

To install a virtual hard disk drive in the VM using Oracle VirtualBox, follow these steps:

1. If necessary, start the Oracle VirtualBox Manager.

2. Click the Windows 7 virtual machine to select it.

3. On the toolbar, click **Settings**. The Windows 7 Settings dialog box displays.

4. In the left pane of the dialog box, click **Storage**. The Storage Tree options are displayed in the center of the dialog box.

5. In the Storage Tree options, right-click **SATA Controller**. In the shortcut menu, click **Add Hard Disk**.

6. A dialog box displays with options for creating a new virtual hard disk. Click **Create new disk**. The Create New Virtual Disk Wizard appears.

7. Select **VHD (Virtual Hard Disk)**, and click **Next**.

8. In the Virtual disk storage details box, click **Dynamically allocated,** and then click **Next**.

9. The options for Virtual disk file location and size display. Under Location, type **NewHardDisk5.**

10. Using the drag ruler, select a size of around 10 GB, and then click **Next**. The Summary dialog box displays.

11. After inspecting the information in the Summary dialog box, click **Create**.

12. When the system is finished creating the virtual disk, it displays the Storage Tree options with the newly created virtual hard disk, as shown in Figure 10-4. Click **OK** to close the dialog box.

Proceed to Part 4 to use the new virtual hard drive installed in your VM.

Source: Oracle VirtualBox

Figure 10-4   Oracle VirtualBox VM settings displaying the Storage Tree with newly created virtual hard drive

PART 3: USE WINDOWS VIRTUAL PC TO INSTALL A SECOND HARD DRIVE IN A VM

To install a virtual hard disk drive in the VM using Windows Virtual PC, follow these steps:

1. If the Virtual Machines folder in Windows Explorer is not already open, open it.

2. Click on the Windows 7 VM to select it. (Do not open the VM.)

3. Click **Settings** in the toolbar. The Settings dialog box for this VM opens.

4. Click **Hard Disk 2**. In the right pane, click **Virtual hard disk file** (see Figure 10-5).

5. Click **Create**. In the box that appears, click **Dynamically expanding**. For the name of the hard disk, enter **HDD2**, and click **Next**.

6. For the size of the disk, enter **10000 MB**, and then click **Create**.

7. The new hard disk is added to the VM. Click **OK** to close the Settings dialog box.

Continue to Part 4 to use the new virtual hard disk installed in your VM.

10

Figure 10-5 Create a new virtual hard disk for the VM

PART 4: USE DISK MANAGEMENT TO PREPARE A NEW HARD DRIVE FOR FIRST USE

You have created a new virtual hard disk and added it to the system. Further configuration is required to allow the operating system to acknowledge the drive's existence so that you can begin taking advantage of the newly acquired storage space. To learn more, follow these steps:

1. Start your VM. Windows 7 in the virtual machine starts up and displays the logon screen. Log on to the system. The Windows desktop appears.

2. To open the Computer window, click **Start,** and then click **Computer.** Answer the following questions:

   ◢ How many drives does Windows Explorer display?

   _____

   ◢ Which drive letters have been assigned to the displayed drives, including optical drives?

   _____

3. Close all windows.

When a new hard drive is first installed, neither the Computer window nor Windows Explorer is able to see it. You need to use Disk Management to initialize, partition, and format the drive. Follow these steps:

1. Open the Computer Management console. Click **Disk Management.**

2. The Initialize Disk dialog box displays automatically because the system has detected the presence of a new storage device. In the Initialize Disk dialog box, select **MBR (Master Boot Record),** and click **OK.** The newly installed 10 GB disk is displayed as a Basic disk with unallocated space.

3. Right-click in the unallocated space, and click **New Simple Volume** in the shortcut menu. The New Simple Volume Wizard displays. Click **Next**.

4. In the Specify Volume Size dialog box, leave the size of the volume at the maximum size, and click **Next**.

5. In the Assign Drive Letter or Path dialog box, to the right of *Assign the following drive letter*, select **F** in the drop-down list. (This letter is the default value.) Click **Next**.

6. In the Format Partition dialog box, select **Format this volume with the following settings:** and select **NTFS** for the File system. Select **Default** for the Allocation unit size. Enter your name as the Volume label.

7. If necessary, check the box for **Perform a quick format**, and click **Next**.

8. To close the wizard, click **Finish**. The newly created partition is displayed, as shown in Figure 10-6.

Figure 10-6   Disk Management displays all partitions and volumes

9. Right-click in the New Volume (F:) area. A shortcut menu displays, listing eleven items. List each item in the shortcut menu, and write a brief description of its purpose:

_____

_____

_____

_____

_____

_____

10

_____

_____

_____

_____

10. Close all windows.

11. Open the **Computer** window. How many drives do you see? List the drive letter and size of each drive:

_____

_____

CRITICAL THINKING (ADDITIONAL 20 MINUTES)

In this lab, you installed a 10 GB virtual hard disk and formatted it with the NTFS file system using a single partition (or volume) that used all available space on the disk. Using Disk Management, split the new partition you have just created on the new virtual hard disk. Do the following:

1. Use File Explorer/Windows Explorer or a command prompt window to copy all the files in the \Program Files\Internet Explorer folder to a new folder on the new hard drive named \Copytest. How large is the \Copytest folder?

_____

2. Without erasing the \Copytest folder, use Disk Management to split the partition on the new hard drive into two partitions. Make one partition 6 GB and the other partition 4 GB. Each partition should use the NTFS file system. List the steps you took to split the partition:

_____

_____

_____

_____

REVIEW QUESTIONS

1. What are two reasons to add a second hard disk to a computer?

_____

2. Why is it better to practice installing a second hard disk by using a VM rather than a physical computer?

_____

3. When installing a new virtual hard disk in a VirtualBox VM or a Virtual PC VM, why is it better to use a dynamically expanding virtual hard disk rather than a fixed-size virtual hard disk?

_____

4. What is the purpose of formatting a drive using Disk Management?

_____

5. What must you do in Disk Management so that Windows Explorer can recognize and use a new hard disk?

_____

6. Other than using the Computer Management console, what is another way to access Disk Management?

_____

LAB 10.5 LEARN TO WORK FROM THE COMMAND LINE

OBJECTIVES

The goal of this lab is to explore some commands used when working from the command line. In this lab, you change and examine directories and drives, and then perform a copy operation. You also learn how to use the command-line Help feature and how to read Help information. After completing this lab, you will be able to:

◢ Create a file and folder with Notepad and Computer

◢ Examine directories

◢ Switch drives and directories

◢ Use various commands at the command prompt

MATERIALS REQUIRED

This lab requires the following:

◢ Windows 8 or Windows 7 operating system

◢ A USB flash drive

LAB PREPARATION

Before the lab begins, the instructor or lab assistant needs to do the following:

◢ Verify Windows starts with no errors

ACTIVITY BACKGROUND

Experienced technicians use the command line for tasks that just can't be done in a graphical interface, especially when troubleshooting a system. For most tasks, however, you'll rely on a graphical interface, such as File Explorer. In this lab, you use File Explorer in Windows 8 or Windows Explorer in Windows 7 to create a new folder and a new file. Then you use the command line to delete that file. In this lab, it's assumed that Windows is installed on the C: drive. If your installation is on a different drive, substitute that drive letter in the following steps.

10

Activity

To create a new folder and text file using File Explorer or Windows Explorer, follow these steps:

1. Open File Explorer or Windows Explorer, and double-click **drive C** in the left pane. The contents of the drive C: root appear in the right pane.

2. Right-click anywhere in the blank area of the right pane, point to **New** in the shortcut menu, and then click **Folder**. A new folder icon appears with "New folder" highlighted as the default name, ready for you to rename it.

3. To rename the folder, type **Tools**, and press **Enter**.

4. To create a file in the Tools folder, double-click the **Tools** folder icon, and then right-click anywhere in the blank area of the Tools pane. Point to **New**, and then click **Text Document**. A new file icon appears in the Tools pane with "New Text Document" highlighted, indicating it's ready for renaming.

5. Double-click the **New Text Document.txt** icon to open the file in Notepad.

6. On the Notepad menu, click **File**, and then click **Save As**.

7. In the Save As dialog box, name the file **Deleteme**, and make sure the selection in the Save as type drop-down list is **Text Documents**. Click the **Save** button.

8. Close Notepad.

9. In the Computer window, right-click **New Text Document.txt**, and then click **Delete** in the shortcut menu. Click **Yes** to confirm the deletion.

10. Close all open windows.

To practice using the command-line environment, follow these steps:

1. Open the command prompt window, and notice that the cursor is flashing at the command prompt.

2. The title bar of the command prompt window varies with different versions of Windows, and depends on the user name of the person currently logged in, for example:

   C:\Users\James Clark>

   The command prompt indicates the working drive (drive C:) and the working directory (for example, the \Users\James Clark directory). Commands issued from this prompt apply to this folder unless you indicate otherwise.

3. Type **DIR** and press **Enter**. Remember that DIR is the command used to list a directory's contents. If the list of files and directories that DIR displays is too large to fit on one screen, you see only the last few entries. Entries with the <DIR> label indicate that they are directories (folders), which can contain files or other directories. Also listed for each directory and file are the time and date it was created, and the number of bytes a file contains. (This information is displayed differently depending on which version of Windows you're using.) The last two lines in the list summarize the number of files and directories in the current directory, the space they consume, and the free space available on the drive.

As you'll see in the next set of steps, there are two ways to view any files that aren't displayed because of the length of the list and the window size. To learn more about displaying lists of files in the command-line environment, perform the following steps:

1. First, you'll go to a particularly large directory so you have more files to experiment with. Type **CD C:\Windows** and press **Enter**. The new command prompt should look like this: C:\Windows>.

2. Maximize the command prompt window.

3. Type **DIR /?** and press **Enter** to display Help information for the directory command. You can view Help information for any command by entering the command followed by the /? parameter (also called a "switch").

4. Type **DIR /W** and press **Enter**. What happened?

5. Type **DIR /P** and press **Enter**. What happened?

6. Type **DIR /OS** and press **Enter**. What happened?

7. Type **DIR /O-S** and press **Enter**. What happened? What do you think the hyphen between O and S accomplishes?

8. Insert a USB flash drive in a USB port.

9. Open File Explorer/Windows Explorer, and find out what drive letter Windows assigned to the flash drive. (The drive will be listed in the left pane with the assigned drive letter in parentheses.) What is that drive letter? The following steps assume that the drive letter is H:, but your drive letter might be different.

10. Close File Explorer/Windows Explorer. In the command prompt window, type **H:** and press **Enter**. The resulting prompt should look like this: H:\>. What does the H: indicate?

11. What do you think you would see if you issued the DIR command at this prompt?

12. Type **DIR** and press **Enter**. Did you see what you were expecting?

13. Change back to the C: drive by typing **C:** and then pressing **Enter**.

14. Type **DIR C:\Tools** and press **Enter**. This command tells the computer to list the contents of a specific directory without actually changing to that directory. In the resulting file list, you should see the file you created earlier, Deleteme.txt.

10

File attributes are managed by using the Attrib command. Follow these steps to learn how to view and manage file attributes:

1. To make C:\Tools the default directory, type **CD C:\Tools** and press **Enter**.

2. To view the attributes of the Deleteme.txt file, type **Attrib Deleteme.txt** and press **Enter**.

3. To change the file to a hidden file, type **Attrib +H Deleteme.txt** and press **Enter**.

4. View the attributes of the Deleteme.txt file again.

   ◢ What command did you use?

   _____

   ◢ How have the attributes changed?

   _____

5. To view the contents of the C:\Tools directory, type **DIR** and press **Enter**. Why doesn't the Deleteme.txt file show in the directory list?

   _____

6. To change the attributes so that the file is a system file, type **Attrib +S Deleteme.txt** and press **Enter**. What error message did you get?

   _____

7. Because you can't change the attributes of a hidden file, first remove the hidden attribute by typing **Attrib -H Deleteme.txt** and then pressing **Enter**.

8. Now try to make the file a system file. What command did you use?

   _____

9. Use the DIR command to list the contents of the C:\Tools directory. Are system files listed?

   _____

10. To remove the file's system attribute, type **Attrib -S Deleteme.txt** and press **Enter**.

11. To move to the root directory, type **CD C:** and press **Enter**.

To learn how to delete a file from the command prompt, follow these steps:

1. Type **DEL Deleteme.txt** and press **Enter** to instruct the computer to delete that file. You'll see a message stating that the file couldn't be found because the system assumes that commands refer to the working directory unless a specific path is given. What command could you use to delete the file without changing to that directory?

   _____

2. The current prompt should be C:\>. The \ in the command you typed indicates the root directory.

3. Type **CD Tools** and press **Enter**. The prompt now ends with "Tools>" (indicating that Tools is the current working directory).

4. Now type **DEL Deleteme.txt /p** and press **Enter**. You're prompted to type **Y** for Yes or **N** for No to confirm the deletion. If you don't enter the /p switch (which means "prompt for verification"), the file is deleted automatically without a confirmation message. It's a good practice to use this /p switch, especially when deleting multiple files with wildcard characters. Also, when you delete a file from the command line, the file doesn't go to the Recycle Bin, as it would if you deleted it in File Explorer/Windows

Explorer or the Computer window. Because deletion from the command line bypasses the Recycle Bin, recovering accidentally deleted files is more difficult.

5. Type **Y** and press **Enter** to delete the Deleteme.txt file. You're returned to the Tools directory.

To display certain files in a directory, you can use an asterisk (*) or a question mark (?) as wildcard characters. Wildcard characters are placeholders that represent other unspecified characters. The asterisk can represent one or more characters, and the question mark represents any single character. The asterisk is the most useful wildcard, so it's the one you'll encounter most often. To learn more, follow these steps:

1. Return to the root directory. What command did you use?

2. Type **DIR *.*** and press **Enter**. How many files are displayed? How many directories are displayed?

3. Type **DIR U*.*** and press **Enter**. How many files are displayed? How many directories are displayed?

4. Explain why the results differed in the previous two commands:

CRITICAL THINKING (ADDITIONAL 30 MINUTES)

Follow these steps to practice using additional commands at the command prompt:

1. Copy the program file Notepad.exe from the \Windows to the \Tools directory. What command did you use?

2. Rename the file in the \Tools directory as **Newfile.exe**. What command did you use?

3. Change the attributes of Newfile.exe to make it a hidden file. What command did you use?

4. Type **DIR** and press **Enter**. Is the Newfile.exe file displayed?

5. Unhide **Newfile.exe**. What command did you use?

6. List all files in the \Windows directory that have an .exe file extension. What command did you use?

10

7. Create a new directory named **\New** in the root directory of drive C:, and then copy **Newfile.exe** to the \New directory. What commands did you use?

_____

_____

8. Using the /p switch to prompt for verification, delete the **\New** directory. What commands did you use?

_____

_____

9. Open Windows Help and Support. Use the Search text box or the Internet to answer the following questions:

◢ What is the purpose of the Recover command?

_____

_____

◢ What is the purpose of the Assoc command?

_____

_____

REVIEW QUESTIONS

1. What command/switch do you use to view Help information for the DIR command?

_____

2. What do you add to the DIR command to list the contents of a directory that's not the current working directory?

_____

3. What command do you use to change directories?

_____

4. What command do you use to delete a file?

_____

5. What command do you use to switch from drive A: to drive C:?

_____

LAB 10.6 USE THE XCOPY AND ROBOCOPY COMMANDS

OBJECTIVES

The goal of this lab is to observe differences in the Xcopy and Robocopy commands. After completing this lab, you will be able to:

◢ Copy files and folders with the Xcopy or Robocopy command

MATERIALS REQUIRED

This lab requires the following:

◢ Windows 8 or Windows 7 operating system

◢ A USB flash drive or another form of removable media

LAB PREPARATION

Before the lab begins, the instructor or lab assistant needs to do the following:

◢ Verify Windows starts with no errors

ACTIVITY BACKGROUND

The Copy command allows you to copy files from one folder to another folder. Using a single Xcopy command, you can copy files from multiple folders, duplicating an entire file structure in another location. The Robocopy command is basically a new version of Xcopy, with a few more features, including the ability to schedule copying to run automatically and the ability to delete the source files when the copying is finished. In this lab, you learn to copy files using either of these commands.

ESTIMATED COMPLETION TIME: 30 MINUTES

Activity

Before you begin using the Xcopy and Robocopy commands, you need to create a test directory to use when copying files. Follow these steps:

1. Open a command prompt window, and make the root of drive C: the current directory. The quickest way to change to the root of a drive is to type **T:** (where T is the drive letter), and then press **Enter.**

2. Make a directory in the drive C: root called **copytest.**

Now you can begin experimenting with the Xcopy command. Follow these steps:

1. Type **Xcopy /?** and press **Enter.** Xcopy Help information is displayed. Notice all the switches you can use to modify the Xcopy command. In particular, you can use the /e switch to instruct Xcopy to copy all files and subdirectories in a directory, including any empty subdirectories, to a new location.

2. Type **Robocopy /?** and press **Enter.** What are some new features unique to Robocopy?

_____

_____

_____

_____

3. Type **Xcopy "C:\program files\internet explorer" C:\copytest /e** and then press **Enter.** (You must use quotation marks in the command line to surround a path, file name, or folder name containing spaces.) You'll see a list of files scroll by as they are copied from the C:\program files\internet explorer folder to the C:\copytest folder.

4. When the copy operation is finished, check the copytest folder to see that the files have been copied and the subdirectories created.

10

5. Enter a DIR command with switches that will give you the total size of the copytest directory, including all the files in the directory and its subdirectories.

   ◢ What command did you use?

   _____

   ◢ What is the total size of the copytest directory in bytes, including all files in the directory and its subdirectories?

   _____

   ◢ What is the total size in MB? In GB?

   _____

6. Insert a USB flash drive or attach an equivalent removable device. To find the capacity of your USB flash drive, enter the command DIR H:. (You might have to substitute the drive letter assigned to your storage device for H:) Add the bytes of used space and free space to determine the capacity of the drive.

   ◢ What is the drive capacity of your USB flash drive in MB? In GB?

   _____

   ◢ What is the free space on your USB flash drive?

   _____

   ◢ Will all the files in the C:\copytest directory fit on your flash drive?

   _____

7. Type **MD H:\copytest**, and then press **Enter**. This command creates a directory named copytest on the H: drive. (Remember to use the letter for the drive assigned to your media device.)

8. To copy all files in the copytest directory on the hard drive to the copytest directory on drive H:, type **Xcopy C:\copytest H:\copytest** and then press **Enter**.

9. The system begins copying files. If the flash drive does not have enough free space to hold the entire C:\copytest directory, the system displays a message stating that the device is out of space and asking you to insert another device. Did you get this error message? If so, what is the exact error message?

   _____

   _____

10. If you don't have enough free space, stop the copying process. To do that, press **Ctrl+Pause/Break**. You're returned to the command prompt.

REVIEW QUESTIONS

1. Can a single Copy command copy files from more than one directory?

   _____

2. What switch do you use with Xcopy or Robocopy to copy subdirectories?

   _____

3. Why might you want to schedule a Robocopy command to occur at a later time?

_____

_____

4. Which Xcopy switch suppresses overwrite confirmation?

_____

10

Optimizing Windows

Labs included in this chapter:

- **Lab 11.1:** Use the Microsoft Management Console
- **Lab 11.2:** Analyze a System with Event Viewer
- **Lab 11.3:** Use Task Manager
- **Lab 11.4:** Edit the Registry with Regedit
- **Lab 11.5:** Identify a Hard Drive Bottleneck by Using Performance Tools
- **Lab 11.6:** Use the System Configuration Utility
- **Lab 11.7:** Critical Thinking: Use Windows Utilities to Speed Up a System

LAB 11.1 USE THE MICROSOFT MANAGEMENT CONSOLE

OBJECTIVES

The goal of this lab is to add snap-ins and save settings using the Microsoft Management Console (MMC) to create a customized console. After completing this lab, you will be able to:

- ◢ Use the MMC to add snap-ins
- ◢ Save a customized console
- ◢ Identify how to launch a console from the Start menu

MATERIALS REQUIRED

This lab requires the following:

- ◢ Windows 8 or Windows 7 operating system, Professional edition or higher
- ◢ An account with administrator privileges

> **Notes** This lab works great in a Windows 8 or Windows 7 virtual machine.

LAB PREPARATION

Before the lab begins, the instructor or lab assistant needs to do the following:

- ◢ Verify Windows starts with no errors
- ◢ Verify each student has access to a user account with administrator privileges

ACTIVITY BACKGROUND

The Microsoft Management Console (MMC) is a standard management tool you can use to create a customized console by adding administrative tools called snap-ins. You can use snap-ins provided by Microsoft as well as those from other vendors. Many of the administrative tools you have already used (such as Device Manager) can be added to a console as a snap-in. The console itself serves as a convenient interface that helps you organize and manage the administrative tools you use most often. In this lab, you use the MMC to create a customized console.

> **ESTIMATED COMPLETION TIME: 30 MINUTES**

 Activity

Follow these steps to build a customized console:

1. Log on to Windows as an administrator.

2. In the Run box, type **mmc**, and then press **Enter**. If Windows needs your permission to continue, click **Yes**. An MMC window for Console1 opens. The left pane displays the list of snap-ins in the console. Currently, nothing appears in this list because no snap-ins have been added to Console1 yet.

3. On the Console1 menu bar, click **File**, and then click **Add/Remove Snap-in**. The Add or Remove Snap-ins dialog box opens. Available snap-ins are listed on the left side of this dialog box (see Figure 11-1). Note that this list includes some administrative tools you have already used, such as Device Manager and Event Viewer. To add Device Manager as a snap-in, click **Device Manager**, and then click **Add**.

Figure 11-1 Adding snap-ins to the Microsoft Management Console

4. The Device Manager dialog box opens, and you can specify here which computer you want this Device Manager snap-in to manage. You want it to manage the computer you're currently working on, so verify the **Local computer** button is selected, and then click **Finish**.

5. Next, you add Event Viewer as a snap-in. Click **Event Viewer** in the Available snap-ins list, and then click **Add**. The Select Computer dialog box opens.

6. Verify the **Local computer** button is selected, and then click **OK**.

7. Click **OK** to close the Add or Remove Snap-ins dialog box. The two new snap-ins are listed in the left and middle panes of the Console1 window.

You have finished adding snap-ins for the local computer to your console. Next, you add another Event Viewer snap-in to be used on a network computer. If your computer isn't connected to a network, you can read the following set of steps, but you won't be able to perform them because Windows won't be able to find any networked computers. If your computer is connected to a network, follow these steps:

1. Add another Event Viewer snap-in, and then click the **Another computer** button in the Select Computer dialog box. Now you need to specify the name of the computer to which you want this Event Viewer snap-in to apply. You could type the name of the computer, but it's easier to select the computer by using the Browse button.

2. Click the **Browse** button. A different Select Computer dialog box opens. Click **Advanced** to open a third Select Computer dialog box. Click **Find Now** to begin searching the network for eligible computers. Eventually, a list of eligible computers is displayed.

3. Click the name of the computer to which you want to apply this Event Viewer snap-in, and then click **OK**. The third Select Computer dialog box closes, and you return to the second Select Computer dialog box.

4. Click **OK** twice to close the two remaining Select Computer dialog boxes. Close the Add or Remove Snap-ins box. A second Event Viewer snap-in is added below the first. The new Event Viewer listing is followed by the name of the remote computer in parentheses. Note: If the second Event Viewer snap-in does not show up and you get an error message

11

instead, write the error message here and continue with the rest of the lab. The remote computer might not be configured to allow event logging on the network.

You're finished adding snap-ins and are ready to save your new, customized console so you can use it whenever you need it. Follow these steps:

1. Verify the left pane of the Console Root folder now contains the following items: Device Manager on local computer, Event Viewer (Local), and, if you were able to complete the network portion, Event Viewer (*remote computer name*).

2. On the Console1 window menu bar, click **File**, and then click **Save As**. The Save As dialog box opens. Unless the location was previously changed, the default location is set to the Administrative Tools folder in your user profile. In Windows 7, if you save your customized console in this location, Administrative Tools is added to your Start menu. Instead, in Windows 8, choose **Desktop** for the Save in location, and in Windows 7, in the Save in drop-down list, choose the **Start Menu** folder in your user profile. This folder is two levels up from the default Administrative Tools folder.

3. Name the console **Custom.msc**, and then click **Save**. The Save As dialog box closes. What is the exact path and file name to the console?

---

4. Close the Console window.

Follow these steps to open and use your customized console:

1. In Windows 8, open the Custom console from the Desktop. In Windows 7, click **Start**, point to **All Programs**, and then click **Custom**. If the UAC dialog box opens, click **Yes**. Your customized console opens in a window named Custom - [Console Root].

2. Maximize the console window, if necessary.

3. In the left pane, click **Device Manager on local computer**, and observe the options in the middle pane.

4. In the left pane, click the arrow next to Event Viewer (Local). Subcategories are displayed below Event Viewer (Local). List the subcategories you see:

---

5. Click **Event Viewer** (*remote computer name*), and observe that the events displayed are events occurring on the remote computer.

6. On the Custom - [Console Root] menu bar, click **File**, and then click **Exit**. A message box opens, asking if you want to save the current settings.

7. Click **Yes**. The console closes.

8. Launch the customized console again, and record the items listed in the middle pane when the console opens:

REVIEW QUESTIONS

1. What term is used to refer to the specialized tools you can add to a console with the MMC? What are they used for?

_____

_____

2. Suppose you haven't created a customized MMC yet. How would you start the MMC?

_____

_____

3. How can a customized console be used to manage many computers from a single machine?

_____

_____

4. Why might you want the ability to manage a remote computer through a network?

_____

_____

5. In Windows 7, in what folder do you put a console so that it appears in the Start menu when you log on to your user account?

_____

6. In Windows 7, in what folder do you put a console so that it appears in the Start menu for all users?

_____

LAB 11.2 ANALYZE A SYSTEM WITH EVENT VIEWER

OBJECTIVES

The goal of this lab is to learn to work with Windows Event Viewer. After completing this lab, you will be able to use Event Viewer to:

▲ View Windows events

▲ Save events

▲ View event logs

▲ Compare recent events with logged events

MATERIALS REQUIRED

This lab requires the following:

▲ Windows 8 or Windows 7 operating system

▲ Network access

▲ An account with administrator privileges

11

LAB PREPARATION

Before the lab begins, the instructor or lab assistant needs to do the following:

⊿ Verify Windows starts with no errors

⊿ Verify each student has access to a user account with administrator privileges

ACTIVITY BACKGROUND

Most of what your computer does while running Windows 8 or Windows 7 is recorded in a log. In this lab, you will take another look at the Event Viewer tool, which provides information on various operations and tasks (known as events) in Windows. Event Viewer notes the occurrence of various events, lists them chronologically, and gives you the option of saving the list so you can view it later or compare it with a future list. You can use Event Viewer to find out how healthy your system is and to diagnose nonfatal startup problems that still allow Windows to start. (Fatal startup problems that prevent a successful startup don't allow you into Windows far enough to use Event Viewer.)

ESTIMATED COMPLETION TIME: 30 MINUTES

 Activity

Follow these steps to begin using Event Viewer:

1. Log on as an administrator.

2. Open the Control Panel window.

3. Click **Administrative Tools**. The Administrative Tools window opens.

4. Double-click **Event Viewer** to open the Event Viewer window. The console tree is shown in the left pane, with Event Viewer (Local) listed at the top. If necessary, click **Event Viewer (Local)** to select it. The Overview and Summary section is in the center pane, with available Actions in the right pane (see Figure 11-2). Maximize the Event Viewer window to see more information in the middle pane.

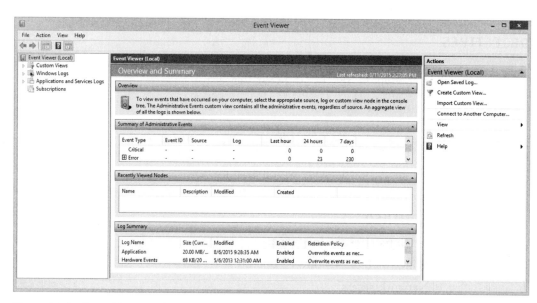

Figure 11-2 Event Viewer tracks failed and successful events

5. You can drag the lines separating the panes to widen or narrow each pane. Widen the center pane because it contains the most useful information.

6. In the console tree, expand **Windows Logs**, and then click **System** in the Windows Logs group. The System log appears in the center pane. In the center pane, if necessary, you can drag the bar between the boxes down so you can see more of the list of events in the top box. The symbols to the left of each event indicate important information about the event. For example, a lowercase "i" in a white circle indicates an event providing information about the system, and an exclamation mark in a yellow triangle indicates a warning event, such as a disk being near its capacity. An exclamation mark in a red circle is an error, and an X in a red circle is a critical event. Each event entry includes the time and date it occurred. Click on several events to see what information changes in various parts of the Event Viewer window when selecting different events.

   For each of the four most recent events, list the source (what triggered the event), the time, and the date:

   _____

   _____

   _____

   _____

7. Double-click the top (most recent) event. The Event Properties dialog box opens. What additional information does this dialog box provide?

   _____

   _____

   _____

8. Close the Event Properties dialog box.

Because Event Viewer provides so much information, it can be difficult to find what you need; however, events can be sorted by clicking the column headings. Do the following to find the most important events:

1. To sort by Level, click **Level**. Events are listed in the following order: Critical, Error, Warning, and Information.

2. To sort events by Date and Time, click **Date and Time**.

3. To see a list of only Critical, Error, and Warning events, expand **Custom Views** in the console tree, and then select **Administrative Events**. How many Critical, Error, and Warning events are recorded on your system?

   _____

You can save the list of events shown in Event Viewer to a log file. When naming a log file, it's helpful to use the following format: *Typelog*EV*mm-dd-yy*.evtx (*mm* = month, *dd* = day, and *yy* = year). For example, you would name a log file of System events saved on January 27, 2016 as SystemEV01-27-16.evtx. After you create a log file, you can delete the current list of events from Event Viewer, allowing the utility to begin creating an entirely new list of events. A short log and resulting log file is easier to view and easier to send to other support technicians when you need help.

11

Follow these steps to save the currently displayed events as a log file, and then clear the current events:

1. Open File Explorer/Windows Explorer, and create a folder called **Logs** in the root directory of drive C:.

2. Leaving File Explorer/Windows Explorer open, return to Event Viewer, and then click **System** in the console tree in the left pane. The System log is selected but no particular event is selected. How many events are there in this log?

_____

3. To save the System log to a log file, on the menu bar, click **Action**, and then click **Save All Events As**.

4. Navigate to the **Logs** folder created in Step 1. Name the file **SystemEV*mm-dd-yy*** (remember to replace the italicized portion with today's date), click **Save**, and then click **OK**. What is the name of your log file, including the file extension?

_____

5. Now you're ready to clear the current list of events from Event Viewer. With the System log still selected, click **Action**, and then click **Clear Log**.

6. When asked if you want to save the System log, click **Clear**. The Event Viewer window now displays only one event. What is this event?

_____

7. Close Event Viewer.

It can be useful to save a log that shows the events of a successful, clean boot, so you can use it as a reference when you have a problem with a boot. You can compare the two logs to help you identify a problem. To save a log of a boot, follow these steps:

1. With your System events log recently cleared, reboot your computer.

2. Return to Event Viewer. How many events are now recorded in your System log?

_____

3. Does this list of events include any Warning or Error events? If so, describe these events here:

_____

4. Save a new file of System events to your Logs folder, and name the file **SystemBootEV*mm-dd-yy***. What is the name of the log file, including the file extension?

_____

5. Now, with the System log still selected, clear the System log.

6. Close Event Viewer.

Next, you create an intentional problem by disconnecting the network cable from your computer. Then, you observe how the resulting errors are recorded in Event Viewer. Do the following:

1. Carefully disconnect the network cable from the network port on the back of your computer.

2. Open Internet Explorer, and try to surf the web.

3. Close Internet Explorer, and then open Event Viewer. How many new events are displayed?

_____

4. List the source, date, and time for any Error or Warning events you see:

_____

5. Click each error or warning event, and read the details. How does Event Viewer describe what happened when you unplugged the network cable?

_____

To restore the network connection and verify the connection is working, follow these steps:

1. Reconnect the network cable to the network port on the back of your computer. Open Internet Explorer. Can you surf the web?

_____

2. In the center pane of the Event Viewer window, the System log reports that new events are available. To see these events, on the menu bar, click **Action**, and then click **Refresh**. How many events are now listed?

_____

When troubleshooting a system, comparing current events with a list of events you previously stored in a log file is often helpful because you can spot the time when a particular problem occurred. Follow these steps to compare the current list of events with the log you saved earlier:

1. Use Windows Explorer to locate the System log files in the C:\Logs folder you created earlier in this lab. Double-click one of these log files. A second instance of Event Viewer opens displaying this log file. Notice in this new window the saved log file is listed in the console tree under Saved Logs.

   ◢ List all the saved logs that are displayed:

   _____

   ◢ What happens when you click on a saved log?

   _____

2. To compare two logs, you can position the two Event Viewer windows side by side. Snap one Event Viewer window to the right of your screen by dragging the window to the right edge of the screen, and then snap the other Event Viewer window to the left of your screen.

3. Widen or narrow the panes in each window so you can see the events listed in each window. In a troubleshooting situation, you would look for differences in the two logs to help you find the source of a problem.

4. Close both Event Viewer windows.

REVIEW QUESTIONS

1. Judging by its location in Control Panel, what type of tool is Event Viewer?

_____

2. What is the file extension that Event Viewer assigns to its log files?

_____

3. How can you examine events after you have cleared them from Event Viewer?

_____

_____

4. Explain how to compare a log file with the current set of listed events:

_____

_____

11

5. Why might you like to keep a log file of events that occurred when your computer started correctly? List the steps to create a log of a successful startup:

_____

_____

_____

_____

_____

LAB 11.3 USE TASK MANAGER

OBJECTIVES

The goal of this lab is to use Task Manager to examine your system. After completing this lab, you will be able to:

◢ Identify applications that are currently running

◢ Launch an application

◢ Display general system performance and process information in Task Manager

MATERIALS REQUIRED

This lab requires the following:

◢ Windows 8 or Windows 7 operating system, Professional edition or higher

◢ Installed CD/DVD drive, installed/onboard sound card, and an audio CD

◢ An account with administrator privileges

LAB PREPARATION

Before the lab begins, the instructor or lab assistant needs to do the following:

◢ Verify Windows starts with no errors

◢ Verify a CD drive and sound card have been installed on all student computers

◢ Verify each student has access to a user account with administrator privileges

ACTIVITY BACKGROUND

Task Manager is a useful tool that allows you to switch between tasks, end tasks, and observe system use and performance. In this lab, you use Task Manager to manage applications and observe system performance.

ESTIMATED COMPLETION TIME: 30 MINUTES

 Activity

Follow these steps to use Task Manager:

1. Log on to Windows as an administrator.

2. Press **Ctrl+Alt+Del**, and then click **Task Manager** in Windows 8 or **Start Task Manager** in Windows 7. Alternatively, you can right-click any blank area on the taskbar, and then click **Task Manager** in Windows 8 or **Start Task Manager** in Windows 7 in the shortcut menu. The Task Manager window opens, with tabs you can use to find information about applications, processes, and programs running on the computer and information on system performance.

3. If necessary, click the **Processes** tab in Windows 8 or the **Applications** tab in Windows 7. What groups of processes or applications are currently listed in the Task list box?

_____

_____

_____

4. Open Windows Help and Support, and then observe the change to the list of processes or applications. What change occurred in the list?

_____

_____

5. In Windows 8, click **File** on the menu bar, and then click **Run new task**. In Windows 7, click the **New Task** button in the lower-right corner of the window. The Create new task dialog box opens, showing the last command entered.

6. Replace whatever command is in the Open text box with **cmd**, and then lick **OK**. A command prompt window opens. Examine the applications listed in Task Manager, and note that C:\Windows\system32\cmd.exe now appears in the list. In Windows 8, expand the Windows Command Processor to view the process listed.

7. Click the title bar of the command prompt window, and drag the command prompt window so it overlaps the Task Manager window. The command prompt window is the active window and appears on top of Task Manager.

You can customize Task Manager to suit your preferences. Among other things, you can change the setting that determines whether Task Manager is displayed on top of all other open windows, and you can change the way information is displayed. To learn more about changing Task Manager settings, make sure the command prompt window is still open and is on top of the Task Manager window. Follow these steps:

1. In Task Manager, click **Options** on the menu bar. A menu with a list of options opens. Note that the check marks indicate which options are currently applied. Check **Always On Top**, which keeps the Task Manager window on top of all other open windows. List other options in the Options menu here:

_____

_____

_____

2. Click the command prompt window in the taskbar. What happens?

_____

_____

_____

11

3. On the Task Manager menu bar, click **View**. You can use the options on the Update Speed submenu to change how quickly the information is updated. List the available and current settings:

_____

_____

_____

Follow these steps in Task Manager to end a task and observe system use information:

1. Notice the information listed in columns in Windows 8, and in the bar at the bottom of Task Manager in Windows 7. What information do you see, and what are their values?

_____

_____

_____

2. While observing these values, move your mouse around the screen for several seconds and then stop. Did any of the values change?

_____

3. Next, move your mouse to drag an open window around the screen for several seconds, and then stop. How did this affect the values?

_____

4. End the Help and Support process using Task Manager. _Caution_: Be careful about ending processes; ending a potentially essential process (which is one that other processes depend on) could have serious consequences. Because Help and Support is not critical to core Windows functions, it's safe to end this process. In the list of applications, click **Microsoft Help and Support** or **Windows Help and Support**, and then click the **End Task** button.

5. Compare the current number of processes, CPU usage, and commit charge (memory usage) with the information recorded in Step 1. How much memory was Windows Help and Support using?

_____

Follow these steps in Task Manager to observe performance information:

1. Click the **Performance** tab, which displays CPU usage and memory usage in bar graphs. What other categories of information are displayed on the Performance tab?

_____

_____

2. Insert and play an audio CD. Observe the CPU and page file or memory usage values, and record them here:

_____

_____

3. Stop the CD from playing, and again observe the CPU usage and page file or memory usage. Compare these values with the values from Step 2. Which value changed the most?

_____

4. When you're finished, close all open windows.

REVIEW QUESTIONS

1. Record the steps for one way to launch Task Manager:

_____

2. Which Task Manager tab do you use to switch between applications and end a task?

_____

3. Why could it be dangerous to end a process with Task Manager?

_____

_____

4. How can you tell whether the processor had recently completed a period of intensive use but is now idle?

_____

5. Did the playback of an audio CD use more system resources than moving the mouse? Explain:

_____

_____

LAB 11.4 EDIT THE REGISTRY WITH REGEDIT

OBJECTIVES

The goal of this lab is to learn how to save, modify, and restore the Windows registry. After completing this lab, you will be able to:

◢ Back up and modify the registry

◢ Observe the effects of a modified registry

◢ Restore the registry

MATERIALS REQUIRED

This lab requires the following:

◢ Windows 8 or Windows 7 operating system

| Notes | This lab works great in a Windows 8 or Windows 7 virtual machine.

11

LAB PREPARATION

Before the lab begins, the instructor or lab assistant needs to do the following:

◢ Verify Windows starts with no errors

ACTIVITY BACKGROUND

The registry is a database of configuration information stored in files called hives. Each time Windows boots, it rebuilds the registry from the configuration files and stores it in RAM. When you need to modify the behavior of Windows, you should consider editing the registry only as a last resort. Errors in the registry can make your system inoperable, and there's no way for Windows to inform you that you have made a mistake. For this reason, many people are hesitant to edit the registry. If you follow the rule of backing up the system before you make any change, however, you can feel confident that even if you make a mistake, you can restore the system to its original condition. In this lab, you back up, change, and restore the registry.

ESTIMATED COMPLETION TIME: 45 MINUTES

 Activity

Windows allows you to create a restore point so that you can restore Windows to a time before any changes were made. Follow these directions to back up the system (including the registry):

1. In Control Panel, open the System window. In the System window, click **System protection**. The System Properties dialog box opens.

2. Select drive **C**.

3. Click **Create**, and then type a name for your restore point. The current time and date will be added automatically. Click **Create** again to create the restore point.

4. When the restore point is completed, close all open windows and dialog boxes.

5. Open the System Properties dialog box again, and then click **System Restore** on the System Protection tab. In the System Restore Wizard, click **Next**, and check the **Show more restore points** check box. Make sure the name and description of the backup you just created are listed by checking the date and time the file was created. Record the name, date, and time of this file:

_____

6. Click **Cancel** to close the System Restore Wizard, and then click **Cancel** again to exit from System Properties.

7. Close any open windows.

As you know, you can use Windows tools such as Control Panel to modify many Windows settings, ranging from the color of the background to power-saving features. Control Panel provides a safe, user-friendly graphical interface that modifies the registry in the background. Sometimes, however, the only way to edit the registry is to do it yourself. These modifications are sometimes referred to as registry tweaks or hacks. In these steps, you will make a relatively small change to the registry by editing the name of the Recycle Bin. To open the registry using the registry editor, do the following:

1. In the Run box, type **regedit**, and then press **Enter**.

2. If Windows presents a UAC dialog box, click **Yes**. The Registry Editor opens, displaying the system's registry hierarchy in the left pane along with any entries for the selected registry item in the right pane.

The registry is large, and searching through it requires a little bit of practice. The section of the registry that governs the naming of the Recycle Bin is HKEY_CURRENT_USER\Software\Microsoft\Windows\CurrentVersion\Explorer\CLSID\{645FF040-5081-101B-9F08-00AA002F954E}. See Figure 11-3.

Figure 11-3 The status bar at the bottom of the Registry Editor window shows the currently selected key

To navigate to this section and rename the Recycle Bin, follow these steps:

1. Click the arrow on the left side of the **HKEY_CURRENT_USER** hive.

2. Click the arrows next to **Software**, and then **Microsoft**. Scroll down the list, and then click the arrows next to **Windows, CurrentVersion, Explorer**, and, finally, **CLSID**.

3. Click **{645FF040-5081-101B-9F08-00AA002F954E}** to select it.

4. In the right pane, double-click **Default**, and the Edit String dialog box displays.

5. To rename the Recycle Bin as Trash Bin, in the Value data box, type **Trash Bin,** and then click **OK**.

6. Notice that Trash Bin now displays under the Data column.

7. To close the Registry Editor, on the menu bar, click **File**, and then click **Exit**. You weren't prompted to save your changes to the registry because they were saved the instant you made them. This is why editing the registry is so unforgiving: There are no safeguards. You can't undo your work by choosing to exit without saving changes, as you can, for instance, in Microsoft Word.

8. Right-click the desktop, and click **Refresh** in the shortcut menu. Note that the Recycle Bin icon is now named Trash Bin.

Finally, you need to undo your changes to the Recycle Bin. Follow these steps to use System Restore to restore the registry's previous version:

1. Open the System Properties dialog box again, and then click **System Restore** on the System Protection tab. In the System Restore Wizard, click **Next**. Check the **Show more restore points** check box.

2. Choose the restore point you created earlier, and then click **Next**.

3. When you're asked to confirm your restore point, click **Finish**. Click **Yes** when the system warns you that a system restore cannot be undone.

4. After the system restore, the computer will have to reboot.

5. After the boot is completed, notice that the name of the Recycle Bin has been restored.

11

Use Windows Help and Support or the Internet to answer the following questions about the registry:

◢ How often does Windows save the registry automatically?

_____

◢ Where are registry backups usually stored?

_____

◢ What files constitute the Windows 8/7 registry? What type of file are they saved as during backup?

_____

_____

REVIEW QUESTIONS

1. Why does Windows automatically save the registry?

_____

_____

2. Where is the registry stored while Windows is running?

_____

3. What type of safeguards does the Registry Editor have to keep you from making mistakes?

_____

4. What are the files that make up a system registry called?

_____

5. In this lab, how did you check to make sure your registry was restored?

_____

LAB 11.5 IDENTIFY A HARD DRIVE BOTTLENECK BY USING PERFORMANCE TOOLS

OBJECTIVES

The goal of this lab is to learn to use the performance monitoring tools in Windows to identify bottlenecks in the system caused by the hard drive or the applications using it. After completing this lab, you will be able to:

◢ Use the Windows 7 Experience Index

◢ Use the Windows Performance Monitor

◢ Identify a hard drive performance bottleneck

MATERIALS REQUIRED

This lab requires the following:

◢ Windows 7 operating system

◢ Internet access

◢ An account with administrator privileges

LAB PREPARATION

Before the lab begins, the instructor or lab assistant needs to do the following:

◢ Verify Windows starts with no errors

◢ Verify Internet access is available

◢ Verify each student has access to a user account with administrator privileges

ACTIVITY BACKGROUND

A problem with slow Windows performance can be caused by hardware or software. Key hardware components that can cause a bottleneck include the processor, memory, and the hard drive. Several factors can affect hard drive performance: the speed of the drive, the amount of free space on the drive, file fragmentation on the drive, hard drive thrashing, and applications that make excessive demands on the drive. In this lab, you determine if the hard drive is a bottleneck to your system by examining all these factors.

Performance Monitor offers hundreds of counters used to examine various aspects of the system related to performance. Two hard drive counters you will use in this lab are the % Disk Time counter and the Avg. Disk Queue Length counter. The % Disk Time counter represents the percentage of time the hard drive is in use. The Avg. Disk Queue Length counter represents the average number of processes waiting to use the hard drive. If the Avg. Disk Queue Length is above two and the % Disk Time is more than 80%, you can conclude that the hard drive is working excessively hard and processes are slowed down waiting on the drive. Anytime a process must wait to access the hard drive, you are likely to see degradation in overall system performance.

ESTIMATED COMPLETION TIME: 45 MINUTES

 Activity

The Windows Experience Index can give you a quick overview of any bottleneck that might be affecting system performance. To view the Windows Experience Index, follow these steps:

1. Log on to the Windows 7 system using a user account with administrative privileges.

2. In the taskbar, click the **Action Center flag.** In the small box that opens, click **Open Action Center.**

3. In the left pane of the Action Center, click **View performance information.** Answer these questions:

   ◢ What is the Base score of the Windows Experience Index?

   _____

   ◢ What component yielded this base score?

   _____

11

4. Click **View and print detailed performance and system information.** A second Performance Information and Tools window opens. Answer these questions:

◢ What is the total amount of system memory?

_____

◢ What is the number of processor cores?

_____

◢ Will this processor support 64-bit computing?

_____

◢ Is the currently installed operating system a 32-bit or 64-bit system?

_____

◢ What is the total size of the hard drive?

_____

◢ What is the amount of free space on the hard drive?

_____

◢ What is the total available graphics memory? Dedicated graphics memory?

_____

◢ Based on the information you have just recorded, what one recommendation do you have to improve system performance?

_____

5. Close the Performance Information and Tools window that was opened in Step 4.

Performance Monitor, which can be configured to measure how well the hard drive is performing, works by displaying counters related to hardware and software components. Follow these steps to use the Performance Monitor to display two counters related to the hard drive:

1. In the left pane of the Performance Information and Tools window, click **Advanced tools.** On the Advanced Tools window, click **Open Performance Monitor.** The Performance Monitor window opens. (Note that you can also open the window by typing *perfmon.exe* in the Search programs and files box.)

> **Notes** Performance Monitor is also available in Windows 8.

2. If necessary, click the triangle to the left of Monitoring Tools to expand this category. Under Monitoring Tools, click **Performance Monitor.**

3. By default, current activity of the processor information object displays in a line graph and the line is red (see Figure 11-4). The list of counters currently selected for display appears at the bottom of the window. In the figure, the one counter selected is % Processor Time. You need to delete any counters you do not need so that you will not unnecessarily use system resources to monitor these counters. To delete the % Processor Time counter, click somewhere in the row to select it. Next, click the **red X** above the graph to delete the counter from the graph. The graph is now empty.

Figure 11-4 Performance Monitor displays current activity of the processor information object

4. To add a new object and counter to the graph, click the **green plus sign** above the graph. The Add Counters box opens.

5. To add a counter for hard drive activity, under *Available counters*, scroll to and click the down arrow to the right of the **PhysicalDisk** object. The counters under the PhysicalDisk object appear, and all these counters are selected. In the list of counters, click **% Disk Time**. This action causes all the other counters to be deselected and this one counter to be selected. Click **Add**. The % Disk Time counter appears in the Added counters area.

6. In the list of counters, click **Avg. Disk Queue Length,** and then click **Add**. The Avg. Disk Queue Length counter appears in the Added counters area. To close the box, click **OK**.

7. The two hard drive counters now appear in the Performance Monitor line graph. Answer these questions:

    ◢ What is the color of the line for the % Disk Time counter?

    _____

    ◢ What is the color of the line for the Avg. Disk Queue Length counter?

    _____

8. Keep the Performance Monitor window open as you perform other activities on your computer. In a real-life situation, you would open the applications a user normally uses and work as the user would normally work to attempt to produce a typical working environment needed to monitor performance. In this lab, try playing a game or surfing the web, keeping both the game and the browser open at the same time. As you work, watch the Performance Monitor window as it shows peaks in both counters.

9. Reading the counters by watching peaks is not as accurate as reading the actual data. To read actual values of the counters, mouse over the line and read the counter value that appears in a bubble window.

10. Performance Monitor also records the average, minimum, and maximum counter values under the graph. In the list of counters at the bottom of the Performance Monitor window, select the **% Disk Time** counter and answer these questions:

11

◢ What is the maximum value for the % Disk Time counter?

_____

◢ Select the **Avg. Disk Queue Length** counter. What is the maximum value for this counter?

_____

    11. Close the Performance Monitor window and the Advanced Tools window.

Follow these steps to use Task Manager to identify a process that might be hogging hard drive resources:

    1. To open Task Manager, right-click the **taskbar,** and then select **Start Task Manager** in the shortcut menu. The Windows Task Manager window opens.

    2. Click the **Processes** tab. Task Manager does not normally monitor disk usage, but you can configure it to do so. Click **View** on the menu bar, and then click **Select Columns**. The Select Process Page Columns dialog box opens.

    3. Scroll through the list of columns that appear on the Task Manager Processes tab. Deselect all items that are currently selected.

    4. In the list, select three items: **I/O Read Bytes, I/O Write Bytes,** and **Description.** Click **OK** to close the dialog box.

    5. Any process listed in Task Manager that shows either the I/O Read Bytes column or the I/O Write Bytes column constantly changing indicates this process is hogging hard drive resources. Search the Task Manager processes for constantly changing values and answer these questions:

      ◢ List the processes that show constantly changing values, and include in your list the description of the process:

_____

_____

_____

_____

      ◢ Of the processes you listed, which processes belong to Windows?

_____

_____

      ◢ Of the processes you listed, which processes do not belong to Windows?

_____

_____

    6. Close the Windows Task Manager window.

If processes that belong to Windows are constantly changing, most likely the problem is caused by hard drive thrashing. Hard drive thrashing happens when the system is short on memory and must, therefore, constantly swap data from memory to the page file and back to memory. This situation can best be corrected by installing more memory.

If a particular process that belongs to an application is hogging resources, consider upgrading or replacing the application with a more efficient version or product.

If you suspect the hard drive is a performance bottleneck, you should investigate whether the drive has enough free space and whether files on the drive are fragmented. Follow these steps to check these two possibilities:

1. A hard drive needs a minimum of 15% free space on the drive. Looking back at the hard drive information you gathered earlier in this lab, answer these questions:

   ◢ What is the total size of the hard drive?

   _____

   ◢ What is the free space on the hard drive?

   _____

   ◢ What is the percentage of free space on the hard drive?

   _____

2. Examine the hard drive and answer these questions:

   ◢ How much space can be cleared up on the drive by performing a complete disk cleanup?

   _____

   ◢ Describe how you found your answer:

   _____

   _____

3. Fragmented files can also slow down hard drive performance. If the default setting has not been changed, Windows 7 automatically defrags the hard drive weekly. Answer these questions:

   ◢ Is Windows 7 configured to defragment the drive weekly?

   _____

   ◢ What day of the week and time of day is defragmentation scheduled?

   _____

   _____

   ◢ Describe how you found your answers:

   _____

   _____

After eliminating processes hogging hard drive resources and determining that you have adequate free space on the hard drive, if you still suspect the hard drive is a performance bottleneck, you might consider upgrading the hard drive to a faster or larger drive. Follow these steps to determine the speed of your drive:

1. Open **Device Manager**. In the Device Manager window, expand the **Disk drives** category. Answer this question:

   ◢ What is the brand and model of your hard drive?

   _____

2. Open your browser and go to **google.com**. In the Google search box, enter the brand and model number of your drive exactly as it appears in the Device Manager window.

11

Click links to find the website of the hard drive manufacturer or other sites where you can find specifications for your drive. Answer these questions:

▲ Is the drive a solid-state drive or a magnetic drive?

_____

▲ If the drive is a magnetic drive, what is the RPM rating for the drive?

_____

▲ Standard RPM ratings for a hard drive for personal computers are 5400, 7200, and 10,000 RPM. Do you consider your drive a slow, moderate, or fast drive?

_____

3. Close all open windows.

Challenge Activity (Additional 15 Minutes)

The Windows Experience Index is often thought to have disappeared with Windows 8; however, it is still there, you just have to know how to find it. To access the Windows Experience Index scores in Windows 8, complete the following steps:

1. Open a command prompt with administrator privileges. Enter **winsat prepop** and then press **Enter**. This command runs a benchmark utility and stores the results in an XML file.

2. Next, open Windows PowerShell, enter **Get-WmiObject -Class Win32_WinSAT** and then press **Enter**. This command analyzes the results of the benchmark utility and then displays the results as scores, similar to the Windows Experience Index seen in Windows 7.

▲ After performing these steps on a Windows 8 system, what is the system's base score?

_____

▲ What are the scores for each category?

▲ Processor score: _____

▲ 3D graphics capabilities score: _____

▲ Hard disk score: _____

▲ Graphics score: _____

▲ Memory score: _____

REVIEW QUESTIONS

1. If you determine that the hard drive is experiencing excessive use, but the Windows Experience Index says that memory is the system bottleneck, which component do you upgrade first, memory or the hard drive? Why?

_____

_____

_____

_____

2. What values for the % Disk Time and Avg. Disk Queue Length counters of Performance Monitor collectively indicate the hard drive is a performance bottleneck?

_____

_____

3. Based on the maximum values for both hard drive counters you measured using Performance Monitor in this lab and the criteria for the two counters given in the Activity Background section of this lab, is the hard drive a performance bottleneck in your system? Why or why not?

_____

_____

_____

4. What can you conclude if a Windows process is constantly reading and writing to the hard drive?

_____

_____

5. How much free space does a hard drive need to prevent a performance slowdown?

_____

_____

LAB 11.6 USE THE SYSTEM CONFIGURATION UTILITY

OBJECTIVES

The goal of this lab is to learn to diagnose problems using the System Configuration utility. After completing this lab, you will be able to:

◢ Use options in System Configuration that can later help you troubleshoot Windows startup problems

◢ Explore the startup functions of Windows

MATERIALS REQUIRED

This lab requires the following:

◢ Windows 8 or Windows 7 operating system

◢ For Windows 7, two or more applications installed that appear in the Start, All Programs menu (for example, Adobe Reader, Microsoft Security Essentials, or other freeware)

◢ An account with administrator privileges

LAB PREPARATION

Before the lab begins, the instructor or lab assistant needs to do the following:

◢ Verify Windows starts with no errors

11

◢ For Windows 7, verify two or more applications are installed that appear in the Start, All Programs menu

◢ Verify each student has access to a user account with administrator privileges

ACTIVITY BACKGROUND

Windows offers many wizards and utilities that technicians use to troubleshoot a malfunctioning computer. One of these utilities, the System Configuration utility (also called Msconfig), is used to troubleshoot Windows startup problems. This utility allows you to make changes to boot files and startup parameters, which can help you determine which boot file, startup parameter, or startup program is causing a problem.

In this lab, you work with the features included in System Configuration to learn how to detect problems that might occur when a Windows service, application service, or application fails to load at Windows startup.

ESTIMATED COMPLETION TIME: 30 MINUTES

 Activity

Follow these steps to learn about two methods to start the System Configuration utility:

1. Log on to Windows using an administrator account. An administrator account is required to use all the features of System Configuration.

2. To launch System Configuration, in the Run box type **msconfig.exe** and then press **Enter**. The System Configuration dialog box opens (see Figure 11-5).

Figure 11-5   The System Configuration utility with the General tab open

3. A technician needs to know more than one method to reach utilities and tools in an operating system. To see an alternate way to open the System Configuration utility, close the System Configuration dialog box, and then open **Control Panel**.

4. In Control Panel, click **Administrative Tools**, and then double-click **System Configuration**. The System Configuration dialog box opens. Answer the following questions:

⊿ Of the three startup selections listed on the General tab, which one loads all device drivers and services set to load when Windows starts?

_____

⊿ Which startup selection loads only basic devices and services?

_____

⊿ Which startup selection allows you to load only system services and no startup applications?

_____

⊿ Which startup selection is currently selected?

_____

Diagnostic startup allows you to start the computer with only the most basic devices and services that are needed for the computer to run. This clean environment can help with Windows troubleshooting. Do the following to find out more:

1. To perform a diagnostic startup, click **Diagnostic startup** on the General tab, and then click **Apply**. The wait icon appears while Windows processes this change. If it encounters a problem, it rejects Diagnostic startup and reverts to Selective startup. Which startup selections are chosen when the wait icon disappears?

_____

2. If Diagnostic startup is not still selected, select **Diagnostic startup**. Click **OK** to close the System Configuration dialog box. A new System Configuration dialog box appears saying that your computer must be restarted to apply this change. Click **Restart**.

3. As Windows restarts, log back on to Windows as an administrator, and watch carefully for error messages.

⊿ Record any problems or error messages you see during the restart:

_____

⊿ What changes do you notice to your Windows desktop, video, and taskbar?

_____

⊿ If the system gives an error message using this bare-bones startup method, how might that be helpful when troubleshooting the system?

_____

4. Open the System Configuration utility. Record any differences you noted when starting the utility compared with how it started earlier in the lab:

_____

Now let's explore the Selective startup option, which can be used to limit Windows startup only to services, but not other programs. Doing so can help you eliminate startup programs that are not services from the types of programs that might be causing a Windows startup problem. Follow these steps to find out more:

1. Click **Selective startup**. Check the **Load system services** check box. Uncheck **Load startup items**. Click **OK**. In the new dialog box that appears, click **Restart**.

11

2. Windows restarts. Log back on to the system as an administrator. Record any problems or error messages you see during the restart, and record any differences in the video, desktop, and taskbar compared with a normal startup:

_____

_____

3. Open the System Configuration utility again. Record any differences you noted when starting the utility compared with how it started at the beginning of this lab:

_____

Now let's explore the Services tab of System Configuration. The Services tab can help you troubleshoot problems related to system and application services that load at startup. Follow these steps:

1. To reset startup settings, on the General tab, click **Normal startup**.
2. Click the **Services** tab. On this tab, check the **Hide all Microsoft services** check box. List the non-Microsoft services installed on this machine and the status of each:

_____

_____

_____

_____

_____

3. To disable all the non-Microsoft services, click **Disable all**. To restart the system using this setting, click **OK**. In the next dialog box, click **Restart**.
4. Windows restarts. Log on again as an administrator. What do you notice about the system that is different from a normal startup?

_____

In a real troubleshooting situation, you would not need to disable all Microsoft services except in the most extreme situations. In many cases, you might choose to disable all non-Microsoft services and only disable a particular system service that you suspect is causing a problem. To practice disabling system services, follow these steps to disable all non-Microsoft and system services:

1. Open the System Configuration utility again. Go to the **Services** tab, and uncheck the **Hide all Microsoft services** check box. Click **Disable all**, and then click **OK**. In the dialog box that appears, click **Restart**.
2. Windows restarts. Log on as administrator. Carefully watch what happens as the Windows desktop loads. Record any error messages and differences in the video, desktop, or taskbar compared with a normal startup:

_____

3. Because many system services are not running, Windows functions differently than it does during a normal startup. To see some of these differences, open **Control Panel** and the **Network and Sharing Center**. Describe any differences you notice in these tools compared with a normal startup:

_____

_____

4. Open the System Configuration utility, and return startup to a Normal startup with all services enabled. Click **OK** and restart the system. Windows restarts normally. Log on to the system as an administrator.

5. Open the System Configuration utility, and select the **Boot** tab. List each operating system installed and the drive and folder where it is installed:

_____

Here is an explanation of each option on the Boot tab:

Safe boot: Minimal. Boots to Safe Mode with networking disabled.

Safe boot: Alternate shell. Boots to a Windows command prompt in Safe Mode; networking is disabled.

Safe boot: Active Directory repair. Boots to Safe Mode; used to repair Active Directory on a domain.

Safe boot: Network. Boots to Safe Mode with Networking.

No GUI boot. No Windows splash screen is displayed when booting.

Boot log. Boot logging is stored in *%SystemRoot%*Ntbtlog.txt.

Base video. Boots to minimal VGA mode.

OS boot information. Displays driver names as the drivers are loaded during the boot.

Make all boot settings permanent. Changes you have made in System Configuration are permanent; you cannot roll back your changes by selecting Normal startup on the General tab.

The Startup tab lists applications launched at startup, including how they are launched from a startup folder or registry key. This information can be really useful when you are investigating how a program is launched at startup. For example, malware that launches at startup might not be found by anti-malware software. You can use this tab to find the folder or registry key where a program is launched so that you can delete the entry. Follow these steps to find out more:

1. Select the **Startup** tab. In Windows 8, you need to click the link to view Startup items in Task Manager. In Windows 7, it might be necessary to select the first item in the list to view the Command column. Record the following for the first item in the list:

◢ Startup item:

_____

◢ Publisher/manufacturer:

_____

The Tools tab provides a convenient list of diagnostic tools and other advanced tools that you can run from System Configuration. Follow these steps to find out more:

1. Click the **Tools** tab, and then click **Action Center**. What is the path and program name of the Action Center?

_____

2. Click the **Launch** button. What was the result of your action?

_____

3. Close all windows and the System Configuration utility.

11

REVIEW QUESTIONS

1. Which tab in System Configuration can you use to find out if the computer is using a dual-boot configuration? What information on this tab tells you that two operating systems are installed?

2. How can enabling and disabling items listed on the Startup tab be useful when you are troubleshooting a problem boot?

3. Which tab in System Configuration can be used to restart the system in Safe Mode?

4. Which tab in System Configuration can you use to find out if a service is currently running?

5. How can the Tools tab in System Configuration be useful to a technician?

LAB 11.7 CRITICAL THINKING: USE WINDOWS UTILITIES TO SPEED UP A SYSTEM

OBJECTIVES

The goal of this lab is to learn how to clean up processes that might slow Windows performance. After completing this lab, you will be able to:

⊿ Use Windows tools to clean up startup

⊿ Investigate processes that are slowing down Windows

⊿ Configure the system to keep it clean and free of malware

MATERIALS REQUIRED

This lab requires the following:

⊿ Windows 8 or Windows 7 operating system

⊿ An account with administrator privileges

⊿ Internet access

LAB PREPARATION

Before the lab begins, the instructor or lab assistant needs to do the following:

⊿ Verify Windows starts with no errors; for the best student experience, try to use systems that are not optimized and need the benefits of this lab. For example, you can do this lab using your own or a friend's computer, or one your instructor assigns to you that gets heavy student use.

⬦ Verify each student has access to a user account with administrator privileges

⬦ Verify Internet access is available

ACTIVITY BACKGROUND

A troubleshooting problem you'll often face as an IT support technician is a sluggish Windows system. Customers might tell you that when their Windows computer was new, it ran smoothly and fast, with no errors, but that it now hangs occasionally, is slow to start up or shut down, and is slow when working. One particular problem doesn't stand out above the rest. The customer just wants you to make the system work faster. When solving these types of general problems, it helps to have a game plan. This activity gives you just that. You'll learn how to speed up Windows, ridding it of unneeded and unwanted processes that are slowing it down.

ESTIMATED COMPLETION TIME: 60 MINUTES

 Activity

Use an administrator account to log on to the system each time you need to log on during this lab. Before you make any changes to the system, first get a benchmark of how long it takes for Windows to start up. Do the following:

1. Power down the computer, and then turn it back on. Using a watch with a second hand, note how many minutes it takes the system to start. Startup is completed after you have logged on to Windows, the hard drive activity light has stopped, and the mouse pointer looks like an arrow. How long does startup take?

   _____

2. Describe any problems you observed during startup:

   _____

   _____

This lab assumes that Windows might be slow starting, but that it does start up without errors. If you see error messages on screen or the system refuses to boot, you need to solve these problems before you continue with a general cleanup in the following steps.

When you're ready to begin a general cleanup, do the following:

1. If valuable data on the hard drive is not backed up, back up that data now.

2. Run anti-malware software. Here are your options:

   ⬦ If anti-malware software is not installed and you have the anti-malware software setup CD, install it. If it fails to install (some malware can block software installations), boot into Safe Mode, and install and run it from there.

   ⬦ If you don't have access to the anti-malware software setup CD, you can download software from the Internet. If your computer cannot connect to the Internet (possibly because Internet access is being blocked by malware), try to connect to the Internet using the Safe Mode with Networking option on the Advanced Boot Options menu. (This option might disable malware that is preventing Internet access.) If that doesn't work, then download the software on another computer, and burn a CD with the downloaded file.

11

◢ If you don't have anti-malware software installed and don't have access to an anti-malware software setup CD, but you can connect the computer to the Internet, you can run an online anti-malware scan from an anti-malware website. For example, Trend Micro (*trendmicro.com*) offers a free online anti-malware scan. (This free online scan has been known to find malware that other scans do not.)

◢ List the steps you took to run the anti-malware software:

_____

_____

_____

◢ List any malware the anti-malware software found:

_____

_____

_____

3. Reboot the system. Is there a performance improvement? How long does startup take?

_____

_____

4. If the system is still running so slowly you find it difficult to work, you can temporarily turn off startup processes that are hogging system resources. In Windows 8, use Task Manager to manage startup processes, and in Windows 7, use the System Configuration utility.

5. You can keep services from starting by unchecking them on the Startup tab. List all of the services that are run at startup, and use the Internet to determine the purpose of each of them:

_____

_____

_____

_____

_____

_____

_____

_____

6. Uncheck all the services except the ones associated with your anti-malware program. Reboot the system to cause these changes to take effect.

7. Is there a performance improvement? How long does startup take?

_____

8. Clean up the hard drive. Delete temporary files, and check the drive for errors. If the system is slow while doing these tasks, do them from Safe Mode. Note that you need about 15 percent free hard drive space to defragment the drive. If you don't have that much free space, find some folders and files you can move to a different media. Windows requires this much free space to run well.

9. Reboot the system. Is there a performance improvement? How long does startup take?

_____

10. Check Device Manager for hardware devices that are installed but not working as well as those devices that are no longer needed and should be uninstalled. Did you find any devices that need fixing or uninstalling? How did you handle the situation?

_____

_____

🖐 Challenge Activity (Additional 15 Minutes)

Task Manager in Windows 8 and System Configuration in Windows 7 do not necessarily show all the processes that run at startup. So, to get a more thorough list, you need to use a more powerful startup manager such as Autoruns from Sysinternals.

1. Go to **http://technet.microsoft.com/en-us/sysinternals/bb963902**, and download and install the latest version of Autoruns.

2. Run Autoruns, and then select the **Logon** tab, as shown in Figure 11-6.

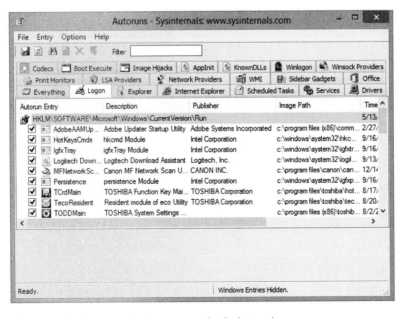

Figure 11-6 Autoruns startup manager by Sysinternals

11

3. How does the list of startup processes differ from the list generated by System Configuration? List any additional processes identified:

_____

_____

_____

_____

REVIEW QUESTIONS

1. If anti-malware software is not installed and you don't have access to the Internet, how can you install it?

_____

2. Which window or dialog box is used to check a hard drive for errors?

_____

3. What two folders can contain programs to be launched when a specific user logs on to the system?

_____

4. When cleaning up startup, why should you not delete a program file you find in a startup folder?

_____

5. What utility lists all currently running processes?

_____

Supporting Customers and Troubleshooting Windows

Labs included in this chapter:

- **Lab 12.1:** Understand IT Codes of Ethics
- **Lab 12.2:** Provide Customer Service
- **Lab 12.3:** Practice Help-Desk Skills
- **Lab 12.4:** Practice Good Communication Skills
- **Lab 12.5:** Understand How to Create a Help-Desk Procedure
- **Lab 12.6:** Apply a Restore Point
- **Lab 12.7:** Update Drivers with Device Manager
- **Lab 12.8:** Find a Driver for an Unknown Device
- **Lab 12.9:** Research Data Recovery Software
- **Lab 12.10:** Use the Problem Steps Recorder

LAB 12.1 UNDERSTAND IT CODES OF ETHICS

OBJECTIVES

The goal of this lab is to become familiar with the concept of a code of ethics for IT professionals. After completing this lab, you will be able to:

▲ Examine a code of ethics for IT professionals

▲ Consider different values when making an ethical decision

MATERIALS REQUIRED

This lab requires the following:

▲ A Windows 8 or Windows 7 workstation

▲ Internet access

▲ A workgroup of two to four students

LAB PREPARATION

Before the lab begins, the instructor or lab assistant needs to do the following:

▲ Read through the IEEE code of ethics and be prepared to discuss it with each group

▲ Verify Windows starts with no errors

▲ Verify Internet access is available

ACTIVITY BACKGROUND

Most companies and professional organizations have a code of ethics or a code of conduct that they expect their employees or members to uphold. The code typically outlines the rights and responsibilities of employees/members as well as their customers. Certain practices, such as respecting confidentiality and avoiding conflicts of interest are common to most codes, while other behaviors are industry specific. In addition, many businesses publish a Statement of Values that outlines the values or qualities that guide their actions. In this lab, you examine a code of ethics developed by the Institute of Electrical and Electronics Engineers (IEEE), and consider the values it represents.

ESTIMATED COMPLETION TIME: 60 MINUTES

 Activity

To develop your own code of ethics that you think professionals in the computer industry should follow, complete these steps:

1. In your opinion, what are the three most important ethical issues professionals in the computer industry regularly face?

_____

_____

_____

2. Develop an ethical standard that professionals in the computer industry should use when faced with each of the three issues you identified above:

_____

_____

_____

3. Discuss your ideas in your workgroup, and, as a group, create a code of ethics using the five ethical standards your group thinks are most important for professionals in the computer industry:

_____

_____

_____

_____

To learn more about computer industry ethics and values, follow these steps:

1. To begin, go to the IEEE website (**ieee.org**) and search for the IEEE code of ethics. Review the code, and then do the following:

◢ Discuss this code with your group. What do you, as a group, consider to be the most important guideline in the list?

_____

_____

◢ Describe any significant similarities or differences between the IEEE code and the code of ethics your workgroup created:

_____

_____

_____

◢ Find at least one other technological organization or company that posts a code of ethics on its website. Write down the name of the organization and its URL below:

_____

_____

◢ Describe any significant similarities or differences between the IEEE code and the code from the other technological organization:

_____

_____

_____

12

Ethical decisions are often constructed around a set of priorities or values, such as fairness, equality, and honesty. Further evaluate values by following these steps:

1. On your own, write down as many unique values as you can come up with in 10 minutes. You might want to research "ethical values" on the Internet for inspiration.

_____

_____

_____

_____

_____

2. When you're finished, share your list of values with your group, and try to agree on what you consider to be the seven most important values for aiding ethical decision making. Remember that there are no right or wrong answers; you're just trying to determine what's most important to the members in your group.

◢ List the values below:

1. _____

2. _____

3. _____

4. _____

5. _____

6. _____

7. _____

3. What values from your group's list are also represented by the IEEE code of ethics?

_____

_____

_____

Case study: You are working in the IT Department of a large company. Your employer has asked you to monitor the email and Internet activity of select individuals in the company, and to submit a report on those activities at the end of the week. Answer the following questions:

1. Does your employer have the right to monitor this information? Does it have a responsibility to do so? Explain your answer:

_____

_____

_____

2. Does your employer have a responsibility to inform its employees that their email and Internet activity are being monitored? Explain your answer:

_____

_____

3. What should you do if you discover an illegal activity during your investigation? What if your employer doesn't agree with your decision?

_____

_____

_____

4. What would you do if you discovered that your employer was engaged in illegal activity, such as using pirated software?

_____

_____

_____

5. If a coworker who is a close friend is found to be using the Internet for job hunting, would you mention it in your report? Explain your answer:

_____

_____

_____

REVIEW QUESTIONS

1. Did your group have any trouble agreeing on the seven most important values? Why did you agree or disagree?

_____

_____

2. Do you think having a company code of ethics makes ethical decisions any easier? Why?

_____

_____

3. Do you think most people share a fundamental set of values? Why?

_____

_____

4. What can you do in cases where your personal values conflict with the values of your employer?

_____

_____

12

LAB 12.2 PROVIDE CUSTOMER SERVICE

OBJECTIVES

The goal of this lab is to develop an understanding of some of the issues involved in providing excellent customer service. After completing this lab, you will be able to:

◢ Evaluate the service needs of your customers

◢ Plan for good customer service

◢ Respond to customer complaints

MATERIALS REQUIRED

This lab requires the following:

◢ A workgroup of two to four students

LAB PREPARATION

Before the lab begins, the instructor or lab assistant needs to do the following:

◢ Read through the customer service scenarios and be prepared to discuss them with each group

ACTIVITY BACKGROUND

An IT technician needs to be not only technically competent, but also skilled at providing excellent customer service. Acting in a helpful, dependable, and, above all, professional manner is a must—whether the technician deals directly with customers or works with other employees as part of a team.

To complete this lab, work through the following customer service scenarios. When you are finished, compare your answers with the rest of your group and see whether you can arrive at a consensus. Keep in mind that there might not be a single right answer to each question.

ESTIMATED COMPLETION TIME: 60 MINUTES

 Activity

Working with a group, review the following customer service scenarios, and answer the accompanying questions:

1. A customer returns to your store complaining that the upgraded computer he just picked up doesn't boot. You remember testing the computer yourself before the pickup, and everything was fine.

   ◢ What can you do to remedy the situation?

   _____

   _____

   ◢ How can you avoid this kind of problem in the future?

   _____

   _____

2. You're working in a call center that provides support to customers who are trying to install your company's product at home. While working with an inexperienced customer over the telephone, you realize that she's having trouble following your directions.

 ◢ What are some ways you can help customers even when they can't see you in a face-to-face environment?

 _____

 _____

 _____

 _____

 ◢ How can you communicate clearly with your customers while avoiding the impression that you're talking down to them?

 _____

 _____

 _____

3. You arrive on a service call, and the overly confident office supervisor shows you the malfunctioning computer. She begins to explain what she thinks is the problem, but you can tell from the computer's operation that it's something else. You suspect that the office supervisor might have caused the malfunction.

 ◢ How can you troubleshoot the problem without offending your customer?

 _____

 _____

 ◢ Would it be a mistake to accuse the customer of causing the problem? Why?

 _____

 _____

4. An irate customer calls to complain that he's not satisfied with service he has received from your company, and he tells you he plans to take his future business elsewhere.

 ◢ Should you apologize even if you don't think your company acted improperly?

 _____

 _____

 ◢ How can you give the customer the impression that you and your company are listening to his complaints?

 _____

12

REVIEW QUESTIONS

1. What other viewpoints did the other members of your group have that you hadn't considered?

_____

_____

_____

2. Did you have any trouble coming to a consensus about how to deal with each situation? Explain your answer:

_____

3. Why is an understanding of good customer service important for a technician who doesn't work directly with customers?

_____

_____

4. How can you improve your listening skills when working with customers?

_____

_____

_____

LAB 12.3 PRACTICE HELP-DESK SKILLS

OBJECTIVES

The goal of this lab is to learn how to work with a customer via a chat session and a telephone conversation. After completing this lab, you will be able to:

◢ Use help-desk skills in a chat session and on the phone to solve customer problems

MATERIALS REQUIRED

This lab requires the following:

◢ Two or more Windows 8 or Windows 7 operating systems

◢ Internet access

◢ Access to instant messaging software such as Skype

◢ A phone (or cell phone) for each student

LAB PREPARATION

Before the lab begins, the instructor or lab assistant needs to do the following:

⊿ Verify Windows starts with no errors

⊿ Verify Internet access is available

⊿ Verify messaging software is available

⊿ Instruct students to bring their cell phones to the lab, or provide telephones in the lab

ACTIVITY BACKGROUND

In the past, help-desk support was provided solely by telephone; however, most hardware and software companies now also offer technical support for their products through chat sessions with the company's help-desk staff. Help-desk personnel need to know how to ask questions, connect with customers in a friendly and personal tone, and solve problems via a telephone conversation or a chat session. Typically, a customer can initiate a chat session by clicking a link on a company's website. For example, in Figure 12-1, you can see where to click to start a live chat session with NETGEAR support.

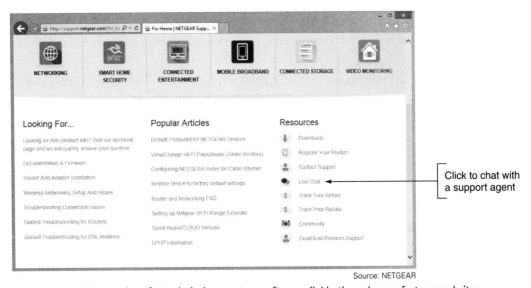

Source: NETGEAR

Figure 12-1 Chat sessions for technical support are often available through manufacturer websites

ESTIMATED COMPLETION TIME: 60 MINUTES

 Activity

Imagine that Jesse is having problems securing his home wireless network. The router that serves as his wireless access point was not working, so he pressed the Reset button on the router. The router began working, but Jesse then discovered he had reset the router back to the factory default settings, undoing all his wireless security settings. When Jesse tried to reconfigure the router, he could not find the router documentation, which included the user name and password to the router firmware utility. After giving up his search for the documentation, he has decided to contact NETGEAR for help.

Jesse goes to the NETGEAR website and clicks the Support link, which opens the page shown earlier in Figure 12-1. He clicks the Live Chat link, and on the next page, enters his name, phone number, email address, and product name. After he submits this information, a chat window opens, similar to the one in Figure 12-2. Farly is working the help desk at NETGEAR and responds to Jesse.

12

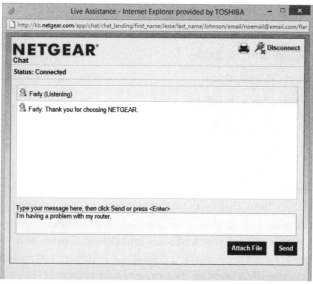

Source: NETGEAR

Figure 12-2 Sample technical support chat window

Working with a partner in your workgroup, use network and chat software such as Skype, and complete the following steps:

1. Select one person in your workgroup to play the role of Jesse, the customer. Select another person to play the role of Farly, the help-desk technician.

2. Jesse initiates a chat session with Farly. What is the first thing Farly says to Jesse in the chat session?

3. In your chat session between Jesse and Farly, communicate the following:

   Farly asks Jesse for the serial number of the router. This number is embedded on the bottom of the router.

   Farly knows that the default user name for this router is a blank entry with "admin" for the password. Farly wants Jesse to know it would have been better for him to have reset the router by unplugging it and then plugging it back in, rather than using the Reset button. Farly also tells Jesse that, for security reasons, he needs to enter a new user name and password for the router.

4. Print the chat session. If your chat software does not have a print option, then copy and paste the chat session text into a document, and print the document. As a courtesy, many companies send the customer a transcription of the chat session via email.

5. Critique the chat session with others in your workgroup. Make suggestions that might help Farly to be more effective, friendly, and helpful.

Use telephones to simulate a help-desk conversation. Use the same troubleshooting scenario, but this time, switch players between Jesse and Farly. Do the following:

1. Jesse calls Farly, and Farly answers, "Hello, this is Farly Jackson with the NETGEAR help desk. May I please have your name, the product you need help with, your phone number, and email address?"

2. After the necessary information is collected, Farly allows Jesse to describe the problem and then steps him through the solution.

3. When the problem is solved, Farly ends the call politely and positively.

4. Ask your workgroup to make suggestions that might help Farly to be more effective, friendly, and helpful.

In the next help-desk session, Joy contacts technical support for her company, complaining of too many pop-up ads on her desktop. Do the following:

1. Select someone to play the role of Joy and another person to play the role of Sam, the help-desk technician. Assume that Joy is a novice user who needs a little extra help with keystrokes.

2. Using chat software, Joy starts a chat session with Sam, and Sam solves the problem.

3. Sam decides to have Joy turn on the Internet Explorer pop-up blocker, use previously installed anti-malware software to scan for viruses, and in Windows 8 run Windows Defender and in Windows 7 download, install, and run Microsoft Security Essentials software from the Microsoft website.

4. Print the chat session, and discuss it with your workgroup. Do you have any suggestions for Sam to improve his help-desk skills?

_____

_____

5. Using telephones, switch players for Joy and Sam, and solve the same problem. Do you have any suggestions for Sam to improve his help-desk skills?

_____

_____

CHALLENGE ACTIVITY (ADDITIONAL 30 MINUTES)

Do the following to get more practice supporting users on the phone:

1. Think of a computer problem you or a friend has encountered that you or your friend could not quickly solve. Describe the problem as a user would describe it when he first calls a help desk:

_____

_____

2. Working with a partner, the partner plays the role of a help-desk technician and you play the role of the user. Call the "help desk," and describe your problem. Work with your partner toward a solution. Answer the following questions:

◢ Was your partner able to help you solve the problem?

_____

◢ Assess how well your partner handled the call. How would you assess the service you received?

_____

_____

3. Switch roles with your partner, and repeat Steps 1 and 2. You become the help-desk technician as your partner gets help with a problem she or a friend has encountered in real life.

12

REVIEW QUESTIONS

1. After doing your best, but finding you still cannot solve a customer's problem, what is the appropriate next step?

_____

_____

2. Your cell phone rings while working with a customer. You look at the incoming number and realize it's your sister calling. How do you handle the call?

_____

_____

_____

3. Why is it not a good idea to tell a customer about the time you were able to solve the computer problem of a very important person?

_____

_____

4. A customer is angry and tells you he will never buy another product from your company again. How do you respond?

_____

_____

LAB 12.4 PRACTICE GOOD COMMUNICATION SKILLS

OBJECTIVES

The goal of this lab is to help you learn how to be a better communicator. After completing this lab, you will be able to:

◢ Listen better

◢ Work with a customer who is angry

◢ Act with integrity toward customers

MATERIALS REQUIRED

This lab requires the following:

◢ Paper and pencil or pen

◢ A workgroup of two or more students

LAB PREPARATION

No lab preparation is necessary.

ACTIVITY BACKGROUND

IT support technicians are expected to be good communicators; however, technical people often find this to be a difficult skill to master, so practice and training are very important. In this lab, you discover some ways to be an active listener and a better communicator.

ESTIMATED COMPLETION TIME: 60 MINUTES

 Activity

Work with a partner to learn to be a better listener. Do the following:

1. Sit with paper and a pencil in front of another student who will play the role of a customer. As the customer describes a certain computer problem he or she is having, take notes as necessary.

2. Describe the problem back to the customer. Were you able to describe the problem accurately, without missing any details? Have the customer rate you from one to ten, with ten being the highest rating, for good listening skills. What rating did you receive?

_____

3. Switch roles as you, the customer, describe a problem to the support technician. Then have the technician repeat the problem and its details. Rate the technician for good listening skills on a scale of one to ten.

4. Choose a somewhat more difficult problem, with more details, and describe it to the support technician. Rate the technician on a scale of one to ten for good listening skills.

5. Switch roles, and listen as the customer describes a more detailed and difficult problem. Then repeat the problem and its details back to the customer, and have the customer rate your listening skills. What rating did you receive?

_____

Being a good communicator requires being able to deal with people who may be angry and difficult. Make suggestions as to the best way to handle these situations:

1. An angry customer calls to tell you that she has left you numerous phone messages that you have not answered. She is not aware that you receive about 25 voice messages each day and are trying hard to keep up with the workload. What do you say?

_____

_____

2. A customer who is frustrated and angry begins to use abusive language. What do you say?

_____

_____

3. You have tried for over two hours, but you cannot fix the customer's boot problem. You think the motherboard has failed, but you are not sure. Before you make your conclusions, you want to try a POST diagnostic card. The customer demands that you fix the problem immediately, before she leaves the office at 4:45 p.m.—about 10 minutes from now. What do you say to her?

_____

_____

12

Discuss in your workgroup the ethical thing to do in each situation below. Write down the group consensus to each problem:

1. You work on commission in a computer retail store. One day, you spend over an hour working with a very difficult customer who then leaves without buying anything. As he walks out the door, you notice he dropped a twenty-dollar bill near where you were talking. What do you do?

   _____

   _____

2. A customer is yelling at a coworker in a retail store. You can see that your coworker does not know how to handle the situation. What do you do?

   _____

   _____

3. You are working in a corporate office as a technical support person, trying to fix a scanner problem at an employee's workstation. You notice the employee has left payroll database information displayed on the screen. You know this employee is not authorized to view this information. What do you do?

   _____

   _____

4. Your supervisor has asked you to install a game on his computer. The game is on a CD-R and is obviously a pirated copy. What do you do?

   _____

   _____

5. You work for a retail store that sells a particular brand of computers. A customer asks your opinion of another brand of computer. What do you say?

   _____

   _____

6. You are asked to make a house call to fix a computer problem. When you arrive at the appointed time, a teenage girl answers the door and tells you her mother is not at home, but will return in a half hour. What do you do?

   _____

   _____

Have a little fun with this one! Working in a group of three, one member of the team plays the role of tech support. A second team member writes down a brief description of a difficult customer and passes the description to a third team member. (The tech support person cannot see this description.) The third team member plays out the described customer role. Use the following scenarios or make one up:

1. A customer calls to say his notebook will not start. The LCD panel was broken when the customer dropped the notebook, but he does not willingly disclose the fact that the notebook was dropped.

2. A customer complains that her CD drive does not work. The CD is in the drive upside down, and it is clear that the customer sees herself as a techie and does not want the tech to ask her about such a simple issue.

REVIEW QUESTIONS

1. When working at a retail store that also fixes computers, what five pieces of information should you request when a customer first brings a computer to your counter?

_____

_____

_____

_____

_____

2. List three things you should not do while at a customer's site:

_____

_____

_____

3. When is it acceptable to ask a customer to refrain from venting about a problem?

_____

_____

_____

4. When is it appropriate to answer a cell phone call while working with a customer?

_____

_____

5. When is it appropriate to install pirated software on a computer?

_____

_____

LAB 12.5 UNDERSTAND HOW TO CREATE A HELP-DESK PROCEDURE

OBJECTIVES

The goal of this lab is to explore the process of creating help-desk procedures. After completing this lab, you will be able to:

▲ Identify problems that would prevent users from browsing the network

▲ Determine which types of problems can be solved over the telephone

12

◢ Decide which types of problems require administrative intervention

◢ Create a help-desk procedure that includes a support matrix for telephone instruction

MATERIALS REQUIRED

This lab requires the following:

◢ Windows 8 or Windows 7 operating system

◢ A network connection

◢ Paper and pencil or pen

◢ Internet access (optional)

◢ Two workgroups, with two to four students in each group

LAB PREPARATION

Before the lab begins, the instructor or lab assistant needs to do the following:

◢ Verify Windows starts with no errors

◢ Verify the network connection is available

◢ Verify Internet access is available (optional)

ACTIVITY BACKGROUND

When a company sets up a help desk for computer users, it establishes a set of procedures to address common troubleshooting situations. Well-written help-desk procedures ensure that help-desk workers know each and every step to perform in a given situation, which means they can solve problems more quickly and confidently. These procedures should include instructions that the average user can be expected to carry out with telephone support from help-desk staff. In this lab, you create help-desk procedures for resolving a common problem: the inability to connect to a network. Assume you're working at a company help desk. If you can't solve the problem, you escalate it to the network administrator or an onsite technician who actually goes to the computer to fix the problem.

ESTIMATED COMPLETION TIME: 60 MINUTES

 Activity

Work with a group to better understand how to create help-desk procedures. Do the following:

1. Assume that your company network is designed according to the following parameters. (Note that your instructor might alter these parameters so that they more closely resemble your network's parameters.)

   ◢ Ethernet LAN is using only a single subnet

   ◢ TCP/IP is the only protocol

   ◢ The workgroup name is ZEBRA

   ◢ The DHCP server assigns IP information

2. Assume that all users on your company network use computers with the following parameters. (Note that your instructor might alter these parameters so that they more closely resemble your computer.)

   ◢ Core i7 2.9 GHz

   ◢ Windows 8 operating system

◢ Internal NIC

◢ Category 5e cabling with RJ-45 connectors

3. As a group, discuss the reasons a user might not be able to connect to the network, and then make a list of the four most common reasons. In your list, include at least one problem that would be difficult to solve over the phone and would require the network administrator or another technician to go to the computer to solve the problem. Order the four problems from the least difficult to solve to the most difficult to solve. The one problem that requires administrator intervention should be Problem 4. If your group has trouble completing the list, ask your instructor or search the web for ideas. List the source of these problems, both hardware and software, on the following lines:

◢ Source of Problem 1:

_____

◢ Source of Problem 2:

_____

◢ Source of Problem 3:

_____

◢ Source of Problem 4:

_____

For each problem, describe the symptoms as a user would describe them:

◢ Symptoms of Problem 1:

_____

_____

◢ Symptoms of Problem 2:

_____

_____

◢ Symptoms of Problem 3:

_____

_____

◢ Symptoms of Problem 4:

_____

_____

As a group, decide how to solve each problem by following these steps:

1. On separate sheets of paper, list the steps to verify and solve each problem. (This list of steps is sometimes referred to as a procedure, support matrix, or job aid.)

2. Double-check the steps by testing them on your computer. (In real life, you would test the steps using a computer attached to the network you're supporting.) When making your list of steps, allow for alternatives, based on how the user responds to certain

12

questions. For example, you might include one list of steps for situations in which the user says others on the network are visible in the Network window and another list of steps for situations in which the user says no remote computers can be seen in the Network window.

3. For any problem that can't be solved by the procedure, the last step should be for help-desk personnel to escalate the problem. In your procedure, include questions to the user when appropriate. As you work, you might find it helpful to use a diagram or flowchart of the questions asked and decisions made. Here's an example of one step that involves a question:

◿ Question: Is your computer on?

◿ Answer: Yes, go to Step 3; no, go to Step 2.

Now it is time to test your help-desk procedures by using them on another workgroup. Follow these steps:

1. Introduce one of your four problems on a computer connected to a network.

2. Have someone from another workgroup sit at your computer. The remaining steps in this step sequence refer to this person as "the user."

3. Sit with your back to the user so that you can't see what he or she is doing. Place your step-by-step procedures in front of you, either on paper or on screen. (It's helpful if you can sit at a computer connected to the network so that you can perform the same steps you ask the user to perform. However, make sure you can't see the other computer screen or see what the user is doing.)

4. The user should attempt to access the network and then "call" your help desk for assistance.

5. Follow your procedure to solve the problem.

6. Revise your procedure as necessary.

7. Test all four help-desk procedures.

REVIEW QUESTIONS

1. Can all users' computer problems be solved with remote help-desk support? Why or why not?

_____

_____

2. After you design and write your help-desk procedures to solve problems, what should you do next?

_____

3. How should help-desk procedures address complex problems that require administrative intervention?

_____

_____

_____

4. How should you write your procedures based on your users' technical experience?

_____

5. Why do you need to consider what the network and computer configuration are when creating your procedures?

6. What has been your experience when calling a help desk? How well did the technician walk you through the process of solving your problem?

LAB 12.6 APPLY A RESTORE POINT

OBJECTIVES

The goal of this lab is to restore the system state on a Windows 8 or Windows 7 computer. After completing this lab, you will be able to:

◢ Create a restore point by using System Restore

◢ Change system settings

◢ Restore the system state with the restore point you created

MATERIALS REQUIRED

This lab requires the following:

◢ Windows 8 or Windows 7 operating system

LAB PREPARATION

Before the lab begins, the instructor or lab assistant needs to do the following:

◢ Verify Windows starts with no errors

ACTIVITY BACKGROUND

Using the System Restore tool in Windows, you can restore the system to the state it was in when a snapshot, called a "restore point," was taken of the system state. The settings recorded in a restore point include system settings and configurations and files needed for a successful boot. When the system state is restored to a restore point, user data on the hard drive isn't affected, but software and hardware might be. Restore points are useful if, for example, something goes wrong with a software or hardware installation and you need to undo these changes. In this lab, you create a restore point, make changes to system settings, and then use the restore point to restore the system state.

12

Activity

To use the System Restore tool to create a restore point, follow these steps:

1. Click **Start, All Programs, Accessories, System Tools,** and, finally, **System Restore.** The System Restore dialog box opens.

2. In Windows 8, use the information on this screen or search Windows Help and Support. In Windows 7, click **Is this process reversible?** to open Windows Help and Support. Answer the following questions:

   ◢ Can changes made by System Restore be undone?

   _____

   ◢ What type of data does System Restore leave unaffected?

   _____

   _____

3. Close Windows Help and Support if necessary. In the System Restore box, click **Next.** Check **Show more restore points.** (If this check box is not available, your system has no more restore points to show.)

   ◢ What are the dates of the three most recent restore points?

   _____

   ◢ What types of recent events prompted Windows to automatically create restore points?

   _____

   _____

4. To create a new restore point, open **Control Panel** and click **System.** Click **System protection** in the left pane of the System window to open the System Properties dialog box.

5. To create a restore point, click **Create.** Name your restore point, and then click **Create.** A restore point is created.

6. Close any open windows.

Next, you make a change to the system by changing the display settings. Follow these steps:

1. Open **Control Panel** and click **Personalization.** Using the Personalization window, change the desktop background or the desktop theme.

2. Close the Control Panel window. Notice that the desktop background or desktop theme has changed to the one you selected.

Follow these steps to use the restore point you created to restore the system state:

1. Open the **System Restore** tool. Click **Next.**

2. Select the restore point you created earlier in the lab, and then click **Next.**

3. When a confirmation window is displayed, click **Finish** to continue. If necessary, click **Yes** to proceed.

◢ Describe what happens when you proceed with a restore:

_____

_____

4. After the system restarts, log on to the Windows desktop. A message is displayed stating that the restoration is complete. Click **Close**.

◢ Did the display settings change back to their original settings?

_____

REVIEW QUESTIONS

1. List three situations in which you might want to create a restore point:

_____

_____

_____

2. What types of restore points are created by the system, and what types are created by users?

_____

_____

3. How often does the system create restore points automatically?

_____

4. Can more than one restore point be made on a specific date?

_____

5. Does Windows track more than one restore point? Why?

_____

_____

_____

LAB 12.7 UPDATE DRIVERS WITH DEVICE MANAGER

OBJECTIVES

The goal of this lab is to explore the functions of Device Manager. After completing this lab, you will be able to:

◢ Use Device Manager to find information about your display adapter and update the display adapter drivers

◢ Explore alternative methods to update a driver

12

MATERIALS REQUIRED

This lab requires the following:

◢ Windows 8 or Windows 7 operating system

◢ Updated driver files for the display adapter (optional)

◢ Internet access

LAB PREPARATION

Before the lab begins, the instructor or lab assistant needs to do the following:

◢ Verify Windows starts with no errors

◢ Verify Internet access

◢ Locate or download updated driver files for the display adapter or video card, if newer driver files are available

ACTIVITY BACKGROUND

With Device Manager, you can update device drivers as well as monitor resource use. If you find a new driver for a device, you can use Device Manager to select the device and update the driver. In this lab, you use Device Manager to update the driver for your display adapter.

ESTIMATED COMPLETION TIME: 30 MINUTES

 Activity

In this lab, you first use Device Manager to update a driver, and then you explore alternative ways to update drivers.

PART 1: USE DEVICE MANAGER TO UPDATE A DRIVER

1. To open Device Manager, open **Control Panel**, and then click **Device Manager**.

2. Click the arrow next to **Display adapters** to expand this category, and then click your display adapter to select it. What is the name of your display adapter?

   _____

3. To open the Properties dialog box for your display adapter, right-click the **adapter** and select **Properties**. What is the manufacturer of your display adapter?

   _____

4. Click the **Driver** tab, and answer the following questions:

   ◢ What company is the provider for your driver?

   _____

   ◢ What is the driver date?

   _____

   ◢ What is the driver version?

   _____

5. Click the **Driver Details** button, and answer the following questions:

   ◢ Which folders contain the drivers used by your display adapter?

   _____

   _____

   _____

◢ What is the file version?

6. Click **OK** to return to the Driver tab in the display adapter's Properties dialog box. Click **Update Driver**. A dialog box appears asking where to find the drivers (see Figure 12-3).

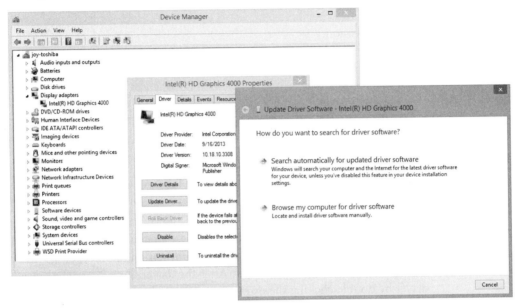

Figure 12-3 Use Device Manager to find and update drivers

7. If your instructor has provided the updated driver in a specific location on your computer, click **Browse my computer for driver software**. If your instructor has not provided the drivers, you can allow Windows to search the web for the drivers. To do so, click **Search automatically for updated driver software**.

8. If you are using the web to update your driver, follow the on-screen instructions to search for and install drivers. If your driver is already up to date, Windows displays a message saying the best driver software for your device is already installed. If Windows finds a newer version, it installs the update. When the update is finished, you might be asked to restart your computer. Then, proceed to Part 2 of this lab.

9. If your instructor has provided the drivers, type the location of the driver installation file, or click the **Browse** button to select the location your instructor has designated. After you have specified a location, click **Next**. Windows searches the location and reports its findings.

10. If the wizard indicates it has found a file for the display adapter, click **Next** to continue. If the wizard reports that it can't find the file, verify you have entered the installation file's location correctly.

11. After Windows locates the drivers, it copies the driver files. If a file being copied is older than the file the system is currently using, you're prompted to confirm that you want to use the older file. Usually, newer drivers are better than older drivers. However, you might choose to use an older driver if you experience problems after updating drivers. In this case, you might want to reinstall the old driver that wasn't causing problems.

12. When the files have been copied, click **Finish** to complete the installation.

13. Close all open windows, and restart the computer if prompted to do so.

12

PART 2: EXPLORE ALTERNATIVE WAYS TO UPDATE DRIVERS

1. Device Manager should now show updated driver information for your display adapter. Return to Device Manager. Record the new driver information below, and compare it with the information you collected earlier.

   ◢ Driver date:

   _____

   ◢ Driver version:

   _____

   ◢ File version:

   _____

Windows will not always have access to drivers through Device Manager, especially drivers for accessories or other after-market hardware. In these situations, you can do one of the following:

   ◢ Install a driver from a disc that comes with the new hardware. You can use the Browse option in Device Manager, as described above, or you can open File Explorer/Windows Explorer and double-click an installation program on the disc.

   ◢ Download a driver directly from the hardware manufacturer's website. To install a driver from a manufacturer's website, you need information about your system in order to search online for the correct driver. After the driver file is downloaded, you install the driver by double-clicking the downloaded file and following the on-screen directions.

To collect the information you need to find a driver online, follow these steps:

1. In the Run box, type **msinfo32** and press **Enter**.
2. Using the System Information dialog box, collect the following information:
   ◢ OS name: _____
   ◢ System manufacturer:_____
   ◢ System model: _____
   ◢ System type: _____

When downloading and running a program from the web, always download the file to your hard drive and then use File Explorer/Windows Explorer to execute the downloaded file. To avoid accidentally installing malware, do not run the file from your browser. Also, always reboot your system after installing a new driver, even if not instructed to do so. This last precaution helps identify any problems with the boot process or with Windows that might be caused by a new device or driver.

CRITICAL THINKING (ADDITIONAL 30 MINUTES)

Open Device Manager, and select other devices to update. Device drivers that you might want to update include your motherboard and audio drivers. If an update does not work properly, you can use the Roll Back Driver button on the Driver tab of the device's Properties dialog box to return the device to a previously installed driver.

REVIEW QUESTIONS

1. Describe the steps to access Device Manager:

   _____

   _____

2. What are the steps to view the properties of a device using Device Manager?

_____

_____

3. What tab in the Properties dialog box do you use to update a driver?

_____

4. Besides typing the path, what other option can you use to specify a driver's location?

_____

_____

5. Why might you want to use an older driver for a device rather than the latest driver?

_____

_____

LAB 12.8 FIND A DRIVER FOR AN UNKNOWN DEVICE

OBJECTIVES

The goal of this lab is to learn how to find the drivers for an unknown device. After completing this lab, you will be able to:

◢ Use third-party software to determine brand and model information of an unknown device

◢ Use the Internet to find and download a driver

MATERIALS REQUIRED

This lab requires the following:

◢ A Windows 8 or Windows 7 computer designated for this lab

◢ Internet access

◢ A burnable CD and a marker to label the CD

◢ A USB flash drive with at least 1-GB capacity (all data on the flash drive will be erased in this lab) (optional)

LAB PREPARATION

Before the lab begins, the instructor or lab assistant needs to do the following:

◢ Verify Windows starts with no errors

◢ Verify Internet access is available

◢ Download files before the lab starts and make these files available to students

> **Notes** The instructor or lab assistant is encouraged to download the required files to a local server and make these available to students locally so students are not required to perform this long download during the lab.

12

ACTIVITY BACKGROUND

Someone has come to you for help with her computer. She is unable to connect to the Internet and is not sure why. After some investigation, you realize that she has just replaced her computer's network adapter, but has lost the driver CD for the adapter, along with its documentation. Windows does not recognize the device type and there is no model information on the device itself. To find the correct drivers on the web, you need to know the exact brand and model of the device.

Software that runs from a bootable CD or USB flash drive sometimes does a better job of identifying an unknown device than software installed in Windows. In this lab, you use Hiren's BootCD to identify your network adapter. To save time in this lab, your instructor might have already downloaded the program. Ask your instructor if the file is available, and record its location and file name here:

> **Notes** The Hiren's BootCD software sometimes causes anti-malware software to give a false positive alert. The software, however, is safe to use.

ESTIMATED COMPLETION TIME: 45 MINUTES (NOT INCLUDING DOWNLOAD TIME)

 Activity

In this lab, you create and use the Hiren's BootCD to find out the brand and model of an unknown device. This tool can be a valuable utility to add to your computer repair kit, and it can be installed on a burnable CD or a USB flash drive. Follow these steps to create and use a bootable CD using the Hiren's BootCD software:

1. Later in the lab, you use Hiren's BootCD to identify the network adapter installed on your computer. So that you can later compare its results with what Windows reports, open **Device Manager**.

2. Find your network adapter, and open its **Properties** dialog box. Find the tab that displays the brand and model of your NIC and the provider and version number of its driver. Record the following information:

    ◢ What is the brand and model of your NIC?

    ◢ Who is the driver provider, and what is the version number of the driver?

---

3. If your instructor has made the Hiren's BootCD download file available, skip to Step 4. If you need to download the file, go to the Hiren's BootCD download page at **hirensbootcd.org/download** and download the Hiren's BootCD Zip file. (For version 15.2, the file name is **Hirens.BootCD.15.2.zip**, although the current version might be different. The link to download the file is located near the bottom of the page. Be careful to not download other free software from this website.) This file is large and will take a while to download. Save the file in your Downloads folder or on your desktop. Answer the following:

    ◢ What is the exact path, file name, and file extension of the downloaded file?

---

4. The downloaded file is a Zip file. Extract the contents of the Zip file, and open the extracted folder in File Explorer/Windows Explorer. Compare the contents of the folder with the list shown in Figure 12-4 in the right pane of Explorer.

Source: Hiren's BootCD

Figure 12-4   Contents of the extracted Hiren's BootCD folder

◢ Do the contents of your extracted folder differ from the list shown in the figure? If so, record the differences here:

_____

◢ One of the files extracted is an ISO disc image, which has an .iso file extension. When using version 15.2, that file name is Hiren's.BootCD.15.2.iso. What is the name of the ISO file in your extracted folder?

_____

◢ In these instructions, we are using version 15.2. What version of the Hiren's BootCD are you using?

_____

5. With Windows 8 or Windows 7, you can burn an .iso disc image to a CD. To do so, in Windows 8, right-click the Hiren's.BootCD.15.2.iso file, and select **Burn disc image** in the shortcut menu. In Windows 7, right-click the **Hiren's.BootCD.15.2.iso** file, and select **Open with** in the shortcut menu. The Open with dialog box appears. Click **Windows Disc Image Burner**, and then click **OK**. The Windows Disc Image Burner Wizard opens.

> **Notes** If you don't see Windows Disc Image Burner listed in the Open with dialog box, another disc image burner program is probably installed on your computer. You can uninstall that program in order to enable the Windows disc image burner, or you can use the other program to burn the image.

12

6. Insert a blank CD in the optical drive, check **Verify disc after burning**, and then click **Burn**. The CD is burned. Click **Close** when finished, and then close any open windows.

7. If your computer automatically ejects the CD when the burn is complete, reinsert the CD into your disc drive. If necessary, close the AutoPlay dialog box.

8. Reboot the computer from the CD. To boot from a CD, you might need to access the UEFI/BIOS setup and change the boot sequence to list the optical drive first in the boot priority order.

9. When the computer boots from the CD, the Hiren's BootCD menu appears. In this menu, select **Mini Windows Xp**, and then press **Enter**. The computer displays a graphical user interface similar to that of Windows XP.

10. From the desktop, click **Start**, and then click **HBCD Menu**. The Hiren's BootCD 15.2 – Program Launcher dialog box appears.

11. On the menu bar, click **Programs**, and then answer the following questions:

    ◢ What are two utilities included on the CD for partitioning hard drives?

    _____

    _____

    ◢ Name three utilities on the CD that provide system information:

    _____

    _____

    _____

    ◢ What are two utilities included for backup of data?

    _____

    _____

12. From the Program menu, point to **Device Drivers**, and then click **UnknownDevices (device info)**. This program scans your computer hardware and displays a report in the Unknown Devices window. Use this window to find the make and model number of the NIC installed in your system, and record that information:

    _____

    _____

13. Close all open windows, remove the CD, and reboot your system. Using a permanent marker, label the CD **Hiren's BootCD**, and include the version number that you downloaded.

14. Using the information you collected from the Hiren's BootCD about your NIC, search the web for the correct NIC driver. What is the name of this driver, and where did you find it on the web?

    _____

    _____

15. Earlier in the lab, you recorded the information that Windows offered about the make and model of your NIC and the current driver installed on your computer.

⊿ Do the make and model of the NIC reported by Windows and the Hiren's BootCD match? Describe any differences.

_____

⊿ Does the driver information you collected by your research match the driver currently installed on your system? Describe any differences.

_____

CHALLENGE ACTIVITY (ADDITIONAL 60 MINUTES)

As you build your arsenal of tools that can take your diagnostic skills to the next level, you might find that creating a version of the Hiren's BootCD on a USB flash drive is not only convenient but necessary in case you are called on to troubleshoot a computer that does not have an optical drive. Follow these steps to create a bootable Hiren's BootCD on a USB flash drive:

1. Connect a 1-GB or larger USB flash drive to your computer. (Be aware that all data on the flash drive will be erased.)

2. Using File Explorer/Windows Explorer, right-click on the flash drive. In the shortcut menu, click **Format**. The Format Wizard opens.

3. Leave Capacity at its default setting, select **FAT32** for File system, select **4096 bytes** (or the next closest size) for Allocation unit size, and then type **USB DISK** for Volume label. In the Format options, unselect **Quick Format** and then click **Start**. If a warning displays indicating that all the information will be deleted, click **OK**. A progress bar is displayed right above where you clicked Start. When formatting is complete, click **OK** and then close the Format Wizard box.

4. Next you'll need to prepare your flash drive with an MBR (Master Boot Record) environment, which makes it bootable. Using your web browser, go to one of these URL locations to download the Zip file named grub4dos.zip:

⊿ **hirensbootcd.org/files/grub4dos.zip**

⊿ **hirensbootcd.org/usb-booting/**

5. Once the file is downloaded, extract the contents of the folder to your desktop.

6. Open the **grub4dos** folder created on your desktop, and double-click **gubinst_gui. exe**. If a UAC dialog box appears, click **Yes** to continue. The Grub4Dos Installer 1.1 displays.

7. Under Device Name, select **Disk**. In the drop-down list beside Disk, select your flash drive. To determine which disk is your flash drive, match the size of the disk to the size of your flash drive.

8. To the right of Part List, click **Refresh**.

Notes If you receive an error message like the one on the right side of Figure 12-5, it means that your flash drive has an MBR record that Grub4dos does not recognize. (Most likely this is because your flash drive has a large capacity.) To get around the problem, first click OK to close the message box, and then type skip-mbr-test in the Extra box, as shown on the left side of Figure 12-5.

12

Source: Grub4Dos

Figure 12-5 Grub4Dos does not recognize the MBR record on the flash drive

9. In the drop-down list beside Part List, select **Whole disk (MBR)**. Click **Install**. A command window displays. Press **Enter** to close this window. In the Grub4Dos Installer dialog box, click **Quit**. The dialog box closes.

10. Insert the previously created Hiren's BootCD into your CD drive. Copy all files and folders from the Hiren's BootCD to the flash drive.

> **Notes** Alternately, you can mount the Hiren's BootCD image using an ISO disk mounting utility such as MagicDisc, ISODisk, or slysoft Virtual Clone Drive.

11. Now you need to give the bootable flash drive a boot loader program and a startup menu. Open the HBCD folder in the Hiren's BootCD, and copy and paste the following files to the root folder of your flash drive.

   ◢ grldr

   ◢ menu.lst

Figure 12-6 shows all the correct files on the USB flash drive.

Figure 12-6 Final view of USB flash drive contents

12. Close all open windows, and remove the Hiren's BootCD disc from the optical drive. Shut down your computer.

13. Boot the computer from the USB flash drive. To do so, you might need to change the boot priority sequence using the UEFI/BIOS setup. (Some older computers do not provide USB boot capability, so you might not be able to boot from the USB device.)

14. Using the Hiren's BootCD menu, launch Mini Windows Xp, and verify the desktop loads. Then shut down the system.

15. After removing the USB flash drive, label it with a tag (or write directly on the casing), using the name Hiren's BootCD, and give the version number you used.

REVIEW QUESTIONS

1. When trying to identify an unknown device, what are some advantages to using a boot CD over running diagnostic programs in Windows?

2. What are ISO images, and can Windows use them to burn a CD or DVD without additional software?

3. Other than the situation described in this lab, describe two other situations in which the Hiren's BootCD would be useful:

4. How much does the Hiren's BootCD software cost?

5. When you need to boot from the optical drive or a USB flash drive, what must you do to prevent the computer from booting from Windows on the hard drive?

12

LAB 12.9 RESEARCH DATA RECOVERY SOFTWARE

OBJECTIVES

The goal of this lab is to explore different methods of recovering deleted data from a hard disk drive. After completing this lab, you will be able to:

◢ Restore files from the Recycle Bin

◢ Identify the benefits of third-party data recovery software and services

◢ Recover deleted files using Recuva (optional)

MATERIALS REQUIRED

This lab requires the following:

◢ Windows 8 or Windows 7 operating system

◢ An account with administrator privileges

◢ Internet access

LAB PREPARATION

Before the lab begins, the instructor or lab assistant needs to do the following:

◢ Verify Windows starts with no errors

◢ Verify each student has access to a user account with administrator privileges

◢ Verify Internet access is available

ACTIVITY BACKGROUND

A client has contacted you because she accidentally deleted a group of files that hold very important financial information. She is unable to find the files in the Recycle Bin and is panicked because her job may depend on retrieving the files, which contain sensitive financial information. To retrieve the data, you will need to install third-party data recovery software to scan the drive and attempt retrieval.

ESTIMATED COMPLETION TIME: 30 MINUTES

 Activity

Let's first see how to recover files from the Recycle Bin. To begin, you need to create a folder and files. Follow these steps to create the folder and files, delete them, and then recover them from the Recycle Bin:

1. To create a new folder on your desktop, right-click your desktop, and in the shortcut menu select **New** and then click **Folder**. A new folder is created. Name the newly created folder **Important Files**.

2. Double-click the **Important Files** folder to open it. Right-click in the white space in the right pane of File Explorer/Windows Explorer, select **New** in the shortcut menu, and then click **Text Document**. Name this document **Monthly budget**. Open the text file, type your name in the document, and close the file, saving your changes.

3. Create a second text document, naming this document **Financial statement**. Enter some text in the document, and then save and close the document.

4. Select both files and right-click your selection. In the shortcut menu, click **Delete**. If necessary, confirm your deletion. The files are deleted and placed in the Recycle Bin.

5. Double-click the Recycle Bin on your desktop, and search for the deleted files. In Windows 8, you can use the View ribbon to change the Sort by selection and the View selection to more easily find your deleted files. In Windows 7, click a column heading to sort by that field. Right-click one of the files you just deleted. In the shortcut menu, click **Restore**. The file is restored to the Important Files folder. Restore the second file in the same way.

6. Check the Important Files folder and confirm the two files are restored. You may need to click the Refresh icon in File Explorer/Windows Explorer.

Sometimes deleted files cannot be found in the Recycle Bin. In this situation, third-party data recovery software, such as Recuva by Piriform, might help. To learn about the Recuva (pronounced recover) data recovery software, follow these steps:

1. Open your browser and go to **piriform.com/recuva**.

2. Review the features and information provided about Recuva, and answer the following questions:

   ◢ What is a deep scan?

   _____

   _____

   ◢ How can you use a portable version of Recuva if you can't or don't want to install the software on the computer on which you're trying to recover files?

   _____

   _____

   ◢ What are the editions of Recuva and their respective prices?

   _____

   _____

   _____

3. Save this website to your browser's Favorites or Bookmarks under a new folder called Recovery Programs.

Another company that offers data recovery software is Paragon. To learn about this third-party software, follow these steps:

1. Go to **paragon-software.com/home/rk-free**.

2. Review the features and information provided, and answer the following questions:

   ◢ Does your computer meet the minimum system requirements? If not, explain why.

   _____

   _____

12

◢ Paragon's Rescue Kit offers an ISO image. Why is this significant when considering data recovery?

_____

_____

_____

◢ Are you allowed to use this free software on your personal computer? Can you use it in a corporate environment?

_____

_____

3. Add the website to your list of Favorites or Bookmarks in the Recovery Programs folder.

Sometimes, storage devices experience mechanical failure or are damaged by fire or a natural disaster. Occasionally, someone even intentionally tries to destroy data to cover a crime. Third-party software might not be able to retrieve data that has been damaged to this point. In these situations, special, almost surgical, procedures are needed to retrieve the data. To learn about these processes, follow these steps:

1. Go to **drivesaversdatarecovery.com**.

2. Point to **Why DriverSavers?** on the menu bar, and then click **Data Recovery You Can Trust**.

◢ What level of clean room does DriveSavers maintain?

_____

◢ What security compliance qualifies DriveSavers to handle confidential medical records?

_____

3. Point to **Why DriveSavers?** on the menu bar, click **Virtual Tour**, and then play the virtual tour video. Answer the following questions:

◢ What are two kinds of devices that DriveSavers can recover data from?

_____

_____

◢ If DriveSavers opens your hard drive, what happens to your manufacturer's warranty?

_____

_____

4. Point to **Data Recovery Services** on the menu bar, and then click **Data Recovery Service Plans**. What is one Security Type offered by DriveSavers?

_____

CHALLENGE ACTIVITY (ADDITIONAL 45 MINUTES)

Recuva is a powerful freeware utility that can be used to restore files that have been deleted and cannot be restored from the Recycle Bin. To practice using Recuva, follow these steps:

1. Create a new Microsoft Word Document in the Important Files folder titled **My Resume**. (If you don't have Microsoft Word installed, create a Text Document file instead.) Open the file, type **This is a test of My Resume**, and then save and close the file.

2. Delete the **My Resume** file in the Important Files folder.

3. To empty the Recycle Bin, right-click the **Recycle Bin** on your desktop. In the shortcut menu, click **Empty Recycle Bin**. When prompted to confirm deletion, click **Yes**.

4. Open your browser and go to **piriform.com**. Download the latest version of Recuva and install it. As you install it, be careful to not install other freeware offered during the installation. Close all open windows.

5. Launch Recuva. If a UAC dialog box appears, click **Yes**. The Recuva Wizard opens. Click **Next**. If you created a Microsoft Word Document file, select **Documents** for the File type. If you created a Text Document file, select **All Files** for the File type. Click **Next**.

6. On the next screen in the wizard, select **In the Recycle Bin** for the file location (see Figure 12-7). Click **Next**.

Source: Recuva

Figure 12-7 Recuva asks where to search for files to recover

7. Click **Start**. Recuva will run a scan on your computer, which might take several minutes depending on the size of your drive(s). If Recuva does not find any files, it offers to perform a deep scan. If you see this message, you can click **Yes** to allow a deep scan. If this was not an option, close and then relaunch Recuva. Rescan your computer using the deep scan option available on the final screen, where you click Start.

8. When the program presents its scan results, look for a .docx or .txt file created at the same time you created the My Resume file. Figure 12-8 shows one search results window, but yours might look different. The file name might be an unintelligible mix of letters, numbers, and symbols, but you can identify the correct file by checking the date and time it was last modified. (To sort the list by date last modified, click the Last Modified column heading.) Check the box next to the file, and then click **Recover**.

9. In the Browse For Folder dialog box, select the **Important Files** folder, and then click **OK**. When asked if you want to restore to the same drive, click **Yes**. When the operation is completed, click **OK**.

10. Go back to the Important Files folder in File Explorer/Windows Explorer, and double-click the recovered file. Confirm that the text you typed in the file earlier has been successfully recovered.

Source: Recuva

Figure 12-8   In this example, the file name is the same as the original, but sometimes it is altered

> **Notes** Sometimes the data in a deleted file is corrupted and cannot be recovered easily by Recuva. A red dot next to the file indicates it is corrupted, and a green dot indicates a good file. If your file has a red dot, you can still go through the steps of recovering the file, but you will get an error message when you try to open the file.

REVIEW QUESTIONS

1. What happens to files when you delete them?

   _____

   _____

2. How do you recover a deleted file using the Recycle Bin?

   _____

   _____

3. What is a clean room, and how is it used by data recovery services?

   _____

   _____

4. What are three methods of restoring data you learned about in this lab?

   _____

   _____

   _____

LAB 12.10 USE THE PROBLEM STEPS RECORDER

OBJECTIVES

The goal of this lab is to use the Windows 8 Steps Recorder. After completing this lab, you will be able to:

◢ Record steps using Steps Recorder

◢ Review steps recorded

MATERIALS REQUIRED

This lab requires the following:

◢ Windows 8 operating system

LAB PREPARATION

Before the lab begins, the instructor or lab assistant needs to do the following:

◢ Verify Windows starts with no errors

ACTIVITY BACKGROUND

When you're troubleshooting a problem in Windows, recording the steps you take can be crucial to proper documentation. Recording steps is also helpful when you're documenting how to do something or when a user needs to show you what he or she is doing. Fortunately, Microsoft provides Steps Recorder to record steps and generate a report with all actions recorded.

ESTIMATED COMPLETION TIME: 20 MINUTES

 Activity

Follow these steps to use Steps Recorder:

1. On the Start screen, start typing **Steps Recorder**. Click **Steps Recorder** in the search results. The Steps Recorder program opens on the desktop.

2. Click **Start Record**. The Steps Recorder begins recording all actions taken on the computer.

3. Return to the **Start** screen, and type **paint**. Click **Paint** in the search results. The Paint program opens on the desktop. Note that when you click, a red dot appears. This indicates that this action was recorded.

4. Draw a mark or shape on the Paint window.

5. In the Steps Recorder program, click **Stop Record**. The Steps Recorder automatically opens a file containing all the steps and information that was recorded. See Figure 12-9. Scroll down the window to review the scripted steps and images that were recorded while you opened the Paint program and drew an image in the Paint window.

6. In the Steps Recorder window showing the file containing the steps, click **Save**.

7. Save this report to your computer, and name it **UsingPaint.zip**. Close the Steps Recorder and Paint windows (no need to save changes in Paint).

8. Open the UsingPaint.zip file, and then open the recording file. Review your recording, and close the file.

12

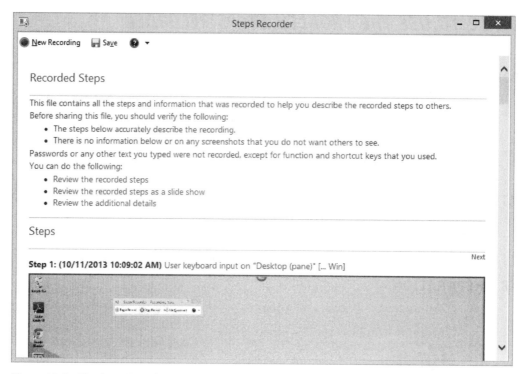

Figure 12-9   The Steps Recorder records screen captures and detailed steps of user activity

REVIEW QUESTIONS

1. How do you know an action using the mouse is recorded?

2. What type of folder contains the file of recorded steps?

3. What type of file contains the recorded steps? By default, which program is used to view the file?

4. Does Steps Recorder record a script of the actions taken or images of the actions taken?

5. Imagine you have a job working on a help desk. What is a possible situation in which you might use the Steps Recorder?

CHAPTER
13

Troubleshooting Windows Startup

Labs included in this chapter:

- **Lab 13.1:** Investigate Startup Processes
- **Lab 13.2:** Explore Tools to Solve Windows 8 Startup Problems
- **Lab 13.3:** Create and Use a Custom Refresh Image
- **Lab 13.4:** Create a Windows 7 Repair Disc
- **Lab 13.5:** Explore the Repair Disc and Windows Recovery Environment (RE)
- **Lab 13.6:** Reimage the Windows Volume
- **Lab 13.7:** Recover Data from a Computer That Will Not Boot
- **Lab 13.8:** Critical Thinking: Sabotage and Repair Windows

LAB 13.1: INVESTIGATE STARTUP PROCESSES

OBJECTIVES

The goal of this lab is to identify malicious software running on your computer by examining all running processes. After completing this lab, you will be able to:

- Identify all processes running on your computer at startup
- Use the Internet to determine the function of each process

MATERIALS REQUIRED

This lab requires the following:

- Windows 8 or Windows 7 operating system
- An account with administrator privileges
- Internet access

LAB PREPARATION

Before the lab begins, the instructor or lab assistant needs to do the following:

- Verify Windows starts with no errors
- Verify each student has access to a user account with administrator privileges
- Verify Internet access is available

ACTIVITY BACKGROUND

As more add-ons, utilities, and applications are installed on a system over time, they can cause Windows to slow down and give errors. When a program automatically launches at startup, it takes up valuable computer resources behind the scenes and can cause startup errors. In this lab, you learn to investigate all the startup processes on your computer and to identify those you should remove.

ESTIMATED COMPLETION TIME: 45 MINUTES

 Activity

Follow these steps to investigate the startup processes on your computer:

1. Restart your computer, and log on as an administrator.
2. Use Task Manager to display all the running processes on your machine. In Windows 8, use the Details tab in Task Manager, and in Windows 7, use the Processes tab. Be sure to show processes for all users.
3. How many processes are running? Note that many processes are listed twice, but you should count each process only once. To help you identify processes listed more than once, click the **Name** column in Windows 8, or the **Image Name** column in Windows 7 to sort the processes by process name. Figure 13-1 shows the running processes for one system, but yours will be different. On a separate piece of paper, make a list of each process running on the computer, or create and print screen shots that show these processes.

> **Notes** To change which columns are displayed, right-click a column heading, and then click **Select columns.**

Figure 13-1 The Name and Image path name columns on the Details tab can help you identify a process and how it is loaded

4. Now reboot the computer in Safe Mode, and use Task Manager to list the running processes for all users again. How many processes are running now? (Remember: Count each process only once.)

   _____

5. Which processes didn't load when the system was running in Safe Mode?

   _____

   _____

   _____

6. Research each process identified in Step 5 on the web, and write a one-sentence explanation of each process on a separate piece of paper.

   ◢ Did you find any malicious processes running? If so, list them:

   _____

   _____

◢ Did you find any programs that should be uninstalled from the system? If so, list them:

_____

_____

_____

◢ Suppose one of the processes running on your computer is named whAgent.exe. What program is associated with this process?

_____

◢ How could you use the System Configuration utility to temporarily disable a process?

_____

_____

◢ List the steps you could take to remove this program from your computer:

_____

_____

_____

_____

7. To improve the computer's performance, use the System Configuration utility to temporarily disable any program that you decide is not necessary. Which program, if any, did you disable?

_____

8. If the system works fine with the program disabled, go ahead and uninstall the program. Which program, if any, did you uninstall?

_____

REVIEW QUESTIONS

1. Why is it a good idea to temporarily disable a program before removing it altogether?

_____

2. Why might anti-malware software not detect malicious software?

_____

_____

3. Why would you expect fewer processes to be running in Safe Mode?

_____

_____

4. Why is disabling the Lsass.exe process not a good idea?

_____

5. What key do you press during startup to launch Safe Mode?

_____

LAB 13.2 EXPLORE TOOLS TO SOLVE WINDOWS 8 STARTUP PROBLEMS

OBJECTIVES

The goal of this lab is to explore tools to solve Windows 8 startup problems. After completing this lab, you will be able to:

- Find troubleshooting tools for Windows startup problems
- Use the Startup Repair process
- Enable and disable the Advanced Boot Options menu
- Boot to Safe Mode with Networking

MATERIALS REQUIRED

This lab requires the following:

- Windows 8 operating system
- Windows 8 setup DVD or recovery drive
- An account with administrator privileges
- Internet access

LAB PREPARATION

Before the lab begins, the instructor or lab assistant needs to do the following:

- Verify Windows starts with no errors and the Windows 8 setup DVD or a recovery drive is available
- Verify each student has access to a user account with administrator privileges
- Verify Internet access is available

ACTIVITY BACKGROUND

Startup problems can be annoying, and Windows 8 has taken great effort to minimize this pain. Windows 8 is one of the most stable operating systems with the fewest errors at startup. On the third sequential reboot, Windows 8 automatically starts a self-healing process. If you still encounter a hang-up, error message, stop error, or hardware error after Windows 8 has attempted to heal itself, you can use the startup repair tools discussed in this lab to help you resolve startup problems.

ESTIMATED COMPLETION TIME: 45 MINUTES

 Activity

This lab is divided into two parts. In Part 1, you use the charms bar to explore several Windows 8 tools used to fix startup problems. You also use the Startup Repair tool, and you boot into Safe Mode with Networking. In Part 2 of the lab, you enable the Advanced Boot Options menu and boot into Safe Mode with Networking. As you work through this lab, reference Figure 13-2 to keep track of where you find each of the startup troubleshooting tools.

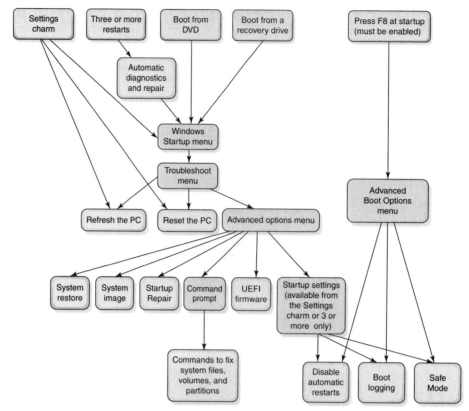

Figure 13-2 Methods to boot the system, including menus and tools for troubleshooting startup problems

PART 1: FIND TOOLS TO FIX STARTUP PROBLEMS

Follow these steps to locate startup repair tools:

1. Sign in to your system with an administrator account.

2. On the **charms bar**, select the **Settings** charm. Click **Change PC settings**.

3. On the PC settings page, click **Update and recovery** in the left pane.

4. On the Update and recovery page, click **Recovery** in the left pane. List the options for recovering your computer that can be accessed through the Settings charm, and briefly describe the purpose of each one:

_____

_____

_____

_____

5. Click **Restart now** under the Advanced startup option. Your computer restarts. When given an option, click **Troubleshoot**, and then click **Advanced options**. List the tools available under Advanced options for troubleshooting startup problems, and briefly describe the purpose of each:

_____

_____

_____

6. Select **Startup Repair**. Your computer restarts into Startup Repair.

7. Choose your account name, and enter your password. Click **Continue**.

8. Startup Repair diagnoses your system, and reports its findings. Click **Advanced options**. This returns you to the Windows Startup menu.

9. Click **Troubleshoot**, and then click **Advanced options**.

10. Click **Startup Settings**, and then click **Restart**.

11. Listed are options for changing startup behavior. Press **5** or **F5** on your keyboard to select **Enable Safe Mode with Networking**. The system reboots. After you sign in, Safe Mode with Networking loads.

12. Open **Internet Explorer**, and make sure the Internet is available.

13. On the charms bar, click the **Settings** charm, and then click **Restart**.

If the hard drive is so corrupted you cannot boot to it, you must boot from another bootable media. Follow these steps to explore the troubleshooting tools available when booting from other bootable media:

1. Boot from the Windows setup DVD or a recovery drive, and select your language and keyboard layout. (Before you can boot to media other than the hard drive, you might need to first change the boot priority order in UEFI/BIOS setup.)

2. When the Windows Setup screen appears, click **Repair your computer**. On the next screen, select your keyboard layout. Next, select the correct troubleshooting options on each screen until you reach the Advanced options screen.

   ◢ List the tools available under Advanced options:

   _____

   _____

   _____

   _____

   ◢ Which tool is not available on this screen that was available in Step 5, when you used the Settings charm to restart the system?

   _____

3. Launch Windows 8 normally, and remove the bootable media from your computer.

PART 2: ENABLE AND USE THE ADVANCED BOOT OPTIONS MENU

Safe Mode can be extremely useful when you're trying to solve a problem with a corrupted device driver or a problem caused by a malware infection because the malfunctioning driver or the malware may not load when Safe Mode is launched. By default in Windows 8, Safe Mode is launched only from the Settings charm. If you cannot start Windows properly, you cannot use the Settings charm to access Safe Mode.

> **Notes** This part of the lab will not work if your computer is set for dual boot.

Another way to launch Safe Mode is to press F8 at startup. This allows you to access the Advanced Boot Options menu. By default, this option is disabled. To use F8 at startup, you must enable it before you encounter a startup problem. Follow these steps to enable the use of F8 during startup:

1. On the Start screen, type **command**. Right-click the **Command Prompt** tile that appears, and select **Run as administrator** in the status bar. Respond to the UAC dialog box. The command prompt window opens on the desktop with administrator privileges.

2. In the command prompt window, enter this command: **bcdedit /set {default} bootmenu-policy legacy**. Press **Enter**.

3. Restart your system. When Windows first starts to load, press **F8** to access the Advanced Boot Options menu. List the options available to change the boot behavior:

_____

_____

_____

_____

_____

_____

4. Select **Safe Mode with Networking**, and press **Enter**. The system reboots. After you sign in, Safe Mode with Networking loads.

5. On the charms bar, click the Settings charm, and then click **Restart**.

If your instructor asks you to disable the use of F8 at startup, follow these steps to disable the F8 option:

1. Open a command prompt window with administrator privileges.

2. In the command prompt window, enter this command: **bcdedit /set {default} bootmenu-policy standard**. Press **Enter**.

3. Close all open windows.

REVIEW QUESTIONS

1. Why is Windows 8 considered to be a more stable system than previous Windows editions in terms of startup problems?

_____

_____

2. List the steps you take to find the Refresh the PC option using the charms bar:

_____

_____

_____

_____

3. What is the difference between a refresh and a reset?

_____

_____

_____

4. Why would you want the F8 option at startup enabled on a system?

_____

_____

5. What is the command line you enter into the command prompt window to disable the F8 option at startup?

_____

6. If the hard drive is so corrupted that pressing F8 at startup cannot load the Advanced Boot Options menu, how should you boot the system so you can attempt to repair the Windows installation?

_____

LAB 13.3 CREATE AND USE A CUSTOM REFRESH IMAGE

OBJECTIVES

The goal of this lab is to create and use a custom refresh image. After completing this lab, you will be able to:

◢ Create a custom refresh image

◢ Refresh your system using your custom refresh image

MATERIALS REQUIRED

This lab requires the following:

◢ Windows 8 operating system

◢ Internet access

◢ An account with administrator privileges

LAB PREPARATION

Before the lab begins, the instructor or lab assistant needs to do the following:

◢ Verify Windows starts with no errors

◢ Verify Internet access is available

◢ Verify each student has access to a user account with administrator privileges

ACTIVITY BACKGROUND

If your system isn't running well, you might want to refresh or reset it. A refresh is preferred to a reset because a refresh retains user settings, data, and Windows 8 apps. A refresh works even better if you have created a custom refresh image to use during the refresh. Using the image, the system is restored to the point it was when the image was created, and then any user settings, data, or Windows 8 apps that were installed or changed since the image was created are also restored. After you refresh your system using a custom refresh image, you will need to reinstall any desktop applications that were not installed at the time you created the custom refresh image.

Best practice is to create a custom refresh image after you have the system configured just the way you want it. A custom refresh image takes a snapshot or image of the current system and stores in the image the Windows installation, all installed applications, and user settings and data.

In this lab, you make some changes to user settings, data files, and installed apps. Then, you create a custom refresh image, and make additional changes to user settings, data files, and installed apps. Next, you refresh the system, and then examine the system to find out which changes are retained by the refresh. By working your way through this lab, you can be confident you understand exactly how a refresh works and what to expect from one.

ESTIMATED COMPLETION TIME: 60–120 MINUTES

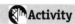**Activity**

Follow these steps to customize your computer:

1. Sign in using an administrator account.

2. From the Start screen, on the **charms bar**, click the **Settings** charm. Click **Personalize**. Select a picture for the Start screen background, and then select a **Background color**. Describe the picture and color you selected:

   _____

3. Visit **google.com/chrome**, and download and install the free web browser, Google Chrome.

4. Create a new document, and save it in your Documents folder. What is the file name and the path to your document?

   _____

Follow these steps to create a custom refresh image:

1. On the Start screen, move your pointer to the bottom of the screen, and click the **down arrow**. On the Apps screen, scroll to the right, and in the Windows System section, find the Command Prompt tile. Right-click **Command Prompt**. In the status bar, click **Run as administrator**. Respond to the UAC dialog box. The command prompt window opens.

2. Enter this command, substituting any drive and folder for that shown in the command line:

   recimg /createimage C:\MyImage

3. The image is created and registered. In the command prompt, enter this command:

   recimg /showcurrent

4. The location of the image is displayed. Write down the location of the image:

   _____

5. Close the command prompt window. Open File Explorer, and browse to the image file. What is the location given in your address bar? What is the size of the image file?

   _____

Follow these steps to make additional changes to your system:

1. From the Start screen, open the **Settings** charm, and click **Personalize**. Select a picture for the Start screen background and a background color different from those you selected at the beginning of this lab. Describe the new picture and color you selected:

———————————————————————————————

2. Go to **mozilla.org/firefox**, and download and install the Mozilla Firefox browser.

3. Open the Store app, and install a Windows 8 app. Which application did you install?

———————————————————————————————

4. Delete the file you stored in your Documents folder earlier in the lab.

Follow these steps to refresh the system using the custom refresh image you created earlier:

1. On the **charms bar**, select the **Settings** charm, and then click **Change PC settings**.

2. On the PC settings page, click **Update and recovery** in the left pane.

3. On the Update and recovery page, click **Recovery** in the left pane.

4. Under Refresh your PC without affecting your files, click **Get started**.

5. On the Refresh your PC screen, review what will happen when you perform a refresh. Click **Next**.

6. Click **Refresh**. During the refresh process, your system restarts.

Do the following to find out the results of the refresh:

1. Sign in to your system, and answer the following questions:

   ◢ Does the Start screen use the latest picture and background color you selected? Why or why not?

   ———————————————————————————————

   ◢ Is the app you installed from the Windows Store still installed? Why or why not?

   ———————————————————————————————

   ◢ Is the file you stored in your Documents folder there? Why or why not?

   ———————————————————————————————

   ◢ Is Google Chrome installed as a desktop app? Why or why not?

   ———————————————————————————————

   ◢ Is Mozilla Firefox installed as a desktop app? Why or why not?

   ———————————————————————————————

2. Browse to the root of drive C:. What is the size of the Windows.old folder?

   ———————————————————————————————

3. Open the file stored on the Windows desktop that lists the desktop applications that were removed from your computer during the refresh. Which application(s) were removed during the refresh?

   ———————————————————————————————

Now it's time to clean up the system. Do the following:

1. To keep your hard drive clean, it's best to delete the Windows.old folder after you have confirmed that the refresh was successful. Delete the **Windows.old** folder.

2. Uninstall any Windows 8 apps or desktop applications that you installed in this lab that are still installed.

3. If your instructor requests it, delete the custom refresh image you created in this lab.

REVIEW QUESTIONS

1. What command line can you enter into the command prompt window to view the location of the active recovery image?

_____

2. What is the file name of the refresh image?

_____

3. When you perform a system refresh, how will your computer settings be changed?

_____

4. When you perform a system refresh without the help of a custom refresh image, some apps are kept and some are removed. Which apps are kept? Which are removed? How do you know which apps were removed?

_____

_____

_____

LAB 13.4 CREATE A WINDOWS 7 REPAIR DISC

OBJECTIVES

The goal of this lab is to learn to create a Windows 7 repair disc, which can be used in the event the hard drive will not boot and the Windows 7 setup DVD is not available. After completing this lab, you will be able to:

◢ Create a Windows 7 repair disc

◢ Verify the disc boots without errors

MATERIALS REQUIRED

This lab requires the following:

◢ Windows 7 operating system

◢ A computer with a CD-R drive or other optical drive that will burn a CD

◢ Blank CD-R disc

◢ Permanent marker to label the disc

LAB PREPARATION

Before the lab begins, the instructor or lab assistant needs to do the following:

◢ Verify Windows starts with no errors

◢ Verify the boot priority order in UEFI/BIOS is set so that the system can boot to a CD before turning to the hard drive; if you expect the students to change the boot priority order during the lab, verify the key to press at startup to access setup UEFI/BIOS.

ACTIVITY BACKGROUND

Windows 7 allows you to create a bootable repair disc that holds the Windows Recovery Environment (RE). The repair disc can be used in place of the Windows 7 setup DVD to fix a corrupted Windows installation. When Windows creates the repair disc, a 32-bit version of Windows creates a 32-bit version of Windows RE, and a 64-bit version of Windows creates a 64-bit version of Windows RE. These discs are not interchangeable; you must use a 32-bit repair disc to repair a 32-bit installation of Windows, and a 64-bit repair disc must be used to repair a 64-bit installation. You can, however, use a repair disc created by one edition of Windows 7 to repair another edition. For example, a repair disc created by Windows 7 Home Premium can be used to repair a Windows 7 Ultimate installation.

In this lab, you create the repair disc. Then in the next lab, you will use the repair disc to explore Windows RE.

ESTIMATED COMPLETION TIME: 15 MINUTES

 Activity

Follow these steps to create a Windows 7 repair disc:

1. To find out if your version of Windows 7 is a 32-bit or 64-bit OS, open the System window, and answer these questions:

   ◢ Is your system type a 32-bit operating system or a 64-bit operating system?

   _____

   ◢ What edition of Windows 7 is installed?

   _____

2. Insert a blank CD in your CD-R drive or other optical drive that has the ability to burn a CD.

3. There are several ways to launch the utility to build the repair disc. In this lab, you use the Backup and Restore window. Click **Start**, type **Backup and Restore** in the Search box, and then press **Enter**. The Backup and Restore window opens.

4. In the left pane, click **Create a system repair disc**, and follow the on-screen directions to create the disc.

5. When the process is finished, remove the CD from the drive, and label it "Windows 7 32-bit Repair Disc" for a 32-bit version of Windows or "Windows 7 64-bit Repair Disc" for a 64-bit version of Windows. Also include on the label the edition of Windows 7 used to create the disc.

Follow these steps to test the repair disc, verifying you can use it to boot the system and launch Windows RE:

1. Insert the repair disc in the optical drive, and restart the system. A message might appear that says, "Press any key to boot from DVD or CD." If so, press any key.

2. If the system does not boot from the disc, chances are UEFI/BIOS setup is configured to look first to the hard drive before turning to the optical drive for a boot device. Check UEFI/BIOS setup, and change the boot sequence so that it looks to the optical drive before it turns to the hard drive for an OS. The method for accessing UEFI/BIOS setup varies, depending on your computer. Look for a message that says "Press Del to access setup" or "Press F2 for setup," or a similar message when the system is first started. After you have made your changes, save your UEFI/BIOS settings and reboot. This time you should be able to boot from the disc.

3. After you have booted from the CD, the first screen shows the System Recovery Options window where you can select your keyboard input method. When you see this window, you know you have successfully created a bootable repair disc.

4. Remove the disc, and restart the system to the Windows 7 desktop.

5. Save the repair disc to use in the next lab.

REVIEW QUESTIONS

1. What Windows utility is used to create a Windows 7 repair disc?

   _____

2. Is your system a 32-bit or 64-bit operating system?

   _____

3. Why do you think it is important to label the Windows repair disc as a 32-bit or 64-bit version?

   _____

   _____

4. Sometimes a computer boots directly to the hard drive even when a bootable CD is inserted in the optical drive. Explain why this happens and how you can fix the problem so that the computer boots from the CD:

   _____

   _____

   _____

   _____

5. What key on your computer do you press to access UEFI/BIOS setup to change the boot sequence?

   _____

LAB 13.5 EXPLORE THE REPAIR DISC AND WINDOWS RECOVERY ENVIRONMENT (RE)

OBJECTIVES

The goal of this lab is to learn how to use the repair disc and the Windows Recovery Environment (RE) to solve problems with Windows startup. After completing this lab, you will be able to:

◢ Boot to the Windows RE user interface using two methods

◢ Use the tools in Windows RE to solve startup problems

MATERIALS REQUIRED

This lab requires the following:

◢ Windows 7 operating system

◢ An account with administrator privileges

◢ Repair disc created in the previous lab

LAB PREPARATION

Before the lab begins, the instructor or lab assistant needs to do the following:

◢ Verify Windows boots with no errors

◢ Verify each student has access to a user account with administrator privileges

◢ Verify the repair disc created in the previous lab is available

ACTIVITY BACKGROUND

Windows RE is an operating system designed to be used to recover from a corrupted Windows installation. Windows RE can be loaded from the Windows setup DVD, the repair disc, or the hard drive. It contains graphical and command-line tools used to troubleshoot a failed Windows startup. In a real troubleshooting situation, first try to load Windows RE from the hard drive using the Advanced Boot Options menu. If that does not work, you can start Windows RE from the Windows setup DVD or the repair disc.

ESTIMATED COMPLETION TIME: 45 MINUTES

 Activity

Even if Windows will not start, you can load Windows RE from the hard drive if the hard drive is still healthy. Follow these steps to load the Windows RE operating system from the hard drive using the Advanced Boot Options menu:

1. If necessary, shut down the computer.

2. Start the computer, and, as it boots up, press **F8**. The Advanced Boot Options menu appears. (In a real troubleshooting situation, the menu might not appear if the hard drive is badly corrupted.)

> **Notes** If the F8 option has been disabled on your computer, open an elevated command prompt, and use this command to enable the F8 option: **bcdedit /set {default} bootmenupolicy legacy.**

3. On the Advanced Boot Options menu, use the arrow keys to highlight **Repair Your Computer**, and then press **Enter**. Windows RE loads and the System Recovery Options menu appears. Click **Next**.

4. On the next screen, enter a password to an administrator account.

5. The System Recovery Options menu appears (see Figure 13-3). Click **Shut Down** to shut down the system. (You will explore the System Recovery Options menu later in this lab.)

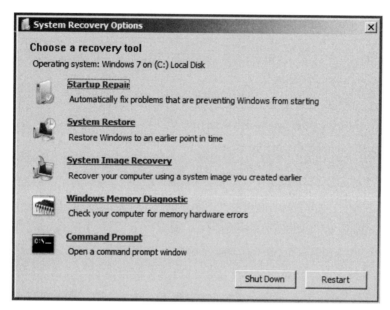

Figure 13-3   The System Recovery Options window lists troubleshooting tools

Starting Windows RE from the hard drive will not work if the hard drive is corrupted. In this situation, you must use either the repair disc or the Windows setup DVD to load Windows RE. Follow these steps to use the repair disc you created in the previous lab to launch Windows RE:

1. Insert the repair disc in the optical drive, and power up the system. A message might appear that says, "Press any key to boot from DVD or CD." If so, press any key.

2. If the system does not boot from the disc, reboot the system, press a key to launch setup UEFI/BIOS, and change the boot sequence to list the optical drive first. Then reboot using the disc.

3. On the first screen, click **Next**. Windows RE searches for Windows installations.

4. On the next screen, Windows RE lists the installations of Windows it was able to detect. (If Windows cannot detect an installation, it gives you the option to restore the system from a previously created system image.) Select your installation, and confirm that the **Use recovery tools that can help fix problems starting Windows** option is selected. Click **Next**. The System Recovery Options menu appears, as shown earlier in Figure 13-3.

5. The first tool to try in almost every troubleshooting situation is Startup Repair, which examines key system files used to start the system and replaces or rebuilds them if a problem is detected. It's easy to use, and you can't do any harm using it. Click **Startup Repair**.

6. The system is checked for errors, and an error report is generated. Click **Finish** to return to the System Recovery Options window.

7. Sometimes a problem can be resolved by applying a restore point. To explore this option, click **System Restore**, and then click **Next**. A list of restore points appears.

⬥ What types of problems can you solve by successfully applying a restore point?

_____

_____

⬥ What problems might you create when you successfully apply a restore point?

_____

_____

8. To continue without applying a restore point, click **Cancel**. You are returned to the System Recovery Options window.

9. In a troubleshooting situation, you might decide to completely restore the volume on which Windows is installed to the time the last system image was created. To explore this option, click **System Image Recovery**. If a system image is found, information about the system image appears, and you can continue with the restore. Describe what changes you would make to the system if you continued with the System Image Recovery:

_____

_____

10. If no system image is found, a message indicating that appears. Click **Cancel** to close the message. Another window appears, giving you another opportunity to provide the backup media that contains a system image. Click **Cancel** to return to the System Recovery Options window.

11. Problems with memory can often present themselves as Windows or application problems. To test memory for errors, click **Windows Memory Diagnostic**. A message appears saying that the utility wants to restart the system to test memory.

⬥ What type of symptoms might a system exhibit if memory is bad?

_____

_____

⬥ If Windows Memory Diagnostic reports bad memory, what should you do next?

_____

12. Click **Cancel** to skip performing the memory test.

13. Some problems can be resolved by using commands in a command prompt window. To explore the command prompt window, click **Command Prompt**. A command prompt window opens where you can enter commands.

⬥ What is the default drive and path showing in the command prompt?

_____

14. At the command prompt, enter the command to list the contents of the current folder. What command did you use?

_____

15. Enter the command to move up one level in the directory tree to the parent folder of the current folder. What command did you use?

_____

16. Enter the command to close the command prompt window. What command did you use?

_____

17. In the System Recovery Options window, click **Restart** to restart the system and load the Windows desktop.

REVIEW QUESTIONS

1. Which System Recovery Option should you use to solve a problem with a corrupted device driver that was just installed and causes the system to not boot?

_____

2. Which System Recovery Option should you use if Microsoft Word documents continue to get corrupted?

_____

3. Suppose that after you insert the repair disc in the drive and restart the system, the Windows desktop loads. Why did the system not boot from the disc?

_____

4. Which System Recovery Option should you use if the system hangs at odd times and is generally unstable?

_____

5. What can you conclude if you cannot load the Advanced Boot Options menu by pressing F8 at startup, but you can load Windows RE by booting from the repair disc?

_____

_____

6. Which System Recovery Option will make the least intrusive changes to the system, System Restore or Startup Repair?

_____

LAB 13.6 REIMAGE THE WINDOWS VOLUME

OBJECTIVES

The goal of this lab is to learn how to create a system image and use it to restore the Windows volume. After completing this lab, you will be able to:

◢ Create a system image using a second hard drive installed in a system

◢ Use the system image to reimage the Windows volume

MATERIALS REQUIRED

This lab requires the following:

◢ Windows 7 operating system

◢ A second internal or external hard drive

◢ Alternately, you can use Windows 7 installed in a virtual machine (If you are using a VM, this lab creates a second virtual hard drive in the VM. Instructions in this lab are given for both Windows Virtual PC and Oracle VirtualBox.)

LAB PREPARATION

Before the lab begins, the instructor or lab assistant needs to do the following:

◢ Verify Windows starts with no errors and a second hard drive is available

◢ Alternately, if you plan to use a VM for this lab, verify Windows 7 is installed in the VM

ACTIVITY BACKGROUND

A system image backs up the entire Windows volume and can be stored on an external or internal hard drive or on DVDs. (For Windows 7 Professional, Ultimate, and Enterprise editions, you can install the system image on a network location.) When the Windows volume is corrupted or data on the drive is totally lost, you can use a system image to restore the entire Windows volume to the time the system image was last updated.

You can do this lab using a Windows 7 computer with a second hard drive. Alternately, you can use Windows 7 installed in a virtual machine and create a second hard drive in the VM. Directions for both methods are included.

ESTIMATED COMPLETION TIME: 45 MINUTES

 Activity

If you are using a Windows 7 computer and a second hard drive, follow the steps in Part 1 of this lab. If you are using Windows 7 in a VM, follow the steps in Part 2 of this lab.

PART 1: USE A WINDOWS 7 COMPUTER TO CREATE AND USE A SYSTEM IMAGE

1. Plug in an external hard drive or install a second internal hard drive in your computer.

2. If the hard drive is new and needs to be partitioned and formatted, open Disk Management, and partition and format the hard drive using the NTFS file system.

3. Using Windows Explorer, find out how much space is used on drive C:. Find out how much space is free on the second hard drive. The free space needed to hold the system image on the second hard drive will be about 80 percent of the space used on drive C:.

   ◢ How much space is used on drive C:?

   _____

   ◢ How much space is free on the second hard drive? Do you have enough room on the second drive for the system image?

   _____

4. To create the system image, open the Backup and Restore utility, and then click **Create a system image**. Follow the on-screen directions to create the image.

▲ Other than the second hard drive, what locations or devices can you use for the image?

_____

▲ What is the name of the subfolder in the WindowsImageBackup folder that holds the system image? What is the size of this subfolder?

_____

5. Now let's make some changes to the Windows volume. Use Windows Explorer to go to your user profile in C:\Users*username*. Record below the exact path to your My Documents, My Music, My Pictures, and My Videos folders, and then delete these four folders.

_____

_____

6. Shut down Windows.

7. Boot up the computer, and load the Advanced Boot Options menu. Click **Repair Your Computer** to launch Windows RE. What responses did you need to make to launch Windows RE?

_____

8. In the System Recovery Options window, click **System Image Recovery**. Follow the on-screen directions to reimage the drive. What decisions and responses did you need to make during this process?

_____

_____

_____

9. When the imaging is complete, Windows restarts and the Windows desktop loads. Look in your user profile. Are the deleted folders restored?

_____

PART 2: USE WINDOWS 7 IN A VM TO CREATE AND USE A SYSTEM IMAGE

1. Using Windows Virtual PC or Oracle VirtualBox, select a VM that has Windows 7 installed. If necessary, install in the VM a second virtual hard drive (VHD). Make the VHD a dynamically expanding drive with a maximum capacity of at least 50 GB.

2. Start the VM. If you have just installed a new VHD, use Disk Management to partition and format this drive using the NTFS file system.

3. Open Windows Explorer or Disk Management to help you answer these questions:

▲ How much space is used on drive C:?

_____

◢ How much space is free on the second hard drive? Do you have enough room on the second drive for the system image?

_____

4. Open the Backup and Restore utility, and use it to create a system image on the second hard drive.

◢ What other locations or devices can you use for the image other than the second hard drive?

_____

◢ What is the name of the subfolder in the WindowsImageBackup folder that holds the system image? What is the size of this subfolder?

_____

5. Now let's make some drastic changes to the Windows volume. List the exact paths to several folders on drive C:, and then delete these folders. Include Windows subfolders and Users subfolders in your list of folders to delete.

_____

_____

_____

6. Shut down the Windows 7 VM.
7. Start the VM again and load the Advanced Boot Options menu. Launch Windows RE. What responses did you need to make to launch Windows RE?

_____

8. In the System Recovery Options window, click **System Image Recovery**. Follow the on-screen directions to reimage the drive. What decisions and responses did you need to make during this process?

_____

_____

_____

9. When the imaging is complete, the VM restarts and the Windows desktop loads. Did Windows launch successfully? Are the deleted folders restored?

_____

CHALLENGE ACTIVITY (ADDITIONAL 20 MINUTES)

Interestingly enough, Windows stores the system image in a VHD. If you drill down into the WindowsImageBackup subfolders, you will find a very large VHD file, which contains the image. Mount (attach) this VHD file as a virtual hard drive installed on your computer or virtual machine. Then, use Windows Explorer to explore the VHD. Copy a file from the C:\Users\Public\Public Music\Sample Music folder in the system image to the Windows desktop.

Answer the following questions:

◢ What utility did you use to attach the VHD file to your system as an installed virtual hard drive? What drive letter did Windows assign the VHD?

_____

◢ What is the size of the VHD file in the WindowsImageBackup folder that holds the system image you created in this lab?

_____

◢ Why is it unreasonable to ask you the name of the VHD file?

_____

REVIEW QUESTIONS

1. If you were using single-sided recordable DVDs to hold the system image you created in this lab, how many DVDs would be required? How did you arrive at your answer?

_____

_____

2. What Windows utility is used to create a system image? To restore the system using a system image? To mount a VHD to the Windows system?

_____

_____

_____

3. Why is it useful to know that you can mount into the Windows system the VHD that holds the system image?

_____

_____

4. Describe one situation in the field when you might want to recover the Windows volume using the system image. Describe a situation when you might want to mount into the Windows system the VHD that holds the system image:

_____

_____

LAB 13.7 RECOVER DATA FROM A COMPUTER THAT WILL NOT BOOT

OBJECTIVES

The goal of this lab is to learn how to recover data from a computer that will not boot. After completing this lab, you will be able to:

◢ Copy data from a nonbooting computer

MATERIALS REQUIRED

This lab requires the following:

▲ Two Windows 8 or Windows 7 computers designated for this lab

▲ An account with administrator privileges

▲ Internet access

LAB PREPARATION

Before the lab begins, the instructor or lab assistant needs to do the following:

▲ Verify Windows works with no errors

▲ Verify each student has access to a user account with administrator privileges

▲ Verify Internet access is available

ACTIVITY BACKGROUND

If Windows is corrupted and the system will not boot, recovering your data might be your first priority. One way to get to the data is to remove your hard drive from your computer and install it as a second nonbooting hard drive in another working system. After you boot up the system, you should be able to use File Explorer/Windows Explorer to copy the data to another medium, such as a USB flash drive. If the data is corrupted, you can try to use data recovery software. In this lab, you will remove the hard drive from a computer and attempt to recover information from it.

ESTIMATED COMPLETION TIME: 45 MINUTES

 Activity

First you need to create some data on the first computer that will need to be rescued:

1. Boot the first computer, and log on as administrator.

2. Using Control Panel, create a new user called **User1**.

3. Log on as User1.

4. You will now create some files to represent important information that might be saved in various locations on this computer. Use Notepad to create three text files, named **file1.txt**, **file2.txt**, and **file3.txt**, and save one in each of the following locations:

   ▲ Save **file1.txt** in User1's My Documents folder.

   ▲ Save **file2.txt** in the Public Documents subfolder in the \Users\Public folder.

   ▲ Save **file3.txt** in the root (probably C:\).

5. Open Internet Explorer, and bookmark at least three locations on the web.

6. Log off and shut down this computer.

Now pretend this computer is no longer able to boot. Because a backup or restore point has not been created recently, you will remove the hard drive and attempt to recover your important files before attempting to determine why the computer won't boot.

1. Remove the main hard drive, and install it as a second hard drive in another Windows machine. If you are not trained to work inside a computer, ask your instructor for assistance.

> **Notes** You can save time by purchasing an external IDE/SATA-to-USB converter kit (for about $30), which can be used to temporarily connect a hard drive to a USB port on a working computer.

2. Boot this computer, and log on as an administrator.

3. Use File Explorer/Windows Explorer to locate the three text files on the hard drive you just installed.

4. List the path where each of these files can be found:

   ◢ file1.txt

   _____

   ◢ file2.txt

   _____

   ◢ file3.txt

   _____

5. Determine the name and location of the file containing your Internet Explorer bookmarks:

   _____

6. Can you think of any other locations that could contain information a user might want to recover?

   _____

   _____

In some cases, the files you are trying to recover might be corrupt, or you might not be able to access the drive at all. In these cases, you can attempt to use file-recovery software.

1. Open a command prompt window. Use the chkdsk command to check the hard drive on which you have important data for errors, and attempt to fix them. What chkdsk command line did you use?

   _____

2. Shut down the system you're using and return the hard drive to its original computer.

3. Boot both computers back up, and ensure that everything is working before shutting them both down.

CHALLENGE ACTIVITY (ADDITIONAL 45 MINUTES)

You can simulate this lab using two virtual machines. Go through the steps in the lab again using Windows 8 or Windows 7 installed in a virtual machine using either Virtual PC or VirtualBox. Then "move" the virtual hard drive (VHD) to a second VM that has Windows 8 or Windows 7 installed. Install the VHD as the second hard drive in this VM. Then use Windows 8 or Windows 7 on this second VM to recover the data on your virtual hard drive. Finally, return the VHD to the original VM, and start up both VMs to make sure everything is working as it should. Answer the following questions:

1. List the steps you took to "move" the VHD in the first VM to the second VM:

   _____

   _____

   _____

2. List the steps you took to locate and use the second virtual hard drive when you started the second VM:

_____

_____

_____

3. List the steps you took to return the VHD to the first VM:

_____

_____

_____

4. What problems did you encounter while performing this Challenge Activity, and how did you solve them?

_____

_____

REVIEW QUESTIONS

1. Why might you want to recover lost data before attempting to resolve a boot problem?

_____

_____

2. How could scheduled backups save you a lot of time if your system will not boot?

_____

_____

3. What type of errors might cause a computer to not boot? List three possible causes:

_____

_____

_____

4. If you suspect the first computer is not booting because it is infected with a virus, what should you ensure before installing its hard drive in a second computer?

_____

_____

LAB 13.8 CRITICAL THINKING: SABOTAGE AND REPAIR WINDOWS

OBJECTIVES

The goal of this lab is to learn to troubleshoot Windows by repairing a sabotaged system. After completing this lab, you will be able to:

⊿ Troubleshoot and repair a system that isn't working correctly

MATERIALS REQUIRED

This lab requires the following:

⊿ Windows 8 or Windows 7 installed on a computer designated for sabotage

⊿ Windows 8 or Windows 7 setup DVD or installation files

⊿ A workgroup of two to four students

> **Notes** This lab works great on Windows 8 or Windows 7 installed in a VM.

LAB PREPARATION

Before the lab begins, the instructor or lab assistant needs to do the following:

⊿ Verify Windows starts with no errors

⊿ Provide each workgroup with access to the Windows 8 or Windows 7 installation files, if needed

ACTIVITY BACKGROUND

You have learned about several tools and methods you can use to recover Windows when it fails. This lab gives you the opportunity to use these skills in a troubleshooting situation. Your group will sabotage another group's system while that group sabotages your system. Then your group will repair its own system.

ESTIMATED COMPLETION TIME: 45 MINUTES

 Activity

Follow these steps to sabotage a Windows 8 or Windows 7 system for another group, and then repair your Windows 8 or Windows 7 system that the other group has sabotaged:

1. If your system's hard drive contains important data, back it up to another medium. Is there anything else you would like to back up before another group sabotages the system? Record the name of that item here, and then back it up:

   _____

2. Trade systems with another group, and sabotage the other group's system while they sabotage your system. Do one thing that will cause the system to fail to boot, display errors after the boot, or prevent a device or application from working. The following list offers some sabotage suggestions. Do something in the following list, or think of another option. (Do not alter the hardware.)

◢ Find a system file in the root directory that's required to boot the computer, and rename it or move it to a different directory. (Don't delete the file.)

◢ Using the Registry Editor (Regedit.exe), delete several important keys or values in the registry.

◢ Locate important system files in the Windows folder or its subfolders, and rename them or move them to another directory.

> **Notes** To move, delete, or rename a Windows system file, you might need to first take ownership of the file using the takeown and icacls commands. The Microsoft Knowledge Base Article 929833 at *support.microsoft.com* explains how to use these two commands.

◢ Put a corrupted program file in the Windows folder that will cause the program to launch automatically at startup. Record the name of that program file and folder here:

_____

◢ Use display settings that aren't readable—such as black text on a black background.

◢ Disable a critical device driver or Windows service.

3. Reboot the system and verify a problem exists.

4. How did you sabotage the other team's system?

_____

_____

5. Return to your system and troubleshoot it.

6. Describe the problem as a user would describe it to you if you were working at a help desk:

_____

_____

_____

7. What is your first guess as to the source of the problem?

_____

8. As you troubleshoot the system, list the high-level steps you are taking in the troubleshooting process:

_____

_____

_____

_____

9. How did you finally solve the problem and return the system to good working order?

_____

_____

REVIEW QUESTIONS

1. What would you do differently the next time you encountered the same symptoms that you encountered in this lab?

_____

_____

2. What Windows utilities did you use—or could you have used—to solve the problem in the lab?

_____

3. What might cause the problem in the lab to occur in real life? List three possible causes:

_____

_____

_____

4. If you were the IT support technician responsible for this computer in an office environment, what could you do to prevent this problem from happening in the future or at least limit its impact on users if it did happen?

_____

_____

CHAPTER 14

Connecting To and Setting Up a Network

Labs included in this chapter:

- **Lab 14.1:** Understand the OSI Model
- **Lab 14.2:** Convert Binary and Hexadecimal Numbers
- **Lab 14.3:** Network Two Computers
- **Lab 14.4:** Demonstrate Homegroup Security
- **Lab 14.5:** Set Up a Wireless Router
- **Lab 14.6:** Secure a Wireless LAN

LAB 14.1 UNDERSTAND THE OSI MODEL

OBJECTIVES

The goal of this lab is to understand some of the concepts and principles of networking technology. After completing this lab, you will be able to:

- ◢ Describe the OSI layers
- ◢ Apply the OSI layer principles to networking

MATERIALS REQUIRED

This lab requires the following:

- ◢ Windows 8 or Windows 7 operating system
- ◢ Internet access

LAB PREPARATION

Before the lab begins, the instructor or lab assistant needs to do the following:

- ◢ Verify Windows starts with no errors
- ◢ Verify Internet access is available

ACTIVITY BACKGROUND

Network architects use a variety of principles and concepts for communication when designing and implementing networks. Collectively, this architectural model is called the OSI (Open Systems Interconnection) model. The OSI model consists of seven layers. As an IT support technician, you do not need to understand network architecture. However, you might find it interesting to know a little about these fundamental concepts, which can help you better understand how the TCP/IP protocols work. Understanding these concepts will also help you better communicate with network specialists.

ESTIMATED COMPLETION TIME: 30 MINUTES

 Activity

Using the Internet for your research, answer the following questions:

1. What are the seven OSI layers? Enter their names in the empty boxes on the left side of Table 14-1.

2. The OSI model is easier to understand if you memorize the seven layers. You can use a phrase mnemonic, in which the beginning letter of each layer is used to create a memorable phrase, to help you with this task. Research online for a mnemonic to help you memorize the OSI layers, and record it here:

_____

3. TCP/IP is a suite of protocols that follow the concepts of the OSI model. The four layers of the TCP/IP model are shown on the right side of Table 14-1. Email is one example of a TCP/IP application that works at the Application layer. What are two more examples of applications that work at this layer?

_____

OSI Layer	TCP/IP Protocol Stack Layer
7	**Application layer** (For example, email using SMTP and IMAP protocols)
6	
5	
4	**Transport layer** (TCP protocol)
3	**Internet layer** (IP protocol)
2	**Network interface layer** (Network card using Ethernet protocol)
1	

Table 14-1 Describing the OSI model and the TCP/IP model

4. The TCP protocol works at the Transport layer of TCP/IP. Briefly describe the function of the TCP protocol as used in Internet communications:

_____

_____

5. The IP protocol, working at the Internet layer, is responsible for locating the network and host for a data packet being transmitted by TCP. What type of address does the IP protocol use to identify a unique network and host?

_____

6. Other than a network card (NIC), what is an example of a device that works at the Network layer of the TCP/IP stack?

_____

7. Other than IP, what is an example of a protocol that works at the Internet layer of TCP/IP?

_____

8. At which TCP/IP layer does a MAC address function?

_____

9. At which TCP/IP layer does the TLS protocol work?

_____

10. At which TCP/IP layer does the HTTPS protocol work?

_____

11. Why do you think TCP/IP is often called a protocol stack rather than a protocol suite?

_____

_____

REVIEW QUESTIONS

1. What mnemonic can you use to help you remember the seven OSI layers?

_____

2. List all of the OSI layers used when an email client requests email over the Internet:

_____

_____

3. What protocol does a web browser normally use? At which OSI layer does this protocol work?

_____

4. When more than one application is running on a server, how does IP know which service should be presented an incoming data packet?

_____

5. When configuring a network connection to the Internet, you might need to enter the IP address of the computer, the DNS server, the subnet mask, and the default gateway. Of these four items, which are used to determine whether a remote computer is on the same network or a remote network?

_____

_____

6. Of the four items listed in Question 5, which is used to relate a domain name to an IP address?

_____

LAB 14.2 CONVERT BINARY AND HEXADECIMAL NUMBERS

OBJECTIVES

The goal of this lab is to practice converting numbers between decimal, binary, and hexadecimal forms. After completing this lab, you will be able to:

◢ Convert decimal numbers (base 10) to hexadecimal and binary form

◢ Convert hexadecimal numbers (base 16) to binary and decimal form

◢ Convert binary numbers (base 2) to decimal and hexadecimal form

MATERIALS REQUIRED

This lab requires the following:

◢ A pencil and paper and/or Windows Calculator

14

⊿ Access to the online content "The Hexadecimal Number System" that accompanies this lab manual; for instructions on how to access this content at *cengagebrain.com*, see the Preface.

⊿ Windows 8 or Windows 7 operating system

LAB PREPARATION

Before the lab begins, the instructor or lab assistant needs to do the following:

⊿ Announce to students that, before they come to lab, they should read the online content "The Hexadecimal Number System." It is also suggested that students bring this content to class in printed form.

ACTIVITY BACKGROUND

Sometimes you need to know what resources, such as memory addresses, are being reserved for a device. This information is often displayed on a computer using the binary or hexadecimal (hex) number system, which, while useful to the computer, is difficult for humans to read and understand. In another example, IPv4 addresses are displayed and written in decimal and often need to be converted to binary. In addition, IPv6 addresses are written and displayed in hex, and you need to write them in binary or decimal. It's also interesting to know that MAC addresses are displayed in hex.

As an IT support technician, you are likely to encounter the need to convert numbers from one number system to another, such as when you are comparing an IP address with a subnet mask in order to decide if the IP address is in a particular subnet. This lab gives you that practice.

ESTIMATED COMPLETION TIME: 60 MINUTES

 Activity

Follow these steps to practice converting numbers from one number system to another:

1. Convert the following decimal numbers to binary numbers using a calculator or by following the instructions in the online content "The Hexadecimal Number System." (To access Windows Calculator in Windows 8, press **Win+S**, type **calculator**, and press **Enter**. To access Windows Calculator in Windows 7, click **Start**, **All Programs**, **Accessories**, and then click **Calculator**. If necessary, click **View** on the Calculator menu bar, and then click **Programmer** to access the function you need to perform the conversions in these steps.)

⊿ 14 = _____

⊿ 77 = _____

⊿ 128 = _____

⊿ 223 = _____

⊿ 255 = _____

2. Convert the following decimal numbers to hexadecimal notation:

⊿ 13 = _____

⊿ 240 = _____

⊿ 255 = _____

⊿ 58880 = _____

⊿ 65535 = _____

3. Convert the following binary numbers to hexadecimal notation:
   - 100 = _____
   - 1011 = _____
   - 111101 = _____
   - 11111000 = _____
   - 10110011 = _____
   - 00000001 = _____

4. Hexadecimal numbers are often preceded by "0x." However, when converting a hexadecimal number, do not include the "0x" in the entry on the calculator. Convert the following hexadecimal numbers to binary numbers:
   - 0x0016 = _____
   - 0x00F8 = _____
   - 0x00B2B = _____
   - 0x005A = _____
   - 0x1234 = _____

5. Convert the following hexadecimal numbers to decimal:
   - 0x0013 = _____
   - 0x00AB = _____
   - 0x01CE = _____
   - 0x812A = _____

6. Convert the following binary numbers to decimal:
   - 1011 = _____
   - 11011 = _____
   - 10101010 = _____
   - 111110100 = _____
   - 10111011101 = _____
   - 11111000001111 = _____

A network card, also called a network adapter or NIC, is assigned a MAC address (or physical address) at the factory. Windows assigns to a network connection an IPv4 address, a subnet mask, and possibly an IPv6 address each time the connection is created. In the following steps, you find these assigned values for your computer, and then convert them to binary numbers:

1. Open the command prompt window, type **ipconfig /all**, and then press **Enter**.

2. Write down the following information for your system's active network connection (most likely either Ethernet or Wi-Fi):
   - Physical address in paired hexadecimal form:

     _____

   - Physical address expressed in binary pairs:

     _____

   - IPv4 address in decimal form:

     _____

   - IPv4 address expressed as four octets in binary form:

     _____

◢ Subnet mask in decimal form:

_____

◢ Subnet mask expressed as four octets in binary form:

_____

◢ IPv6 address in decimal form:

_____

◢ IPv6 address expressed as eight blocks of hexadecimal numbers (some of these blocks might contain a zero):

_____

◢ IPv6 address expressed as eight blocks of binary numbers:

_____

Memory addresses are displayed in hexadecimal form. Do the following to find out the memory address range assigned to the NIC on your computer, and then convert this range to decimal:

1. Open **Device Manager,** and then open the **Properties** dialog box for the network adapter. Click the **Resources** tab. What is the memory address range for the NIC?

_____

2. Convert the numbers in the network adapter's memory range, and determine how many bytes, expressed in a decimal number, are in its memory address range:

_____

CRITICAL THINKING (ADDITIONAL 15 MINUTES)

1. A typical video card uses a color depth of 8 bits to define the screen color in Safe Mode. Eight bits can form 256 different numbers from 00000000 to 11111111 in binary (0 to 255 in decimal) so 256 different colors are possible. How many colors are available with a 16-bit color depth? How many are available with a 24-bit or a 32-bit depth?

_____

_____

_____

REVIEW QUESTIONS

1. How long, in bits, is a typical MAC address?

_____

2. Computers often express numbers in _____ format, which is a base 16 number system.

3. Most people are more comfortable working with a(n) _____, or base 10, number system.

4. In the hexadecimal system, what decimal value does the letter A represent?

_____

5. Hexadecimal numbers are often preceded by _____ so that a value containing only numerals is not mistaken for a decimal number.

6. Write the following IPv6 address using a short hand method: 2001:0:4147:0:0:1c32:0:fe99.

_____

7. The IP address of Computer 1 is 192.168.200.10, and it has a subnet mask of 255.255.240.0. The IP address of Computer 2 is 192.168.195.200, and the IP address of Computer 3 is 192.168.230.40.

a. How many bits of the IP address for Computer 1 are used to define its subnet?

b. Are Computer 1 and Computer 2 part of the same subnet? Explain your answer.

c. Are Computer 1 and Computer 3 part of the same subnet? Explain your answer.

_____

_____

_____

_____

_____

LAB 14.3 NETWORK TWO COMPUTERS

OBJECTIVES

The goal of this lab is to install and configure a network interface card (NIC) and configure the TCP/IP settings to connect two computers. After completing this lab, you will be able to:

◢ Uninstall and install a NIC

◢ Configure TCP/IPv4 settings

◢ Share files and folders between two computers

◢ Configure IP addressing

MATERIALS REQUIRED

This lab requires the following:

◢ Windows 8 or Windows 7 operating system

◢ An account with administrator privileges

◢ A wireless NIC and the associated drivers

◢ Wi-Fi network access

◢ A workgroup partner

LAB PREPARATION

Before the lab begins, the instructor or lab assistant needs to do the following:

◢ Verify Windows starts with no errors

◢ Verify each student has access to a user account with administrator privileges

◢ Verify drivers for the NIC and wireless equipment to connect two computers are available

ACTIVITY BACKGROUND

Computers on a network have the ability to communicate with one another and share resources, such as files and devices. A computer connects to a network through a network interface card (NIC). In this lab, you install a NIC, configure necessary network settings, and verify the NIC is functioning correctly. Working with a partner, you create a simple network of two computers and work through the basics of networking.

ESTIMATED COMPLETION TIME: 45 MINUTES

 Activity

As an IT technician, you need to be able to set up, configure, and troubleshoot the hardware involved in networking. A key hardware piece is the network interface card (NIC). This card allows the computer to communicate on the network. Follow these steps to learn to uninstall and reinstall the NIC:

1. Power on your computer, and then sign in to Windows.

2. Disconnect any network cable, and then disable Wi-Fi.

3. Open **Device Manager**. Expand the **Network adapters** listing. What are the names of the network adapters installed on your system?

_____

4. Right-click the **Wi-Fi network adapter,** and then click **Uninstall** in the shortcut menu. Click **OK** to confirm the device uninstall.

5. Restart the computer, and install the NIC. The installation process might take a few minutes because there might be several layers to the drivers.

6. After installation is complete, return to **Device Manager,** and verify your NIC has been reinstalled and that Device Manager reports no problems with the device.

Now that the network adapter is working, you need to configure the computer to gain access to shared resources on the network. It is important for you to know where to locate and how to modify settings that control network communication. These settings make your computer unique on the network and easily identified by other computers. Let's explore the configuring of the network settings.

To verify and configure the current TCP/IP settings, follow these steps:

1. Open **Network and Sharing Center** (see the left side of Figure 14-1). In the left panel, click **Change adapter settings**. Right-click **the Wi-Fi network connection,** and click **Properties** in the shortcut menu. The Wi-Fi Properties dialog box opens.

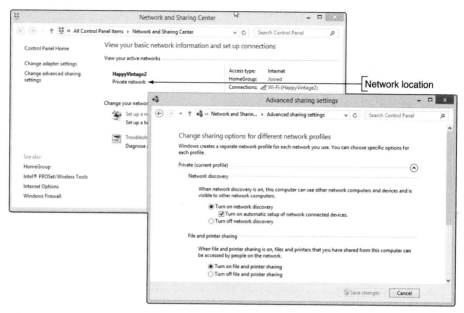

Figure 14-1 The Network and Sharing Center reports the network location and gives options for adjusting the network profile

2. In the list of connection items, click **Internet Protocol Version 4 (TCP/IPv4)**, and then click **Properties**. The Properties dialog box that opens can be used to configure the IP settings for the connection.

3. For this part of the lab, you use static IP addressing. With your lab partner, determine who will use the Partner #1 information in the grid below and who will use the Partner #2 information:

	Partner #1	**Partner #2**
IP address	192.168.1.1	192.168.1.2
Computer name:	Lab1	Lab2
Workgroup name:	NIC LAB	NIC LAB

4. Select the **Use the following IP address** option, and then enter your chosen IP address.

5. Use the **Tab** key to move to the Subnet mask box. If Windows doesn't automatically populate the subnet mask, enter a subnet mask of 255.255.255.0.

6. Click **OK**, and then close all windows.

Now that your computer has a unique IP address on the network, it is time to assign a computer name and workgroup name to your computer. These assignments will give the computer an identity on the network. Follow these steps:

1. Open the System window. In the Computer name, domain, and workgroup settings area, click **Change settings**. The System Properties dialog box opens.

2. Click **Change**. The Computer Name/Domain Changes dialog box opens.

3. Enter the computer name for your machine from the chart.

4. If necessary, click **Workgroup** to select it. Enter the Workgroup name from the chart. Other than Workgroup, what is a second choice for membership?

5. Click **OK**. A Welcome to the workgroup dialog box appears. Click **OK**. Windows displays a message with instructions about applying the change. What must you do next to apply the change?

_____

6. Click **OK**, and close all windows. Restart your computer, and then sign in to Windows.

7. Connect the computer to the Wi-Fi network. Make sure to configure the connection as a public network. In Windows 8, set the connection as public by clicking **No** when asked if you want to find PCs and other devices and content on the network. In Windows 7, set the connection as public by clicking **Public network** in the Set Network Location dialog box. Refer to the chapter, "Survey of Windows Features and Support Tools," for details on how to change this setting in either Windows 8 or Windows 7.

8. Open the **Network and Sharing Center**, and then click **Change advanced sharing settings** (see the right side of Figure 14-1). The Advanced sharing settings window opens. Here you can change your network profiles for each network location.

9. At the top of this window, hide the profile for Private in Windows 8 or for Home or Work in Windows 7, and expand the profile for Guest or Public in Windows 8 or for Guest in Windows 7. Verify the Guest or Public profile (in Windows 8) or the Public profile (in Windows 7) is labeled as the current profile.

10. Under Network discovery, select **Turn on network discovery**.

11. Under File and printer sharing, select **Turn on file and printer sharing**.

12. In Windows 8, expand the All Networks profile. In either Windows 8 or Windows 7, under Public folder sharing, select **Turn on sharing so anyone with network access can read and write files in the Public folders**.

13. Under Password protected sharing, select **Turn off password protected sharing**.

14. Click **Save changes**.

15. Open File Explorer or Windows Explorer. In the left pane, scroll down and then click **Network**.

◢ What machines show up in the Computer section?

_____

16. Close all windows.

Now let's see what happens when there is a conflict in IP addresses on your small network. Follow these steps:

1. Partner #1: Return to your Internet Protocol Version 4 (TCP/IPv4) Properties dialog box, and change the IP address of your machine to **192.168.1.2**.

2. Partner #1: Click **OK** and close all windows. If you're using a Windows 7 computer, what is the error message that appears on the Partner #1 computer?

_____

If you're using a Windows 8 computer, you have to do a little more detective work (which can also be done on a Windows 7 computer). With either Windows 8 or Windows 7, open a command prompt window, type **ipconfig**, and then press **Enter**. What is the IPv4 address for your computer? What does this information tell you?

_____

_____

3. Partners #1 and #2: Close all windows, reboot your computers, and sign in. If necessary, connect to the network. Wait for the Network icon in the taskbar to finish processing network discovery.

4. Partners #1 and #2: Open File Explorer or Windows Explorer, and drill down into the **Network** group.

   ◢ What computers have been discovered? (You might need to refresh this screen a couple of times. To refresh a selected window, press **F5**.)

   _____

   ◢ Explain the importance of using correct IP addressing when networking computers.

   _____

   _____

5. Partner #1: Return your IP address to 192.168.1.1, reboot your computer, and sign in. If necessary, connect to the network.

With the computers communicating with each other on the network, you can now view shared resources on each other's computer through the network. Follow these steps:

1. Open File Explorer or Windows Explorer, and drill down into the **Network** group. What computers are identified in the right pane?

   _____

2. Double-click your partner's computer icon to open that computer. What folder is presented to you?

   _____

3. Open the folder from Step 2. What folders are now presented to you?

   _____

4. Open the **Public** folder, and then open **Public Documents**.

   ◢ What files or folders do you find inside?

   _____

   ◢ What files or folders do you find in the Public Pictures folder?

   _____

5. Close all windows.

6. To open WordPad, type **WordPad** in the Search box, and then press **Enter**. Using WordPad, create a document with a single line of text, and save this document in your **Documents** library with a name of **Test Document**. What file extension did WordPad automatically assign the file?

   _____

7. Display your partner's computer in the Network listing of the Computer window.

8. Explore your partner's computer.

   ◢ Are you able to see your partner's WordPad document?

   _____

◢ What theory do you have as to why you can or cannot see the document?

_____

Follow these steps to find out what changes are made to shared resources when you turn off Public folder sharing:

1. Return to the **Network and Sharing Center**, and access **Advanced sharing settings**.

2. Under Public folder sharing, select **Turn off Public folder sharing**, and save your changes.

3. Using File Explorer or Windows Explorer, look in the **Network** group for your partner's computer. Explore the user profile folders for your partner's user account. What has changed?

_____

Follow these steps to find out what happens to shared resources when you change the network location:

1. To change the network location on a Windows 8 computer, open PC Settings, and click **Network, Connections,** and then click the name of the network. Turn on Find devices and content to change the network location to the private profile. Alternatively, force the computer to forget the network, and then re-create the network connection. On a Windows 7 computer, return to the **Network and Sharing Center**. In the View your active networks section, change the network location to **Work network**. Close all open windows.

2. Open File Explorer or Windows Explorer and view your partner's computer folders in the Network group. What has changed when viewing your partner's resources?

_____

_____

Now let's configure each computer to use dynamic IP addressing. If there is no DHCP server available to provide an IP address to your computer and Windows is set for dynamic IP addressing, Windows will use Automatic Private IP Addressing (APIPA). Follow these steps to investigate this situation:

1. Open an elevated command prompt window. List the exact steps you took to do so:

_____

_____

_____

2. At the command prompt, enter **ipconfig /all** and press **Enter**. What are the following values for your network connection?

◢ IPv4 address: _____

◢ Subnet mask: _____

◢ Default gateway: _____

◢ DNS server: _____

3. Close the command prompt window.

4. Open the Internet Protocol Version 4 (TCP/IPv4) Properties dialog box.

5. Select **Obtain an IP address automatically** and **Obtain DNS server address automatically**. Click **OK**, and close all windows.

6. Reboot the computer and launch a command prompt window. Enter the **ipconfig /all** command, and record the results here:

   ◢ IPv4 address: _____

   ◢ Subnet mask: _____

   ◢ Default gateway: _____

   ◢ DNS server: _____

7. Compare these results with those recorded in Step 2. What are your conclusions about the TCP/IP values assigned to your computer?

   _____

   _____

REVIEW QUESTIONS

1. What dialog box do you use to configure TCP/IPv4 settings for the network adapter?

   _____

2. What are the two types of addresses or names used in this lab that can uniquely identify a computer on the network?

   _____

   _____

3. If there is no DHCP server to provide a computer a unique IP address, how is a computer able to acquire an IP address?

   _____

4. What is the exact path to the Documents folder (My Documents folder in Windows 7) for a user named John Smith?

   _____

5. What is the name of the window you can use to configure the network discovery and file sharing settings?

   _____

LAB 14.4 DEMONSTRATE HOMEGROUP SECURITY

OBJECTIVES

The goal of this lab is to learn how a Windows homegroup is used to provide security for shared resources on a small network. After completing this lab, you will be able to:

◢ Create and use a homegroup

◢ Change the homegroup settings

MATERIALS REQUIRED

This lab requires the following:

◢ Two computers using Windows 8 or Windows 7, networked together

◢ An account with administrator privileges

◢ A workgroup of two students

LAB PREPARATION

Before the lab begins, the instructor or lab assistant needs to do the following:

◢ Verify both computers start with no errors

◢ Verify the local network is working

◢ Verify students have access to a user account with administrator privileges

ACTIVITY BACKGROUND

Earlier versions of the Windows operating system (prior to Windows 7) support Windows workgroups to secure networked resources on a peer-to-peer network. Windows 7 and Windows 8 support both workgroups and homegroups. A homegroup is an easy method of sharing folders and printers on a small peer-to-peer network. The primary difference between a homegroup and a workgroup is that a password is assigned to the homegroup, and the password applies to all computers in the homegroup. In contrast, in a workgroup, a password is assigned to each user of a computer in the workgroup.

In this lab, you and your partner set up a homegroup between two computers and see how shared resources are managed by the homegroup. In Part 1 of this lab, you set up two user accounts, each on a different computer. In Part 2, you join Computer1 to the homegroup, and in Part 3, you join Computer2 to the homegroup.

ESTIMATED COMPLETION TIME: 45 MINUTES

 Activity

PART 1: SET UP USER ACCOUNTS

In this part of the lab, you set up two user accounts: User1 on Computer1 and User2 on Computer2. Working with a partner, designate one computer as Computer1 and the other computer as Computer2. Follow these steps to set up a user account on each computer:

1. Sign in to Computer1 and Computer2 with user accounts that have administrator privileges.

2. If Computer1 is running Windows 8, open PC Settings, click **Accounts, Other accounts,** and then **Add an account.** Click **Sign in without a Microsoft account (not recommended),** and then click **Local account.** If Computer1 is running Windows 7, open Control Panel, and then click **Add or remove user accounts.** For either Windows 8 or Windows 7, follow the on-screen instructions to create a Standard user account named **User1.**

3. On Computer2, create a Standard user account named **User2.**

PART 2: JOIN COMPUTER1 TO THE HOMEGROUP

Follow these steps to set up a new homegroup or join Computer1 to an existing homegroup:

1. On Computer1, in the Search box, type **homegroup**, and then click **HomeGroup** in the search results. The HomeGroup window opens. If the window reports the computer already belongs to a homegroup, click **Leave the homegroup**. On the next screen, click **Leave the homegroup** again. Click **Finish**, and close all windows.

2. On Computer2, if the computer already belongs to a homegroup, leave the homegroup, and close all windows.

3. To create or join a homegroup, the network location must be set to Private on a Windows 8 computer or Home on a Windows 7 computer. On Computer1, to verify the network location, open the **Network and Sharing Center**.

The network location is reported under the View your active networks category. For example, in Figure 14-1 shown in the previous lab, the network location is a Private network.

If the network location is a Private (Windows 8) or Home (Windows 7) network, follow these steps to create a homegroup or join an existing homegroup, and then verify the homegroup settings:

1. In the left pane of the Network and Sharing Center window, click **HomeGroup**. The HomeGroup window opens (see Figure 14-2). If the window reports "There is currently no homegroup on the network," click **Create a homegroup**, and proceed to Step 2. If Windows detects and reports a homegroup on the network, go to Step 5 to join the existing homegroup.

Figure 14-2 The computer does not belong to a homegroup that exists on the network

2. For Windows 8 systems, click **Next**. For either Windows 8 or Windows 7, you can select what you want to share in the homegroup. Make sure that **Documents, Pictures, Music, Videos**, and **Printers** are all shared, and then click **Next**.

3. The next screen provides a suggested password to the homegroup.

   ◢ Write down the password, being careful to record the correct case because the password is case sensitive:

4. Click **Finish**. Proceed to Part 3 of this lab, "Join Computer2 to the Homegroup."

5. If Windows detected a homegroup on the network, click **Join now**.

6. For Windows 8 systems, click **Next**. On either Windows 8 or Windows 7, verify the **Documents, Pictures, Music, Videos**, and **Printers** resources are shared with the homegroup, and then click **Next**.

7. On the next screen, enter the password for the existing homegroup, click **Next**, and then click **Finish**. If you don't know the password, go to another computer on the network that belongs to the homegroup, open the **Network and Sharing Center** window, click **HomeGroup**, and then click **View or print the homegroup password**.

   ◢ What is the password of the existing homegroup?

If the current network is a Public network or Work network, follow these steps:

1. Change the network location to a Private network (Windows 8) or Home network (Windows 7), as you learned how to do in the previous lab.

2. Join an existing homegroup or create a new one, as described above.

PART 3: JOIN COMPUTER2 TO THE HOMEGROUP

1. On Computer2, sign in with the User2 account, verify the network location is a **Private or Home network**, and join the homegroup using the password you recorded earlier in this lab. Share **Documents, Pictures, Music, Videos**, and **Printers** with the homegroup.

2. On Computer1, still signed in as an administrator, open File Explorer or Windows Explorer. Under Libraries, click **Pictures**, and notice the Shared status for this library in the status bar at the bottom of the Explorer window.

3. To see how and with whom this library is shared, right-click **Pictures**, point to **Share with** in the shortcut menu, and then click **Specific people**. The File Sharing dialog box appears. Answer these questions:

   ◢ What permission level does the homegroup have for this library?

   ◢ Based on the current homegroup security, can a user on Computer2 copy a file to this library?

---

4. Close the File Sharing dialog box.

5. Using File Explorer or Windows Explorer, remove the Pictures library from the homegroup. List the steps you took to accomplish this:

---

6. Still in File Explorer or Windows Explorer, click **Homegroup** in the left pane. Record the resources you see available in the homegroup:

_____

_____

_____

_____

7. Using File Explorer or Windows Explorer, create a folder named Data under the C root directory.

8. Add the Data folder to the homegroup, giving the homegroup users permission to read and write to the folder. List the steps you took to accomplish that:

_____

_____

_____

_____

_____

_____

Follow these steps to see how User1 can access resources in the homegroup:

1. On Computer1, sign in to the system as **User1** (rather than as an administrator).

2. Open File Explorer or Windows Explorer. In the left pane, click **Music**, and notice in the status bar this Music folder is not shared with the homegroup.

3. Click **Homegroup**. Record the resources you see available to User1 in the homegroup:

_____

_____

_____

_____

_____

_____

4. Based on what you have learned in this lab about homegroups, answer the following questions:

   ◢ Can any user signed in to a computer in a homegroup access resources shared with the homegroup?

   _____

   ◢ If an administrator shares her Documents folder with the homegroup, will the Documents folders of all the users of this computer also be shared with the homegroup? Why or why not?

   _____

   ◢ If one user on a computer shares his libraries or folders with the homegroup, will another user of the same computer be able to access these resources?

   _____

5. Close all open windows on Computer1 and Computer2.

REVIEW QUESTIONS

1. List the steps to change the password to the homegroup:

   _____

   _____

   _____

   _____

   _____

   _____

2. What type of network location is required for a homegroup in Windows 8? In Windows 7?

   _____

3. What five resources can be shared by default in a homegroup?

   _____

   _____

4. How does Windows indicate in File Explorer or Windows Explorer that a folder is shared?

   _____

   _____

5. How many homegroups can you have on a local network?

   _____

LAB 14.5 SET UP A WIRELESS ROUTER

OBJECTIVES

The goal of this lab is to install and configure a wireless router. After completing this lab, you will be able to:

◢ Install and configure a wireless router

◢ Configure computers to connect to a wireless router

MATERIALS REQUIRED

This lab requires the following:

◢ Windows 8 or Windows 7 computer designated for this lab

◢ An account with administrator privileges

◢ A wireless router with setup CD or user's manual

◢ A USB wireless NIC is recommended for this lab

LAB PREPARATION

Before the lab begins, the instructor or lab assistant needs to do the following:

⊿ Verify Windows starts with no errors

⊿ Verify each student has access to a user account with administrator privileges

⊿ Verify a network connection is available

ACTIVITY BACKGROUND

A small office/home office (SOHO) router is the best device to use to set up a small network. A router can provide these basic functions on the network:

⊿ It can serve as a gateway to the Internet. The router stands between the networked computers and a DSL or cable modem used for a broadband connection to an ISP and to the Internet.

⊿ The router can add additional security by providing a hardware firewall and limiting access to the Internet.

⊿ A router can provide wired and wireless access to the network.

⊿ The router can serve other purposes, such as functioning as a DHCP server.

In this lab, you set up and configure a wireless router, and then connect to it from a remote computer.

ESTIMATED COMPLETION TIME: 30 MINUTES

 Activity

Follow these steps to set up your router:

1. If your router comes with a setup CD (see Figure 14-3), run the setup program on one of your computers on the network (it doesn't matter which one). Follow the instructions on the setup screen or in the accompanying user's manual to use network cables to physically connect the computer to the router, plug in the router, and turn it on either before or after you run the setup CD. A computer can connect directly to a network port (Ethernet port) on the router (see Figure 14-4), or you can connect through a switch or hub to the router.

For this router, you run the setup CD before you connect the computer and the router

Figure 14-3 A typical SOHO router with a setup CD

Figure 14-4 Connectors and ports on the back of a Cisco SOHO router

2. Connect the other computers on your network to the router.

3. Firmware on a router (which can be flashed for updates) contains a configuration program that you can access using a web browser from anywhere on the network. In your browser address box, enter the IP address of the router (for many routers, that address is 192.168.0.1 or 192.168.1.1), and then press **Enter**. What is the name and IP address for your router?

_____

4. You'll probably be required to sign in to the router firmware utility using a default password. The first thing you want to do is reset this password so that others cannot change your router setup. What is your new router password?

_____

5. After you change the password, a Setup or Quick Setup window appears, as shown in Figure 14-5. For most situations, the default settings on this and other screens should work without any changes required. The setup program will take you through the process of configuring the router. After you've configured the router, you might have to turn your cable or DSL modem off and back on so that it correctly syncs up with the router. What basic steps did the setup program have you follow to configure the router?

_____

_____

_____

_____

Figure 14-5 Quick Setup screen used to configure a TP-Link router

Source: TP-LINK Technologies Co., Ltd.

6. Spend some time examining the various features of your router. What security features does it have?

_____

_____

_____

7. What is the IP address of the router on the ISP network?

_____

8. Why is it necessary for the router to have two IP addresses?

_____

_____

Follow these steps to create a wireless connection to your wireless router from another computer:

1. Make sure you are signed in to Windows as an administrator. If you are using a wireless USB NIC, plug it into an available USB port. If necessary, install the drivers.

2. After the NIC has finished installing, click the **Network** icon in your taskbar. (If you don't see the Network icon, click the up arrow on the right side of the taskbar, and then click the **Network** icon, as shown in Figure 14-6a.)

3. Windows displays a list of wireless networks that are broadcasting availability (see Figure 14-6b for Windows 8). List all the networks that are available on your computer:

_____

4. Select the name of the network you would like to connect to. If you are comfortable with Windows automatically connecting to this network in the future, check **Connect automatically**, and then click **Connect**. If you are attempting to connect to a secured network, Windows will prompt you for the security key.

Figure 14-6   Use the Network icon to make a network connection

5. Windows reports the connection is being made. To see the network to which you are connected, click the **Network** icon in the taskbar or in the hidden icons box.

> **Notes** To add the Network icon to the taskbar, right-click the taskbar, and select **Properties**. In the Taskbar and Navigation properties dialog box (Windows 8) or Taskbar and Start Menu Properties dialog box (Windows 7), click **Customize**. In the Notification Area Icons window, select the option to show the Network icon, and then click **OK**.

6. Open the **Network and Sharing Center**. Verify Windows has configured the network as a Public network (see Figure 14-7). Click **Change advanced sharing settings** in the left pane.

Figure 14-7   Network and Sharing Center

7. The Advanced sharing settings window appears. Verify that Network discovery, File and printer sharing, and Public folder sharing settings are all turned off.

8. To see the status of your wireless connection, click the **Back** arrow to return to the Network and Sharing Center. In the View your active networks section, click the wireless network connection.

◢ What speed is your wireless connection?

_____

◢ Fast Ethernet runs at 100 Mbps, and Gigabit Ethernet runs at 1000 Mbps. How does your wireless network speed compare with these two types of wired networks?

_____

_____

9. Open your browser to test the connection.

10. When you're finished, reset and uninstall the wireless router and NIC.

REVIEW QUESTIONS

1. What are some of the additional features available on your router that you would implement if you were setting up a small wired and wireless network?

_____

_____

2. Name two ways your router can limit Internet access:

_____

_____

3. Name one advantage and one disadvantage of a wireless connection compared with a wired connection:

_____

_____

4. Most wireless routers have a reset switch. Give an example of when this might be useful:

_____

_____

LAB 14.6 SECURE A WIRELESS LAN

OBJECTIVES

The goal of this lab is to learn how to set up and configure security options on a wireless router. After completing this lab, you will be able to:

◢ Download a manual for a wireless router

◢ Explain how to improve wireless security

◢ Describe a few methods for securing a wireless LAN

MATERIALS REQUIRED

This lab requires the following:

◢ Windows 8 or Windows 7 operating system

◢ Internet access

◢ Adobe Acrobat Reader installed for viewing PDF files

◢ Wireless router (optional)

◢ Laptop or desktop with compatible wireless access (optional)

LAB PREPARATION

Before the lab begins, the instructor or lab assistant needs to do the following:

◢ Verify Windows starts with no errors

◢ Verify Internet access is available

ACTIVITY BACKGROUND

Wireless networks are a simple way to include computers in a home or small office network. Without adequate security, however, you can open up your network to a wide range of threats. In this lab, you learn how to enable and configure some security features of a wireless router.

If you have a router, use your router in this lab. If you don't have a router to do this lab, you can still complete the lab. To do so, assume that your router is the Linksys EA4500 router, similar to the one shown earlier in Figure 14-3. If you are not using the Linksys EA4500 router, what router brand and model are you using?

_____

ESTIMATED COMPLETION TIME: 45 MINUTES

 Activity

1. Open your web browser, and locate the support page for your router provided by the router manufacturer. For the Linksys EA4500 router, you go to the Linksys site for home routers at *linksys.com/us/shop-linksys/* and then search on the router model number.

   Follow links to view or download the user guide for your router. You might also find the user guide on the setup CD for your router. If you cannot find a user guide, then search the support documentation provided for the router on the manufacturer's website. Using any of these sources, answer the following questions:

   ◢ Most wireless routers can be configured with a web-based utility by entering the router's IP address in the browser address box. What's the default IP address of this router?

   _____

   ◢ Describe how you would log on to the router for the first time:

   _____

_____

_____

Most routers are easily configured with a setup utility that asks a series of questions about your network and your Internet service provider. The default settings, however, might not enable all your router's security features. Here are the four most important steps in securing your LAN:

◢ Update the router's firmware from the manufacturer's website so that any known security flaws are fixed.

◢ Set a password on the router itself so that other people can't change its configuration.

◢ Disable remote configuration of the router.

◢ Use some kind of wireless encryption. (WEP is better than nothing; WPA is better; and WPA2 is better still.)

Here are two more ways to secure a router. They are not considered strong security measures because they are easily hacked:

◢ Change the wireless network's name (called a service set identifier—SSID) and turn off the SSID broadcast to anyone who's listening.

◢ Enable MAC filtering so that only the computers whose MAC addresses are listed in your router table can access the network.

Continue to use the manual to answer the following additional questions:

◢ Which window in the router's web-based utility do you use to change the password needed to configure the router?

_____

◢ List the steps for changing the router's SSID:

_____

_____

_____

_____

◢ Does the router support Wi-Fi Protected Setup? If so, on which screen can it be enabled?

_____

◢ Describe the steps to limit access through MAC filtering to everything but the computer you are now using:

_____

_____

CHALLENGE ACTIVITY (ADDITIONAL 30 MINUTES)

If you have access to a wireless router, set up a secure wireless connection by following these steps:

1. Set up a nonsecure wireless connection with the router, as covered in the previous lab.

2. Go to the router manufacturer's website, and update the router's firmware (if necessary) to the latest version. Did your router require an update? What version of the firmware is it now running?

_____

3. Set a strong password for the router. What password did you use?

_____

4. Disable remote configuration for the router so the router cannot be configured wirelessly. List the steps you went through to complete this task:

_____

_____

_____

_____

5. Change the router's name (SSID). What was the router's default name, and what did you change it to?

_____

6. Disable the broadcast of the new SSID.

7. Set up some kind of wireless encryption on the router. What form of encryption did you use?

_____

8. Enable MAC filtering so that only the computer you are using can connect. How did you determine the MAC address of your computer?

_____

_____

9. Test your network connection by opening your browser and surfing the web.

10. When you're finished, reset the router to undo any changes you made to it.

REVIEW QUESTIONS

1. What client application on your computer is used to configure a home router?

_____

2. Why should you update your router's firmware before making any other security changes?

_____

_____

3. How could not changing your router's password compromise all of your other security changes?

_____

_____

4. Why wouldn't "password" or "Linksys" make a good password for your router?

_____

5. How can you configure your router once you've disabled remote configuration?

_____

_____

Supporting Network Hardware

Labs included in this chapter:

- **Lab 15.1:** Inspect Cables

- **Lab 15.2:** Compare Options for a Small Office or Home Office LAN

- **Lab 15.3:** Create a Straight-Through Cable

- **Lab 15.4:** Create a Crossover Cable

- **Lab 15.5:** Set Up Advanced IP Scanner and Wake-on-LAN

- **Lab 15.6:** Troubleshoot with TCP/IP Utilities

- **Lab 15.7:** Sabotage and Repair a Network Connection

LAB 15.1 INSPECT CABLES

OBJECTIVES

The goal of this lab is to visually inspect a set of cables and use a multimeter to test them. After completing this lab, you will be able to:

◢ Identify two CAT-5e or CAT-6 wiring systems

◢ Test cables with a multimeter

◢ Draw pinouts for cable connectors

◢ Determine whether a cable is a patch cable (also known as a straight-through cable) or a crossover cable

◢ Visually inspect cables and connectors

MATERIALS REQUIRED

This lab requires the following:

◢ A variety of cables, including a patch cable and a crossover cable

◢ A multimeter

◢ Internet access

◢ Access to a printer (optional)

LAB PREPARATION

Before the lab begins, the instructor or lab assistant needs to do the following:

◢ Verify Internet access is available

ACTIVITY BACKGROUND

For a network connection to function properly, the cables must be wired correctly and be without any defects. In this lab, you physically inspect cables and the connector, and then test the cable's pinouts and continuity using a multimeter.

ESTIMATED COMPLETION TIME: 45 MINUTES

 Activity

1. Open your web browser, and go to **lanshack.com**. You can also search the web for information about a patch cable diagram, a crossover cable diagram, and a CAT-5e or CAT-6 wiring diagram. List the two standards for unshielded twisted-pair (UTP) wiring schemes. Which website did you use?

2. For both wiring schemes, print or draw on a separate sheet of paper a pinout diagram for a patch cable and a crossover cable.

Follow these steps to visually inspect cables:

1. Examine the length of the cable for obvious damage, such as a cut or abrasion in the outer sleeve with further damage to the twisted pairs inside. A completely cut strand is an obvious problem, but the conductor inside the cable might be broken even if the insulator is intact. Any visible copper is an indication you need a new cable.

2. Inspect the RJ-45 connectors. In particular, look for exposed twisted pairs between the clear plastic connector and the cable sleeve or jacket. This indicates that the cable was assembled improperly or excessive force was used when pulling on the cable. The cable sleeve should be crimped inside the RJ-45 connector. Sometimes you can identify a nonconforming wiring scheme by noting the color of the insulation through the clear connector, but you should check the cable with a multimeter to verify its condition.

3. Next, verify the retaining clip on the connector is present. When an assembled cable is pulled, this clip often snags on carpet or other cables, and breaks off. This results in a connector that's likely to become loose or fall out of the jack. Worse still, this connection might be intermittent. Some cables have boots to prevent the clip from snagging when pulled, but these boots can cause problems when seating the connector in the jack if the boot has slid too far toward the end of the cable.

4. Test your cables with a multimeter, and fill in Table 15-1. For each cable, you need to identify which pin at one end of a cable connects to which pin at the other end of the cable. To do so, you use the multimeter to systematically determine continuity between pins. For example, start with pin 1 of cable 1. First record the insulator color for this pin. Then check for continuity between it and each of the pins at the other end of the cable. Which pin connects to pin1? Record that information (insulator color and pin position) in the first row of the table. Then continue to the other pins and cables until the table is completed. What settings on the multimeter did you use when testing the cables?

	End A			End B			Questions About the Cable
	Pin #	Insulator color	Pin tied to pin at End B	Insulator color	Pin tied to pin at End A		Is the cable good or bad?
Cable 1	1						
	2						Wired with what scheme?
	3						
	4						
	5						Is the cable a crossover or patch cable?
	6						
	7						
	8						

Table 15-1   Pin connections for selected cables (continues)

	End A		End B		Questions About the Cable
Pin #	**Insulator color**	**Pin tied to pin at End B**	**Insulator color**	**Pin tied to pin at End A**	**Is the cable good or bad?**
1					
2					**Wired with what scheme?**
3					
4					
5					**Is the cable a crossover or patch cable?**
6					
7					
8					
Pin #	**Insulator color**	**Pin tied to pin at End B**	**Insulator color**	**Pin tied to pin at End A**	**Is the cable good or bad?**
1					
2					**Wired with what scheme?**
3					
4					
5					**Is the cable a crossover or patch cable?**
6					
7					
8					

(Left margin labels: Cable 2 for the top section, Cable 3 for the bottom section)

Table 15-1 Pin connections for selected cables

REVIEW QUESTIONS

1. If you can see a copper conductor in a cable, what should you do with the cable?

   _____

2. What type of connector is used with CAT-5e and CAT-6 cables?

   _____

3. Based on your research, which cabling scheme is more common: straight-through or crossover?

   _____

4. On a patch cable, pin 3 on one end connects to pin _____ on the other end of the cable.

5. On a crossover cable, pin 2 on one end connects to pin _____ on the other end of the cable.

LAB 15.2 COMPARE OPTIONS FOR A SMALL OFFICE OR HOME OFFICE LAN

OBJECTIVES

The goal of this lab is to research the costs and capabilities of upgrading wired and wireless home local area networks (LANs). After completing this lab, you will be able to:

⊿ Research wired and wireless Ethernet

⊿ Research 802.11 standards

⊿ Identify components to build the network

MATERIALS REQUIRED

This lab requires the following:

⊿ Internet access

LAB PREPARATION

Before the lab begins, the instructor or lab assistant needs to do the following:

⊿ Verify Internet access is available

ACTIVITY BACKGROUND

As the prices of equipment and computers fall, installing a home LAN has become increasingly popular. SOHO (small office or home office) is a term that often refers to a virtual office, which has many of the same components as a brick-and-mortar office, such as computer and communication equipment to provide data storage and support device sharing. Even though a SOHO tends to be relatively small in scope, it still demands sophisticated software and networking hardware to support a variety of office applications and functions. In this lab, you research wireless and wired Ethernet, and determine which option is best in a SOHO environment.

ESTIMATED COMPLETION TIME: 30 MINUTES

 Activity

Use your favorite search engine to investigate and answer the following questions about wireless LAN standards:

1. The current Wi-Fi wireless standard is 802.11ac. Answer the following questions about this standard compared with Ethernet wired standards:

⊿ What is the theoretical throughput of 802.11ac?

_____

⊿ What is the theoretical range of 802.11ac?

_____

⊿ What frequency does 802.11ac use?

_____

◢ What is an advantage of the frequency used by 802.11ac on a network?

_____

_____

◢ Why might a wireless router have two or more antennas rather than just one?

_____

_____

◢ What is the speed of 802.11n wireless?

_____

◢ What is the speed of Fast Ethernet?

_____

◢ What is the speed of Gigabit Ethernet?

_____

◢ How does the speed of 802.11ac compare with the speed of 802.11n?

_____

◢ How does the speed of 802.11ac compare with the speed of Fast Ethernet?

_____

◢ How does the speed of 802.11ac compare with the speed of Gigabit Ethernet?

_____

2. In a small office, there are five computers, a network printer, and a broadband connection to the Internet. What devices are needed to set up a wired network for these five computers, the network printer, and the broadband connection?

_____

_____

_____

_____

3. Which device connects wireless users to a wired network?

_____

4. What is the function of a router?

_____

_____

_____

5. Search the web to find two routers that could be used to build your SOHO Gigabit Ethernet network, and list their distinguishing characteristics and prices:

Router #1:

_____

_____

Router #2:

_____

_____

6. If a computer in the home office doesn't have Gigabit Ethernet, how would you add that feature?

_____

7. Research and find two Gigabit Ethernet network adapter interface cards that you could add to a workstation. Include key features and prices:

Adapter # 1:

_____

_____

Adapter # 2:

_____

_____

8. Research and find two USB wireless Wi-Fi adapters that you could add to a workstation. List the key features and prices:

Adapter # 1:

_____

_____

Adapter # 2:

_____

_____

9. If you were to include in a home office setup a laptop that has an onboard Fast Ethernet port, how could you upgrade to Gigabit Ethernet?

_____

_____

10. Research and find two Gigabit Ethernet upgrades for your laptop. List key characteristics and prices:

Adapter # 1:

_____

_____

Adapter # 2:

_____

_____

11. What happens to the connection speed if you connect your laptop or workstation with Fast Ethernet to a Gigabit Ethernet router?

_____

12. Based upon the previous question, in order to get the fastest connection speed between routers and computers, how must the devices be set up?

_____

13. In a wired network, you will need cables to connect the devices. What cabling is needed to upgrade to a Gigabit Ethernet network?

_____

14. Does this cabling require different RJ-45 connectors? Why?

_____

15. Research and find Gigabit Ethernet 25-foot network cables. Record the source and price:

_____

16. A home office in a medium-sized room has the following setup:
    ◢ One desktop computer with a Fast Ethernet NIC
    ◢ One desktop computer with a Gigabit Ethernet NIC
    ◢ One laptop with a Fast Ethernet NIC
    ◢ Gigabit router with four ports; compliant with the 802.11n standard
    ◢ All-in-one wireless printer that has a USB connection and an onboard Fast Ethernet NIC

    Your mission is to upgrade the setup to Gigabit Ethernet for the fastest network connection speed (without using fiber optics). From your research above, list the components you would use along with an approximate total price of the upgrade:

    _____

    _____

    _____

    _____

    _____

    Total Price: _____

REVIEW QUESTIONS

1. What is the least expensive way to connect five computers using a wired network to a router that has only four network ports?

_____

2. Theoretically, which is faster: the current Wi-Fi standard or Gigabit Ethernet (1000BaseT)? What real-world issues might affect actual speeds for each technology?

_____

_____

_____

3. What is the name for a cable that connects a computer to another computer to create a two-node network?

_____

4. What determines the speed of devices on a LAN that consists of both 100-Mbps and 1000-Mbps devices?

_____

_____

5. Could you combine a wireless and wired LAN in the same home? Why would you?

_____

_____

_____

LAB 15.3 CREATE A STRAIGHT-THROUGH CABLE

OBJECTIVES

The goal of this lab is to create a straight-through cable (also called a patch cable). After completing this lab, you will be able to:

- Identify the color scheme for T568A and T568B wiring
- Understand the process of crimping cables
- Identify the tools needed to create a straight-through cable and create the cable
- Test a cable using a cable tester

MATERIALS REQUIRED

This lab requires the following:

- One meter of CAT-5 cable
- Up to eight RJ-45 connectors
- Wire cutter or electrician snips
- Wire-stripping tool
- Crimping tool
- Cable tester

LAB PREPARATION

Before the lab begins, the instructor or lab assistant needs to do the following:

◢ Verify CAT-5 cable is available

◢ Verify RJ-45 connectors are available

◢ Verify wire cutters or electrician snips are available

◢ Verify a wire-stripping tool is available

◢ Verify a wire crimper is available

◢ Verify a cable tester is available

ACTIVITY BACKGROUND

Industry standards have been established to make sure that everyone who deals with the same type of technology can ensure interconnectivity. You can think of standards as agreements by which everyone abides. The Electronics Industries Alliance (EIA) began the work of developing standards for telecommunications cabling, and later turned the job over to the Telecommunications Industry Association (TIA), which currently develops voluntary, consensus-based industry standards for a variety of situations used in communication and information technology (IT) applications. (The areas of IT that apply to communication are sometimes called the information and communication technology [ICT] segment of IT.) One set of TIA standards applies to network and telecommunications cabling standards for commercial buildings. The wiring standards that govern wiring category (CAT) cable or patch cable are referred to as EIA/TIA-568. There are two types of wiring standards: T568A and T568B. These standards outline the wiring scheme for the RJ-45 connectors and wall jacks. For commercial applications, the most common wiring scheme is T568B. In government buildings, the most common wiring scheme is T568A.

As an IT repair technician, you need to know how to create, repair, and test the different types of cables used to connect computers, switches, routers, and other network devices using both the T568B and T568A standards.

ESTIMATED COMPLETION TIME: 40 MINUTES

 Activity

Having the right cable for the job is essential. A straight-through cable is used to connect a computer to a switch, a computer to a hub, or a switch or hub to a router. Both ends of a straight-through cable are terminated the same in agreement with either T568A or T568B standard. Table 15-2 shows the T568A standard, and Table 15-3 shows the T568B standard.

RJ-45 Pin Number	Wire Color (T568A)
1	White/green
2	Green
3	White/orange
4	Blue
5	White/blue
6	Orange
7	White/brown
8	Brown

Table 15-2 T568A wiring standard for a network cable

RJ-45 Pin Number	Wire Color (T568B)
1	White/orange
2	Orange
3	White/green
4	Blue
5	White/blue
6	Green
7	White/brown
8	Brown

Table 15-3 T568B wiring standard for a network cable

To create a straight-through cable using the T568B standard, follow these steps:

1. Cut the desired length of the CAT-5 cable plus six or eight extra inches (needed for trimming).

2. Use wire strippers to strip away about two inches of the plastic jacket from one end of the cable. The four twisted pairs of the cable are exposed.

3. Use wire cutters to start a cut into the jacket. Then pull the rip cord up into the cut, and rip back about two inches of the jacket (see Figure 15-1). Cut off this extra jacket and the rip cord. You take this extra precaution in case you nicked the insulation around a wire when you were using the wire strippers.

Figure 15-1 Rip back the jacket, and then cut off the extra jacket and rip cord

4. Separate each wire from its pair, and extend them away from each other.

5. Straighten each wire as much as possible by stretching it out and smoothing it between your fingers.

6. Grip the base of the white/orange wire with your left thumb and index finger (reverse if you are left handed), and use your right hand to extend the wire, stretching it out until it is perfectly straight.

7. Continue to hold the white/orange wire from the base, and bring the orange wire into your grip.

8. Continue to hold the previous two wires, and bring into your grip the white/green wire. Wiggle the three wires up and down and side to side to get them as close together as possible.

9. Continue to hold the previous three wires, and bring into your grip the blue wire. Wiggle the wires up and down and side to side to get them as close together as possible.

10. Continue to hold the previous four wires, and bring into your grip the white/blue wire, wiggling them up and down and side to side to get them as close together as possible.

11. Continue to hold the previous five wires, and bring into your grip the green wire, wiggling them up and down and side to side to get them as close together as possible.

12. Continue to hold the previous six wires, and bring into your grip the white/brown wire. Wiggle them up and down and side to side to get them as close together as possible.

13. Continue to hold the previous seven wires, and bring into your grip the brown wire, wiggling the wires up and down and side to side to get them as close together as possible.

15

14. Holding the wires in a flat and straight position, cut the wires to about half an inch away from the insulation. You can judge the exact length by holding the RJ-45 connector up to the wires. You want to leave enough jacket to go inside the connector. See Figure 15-2.

Figure 15-2 Evenly cut off wires measured to fit in the RJ-45 connector with the jacket protruding into the connector

15. Hold the RJ-45 connector with the clip toward the bottom and insert the wires into the connector. Push the wires all the way to the front of the connector, making sure that you can see the ends of the wires touch the plastic at the front of the connector. Also make sure the cable jacket goes into the back of the connector far enough so that when you crimp it, the plastic wedge can put pressure on the jacket, to help hold the cable in place.

16. Insert the RJ-45 connector into the RJ-45 hole on the crimping tool. Use one hand to push the cable into the hole while you use the other hand to crimp the connector. See Figure 15-3. After the cable is partially crimped, you can use both hands to apply a stronger force to completely crimp the connector.

Figure 15-3 Use the crimper to crimp the connector to the cable

17. Remove the cable from the crimper. Use moderate (not too strong) force to try to pull the connector off the cable to make sure it is solidly crimped. If the connector comes off the cable, throw it away, and try again.

18. Examine the connector, which should look like the one in Figure 15-4.

◢ Do you see the crimp holding the cable jacket securely?

_____

◢ Do you see the eight wires pierced through with eight blades near the front of the connector?

_____

◢ Do you see the eight wires each in their correct positions at the end of the connector?

_____

The cable is crimped here

Blades pierce through to each wire

Figure 15-4 The crimper crimps the cable, and the eight blades pierce the jacket of each individual copper wire

19. Repeat the process on the other end of the cable.

20. Test the cable using a cable tester. If the cable does not pass the test, carefully examine each connector to decide which one is bad. Cut the bad connector off the cable, and try again with a new connector.

◢ Did the cable tester show that the cable was made correctly?

_____

◢ What indicator did the tool use to let you know the cable was correctly wired?

_____

21. Wiring jobs can create a mess. Take a few minutes to clean up. Be sure and save as a souvenir your first network cable!

Suppose a client requires 20 network cables that are each 10 feet long. Follow these steps to compare the prices of making the network cables versus buying ready-made cables:

1. Don't forget to include extra wiring and connectors, which are needed when making cables. Using the web, search for these prices:

◢ The price of 220 feet of CAT-5e network cabling:

_____

◢ The price of 40 or more RJ-45 connectors and boots:

_____

◢ The price of 20 straight-through cables that are each 10 feet long:

_____

2. Calculate and compare the prices:

◢ For one hand-made 10-foot cable:

_____

◢ For one ready-made 10-foot cable:

_____

◢ For this cable job, which is less expensive, hand-made network cables or ready-made cables?

_____

REVIEW QUESTIONS

1. What is the difference in typical usage between T568A and T568B standards?

_____

_____

2. What is TIA, and what is it responsible for?

_____

_____

3. Which devices can be connected using a straight-through cable?

_____

_____

_____

4. What is the color scheme for T568B wiring?

_____

_____

_____

_____

5. Why is it advisable to rip back the jacket and cut it from the cable even after you have already stripped the jacket?

_____

_____

6. What was the most difficult part of this lab as you created a straight-through cable?

_____

_____

LAB 15.4 CREATE A CROSSOVER CABLE

OBJECTIVES

The goal of this lab is to create a crossover cable. After completing this lab, you will be able to:

◢ Identify the color scheme for T568A and T568B wiring

◢ Understand the process of crimping cables

◢ Create a crossover cable

◢ Test a cable

MATERIALS REQUIRED

This lab requires the following:

◢ One meter of CAT-5 cable

◢ Up to eight RJ-45 connectors

◢ Wire cutter or electrician snips

◢ Wire-stripping tool

◢ Crimping tool

◢ Cable tester

LAB PREPARATION

Before the lab begins, the instructor or lab assistant needs to do the following:

◢ Verify CAT-5 cable is available

◢ Verify RJ-45 connectors are available

◢ Verify wire cutters or electrician snips are available

◢ Verify wire strippers are available

◢ Verify a wire crimper is available

◢ Verify a cable tester is available

ACTIVITY BACKGROUND

As with straight-through CAT cable, industry standards exist for crossover cable. A crossover cable is wired differently than a straight-through cable, and its transmit and receive lines are reversed so that one device receives off the line to which the other device transmits. Crossover cables were required when using Fast Ethernet to connect a hub to a hub or a switch to a switch. Using Gigabit Ethernet, straight-through cables can be used for these connections because Gigabit switches use auto-uplinking. Today, a crossover cable is mostly used when you want to connect two computers in the simplest network of all. A crossover cable for Fast Ethernet is wired differently than a crossover cable for Gigabit Ethernet.

For Fast Ethernet, if you use T568A wiring on one end of the cable and T568B on the other end of the cable, you have a crossover cable (see Figure 15-5a). For Gigabit Ethernet that transmits data on all four pairs, you must cross not only the green and orange pairs, but also the blue and brown pairs to make a crossover cable (see Figure 15-5b).

(a) Crossover wiring for Fast Ethernet   (b) Crossover wiring for Gigabit Ethernet

Figure 15-5 (a) Two crossed pairs in a crossover cable compatible with Fast Ethernet; (b) four crossed pairs in a crossover cable compatible with Gigabit Ethernet

It will be useful to you to know how to create, repair, and test the different types of cables used to connect computers, switches, routers, and other network devices.

ESTIMATED COMPLETION TIME: 40 MINUTES

Activity

A crossover cable for Fast Ethernet has a T568A termination on one end and a T568B termination on the other. Refer to Tables 15-2 and 15-3 for the T568A and T568B wiring standards, respectively.

To create a Fast Ethernet crossover cable, first wire one end using the T568B standard as follows:

1. Cut the desired length of the CAT5 cable, plus a few inches.

2. Choose one end of the cable, and strip away about two inches of the jacket to expose the four pairs of cables.

3. Start a cut into the jacket, and use the rip cord to pull back about two inches of the jacket. Cut off the extra jacket and rip cord.

4. Separate each wire from its pair, and extend them away from each other. Extend the wire straight by stretching it out as much as possible.

5. Using the method you learned in the previous lab, grip the white/orange wire from the base with your left thumb and index finger (reverse if you are left handed), and use your right hand to extend the wire straight.

6. Continue to hold the white/orange wire from the base, and bring the orange wire into your grip.

7. Bring into your grip the white/green wire.

8. Bring into your grip the blue wire.

9. Bring into your grip the white/blue wire.

10. Bring into your grip the green wire.

11. Bring into your grip the white/brown wire.

12. Bring into your grip the brown wire.

13. Holding the wires in a straight position, cut the wires to about half an inch away from the end of the insulation.

14. Hold the RJ-45 connector with the clip toward the bottom, and insert the wires into the connector, making sure that you can see the copper touch the plastic inside the front of the connector. Make sure that the cable jacket goes into the back of the connector far enough so that when you crimp it, the plastic wedge can put pressure on the jacket, to help hold the cable in place.

15. Insert the RJ-45 connector in the crimping tool for the appropriate connector. Push the cable into the crimper as you crimp the connector.

16. Test the crimp by trying to moderately pull on the connector. If it comes off the cable, throw it away, and try again.

17. Repeat the process this time using the T568A wiring scheme.

18. Test the cable using a cable tester. What were the results of the cable tester?

A Gigabit Ethernet crossover cable has four pairs of wires crossed. Do the following to create a Gigabit Ethernet crossover cable:

1. Fill in the following chart showing the color for each pin on each end of this type of cable:

Pin	Color for End 1	Color for End 2
1		
2		
3		
4		
5		
6		
7		
8		

2. Create the Gigabit Ethernet crossover cable.

3. Test the cable with a cable tester.

   ◢ What indicator did the tool use to let you know the cable was correctly wired?

4. Wiring jobs can create a mess. Take a few minutes to clean up.

REVIEW QUESTIONS

1. Which wires get switched by wiring one end T568A and the other end T568B? What type of crossover cable is created using this wiring scheme?

2. How many pairs of wires get switched when making a Gigabit Ethernet crossover cable? Which wires are switched?

3. Which devices can be connected using a crossover cable?

_____

_____

4. Which step was the most difficult when creating a crossover cable?

_____

_____

5. What is the wiring scheme for the T568A standard?

_____

_____

LAB 15.5 SET UP ADVANCED IP SCANNER AND WAKE-ON-LAN

OBJECTIVES

The objective of this lab is to set up and use Advanced IP Scanner to remotely power on a computer. After completing this lab, you will be able to:

◢ Set up Wake-on-LAN

◢ Remotely power on a computer

MATERIALS REQUIRED

This lab requires the following:

◢ Windows 8 or Windows 7 workstation with Wake-on-LAN feature

◢ Internet access

◢ Two or more computers on the same wired network (not wireless)

LAB PREPARATION

Before the lab begins, the instructor or lab assistant needs to do the following:

◢ Set up a simple network with two or more computers

◢ Provide Internet access in the lab, or provide students with the Advanced IP Scanner utility

◢ Verify the Wake-on-LAN feature can be enabled on one or more machines

ACTIVITY BACKGROUND

Often, a technician needs to be able to identify and control machines on a network. Modern motherboards often have a Wake-on-LAN feature, which enables a technician to control that machine without having to be at the machine. This increases the efficiency of managing machines and decreases the time needed to complete support activities.

Activity

Follow these steps to set up Wake-on-LAN:

1. Select one of the lab machines to use as a test for the Wake-on-LAN feature.

2. Boot that machine, and enter UEFI/BIOS setup of that machine.

3. Locate in UEFI/BIOS the Wake-on-LAN feature, and enable that function. Save the setting change, and reboot the machine.

4. Record the IP address of that machine by opening a command prompt window and issuing the **ipconfig /all** command.

   Write down the IP address: _____

5. Close the command prompt window.

6. Next, you enable Wake-on-LAN in Windows. Open **Control Panel**, and click **Network and Sharing Center**.

7. In the left pane, click **Change adapter settings**.

8. Right-click the network adapter for the wired connection, and then click **Properties**.

9. Click **Configure**, and then select the **Power Management** tab.

10. Make sure that the **Allow the computer to turn off this device to save power** option is selected. This enables power management in Windows.

11. Check **Allow this device to wake the computer**.

12. Click **OK**.

Go to the other workstation, and install the Advanced IP Scanner utility. Follow these steps:

1. Using your web browser, go to **advanced-ip-scanner.com**, and download and install the software utility, **Advanced IP Scanner**.

2. Open Advanced IP Scanner.

3. After Advanced IP Scanner loads, click the **Scan** button to scan your network. As the scanning progresses, the lower pane shows network devices and machines that the utility discovers. See Figure 15-6.

Source: Famatech

Figure 15-6 Advanced IP Scanner detects devices on a network

4. In the Status column, select one of the machines listed, and expand it to view the contents. You can access shared folders and devices by double-clicking items listed under a machine.

5. Use the IP address information (which appears in the Name column) to find and select the machine on which you enabled the Wake-on-LAN feature.

6. At the top of the Advanced IP Scanner window, click **Actions**, and then click **Shut down**. If needed, provide a user name and password for the remote machine.

   ◢ Did the machine shut down?

   _____

7. In the Actions menu, click **Wake-on-LAN** to send Wake-on-LAN packets.

   ◢ Did the machine boot up?

   _____

REVIEW QUESTIONS

1. If you want to turn on a machine remotely, what motherboard feature must be enabled to make this happen?

   _____

2. When using the scan feature of Advanced IP Scanner, what information does it provide about the network?

   _____

   _____

3. As an IT technician in the field, how might you use this utility?

   _____

   _____

4. The Advanced IP Scanner utility has a print function. How can this be useful?

   _____

   _____

LAB 15.6 TROUBLESHOOT WITH TCP/IP UTILITIES

OBJECTIVES

The goal of this lab is to use Windows TCP/IP utilities to troubleshoot connectivity problems. After completing this lab, you will be able to:

◢ Use the ipconfig utility

◢ Use the ping utility

◢ Use the tracert utility

◢ Use the nslookup utility

◢ Use the netstat utility

MATERIALS REQUIRED

This lab requires the following:

◢ Windows 8 or Windows 7 operating system

◢ An account with administrator privileges

◢ A DHCP server

◢ Internet access

LAB PREPARATION

Before the lab begins, the instructor or lab assistant needs to do the following:

◢ Verify Windows starts with no errors

◢ Verify Internet access is available

◢ Verify students can sign in to their computers with administrator privileges

ACTIVITY BACKGROUND

Loss of network connectivity can be frustrating to users and can be costly to a business. As an IT technician, you might be asked to restore these connections, and sometimes you even have to deal with several failed connections at one time. When troubleshooting network connections, it helps to know whether many users in one area of a network are having the same connection problem. That information can help you narrow down the source of the problem. After you have an idea of which machine is causing the problem, you can use a few TCP/IP utilities to test your theory without physically checking the system. In this lab, you learn to use TCP/IP utilities to isolate connection problems.

> **ESTIMATED COMPLETION TIME: 30 MINUTES**

 Activity

Follow these steps to display IP settings in Windows:

1. Open the Network and Sharing Center.

2. In the left pane, click **Change adapter settings**. Right-click the active network connection (whether Ethernet or Wi-Fi), and select **Properties** in the shortcut menu. The connection's properties dialog box opens.

3. Click **Internet Protocol Version 4 (TCP/IPv4)**, and then click the **Properties** button. The Internet Protocol Version 4 (TCP/IPv4) Properties dialog box opens. Notice the different options. What two ways can you set up the IP configuration?

   _____

   _____

4. Select **Obtain an IP address automatically** if it is not already selected.

5. Click **OK** to close the Internet Protocol Version 4 (TCP/IPv4) Properties dialog box, and then close any open windows.

By default, the command prompt window cannot be made very wide on the monitor screen. Follow these steps to adjust the command prompt display so that you can view more information in the window:

1. Open a command prompt window.

2. Right-click the title bar of the command prompt window, and select **Properties** in the shortcut menu. The Command Prompt Properties dialog box opens.

3. On the Layout tab in the Screen Buffer Size section (see Figure 15-7), enter **150** for width and **300** for height. These settings enable you to scroll in the command prompt window, and view 300 lines and 150 characters per line. Click **OK** to save the settings. You can now widen the command prompt window.

Figure 15-7   Adjust the command prompt window display settings

> **Notes** You might want to further customize the command prompt window and make these changes permanent. To do so, right-click the title bar of the window, and then click **Defaults**. Changes you make in the Console Windows Properties dialog box are retained and can include the Screen Buffer Size, font color, and background color of the command prompt window.

Follow these steps to learn how to display IP information from the command line:

1. At the command prompt, type **ipconfig /?** and press **Enter**. What are the available parameters for ipconfig?

_____

_____

_____

2. Type **ipconfig** and press **Enter**. What is the IP address and subnet mask for the active network connection?

_____

3. To get more information about your IP settings, type **ipconfig /all** and press **Enter**. Answer these questions:

   ◢ What is the physical address (MAC)?

   _____

   ◢ What is the address of the default gateway?

   _____

   ◢ What is the purpose of DHCP? (You can use the Windows Help and Support feature to find this answer.)

   _____

   ◢ What is the address of the DHCP server?

   _____

   ◢ What is the address of the DNS server?

   _____

4. Because your system is using DHCP to obtain an IP address, you can ask DHCP to renew the IP address. To do so, first release the existing IP address lease. Type **ipconfig /release** and press **Enter**. Then request a new IP address lease; type **ipconfig /renew** and press **Enter**. The command prompt window again displays IP information.

5. Again, type **ipconfig /all** and press **Enter**. Compare the earlier IP address lease information to the information on the screen. What information changed?

   _____

6. Once again, type **ipconfig /release** and press **Enter**. Note that your adapter has no IP address and no subnet mask. These two parameters are necessary to communicate with TCP/IP. How do you predict this command will affect connectivity?

   _____

   _____

7. The ping command tests if an IP address is accessible by sending four packets to the IP address and recording the time required for the round trip. To use the ping command, type **ping course.com** in the command prompt. Press **Enter**. What message is displayed?

   _____

8. Attempt to ping the DHCP server and the DNS server IP addresses you recorded in Step 3. What are the results?

   _____

9. Type **ipconfig** and press **Enter**. What IPv4 address is listed for the active network adapter now? How did your computer obtain this IP address? How do you know?

   _____

   _____

10. To get an IP address lease from the DHCP server again, type **ipconfig /renew** and press **Enter**. New IP information, which might be the same address as before, is assigned.

11. Find your new IP address lease information (time obtained and time it will expire). List the command you used to find this information and the lease information:

_____

_____

Follow these steps to determine what route your packets take to reach an Internet address:

1. If necessary, open a command prompt window.

2. Type **tracert** followed by a single space and then a domain name on the Internet (for example, type **tracert course.com**). Press **Enter**.

3. The DNS server resolves the domain name to an IP address. When the tracert command reports the name of a DNS server, you know your packets traveled at least as far as this server. Also, each hop (or router your packet passes through) is listed with the time in milliseconds that the packet took to reach its destination. How many hops did the packets take to reach the domain you specified?

_____

4. Now use the tracert command with an illegitimate domain name (for example, type **tracert mydomain.c**). What are the results of this command?

_____

5. When you're finished, close any open windows.

When you first type the URL _course.com_ into your browser, your computer does not know the actual IP address of that website. Without the IP address, it cannot create packets at the Network layer because all packets must contain a source IP address and a final destination IP address. To find the destination IP address, your computer requests it from a Domain Name Service (DNS) server. The job of the DNS server is to resolve IP addresses to domain names. The nslookup command gives information about DNS and can run in interactive mode or noninteractive mode. To learn more, follow these steps:

1. Open an elevated command prompt window.

2. At the command prompt, type **nslookup** and then press **Enter**. The name and IP address of the default DNS server appear, and nslookup starts up in interactive mode.

◢ What new command prompt appears?

_____

◢ What is the name of the DNS server?

_____

◢ What is the IP address of the DNS server?

_____

3. At the nslookup command prompt, type **help** and then press **Enter**. A list of nslookup commands appears.

4. To find out the IP address of the web server for _course.com_, type **course.com** and press **Enter**. What is the IP address?

_____

5. To exit nslookup interactive mode, type **exit** and then press **Enter**. The normal command prompt appears.

6. To use nslookup in noninteractive mode, at the command prompt, type **nslookup course.com** and then press **Enter**. Describe any output differences between nslookup in interactive mode and nslookup in noninteractive mode:

_____

_____

15

The local computer does not need to go back to the DNS server to resolve an IP address every time you request the same webpage. Instead, your local computer stores a list of previously resolved IP addresses in a local cache. To display the cached list of previously resolved domain names to IP addresses, follow these steps:

1. Open your browser, and go to **cengage.com**. Then go to **course.com**. Close your browser. To access these webpages, the computer needed to resolve the domain names and IP addresses; it then stored this information in the local cache.

2. At the command prompt, type **ipconfig /displaydns** and then press **Enter**.

3. Browse through the results and observe any cached results for *course.com* or *cengage.com*.

4. Close all open windows.

At the Transport layer, segments are labeled as TCP data packets when a delivery confirmation is required or as UDP datagrams when a delivery confirmation is not required. As an IT technician, you might have to monitor TCP and UDP traffic. The netstat command can help. To learn more about this command, follow these steps:

1. Open an elevated command prompt window.

2. Type **netstat** and then press **Enter**. A list of active connections appears. The protocol for each connection (for example, TCP or UDP) appears in the first column of this list. Answer the following questions:

   ◢ What protocol is used for the first connection in the list?

   _____

   ◢ What is the foreign address of this connection and the state of the connection?

   _____

3. At the command prompt, type **netstat –s** and then press **Enter**. Answer the following questions:

   ◢ What is the purpose of the –s parameter used with the netstat command?

   _____

   ◢ In the TCP Statistics for IPv4 section, what is the number of current connections?

   _____

   ◢ In the UDP Statistics for IPv4 section, what is the number of datagrams sent?

   _____

4. At the command prompt, type **netstat –a** and then press **Enter**. Describe the difference in the output when using the –s parameter with the netstat command versus using the –a parameter with the netstat command:

   _____

   _____

5. Close all open windows.

REVIEW QUESTIONS

1. List four additional types of information that the ipconfig command with the /all parameter provides that the ipconfig command without the parameter does not:

   _____

   _____

   _____

   _____

2. What type of server resolves a domain name to an IP address?

   _____

3. What command discards the IP address?

   _____

4. What command do you use to determine whether you can reach another computer on the local network? Would this command work if the default gateway were down?

   _____

5. When troubleshooting problems with resolving domain names to IP addresses, flushing the DNS cache can sometimes help so that the local computer must build the cache again. What is the command to flush the DNS cache?

   _____

LAB 15.7 SABOTAGE AND REPAIR A NETWORK CONNECTION

OBJECTIVES

The goal of this lab is to troubleshoot and remedy common network connectivity problems. After completing this lab, you will be able to:

▲ Diagnose and solve connectivity problems

▲ Document the troubleshooting process

MATERIALS REQUIRED

This lab requires the following:

▲ Windows 8 or Windows 7 operating system

▲ A computer connected to a network and to the Internet

▲ Windows installation CD/DVD or installation files

▲ A computer toolkit with ESD strap

▲ A workgroup partner

LAB PREPARATION

Before the lab begins, the instructor or lab assistant needs to do the following:

◢ Verify Windows starts with no errors

◢ Provide each student with access to the Windows installation files in case a student needs to repair the Windows installation during the lab

ACTIVITY BACKGROUND

To a casual user, Internet and network connections can be confusing. When users have a connectivity problem, they usually have no idea how to remedy the situation. In this lab, you introduce and solve common connectivity problems.

ESTIMATED COMPLETION TIME: 60 MINUTES

🕸 Activity

1. Verify your network is working correctly by browsing the network and connecting to a website.

2. Do one of the following:

   ◢ Change your computer's IP address.

   ◢ Change your computer's subnet mask.

   ◢ Remove your computer's network cable.

   ◢ Remove TCP/IP from your computer.

   ◢ Uninstall your computer's network adapter in the active connection's properties dialog box.

   ◢ Unseat or remove your computer's NIC, but leave it installed in the active connection's properties dialog box.

   ◢ Disable your computer's NIC in Device Manager.

   ◢ Release your computer's IP address (if DHCP is enabled).

3. Swap computers with your partner, and troubleshoot the network connection on your partner's computer.

4. Answer these questions about the problem you solved (additional paper might be needed):

   ◢ What is the initial symptom of the problem as a user might describe it?

   _____

   ◢ What steps did you take to discover the source of the problem?

   _____

   _____

   ◢ What steps did you take to solve the problem?

   _____

5. Repeat Steps 1 through 4 until you and your partner have used all the options listed in Step 2. Be sure to answer the questions in Step 4 for each troubleshooting situation.

REVIEW QUESTIONS

1. What type of network connectivity problem can be solved by using Device Manager?

   _____

   _____

2. Which problem (or problems) might require you to reboot the computer after repairing it?

   _____

3. When configuring TCP/IP, what two values are necessary when using static IP addressing?

   _____

   _____

4. What TCP/IP utility was the most useful, in your opinion, for troubleshooting the problems in this lab? Why?

   _____

   _____

5. Why should you always check for physical problems like unplugged network cables before considering logical problems like missing drivers?

   _____

CHAPTER

16

Supporting Mobile Operating Systems

Labs included in this chapter:

- **Lab 16.1:** Research the Latest Smart Phones
- **Lab 16.2:** Research Android Apps and Use Dropbox
- **Lab 16.3:** Explore How Android Apps Are Developed and Tested
- **Lab 16.4:** Configure Email and Dropbox on Mobile Devices
- **Lab 16.5:** Research Xcode and the iOS Simulator

LAB 16.1 RESEARCH THE LATEST SMART PHONES

OBJECTIVES

The goal of this lab is to explore the similarities and differences among iOS, Android, and Windows smart phones. Understanding the characteristics of different smart phones can help you make wise purchasing decisions for yourself or on behalf of a client. After completing this lab, you will be able to:

◢ Research different types of smart phones

◢ Summarize and compare the major features and capabilities of an Android, iOS, and Windows smart phone

MATERIALS REQUIRED

This lab requires the following:

◢ Windows 8 or Windows 7 computer

◢ Internet access

LAB PREPARATION

Before the lab begins, the instructor or lab assistant needs to do the following:

◢ Verify Windows starts with no errors

◢ Verify Internet access is available

ACTIVITY BACKGROUND

Smart phones are becoming more available and accessibly priced every day. New smart phones are constantly being released, and when you are ready to upgrade your phone, you need to do research to find the best option available to meet your needs. In addition, as a support technician, you will likely be called on to help a client decide which technology to purchase. Therefore, you need to be familiar with the technologies and options a client might want or need.

Deciding factors to consider when selecting your own smart phone or presenting options to a client are brand, capabilities, features, support provided by a manufacturer or apps vendor, and price. In this lab, you research iOS, Android, and Windows smart phones.

ESTIMATED COMPLETION TIME: 30 MINUTES

 Activity

In this lab, you research specifications for three different smart phones for comparison:

1. Use the Internet to research one example of a smart phone for each of the mobile operating systems named at the top of the columns of Table 16-1. You might find these phones on the manufacturers' websites or on service provider websites. Record in the table the specifications for each of the smart phones.

2. Use the Internet to research reviews for each of the phones that you selected in Step 1. Record the highlights of those reviews, as detailed below:

◢ Android advantages:

_____

_____

Specification	Android	iOS	Windows
Brand or manufacturer			
Model			
Price			
Version of OS installed			
Processor			
Types of network connections			
Storage capacity			
Screen size			
Screen resolution			
Camera pixels			
Website for cloud storage and app purchases			
Amount of free cloud storage			
Unique features			

Table 16-1 Fill in the specifications for three smart phones

▲ Android disadvantages:

_____

_____

▲ iOS advantages:

_____

_____

▲ iOS disadvantages:

_____

_____

▲ Windows advantages:

_____

_____

▲ Windows disadvantages:

_____

_____

3. Close all open windows.

REVIEW QUESTIONS

1. Assume that you are in the market to buy a new smart phone. Which of the smart phones you researched would you purchase? Why would you choose this smart phone over the other two smart phones?

   _____

   _____

   _____

2. What are some methods service providers use to offer lower prices on the devices they sell?

   _____

   _____

3. Some smart phones provide more flexible options for updating hardware than do others. Of the smart phones you researched, which (if any) allow for the battery to be replaced?

   _____

4. Other than the criteria given in this lab, what criteria might influence which smart phone you would purchase?

   _____

   _____

5. Give two reasons why you should research information about related apps and app stores when deciding which smart phone to buy:

   _____

   _____

LAB 16.2 RESEARCH ANDROID APPS AND USE DROPBOX

OBJECTIVES

The goals of this lab are to research and compare Android apps and to explore how to sync data between two sources using an Android app. This exploration is useful because, as an A+ certified technician, you will be expected to know how to service Android mobile devices and the apps installed on them. This service includes knowing how to sync data between two sources and back up data on an Android device. Android offers many data sync options to choose from, including the very popular Dropbox app. After completing this lab, you will be able to:

◢ Use the Google Play Store to research apps

◢ Find additional information on apps using other resources

◢ Install Dropbox, an Android-compatible app, on your computer

◢ Sync data between two sources using Dropbox

MATERIALS REQUIRED

This lab requires the following:

◢ Windows 8 or Windows 7 operating system

⊿ An account with administrator privileges

⊿ Internet access

⊿ Email account

⊿ Email addresses for your instructor and a classmate

LAB PREPARATION

Before the lab begins, the instructor or lab assistant needs to do the following:

⊿ Verify Windows starts with no errors

⊿ Verify each student has access to a user account with administrator privileges

⊿ Verify Internet access is working

⊿ Verify Dropbox is not already installed

ACTIVITY BACKGROUND

Because Android is open source software, Android-compatible apps are available from many different developers. It's not unusual to find several apps that do essentially the same tasks. Some developers produce excellent apps, and some produce only mediocre ones. Therefore, research is important in finding the best app for the job.

Most Android apps are available through the Google Play Store (*play.google.com/store/apps*) as seen in Figure 16-1, and this is a central location for information about those apps. Each app listed contains information on what access privileges the app needs, who the developer is, how much memory the app requires, and what other users think of the app. The 5-star rating system and the user reviews provide a wealth of feedback on the functionality and performance of apps, including how to address problems with the app features or installation.

One widely used file-sharing program available for Android is Dropbox. You can install Dropbox on nearly any current Windows, Mac, Linux, BlackBerry, or Android device, and share files between all those devices. Files saved in your Dropbox account are stored in

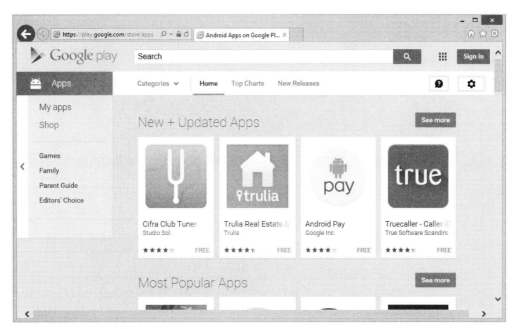

Source: Google, Inc.

Figure 16-1   The Google Play Store is one of many sources of Android apps the cloud, and Dropbox automatically syncs these files with all of your Dropbox-enabled devices. Your Dropbox folders can be managed directly from any of these devices or through your online dashboard using a personal computer.

In this lab, you investigate some Android apps, and then you install and use the Dropbox software on your personal computer. If you have access to an Android device, you can also install and use the Dropbox app to sync data on your device with your other devices and computers, and with other users.

ESTIMATED COMPLETION TIME: 45 MINUTES

 Activity

The flashlight app can turn your smart phone or tablet into a flashlight. To collect information on flashlight apps, follow these steps:

1. Using a browser, go to Google Play at **play.google.com/store/apps**.

2. Click the **Categories** tab, and then click **Tools**.

3. Find three different flashlight apps, and collect the following information on these apps, as detailed in Table 16-2:

Specification	App 1	App 2	App 3
App name			
Rating			
Number of reviews			
Date last updated			
Three key features			
One negative issue raised by reviewers			

Table 16-2   Fill in the specifications for three apps

4. If you were to choose one of these flashlight apps, which one would you choose and why?

_____

_____

_____

5. Third-party websites can be an excellent source of information on apps you're researching. Do a quick search on **google.com** for the flashlight app you chose in Step 4; be sure to select **Past year** in the Search tools menu to ensure you find the latest information on the app. Is your selected app also available in the iTunes App Store?

_____

6. Next, research a different kind of app. A chromatic tuner is a device used by musicians to tune instruments. Do a Google search for chromatic tuner apps for Android, and answer the following questions:

◢ Based on your Google search results, what are three apps that can be used to tune a musical instrument?

_____

_____

_____

◢ Besides Google Play, what is another source for one of the tuner apps you listed?

_____

16

> **Notes** Different apps work with different devices. App listings online include a list of which devices are compatible with that app. However, when you surf the Play Store directly from your Android phone, only device-compatible apps show up in your search.

To install Dropbox on a mobile device, you download the Dropbox app from the device's primary application source (Google Play Store for an Android device or the App Store for an iOS device). To install Dropbox on your computer, do the following:

1. Go to **dropbox.com**, and click **Download the app**, as shown in Figure 16-2, and then save the download. What is the name of the downloaded file?

_____

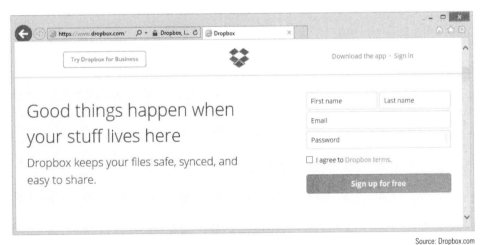

Source: Dropbox.com

Figure 16-2 At the time of this writing, you can get up to 2 GB of free online storage space with Dropbox

2. Locate the downloaded file, and install Dropbox.

3. In the Dropbox Setup dialog box, click **Sign up**, and enter the requested information to create an account. Write down the email address and password for your account:

_____

4. Complete the installation process, and then click **Open my Dropbox**. In the Welcome to Dropbox dialog box, click **Get Started**. Proceed through the tour slides, and then click

Finish. Dropbox opens automatically in File Explorer/Windows Explorer. What item is included in your Dropbox folder by default? In the left pane of Explorer, where is the Dropbox shortcut located?

_____

_____

You can share Dropbox files and folders with other people. Anyone who has the link to a particular file or folder can view that item in a browser, even without using a Dropbox account. It's important to note that you have no control over who can use the link, so be sure you don't put private information in a shared folder. To practice sharing a file, do the following:

1. Create a text file using Notepad, and type a couple of lines of text. Click **File**, and then click **Save**. In the left pane of the Save As window, click **Dropbox** under Favorites. Name the file **MeetingNotes.txt**, and then click **Save**.

2. Close the file. Using File Explorer/Windows Explorer, find your file in the Dropbox folder.

3. Ensure the file shows a green check on its icon, indicating the file has been fully synced with Dropbox (see Figure 16-3). If the green check has not yet appeared, wait for the file to finish syncing.

Figure 16-3 The green check shows that the file is fully synced

4. Right-click the **MeetingNotes.txt** file, and click **Share Dropbox link**, as shown in Figure 16-4. The link is copied to your Clipboard.

Figure 16-4 Copy the file's Dropbox link to your Clipboard

5. Paste the link into an email message to your instructor and to a classmate, and then send the email. When you receive your classmate's email, click the link. The file opens in your browser. Notice that you cannot change the text of your classmate's file, but you can copy the file to your computer and edit it there. You can also make comments on the file, and subscribe to notifications of future changes to the file.

Files placed in your Dropbox are automatically synced with your Dropbox on other devices linked to your account. To share files in your Dropbox with other people, it is not necessary to share your Dropbox account information. When you invite other Dropbox users to one of your folders, this folder, including all of its files and subfolders, is synced in their accounts and in your account (however, other folders in your Dropbox remain private unless you share them). To invite a classmate to one of your Dropbox folders, do the following:

1. Return to your Dropbox folder in File Explorer/Windows Explorer. Click **New folder**, and name the folder **Computer class**.

2. Right-click the folder you just created, and click **Share this folder**, as shown in Figure 16-5.

Figure 16-5 Share any folder directly under your Dropbox folder

3. The first time you associate your email address with Dropbox, Dropbox takes you to the Dropbox website and requests verification of your email address in order to share folders (see Figure 16-6). To verify your email address, click **Send Email**. Open the email sent by Dropbox (be sure to check your junk folder if you don't see the Dropbox email in your inbox), and click **Verify your email**. The Dropbox - Sign in webpage opens. Close the website (it's not necessary to sign in). Now that your email address is verified, repeat Step 2 to share the Computer class folder.

Figure 16-6 Access to your email account is needed to complete verification

4. In the Dropbox - Share Folder dialog box, enter a classmate's email address, and then click **Invite**. An invitation email is sent to your classmate. When your classmate accepts your invitation, you should receive a confirmation email.

5. To accept a Dropbox folder shared by your classmate, click the **View folder** link in the invitation email that you receive. Sign in if necessary, and then click **Accept** to add the folder to your Dropbox. Because you should now have two folders with the name Computer class, the new one will have a version number behind the name, such as Computer class (1).

> **Notes** Be aware that shared folders count toward a user's storage quota. Also, once a folder is shared, you cannot change the name or location of that folder as it is listed in another Dropbox. However, you can change the name or location of the folder in your own Dropbox.
> To unshare a folder, sign in on the Dropbox website. Open the folder, and then click **Settings**. Click **Unshare folder**. You can choose whether to allow collaborators to keep a copy of the files, and then click **Unshare folder**.

6. Take a moment to explore the online Dropbox dashboard. In the left pane, click **Get Started**. What steps do you still need to complete in order to earn extra, free storage space?

_____

_____

7. Next to your name, click the drop-down arrow, and then click **Settings**. Where can you find a listing of the devices linked to your account?

_____

8. Create a new text file using Notepad, and save the file to your shared 'Computer class' folder. Give it a silly name and write it here:

_____

9. Have your classmate execute Step 8 as well. When you receive your classmate's file in his or her shared Dropbox folder, write the name of that file here:

_____

10. Close any open windows.

If you want to use your Dropbox on a computer that has already been linked to another user's Dropbox, you can unlink the computer and add your own account. Follow these steps to set up your Dropbox account on another computer:

1. Go to another computer in the lab that has Dropbox installed. Click the **Dropbox** icon in the taskbar, click the cog settings icon, and then select **Preferences**.

2. From the Dropbox Preferences box, select **Account**. The email address currently linked to Dropbox on this computer appears. Click **Unlink This Dropbox,** and click **OK**. The Unlink Dropbox? dialog box opens.

3. Click **OK** to confirm that you want to unlink the computer from Dropbox. The Dropbox Setup dialog box, which you used earlier to create your account, opens. You can use this setup box to create a new Dropbox account or set up an existing Dropbox account on the computer. Follow directions on screen to set up your existing Dropbox account on this computer. Verify your Dropbox folders and files are present.

4. If you're working on a lab computer or public computer, go to the Programs and Features window in Control Panel and uninstall Dropbox.

5. Close any open windows.

REVIEW QUESTIONS

1. Besides apps and games, what other kinds of files can you download from Google Play?

_____

2. Downloading apps on a mobile device can drain a user's cellular data allotment quickly. What is one way to avoid data charges when downloading apps?

_____

_____

3. In your online Dropbox dashboard, where can you find a record of the date and time you shared your folder with your classmate in Dropbox? *Hint:* Check the Dropbox menu in the left pane.

_____

_____

4. A file placed in a shared Dropbox folder is accessible by anyone with a link to that folder, no matter how they obtained the link. How can you remove the file from public access?

_____

_____

5. Do a quick Google search for another app other than Dropbox that can sync files between a mobile device and a personal computer. Which app did you find?

_____

LAB 16.3 EXPLORE HOW ANDROID APPS ARE DEVELOPED AND TESTED

OBJECTIVES

The goal of this lab is to learn how Android apps are developed and tested using the Android Software Development Kit (SDK) and the Android emulator. If you have never used an Android device, this is your chance to learn about Android, by using an Android virtual device in the Android emulator. After completing this lab, you will be able to:

◢ Describe the tools and procedures used to develop and test Android apps

◢ Install and use the Android emulator to run an Android virtual device

MATERIALS REQUIRED

This lab requires the following:

◢ Windows 8 or Windows 7 operating system

◢ Internet access

LAB PREPARATION

Before the lab begins, the instructor or lab assistant needs to do the following:

◢ Verify Windows starts with no errors

◢ Verify Internet access is available

ACTIVITY BACKGROUND

The Android website at *android.com* by Google offers tools to develop and test Android apps. The process can be fun to learn but does require you download and install multiple pieces of software. The Android Software Development Kit (SDK) depends on Java to run. In this lab, you won't actually write an Android app, but you will learn much about the tools used and how the process works.

> **ESTIMATED COMPLETION TIME: 60 MINUTES**

 Activity

How do you best like to learn a new computer skill? You might prefer to watch a video, read a book, search for online discussions or tutorials, or discuss and investigate the topic with your friends. The following steps will help you explore online videos and websites related to developing Android apps:

1. Go to **youtube.com** and search for tutorial videos. Possible search strings are "android application development," "make your first android app," and "android application tutorials."

2. Search the web for additional information and tutorials. Good search strings to use are "android app tutorial for beginners" and "how to develop android apps."

3. Explore websites that might help you with your research. Try researching on these useful websites: *techradar.com* and *androidcommunity.com*.

   ◢ What is Android Studio and where can you get it?

   _____

   _____

◢ What software should you install before you can install Android Studio?

_____

◢ What is the Android Emulator and how would you use it when developing an Android app?

_____

_____

◢ What programming language is used to write Android apps?

_____

◢ What file extension is used to hold an Android app after it is developed so that it can be tested in the Android Emulator?

_____

◢ What tool can you use to add an app to the Android Emulator?

_____

16

> **Notes** To run the Android Emulator on your computer, virtualization technology must be enabled in UEFI/BIOS, and Hyper-V must be disabled, which can be done through Programs and Features.

Now you're ready to install the software you need to run the Android Emulator. Android Studio requires Java Standard Edition (Java SE) Development Kit (also called JDK) to run. To download and install Java SE and Android Studio, follow these steps:

1. Go to **java.oracle.com** and drill down to the Java SE download page. Click the **Java Platform (JDK)** download link. Accept the license agreement, and download and install the Windows version of the JDK. Be sure you download the correct version for your Windows installation: 32-bit Windows or 64-bit Windows (see Figure 16-7). At the time of this writing, the link to the download is **oracle.com/technetwork/java/javase/downloads/jdk8-downloads-2133151.html**. However, your link might be different. After you download the file, double-click it to install the software, accepting all defaults, and then close all open windows.

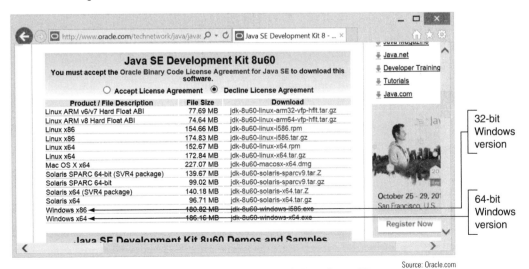

Source: Oracle.com

Figure 16-7 Download a 32-bit or 64-bit Windows installation of Java SE

2. Open File Explorer/Windows Explorer and locate the folder that contains the software. The folder name includes the version of Java SE installed. For the current version of Java, the folder is C:\Progam Files\Java\jdk1.8.0_60, but your Java version might install differently. What is the path to the Java software?

An environment variable is a string stored in the Windows registry that software can use to find other software or to know where to store its data. The Android SDK uses an environment variable to know where to look to find Java SE. Follow these steps to use the Environment Variables dialog box to create an environment variable that applies to the currently signed-on user and points to the Java SE path:

1. Open the System window of your computer, and click **Advanced system settings**. The System Properties box opens with the Advanced tab selected. Click **Environment Variables**. In the Environment Variables box, click **New** in the User variables group. The New User Variable box opens.

2. Enter **JAVA_HOME** as the Variable name and **C:\Program Files\Java\1.8.0_60** as the Variable value, substituting the path you recorded in Step 2 in the previous step sequence. See Figure 16-8. Click **OK** three times to close all boxes. Close the System window. The registry is immediately updated with this variable name and value.

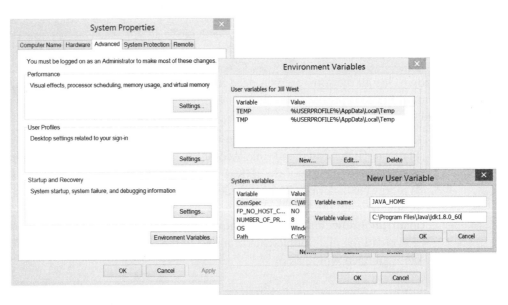

Figure 16-8   Create a user variable to point to the Java software

Follow these steps to download and install Android Studio:

1. Go to **developer.android.com** and locate and download Android Studio for Windows. What is the exact URL where you found the download? List the steps you took to download and install Android Studio, accepting all default settings:

2. Android Studio automatically launches and opens to the setup wizard (see Figure 16-9). If it does not launch, you can launch it from the Start screen (Windows 8) or the Start menu (Windows 7).

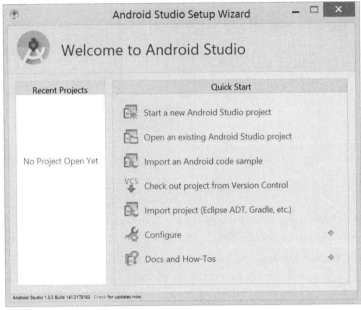

Source: Android Studio

Figure 16-9 Configure the Android Studio installation through the Android Studio Setup Wizard

3. To complete setup, in the Android Studio Setup Wizard dialog box, click **Configure**, and then click **SDK Manager**. The Android SDK Manager window opens with several packages selected by default. If your motherboard is made by Intel, you need one more item. Scroll down to the section under Extras, and select the **Intel x86 Emulator Accelerator** item. Click **Install packages** to install all the checked packages. Follow directions on screen to complete the installation, and then close the Android SDK Manager window.

4. Close the Android Studio Setup Wizard window and all other open windows.

5. To complete installation of the HAXM software on a system with an Intel motherboard, locate the application file in File Explorer/Windows Explorer. By default, the location is C:\Users*username*\AppData\Local\Android\sdk\extras\intel\Hardware_Accelerated_Execution_Manager. (The file's location in your system might be different.) Double-click **intelhaxm-android.exe**, and follow the on-screen instructions. You do *not* need to launch the Intel HAXM documentation when you finish setup. After installation, close all open windows.

The AVD Manager is used to create and manage an Android Virtual Device (AVD), and is included in the Android SDK. Android app developers test an app on several AVDs, one for each type of Android device they expect the app to use. To access the AVD Manager, you first create a new project and then configure the virtual device. Follow these steps to use the AVD Manager program to set up an Android Virtual Device (AVD):

1. Open Android Studio, close the Tip of the Day box, and click **Start a new Android Studio project**. Follow the on-screen directions, accepting all default settings for your new app called My Application. Once your project is created, the My Application window shows an Android device (see Figure 16-10).

SDK Manager

AVD Manager

Source: Android Studio

Figure 16-10 Android Studio shows the new application on the virtual device's screen

2. Click the **AVD Manager** icon in the toolbar. The Android Virtual Device Manager window opens with one default device listed (see the left side of Figure 16-11).

3. Click **Create Virtual Device,** and select a device from the list (see the right side of Figure 16-11). Continue the device-creation process, keeping all default settings. Give your device a name, and click **Finish**. The new virtual device is now listed in the AVD Manager window.

Launch device

Edit device

Source: Android Studio

Figure 16-11 Use the AVD Manager to create a new Android virtual device

For actual development and testing of Android apps, you would install several versions of Android and create one virtual device using each version so that you could test your apps on several Android platforms.

Let's see how a virtual Android device works. To find out, do the following:

1. In the Android Virtual Device Manager window, click the green launch arrow next to the AVD you just created. Depending on your system configuration, you might have to troubleshoot one or more error messages. Research online as necessary to determine the exact settings to use so the emulator will work on your system. For example, you might have to disable using the host GPU, which is enabled by default. Once you've resolved any error messages, relaunch the virtual device and wait a moment while the emulator boots the AVD.

2. Use the emulator as you would an Android device. What happens when you try to use it to surf the web?

_____

3. Use the App Launcher to view the installed apps. See Figure 16-12. What apps are installed on the AVD?

_____

_____

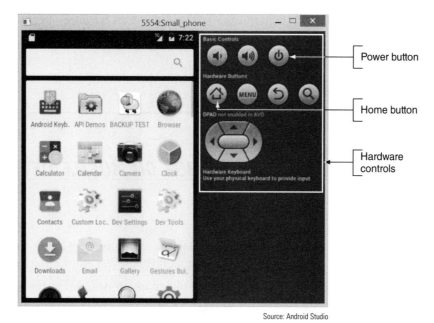

Source: Android Studio

Figure 16-12 The AVD showing installed apps.

4. List the steps to activate the camera on the AVD:

_____

_____

5. Check out the Settings app. Which settings can you adjust on the AVD?

_____

6. Close any open windows.

REVIEW QUESTIONS

1. Why might an app developer want to test his apps on an AVD rather than on actual Android devices?

_____

_____

2. Which programming language is used to write Android apps?

_____

16

3. When installing the Android SDK, what is the purpose of creating a user variable using the Environment Variables dialog box in Windows?

_____

4. Which program is used to create an Android virtual device?

_____

_____

_____

5. What would be the advantage of installing several AVDs when testing Android apps?

_____

_____

_____

LAB 16.4 CONFIGURE EMAIL AND DROPBOX ON MOBILE DEVICES

OBJECTIVES

The goal of this lab is to practice configuring various accounts, such as for email and Dropbox, on an Android device. After completing this lab, you will be able to:

◢ Create a new email account through the Email app on an Android virtual device

◢ Install Dropbox on a smart phone or tablet

◢ Sync Dropbox files from a smart phone or tablet

MATERIALS REQUIRED

This lab requires the following:

◢ Windows 8 or Windows 7 operating system

◢ Internet access

◢ Email account with password

◢ Email address for your instructor

◢ Dropbox account with sign-in information (created earlier in this chapter)

◢ Android Studio, as installed in the previous lab

◢ Android, iOS, or Windows Phone mobile device (optional)

LAB PREPARATION

Before the lab begins, the instructor or lab assistant needs to do the following:

◢ Verify Windows starts with no errors

◢ Verify Internet access is available

◢ Verify Android Studio is correctly installed

ACTIVITY BACKGROUND

Gone are the days when mobile devices had to be connected to a computer by cable in order to sync data. Email, files, and other data can be automatically synced over either Wi-Fi or cellular connections for any current Android, iOS, or Windows Phone mobile device.

In this lab, you add an email account to the Email app on your Android virtual device. Then you install the Dropbox app on your own or a classmate's Android, iOS, or Windows Phone mobile device, and then sync a file to Dropbox on your computer.

ESTIMATED COMPLETION TIME: 30 MINUTES

ACTIVITY

To add an email account on a virtual device in Android Studio, complete the following steps:

1. Open Android Studio. Click the **AVD Manager** icon to open the Android Virtual Device Manager window.

2. Click the green launch arrow on one of the devices listed.

3. After the device boots up, click the **Settings** icon (you might have to swipe to the left to view the second home screen—to swipe, press the mouse button and drag your cursor across the screen). Scroll down and click **Accounts**. Click **Add account**.

4. Click **Personal (IMAP)**, and then follow the on-screen directions to enter your email account information, keeping other default settings.

5. Swipe down to close the Settings app (alternately, click the **Home** hardware button, as shown earlier in Figure 16-12). Click the **Apps Drawer** icon, and then click **Email**.

6. In the Email app, complete any setup steps required. How far back in time did your email account sync on the virtual device?

_____

7. Compose a new email and send it to your instructor.

8. To view server settings for this email account, click the **Menu** icon, scroll down, and then click **Settings**. Click the name of the email account.

9. Under Server settings, click **Incoming settings**. Answer the following questions:

   ◢ What port is the server using?

   _____

   ◢ What does this tell you about the protocol being used?

   _____

   ◢ What port would you have expected the server to be using here? Why?

   _____

10. To protect your privacy, be sure to remove your email account from any virtual devices. The most secure way to do this is to delete the AVD. Describe the steps to do this. Be sure to complete the deletion process so your information is protected.

   _____

   _____

   _____

Dropbox is compatible with many operating systems, including Android, iOS, and Windows Phone. Use your own smart phone or tablet for this portion of the lab, or team up with one or more classmates to use their mobile device(s). Alternatively, pair up with a classmate with a mobile device using a different OS than your own, and install Dropbox on both devices so you both can see how the app works on multiple mobile operating systems.

Complete the following steps:

1. Download Dropbox from your phone's primary app provider.

2. Sign in using the Dropbox account you created earlier in this chapter.

3. Take a screen shot of your phone's display that shows your Dropbox folders on your phone.

4. Open the screen shot, click the **Share** icon, and add the screen shot file to Dropbox. Save it to the Computer class folder you created in the Dropbox lab earlier in this chapter.

5. Open Dropbox on your computer. (If you're using a lab computer and Dropbox is not installed, use the online Dropbox dashboard at **dropbox.com**.) Sign in if necessary.

6. Open the **Computer class** folder. Click on the screen shot file to view it, and then click **Share**. Enter your instructor's email address to send the link, and then click **Send**.

REVIEW QUESTIONS

1. What port number is used by default to receive IMAP email? POP3 email?

   _____

   _____

2. What port numbers are used to receive email by IMAP and POP3 servers when using SSL?

   _____

3. What are the steps to change how far back in time the Email app syncs with the email account?

   _____

   _____

   _____

4. Why should you delete the AVD at the end of the lab?

   _____

LAB 16.5 RESEARCH XCODE AND THE iOS SIMULATOR

OBJECTIVES

The goal of this lab is to explore the features and requirements of Xcode. After completing this lab, you will be able to:

◢ Describe the purpose of Xcode

◢ Explain the use of the Simulator tool in Xcode

MATERIALS REQUIRED

This lab requires the following:

◢ Internet access

LAB PREPARATION

Before the lab begins, the instructor or lab assistant needs to do the following:

◢ Verify Internet access is available

ACTIVITY BACKGROUND

When app developers create apps for iOS devices, they use Apple's Xcode application. The program is available only for Mac computers; however, you can learn about the application without downloading it by going to the iOS Developer website (*developer.apple.com*), which contains a wealth of useful information, resources, and community support. In this lab, you explore some of Apple's app developer tools contained within Xcode.

ESTIMATED COMPLETION TIME: 45 MINUTES

16

ACTIVITY

Do the following to find out more about Xcode:

1. In your web browser, go to **developer.apple.com**, and explore the resources on the main page. If necessary, use a search engine as you answer the following questions, and add the **site:developer.apple.com** tag to limit your search to Apple's website:

◢ How much does the Apple Developer Program individual membership cost?

_____

> **Notes** Some schools qualify for the free iOS Developer University Program, which provides a suite of tools for student development projects and collaboration between students and instructors. Learn more at *developer.apple.com/programs/ios/university*.

◢ What is Xcode? What is the current version of Xcode?

_____

_____

◢ What equipment and OS do you need to get Xcode from the App Store for free?

_____

◢ What is Simulator?

_____

_____

◢ What is Swift?

_____

_____

2. Using your favorite search engine, search for the iOS Simulator User Guide. At the time of this writing, the Simulator User Guide is found at the following webpage: **https://developer.apple.com/library/prerelease/ios/documentation/IDEs/Conceptual/iOS_Simulator_Guide/Introduction/Introduction.html**

Answer these questions:

⊿ What are the two ways to access iOS Simulator in Xcode?

_____

_____

⊿ Other than iOS, what OSs can be simulated in Simulator?

_____

⊿ How are gestures simulated on a virtual device in Simulator?

_____

_____

3. Search for online Xcode tutorial videos on *youtube.com* or by using a search engine. Answer the following questions:

⊿ What is the playground?

_____

⊿ What file type is used to store the code for a new app?

_____

⊿ What is a storyboard?

_____

REVIEW QUESTIONS

1. What programming language does Apple currently use for iOS apps?

_____

_____

2. What OS is used on Apple Watch devices?

_____

3. Xcode is a free app from the App Store, so why might you need to pay for an Apple Developer Program membership?

_____

4. If you were to begin developing apps, which OS would you prefer to work with? Why?

_____

Windows Resources on a Network

Labs included in this chapter:

LAB 17.1 MAP A NETWORK DRIVE AND USE WAKE-ON-LAN

OBJECTIVES

The goal of this lab is to learn to map a network drive and remotely power on your computer. After completing this lab, you will be able to:

- Map a network drive in Windows
- Set up Wake-on-LAN

MATERIALS REQUIRED

This lab requires the following:

- Two or more Windows 7 or Windows 8 computers on the same wired network (not wireless)
- Internet access (optional and used for research only)

LAB PREPARATION

Before the lab begins, the instructor or lab assistant needs to do the following:

- Verify Windows starts with no errors
- Verify Internet access is available
- Set up a peer-to-peer network with two or more computers

ACTIVITY BACKGROUND

When using more than one computer (for example, a laptop and a desktop), it is sometimes necessary to pass files between them. Having a mapped network drive on a computer makes it easy to access the files on another computer. On a small network, you might be accessing a resource on a desktop instead of a server, and the hosting computer might go to sleep. Setting up the Wake-on-LAN allows you to wake up the hosting computer and access your files. This can be useful if you're accessing your files remotely over a VPN from the other side of the country, or if you are just tired of getting up and walking across the room to turn on the computer.

ESTIMATED COMPLETION TIME: 45 MINUTES

 Activity

> **Notes** Sometimes HomeGroup does not play well with others when sharing. Before beginning this lab, open the **Network and Sharing Center**, and click **Change advanced sharing settings**. Make sure HomeGroup is turned off. Also, in Windows 8, open the **Settings** charm, and click **Change PC settings**. Click **Network**, and then click **HomeGroup**. If available, click **Leave**. Repeat these steps on the second computer.

In this lab, Computer 1 is acting as the server that is serving up a network resource (a folder named Downloads), and Computer 2 is acting as the client that is using this shared resource.

1. Begin with two networked Windows computers. Designate one computer to be Computer 1 and the other computer to be Computer 2.

2. On Computer 1, which will be your server, open File Explorer/Windows Explorer, navigate to your C: drive, and display the drive root.

3. To create a new folder in the root of drive C:, on the Home ribbon, click **New folder**, and name it **Resources.**

4. Right-click your new **Resources** folder, select **Share with,** and then click **Specific people** to open the File Sharing window.

5. To grant access to all users, select **Everyone** from the drop-down list, and then click **Add.** Under Permission Level, grant **Read/Write** access, and then click the **Share** button. Windows confirms that the folder is shared.

6. Make sure network discovery and file and printer sharing are turned on. To check these settings in the Network and Sharing Center, click **Change advanced sharing settings.**

7. To see a list of all network shares on this computer, open a command prompt window, and enter the **net share** command at the command prompt. Record on the following lines all the shared resources on the computer. Close the command prompt window.

_____

_____

_____

8. Go to Computer 2, and expand **Network** in the File Explorer/Windows Explorer navigation pane. Computer 1 should be in the list of available computers. If Computer 1 is not in the list, check Computer 1 and make sure its network discovery settings are correct. Record the names of all the computers visible on the network:

_____

9. To view the shared resources on Computer 1, open Computer 1. You might have to enter your user name and password if you haven't previously opened the network resource and saved your credentials.

10. You see a list of the shared resources on Computer 1. Does the list match the list of shared resources you wrote down in Step 7?

_____

11. Right-click the **Resources** folder, and select **Map network drive.** Windows assigns a drive letter by default, starting at Z and working backward through the alphabet. However, you can change this drive letter. What drive letter did you assign to the network drive? Check **Reconnect at sign-in** or **Reconnect at logon** if it is not already checked, and then click **Finish.**

_____

12. To test the functionality of your new network drive, create a test document on the mapped drive.

13. Go back to Computer 1, and verify the test document you created is in the Resources folder in the C: drive.

Now you will activate the Wake-on-LAN functionality. Follow these steps:

1. On Computer 1, open the **Network and Sharing Center.**

2. In the left pane, click **Change adapter settings.**

3. Right-click the network adapter for the wired connection, and select **Properties.**

4. Click **Configure**, and then select the **Power Management** tab. Which boxes are checked on the Power Management tab?

_____

_____

5. Make sure that the **Allow the computer to turn off this device to save power** option is selected. This enables power management in Windows.

6. Check **Allow this device to wake the computer**. Why shouldn't you select _Only allow a magic packet to wake this computer_?

_____

_____

_____

7. Click **OK**.

8. Shut down Computer 1.

9. Boot Computer 1, and access setup UEFI/BIOS. Find the power management configuration screen in UEFI/BIOS, and confirm that Wake-on-LAN is enabled. Did you need to enable Wake-on-LAN?

_____

10. Exit the UEFI/BIOS setup, and start Windows.

11. Put Computer 1 in sleep mode.

12. On Computer 2, go to File Explorer/Windows Explorer and try to open your mapped network drive. What happens?

_____

13. Shut down Computer 1.

14. On Computer 2, go to File Explorer/Windows Explorer and try to open your mapped network drive. What happens?

_____

REVIEW QUESTIONS

1. What is the purpose of the net share command? When network discovery and file and printer sharing are turned off, does the net share command still report a shared folder as shared?

_____

2. What drive letter does Windows first attempt to assign a mapped network drive? What is the second letter used?

_____

3. Why should you map a network drive rather than just access your network resource from the Network group in File Explorer/Windows Explorer?

_____

4. In what two locations must you enable Wake-on-LAN to use it?

_____

_____

5. Why is Wake-on-LAN typically disabled on laptops?

_____

_____

6. Why would you choose to disable the Wake-on-LAN functionality?

_____

_____

LAB 17.2 USE REMOTE DESKTOP

OBJECTIVES

The goal of this lab is to learn how to log on to another computer remotely by using Windows Remote Desktop. After completing this lab, you will be able to:

◢ Configure Remote Desktop

◢ Use Remote Desktop to log on to another computer remotely

MATERIALS REQUIRED

This lab requires the following:

◢ Windows 8 or Windows 7 Professional, Ultimate, or Enterprise edition

◢ An account with administrator privileges

◢ A network workgroup consisting of two or more computers

◢ A team of two or more students

LAB PREPARATION

Before the lab begins, the instructor or lab assistant needs to do the following:

◢ Verify Windows starts with no errors

◢ Verify a network connection is available

◢ Verify each student has access to a user account with administrator privileges

ACTIVITY BACKGROUND

Windows allows users to connect remotely from other Windows machines. With a remote connection, you can control a computer from another location, such as work or home. Remote Desktop is different than Remote Assistance because Remote Desktop does not need the end users' permission to connect their computer. Remote Desktop is also useful for connecting to servers, database servers, file servers, or other machines you access. For example, as a support technician, you might find Remote Desktop useful when you need to update or reset software on a server when you are working at your desk and the server is in the data center.

Remote Desktop is only available in Windows 8 or Windows 7 Professional, Ultimate, and Enterprise versions. Using Home editions of Windows 7, you cannot host the Remote Desktop, but you can remote in to a computer that is hosting Remote Desktop.

Remote Desktop is not enabled by default in the operating system. When enabled, members of the administrators group can connect to the computer from another machine. When you use Remote Desktop, you are logged on to the remote computer as if you were actually sitting in front of that machine with full rights and access. Standard users must be placed on a remote access list to use Remote Desktop.

In this lab, you configure one computer to accept a remote connection, and then allow someone in your class workgroup to connect to it from her machine.

ESTIMATED COMPLETION TIME: 30 MINUTES

Activity

In this lab, you set up your computer to allow a remote connection. Then, you remote it to another computer in your workgroup that is also configured to use Remote Desktop. To configure your computer to accept a remote connection, follow these steps:

1. Log on using an account with administrator privileges.

2. To determine the computer name and IP address, open a command prompt window, and enter the **ipconfig /all** command. Write down the computer name (host name) and IP address:

   _____

3. Open the **System** window, and click **Remote settings** in the left pane. The System Properties dialog box opens with the Remote tab selected.

4. Select the **Allow connections only from computers running Remote Desktop with Network Level Authentication** option. If a dialog box appears warning about a Power Options setting, click **OK** to continue. Click **Apply**.

5. Click **Select Users**. In the Remote Desktop Users dialog box, you can add or remove users who are allowed to use a Remote Desktop connection. The users listed here and the user currently signed in have access to Remote Desktop. On the following line, list those users:

   _____

6. Close all windows.

Follow these steps to connect to a computer using Remote Desktop:

1. Find someone in your group who has set up Remote Desktop on his or her computer. Ask for the computer name and IP address of his or her computer so that you can connect to it using Remote Desktop. What computer name and IP address will you connect to?

   _____

2. In Windows 8, on the Start screen, type and then select **Remote Desktop Connection**. In Windows 7, click **Start, All Programs, Accessories, Remote Desktop Connection**.

Notes All local users are automatically logged off a computer when it is being remotely accessed. Also, only one computer can remotely access a single computer at a time.

3. In the Remote Desktop Connection dialog box, enter the IP address or computer name of the remote computer in the Computer text box, and click **Connect**.

4. A Windows security window appears asking for the logon credentials of the computer you are connecting to. Enter the credentials for one of the user accounts that is allowed access. For the user name, you might need to include the computer name, for example LenovoLaptop\Jean Andrews.

5. An identity warning window might pop up because the system cannot authenticate the certificate. If you see this window, click **Yes** to accept. You can also check the **Don't ask me again for connections to this computer** box so that the warning doesn't appear again.

6. After a moment, the screen of the computer to which you now have remote access appears.

Follow these steps to use the remote machine:

1. Notice the toolbar at the top of the screen. What is the name of the computer that you are accessing?

   _____

2. Open the **Documents** folder. Create a test document on the remote computer. What is the name of the document you created?

   _____

   _____

3. Using Control Panel, adjust the time by a half hour. What is the new time?

   _____

4. Click **OK**, and close all windows.

5. Close the Remote Desktop Connection window, which ends the remote connection session.

6. Log on to the remote machine you just used, change the time back to the correct time, and verify the file has been created.

REVIEW QUESTIONS

1. Describe two situations in which you might want to use Remote Desktop Connection:

   _____

   _____

   _____

2. How can you tell if you are connected remotely to another computer?

   _____

   _____

3. How can you determine the name of the remote computer before connecting? How can you determine the IP address of the remote computer?

   _____

   _____

4. How might other programs, such as firewalls, interfere with a remote connection?

_____

_____

5. When a connection was made to the remote computer in the lab, what changed on that computer?

_____

6. What is the advantage of a host computer not displaying the Windows desktop locally when a Remote Desktop session is active?

_____

_____

LAB 17.3 MANAGE USER ACCOUNTS IN WINDOWS 8

OBJECTIVES

The goal of this lab is to gain experience adding and modifying user accounts by using the PC settings page in Windows 8. After completing this lab, you will be able to:

◢ Add users

◢ Reset passwords

◢ Control user account access

MATERIALS REQUIRED

This lab requires the following:

◢ Windows 8 operating system

◢ An account with administrator privileges

LAB PREPARATION

Before the lab begins, the instructor or lab assistant needs to do the following:

◢ Verify Windows starts with no errors

◢ Verify each student has access to a user account with administrator privileges

ACTIVITY BACKGROUND

Maintaining Windows involves more than just managing physical resources like hard drives; you also need to manage users and their access to these resources. Managing users can be very time consuming, however. Much of this time is typically spent helping users who have forgotten their passwords or entered their passwords incorrectly multiple times, causing Windows to lock their accounts. In this lab, you practice managing user accounts and passwords using the PC settings page and the Manage Accounts window in Control Panel. For more advanced user account management, you can use the Computer Management console, which is not covered in this lab.

Activity

To examine the user account information available via the PC settings page, follow these steps:

1. Sign in using an account with administrator privileges.

2. Open **Control Panel**. Click **User Accounts**, and then click **Manage another account**. The Manage Accounts window opens. Your screen will resemble Figure 17-1.

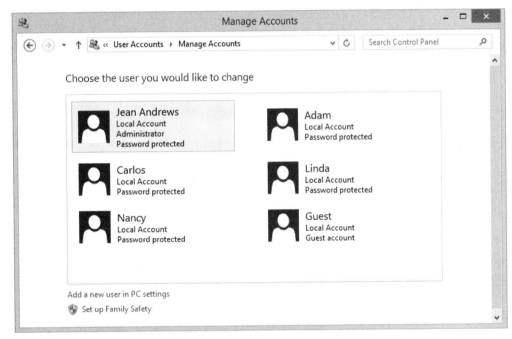

Figure 17-1 The Manage Accounts window lists all available user accounts

3. Examine the Manage Accounts window, click different user names, and answer the following questions:

◢ What types of user accounts are included on a Windows 8 system by default?

_____

_____

_____

◢ Does your system contain any individual user accounts? If so, list them here:

_____

_____

Windows 8 sends you to the PC settings page to add a new user. Add a new user on your local computer by following these steps:

1. In the Manage Accounts window, click **Add a new user in PC Settings**, or using the charms bar, click the **Settings** charm, and then click **Change PC settings**.

2. On the PC settings page, click **Accounts**, and then click **Other accounts**.

3. Click **Add an account**.

4. On the *How will this person sign in?* screen, click **Sign in without a Microsoft account** at the bottom of the screen. Review the two options for signing in, and then select **Local account**.

5. In the User name text box, type **James Clark**.

6. In the Password text box, type **changeme**, and confirm the password in the next text box. Enter a password hint in case the password is forgotten.

7. Click **Finish**.

New users in Windows 8 are set up as Standard user accounts by default. A Standard user account can't create, delete, or change other accounts; make system wide changes; change security settings; or install some types of software. To give the account administrator privileges, do the following:

1. On the Manage other accounts page, select the **James Clark** account, and then click **Edit**.

2. On the Edit account screen, change the account type to **Administrator**.

3. Click **OK**.

4. Sign out your computer, and sign in as James Clark. List the steps you took to accomplish this task:

_____

_____

_____

Occasionally, administrators have to reset user passwords. To reset a user's password, do the following:

1. Sign out of the James Clark account, and sign in again using the original administrator account.

2. Open the Manage Accounts window in Control Panel, and select the James Clark account.

3. Click **Change the password**. What information does a user lose when the password is changed by an administrator?

_____

_____

_____

4. Enter the password as **newpass**, confirm the password, enter a new password hint, and then click **Change password**.

5. Close all open windows, and try to sign in with the James Clark account using the old password. What error do you get? Click **OK**.

_____

6. If a user does not know his or her password, the user might be able to reset it using the sign-in screen. Under the password box on the sign-in screen, click **Reset password**. What does a user need to have to reset a password? Click **OK**.

_____

7. Sign in using the new password.

8. Finally, sign out of the James Clark account, sign in as the administrator, and delete the James Clark account. List the steps that you took to delete the account:

_____

_____

_____

REVIEW QUESTIONS

1. Besides adding, editing, and deleting users, what additional tasks can you perform in the Manage Accounts window of Control Panel in Windows 8?

_____

_____

2. Besides Administrator, Standard, and Guest account types, which are used to assign access, what is the fourth account type available in Windows 8? Why might you use this account type?

_____

_____

_____

_____

_____

3. List the steps to change an account type using the PC settings page:

_____

_____

_____

_____

4. What user accounts management function can be performed on the PC settings page but not in the Manage Accounts window in Control Panel? What functions can be performed both on the PC settings page and in Control Panel?

_____

_____

_____

5. Why is it a good idea to primarily use a Standard account instead of an Administrator account for normal computer activity?

_____

_____

17

LAB 17.4 MANAGE USER ACCOUNTS IN WINDOWS 7

OBJECTIVES

The goal of this lab is to gain experience adding and modifying user accounts by using Control Panel in Windows 7. After completing this lab, you will be able to:

◢ Add users

◢ Control user account access

MATERIALS REQUIRED

This lab requires the following:

◢ Windows 7 operating system

◢ An account with administrator privileges

LAB PREPARATION

Before the lab begins, the instructor or lab assistant needs to do the following:

◢ Verify Windows starts with no errors

◢ Verify each student has access to a user account with administrator privileges

ACTIVITY BACKGROUND

Managing user accounts in Windows 8 is quite different than in Windows 7. In Windows 8, Microsoft moved some of the user management functions to the PC settings page. In Windows 7, you can access most of the necessary functions in just the Manage Accounts window in Control Panel. Because changing the password is almost exactly the same in Windows 7 as it is in Windows 8, you can refer to the previous lab, "Manage User Accounts in Windows 8," for those instructions. In this lab, you practice adding and editing user accounts using the Manage Accounts window in Control Panel. For more advanced user account management, you can use the Computer Management console, which is not covered in this lab.

ESTIMATED COMPLETION TIME: 30 MINUTES

 Activity

To examine the user account information available via Control Panel, follow these steps:

1. Log on using an account with administrator privileges.

2. Click **Start, Control Panel**, and then click **Add or remove user accounts**. The Manage Accounts window appears.

3. Examine the Manage Accounts window, and answer the following questions:

◢ What three types of user accounts are included on a Windows 7 system by default?

_____

_____

_____

◢ Does your system contain any individual user accounts? If so, list them here:

_____

Using the Manage Accounts window, add and configure users on your local computer by following these steps:

1. In the Manage Accounts window, click **Create a new account**.

2. In the New account name text box, type **James Clark**.

3. Click **Standard user**, if it is not selected, and then click **Create Account**.

4. To create a password for the new account, click the **James Clark** account in the Manage Accounts window. Click **Create a password**.

5. In the New password text box, type **newuser**, and confirm the password in the next text box.

6. Click **Create password**, and then close all open windows.

A Standard user account can't create, delete, or change other accounts; make system wide changes; change security settings; or install some types of software. To give the account administrator privileges, do the following:

1. Open the Manage Accounts window in Control Panel, and select the **James Clark** account.

2. Click **Change the account type**, and select **Administrator**.

3. Click **Change Account Type**.

4. Log off your computer, and log on as James Clark. List the steps you took to accomplish this task:

_____

_____

_____

REVIEW QUESTIONS

1. Besides adding, editing, and deleting users, what additional tasks can you perform in the Manage Accounts window of Control Panel in Windows 7?

_____

2. What are the differences between Standard and Administrator accounts?

_____

_____

_____

_____

3. List the steps required to change an account type:

_____

_____

_____

4. Why do you think new user accounts are not automatically assigned administrator privileges?

_____

_____

5. Why might it be a good idea to have users reset their passwords instead of having an administrator do it for them?

_____

_____

LAB 17.5 USE NTFS PERMISSIONS TO SHARE FILES AND FOLDERS

OBJECTIVES

The goal of this lab is to learn to use the advanced sharing and security tools in Windows to give folder permissions to specific local users and to control a network connection sharing specific folders with specific users and/or groups. After completing this lab, you will be able to:

◢ Configure how a network connection is controlled

◢ Share folders with others on the network using NTFS permissions

MATERIALS REQUIRED

This lab requires the following:

◢ Two computers networked together; one computer must use Windows 8 or Windows 7 Professional or higher, and the other computer can use any edition of Windows 8 or Windows 7

◢ An account with administrator privileges

◢ A workgroup of two students

LAB PREPARATION

Before the lab begins, the instructor or lab assistant needs to do the following:

◢ Verify both Windows computers start with no errors

◢ Verify the local network is working

◢ Verify each student has access to a user account with administrator privileges

ACTIVITY BACKGROUND

On a Windows 8 or Windows 7 Professional or higher computer, you can control which specific users or groups have access to specific folders. Microsoft best practices recommend that you set up a user group for each classification of data and assign permissions to a folder or other shared resources according to user groups. Assigning permissions to user groups is easier to maintain than assigning permissions to specific users because you can add or remove users from the group easier than you can change the permissions on each folder.

In this lab, you set up the security for a peer-to-peer network for a doctor's office. Two computers are connected to the small company network; one of these computers (Computer1) acts as the file server for the other computer (Computer2). You create two classifications of data, Financial and Medical. Two workers (Nancy and Adam) require access to the Medical data, and two workers (Linda and Carlos) require access to the Financial folder. In addition, the doctor, Lucas, requires access to both categories of data.

This lab is divided into four parts, which accomplish the following:

◢ Part 1: On Computer1, you create folders named Financial and Medical, and you create five user accounts, for Lucas, Nancy, Adam, Linda, and Carlos. All the accounts belong to the standard user group. You also create two new user groups, Financial and Medical.

◢ Part 2: You set the NTFS permissions on the Financial and Medical folders so that only the members of the appropriate group can access each folder.

◢ Part 3: You test your security settings for local users.

◢ Part 4: For each user on Computer2, you test the access to both folders across the network.

ESTIMATED COMPLETION TIME: 60 MINUTES

 Activity

Working with your partner, perform all four parts of this lab.

PART 1: CREATE FOLDERS, USER ACCOUNTS, AND USER GROUPS

Follow these steps to create the folders, user accounts, and user groups on Computer1 (the file server) that is using Windows 8 or Windows 7 Professional or higher edition:

> **Notes** Before beginning this lab, disable HomeGroup. In Windows 8, use the Network page under PC Settings page to leave the homegroup, and use the Advanced Sharing settings window in the Network and Sharing Center to turn off HomeGroup settings. In Windows 7, use the Network and Sharing Center and the Advanced Sharing settings window to turn off HomeGroup settings.

1. Log on to Computer1 as an administrator.

2. Create two folders: **C:\Financial** and **C:\Medical**. In each folder, create a test document. What is the name of the test document in the Financial folder? In the Medical folder?

   _____

3. To open the Computer Management console, in Windows 8, right-click the **Start** button, and then click **Computer Management**, or in Windows 7, type **Computer Management** in the Search programs and files box, and then press **Enter**.

4. Using the console, create user accounts for Lucas, Nancy, Adam, Linda, and Carlos. To create the first new user, right-click **Users** under **Local Users and Groups**, and then select **New User** in the shortcut menu. Make the password for each user the same as the name of the user. Uncheck the **User must change password at next logon** check box. What are the other three check box options when creating user accounts?

   _____

   _____

   _____

5. Click **Create**. The user will automatically be added to the Users group. Create all the user accounts, and click **Close** after the last user account is created.

6. To create the Financial user group, right-click **Groups** under Local Users and Groups, and then select **New Group** in the shortcut menu. The New Group dialog box appears. Enter **Financial** as the name of the group. Enter the description **Users have access to the Financial folder**.

7. To add members to the Financial group, click **Add**. The Select Users dialog box opens. In the *Enter the object names to select* box, enter the name of a user, and then click **OK**. Add all the user account names that need access to this folder, separated by semicolons, as in **Carlos; Linda; Lucas**. (Alternatively, you can click **Advanced** to open a new dialog box, and then click **Find Now** to view a list of user names. Then, hold down the **Ctrl** key and select multiple names, and then click **OK**.) To create the group, click **Create** in the New Group box.

8. Next, create the **Medical** group, and add Lucas, Nancy, and Adam to the group.

9. Close the Computer Management console.

PART 2: SET NTFS PERMISSIONS ON FOLDERS

Follow these steps to set the permissions for the two folders:

1. Open File Explorer/Windows Explorer, right-click the **Financial** folder, and then select **Properties** in the shortcut menu. The Properties dialog box for the folder appears. Click the **Security** tab (see the right side of Figure 17-2). What groups and users already have access to the C:\Financial folder?

Figure 17-2 Permissions assigned to the Financial folder

2. When you select a user group in the Group or user name section, the type of permissions assigned to that group appears in the Permissions section. Note that the Administrators group has full control of the folder. Also notice the checks under Allow are dimmed. These permissions are dimmed because they have been inherited from the Windows parent object.

3. To remove the inherited status from these permissions so that you can change them, click **Advanced**. The Advanced Security Settings window appears. In Windows 8, click **Disable inheritance** (see Figure 17-3). In Windows 7, click **Change Permissions**. You can now uncheck **Include inheritable permissions from this object's parent**. A Windows Security

warning dialog box, also shown in Figure 17-3, appears. To keep the current permissions, but remove the inherited status placed on them, click **Convert inherited permissions into explicit permissions on this object** in Windows 8, or in Windows 7, click **Add**.

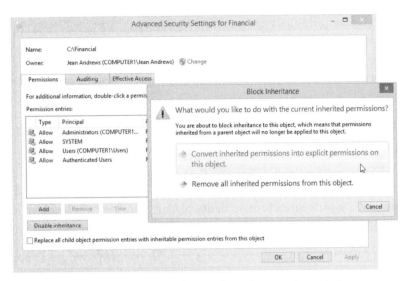

Figure 17-3 Remove the inherited status from the current permissions

4. Click **Apply**, and click **OK** to close the Advanced Security Settings window.

5. In the Financial Properties dialog box, notice the permissions are now checked in black, indicating they are no longer inherited permissions and can be changed. What permissions are allowed to the standard Users group by default?

6. Click **Edit** to change these permissions.

7. The Permissions for Financial dialog box opens (see Figure 17-4). Select the **Users** group, and then click **Remove**. Also remove the **Authenticated Users** group. Don't remove the SYSTEM group or the Administrators group. That way, an administrator can always access the data.

Figure 17-4 Change the permissions of a folder

8. To add a new group, click **Add**. The Select Users or Groups dialog box opens. In the *Enter the object names to select* box, type **Financial**, and then click **OK**. The Financial group is added to the list of groups and users for this folder.

9. In the Permissions for Financial section, check **Allow** for the **Full control** option to give that permission to this user group. Click **Apply**, and then click **OK** twice to close the Properties dialog box.

10. Following the same process, change the permissions of the C:\Medical folder so that Authenticated Users and Users are not allowed access and the Medical group is allowed full control. Don't forget to first disable inheritable permissions in the advanced settings.

PART 3: TEST YOUR SECURITY SETTINGS WITH LOCAL USERS

Do the following to test the share permissions on each shared folder:

1. On Computer1, log off and log back on as **Lucas** with the password set earlier in this lab. Verify Lucas can access both the Medical and Financial folders.

2. Log off and log back on as **Nancy**. Verify Nancy can access the Medical folder but not the Financial folder. What warning pops up when Nancy tries to access the Financial folder?

   _____

   _____

3. Log off and log back on as **Adam**. Verify Adam can access the Medical folder but not the Financial folder.

4. Log off and log back on as **Linda**. Verify Linda can access the Financial folder but not the Medical folder.

5. Log off and log back on as **Carlos**. Verify Carlos can access the Financial folder but not the Medical folder.

PART 4: TEST YOUR SECURITY SETTINGS ON THE NETWORK FOR EACH USER ON COMPUTER2

NTFS permissions and share permissions both control access over the network, and the most restrictive permission setting applies. Best practice is to give full access using share permissions and restrictive access using NTFS permissions. Do the following to set share permissions so that all network users are given full control of both folders:

1. Log on to Computer1 as an administrator. Open the Properties dialog box for the Medical folder, and click the **Sharing** tab. In Windows 8, click **Advanced Sharing**. Check **Share this folder**, and then click **Permissions**. If necessary, add the Everyone group. Select **Everyone**, and check **Allow** next to **Full Control**. Click **Apply**, and then click **OK**. Click **Apply** again, and then click **OK**. In Windows 7, click **Share**. In the drop-down list, select **Everyone** and click **Add**. In the Name column, click **Everyone**, and, in the Permission Level column, select **Read/Write**. Click **Share**. Close the Properties dialog box.

2. In the same way, set share permissions for the Financial folder.

Even though share permissions allow full access, the NTFS permissions set earlier in this lab will limit access. Do the following to test your security settings for network users:

1. On Computer2, log on as an administrator.

2. Create user accounts for Lucas, Nancy, Adam, Linda, and Carlos. Make the password for each account the name of the user.

> **Notes** If Computer2 uses a Windows 8 or Windows 7 Home edition, you must use the PC settings page or Control Panel to create user accounts.

3. Log off and log back on to Computer2 as **Lucas**. Verify Lucas can access both the Medical and Financial folders on Computer1. If you have a problem accessing the folders, go back and check your work, making sure all settings are correct. If you still have a problem, try logging off and logging back on. If that doesn't work, try restarting both computers.

4. Log off and log back on to Computer2 as **Nancy**. Verify Nancy can access the Medical share but not the Financial share on Computer1. What text appears in the Network Error box when Nancy tries to access the Financial share?

_____

_____

5. Log off and log back on to Computer2 as **Adam**. Verify Adam can access the Medical share but not the Financial share on Computer1.

6. Log off and log back on to Computer2 as **Linda**. Verify Linda can access the Financial share but not the Medical share on Computer1.

7. Log off and log back on to Computer2 as **Carlos**. Verify Carlos can access the Financial share but not the Medical share on Computer1.

REVIEW QUESTIONS

1. Why is it necessary that Computer1 run Windows 8 or Windows 7 Professional or higher edition to implement the security used in this lab?

_____

_____

2. When viewing the permissions assigned to a folder, why might these permissions be grayed out so that you cannot change them?

_____

_____

3. When assigning permissions to a folder, why might you allow full permissions to the Administrators group?

_____

4. What is the purpose of turning on the _Use user accounts and passwords to connect to other computers_ setting in the Advanced sharing settings window?

_____

_____

LAB 17.6 WORK WITH OFFLINE FILES

OBJECTIVES

The goal of this lab is to learn to work with offline files. After completing this lab, you will be able to:

▲ Enable offline files in Windows

▲ Make network files available offline

▲ Sync offline files with the network

MATERIALS REQUIRED

This lab requires the following:

◢ Two or more Windows 8 or Windows 7 computers networked together. At least one computer must use Windows 8 or Windows 7 Professional or higher.

◢ Internet access

> **Notes** It is recommended that you complete the first lab in this chapter, "Map a Network Drive and Use Wake-on-LAN," before tackling this lab.

LAB PREPARATION

Before the lab begins, the instructor or lab assistant needs to do the following:

◢ Verify Windows starts with no errors

◢ Verify Internet access is available

◢ Set up a simple network with two or more computers

ACTIVITY BACKGROUND

Sometimes, you need access to network files when the network is not available. Maybe you're traveling and you can't find a wireless connection or maybe the server is being updated and it's temporarily unavailable. Windows allows you to work with offline files and then sync up the changes with the network files later. In this lab, you set up some network files so they can be changed offline.

ESTIMATED COMPLETION TIME: 45 MINUTES

 Activity

In this lab, Computer1 is serving up a folder that is used by Computer2. Computer2 will use offline files to use the folder even when it is not connected to Computer1. Offline files is a feature of Windows 8 Professional or Enterprise editions or Windows 7 Professional, Ultimate, or Enterprise editions. Therefore, Computer2 must be using one of these editions.

1. Begin with two networked Windows computers and test your network connection. What method or utility did you use?

   _____

2. Computer1 will be your server. Using Computer1, create a folder named **Offline Files** in the root of drive C:. Share this folder with the Everyone group. (If you need help sharing the folder, see the first lab in this chapter, titled "Map a Network Drive and Use Wake-on-LAN.") In the folder, create a small text document. What is the exact name and path of your shared folder and file?

   _____

3. Computer2 must be using Windows 8/7 Professional or higher. Log on to Computer2, and create a mapped network drive to the shared folder. If you need help with this step, see the first lab in this chapter, titled "Map a Network Drive and Use Wake-on-LAN."

4. Still using Computer2, open the text file to test your connection.

5. Open the **Computer** window, right-click the drive you just mapped, and select **Always available offline** in the shortcut menu.

6. To open the Sync Center, in Windows 8, on the Start screen type **Sync Center,** and select it from the search results. In Windows 7, click **Start,** type **Sync Center** in the Search box, and then press **Enter.** In the left pane of the Sync Center, click **View sync partnerships,** if it is not already selected. The window reports progress syncing the files (see Figure 17-5). Note any messages or conflicts here:

_____

Figure 17-5   The Sync Center is used to manage your offline files

You can work with offline files by following these steps:

1. Temporarily remove Computer2 from the network by unplugging the network cable or disabling the network adapter. Windows will automatically enable offline files whenever the network is not available.

2. Open File Explorer/Windows Explorer, and open the offline version of the shared text file.

3. Make a small change to this file. What change did you make?

_____

4. In the Sync Center, click **Manage offline files.** The Offline Files dialog box opens. Answer the following questions:

◢ What objects are listed when you click **View your offline files?**

_____

_____

◢ How can you change the amount of space available for storing offline files on your computer?

_____

_____

◢ How can offline files help you when you are experiencing a slow network connection?

_____

_____

5. Now reconnect Computer2 with the network.

6. Windows updates offline files automatically, but not continuously. To make sure the offline file is updated, go to the Sync Center, right-click **Offline Files,** and then click **Sync Offline Files.**

7. After the sync finishes, go to Computer1, and, if necessary, log on. Open the shared file. Did the file update with offline changes made from Computer2?

_____

CHALLENGE ACTIVITY (ADDITIONAL 20 MINUTES)

Suppose you are working with offline files while disconnected from the network and you make a change to the file on your local computer while another change is made to the same file stored on the host computer. What happens when you reconnect to the network and sync your offline files? Which change is kept and which change is lost? Set up this scenario, and describe what happens:

_____

_____

_____

REVIEW QUESTIONS

1. What are some reasons you might choose to set up offline files?

_____

_____

_____

_____

2. How is working with offline files different from simply making a second copy of the files you need to access?

_____

3. Why might encrypting your offline files be necessary? Describe at least one situation when encrypting your offline files might be appropriate:

_____

_____

_____

4. Why might you choose to work with offline files even if the network is available?

_____

_____

Security Strategies

Labs included in this chapter:

- **Lab 18.1:** Monitor Security Events
- **Lab 18.2:** Audit Access to Private Folders
- **Lab 18.3:** Use Encryption
- **Lab 18.4:** Deal with a Rootkit
- **Lab 18.5:** Secure a Workstation
- **Lab 18.6:** Protect Against Malware in Windows 8
- **Lab 18.7:** Download and Use Microsoft Security Essentials in Windows 7

LAB 18.1 MONITOR SECURITY EVENTS

OBJECTIVES

The goal of this lab is to use Event Viewer to monitor security events such as failed attempts to log on to the system or changes to files and folders. Multiple failed attempts at logging on to a system can indicate a potential hacker, and sometimes audit reports can help identify unauthorized use of a file or folder. After completing this lab, you will be able to:

⊿ Use the Local Security Policy tool in Control Panel to set policies to monitor failed logon attempts and changes to files and folders

⊿ Use Event Viewer to monitor the events of failed logons and changes to files and folders

MATERIALS REQUIRED

This lab requires the following:

⊿ Windows 8 operating system, Professional or Enterprise edition or Windows 7 operating system, Professional, Ultimate, or Enterprise edition

⊿ An account with administrator privileges

LAB PREPARATION

Before the lab begins, the instructor or lab assistant needs to do the following:

⊿ Verify Windows starts with no errors

⊿ Verify each student has access to a user account with administrator privileges

ACTIVITY BACKGROUND

As part of its efforts to manage the security of a computer or network, your organization might ask you to report incidents of suspicious events such as failed attempts to log on (indicating a potential hacker) or unauthorized changes to certain files. For example, suppose an employee is suspected of stealing from the company; you might be called on to monitor any changes to the bookkeeping files to which this employee has access but would not normally change.

You can track auditing events by setting policies using the Local Security Policy tool, and then using Event Viewer to monitor the logged events.

The Local Security Policy tool is one of the Administrative tools available in Control Panel. The tool creates security policies that apply only to the local computer. If you needed to set other policies, you would need to use Group Policy, which covers a wider range of policies than does the Local Security Policy tool.

ESTIMATED COMPLETION TIME: 30 MINUTES

 Activity

Repeated failures at logging on to a system might indicate someone is trying to guess a password and gain unauthorized access to a user account. Follow these steps to use Local Security Policy to monitor failures when someone is attempting to log on to the system:

1. Log on as an administrator, and create a new standard user account called **Newuser**. Create a password for this new user account. What is that password?

2. Using Control Panel, open **Administrative Tools**. Double-click **Local Security Policy**. The Local Security Policy window opens.

3. Expand the **Local Policies** group, and select **Audit Policy**. How many policies appear in the right pane for the Audit Policy group?

4. Double-click **Audit account logon events**. The Audit account logon events Properties dialog box opens. Check the **Failure** check box, as shown in Figure 18-1, and then click **OK**. Do the same for the **Audit logon events policy**.

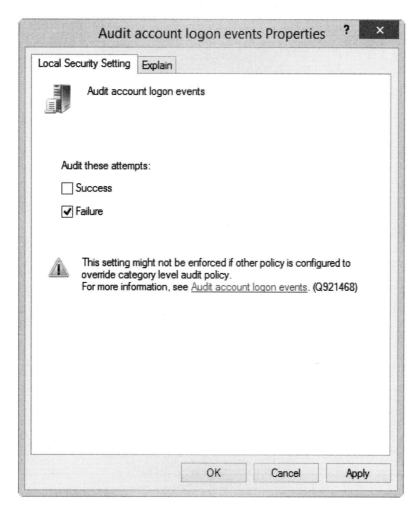

Figure 18-1 Local Security Policy set to audit failed logon events

5. Examine the other Audit Policy policies. Which one would you use to monitor when a password is changed? Close the Local Security Policy window.

6. To see the logged audit events, open **Event Viewer** from the Administrative Tools window. In the left pane, click **Windows Logs**, and then click **Security**. How many events are logged in this group of events? Does Event Viewer currently list any logon failures?

7. Log off, and attempt to log on to the Newuser account using an incorrect password.

8. Now log back on using an administrator account.

9. Open Event Viewer and again click **Security**, as shown in Figure 18-2. What is the date and time that Windows recorded for the failed logon attempt?

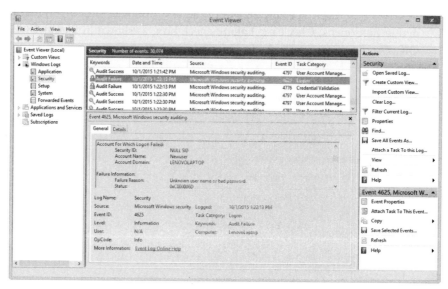

Figure 18-2 Event Viewer displays the failed logon event

Follow these steps to monitor changes to files and folders:

1. Open the Local Security Policy window, and locate the Audit Policy policies, as you did in Steps 2 and 3 earlier in this lab. Double-click **Audit object access**. The Audit object access Properties dialog box opens. Click the **Explain** tab, and answer the following questions:

   ◢ What is a SACL?

   ◢ Which dialog box do you use to set a SACL for a file system object?

2. On the Local Security Setting tab, check the **Success** and **Failure** check boxes, and then click **OK**.

3. Close the Local Security Policy window.

4. Now let's set Windows to audit activity in the Public folder. To do so, in File Explorer/ Windows Explorer, open the **Properties** dialog box of the C:\Users\Public folder, and then click the **Security** tab.

5. Click **Advanced**, select the **Auditing** tab, and then click **Continue**.

6. The Advanced Security Settings for Public dialog box opens. You can now add users or groups that you want to monitor.

7. Click **Add**. In Windows 8, click **Select a principal**. Click **Advanced**, click **Find Now**, select **Newuser**, and then click **OK**.

8. Click **OK** to close the Select User or Group window.

9. In Windows 8, change the Type to **All**, and check **Full Control**. Click **OK** to close the Auditing Entry for Public dialog box. In Windows 7, check the **Full control** check boxes in the Successful and Failed columns, and click **OK** to close the Auditing Entry for Public dialog box. Click **OK** to close the Advanced Security Settings for Public dialog box. If error dialog boxes appear, click **Continue** to close each box.

10. Close all windows, and log off the system.

11. Log on as **Newuser**, and open the C:\Users\Public folder. While you're there, use Notepad to create a short text file and save it to this location. What did you name your text file?

_____

12. Log off as Newuser, and log back on using your administrator account.

13. Open **Event Viewer**. In the left pane, select **Event Viewer (Local)**. In the Summary of Administrative Events section, double-click **Audit Success** to open that group of events. Double-click the first event in the group named **Microsoft Windows security auditing**. Maximize the window so you can easily view information about each event.

14. Explore the recent events in this section until you find the ones that are associated with Newuser's activity in the C:\Users\Public folder. You might need to search other Microsoft Windows security auditing events to find the relevant events. About how many events were created?

_____

15. List one event that is related to the creation of the new text file:

_____

16. Close all open windows.

REVIEW QUESTIONS

1. How can you use the Local Security Policy to determine if someone has tried to hack into a user account?

_____

_____

2. When securing a system, why is it important to audit failed attempts to access files?

_____

_____

3. Which policy would you use to monitor when a user changes her password?

_____

4. In this lab, you monitor the activity of a single user. What would be a more efficient way to monitor the activities of a collection of users?

_____

5. Why does accessing one file create multiple events?

_____

_____

LAB 18.2 AUDIT ACCESS TO PRIVATE FOLDERS

OBJECTIVES

The goal of this lab is to learn how to set up folder auditing so that you can determine if unauthorized users attempt to access a private folder. After completing this lab, you will be able to:

◢ Use a local security policy to require a password for all user accounts

◢ Configure Windows to log attempts to access a private folder

◢ View the event log for folder access attempts

MATERIALS REQUIRED

This lab requires the following:

◢ Windows 8 or Windows 7 operating system, Professional or higher edition

◢ An account with administrator privileges

LAB PREPARATION

Before the lab begins, the instructor or lab assistant needs to do the following:

◢ Verify Windows starts with no errors

◢ Verify each student has access to a user account with administrator privileges

ACTIVITY BACKGROUND

Although auditing of file and folder access is usually not necessary for home computers with only a few trusted users, it can be useful in a networked environment with many users where all users are not trusted with complete access to all resources. You can set up Windows to audit activity on a file or folder so that whenever the file or folder is accessed, this activity is recorded in a log. Each user has a user profile in the C:\Users folder, and a standard user should not be able to access the folders that belong to another user. In this lab, you set up a user profile for a user, configure Windows to audit the folder, attempt to access the folder, and verify the access attempt was logged.

ESTIMATED COMPLETION TIME: 30 MINUTES

 Activity

PART 1: SET A LOCAL SECURITY POLICY TO REQUIRE PASSWORDS FOR USER ACCOUNTS

In the first part of the lab, you set a local security policy to require a password on all accounts. To see the effect of the policy, you create one standard user before you set the security policy in order to verify a password is not required for the account. Then, you create another user after you set the policy and verify a password is now required. Recall that the Local Group Policy Editor is only available in the Professional or Enterprise editions of Windows 8 or the Professional, Ultimate, and Enterprise editions of Windows 7, and can be run only by an administrator. Do the following to create a standard user account:

1. Log on to the computer as an administrator.

2. Using the Computer Management window, create a standard user named **User1**, without a password.

3. Log off and log back on as **User1**. Note that you are not prompted for a password. When a user first logs on, his user profile namespace is created in the C:\Users folder. These folders are private and can be accessed only by the owner of the folder and administrators.

Do the following to set the local security policy:

1. Log off and log back on as an administrator. To start Group Policy in Windows 8, on the Start screen, type **gpedit.msc** and select it from the search results. In Windows 7, click **Start**, type **gpedit.msc** in the Search box, and then press **Enter**. The Local Group Policy Editor console opens.

2. In the left pane, expand **Computer Configuration, Windows Settings, Security Settings,** and **Account Policies,** and then click **Password Policy.**

3. Double-click **Minimum password length** in the right pane. When the Minimum password length Properties window opens, click the **Explain** tab, and read the information about password length.

4. Click the **Local Security Setting** tab, enter a non zero value in the text box, and then click **OK.** Close the Local Group Policy Editor console.

Any new user accounts created will now need a password. Existing user accounts will not be affected until their passwords are created or changed. To verify this, you'll create another user account, and then log on with that account. Follow these steps:

1. Using the Computer Management window, create a standard user named **User2**, without a password. An error message appears saying the minimum password requirement was not met. Add the password, and create the user. Log off the computer.

2. Log on as **User2**.

PART 2: ATTEMPT TO ACCESS A PRIVATE FOLDER

To verify the folders that belong to User1 are not accessible to other users, attempt to access the folders while you are logged on as User2. Follow these steps:

1. In the address bar of File Explorer/Windows Explorer, type **C:\Users\User2** to navigate to the folders that belong to this user. A user has full access to his own private folders.

2. In the address bar of File Explorer/Windows Explorer, type **C:\Users\User1**. A message informs you that you don't have access to the folder. Click **Continue**, and note that you must supply an administrator password to open the folder. Click **No**, and log off the computer.

PART 3: AUDIT FOLDER ACCESS

In this part of the lab, you configure Windows to audit access attempts on the private folders that belong to another user. First, you enable auditing in Group Policy, and then you configure auditing options on a specific folder in the folder's Properties window. Follow these steps:

1. Log on to the computer as an administrator. Use **gpedit.msc** to open the Local Group Policy Editor console again.

2. In the left pane, expand **Computer Configuration, Windows Settings, Security Settings,** and **Local Policies,** and then click **Audit Policy.**

3. Double-click **Audit object access** in the right pane to open the Audit object access Properties dialog box. Note that you can audit successful attempts, failures, or both. For the purposes of this lab, you'll audit failures only. Check the **Failure** check box, and, if necessary, uncheck the **Success** check box. See Figure 18-3. Click **OK.** Close the Local Group Policy Editor console.

Figure 18-3 Audit failed logon attempts

Next, you edit the properties of the C:\Users\User1 folder to enable auditing for that folder. Follow these steps:

1. In File Explorer/Windows Explorer, navigate to C:\Users, and right-click the **User1** folder. If a warning dialog box opens, click **Continue** to access the User1 folder.

2. Select **Properties** in the shortcut menu, and then click the **Security** tab. Click **Advanced**, click the **Auditing** tab, and then click **Continue** to view the folder's auditing properties. The Advanced Security Settings for User1 dialog box opens.

> **Notes** Only administrator accounts are able to use the Advanced Security Settings dialog box.

3. The auditing entries box will be blank because no entries have been added yet. Click the **Add** button, and in Windows 8, click **Select a principal**, type **Everyone** in the Select User or Group dialog box, and then click **OK**.

> **Notes** To delete an auditing entry you find already listed, select it, and then click **Remove**.

4. In Windows 8, change the type to **Fail**. If necessary, click **Show advanced permissions**. Check the **Traverse folder/execute file** check box and the **List folder/read data** check box, as shown in Figure 18-4. In Windows 7, in the Auditing Entry for User1 dialog box, place check marks in the **Failed** column for Traverse folder/execute file and List folder/read data. At the bottom of the dialog box, select the option to apply these auditing settings only to objects and/or containers within this container. Click **OK** four times to close the open dialog boxes. When you click OK to apply the changes, you might receive an Error Applying Security message. Some folders will not allow this audit policy to be applied. Click **Continue** to continue applying the audit policy to other folders. You might have to address this error message several times.

5. Log off the administrator account.

Figure 18-4 Use check marks to indicate types of access to be audited

Next, you attempt to access the User1 folder with an unauthorized account. Then, you view the event that is logged in the Event Viewer. Follow these steps:

1. Log on to the computer as User2, and, as you did before, attempt to navigate to the **C:\Users\User1** folder. You should get the same message informing you that you don't have access to the folder.

2. Log off User2, and log back on as an administrator. Open Event Viewer by typing **Eventvwr.msc** on the Start screen or in the Start search box, or in Windows 8, right-click the **Start** icon and select **Event Viewer**.

3. In the left pane, expand **Windows Logs**, and then click **Security**.

4. In the middle pane, scroll through the list of events (if necessary) and look for an event for which "Audit Failure" appears in the Keywords column and "File System" appears in the Task Category column. There might be more than one event listed.

5. Double-click the event, and read the description in the top section of the General tab of the Event Properties dialog box. (You might need to scroll or resize the window to see all the details.) Note that the account name (User2) and the object name (C:\Users\User1) are both listed, as shown in Figure 18-5.

6. Close any open windows.

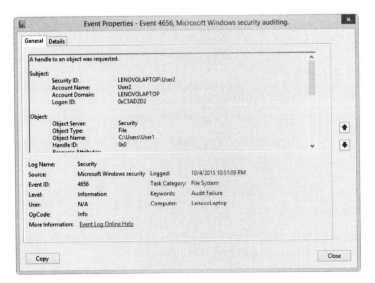

Figure 18-5 Use Event Properties to display details of an event

REVIEW QUESTIONS

1. What is the maximum number of characters that can be used in a Windows password?

_____

2. How can you configure Windows so that passwords are not required for user accounts?

_____

3. How can you configure a folder so that another user can view the files in the folder but not change them?

_____

_____

4. What group policy needs to be set to allow auditing of folder access attempts?

_____

5. Why is it important to require passwords for all user accounts on a computer when you want to audit access to a folder?

_____

6. What prevents a standard user from disabling auditing on a Windows computer?

_____

LAB 18.3 USE ENCRYPTION

OBJECTIVES

The goal of this lab is to work with Windows file and folder encryption. File and folder encryption is one method you can use when you want to secure important and private data. In this lab, you learn how to encrypt a folder and how to back up your encryption key. You also learn what happens when someone tries to use an encrypted file without permission, and how to move encrypted files from one storage device to another and from one computer to another. After completing this lab, you will be able to:

◢ Encrypt a folder

◢ Save files to the encrypted folder

◢ Back up the encryption certificate key

◢ Attempt to access the encrypted files as a different user

◢ Observe what happens when you move or copy an encrypted file or folder to another computer

MATERIALS REQUIRED

This lab requires the following:

◢ Windows 8 operating system, Professional or Enterprise edition or Windows 7 operating system, Professional, Ultimate, or Enterprise edition

◢ An account with administrator privileges

LAB PREPARATION

Before the lab begins, the instructor or lab assistant needs to do the following:

◢ Verify Windows starts with no errors

◢ Verify each student has access to a user account with administrator privileges

ACTIVITY BACKGROUND

Despite your best efforts to set secured permissions to files and folders, unauthorized users might still gain access to sensitive files. To further decrease the possibility of this type of security breach, you can use file encryption, which prevents unauthorized users from being able to view files, even if they do manage to gain access to them. The EFS (Encrypting File System) is a Windows feature that allows a user to store information on her hard drive in an encrypted format.

You can encrypt individual files or entire folders. Encryption is the strongest protection that the operating system offers to keep your information secure. The EFS is available on hard drives that are set up as NTFS drives. In this lab, you create and encrypt a folder and its contents. Then, you test the encryption and back up the encryption certificate key. Finally, you learn how to decrypt a file and move an encrypted file to another computer.

ESTIMATED COMPLETION TIME: 30 MINUTES

18

 Activity

Follow these steps to prepare your system for this lab:

1. Log on as an administrator.

2. Create a new standard user account. Assign a password to the account. List below the name and password of the new account:

_____

3. In File Explorer/Windows Explorer, open the **Documents** folder.

4. Create two folders in the Documents folder named **Normal Test** and **Encrypted Test**.

5. Create a text document in each folder. Name each document **TestFile**.

Now that you have the system prepared, let's work with the Encrypting File System. Follow these steps:

1. In the Documents folder, right-click the **Encrypted Test** folder, and select **Properties** in the shortcut menu.

2. On the General tab of the Encrypted Test Properties dialog box, click **Advanced**.

3. The Advanced Attributes dialog box appears. Check the **Encrypt contents to secure data** check box, and click **OK**.

4. Click **OK** to close the Encrypted Test Properties dialog box.

5. A Confirm Attribute Changes dialog box opens. This dialog box indicates the attribute *encrypt* has been chosen and asks how you want to apply this attribute. Select **Apply changes to this folder, subfolders and files**. Click **OK** to close the dialog box. A taskbar bubble might appear reminding you to back up your file encryption certificate and key.

When you start encrypting information, it is important to back up your encryption certificate. This is your key that unlocks the data. If you lose this key or the key is damaged and you didn't make a backup, the encrypted information can forever remain locked.

Follow these steps to create a backup of the encryption certificate:

1. In Windows 8, on the Start screen, type **certmgr.msc** and select **certmgr** from the search results. In Windows 7, click **Start**, enter **certmgr.msc** in the Search box, and then press **Enter**. The certmgr window opens (see the left side of Figure 18-6).

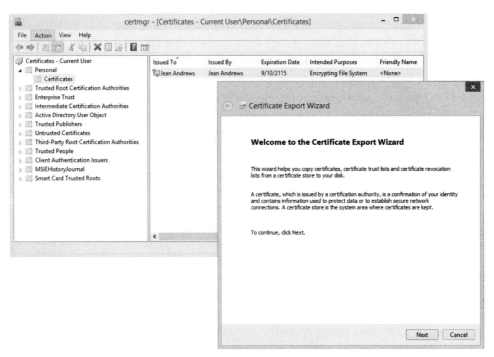

Figure 18-6 Use the certmgr window to back up encryption keys

2. In the left pane, select **Personal**, and then **Certificates**. In the right pane, select the certificate that shows **Encrypting File System** in the Intended Purposes column, as shown in Figure 18-6. If more than one certificate is listed, select them all.

3. On the menu bar, click **Action**, click **All Tasks**, and then click **Export**. The Certificate Export Wizard opens, as shown on the right side of Figure 18-6. Click **Next**.

4. Select **Yes, export the private key**, and click **Next**.

5. Select **Personal Information Exchange** for the file format, and click **Next**. The backup of the key will be saved in a PFX (.pfx) file.

6. Create a password for your key. Click **Next**. Write the password below:

_____

7. Click **Browse**. Navigate to where you want to save the file, name the file **Encryption Key Backup**, and click **Save**. What is the exact path and name of the file, including the file extension?

_____

8. To complete the process, click **Next**, click **Finish,** and then click **OK**.

Now that you have encrypted the folders and backed up the encryption key, let's investigate how an encrypted folder works. Follow these steps:

1. In File Explorer/Windows Explorer, in the Documents folder, what is the new color of the Encrypted Test folder name? What is the color of the file name in this folder?

> **Notes** If the folder is not shown in a different color, you can adjust that setting. To do so, in Windows 8, on the View ribbon, click **Options** to open the Folder Options dialog box. In Windows 7, click **Organize** in the window toolbar, and then click **Folder and search options**. In the Folder Options dialog box, click the **View** tab, and check the **Show encrypted or compressed NTFS files in color** check box (see Figure 18-7). Click **OK**.

Figure 18-7 Change the way folders and files appear in File Explorer/Windows Explorer

2. Verify the file in the Encrypted Test folder is encrypted. How did you verify encryption is applied?

---

3. Copy both the **Normal Test** folder and **Encrypted Test** folder to the root of drive C:. Are the contents of the Encrypted Test folder in the root of drive C: encrypted? How do you know?

---

4. Copy the **Normal Test** folder and the **Encrypted Test** folder to a USB flash drive. Are the contents of the Encrypted Test folder on the USB flash drive encrypted? How do you know?

_____

5. Log off, and then log on using the standard user account you created earlier in this lab.

6. Open File Explorer/Windows Explorer, and locate the **Normal Test** folder in the root of drive C: Describe what happens when you double-click the file in the Normal Test folder:

_____

7. Locate the Encrypted Test folder in the root of drive C:. Describe what happens when you double-click the file in the Encrypted Test folder:

_____

8. Log off, and then log on using your administrator account.

9. Upon reaching the desktop, return to the encrypted folder in the Documents folder.

Let's assume you have moved your files to another computer that supports the Encrypted File System. When you do so, the files are still encrypted. However, you will not be able to use them unless you use your private key to access the files. You must import the private key to the new computer. Follow these steps to see how the process works:

1. To import or install your private key on a computer, you must use the Certificate Import Wizard. To launch it, double-click the **Encryption Key Backup** file you created earlier. The Certificate Import Wizard opens. Click **Next** two times.

2. Enter the password you created to the private key file, and then click **Next**. On the Certificate Store box, click **Next**. Click **Finish**. The wizard reports the import was successful. Click **OK**. Now that your private key is installed, you can use the encrypted files and folders you have moved to this computer.

There are times you may need to decrypt a folder or file to return it to unrestricted use. Follow these steps:

1. In the Documents folder, right-click the **Encrypted Test** folder that you made earlier. Click **Properties**. On the **General** tab, click **Advanced**.

2. In the Advanced Attributes dialog box, uncheck the **Encrypt contents to secure data** check box. Click **OK**. Click **OK** again.

3. To confirm the attribute change, click **OK**. Verify the file in the Encrypted Test folder is no longer encrypted. Explain how you know the file is no longer encrypted:

_____

_____

REVIEW QUESTIONS

1. Which file system must be used to enable encryption?

_____

2. What is necessary so that a USB flash drive can be used to hold encrypted files and folders?

_____

3. When you move an encrypted file from one computer to a second computer, what must you do first before you can open the encrypted file on the second computer?

_____

_____

4. What happens to encryption when you move an encrypted file to a Windows 8 or Windows 7 Home Premium computer? Explain your answer:

_____

_____

5. What is the file extension for an exported certificate backup file?

_____

6. Why is it necessary to back up or export your encryption certificate key?

_____

_____

7. (Challenge Question) Why is encryption available in the NTFS file system and not in the FAT32 file system?

_____

_____

LAB 18.4 DEAL WITH A ROOTKIT

OBJECTIVES

The goal of this lab is to identify and remove a rootkit running on your system. After completing this lab, you will be able to:

◢ Create a bootable device with anti-malware installed that is capable of recognizing and removing rootkits

◢ Use AVG Rescue CD installed on a bootable USB flash drive to scan a computer for rootkits

MATERIALS REQUIRED

This lab requires the following:

◢ Computer capable of booting to a USB flash drive

◢ An account with administrator privileges

◢ EICAR virus test file downloaded from *eicar.org*

◢ Access to the AVG Rescue CD (for USB stick) Zip file, stored on a network share

◢ Internet access (optional–needed to update tool before running scan)

◢ USB flash drive with at least 500 MB free space

LAB PREPARATION

Before the lab begins, the instructor or lab assistant needs to do the following:

- ◢ Download the AVG Rescue CD (for USB stick) Zip file from *avg.com/us-en/download. prd-arl*, and store it on a network share for student access

- ◢ Verify each student or team has a USB flash drive with at least 500 MB free space

- ◢ Download the EICAR virus test file from *eicar.org/85-0-Download.html*, and store it on drive C: on each student computer. You probably need to disable the anti-malware software on each computer so that it does not automatically remove the file.

- ◢ Verify Windows starts with no errors

- ◢ Verify Internet access is available (optional)

- ◢ Verify each student has access to a user account with administrator privileges

ACTIVITY BACKGROUND

A rootkit is a type of malware that uses sophisticated methods to hide itself on the system. Rootkits can prevent Windows components, such as Windows Explorer, Task Manager, or the registry editor, from displaying the rootkit processes. This stealthy behavior makes it difficult for anti-malware software to detect a rootkit. When you have already tried other methods, such as anti-malware software, to clean your system, and you still believe your system might be infected, you can try using antirootkit software.

The best way to detect a rootkit is to scan the hard drive when Windows is not loaded. In addition, a system might be so badly infected that anti-malware software will not install or run. For both situations, you can create a bootable device that contains anti-malware software and use it to scan the system. This method does not require you to boot into Windows or install anti-malware software in Windows. In this lab, you create a bootable AVG Rescue CD (for USB stick), boot to the USB flash drive, and use it to run a scan to detect and remove malware.

The AVG Rescue CD (for USB stick) Zip file has been stored on a network share. Ask your instructor for the location of this file, and record the location here:

ESTIMATED COMPLETION TIME: 75 MINUTES

 Activity

Websites change often. The directions in this lab might need adjusting for changes that AVG makes to its website at *avg.com*.

PART 1: CREATE AND BOOT FROM THE AVG RESCUE USB FLASH DRIVE

Follow these steps to create a bootable USB flash drive that contains the AVG Rescue CD (for USB stick) software:

1. Log on as an administrator.
2. Plug in your USB flash drive. What drive letter did Windows assign to the drive?

---

3. Open your browser, and go to **avg.com/us-en/avg-rescue-cd#content**. Click **System Requirements**. How much RAM and hard disk space is required for this installation?

_____

4. Click the **Free Download** button. What are the types of files available for download?

_____

5. In the real world, you would download the Rescue CD Zip file from the AVG website. To save you time, however, in this lab, the file has been stored on a network share. Copy the Rescue CD (for USB stick) Zip file from the share to your desktop. What is the name of the Zip file?

_____

6. Right-click the Zip file, and select **Extract All** in the shortcut menu. The default extract location is your desktop. Allow this default. Click **Extract**. The extracted folder should now open in a window on your desktop.

7. Double-click the **setup.exe** file. If a SmartScreen error or the UAC dialog box opens, click **Run anyway** or **Yes** to continue. Select the drive letter of the USB flash drive, and then click **Install**. When the installation is complete, the Success dialog box opens. What message appears in the dialog box? Click **OK**.

_____

You are now ready to boot from the USB flash drive, which loads the Linux operating system. You can then use the anti-malware software on the flash drive to scan the system. Follow these steps:

1. Shut down the system, and reboot your computer to the USB flash drive. You might need to go into the UEFI/BIOS setup to change the boot device priority order so you can boot to the USB drive. A USB device might appear in the UEFI/BIOS setup as a Removable Drive.

2. When the system boots to the USB flash drive, an initial menu appears. You can let the menu time out, or press **Enter** to select AVG Rescue CD.

3. "I agree" is selected by default. Press **Enter**. If an information dialog box appears with the message, "Internet connection is not available," highlight **OK**, and press **Enter** to continue. AVG Rescue CD mounts the Windows partitions, and the Main Menu appears (see Figure 18-8).

Source: AVG Rescue CD

Figure 18-8 The main menu of the AVG Rescue CD provides access to utilities and other features

4. In the AVG Rescue CD program, you can use the arrow keys to move through a list and the Tab key to toggle between choices of action. Alternatively, you can enter the first letter (in bold red) of any selection to highlight it. Use the arrow keys to scroll down to **Utilities**. "Select" is highlighted by default. Press **Enter** to open the Utilities Menu. Read through the list of available utilities, and answer the following questions:

◢ Which tool can be used to change a setting in the Windows registry?

◢ Which tool can be used to repair a damaged Master Boot Record?

◢ Which tool can be used to attempt to repair a damaged hard disk?

---

5. If you don't have an Internet connection, skip the steps to update the virus database used by the AVG software. To skip this update, highlight **Return**, and press **Enter**. The Main Menu appears. Go to Part 2.

If you have an Internet connection, follow these steps to update the virus database used by the AVG software:

1. Select **Update** from the Main Menu. Highlight **Select**, and press **Enter**. The Update Type Menu appears (see Figure 18-9). Select **Online**. Highlight **Select**, and press **Enter**.

Source: AVG Rescue CD

Figure 18-9 The Update Type Menu allows you to update the virus database from the Internet

2. The Update Priority Configuration Menu appears. Leave "priority 2" selected to update the virus database. With **OK** highlighted, press **Enter**. The update should take a minute or two to run. When completed, highlight **Continue**, and press **Enter**.

PART 2: SCAN THE SYSTEM FOR MALWARE

The Main Menu is displayed. Do the following to perform the scan:

1. Use the up arrow to highlight **Scan**. With **Select** highlighted, press **Enter**. Verify **Volumes** is highlighted. With **Select** highlighted, press **Enter**.

2. The Scan Volumes Menu opens. You should see at least two volumes. One is your USB flash drive, and one is drive C: on your computer. If there are other partitions,

you might see other volumes, such as a hidden diagnostic partition or a second hard drive, on your computer. What are the types and sizes of the volumes that are shown?

---

3. You should be able to tell which volume is the drive C: partition by the size of the partition. Deselect all partitions except the drive C: partition. Then, highlight **OK**, and press **Enter**.

> **Notes** To deselect or select options, highlight an option, and then press the **Spacebar**. Notice that selected options are those with asterisks.

4. The Scan Options Menu appears. Review (do not change) the Scan Options. With the default options selected, highlight **OK**, and press **Enter**. The scan begins. The scan could take a long time to run, but it should find the EICAR_Test virus right away. After the virus is found, you can let the scan complete or cancel the scan. To cancel the scan, highlight **Cancel**, and press **Enter**.

> **Notes** To save time in this lab, you can point the scan to a specific folder where the EICAR_Test virus is located on drive C:, or you can copy the EICAR_Test virus to your USB flash drive and then search the flash drive.

5. After the scan is completed or is canceled, the results screen appears. It should show at least one infection found. Highlight **Continue**, and press **Enter**. The next page lists all rootkits, malware, and viruses found, and it presents options to deal with them all at once or individually. Verify the EICAR_Test virus is selected (an asterisk appears beside it). Highlight **Action**, and press **Enter**.

6. The Action Menu appears. What are the choices listed for actions?

---

7. Suppose the EICAR_Test file is a dangerous file you don't want on your system. To delete it, arrow down to **Delete**, highlight **Select**, and then press **Enter**. To confirm the deletion, highlight **OK**, and press **Enter**. The Scan Type Menu appears in case you want to scan other volumes or directories. We are finished, so right-arrow to **Return**, and press **Enter**. Right-arrow to **Exit**, and press **Enter**. Press **Enter** to verify you want to quit. If an Info window appears, highlight **OK**, and press **Enter**. This will take you to the Linux command prompt.

8. Press **Ctrl+Alt+Delete** to reboot your system. You might need to go back into the UEFI/BIOS setup to fix your boot settings so that you can start the system from the computer's hard drive.

9. Verify the EICAR_Test virus file is no longer on your drive C:.

10. Close any open windows.

REVIEW QUESTIONS

1. How are rootkits different from other forms of malware?

_____

_____

2. Why does running anti-malware software from another operating system (such as a Rescue CD/USB stick) do a better job than running the anti-malware software from Windows?

_____

_____

3. Which operating system does the AVG Rescue CD software use?

_____

_____

4. Why are kernel-mode rootkits more dangerous than user-mode ones?

_____

_____

5. Why should all other applications be closed before scanning for rootkits?

_____

_____

LAB 18.5 SECURE A WORKSTATION

OBJECTIVES

The goal of this lab is to learn how to secure a Windows 8 or Windows 7 workstation. After completing this lab, you will be able to:

◢ Require all users press Ctrl+Alt+Del to log on

◢ Require a password after the computer goes to sleep or screen saver mode

◢ Set a Local Security Policy

MATERIALS REQUIRED

This lab requires the following:

◢ A computer running Windows 8 or Windows 7 operating system, Professional or higher edition

◢ An account with administrator privileges

LAB PREPARATION

Before the lab begins, the instructor or lab assistant needs to do the following:

◢ Verify Windows starts with no errors

◢ Verify each student has access to a user account with administrator privileges

ACTIVITY BACKGROUND

Securing a workstation is one of the most important tasks you can perform when setting up security for an organization or individual. Windows provides some default security settings; however, these default settings are often exploited by malicious programs, thieves, and hackers. A few simple tweaks to your computer's security policy greatly improves the security of your system.

ESTIMATED COMPLETION TIME: 45 MINUTES

 Activity

Follow these steps to require that a user press Ctrl+Alt+Del to log on:

1. In Windows 8, on the Start screen, type **netplwiz**, and select it from the search results. In Windows 7, click **Start**, and in the Search box, type **netplwiz**, and press **Enter**. The User Accounts dialog box opens. Write down the user names displayed in the User Accounts dialog box:

_____

_____

2. Select the **Advanced** tab, and under "Secure sign-in" or "Secure logon," check the **Require users to press Ctrl+Alt+Delete** check box.

3. Apply the changes. Restart the computer to confirm the change has taken effect.

Follow these steps to secure the computer using a screen saver and sleep mode:

1. Open **Control Panel**. Select **Power Options**, and select **Require a password on wakeup** or **Require a password when the computer wakes**.

2. Under "Password protection on wakeup," make sure **Require a password (recommended)** is selected. If you need to change this setting, you might need to first click **Change settings that are currently unavailable**.

3. Save your changes, and close all windows.

4. In Windows 8, from the Start screen, type **Screen Saver**, and select **Change screen saver** from the search results. In Windows 7, click **Start**, and in the Search box, type **Screen Saver**, and press **Enter**. The Screen Saver Settings dialog box opens.

5. Select a screen saver from the drop-down menu to activate the screen saver function.

6. Check the **On Resume, display logon screen** check box. Apply your changes, and close all windows.

Follow these steps to require that all users have a password:

1. In Windows 8, from the Start screen, type **gpedit.msc**, and select it from the search results. In Windows 7, click **Start**, and in the Search box, type **gpedit.msc**, and press **Enter**. The Local Group Policy Editor console opens.

2. Navigate to **Computer Configuration, Windows Settings, Security Settings, Account Policies**, and, finally, **Password Policy** group.

3. Change the Minimum password length policy to a value higher than zero. How many characters did you require?

_____

18

Follow these steps to secure the computer using UEFI/BIOS settings:

1. Restart the computer, and access the UEFI/BIOS setup. To access the UEFI/BIOS setup, you need to press a key or combination of keys at the beginning of the boot. Look for a message to tell you which key(s) to press (for example, F2, Del, or F12).

2. After you are in the UEFI/BIOS setup utility, find the screen to change the security settings.

3. Enter a value for the password that must be entered in order to boot up the computer. This password might be called the power-on password, system password, boot password, or another name. Write down the name for this password given on your UEFI/BIOS setup screen and the password you assigned:

_____

4. Enter a value for the password that must be entered in order to make changes to the UEFI/BIOS settings. This password might be called the admin password, the supervisor password, or another name. Answer the following questions:

   ◢ What is the name for the admin password as described on your UEFI/BIOS setup screen and what is the password you assigned to it?

   _____

   ◢ Does your UEFI/BIOS setup support encrypting the hard drive? If so, describe the feature in UEFI/BIOS setup:

   _____

   _____

   ◢ What other passwords does your UEFI/BIOS setup offer that can be used to secure the computer? Name and describe each password:

   _____

   _____

   _____

5. Save your changes, and restart the computer.

Do the following to test the security settings you created in this lab and record the results of your test:

1. When the computer starts up, what is the message that appears asking you for the power-on password?

   _____

2. Were you required to press Ctrl+Alt+Del before you could see the Windows logon screen?

   _____

3. After you reach the Windows desktop, put the computer in sleep mode. Were you required to enter your Windows password before you could wake up the computer?

   _____

4. Use the Computer Management window to create a new user account with no password. Then, log off and log back on using the new user account. At what point in this

process did you receive a message that required you to create a password for the user account?

_____

5. Did any of the security measures you implemented in this lab fail during this testing process? If so, what was the cause of the problem?

_____

REVIEW QUESTIONS

1. Why is it preferable to require the Ctrl+Alt+Del key combination for logon?

_____

_____

2. Why would you want to require a password to log on after the screen saver activates or the computer comes back on from sleep mode?

_____

_____

3. How many characters should the minimum password length be for best security practice?

_____

4. What does setting the admin password (sometimes called the supervisor password) in UEFI/BIOS accomplish?

_____

5. Why would you want a power-on password?

_____

_____

_____

6. Should you rely only on the Windows password to protect your sensitive data stored on the hard drive? Explain your answer:

_____

_____

_____

_____

_____

_____

18

LAB 18.6 PROTECT AGAINST MALWARE IN WINDOWS 8

OBJECTIVES

The goal of this lab is to verify your computer is clean of malicious programs using Windows Defender or free malware removal software. After completing this lab, you will be able to:

⊿ Make sure Windows Defender is turned on

⊿ Check for and install the latest Windows Defender updates

⊿ Scan for spyware or other malicious software infecting your computer

MATERIALS REQUIRED

This lab requires the following:

⊿ Windows 8 operating system

⊿ Internet access

LAB PREPARATION

Before the lab begins, the instructor or lab assistant needs to do the following:

⊿ Verify Windows starts with no errors

⊿ Verify Internet access is available

⊿ Perform a backup of important files if necessary

ACTIVITY BACKGROUND

Malware removal software is one of the largest growing technology sectors today, as new malicious programs continually flood the Internet. Malware removal software is useful because malware hides from the user and is difficult to detect. As a user surfs the web, malware can be downloaded and installed without the user's knowledge or consent.

Microsoft Windows offers Windows Defender to protect a system against spyware, viruses, and other malware. Once you turn on Windows Defender, it will run automatically to scan for malware or other unwanted programs. Definitions need to be updated daily to keep up with new malware.

ESTIMATED COMPLETION TIME: 15 MINUTES

 Activity

Windows Defender will not run if other anti-malware software is running on your system. Follow these steps to turn off other anti-malware software, and then explore how Windows Defender works:

1. To find out if anti-malware software other than Windows Defender is running on your computer, go to the **Windows desktop**, click the **Action Center** flag in the taskbar, and then click **Open Action Center**. The Action Center opens.

2. Click the **Security** title to expand the Security section. If you find in the Security section that anti-malware software other than Windows Defender is running, turn off this anti-malware program. Close the Action Center.

3. To open the Windows Defender window, go to the **Start** screen, and type **defender**. Click the **Windows Defender** tile. The Windows Defender window opens (see Figure 18-10). In the figure, Windows Defender shows the computer is potentially unprotected.

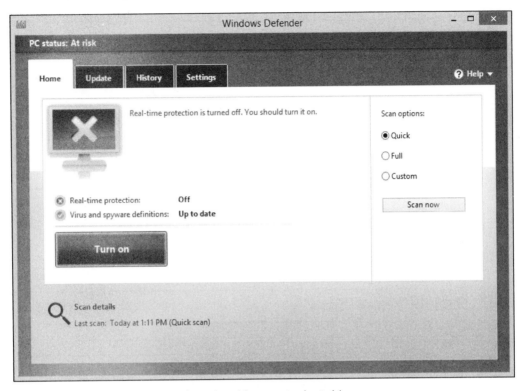

Figure 18-10 Windows Defender alerts that this computer is at risk

4. If your Real-time protection is off, click the **Turn on** button.

5. Click the **Update** tab, and then click **Update** to update your definitions.

After the virus and spyware definitions have finished updating, you are able to scan your computer with the most recent defenses against malware that Windows Defender offers. To scan your computer, follow these steps:

1. Return to the **Home** tab. With **Quick** selected as the scan option in the right pane, click the **Scan now** button.

2. After the scan is completed, you can see results from the scan. If any malicious software is found, complete the action requested by Windows Defender to remove the threat.

3. Repeat the scan, and remove any newly detected threats.

4. Keep repeating the scan until no threats are detected.

To change scan settings and delete quarantined items, follow these steps:

1. To change the scan settings, click the **Settings** tab. Explore the different setting groups in the left pane, and then click the **Advanced** group.

2. Select the boxes you want Windows Defender to use in future scans. If you made any changes, click the **Save changes** button.

3. To remove quarantined items from your computer, click the **History** tab. If necessary, with **Quarantined items** selected, click the **View details** button.

4. Select the items to delete, and click **Remove**, or to delete all quarantined items, click **Remove all**.

REVIEW QUESTIONS

1. Why is it important to use a malware removal program, such as Windows Defender, rather than just being careful while surfing the web?

   _____

   _____

   _____

2. Why is it important to update virus and spyware definitions on malware removal programs, and how often should they be updated?

   _____

   _____

3. Why would you want to quarantine malware, and how do you delete quarantined malware from your system? Why could this be important?

   _____

   _____

   _____

   _____

   _____

4. What are the options available in the Windows Defender settings? Why is the Real-time protection option important?

   _____

   _____

   _____

   _____

LAB 18.7 DOWNLOAD AND USE MICROSOFT SECURITY ESSENTIALS IN WINDOWS 7

OBJECTIVES

The goal of this lab is to learn how to use Microsoft Security Essentials to protect a computer from malware such as viruses, spyware, rootkits, and worms. After completing this lab, you will be able to:

◢ Download and install Microsoft Security Essentials

◢ Configure and use Microsoft Security Essentials

◢ Use the EICAR anti-malware test file to confirm anti-malware protection is active

MATERIALS REQUIRED

This lab requires the following:

⊿ Windows 7 operating system

⊿ An account with administrator privileges

⊿ Internet access

LAB PREPARATION

Before the lab begins, the instructor or lab assistant needs to do the following:

⊿ Verify Windows starts with no errors

⊿ Verify Internet access is available

⊿ Verify each student has access to a user account with administrator privileges

ACTIVITY BACKGROUND

As an IT support technician, you need to make certain that every computer you support has anti-malware software installed and that it is configured to receive automatic updates and run in the background. Many free and paid-by-subscription anti-malware software products are available and can be downloaded from the Internet. Among the free products, Microsoft Security Essentials is well rated and does a good job of protecting a system against malware. In this lab, you learn to download the software, install it, configure it, and make sure it is running in the background to protect a system against malware.

18

> **ESTIMATED COMPLETION TIME: 20 MINUTES**

 Activity

> **Notes** Websites change from time to time, so you might need to adjust the following steps to accommodate changes to the Microsoft site.

Follow these steps to download and install Microsoft Security Essentials:

1. Log on to Windows using an account with administrator privileges.

2. Using your browser, navigate to **windows.microsoft.com/mse**.

3. Click **Free download**.

4. Internet Explorer asks if you want to run or save mseinstall.exe. Select **Save**, and Internet Explorer will automatically save the file to the Downloads folder in the current user's home directory. When the download is complete, click **View downloads**.

5. In the View Downloads window, click **Downloads** beside the file name you just down-loaded.

   ⊿ What is the path and file name (including file extension) of the downloaded file? What is the size of the file?

   _____

6. Close your browser.

7. To execute the downloaded file, double-click the file you just downloaded to your Downloads folder. If necessary, respond to the UAC dialog box.

8. The Microsoft Security Essentials window appears. Click **Next**.

9. On the next screen, click **I accept** to agree to the license agreement.

10. On the next screen, choose whether or not you would like to participate in the Microsoft Customer Experience Improvement Program, and then click **Next**.

11. When the "If no firewall is turned on, turn on Windows Firewall (Recommended)" option appears, leave this box checked, and click **Next**.

12. On the next screen, click **Install**.

13. On the next screen, uncheck the **Scan my computer for potential threats after getting the latest updates** check box. Click **Finish**.

14. The Microsoft Security Essentials window opens with the Update tab active and the update process already running. This process installs the latest virus and spyware definitions, and then scans your computer for malware. Wait for the entire process to complete, which might take several minutes.

15. If necessary, click the **Home** tab. On the Home tab, look for the large green check mark, which indicates that the software is configured to automatically scan for malware and that the software is up to date (see Figure 18-11).

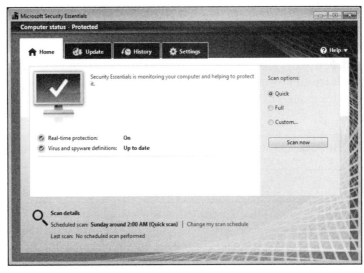

Figure 18-11   Microsoft Security Essentials is up to date with the latest virus and spyware definitions

16. Click the **History** tab. List below any suspicious items the scan recorded:

_____

_____

_____

17. Click the **Settings** tab. Answer the following questions:

▲ On what day of the week and time of day is a scan scheduled?

_____

▲ Is the software configured to check for the latest updates before running a scan?

_____

18. Click **Real-time protection**. What is the purpose of having real-time protection enabled?

_____

_____

19. List the steps to configure the software to scan removable drives:

_____

_____

_____

20. Close the Microsoft Security Essentials window.

21. To clean up your computer, delete the downloaded file in your Downloads folder. Which file did you delete?

_____

The EICAR anti-malware test file can be used to confirm your anti-malware software is working. Follow these steps to find out more:

1. Open Internet Explorer and navigate to **eicar.org/86-0-Intended-use.html**.

2. After reading the instructions for the use of the test file, scroll down the page and copy the ASCII string to your Windows Clipboard.

3. Open Notepad. Paste the string into Notepad, and save the file. What happens when you save the file?

_____

4. Open the Microsoft Security Essentials window, and click the **History** tab. Note any changes from when you viewed the list in Step 16 earlier in this lab:

_____

_____

REVIEW QUESTIONS

1. Why does EICAR release the anti-malware test string?

_____

_____

2. What is the name of the executable program file for Microsoft Security Essentials (not the downloaded file)?

_____

3. Why does Microsoft Security Essentials prompt you to activate Windows Firewall if a firewall is not active?

_____

4. Which tab on the Microsoft Security Essentials window do you use to find out the Virus definitions version and the Spyware definitions version?

_____

18

CHAPTER
19

Supporting Printers and Customizing a System

Labs included in this chapter:

- **Lab 19.1:** Install and Share a Local Printer
- **Lab 19.2:** Install a Network Printer
- **Lab 19.3:** Update Printer Drivers
- **Lab 19.4:** Maintain and Troubleshoot a Printer
- **Lab 19.5:** Manage Print Jobs
- **Lab 19.6:** Sabotage and Repair a Printer
- **Lab 19.7:** Compare Costs of Systems
- **Lab 19.8:** Plan a Customized System

LAB 19.1 INSTALL AND SHARE A LOCAL PRINTER

OBJECTIVES

The goal of this lab is to install and share a printer. After completing this lab, you will be able to:

◢ Install a local printer on a computer

◢ Share a local printer with other users on the network

◢ Using another computer on the network, install and use a shared network printer

MATERIALS REQUIRED

This lab requires the following:

◢ A USB printer and its printer drivers

◢ Two or more Windows 8 or Windows 7 computers connected to a network

◢ Access to the printer manual

LAB PREPARATION

Before the lab begins, the instructor or lab assistant needs to do the following:

◢ Verify Windows starts with no errors

◢ Verify one or more USB printers with printer drivers are available

◢ Verify the printer manual is available or that students have Internet access so they can locate the manual on the web

> **Notes** You can install drivers for a printer even when the printer is not available. If you are working in a computer lab that has no printer, most of this lab can still be done. You just won't be able to print a test page.

ACTIVITY BACKGROUND

A network printer connects directly to a wired or wireless network, and any computer on the network can access it. A local printer connects directly to a computer by way of a USB port, wireless Bluetooth, or other type of connection, and can be shared with other computers on a network. In order for the printer to appear as a network printer on the network, the computer with the printer physically connected to it must have file and printer sharing turned on.

In this lab, you install and share a printer, and then another computer on the network uses the shared printer.

ESTIMATED COMPLETION TIME: 45 MINUTES

 Activity

First, follow these steps to install a USB printer on one computer:

1. If the USB printer is connected to the computer, disconnect it.

2. To make sure the printer is not already installed in Windows, open **Control Panel**, and then click **Devices and Printers** (in Windows 7, you can click **Devices and Printers** directly in the Start menu). The Devices and Printers window opens.

◢ What make and model of printer are you using?

_____

_____

◢ Is the printer already installed in Windows?

_____

3. If the printer is already listed as an installed printer, right-click the printer icon, and select **Remove device** in the shortcut menu. Click **Yes** to remove the device.

4. With the printer turned off, connect the printer to the USB port on your computer. Next, turn on the printer. Windows has embedded USB printer drivers and automatically begins the process of installing the printer.

◢ Does the printer installation begin automatically?

_____

◢ Describe the messages that appear in Windows as the printer installs:

_____

_____

5. In the Devices and Printers window, a green check mark indicates the printer is the default printer. If it is not the default printer, make it the default printer.

◢ If a printer is not the default printer, how do you make it the default printer?

_____

_____

19

6. To verify the installation, print a Windows test page.

◢ List the steps you took to print the test page:

_____

_____

◢ Describe the type of information that prints on the Windows test page:

_____

_____

7. Close any open windows.

If you are troubleshooting a printing problem and the Windows test page does not print, the next step in the troubleshooting process is to print a test page at the printer. If the printer test page prints successfully, you have proven the problem is not with the printer itself. Do the following:

1. Disconnect the printer from the USB port.

2. List the steps you must take to print a test page at the printer. If you need help printing the test page, see the printer manual. If the manual is not available, search the web

for the printer manufacturer and model to find directions on how to use the printer.
Table 19-1 can help you find the correct website.

Printer Manufacturer	Website
Brother	brother.com
Canon	canon.com
Dell	dell.com
Epson	epson.com
Hewlett-Packard	hp.com
IBM	ibm.com
Lexmark	lexmark.com
OKI Data	okidata.com
SATO	satoamerica.com
TallyGenicom	tally.com
Xerox	xerox.com

Table 19-1   Printer manufacturers and their websites

3. Print a printer test page.

4. What type of information prints on the printer test page that does not print on the
   Windows test page?

5. Reconnect the printer to the computer.

If you are working in a lab that does not have a printer, follow these steps to install drivers for a printer:

1. Open the Devices and Printers window. Click **Add a printer**. In the Add Printer dialog
   box on a Windows 8 system, click **The printer that I want isn't listed** (you don't have
   to wait for the search to finish). Select the option **Add a local printer or network
   printer with manual settings**, and then click **Next**. On a Windows 7 computer, in the
   Add Printer box, click **Add a local printer**. On either Windows 8 or Windows 7, select
   Create a new port, and, if necessary, select **Local Port** from the drop-down menu.
   Click **Next**.

2. For the port name, type **VirtualUSB**, and then click **OK**.

3. Select a printer manufacturer and printer model, and then click **Next**. Click **Next** again.

4. Select **Do not share this printer**, and then click **Next**.

5. If available, check **Set as the default printer**, and then click **Finish**.

After the printer is installed, you need to make it possible for other computers in the network to access it.
Follow these directions to share the printer with other computers on the network:

1. Using the computer with the locally installed printer, open the **Devices and Printers**
   window. Right-click the printer, and click **Printer properties** in the shortcut menu.

2. Click the **Sharing** tab. Check **Share this printer,** and type a share name for the printer. Usually the share name is the name of the printer or the physical location of the printer. Make sure **Render print jobs on client computers** is selected.

▲ What is the share name?

_____

▲ What is the computer name?

_____

▲ List the steps you took to find the computer name:

_____

_____

_____

▲ What is the exact name of the shared printer on the network, including the computer name (include backslashes in your answer)?

_____

▲ Describe what happens to print jobs when the "Render print jobs on client computers" option is not selected:

_____

_____

3. Click **Additional Drivers.** Answer these questions:

▲ In the Additional Drivers dialog box (see Figure 19-1), which type of processor is selected?

_____

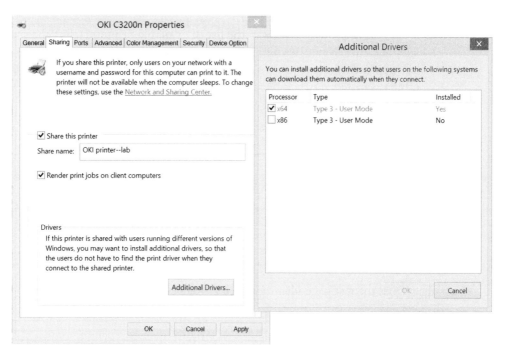

Figure 19-1 Decide which printer drivers Windows can make available to other computers that use the shared printer

⊿ What is the advantage of selecting both x64 and x86 processors?

_____

_____

⊿ Which option should be selected in the Additional Drivers dialog box if other computers on the network that have a 32-bit version of Windows installed will require the
printer drivers?

_____

4. Click **OK** to close the Additional Drivers dialog box. Close the printer properties dialog
   box, saving your changes. Using the Devices and Printers window, describe how you can
   tell that the printer is shared:

_____

The next step in ensuring that the printer appears as a network printer on the network is to configure
Windows to allow file and printer sharing. Follow these steps:

1. Open the Network and Sharing Center window, and click **Change advanced sharing
   settings.**

2. If necessary, turn on file and printer sharing. Save your changes and close all windows.

Before a remote computer can use the printer, printer drivers must be installed on the remote
computer. You can install a shared printer on a remote computer using the Devices and Printers
window in Control Panel or the Network window in File Explorer or Windows Explorer. Using
another computer on the network, follow these steps to install the shared printer using the Devices
and Printers window:

1. Open the Devices and Printers window, and then click **Add a printer**. On a Windows
   8 computer, wait for Windows to complete its search. On a Windows 7 computer, in
   the Add Printer box, click **Add a network, wireless or Bluetooth printer**, and wait for
   Windows to complete its search.

2. If the shared printer appears in the list of available printers, select the shared printer,
   and then click **Next,** (If you don't see the shared printer, skip to Step 3.) If a warning
   box appears asking if you trust this printer (see Figure 19-2), click **Install driver**. The
   printer is installed. Click **Next**. In the next dialog box, you are given the opportunity to
   print a Windows test page. Print the test page, and close all windows.

   ⊿ Did the Windows test page print successfully?

_____

   ⊿ On the Windows test page, what is the computer name?

_____

   ⊿ What is the complete printer name listed on the test page?

_____

   ⊿ Does the test page identify which remote computer printed the test page?

_____

Figure 19-2 Drivers for the printer will be copied from the computer that is sharing the printer to this Windows 7 computer

3. If the printer is not listed among available printers, click **The printer that I want isn't listed** (see the middle of Figure 19-2). On the next screen (see Figure 19-3 for both Windows 8 and Windows 7), select **Select a shared printer by name**, and then click **Browse**. Drill down to the computer that is sharing the printer, and then select the printer. Click **Select**, and then click **Next** to continue the printer installation.

(a)   (b)

Figure 19-3 In (a) Windows 8 or (b) Windows 7, browse to find a printer shared by a computer on the network

To see how you can use the Network window to install a shared printer, follow these steps using the same remote computer on the network:

1. First, use the Devices and Printers window to remove the printer.

2. On the same or another remote computer on the network, open the **Network** window.

3. In the group of computers on the network, drill down to the computer that is sharing the printer. Right-click the shared printer, and click **Connect**.

4. Return to the Devices and Printers window. Is the printer listed as an installed printer?

REVIEW QUESTIONS

1. Where would a 32-bit installation of Windows find drivers for a shared USB printer when the printer is being shared by a computer that has a 64-bit installation of Windows installed? Will these drivers be 32-bit drivers or 64-bit drivers?

_____

_____

2. When troubleshooting a printing problem, what advantages does printing a Windows test page from the printer properties dialog box in Windows have over printing a test page using buttons at the printer?

_____

_____

_____

3. Can you still print on a shared printer from a remote computer when the host computer is shut down?

_____

4. What two characters precede a computer name on the network?

_____

5. What two windows can be used to install a shared printer?

_____

_____

LAB 19.2 INSTALL A NETWORK PRINTER

OBJECTIVES

The goal of this lab is to install a network printer and then print to it from a remote computer on the network. After completing this lab, you will be able to:

⊿ Install a network printer

⊿ Test the printer across the network

MATERIALS REQUIRED

This lab requires the following:

⊿ Windows 8 or Windows 7 operating system

⊿ Network printer, patch cable, printer driver files, and documentation

⊿ A functioning network

⊿ A workgroup of two to four students

LAB PREPARATION

Before the lab begins, the instructor or lab assistant needs to do the following:

⬦ Verify Windows starts with no errors

⬦ Verify the network printer, patch cable, printer drivers, and printer documentation are present and working

⬦ Verify the network is working

ACTIVITY BACKGROUND

A network printer connects directly to the network and doesn't require a host computer. After you connect a network printer directly to the network, any computer on the network can install it if they have the printer drivers. In this setup, each computer is responsible for managing the printer and its print queue.

In a large organization, where many users share a network printer, a network administrator might want more control over the network printer. She can set up one computer on the network as the print server. This one computer installs the network printer and shares the printer. Then other computers on the network install the printer by connecting to the shared printer. The result is that all print jobs must flow through this one computer. The network administrator can monitor and manage the use of the printer from this central location.

In this lab, you learn to install a network printer and connect to it from other computers on the network. In this lab, it is assumed that the network printer and all the networked computers belong to the same subnet. Printing across subnets is not covered in this lab.

ESTIMATED COMPLETION TIME: 30 MINUTES

19

 Activity

The following steps describe the default method for installing a network printer. However, printer manufacturers often provide specialized steps and/or software for installing their devices. In that case, you should follow the steps your printer manufacturer prescribes rather than the steps listed here.

A network printer can be identified on the network by its IP address or printer name. Follow these steps to install a network printer using its IP address:

1. Attach your printer to the network using a network patch cable. Turn the printer on. The printer should indicate in some way that it is connected to the network. For example, many network printers have a control panel that says "Ready" or "Online."

   ⬦ How does your printer indicate that it is connected to the network?

   _____

   ⬦ Most printers can print a status page telling you their IP addresses or can display the IP address in the control panel. Consult the printer's documentation or the web to figure out how to determine the IP address of your printer. How did you determine the IP address for your printer, and what is it?

   _____

   _____

   _____

Go to a computer on the network, and follow these steps to install the network printer using Windows 8 or Windows 7:

1. Open the **Devices and Printers** window, and launch the Add Printer Wizard, as you did in the previous lab. In Windows 7 only, click **Add a network, wireless or Bluetooth printer**, and then click **Next** if necessary.

2. Notice that Windows will begin to search the network for available printers. If your printer is displayed, select it, and then click **Next**. Follow the on-screen directions to install the network printer and print a Windows test page to confirm the installation.

3. If the printer is not listed, click **The printer that I want isn't listed**. The dialog box shown earlier in Figure 19-3 (for either Windows 8 or Windows 7) appears. If another computer, such as a print server, were sharing the printer, you could browse to find the shared printer or identify the shared printer by name. Because your printer is connected directly to the network, select **Add a printer using a TCP/IP address or hostname**, and click **Next**.

4. Enter the IP address assigned to your printer, and then click **Next**. Follow the on-screen instructions to complete the installation.

5. When the installation is complete, print a test page to test your printer.

When installing a network printer using its IP address, the printer must use the same IP address each time it connects to the network. Follow these steps to learn more:

1. Turn off the printer, and then turn it back on. What is the new IP address of the printer? Did the IP address change?

_____

2. Using controls at the printer, determine if the printer is set to use static IP addressing or dynamic IP addressing, and make note of the address configuration below:

_____

3. For best results, a network printer should be configured for static IP addressing. However, you might encounter a situation in the field where a printer is using dynamic IP addressing. If the printer is using dynamic IP addressing, the DHCP server (for example, a router that provides this service) might be serving up the same IP address to this printer each time it connects to the network. For that to happen, the DHCP server must know the MAC address of the printer. Using controls at the printer, find the MAC address of the printer, and list the MAC address here:

_____

> **Notes** For easier printer installations, a network printer and all the computers that use it should be on the same subnet.

Some network printers serve up a browser-based utility that can be used to configure and manage the printer. Follow these steps to learn more:

1. Open a browser, and enter the IP address of the printer in the address box of the browser. Did the printer serve up a printer utility?

2. If the printer provides the utility, log on to the printer, and answer the following questions:

   ◢ Can you configure the IP address of the printer using the utility? If so, how is the IP address currently configured?

_____

◢ Outdated firmware on a network printer can sometimes cause problems. The printer's browser-based utility might provide a way to update the firmware. Search the utility for this feature. Did you find the ability to update the printer firmware? What is the version number of the current firmware?

_____

◢ List three other functions available in the utility. For each function, describe one way the function might be useful when managing the printer:

_____

_____

_____

Sometimes when you are having a problem installing a network printer, the solution is to use the setup program provided by the printer manufacturer. Follow these steps to learn more:

1. Using the Devices and Printers window, remove the network printer.

2. If you have the CD that contains the printer drivers, use this CD to install the printer.

3. If you don't have the CD that contains the printer drivers, use the web to search for the printer drivers on the printer manufacturer's website. Use Table 19-1 to help find the correct website.

◢ What is the network printer brand and model?

_____

◢ What is the website of the printer manufacturer?

_____

◢ What is the name of the file(s) you downloaded and used to install the printer?

_____

◢ Describe how the installation using the printer setup program differed from the installation using the Devices and Printers window:

_____

_____

_____

REVIEW QUESTIONS

1. A printer is connected locally on Computer1 and is shared on the network. Computer2 installs the shared printer and connects to it. Computer1 considers the printer to be a(n) _____ printer, and Computer2 considers the printer to be a(n) _____ printer.

2. Why should you use the manufacturer's prescribed method for installing its printer even if it differs from the default Windows method?

_____

3. Is it possible for a single printer to be both a local and a network printer? Why or why not?

_____

_____

_____

4. How can you determine the IP address of a network printer?

_____

_____

5. What would be the advantage of connecting a printer to a network server locally rather than having users connect to it directly through the network?

_____

_____

LAB 19.3 UPDATE PRINTER DRIVERS

OBJECTIVES

The goal of this lab is to practice updating printer drivers. After completing this lab, you will be able to:

- Identify driver information
- Locate new drivers
- Install new drivers
- Test printer drivers for functionality

MATERIALS REQUIRED

This lab requires the following:

- Windows 8 or Windows 7 operating system
- Internet access
- A local printer

LAB PREPARATION

Before the lab begins, the instructor or lab assistant needs to do the following:

- Verify Windows starts with no errors
- Verify Internet access is available

ACTIVITY BACKGROUND

Printer manufacturers often release new drivers for their existing printers to fix problems with earlier drivers, add new functions, support new applications, and accommodate new operating system features. An IT support technician needs to know how to update printer drivers as they become available. The process of updating printer drivers is similar to that for other devices. You must gather information about the device and the currently installed drivers, download the new drivers, and install them. As with other devices, after printer drivers are installed, you should test the printer to be certain it's functioning correctly before turning it over to end users. The process of updating printer drivers is similar across different Windows platforms and printer manufacturers.

This lab gives you general instructions for updating printer drivers. Modify these instructions to fit your situation and printer.

ESTIMATED COMPLETION TIME: 30 MINUTES

Activity

The first step in updating printer drivers is to gather information about your current printer and drivers. Use the Devices and Printers window and any other resources at your disposal to research and answer the following questions:

1. How is your printer generally used (for example, text, photographs, or graphics)?

_____

2. What operating system are you using? Are you using a 32-bit or 64-bit installation?

_____

_____

3. Who is the printer manufacturer?

_____

4. What is the model of the printer?

_____

5. What is the printer interface (USB, parallel, network, other)?

_____

6. Printers typically have many setup options that deal with print quality and paper handling. Open the Devices and Printers window, right-click the printer, and click **Printer properties** in the shortcut menu. Note any customized printer settings; you'll probably need to reapply them after the driver is updated. (Tabs on the properties dialog box might differ from one printer to another.)

_____

_____

_____

7. To identify the printer drivers, click the **Advanced** tab of the printer properties dialog box. What's the name of the driver listed in the Driver drop-down list?

_____

8. When you're finished, close any open windows.

Follow these general directions to locate available driver updates:

1. Go to the printer manufacturer's website, and locate the driver download section. Use Table 19-1 to help find the website. What's the URL of the driver download page?

_____

2. When you search for the correct driver on the website, you might find more than one driver that will work for your printer, operating system, or application. Generally, you should select the most recent version that matches your printer and operating system. There are exceptions, however. For instance, if a driver is listed as beta, it's still in development and has been released for evaluation. Usually, but not always, the manufacturer has most of the kinks worked out. To be on the safe side, don't download a beta release driver. List up to three drivers, with brief descriptions, for your printer and operating system:

_____

_____

_____

3. What driver did you select to download?

_____

4. Find and list any special installation instructions the manufacturer recommends:

_____

_____

5. Create a folder named **Downloads** on your C drive, if necessary. Then create a subfolder, such as C:\Downloads\Lexmark, named for the manufacturer. What's your folder name?

_____

6. Download the driver you intend to install to that folder.

With any device, it's best to follow the manufacturer's recommended method of installation instead of the Windows method. A good manufacturer tests the driver as well as the installation process. The exception is when you have several printers installed on a system and you think one set of drivers might overwrite files another printer needs. In this case, use the Windows method to update the drivers. Do the following to install the new driver using the manufacturer's installation process:

1. Print an example—a document or a digital picture—of the printer's main use. This printout verifies that your printer is working before you make any changes and is later used for comparison to verify the new drivers are working.

2. In File Explorer or Windows Explorer, double-click the file you downloaded. If it's a compressed file, it self-extracts the files or uses file compression software on your computer to extract the files. If an installation wizard starts after the files are extracted, exit it.

3. Were any files extracted? List the first three files here:

_____

4. Locate any Readme.txt files for late-breaking information about the installation.

5. Double-click the setup or install program. Document the process you used to install the new drivers:

_____

_____

_____

_____

Do the following to test the printer and new drivers:

1. Open the Devices and Printers window, and then print a Windows test page. Did the page print successfully?

_____

2. Apply any customized printer settings you recorded at the beginning of this lab.

3. Reprint the typical document or photograph, and compare it with the one printed before the driver update. List any differences you see:

_____

CHALLENGE ACTIVITY (ADDITIONAL 15 MINUTES)

Suppose you have shared a printer with other computers on the network. The host computer is using a 32-bit version of Windows 8, and you have made available 32-bit printer drivers to be used by other computers on the network when they install the shared printer. List the steps to make available 64-bit printer drivers for other computers on the network that use 64-bit installations of Windows:

_____

_____

_____

_____

_____

REVIEW QUESTIONS

1. List four reasons you might want to update a printer's drivers:

_____

_____

_____

_____

2. List four facts you should know about your printer before you start searching the web for updated drivers:

_____

_____

_____

_____

3. What does the label "beta release" indicate about a driver?

_____

4. Will 32-bit printer drivers work in a 64-bit installation of Windows?

_____

5. List the steps to print a test page in Windows:

_____

_____

LAB 19.4 MAINTAIN AND TROUBLESHOOT A PRINTER

OBJECTIVES

The goal of this lab is to practice supporting printers. After completing this lab, you will be able to:

◢ Use the web to help with printer maintenance

◢ Correct common printer problems

MATERIALS REQUIRED

This lab requires the following:

◢ Internet access

◢ A printer

LAB PREPARATION

Before the lab begins, the instructor or lab assistant needs to do the following:

◢ Verify Internet access is available

ACTIVITY BACKGROUND

Printers require more maintenance than most other peripheral devices. Paper gets jammed, ink cartridges and toner run out, and image or document quality can degrade due to dust and misalignment. Most manufacturers and many models have specific instructions for maintaining ink and toner cartridges, and these instructions apply exclusively to the targeted printers; thus, you must rely on the printer manufacturer for instructions when maintaining a printer. In this lab, you investigate maintenance and troubleshooting instructions for several types of printers.

Activity

Use the web to research how to solve the following problems. The printer is a high-end, color laser printer, the LaserJet Enterprise M750n printer, by Hewlett-Packard (*hp.com*). Answer these questions about routine maintenance for this printer:

1. What is the average number of pages that prints from one black toner cartridge? From one color toner cartridge? You'll need part numbers when ordering toner cartridges. What are the part numbers of the cartridges?

_____

_____

2. Besides toner cartridges, other replaceable printer parts include the paper tray, the fuser, and the parts used in the transfer portion of the printing process, which come as an assembled unit called a transfer kit. Find and list the part numbers for these items that are compatible with the LaserJet Enterprise M750n:

_____

_____

_____

3. What items are included in the transfer kit assembly?

_____

_____

_____

The next printer is an inkjet printer, the HP DeskJet 1010 printer. Answer these questions:

1. Printouts from your printer contain no black ink, but do include the three colors. You know that you replaced the black cartridge recently. Search the HP website, and locate the troubleshooting steps to solve the problem.

2. What is the first thing HP suggests you do when you experience this type of problem?

_____

3. If the ink level is low, HP instructs the user to replace the ink cartridge. What is the last step in replacing the ink cartridge, which might be easy for a user to forget to do?

_____

4. One troubleshooting step that HP suggests is that you clean the cartridge contacts. List the steps to do this on a Windows 7 or Windows 8 computer:

_____

_____

_____

19

5. If the problem isn't fixed, what does HP suggest that you check next?

_____

Next, follow these steps to learn how to perform routine maintenance or troubleshoot problems on your local printer:

1. List the following information to identify your local printer:

   ◢ Printer manufacturer:

   _____

   ◢ Printer model:

   _____

   ◢ Printer interface (USB, Bluetooth, other):

   _____

2. Search the manufacturer's website for troubleshooting and maintenance procedures, and answer the following questions:

   ◢ What types of problems are addressed for your printer?

   _____

   _____

   _____

   ◢ Does the manufacturer offer a printer maintenance kit? If so, what components are included and how much does the kit cost?

   _____

   _____

   _____

   ◢ What maintenance tips for your printer can you find on the website?

   _____

   _____

REVIEW QUESTIONS

1. When a printer isn't working correctly, what are two ways the problem is communicated to users?

   _____

   _____

2. Why do printers require more maintenance than other peripherals?

   _____

3. Besides the toner cartridges, what are three replaceable parts in a laser printer?

_____

4. When replacing an ink cartridge in an inkjet printer, what is the final step, which must be completed through Windows?

_____

LAB 19.5 MANAGE PRINT JOBS

OBJECTIVES

The goal of this lab is to learn how to use the printer queue to manage print jobs. After completing this lab, you will be able to:

◢ Use the printer queue to troubleshoot printing problems

◢ Stop and restart the Print Spooler service

MATERIALS REQUIRED

This lab requires the following:

◢ Two or more Windows 8 or Windows 7 computers connected to a network and belonging to the same Windows workgroup

◢ A local or network printer

◢ A workgroup of two to four students

LAB PREPARATION

Before the lab begins, the instructor or lab assistant needs to do the following:

◢ Verify Windows starts with no errors

◢ Verify a printer is available for each student workgroup

ACTIVITY BACKGROUND

A network administrator is typically responsible for a printer and any problems that might arise with print jobs not printing. One way to make this job easier is to use one computer as a print server, which manages print jobs for all users. In this lab, you can practice managing a printer from a centralized print server.

ESTIMATED COMPLETION TIME: 30 MINUTES

 Activity

For your workgroup of two or more computers, do the following to make sure the printer is available to all computers in your workgroup:

1. Using the knowledge that you've gained from previous labs, install a local or network printer on one computer, and designate this computer as the host computer or print server.

2. Install the printer on other computers in the workgroup. The installation should use the shared printer provided by the host computer.

3. On the host computer, in the Devices and Printers window, double-click the shared printer to view the queue, which will show no documents listed (see Figure 19-4).

Figure 19-4 Use the printer queue window to manage print jobs waiting to print or in the process of printing

> **Notes** When you double-click a printer in the Devices and Printers window, the printer window—where you can manage the print queue and other printer features—should appear. If the printer is not properly installed, a properties dialog box appears instead. The dialog box has only two tabs: the General tab and the Hardware tab. If you see this type of dialog box, go back and troubleshoot the printer installation. Try removing and reinstalling the printer.

4. Print a Windows test page from each computer in your workgroup. As the documents print, observe the printer queue on the host computer. Does every print job sent to the printer appear in the queue?

_____

5. Turn off the printer. On the remote computers, send new print jobs until three jobs are backed up in the queue. How can you tell which print job belongs to which computer or user?

_____

6. In what order are print jobs listed? Delete the first print job queued that has not yet printed.

_____

7. Turn on the printer. Did the other two print jobs print successfully?

_____

8. Remove the paper from the printer, and print a test page from each computer in your workgroup.

◢ What does the printer queue window report on the host computer about the problem?

_____

◢ What does the printer queue window on a remote user's computer report about the problem?

_____

The Windows Print Spooler service is responsible for managing the printer queue. If the queue gets stuck, one thing you can do is stop and restart the Print Spooler service. Do the following to learn more:

1. Verify you still have jobs waiting in the printer queue. Close any open windows, including the Devices and Printers window.

2. Enter **services.msc** in the Windows Search box, and press **Enter**. The Services console window opens. Make sure the **Extended** tab near the bottom of the window is selected (see Figure 19-5).

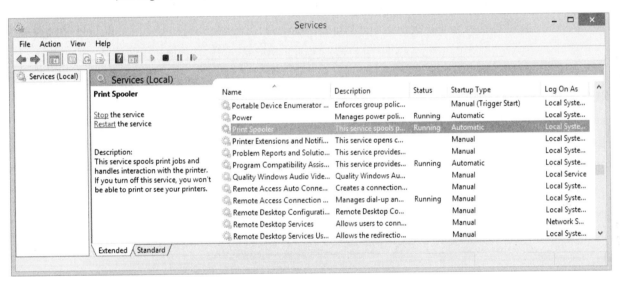

Figure 19-5   Use the Services console to stop and start the Print Spooler service

3. Scroll down to and select **Print Spooler**.

◢ What is the Status of the service?

_____

◢ What is the Startup Type of the service?

_____

4. With the Print Spooler service selected, click **Stop**.

5. Open the Devices and Printers window. Double-click the printer. Can you view the printer queue? Why or why not? Close the window.

_____

_____

6. Return to the Services console, and again select **Print Spooler**. Click **Start**. The spooler starts again.

7. Open the Devices and Printers window, and double-click the printer. Are the print jobs still in the print queue?

_____

8. Close the window.

Stopping and starting the Print Spooler can sometimes solve a print problem. In addition, you can manually delete all jobs in the queue while the service is stopped, which can solve a problem when a print job is corrupted. Follow these steps to learn more:

1. Return to the Services console, and stop the **Print Spooler**.

2. Windows stores queued print jobs in the C:\Windows\System32\spool\PRINTERS folder. Open File Explorer or Windows Explorer, and drill down to this folder. How many files are in the folder?

_____

3. Delete all files in this folder.

4. Use the Services console to start the **Print Spooler**.

5. Return to the Devices and Printers window. Are all jobs removed from the print queue?

_____

REVIEW QUESTIONS

1. If you are responsible for managing and maintaining a network printer, why might you want all print jobs routed through a print server?

_____

_____

2. What are the steps to delete a single print job in the printer queue?

_____

_____

_____

3. Group Policy can be used to prevent a user from installing a network printer and bypassing a host computer serving up the printer. What advantage does this group policy provide?

_____

_____

4. If a network administrator does not want to be called upon frequently to refill the paper in a printer, what can she do to make it easier for users to handle this chore?

_____

5. How do you permanently remove print jobs from the print queue when the Print Spooler service is not running?

_____

LAB 19.6 SABOTAGE AND REPAIR A PRINTER

OBJECTIVES

The goal of this lab is to learn how to troubleshoot problems with a printer. After completing this lab, you will be able to:

⊿ Identify symptoms of common printer problems

⊿ Troubleshoot printing issues

MATERIALS REQUIRED

This lab requires the following:

⊿ Two or more computers connected to a network and belonging to the same Windows workgroup, including one that shares a printer with other computers on the network

⊿ A workgroup of two to four students

LAB PREPARATION

Before the lab begins, the instructor or lab assistant needs to do the following:

⊿ Verify Windows starts with no errors

⊿ Verify a printer is available for each student workgroup

ACTIVITY BACKGROUND

Problems with a network printer are common, and an IT support technician is often called on to solve them. This lab gives you practice solving these types of problems.

ESTIMATED COMPLETION TIME: 45 MINUTES

 Activity

For your workgroup of two or more computers, do the following to make sure the printer is available to all computers in your workgroup:

1. Using the knowledge that you've gained from previous labs, install a local or network printer on one computer and designate this computer as the host computer.

2. Install the printer on other computers in the workgroup. The installation should use the shared printer provided by the host computer.

3. Trade systems with another group, and sabotage the other group's system while that group sabotages your system. The following list has some suggestions for preventing a computer from using the printer. Do something in this list, or think of another option:

   ⊿ On the host computer, remove the sharing option for the printer.

   ⊿ Uninstall the printer on a remote computer.

   ⊿ Pause printing on one or more computers.

   ⊿ Turn the printer off or turn it offline.

19

◢ Disconnect the printer cable from the host computer (for a local printer) or from the network (for a network printer).

◢ Remove paper from the printer.

◢ Introduce an error in the printer configuration on the host computer or a remote computer.

4. What did you do to sabotage the other team's system?

_____

_____

Return to your system and troubleshoot it. Complete the following:

1. Describe the problem as a user would describe it to you if you were working at a help desk:

_____

_____

2. What is your first guess as to the source of the problem?

_____

3. List the steps you took in the troubleshooting process:

_____

_____

_____

_____

4. How did you solve the problem and return the printing system to working order?

_____

_____

5. What might cause this problem to happen again?

_____

_____

_____

REVIEW QUESTIONS

1. How did you initially test the printer to see if it was working?

_____

_____

2. What should you do to make sure the printer itself is printing properly?

_____

3. For a network printer, what TCP/IP command can you enter at a command prompt to verify Windows can communicate with the printer?

_____

4. What would you do differently the next time you encounter the same indications of a printing problem?

_____

LAB 19.7 COMPARE COSTS OF SYSTEMS

OBJECTIVES

The goal of this lab is to compare a preassembled system with the components that could be assembled to build a comparable system. After completing this lab, you will be able to:

⊿ Identify the key components of a preassembled system

⊿ Locate prices for components needed to assemble a comparable system

⊿ Compare the costs of a preassembled system and a self-assembled system

MATERIALS REQUIRED

This lab requires the following:

⊿ Windows 8 or Windows 7 operating system

⊿ Internet access and/or access to printed computer publications

LAB PREPARATION

Before the lab begins, the instructor or lab assistant needs to do the following:

⊿ Verify Windows starts with no errors

⊿ Verify Internet access is available

ACTIVITY BACKGROUND

In this lab, you compare the cost of a brand-name system with the cost of a system having similar specifications but assembled from separate components. Brand-name manufacturers typically build their systems from parts that only they market; these parts are called proprietary parts. Therefore, it's unlikely that you'll be able to find exact matches for brand-name components. However, you can find comparable components. For example, if a Dell computer has a 1-TB, 7200 RPM hard drive installed, find another 1-TB, 7200 RPM hard drive for your list of parts. The idea is to find a close match for each major component so that you can compare the total cost of a brand-name system and a similar system built from parts. Use the Internet and available computer-related publications as your sources for information.

Activity

First you research a preassembled system and record information about its components.

1. Find an advertisement for a complete, preassembled system similar to the one in Figure 19-6. Some manufacturers you might want to check out are Lenovo (*lenovo. com*), Acer (*acer.com*), Dell (*dell.com*), HP (*hp.com*), Asus (*asus.com*), and Gateway (*gateway.com*).

Figure 19-6 The Best Buy website explains the product features of a complete, preassembled system

2. Study the advertisement you found and list the following specifications:
   ◢ Processor brand, model, and speed:

   _____

   ◢ Processor cores and cache:

   _____

   ◢ RAM type, speed, and amount:

   _____

   ◢ OS type and edition:

   _____

◢ HDD (magnetic/SSD/hybrid, SAS or SATA details) capacity, speed, and buffer size (if present):

_____

◢ Monitor:

_____

◢ Video card:

_____

◢ Sound/speakers:

_____

◢ Other drives:

_____

◢ Removable device ports:

_____

◢ Network adapter:

_____

◢ Bundled software:

_____

◢ Total price:

_____

3. Research websites that sell computer parts, such as *tigerdirect.com*, *newegg.com*, or *microcenter.com* and find advertisements similar to those shown in Figure 19-7. Notice that items are grouped by component type.

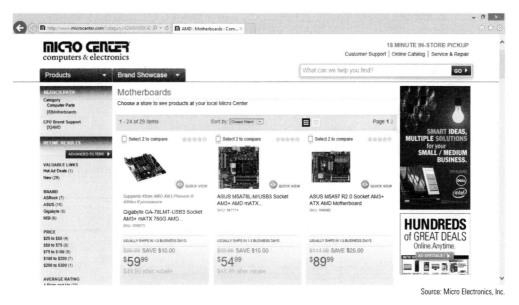

Source: Micro Electronics, Inc.

Figure 19-7   Components for sale

4. Using Table 19-2, list and describe the comparable components, their prices, and the source of your information. You might want to check several sources to find the best price.

> **Notes** Remember, most mail-order or online purchases have shipping costs. If you can determine an exact shipping price for each component, include this information as part of the component's price. If you can't find the exact shipping price, include a 10 percent fee as part of the price for each shipped component. You might have to include tax, depending on the taxing laws that apply. Sometimes the shipping cost is offset by not having to pay sales tax on an item.

Component	Description	Source	Price
Processor/cores/GHz			
Motherboard			
RAM			
Case and power supply			
HDD type and capacity			
CD/DVD-ROM drive			
Other drives			
Removable device ports			
Monitor			
Video adapter			
Sound/speakers			
Bonus items			
Operating system			
Bundled software			
TOTAL SYSTEM PRICE			

Table 19-2 Components for assembling a system

5. When you select computer parts for a system, you need to make sure the parts are compatible. Answer the following questions:

   ◢ Which processors does the motherboard support? Is the processor you selected listed in the motherboard advertisement as a compatible processor?

   _____

   _____

◢ What is the maximum amount of RAM the board can support? What RAM speeds does the board support? Is the type and amount of RAM compatible with the motherboard?

_____

_____

◢ What form factors do the case and motherboard use? Is the case compatible with the motherboard?

_____

_____

◢ What is the wattage rating of the power supply? Does this rating meet the requirements for the system?

_____

◢ What interface does the hard drive use? Does the motherboard have this type of interface?

_____

◢ What interface does the optical drive use? Does the motherboard have this type of interface?

_____

◢ What type of slot does the video adapter use? Does the motherboard have this type of slot?

_____

REVIEW QUESTIONS

1. Which approach to acquiring a system seems to be less expensive?

_____

2. Which single component determines the compatibility of other components in a system?

_____

3. What is the single most expensive component of a system built from separate components?

_____

4. What was the estimated cost of shipping (if any) for the component-built system?

_____

5. What are some potential pitfalls of building your own computer? What are some rewards?

_____

_____

_____

19

LAB 19.8 PLAN A CUSTOMIZED SYSTEM

OBJECTIVES

The goal of this lab is to plan and price a computer system to fit custom needs for function and performance. After completing this lab, you will be able to:

▲ Describe what you want your system to be able to do

▲ Pick components that best meet the design goals

MATERIALS REQUIRED

This lab requires the following:

▲ Windows 8 or Windows 7 operating system

▲ Internet access

▲ Access to computer publications, such as digital magazines on Kindle or another e-reader device or application (optional)

▲ A workgroup of four students

LAB PREPARATION

Before the lab begins, the instructor or lab assistant needs to do the following:

▲ Verify Internet access

▲ Announce that students can bring computer publications on an e-reader application to class (optional)

ACTIVITY BACKGROUND

As an IT technician, you might be in a position to build a system for a customer from separate components to meet particular specifications. Many times, systems are built to meet specific needs with components that will deliver certain performance values. Generally, systems fall within the following groups:

▲ *Gaming computer.* Powerful processor, large amount of RAM, high-end video adapter, high-end sound, and high-end cooling

▲ *Multimedia editing workstation.* Powerful processor, high-end video, maximum RAM, specialized sound, large and fast hard drive, and dual monitors

▲ *Thick or thin client.* Meets basic processor and RAM requirements for running Windows, meets needs of basic applications, affordable video adapter and sound card, and low-demand business uses

▲ *Home or small office computer.* Medium to high-end processor, media streaming and file sharing capabilities, Gigabit NIC, and ability for RAID arrays

In this lab, you research and propose a customized system for a machine that has been assigned to your team. Your team members will act as customers, so prepare to justify your selection.

Activity

Choose and research a custom computer:

1. Each team member selects a different system group from the computer groups listed above. Which system type did you select?

   _____

2. As a team, determine three questions that a customer might ask a technician about the recommendations for a customized system.

   Question 1:

   _____

   _____

   Question 2:

   _____

   _____

   Question 3:

   _____

   _____

Research on the web or in a computer publication for all components needed to build your custom system. Use Table 19-3 following Step 4 to list the components you would like to include in your custom system, the features and cost of each component, and your justification for purchasing it. Use a separate piece of paper if you need more writing space.

1. When selecting parts, begin by selecting the motherboard and processor at the same time.

   ◢ Which motherboard and processor brands and models did you select?

   _____

   _____

   ◢ Which processor socket do they use?

   _____

   ◢ Does the board have onboard video? If so, what type of video port(s) does the board have?

   _____

2. If your system uses a video card, select the card next. Which video card did you select?

   _____

3. Next, select the computer case. Make sure the case uses the form factor of the motherboard, and has the room you need for all internal components. Consider where and how the case will be used. Which case did you select?

   _____

4. You can now select the other components for your system. Be sure you include RAM, at least one hard drive, an optical drive, and an OS. Fill in all details in Table 19-3.

Component Category	Features	Cost	Justification
Processor GHZ/cores			
RAM			
Motherboard			
Hard drives			
Optical drives			
Removable device ports			
Video adapter			
Monitor			
Network adapter			
Sound adapters			
Case			
Additional components			
TOTAL COST			

Table 19-3 Customized system components

After you have completed Table 19-3, join with your team members to discuss your findings.

1. With your team together, have each member present the customized system he or she selected, with other team members playing the role of the customer by asking questions about the system.

   ◢ Which questions were you unable to answer?

   _____

   _____

   ◢ Which questions could you confidently answer?

   _____

   _____

2. Have team members play the role of your technical associates. Have them ask questions about your system to make sure the parts are compatible.

   ◢ List three questions team members asked about your system to determine if parts were compatible:

   _____

   _____

   _____

   ◢ Which parts, if any, did team members discover were not compatible?

   _____

   _____

3. If you discovered the parts were not compatible, go back and select new parts for your system.

4. Have team members decide if your proposal is a good one and make recommendations for improvements. What assessment and recommendations for improvements did the team make?

_____

_____

REVIEW QUESTIONS

1. When investigating the components for your particular customized system, what was your greatest challenge?

_____

_____

_____

2. If you were given a budget for the system, what components would receive the largest share of that budget?

_____

_____

_____

3. What changes would you make if you had to reduce the costs because of budget restrictions, while still meeting the needs of the computer group for your system?

_____

_____

4. What would be the expected life cycle of your customized system before it needs to be upgraded? At the end of the life cycle, what components would need to be upgraded?

_____

_____

19

Virtualization, Linux, and Mac OS X

Labs included in this chapter:

- **Lab 20.1:** Use Oracle VirtualBox to Install and Explore Virtual Machines (VMs)

- **Lab 20.2:** Investigate Operating Systems–Mac OS

- **Lab 20.3:** Investigate Linux and Create a Bootable Ubuntu Flash Drive

- **Lab 20.4:** Compare Operating Systems

- **Lab 20.5:** Use TeamViewer to Remotely Access Another Computer

- **Lab 20.6:** Set Up a VPN

LAB 20.1 USE ORACLE VIRTUALBOX TO INSTALL AND EXPLORE VIRTUAL MACHINES (VMs)

OBJECTIVES

The goal of this lab is to become familiar with the different types of virtual machines currently available, to explore the different features and specifications needed to run these programs, and to explore their use in an enterprise environment. After completing this lab, you will be able to:

◢ Install and configure Oracle VirtualBox

◢ Understand the features of VMware

◢ Install an operating system from an ISO (.iso) file

◢ Contrast virtual machine features and capabilities

MATERIALS REQUIRED

This lab requires the following:

◢ A computer running Windows 8 or Windows 7

◢ A minimum of 2.0 GHz CPU power is advised

◢ A minimum of 4 GB of RAM is advised

◢ A minimum of 20 GB of available hard disk drive space

◢ Internet access

> **Notes** Virtual machine software and virtual machines tend to require heavy system resources. Don't forget that whatever memory you assign to a VM will not be available to the host operating system while the VM is open.

LAB PREPARATION

Before the lab begins, the instructor or lab assistant needs to do the following:

◢ Verify Windows starts with no errors

◢ Verify Internet access is available

◢ Create an ISO (.iso) file of an operating system of your choice, and make this file available to students. Make note of the location for both 32-bit and 64-bit editions, if necessary.

◢ Because of the time it takes to download the VirtualBox software, it is recommended that prior to the lab, the file be downloaded and then made available to students.

ACTIVITY BACKGROUND

Virtual machines are programs that can be installed on operating systems. In this lab, you explore and contrast different types of virtual machines and then install an operating system in a virtual machine using Oracle VirtualBox.

Activity

PART 1: INSTALL AND USE VIRTUALBOX

Oracle VM VirtualBox is a powerful virtualization product. To learn more about it, follow these steps:

1. Open your favorite browser, and go to **virtualbox.org**. Explore the site and familiarize yourself with the available options.

2. Your instructor might have already downloaded the VirtualBox software for your use. If so, locate and execute the downloaded file, and then skip to Step 6. If not, in the left pane of the website, click **Downloads**.

3. Select **VirtualBox 5.0.6 for Windows hosts x86/amd64** or a newer version if available, as shown in Figure 20-1.

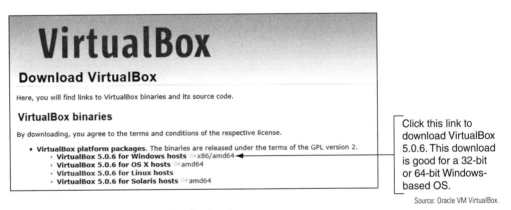

Figure 20-1 Oracle VirtualBox download options

4. Click **Save** when prompted. By default, the file will be downloaded to your Downloads folder.

   ◢ What is the name of the downloaded file and the exact path to the file?

   _____

   ◢ About how many minutes did the file take to download?

   _____

5. Navigate to the Downloads folder, and double-click the file to launch it and install VirtualBox.

6. The Setup dialog box opens. Click **Next**.

7. The Custom Setup options dialog box opens. Leave the default values intact, and click **Next**.

8. The Custom Setup options for shortcuts dialog box opens. Accept the default values, and click **Next** to place a shortcut in the quick launch area of your taskbar and on the desktop.

9. The virtual network interface now needs to be installed. VirtualBox will reset your Internet connection to conduct this installation. Click **Yes** to allow the system to proceed with the network connection installation and reset.

20

10. Click **Install** to allow the wizard to begin the installation. If the UAC dialog box appears, click **Yes**.

11. If Windows Security warning dialog boxes appear, click **Install** for each box. The installation may take several minutes.

12. When done, click **Finish**. VirtualBox launches.

VirtualBox is now ready to create virtual machines. To create a virtual machine using VirtualBox, follow these steps:

1. If VirtualBox is not already open, in Windows 8, from the Start screen, click the **Apps button**. In Windows 7, click **Start**, and then click **All Programs**. Find and open the **Oracle VM VirtualBox** app.

2. To create a new virtual machine, on the toolbar click **New**, as shown in Figure 20-2.

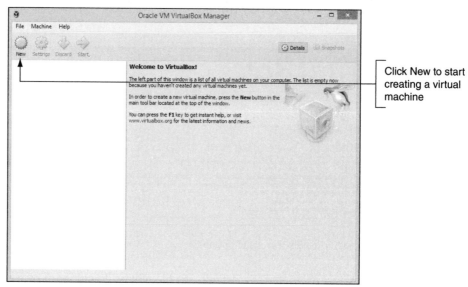

Source: Oracle VM VirtualBox.

Figure 20-2 The Oracle VirtualBox program is ready to create a virtual machine

3. The Create Virtual Machine Wizard opens.

4. Enter the name of the edition of Windows you are installing, such as Windows 8 Professional or Windows 7 Professional. Under Type, Operating System, select **Microsoft Windows**. Under Version, select the version of Windows you are installing (for example, **Windows 8**) and the type of operating system (**32-bit** or **64-bit**). Click **Next**.

5. Select the amount of memory to allocate to your virtual machine based on minimum recommended requirements for the operating system you will install. How much memory did you allocate for your virtual machine? Click **Next**.

6. In the Hard disk box, make sure **Create a virtual hard disk now** is selected, and then click **Create**.

7. For the type of file used to hold your virtual disk, select **VHD** (**Virtual Hard Disk**), and then click **Next**.

8. For the physical hard disk storage details option, select **Dynamically allocated**. Click **Next**.

9. For the size of the virtual disk, select **20 GB**. Click **Next**.

10. Review the summary of the configuration, and click **Create** in the File location and size box. The new virtual machine is now listed in the Oracle VM VirtualBox Manager window.

With the Oracle VM VirtualBox Manager window still open, use the VM help feature to answer the following questions:

◢ How many network cards can VirtualBox virtualize?

_____

◢ Which hardware can be emulated by VirtualBox?

_____

_____

◢ Several aspects of a virtual machine configuration are subject to security considerations. List three of them:

_____

_____

_____

11. Close all open windows.

PART 2: INSTALL AN OPERATING SYSTEM FROM AN ISO FILE

Your instructor has created an ISO file containing an operating system. Ask your instructor for the location of this file. Write down the location of the file here:

_____

To install an operating system from the ISO file to your VirtualBox virtual machine, follow these steps:

1. Open the **Oracle VM VirtualBox** application.

2. Select the virtual machine that you previously created for the operating system you intend to install.

3. On the toolbar, click **Settings**. The Settings dialog box opens. Select the name of the virtual machine you created earlier.

4. On the left pane of the settings windows, click **Storage**.

5. In the Storage Tree area, click the **CD** icon, and then, to the right of Optical Drive in the Attributes area, click the **CD** icon. Click **Choose Virtual Optical Disk File**, as shown in Figure 20-3. The Please choose a virtual optical disk file dialog box opens.

20

Click to add a
CD/DVD device,
which can be a
virtual CD stored
in an ISO file

Source: Oracle VM VirtualBox.

Figure 20-3 Storage Tree options allow you to mount an ISO image as a virtual CD in the virtual machine

6. Browse to the location of the ISO file that was made available by your instructor. Click the file to select it, and then click **Open**. The VM operating system – Settings dialog box opens.

7. In the VM operating system – Settings dialog box, click **OK**. You are returned to the Oracle VM VirtualBox Manager window.

8. On the toolbar, click **Start**. Your virtual machine starts up in its own VirtualBox VM window.

◢ If an Information dialog box appears over this window, write down important information it provides about using the virtual machine:

_____

_____

◢ When you click inside the virtual machine, your keystrokes and mouse actions are captured by the virtual machine. What key do you press to leave the virtual machine?

_____

_____

9. Close any Information dialog boxes that appear. The installation of the operating system begins. Figure 20-4 shows Windows 8 installed in the VirtualBox window.

Figure 20-4 Windows 8 running in a virtual machine using Oracle VirtualBox

Answer the following questions:

◢ When using virtual machine software and virtual machines, what is the host operating system? The guest operating system?

_____

_____

◢ Can Oracle VirtualBox be used to clone images? If so, list the steps here:

_____

_____

_____

◢ How many different operating systems can Oracle VirtualBox support? List them here:

_____

_____

10. Using the Shut down menu in your Windows installation in the virtual machine, shut down the virtual machine. Close the VirtualBox Manager window.

PART 3: EXPLORE VMWARE

Another popular and powerful virtualization program is VMware. To learn more about it, follow these steps:

1. Open your favorite browser, and go to **vmware.com**.

2. Using the options on the website, answer the following questions:

◢ What are three features of VMware Player?

_____

_____

_____

◢ What are three features of VMware vSphere Hypervisor?

_____

_____

_____

◢ What is the purpose of VMware Fusion 8?

_____

_____

3. Close all open windows.

REVIEW QUESTIONS

1. What is the purpose of a virtual machine?

   _____

   _____

2. What is the purpose of a hypervisor?

   _____

   _____

   _____

3. What are the network requirements for virtual machines?

   _____

   _____

4. What are three advantages of using virtual machines?

   _____

   _____

   _____

5. Other than Oracle, what other company makes virtualization software?

   _____

LAB 20.2 INVESTIGATE OPERATING SYSTEMS—MAC OS

OBJECTIVES

The goal of this lab is to become familiar with the various Apple operating systems and the hardware they support. After completing this lab, you will be able to:

⊿ Describe the various Apple operating systems, hardware, and applications

⊿ Research Apple technology on the Apple website *(apple.com)*

MATERIALS REQUIRED

This lab requires the following:

⊿ Internet access

LAB PREPARATION

Before the lab begins, the instructor or lab assistant needs to do the following:

⊿ Verify Internet access is available

ACTIVITY BACKGROUND

Mac operating systems are designed to be used only on Apple Mac computers. Many developers (Apple included) have created applications for Apple products, including applications for the Mac laptop, the iPad, the iPhone, and Apple's other mobile devices. The Apple website *(apple.com)* is the best source of information about its products. In this lab, you investigate different Apple operating systems, hardware, and applications for both computers and mobile devices.

ESTIMATED COMPLETION TIME: 30 MINUTES

  Activity

1. Open your browser and go to **apple.com**. Explore the site, and when you are done, return to the main page. Use the links on the site to answer the questions in this lab (see Figure 20-5).

Source: Apple, Inc.

Figure 20-5   Line of Apple Mac products

2. What is the latest version of the Mac operating system available for a new iMac?

_____

3. What is the cost of upgrading a Mac operating system to the latest version?

_____

Compare the iPhone, iMac, Mac mini, MacBook Pro, and MacBook Air systems available for sale on the Apple website, and answer these questions:

1. What are the speeds or frequencies of the processors in each product?

_____

_____

_____

2. How much does the fastest 27-inch iMac cost?

_____

_____

3. What software comes bundled with an iMac?

_____

_____

4. What is a MacBook?

_____

_____

20

5. How much does the most expensive MacBook Pro cost?

_____

6. What features are included with the least expensive MacBook?

_____

7. Describe the features of an Apple Mighty Mouse:

_____

8. What is the function of an Airport Extreme Base Station?

_____

9. What operating systems are available for Apple mobile devices?

_____

10. What is the latest operating system available for the iPhone?

_____

11. Describe the iCloud service:

_____

_____

12. Describe the purpose of the FaceTime feature for iPhone and iPad:

_____

_____

13. What is the purpose of QuickTime software?

_____

_____

REVIEW QUESTIONS

1. What is one advantage of using an Apple computer instead of a Windows computer?

_____

_____

_____

2. What is one disadvantage of using an Apple computer instead of a Windows computer?

_____

_____

3. Can a Mac OS run on a Windows computer? Explain:

_____

_____

4. Describe the advantages of an iPad:

_____

_____

LAB 20.3 INVESTIGATE LINUX AND CREATE A BOOTABLE UBUNTU FLASH DRIVE

OBJECTIVES

The goal of this lab is to find information about Linux operating systems and use a distribution of Linux to create a bootable USB flash drive. After completing this lab, you will be able to:

◢ Create a bootable Ubuntu flash drive

◢ Explore the different distributions of Linux

◢ Compare Linux to other operating systems

MATERIALS REQUIRED

This lab requires the following:

◢ Internet access

◢ A USB flash drive (thumb drive)

◢ A computer capable of booting from a USB flash drive

LAB PREPARATION

Before the lab begins, the instructor or lab assistant needs to do the following:

◢ Verify Internet access is available

◢ Inform students they will need a flash drive with at least 2 GB capacity for this lab

ACTIVITY BACKGROUND

Linux—a scaled-down version of the UNIX operating system that is provided in basic form, free of charge—allows open access to its programming code. Linux can be used as both a server platform and a desktop platform; additionally, Linux is a portable operating system, meaning that it can be installed on any hardware platform. Ubuntu is one of various Linux distributions.

Imagine the power of having a bootable Linux flash drive that gives you the ability to boot into any computer to perform troubleshooting steps. By the end of this lab, you will have that ability in your hands, using the Ubuntu distribution.

ESTIMATED COMPLETION TIME: 60 MINUTES

 Activity

1. Open a browser and go to **ubuntu.com**. Spend a few minutes exploring the site on your own.

2. Click the **Download** tab.

20

3. Click **Ubuntu Desktop** in the middle of the page.

4. Using the download options in the "Choose your flavour" drop-down menu (see Figure 20-6), choose the bit size you will be working with. If you are not sure which bit size to use, select **32-bit.**

Source: Ubuntu

Figure 20-6 Ubuntu download options

5. Click the **Download** link.

6. On the next page, scroll to the bottom of the page, and then click the **Not now, take me to the download** link. The file automatically begins downloading.

7. Click the **Save** arrow, and then click **Save as.** Save the file to your desktop. Answer the following questions:

◢ What is the size of the downloaded file?

_____

◢ What is the name of the downloaded file?

_____

◢ Depending on the speed of your Internet connection, the download may take a while. How long did the file take to download?

_____

◢ What is the file extension of the downloaded file?

_____

The next step is to download a program called Universal USB Installer. This program is used to make the USB flash drive bootable. We are using the *pendrivelinux.com* website to download the program. Be careful navigating through this website because it contains an excessive number of advertisements. To download the Universal USB Installer program, follow these steps:

1. Open a browser and go to **pendrivelinux.com.** (Websites change often. If this link does not work, perform a Google search for "Universal USB Installer.")

2. On the *pendrivelinux.com* site, click **Universal USB Installer – Easy as 1 2 3**, as shown in Figure 20-7.

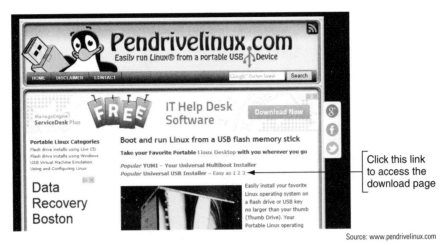

Source: www.pendrivelinux.com

Figure 20-7 Link to USB Installer page

3. Scroll down the page to find the download button for the USB Installer application, located near the middle of the page. At the time of this writing, the button name is DOWNLOAD UUI. Click the **DOWNLOAD UUI** button to download the application. See Figure 20-8.

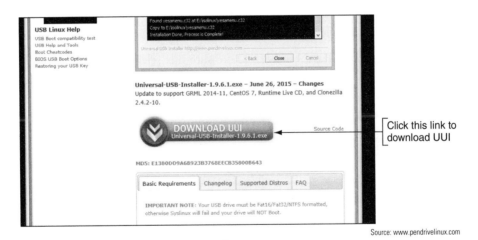

Source: www.pendrivelinux.com

Figure 20-8 Download link to USB Installer program

4. Choose to **Run** the executable file after downloading. If necessary, click **Yes** in the UAC dialog box.

5. If prompted, click **I Agree** to accept the end-user license agreement.

6. The setup dialog box appears. Complete the following (as shown in Figure 20-9):

Source: www.pendrivelinux.com

Figure 20-9   Universal USB Installer setup options

    a. In the drop-down menu for Step 1, select the distribution of Linux you downloaded.

    b. In the Step 2 section, browse to the location of the Ubuntu downloaded file on your desktop. The file has an .iso file extension.

    c. Plug your flash drive into a USB port. (Keep in mind that ALL the data on the flash drive will be deleted.)

    d. Select your USB drive letter. (Make sure this selection is correct.)

    e. Check the **Format F:\ Drive (Erases Content)** check box, indicating you want to format the drive using the FAT32 file system. This option might be different for you after you have selected the USB drive letter.

7. Click **Create**.

8. Confirm your options.

9. When the process completes, click **Close**.

USB Installer will now format and configure your bootable flash drive. The process may take a few minutes to complete. After the process completes, it is time to test your Linux bootable flash drive. To test the drive, follow these steps:

1. Boot into the UEFI/BIOS setup on your computer. (To boot into UEFI/BIOS setup, press a key or key combination at startup. Near the beginning of the boot, look for a message such as "Press Del for setup" or "Press F10 to configure setup.")

2. Using the UEFI/BIOS setup utility, ensure the boot sequence is adjusted to boot from USB first.

3. Exit UEFI/BIOS setup, saving any changes you made, and shut the computer completely off.

4. Plug the USB Linux bootable flash drive into a USB port.

5. Start the computer. Your computer should boot into the Linux operating system. Your desktop should look similar to Figure 20-10.

Source: Ubuntu

Figure 20-10 Typical Linux Ubuntu desktop

6. After Ubuntu boots up, open a browser and make sure you have connectivity to the Internet.

You have just created one of the most powerful tools you can have in your arsenal of software tools. Use it wisely. Ubuntu is not the only distribution of Linux. To learn about other distributions, open a browser and go to *linuxmint.com*. Answer the following questions:

◢ How does Linux Mint compare with Ubuntu?

_____

_____

◢ Linux Mint offers free tutorials. Examine a few, and describe how detailed they are:

_____

_____

_____

◢ What is DuckDuckGo?

_____

_____

◢ What other Linux distributions are popular?

_____

_____

◢ Who is credited with creating Linux?

_____

REVIEW QUESTIONS

1. What are some of the "costs" associated with installing a "free" operating system such as Linux?

   _____

   _____

   _____

2. Why might a company not want to use Linux on its desktop computers?

   _____

   _____

3. What is one advantage of using Linux rather than a Windows operating system on a desktop?

   _____

   _____

4. Based on what you learned from the Linux Mint website, how do you think companies that provide Linux make most of their profit?

   _____

   _____

LAB 20.4 COMPARE OPERATING SYSTEMS

OBJECTIVES

The goal of this lab is to investigate the history of computer operating systems and learn why many of today's operating systems share similar features. After completing this lab, you will be able to:

⏴ Better understand the relationships among operating systems

MATERIALS REQUIRED

This lab requires the following:

⏴ Internet access

LAB PREPARATION

Before the lab begins, the instructor or lab assistant needs to do the following:

⏴ Verify Internet access is available

ACTIVITY BACKGROUND

Modern operating systems, such as Windows, Linux, and Mac OS, have many similar features because they share a common history. Some of them have a direct or indirect connection with earlier operating systems. Figure 20-11 shows some highlights of this history. The arrows indicate a direct or indirect influence from an earlier operating system.

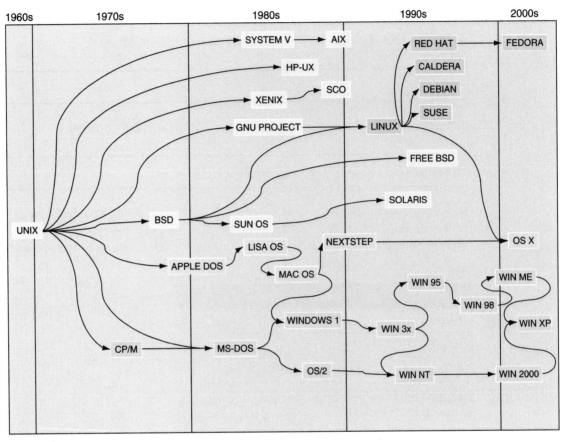

Figure 20-11 Operating system timeline

ESTIMATED COMPLETION TIME: 30 MINUTES

 Activity

Using your favorite search engine, answer the following questions:

1. Search for the "history of operating systems." List the URLs of three sites that you think do a good job of explaining this history:

_____

_____

_____

2. What are two similarities and two differences between the original Mac OS and Windows?

_____

_____

_____

3. How is OS/2 loosely connected to Windows 7?

4. What is the relationship of QDOS to CP/M and MS-DOS?

5. List three mobile device operating systems that are currently popular:

6. Several operating systems have appeared since the year 2000, and they have evolved from Fedora, Mac OS X, or Windows XP. Research new operating systems, and enter your findings in the second column of Table 20-1. (Don't forget about operating systems used on mobile devices.)

Year 2000 OSs	Present Operating System
Fedora	
Mac OS X	
Windows XP	

Table 20-1 Fill in the right column with present operating systems that have evolved from year 2000 operating systems

REVIEW QUESTIONS

Using a search engine, research operating system timelines; then, based on the OS timelines that you find, answer the following questions:

1. Why do you think Linux and UNIX share more commands than Windows 8 and UNIX?

2. Which line of operating systems has recently become more similar to UNIX?

3. Which line of operating systems split into two lines, only to merge again later?

4. Why do you think most versions of Linux and Windows use the cd command to change directories?

LAB 20.5 USE TEAMVIEWER TO REMOTELY ACCESS ANOTHER COMPUTER

OBJECTIVES

The goal of this lab is to explore one method by which computers can be remotely accessed and controlled across an Internet connection. As an IT support technician, you can use TeamViewer when you are called on to support a client's computer remotely. The client can easily give you access to his or her computer if you both have Internet access. TeamViewer is also useful when you are working on a team project and you and your team members need to share information and collaborate about the project from remote locations. After completing this lab, you will be able to:

◢ Download and install TeamViewer

◢ Use TeamViewer to share desktops with other users over the Internet

◢ Use TeamViewer to remotely control other computers over the Internet

◢ Move files between computers over the Internet

MATERIALS REQUIRED

This lab requires the following:

◢ Two computers using Windows 8 or Windows 7 (for best results, the two computers should be sitting side by side)

◢ An account with administrator privileges

◢ Internet access on both computers

◢ Workgroup of two students

LAB PREPARATION

Before the lab begins, the instructor or lab assistant needs to do the following:

◢ Verify Windows starts with no errors

◢ Verify each student has access to a user account with administrator privileges

◢ Verify Internet access is available

ACTIVITY BACKGROUND

TeamViewer is remote control software that is free to noncommercial users. It can be used for such things as tech support, remote maintenance, online presentations and training, team meetings, or simple application and file access. TeamViewer uses 1024-bit key exchange and 256-bit session encryption, thereby providing reasonable security for most situations.

After you have connected to a target computer using TeamViewer, you can take complete control over the computer. For example, an IT support technician tells the story of a client calling to say she lost almost 400 valuable data files on her computer and desperately asking for help to recover them. The technician connected to her computer over the Internet using TeamViewer. He then used this connection to download and install the Recuva software, which you previously learned to use. The technician was able to use the Recuva software to recover 98 percent of her missing files. He became her hero that evening! (True story.)

20

In this lab, you and your partner each download and install the free full version of TeamViewer onto your computers. Then, together you remotely access one computer from the other over the Internet, and explore the settings and capabilities of the software. For best results, the two computers should be side by side, so that you can easily see what happens on each computer after each action is performed. Note that this lab can also be completed by one person using two computers. Each partner should answer all of the questions in his or her own lab manual.

ESTIMATED COMPLETION TIME: 45 MINUTES

 Activity

In this lab, you work with a partner and two computers. The host computer will use TeamViewer to access the target computer. Designate one partner as the host partner using the host computer, and the other partner as the target partner using the target computer.

◢ Who is the host partner?

_____

◢ Who is the target partner?

_____

Note that later in the lab, the host and target roles are reversed and Parts 2–4 are repeated so that each partner has the opportunity to do all the steps in this lab.

PART 1: DOWNLOAD AND INSTALL TEAMVIEWER

Both partners follow these steps to download and install TeamViewer on their computers:

1. Log on to your computer with a user account that has administrator privileges.

2. Using your browser, go to **teamviewer.com**.

   ◢ Besides the free version of TeamViewer, what other versions are available?

   _____

   _____

   _____

   ◢ What is the current version number of the free version available for download?

   _____

3. To download the free versions of TeamViewer, click the **Download** button. Save the downloaded file to your Downloads folder.

4. What is the name of the file that was downloaded?

   _____

5. Double-click the executable file that downloaded to begin the installation. If a Security Warning dialog box appears, click **Run**. Make sure **Basic installation** is selected, select **Personal/Non-commercial use**, and then click **Accept – finish**. If necessary, click **Yes** to respond to the UAC dialog box.

6. You will see the progress bar as TeamViewer is installed in the default program folder. If necessary, review the TeamViewer welcome dialog box, and then click **Close** at the

bottom. TeamViewer opens on your desktop (see Figure 20-12). Minimize any browser windows that are blocking the TeamViewer window. What is the ID number and password displayed in TeamViewer?

Source: TeamViewer

Figure 20-12 TeamViewer displays the ID and password needed for someone to connect to your computer

PART 2: REMOTELY ACCESS TARGET COMPUTER

The host partner uses the host computer to establish access to the target computer. If you are the host partner, follow these steps as the target partner observes:

1. On the host computer, in the Partner ID box in the TeamViewer window, type the ID generated by TeamViewer on the target computer. Click **Connect to partner**. The TeamViewer Authentication dialog box appears. Let's take a few minutes to explore the advanced settings before logging on to the target system. Click **Advanced** in the lower-left corner.

2. Full Access is selected by default. Click **Access control** to open the Access Control Details dialog box. These are the specific settings that can be allowed or denied by choosing one of the three default configurations or by choosing the Custom settings. Notice that with Full Access all of the settings are allowed. Review each of these settings, and then click **Close** to close the Access Control Details dialog box.

3. Click the **Full Access** button. What are the other three choices that appear in the drop-down menu?

4. Select **Confirm all**, and then click **Access control** again. How have the settings changed?

5. Click **Close** to close the Access Control Details dialog box. Click **Confirm all**, and then select **Custom settings**. Click **Access control** again. Notice that each setting now has a customizable drop-down menu for configuring each setting individually. What are the three choices for configuring each setting in the drop-down menu (all settings have the same three choices)?

6. Click **Cancel** to close the Access Control Details dialog box. Using the drop-down menu, change Custom settings back to **Full Access**. Type the TeamViewer password of the target computer, and then click **Log On**.

◢ What happened on the target computer to indicate the session is live?

_____

◢ What happened on the host computer?

_____

Now we will switch the action to the target computer. It is the host partner's turn to observe as the target partner proceeds to Part 3.

PART 3: EXPLORE TEAMVIEWER TARGET CAPABILITIES

If you are the target partner, perform the following steps on the target computer as the host partner observes:

1. On the target computer, notice the session control box in the lower-right corner of the screen (see Figure 20-13). Do *not* click the X; if you do, TeamViewer will close all sessions and disconnect you from the host.

Source: TeamViewer

Figure 20-13 Use the session control box to access tools for TeamViewer

2. Hover the mouse over each icon on the toolbar of the session control box, and list below what each of these five tools does:

_____

_____

_____

_____

_____

3. Click each of the five tool icons one at a time to see what happens. Type a sentence into the chat section, and click **Send**. What happened on the host?

_____

4. Create a text document on your desktop, and use the File Transfer feature to move the file to the host computer. After the document is moved, the host user can right-click the document and download it to any folder on his or her computer (don't do that now).

5. Create a Rich Text document on your desktop, and leave it there. The host user will retrieve it later in this lab. Write down the name of the file:

_____

6. In the Session list section, hover the mouse over the blue arrow icon on the right. What is the purpose of this icon?

_____

7. Sometimes you might want to stop a host user from remotely controlling your computer. To do so, click the **blue arrow**. Then tell the host user to try to do something (like open the Start menu) on your computer from within the TeamViewer host window. Nothing will happen because you have denied the host computer remote control.

_____

Now we will switch the action back to the host computer. It is the target partner's turn to observe again as the host partner proceeds to Part 4.

PART 4: EXPLORE TEAMVIEWER HOST CAPABILITIES

It is possible for a host user to deny a local user of the target computer from using that target computer. To find out how the host can control the target computer, the host partner performs the following steps as the target partner observes:

1. When your target partner gave you access to the target computer earlier in the lab, you had full access, which means you could have locked your target partner out from controlling his or her own computer. Using the host computer, you can lock your partner out now. On the host computer, click the **Actions** menu, and then select **Disable remote input**. Now tell your target partner to try to do something on the target computer. Nothing will happen. Now neither of you can do anything on the target computer.

2. To return control of the target computer to both users, on the host computer, uncheck **Disable remote input**. Ask your partner to uncross the **blue arrow** on the target computer. Each partner should now have access to the target computer.

3. Remember that Rich Text document your partner created on the desktop of the target computer? Rather than asking your partner to move it to the File box so that you can download it, you can just drag and drop it to your desktop. Do that now. Isn't that cool? What pops up when the file transfers?

_____

4. Click the **X** on the pop-up boxes to close them on each computer. Take a few minutes to review each of the options under each of the five menu items on the toolbar (see Figure 20-14).

20

Menu bar displaying available tools

Source: TeamViewer

Figure 20-14   The menu bar displays tools available for TeamViewer

◢ What are the choices under the "View – Quality" setting?

_____

_____

◢ What are the choices under the "Actions – Remote reboot" setting? Warning: Do not click any of them!

_____

5. Click the **Actions** menu, and select **Switch sides with partner**. Whoa! What happened? Now you are the target and your partner is the host.

6. To make your computer the host again, in the Session list section of your session control box, click the small monitor icon, which is on the right, beside the blue arrow. You are now the host again.

7. Now switch roles with your partner and repeat this lab beginning with Part 2.

CHALLENGE ACTIVITY (ADDITIONAL 10 MINUTES)

Using the Extras tab in TeamViewer, set up a meeting and invite a group of three or four users. One user is the host and starts the meeting. The other users then join the meeting. If your computers have webcams, you can use them to see and hear each other during the meeting.

REVIEW QUESTIONS

1. Does TeamViewer have to be running on both the host and the target computer in order to establish a session?

_____

2. What does the host user require from the target user in order to establish a connection?

_____

3. In what general ways can a target user limit the access of the host user?

   _____

   _____

4. After a TeamViewer session is opened, list four types of actions that can be performed between the two computers:

   _____

   _____

   _____

   _____

   _____

   _____

5. Do the ID and password assigned by TeamViewer remain the same after closing and relaunching TeamViewer?

   _____

6. What is a reason the host might need to change the "View – Quality" setting?

   _____

   _____

   _____

   _____

7. Do you think the "Optimize speed" setting makes the actual transfer rate faster? Explain your answer:

   _____

   _____

8. Under what circumstances might you, as the target user, want to limit the access of the host user connecting to your machine?

   _____

   _____

   _____

   _____

   _____

20

9. Under what circumstances might you, as the target user, want to give full access to the host user?

_____

_____

10. What are some useful TeamViewer host tools that a technician might need to use on the target system, and why might they be used?

_____

_____

_____

_____

_____

LAB 20.6 SET UP A VPN

OBJECTIVES

The goal of this lab is to set up a secure VPN. Technicians in the field are often called on to help a client who is traveling or working from home connect to the corporate network using a VPN. After completing this lab, you will be able to:

▲ Set up a VPN in Windows

▲ Use third-party software to securely access the Internet from a public network

MATERIALS REQUIRED

This lab requires the following:

▲ Two Windows 8 or Windows 7 operating systems

▲ An account with administrator privileges

▲ Internet access

▲ VPN server (optional)

▲ Workgroup of two students

LAB PREPARATION

Before the lab begins, the instructor or lab assistant needs to do the following:

▲ Verify Windows starts with no errors

▲ Verify each student has access to a user account with administrator privileges

▲ Verify Internet access is available

▲ Set up a VPN server and record the server's IP address (optional)

▲ Set up a user account on the VPN server, and record the user name and password (optional)

ACTIVITY BACKGROUND

A virtual private network (VPN) offers a very secure connection between two computers. It uses a process called tunneling to form a private connection that encrypts communications independently of the type of network being used. VPNs are often used when a user has to connect to a network over a nonsecure public network such as a wireless hotspot.

This lab presents three options for setting up a VPN connection. In Part 1, you set up a VPN connection between two Windows computers. In Part 2, you set up a VPN connection from a computer to a VPN server. In Part 3, you use software to set up a VPN connection using a third-party server.

ESTIMATED COMPLETION TIME: 60 MINUTES

 Activity

PART 1: VPN CONNECTION USING TWO WINDOWS COMPUTERS

In this part of the lab, you create a VPN connection between two computers connected to the Internet. To do this, you must first set up one computer to host a VPN connection and then allow specific user names to access this connection. Follow these steps to set up an incoming VPN connection to your computer:

1. Log on using an account with administrator privileges.
2. Create a standard user account with a password. Name the standard account **Newuser**, and make the password **newuser**.
3. In Windows 8, right-click the Start button, and then click **Network Connections**. In Windows 7, click **Start**, type **Network and Sharing** in the Search box, and then press **Enter** to open the Network and Sharing Center. Click **Change adapter settings** in the left pane of the Network and Sharing Center.
4. Select your connection, and then press the **Alt** key to display the menu. Click **File** on the menu bar, and then click **New Incoming Connection** to open the "Allow connections to this computer" dialog box.

> **Notes** If you do not see the File button, click **Organize** in the toolbar, select **Layout**, and then click **Menu bar**. The menu bar is now displayed above the toolbar.

5. Click the **Newuser (Newuser)** check box, and then click **Next**.
6. Make sure **Through the Internet** is selected, and click **Next**.
7. Leave the networking software settings at their defaults to use the Internet Protocol Version 4 (TCP/IPv4), and click **Allow access**.
8. The final screen of this setup gives the computer name, which is used to establish the VPN connection. Write down the computer name, and give it to your partner, who will use this VPN connection to your computer. Click **Close**. Close any open windows.

Now that you have set up an incoming VPN connection and granted permission for your partner to use the account Newuser to connect to your computer through this VPN connection, you are ready for your partner to test the connection from his or her computer to yours. Then you can try to connect to your partner's computer using his or her VPN connection. You are only able to do this one at a time. Designate one partner as Partner 1 and the other partner as Partner 2.

20

◢ Who is Partner 1?

_____

_____

◢ Who is Partner 2?

_____

CREATE AN OUTGOING CONNECTION

Partner 1, follow these steps to make an outgoing VPN connection as Partner 2 observes:

1. If necessary, log on using an account with administrator privileges.
2. Open the **Network and Sharing Center** again, and click **Set up a new connection or network**.
3. Select **Connect to a workplace**, and click **Next**, as shown in Figure 20-15.

Figure 20-15   Beginning a VPN setup

4. Click **Use my Internet connection (VPN)**.
5. In the Internet address field, enter the computer name provided by your partner from Step 8 of the previous exercise. What is the name your partner gave you? In Windows 8, click **Create**. In Windows 7, click **Next**.

_____

6. Enter the account name and password for the Newuser account you created at the beginning of this lab to authenticate the VPN connection to your partner's computer. In Windows 8, click **OK**. In Windows 7, click **Connect**.

7. A message says you are connected. In Windows 8, click a blank space on the desktop to close the Networks pane. In Windows 7, click **Close**.

8. In Windows 7, a Set Network Location window appears on both computers. Click **Work network**, and then click **Close**.

9. On both machines, open the **Network and Sharing Center** again, and click **Change adapter settings** in the left pane. Notice the new connections listed on the host machine, as shown in Figure 20-16a. On the other computer, the connections are slightly different, as shown in Figure 20-16b.

(a)

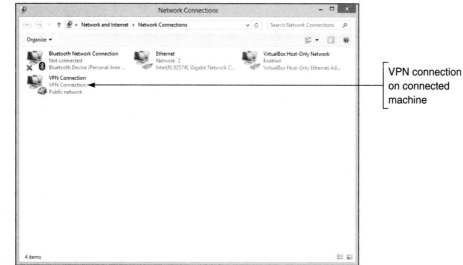

(b)

Figure 20-16 Access the VPN connection from the Network Connections window

Follow these steps to disconnect and delete this outgoing VPN connection:

1. To disconnect, click the network connection icon in the notification area of the taskbar. Click the **VPN Connection**, and then click **Disconnect**.

2. To delete the VPN connection, open the **Network and Sharing Center**.

3. Click **Change adapter settings** in the left pane. Right-click the **VPN Connection** icon, and select **Delete** in the shortcut menu. Click **Yes** to confirm.

Now Partner 2 makes an outgoing connection while Partner 1 observes. Partner 2 should go back to the "Create an Outgoing Connection" heading and follow the steps back to this point in the lab.

PART 2: VPN CONNECTION USING A VPN SERVER (OPTIONAL)

This part of the lab is optional. If your instructor has provided a VPN server, you can follow these steps to connect to it. If a VPN server is not available, please proceed to Part 3 of this lab. To connect to a VPN server in Windows, follow these steps:

1. Log on using an account with administrator privileges.

2. Open the **Network and Sharing Center**, and click **Set up a new connection or network**.

3. Select **Connect to a workplace**, and then click **Next**.

4. Click **Use my Internet connection (VPN)**.

5. Enter the Internet address of the VPN server provided by your instructor. What is the address you used?

   _____

6. Click **Next**. Enter the user name and password provided by your instructor. What user name and password did you use?

   _____

7. Click **Connect**. A message says you are connected. Click **Close**.

8. If a Set Network Location window appears, click **Work network**, and then click **Close**.

9. Disconnect and delete this VPN connection the same way you did the last VPN connection.

PART 3: VPN CONNECTION USING A THIRD-PARTY VPN SERVER

In this part of the lab, you connect a computer to a VPN server using third-party software. Several companies offer programs to secure Internet access from public wireless connections using VPNs. One such program is Hotspot Shield by AnchorFree. To set up a secure connection, follow these steps:

1. Log on using an account with administrator privileges.

2. Open Internet Explorer and go to **hotspotshield.com**.

3. Click the **Free Download** button, and follow the on-screen instructions to install Hotspot Shield. During the installation process:

   ◢ Accept the default configuration.

   ◢ In Windows 7, click **Install**, if any Windows Security windows open.

   ◢ In Windows 8, if a Networks pane opens, click **Yes** to find content on the network.

   ◢ Click **Finish**, when the install completes.

4. When the installation is complete, if necessary, launch Hotspot Shield, and wait for an automatic connection to a VPN server that is provided by AnchorFree to secure your connections.

5. Browse several websites. When Hotspot Shield is running, all your data transmitted or received to and from these websites is secured. How do you know that Hotspot Shield is running?

6. When you're finished, uninstall Hotspot Shield, and close any open windows. How did you uninstall the software?

REVIEW QUESTIONS

1. Will VPNs work on both wired and wireless networks?

2. What process do VPNs use to form a private connection between computers?

3. Why might it be dangerous to do online banking transactions through a public Internet hotspot without using a VPN connection?

4. What type of secure connection does an online banking site usually offer its customers?

5. How does a VPN connection differ from using Remote Desktop? Is a Remote Desktop connection a secured connection?

6. Why is a VPN more secure than other forms of wireless encryption such as WPA2?

7. Why do you think using Hotspot Shield for secured connections slows down response time when surfing the web?

GLOSSARY

100BaseT An Ethernet standard that operates at 100 Mbps and uses twisted-pair cabling up to 100 meters (328 feet). *Also called* Fast Ethernet. Variations of 100BaseT are 100BaseTX and 100BaseFX.

4-pin 12-V connector An auxiliary motherboard connector used for extra 12-V power to the processor.

8-pin 12-V connector An auxiliary motherboard connector used for extra 12-V power to the processor, providing more power than the older 4-pin auxiliary connector.

10-foot user interface Application software used on large screens to control output display menus and other clickable items in fonts large enough to read at a distance of 10 feet.

20-pin P1 connector Used by an older ATX power supply and motherboard and provided +3.3 volts, +5 volts, +12 volts, −12 volts, and an optional and rarely used −5 volts.

24-pin P1 connector Used by the ATX Version 2.2 power supply and motherboard and provides additional power for PCI Express slots.

32-bit operating system Type of operating system that processes 32 bits at a time.

64-bit operating system Type of operating system that processes 64 bits at a time.

1394a *See* FireWire 400.

1394b *See* FireWire 800.

802.11 a/b/g/n/ac The collective name for the IEEE 802.11 standards for local wireless networking, which is the technical name for Wi-Fi.

A+ Certification A certification awarded by CompTIA (the Computer Technology Industry Association) that measures an IT technician's knowledge and skills.

AC adapter A device that converts AC to DC and can use regular house current to power a laptop computer.

Accelerated Processing Unit (APU) An AMD technology that is a combination of a CPU and a graphics processor unit (GPU) in the same processor housing.

accelerometer A type of gyroscope used in mobile devices to sense the physical position of the device.

acceptable use policy (AUP) A document that explains to users what they can and cannot do on the corporate network or with company data, and the penalties for violations.

access control list (ACL) A record or list of the resources (for example, a printer, folder, or file) that a user, device, or program has access to on a corporate network, server, or workstation.

Action bar On an Android device, an area at the bottom of the screen that can contain up to five custom software buttons, called Home touch buttons. The three default buttons are back, home, and overview.

Action Center A tool in Windows 8/7 that lists errors and issues that need attention.

Active Directory A Windows Server directory database and service that is used in managing a domain to allow for a single point of administration for all shared resources on a network, including files, peripheral devices, databases, websites, users, and services.

active partition For Master Boot Record (MBR) hard drives, the primary partition on the drive that boots the OS. Windows calls the active partition the system partition.

active recovery image In Windows 8, the custom refresh image of the Windows volume that will be used when a refresh of the Windows installation is performed. *Also see* custom refresh image.

ActiveX control A small app or add-on that can be downloaded from a website along with a webpage and is executed by a browser to enhance the webpage.

adapter address *See* MAC (Media Access Control) address.

address reservation When a DHCP server assigns a static IP address to a DHCP client. For example, a network printer might require a static IP address so that computers on the network can find the printer.

ad hoc mode A peer-to-peer wireless network between computers where each wireless computer serves as its own wireless access point and is responsible for securing each connection.

administrative share The folders that are shared by default on a network domain that administrator accounts can access.

Administrative Tools A group of tools accessed through Control Panel that you can use to manage the local computer or other computers on the network.

administrator account In Windows, a user account that grants to the administrator(s) rights and privileges to all hardware and software resources, such as the right to add, delete, and change accounts and to change hardware configurations. *Compare with* standard account.

Administrators group A type of user group. When a user account is assigned to this group, the account is granted rights that are assigned to an administrator account.

Advanced Boot Options menu A Windows 7/Vista menu that appears when you press F8 when Windows starts. The menu can be used to troubleshoot problems when loading Windows.

Aero glass *See* Aero user interface.

Aero user interface The Windows 7/Vista 3D user interface that gives a glassy appearance. *Also called* Aero glass.

AES (Advanced Encryption Standard) An encryption standard used by WPA2 and is currently the strongest encryption standard used by Wi-Fi.

AFP (Apple Filing Protocol) An outdated file access protocol used by early editions of the Mac operating system by Apple and is one protocol in the suite of AppleTalk networking protocols.

AirDrop A feature of iOS whereby iPhones and iPads can transfer files between nearby devices. The devices use Bluetooth to detect nearby devices and Wi-Fi to establish connectivity and transfer files.

air filter mask A mask that filters the dust and other contaminants from the air for breathing safety. *Also called* air-purifying respirator.

Airplane mode A setting within a mobile device that disables the cellular, Wi-Fi, and Bluetooth antennas so the device cannot transmit signals.

AirPrint A technology by Apple that allows Apple computers and mobile devices to print to an AirPrint-capable printer without first installing the printer.

air-purifying respirator *See* air filter mask.

all-in-one computer A computer that has the monitor and computer case built together and uses components that are common to both a laptop and a desktop computer.

alternate IP address When configuring TCP/IP in Windows, the static IP address that Windows uses if it cannot lease an IP address from a DHCP server.

alternating current (AC) Current that cycles back and forth rather than traveling in only one direction. In the United States, the AC voltage from a standard wall outlet is normally between 110 V and 115 V. In Europe, the standard AC voltage from a wall outlet is 220 V.

A-Male connector A common type of USB connector that is flat and wide and connects an A Male USB port on a computer or USB hub.

amp (A) A measure of electrical current.

analog A continuous signal with infinite variations. *Compare with* digital, which is a series of binary values—1s and 0s.

Android An operating system used on mobile devices that is based on the Linux OS and supported by Google.

anonymous users User accounts that have not been authenticated on a remote computer.

ANSI (American National Standards Institute) A nonprofit organization dedicated to creating trade and communications standards.

answer file A text file (.bat) that contains information that Windows requires in order to do an unattended installation.

anti-malware software Utility software that can prevent infection, scan a system, and detect and remove all types of general malware, including viruses, spyware, worms, and rootkits.

antistatic bag Static shielding bags that new computer components are shipped in.

antistatic wrist strap *See* ESD strap.

antivirus software Utility software that can prevent infection, scan a system, and detect and remove viruses.

anycast address   Using TCP/IP version 6, a type of IP address used by routers and identifies multiple destinations. Packets are delivered to the closest destination.

APK (Android Application Package)   The format used by Android apps for distributing the app in a package of files wrapped into one file with an .apk file extension.

App Store   The app on an Apple device (iPad, iPhone, or iPod touch) that can be used to download content from the iTunes Store website (*itunes.apple.com*).

Apple ID   A user account that uses a valid email address and password and is associated with a credit card number that allows you to download iOS updates and patches, apps, and multimedia content.

Apple menu   In OS X, the menu that appears when the user clicks the Apple icon in the upper-left corner of the screen.

AppleTalk   An outdated suite of networking protocols used by early editions of the Apple Mac OS, and has been replaced by the TCP/IP suite of protocols.

application virtualization   Using this virtualization, a virtual environment is created in memory for an application to virtually install itself.

Application Virtualization (App-V)   Software by Microsoft used for application virtualization.

Apps Drawer   An Android app that lists and manages all apps installed on the device. By default, this app's icon is in the Favorites tray on an Android screen.

apt-get   A Linux and OS X command to install and remove software packages and install OS updates.

artifact   Horizontally torn image on a computer screen.

ATAPI (Advanced Technology Attachment Packet Interface)   An interface standard, part of the IDE/ATA standards, that allows tape drives, optical drives, and other drives to be treated like an IDE hard drive by the system.

ATA Secure Erase   Standards developed by the American National Standards Institute (ANSI) that dictate how to securely erase data from solid-state devices such as a USB flash drive or SSD drive in order to protect personal privacy.

ATX (Advanced Technology Extended)   The most common form factor for computer systems presently in use, originally introduced by Intel in 1995. ATX motherboards and cases make better use of space and resources than did the earlier AT form factor.

ATX12V power supply   An ATX Version 2.1 power supply that provides an extra 12-V power cord with a 4-pin connector to be used by the auxiliary 4-pin power connector on motherboards used to provide extra power for processors.

audio port   A port that can be used by a microphone, audio in, audio out, and stereo audio out. *Also called* a sound port.

Authenticated Users group   All user accounts that have been authenticated to access the system except the Guest account. *Compare with* anonymous users.

authentication server   A server responsible for authenticating users or computers to the network so they can access network resources.

autodetection   A feature of UEFI/BIOS that detects a new drive and automatically selects the correct drive capacity and configuration, including the best possible standard supported by both the hard drive and the motherboard.

Automatic Private IP Address (APIPA)   In TCP/IP version 4, IP address in the address range 169.254.x.y, used by a computer when it cannot successfully lease an IP address from a DHCP server.

auto-switching   A function of a laptop computer AC adapter that is able to automatically switch between 110-V and 220-V AC power.

Backup and Restore   The Windows 7/Vista utility used to create and update scheduled backups of user data and the system image.

Backup Operators group   A type of Windows user account group. When a user account belongs to this group, it can back up and restore any files on the system regardless of its having access to these files.

ball grid array (BGA)   A connection via a processor that is soldered to the motherboard, and the two are always purchased as a unit.

bandwidth   In relation to analog communication, the range of frequencies that a communications channel or cable can carry. In general use, the term refers to the volume of data that can be transmitted on a bus or over a cable stated in bits per second (bps), kilobits per second (Kbps), megabits per second (Mbps), or gigabits per second (Gbps). *Also called* data throughput or line speed.

barcode reader   Used to scan barcodes on products at the points of sale or when taking inventory.

G

base station A fixed transceiver and antenna used to create one cell within a cellular network.

Bash shell The default shell used by the terminal for many distributions of Linux.

basic disk The term Windows uses that applies to a hard drive when the drive is a stand-alone drive in the system. *Compare with* dynamic disk.

batch file A text file containing a series of OS commands. Autoexec.bat is a batch file.

bcdedit A Windows command used to manually edit the BCD (Boot Configuration Data).

BD-R Stands for BD (Blu-ray Disc) recordable.

BD-RE Stands for BD (Blu-ray Disc) rewriteable.

beamforming A technique supported by the IEEE 802.11ac Wi-Fi standard that can detect the location of connected devices and increase signal strength in that direction.

Berg power connector A type of power connector used by a power cord to provide power to a floppy disk drive.

best-effort protocol *See* connectionless protocol.

biometric authentication To authenticate to a network, computer, or other computing device by means of biometric data, such as a fingerprint or retinal data. Touch ID on an iPhone or face lock on an Android device can perform biometric authentication.

biometric device An input device that inputs biological data about a person; the data can identify a person's fingerprints, handprints, face, voice, eyes, and handwriting.

BIOS (basic input/output system) Firmware that can control much of a computer's input/output functions, such as communication with the keyboard and the monitor. *Compare with* UEFI.

BIOS setup The program in system BIOS that can change the values in CMOS RAM. *Also called* CMOS setup.

BitLocker Drive Encryption A utility in Windows 8/7/Vista that is used to lock down a hard drive by encrypting the entire Windows volume and any other volume on the drive.

BitLocker To Go A Windows utility that can encrypt data on a USB flash drive and restrict access by requiring a password.

bitmap Rows and columns of bits that collectively represent an image.

blue screen error *See* blue screen of death (BSOD).

blue screen of death (BSOD) A Windows error that occurs in kernel mode, is displayed against a blue screen, and causes the system to halt. The error might be caused by problems with devices, device drivers, or a corrupted Windows installation. *Also called* blue screen error or stop error.

Bluetooth A short-range wireless technology used to connect two devices in a small personal network.

Bluetooth PIN code A code that may be required to complete the Bluetooth connection in a pairing process.

Blu-ray Disc (BD) An optical disc technology that uses the UDF version 2.5 file system and a blue laser beam, which is shorter than any red beam used by DVD or CD discs. The shorter blue laser beam allows Blu-ray discs to store more data than a DVD.

BNC connector A connector used with thin coaxial cable. Some BNC connectors are T-shaped and called T-connectors. One end of the T connects to the NIC, and the two other ends can connect to cables or end a bus formation with a terminator.

B-Male connector A USB connector that connects a USB 1.x or 2.0 device such as a printer.

Bonjour An Apple program that is used to interface between computers and devices and share content and services between them. When iTunes is installed on a Windows computer, the installation includes Bonjour.

Boot Camp A utility in OS X that allows you to install and run Windows on a Mac computer.

Boot Configuration Data (BCD) store A small Windows database structured the same as a registry file and contains configuration information about how Windows is started. The BCD file replaces the Boot.ini file used in Windows 2000/XP.

boot loader menu A startup menu that gives the user the choice of which operating system to load, such as Windows 8 or Windows 7, when both are installed on the same system, creating a dual boot.

boot partition The hard drive partition where the Windows OS is stored. The system partition and the boot partition may be different partitions.

booting The process of starting up a computer and loading an operating system.

BootMgr In Windows 8/7/Vista, the boot manager program responsible for loading Windows.

bootrec A Windows command used to repair the BCD (Boot Configuration Data) and boot sectors.

bootsect A Windows command used to repair a dual-boot system.

botnet A network of zombies or robots. *Also see* zombie.

bridge A device that stands between two segments of a network and manages network traffic between them.

broadband A transmission technique that carries more than one type of transmission on the same medium, such as voice and DSL on a regular telephone line.

brownout Temporary reduction in voltage, which can sometimes cause data loss. *Also called* sag.

brute force attack A method to hack or discover a password by trying every single combination of characters.

buffer overflow attack Malicious software that attempts to run its code from an area of memory assigned to another program.

burn-in When a static image stays on a monitor for many hours, leaving a permanent impression of that image on the monitor.

bus The paths, or lines, on the motherboard on which data, instructions, and electrical power move from component to component.

BYOD (Bring Your Own Device) A corporate policy that allows employees or students to connect their own devices to the corporate network.

cable Internet A broadband technology that uses cable TV lines and is always connected (always up).

cable tester A tool used to test a cable to find out if it is good or to find out what type of cable it is if the cable is not labeled.

calibration The process of checking and correcting the graduations of an instrument or device such as an inkjet printer.

call tracking software A system that tracks the dates, times, and transactions of help-desk or on-site IT support calls, including the problem presented, the issues addressed, who did what, and when and how each call was resolved.

CAS Latency A method of measuring access timing to memory, which is the number of clock cycles required to write or read a column of data off a memory module. CAS stands for Column Access Strobe. *Compare with* RAS Latency.

case fan A fan inside a computer case used to draw air out of or into the case.

CAT-3 (Category 3) A rating formally used for unshielded twisted-pair (UTP) cables on a network, and is currently used for phone lines.

CAT-5 (Category 5) A rating used for unshielded twisted-pair (UTP) cables and is rated for Fast Ethernet, but is seldom used today.

CAT-5e (Category 5e) A rating used for unshielded twisted-pair (UTP) cables, rated for Fast Ethernet and Gigabit Ethernet, and is popular today.

CAT-6 (Category 6) A rating used for twisted-pair cables that has less crosstalk than CAT-5e cables. CAT-6 cables might contain a plastic cord down the center of the cable that helps to prevent crosstalk, but is less flexible and more difficult to install than CAT-5e.

CAT-6a (Category 6a) A rating used for twisted-pair cables that is thicker and faster than CAT-6 and rated for 10GBase-T (10-Gigabit Ethernet).

CAT-6e (Category 6e) An unofficial name for CAT-6a.

CAT-7 (Category 7) A rating used for twisted-pair cables that have shielding to almost completely eliminate crosstalk and improve noise reduction.

Category view Default view in Windows Control Panel that presents utilities grouped by category. *Compare with* Classic view.

cd (change directory) The Windows command to change the current default directory.

CD (compact disc) An optical disc technology that uses a red laser beam and can hold up to 700 MB of data.

CDFS (Compact Disc File System) The 32-bit file system for CD discs and some CD-R and CD-RW discs. *Also see* Universal Disk Format (UDF).

CDMA (Code Division Multiple Access) A protocol standard used by cellular WANs and cell phones for transmitting digital data over cellular networks.

CD-ROM Stands for CD-read-only memory.

CD-RW Stands for CD rewriteable.

cellular network A network that can be used when a wireless network must cover a wide area. The network is made up of cells, each controlled by a base station. *Also called* a cellular WAN.

cellular network analyzer Software and hardware that can monitor cellular networks for signal

G

strength of cell towers, wireless access points (WAPs), and repeaters, which can help technicians better position antennas in a distributed antenna system (DAS).

cellular WAN *See* cellular network.

chmod A Linux and OS X command to change modes (or permissions) for a file or directory.

chown A Linux and OS X command to change the owner of a file or directory.

central processing unit (CPU) *Also called* a microprocessor or processor. The component where almost all processing of data and instructions takes place. The CPU receives data input, processes information, and executes instructions.

Centrino A technology used by Intel whereby the processor, chipset, and wireless network adapter are all interconnected as a unit, which improves laptop performance.

Certificate of Authenticity A sticker that contains the Windows product key.

certificate of destruction Digital or paper documentation, which ensures that data has been destroyed beyond recovery.

Certification Authority (CA) An organization, such as VeriSign, that assigns digital certificates or digital signatures to individuals or organizations.

chain of custody Documentation that tracks evidence used in an investigation and includes exactly what, when, and from whom the evidence was collected, the condition of the evidence, and how the evidence was secured while in possession of a responsible party.

channel A specific radio frequency within a broader frequency.

charging In laser printing, the imaging drum is conditioned to contain a high electrical charge.

charm A shortcut that appears in the Windows 8 charms bar.

charms bar A menu that appears on the right side of any Windows 8 screen when you move your pointer to a right corner.

chassis A computer case for any type of computer.

chassis air guide (CAG) A round air duct that helps to pull and direct fresh air from outside a computer case to the cooler and processor.

child directory *See* subdirectory.

chipset A group of chips on the motherboard that controls the timing and flow of data and instructions to and from the CPU.

chkdsk (check disk) A Windows command to verify the hard drive does not have bad sectors that can corrupt the file system.

chkdsk /r A Windows command to check the hard drive for errors and repair the file system.

CIDR notation A shorthand notation (pronounced *"cider notation"*) for expressing an IPv4 address and subnet mask with the IP address followed by a / slash and the number of bits in the IP address that identifies the network. For example, 15.50.35.10/20.

CIFS (Common Internet File System) A file access protocol and the cross-platform version of SMB used between Windows, Linux, Mac OS, and other operating systems. *Also called* SMB2.

Class C fire extinguisher A fire extinguisher rated to put out electrical fires.

Classic view View in Windows Control Panel that presents utilities in small or large icons and are not grouped. *Compare with* Category view.

clean boot A process of starting Windows with a basic set of drivers and startup programs that can be useful when software does not install properly.

clean install Used to install Windows on a new hard drive or to overwrite the existing operating system and applications when installing Windows on a hard drive that already has Windows installed.

client/server Two computers communicating using a local network or the Internet. One computer (the client) makes requests to the other computer (the server), which answers the request.

client-side desktop virtualization Using this virtualization, software installed on a desktop or laptop manages virtual machines used by the local user.

client-side virtualization Using this virtualization, a personal computer provides multiple virtual environments for applications.

clone In Linux and OS X, an image of the entire partition on which the OS is installed.

closed source Software owned by a vendor that requires a commercial license to install and use the software. *Also called* vendor-specific software or commercial license software.

cloud computing A service where server-side virtualization is delegated to a third-party service, and the Internet is used to connect server and client machines.

cloud printing Printing to a printer anywhere on the Internet from a personal computer or mobile device connected to the Internet.

cluster On a magnetic hard drive, one or more sectors that constitute the smallest unit of space on the drive for storing data (*also called* a file allocation unit). Files are written to a drive as groups of whole clusters.

CMOS (complementary metal-oxide semiconductor) The technology used to manufacture microchips. CMOS chips require less electricity, hold data longer after the electricity is turned off, and produce less heat than earlier technologies. The configuration or setup chip is a CMOS chip.

CMOS battery The lithium coin-cell battery on the motherboard used to power the CMOS chip that holds BIOS setup data so that the data is retained when the computer is unplugged.

CMOS RAM Memory contained on the CMOS configuration chip.

coaxial cable A cable that has a single copper wire down the middle and a braided shield around it.

cold boot *See* hard boot.

Cold Cathode Fluorescent Lamp (CCFL) An older backlighting technology that uses one or two fluorescent tubes to light a monitor panel.

commercial license As applied to software, the rights to use the software, which have been assigned to the user by the software vendor. *Also see* closed source.

community cloud Online resources and services that are shared between multiple organizations, but not available publicly.

CompactFlash (CF) card A flash memory device that allows for sizes up to 137 GB, although current sizes range up to 32 GB.

compatibility mode A group of settings that can be applied to older drivers or applications that might cause them to work using a newer version of Windows than the one the programs were designed to use.

Compatibility Support Module (CSM) A feature of UEFI that allows UEFI to be backward compatible with legacy BIOS devices and drivers.

Complete PC Backup A Vista utility that can make a backup of the entire volume on which Vista is installed and can also back up other volumes. *Compare with* system image (Windows 8/7).

Component Services (COM+) A Microsoft Management Console snap-in that can be used to register components used by installed applications.

composite video port A port used by television or by a video card that is designed to send output to a TV. A composite port is round and has only a single pin in the center of the port. *Also called* RGB port.

compressed (zipped) folder A folder with a .zip extension that contains compressed files. When files are put in the folder, they are compressed. When files are moved to a regular folder, the files are decompressed.

computer infestation *See* malicious software.

Computer Management A Windows console (compmgmt.msc) that contains several administrative tools used by support technicians to manage the local computer or other computers on the network.

computer name *See* host name.

connectionless protocol A TCP/IP protocol such as UDP that works at the OSI Transport layer and does not guarantee delivery by first connecting and checking where data is received. It might be used for broadcasting, such as streaming video or sound over the web, where guaranteed delivery is not as important as fast transmission. *Also called* a best-effort protocol. *Also see* UDP (User Datagram Protocol).

connection-oriented protocol In networking, a TCP/IP protocol that confirms a good connection has been made before transmitting data to the other end, verifies data was received, and resends it if it is not. An example of a connection-oriented protocol is TCP.

console A window that consolidates several Windows administrative tools.

contrast ratio The contrast between true black and true white on a screen.

Control Panel A window containing several small Windows utility programs called applets that are used to manage hardware, software, users, and the system.

cooler A cooling system that sits on top of a processor and consists of a fan and a heat sink.

G

copy   The Windows command to copy a single file, group of files, or folder and its contents.

copyright   The right to copy the work that belongs to the creators of the works or others to whom the creator transfers this right.

CPU   *See* central processing unit (CPU).

crimper   A tool used to attach a terminator or connector to the end of a cable.

crossover cable   A cable used to connect two like devices such as a hub to a hub or a computer to a computer (to make the simplest network of all). A crossover cable is not rated for Gigabit Ethernet.

custom installation   In the Windows setup program, the option used to overwrite the existing operating system and applications, producing a clean installation of the OS. The main advantage is that problems with the old OS are not carried forward.

custom refresh image   In Windows 8, an image of the entire Windows volume, including the Windows installation. The image can be applied during a Windows 8 refresh operation.

Dashboard   In OS X, a screen that contains widgets, such as a calendar, a calculator, a clock, and a weather report.

data bus   Lines of the bus, a system of pathways used for communication on the motherboard, used for data.

data cartridge   A full-sized cartridge that holds data and is used in a tape drive.

data loss prevention (DLP)   Methods that protect corporate data from being exposed or stolen; for example, software that filters employee email to verify privacy laws are not accidentally or intentionally being violated.

data path size   The number of lines on a bus that can hold data, for example, 8, 16, 32, and 64 lines, which can accommodate 8, 16, 32, and 64 bits at a time.

data source   A resource on a network that includes a database and the drivers required to interface between a remote computer and the data. *Also see* Open Database Connectivity (ODBC).

Data Sources   A tool in the Administrative Tools group of Control Panel that is used to allow data files to be connected to applications they normally would not use.

data throughput   *See* bandwidth.

Date and Time applet   Accessed through Control Panel, used to set the date and time in Windows.

DB15 port   *See* VGA (Video Graphics Array) port.

DB9 port   *See* serial port.

dd   A Linux and OS X command to copy and convert files, directories, partitions, and entire DVDs or hard drives. You must be logged in as a superuser to use the command.

DDR   *See* Double Data Rate SDRAM.

DDR2   Memory that is faster and uses less power than DDR.

DDR3   Memory that is faster and uses less power than DDR2.

DDR3L   Memory that is faster and uses less power than regular DDR3.

DDR4   Memory that is faster and uses less power than DDR3.

DE15 port   *See* VGA (Video Graphics Array) port.

dead pixel   A pixel on an LCD monitor that is not working and can appear as a small white, black, or colored spot on the computer screen.

default gateway   The gateway a computer on a network uses to access another network unless it knows to specifically use another gateway for quicker access to that network.

default printer   The designated printer to which Windows prints unless another printer is selected.

default program   A program associated with a file extension that is used to open the file.

defrag   The Windows command that examines a magnetic hard drive for fragmented files and rewrites these files to the drive in contiguous clusters.

defragment   A drive maintenance procedure that rearranges fragments or parts of files on a magnetic hard drive so each file is stored on the drive in contiguous clusters.

defragmentation tool   A utility or command to rewrite a file to a disk in one contiguous chain of clusters, thus speeding up data retrieval.

degausser   A machine that exposes a magnetic storage device such as a hard drive or tape drive to a strong magnetic field to completely erase the data on the storage device.

del   The Windows command to delete a file or group of files. *Also called* the erase command.

deployment strategy   A procedure to install Windows, device drivers, and applications on a computer, and can include the process to transfer user settings, application settings, and user data files from an old installation to the new installation.

desktop case A computer case that lies flat and sometimes serves double-duty as a monitor stand.

Destination Network Address Translation (DNAT) When a firewall using Network Address Translation (NAT) allows uninitiated communication to a computer behind the firewall through a port that is normally closed. *Also see* port forwarding.

device driver A small program stored on the hard drive and installed in Windows that tells Windows how to communicate with a specific hardware device such as a printer, network, port on the motherboard, or scanner.

Device Manager The primary Windows tool (devmgmt.msc) for managing hardware.

Devices and Printers window A window used in Windows 8/7 to manage and uninstall printers and other devices.

DHCP (Dynamic Host Configuration Protocol) A protocol used by a server to assign a dynamic IP address to a computer when it first attempts to initiate a connection to the network and requests an IP address.

DHCP client A computer or other device (such as a network printer) that requests an IP address from a DHCP server.

DHCPv6 server A DHCP server that serves up IPv6 addresses.

dictionary attack A method to discover or crack a password by trying words in a dictionary.

digital A signal consisting of a series of binary values—1s and 0s. *Compare with* analog.

digital certificate A code used to authenticate the source of a file or document or to identify and authenticate a person or organization sending data over a network. The code is assigned by a certificate authority such as VeriSign and includes a public key for encryption. Also called digital ID or digital signature.

digital rights management (DRM) Software and hardware security limitations meant to protect digital content and prevent piracy.

digitizer *See* graphics tablet.

digitizing tablet *See* graphics tablet.

DIMM (dual inline memory module) A miniature circuit board installed on a motherboard to hold memory.

dir The Windows command to list files and directories.

direct current (DC) Current that travels in only one direction (the type of electricity provided by batteries). Computer power supplies transform AC to low DC.

direct thermal printer A type of thermal printer that burns dots onto special coated paper as was done by older fax machines.

DirectX A Microsoft software development tool that software developers can use to write multimedia applications, such as games, video-editing software, and computer-aided design software.

disc image *See* ISO image.

discolored capacitor Bulging head or crusty corrosion at the base of a capacitor that might indicate a failing motherboard.

Disk Cleanup A Windows utility to delete temporary files to free up space on a drive.

disk cloning *See* drive imaging.

disk imaging *See* drive imaging.

diskpart A Windows command to manage hard drives, partitions, and volumes.

DisplayPort A port that transmits digital video and audio (not analog transmissions) and is slowly replacing VGA and DVI ports on personal computers. *Also see* Thunderbolt port.

distorted geometry Images are stretched inappropriately on a monitor.

distribution server A file server holding Windows setup files used to install Windows on computers networked to the server.

distribution share The collective files in the installation that include Windows, device drivers, and applications. The package of files is served up by a distribution server.

DMG file In Mac OS X, a disk image file similar to WIM or ISO files in Windows.

DMZ (demilitarized zone) Refers to removing firewall protection from a computer or network within an organization of protected computers and networks.

DNS (Domain Name System or Domain Name Service) A distributed pool of information (called the namespace) that keeps track of assigned host names and domain names and their corresponding IP addresses. DNS also refers to the system that allows a host to locate information in the pool and the protocol the system uses.

G

DNS client When Windows queries the DNS server for a name resolution, which means to find an IP address for a computer when the fully qualified domain name is known.

DNS server A Doman Name Service server that uses a DNS protocol to find an IP address for a computer when the fully qualified domain name is known. An Internet service provider is responsible for providing access to one or more DNS servers as part of the service it provides for Internet access.

dock (1) For an Android device, the area at the bottom of the Android screen where up to four apps can be pinned. (2) For a Mac computer, a bar that appears by default at the bottom of the screen and contains program icons and shortcuts to files and folders.

docking port A connector on a laptop to connect to a port replicator or docking station.

docking station A device that receives a laptop computer and provides additional secondary storage and easy connection to peripheral devices.

domain In Windows, a logical group of networked computers, such as those on a college campus, that share a centralized directory database of user account information and security for the entire domain.

domain account *See* global account.

domain name A name that identifies a network and appears before the period in a website address such as *microsoft.com*. A fully qualified domain name is sometimes loosely called a domain name. *Also see* fully qualified domain name.

Double Data Rate SDRAM (DDR SDRAM) A type of memory technology used on DIMMs that runs at twice the speed of the system clock, has one notch, and uses 184 pins. *Also called* DDR SDRAM, SDRAM II, and DDR.

double-sided A DIMM feature whereby memory chips are installed on both sides of a DIMM.

drive imaging Making an exact image of a hard drive, including partition information, boot sectors, operating system installation, and application software to replicate the hard drive on another system or recover from a hard drive crash. *Also called* disk cloning or disk imaging.

driver store The location where Windows stores a copy of the driver software when first installing a device.

DSL (Digital Subscriber Line) A telephone line that carries digital data from end to end, and is used as a type of broadband Internet access.

dual boot The ability to boot using either of two different OSs, such as Windows 8 and Windows 7. *Also called* multiboot.

dual channels A motherboard feature that improves memory performance by providing two 64-bit channels between memory and the chipset. DDR, DDR2, DDR3, and DDR4 DIMMs can use dual channels.

dual processors Two processor sockets on a server motherboard.

dual rail A power supply with a second +12-V circuit or rail used to ensure the first circuit is not overloaded.

dual ranked Double-sided DIMMs that provide two 64-bit banks. The memory controller accesses first one bank and then the other. Dual-ranked DIMMs do not perform as well as single-ranked DIMMs.

dual voltage selector switch A switch on the back of the computer case where you can switch the input voltage to the power supply to 115 V used in the United States or 220 V used in other countries.

dumb terminal *See* zero client.

dump In Linux, a collection of data that is copied to a backup media.

duplex printer A printer that is able to print on both sides of the paper.

duplexing assembly Used in a duplex printer, a duplexing assembly contains several rollers, turns the paper around, and draws it back through the print process to print on the back of the paper.

DVD (digital versatile disc or digital video disc) A technology used by optical discs that uses a red laser beam and can hold up to 17 GB of data.

DVD-ROM Stands for DVD read-only memory.

DVD-RW Stands for DVD rewriteable memory.

DVD-RW DL Stands for DVD rewriteable memory, dual layers. Dual layers almost double the storage capacity of DVD-RW discs.

DVI (Digital Video Interface) port A port that transmits digital or analog video.

DVI-A A DVI (Digital Visual Interface) video port that only transmits analog data.

DVI-D A DVI (Digital Visual Interface) video port that works only with digital monitors.

DVI-I A DVI (Digital Visual Interface) video port that supports both analog and digital monitors.

dxdiag.exe A Windows command used to display information about hardware and diagnose problems with DirectX.

dynamic disk A way to partition one or more hard drives so that the drives can work together to store data in order to increase space for data or to provide fault tolerance or improved performance. *Also see* RAID. *Compare with* basic disk.

dynamic IP address An IP address assigned by a DHCP server for the current session only, and is leased when the computer first connects to a network. When the session is terminated, the IP address is returned to the list of available addresses. *Compare with* static IP address.

dynamic RAM (DRAM) The most common type of system memory, it requires refreshing every few milliseconds.

dynamic volume A volume type used with dynamic disks by which you can create a single volume that uses space on multiple hard drives.

ECC (error-correcting code) A chipset feature on a motherboard that checks the integrity of data stored on DIMMs or RIMMs and can correct single-bit errors in a byte. More advanced ECC schemas can detect, but not correct, double-bit errors in a byte.

EFI (Extensible Firmware Interface) The original version of UEFI that was first developed by Intel.

EFI System Partition (ESP) For a GPT hard drive, the bootable partition used to boot the OS and contains the boot manager program for the OS.

electrostatic discharge (ESD) Another name for static electricity, which can damage chips and destroy motherboards, even though it might not be felt or seen with the naked eye.

elevated command prompt window A Windows command prompt window that allows commands that require administrator privileges.

email filtering To search incoming or outgoing email messages for matches kept in databases, searching for known scams and spammers to protect against social engineering.

email hoax An email message that is trying to tempt you to give out personal information or trying to scam you.

embedded MMC (eMMC) Internal storage used instead of using a solid-state drive (SSD) in inexpensive mobile devices such as cell phones, tablets, and laptops.

emergency notifications Government alerts, such as AMBER alerts, that are sent to mobile devices in an emergency.

emulator A virtual machine that emulates hardware, such as the hardware buttons on a smart phone.

Encrypted File System (EFS) A way to use a key to encode a file or folder on an NTFS volume to protect sensitive data. Because it is an integrated system service, EFS is transparent to users and applications.

End User License Agreement (EULA) A digital or printed statement of your rights to use or copy software, which you agree to when the software is installed.

enterprise license A license to use software that allows an organization to install multiple instances of the software. *Also called* site license.

entry control roster A list of people allowed into a restricted area and a log of any approved visitors that is used and maintained by security guards.

erase *See* del.

e-reader A mobile device that holds digital versions of books, newspapers, magazines, and other printed documents, which are usually downloaded to the device from the web.

escalate Assigning a problem to someone higher in the support chain of an organization. This action is normally recorded in call tracking software.

ESD mat A mat that dissipates electrostatic discharge (ESD) and is commonly used by technicians who repair and assemble computers at their workbenches or in an assembly line. *Also called* ground mat.

ESD strap A strap you wear around your wrist that is attached to the computer case, ground mat, or another ground so that electrostatic discharge (ESD) is discharged from your body before you touch sensitive components inside a computer. Also called antistatic wrist strap or ground bracelet.

Ethernet over Power (EoP) *See* powerline networking.

Ethernet port *See* network port.

Event Viewer A Windows tool (eventvwr.msc) useful for troubleshooting problems with Windows, applications, and hardware. It displays logs of significant events, such as a hardware or

G

network failure, OS failure, OS error messages, a device or service that has failed to start, or General Protection Faults.

Everyone group   In Windows, the Authenticated Users group as well as the Guest account. When you share a file or folder on the network, Windows, by default, gives access to the Everyone group.

Execute Disable Bit (EDB)   A processor security feature that can work with the operating system to designate an area of memory for holding data or instructions.

executive services   In Windows, a group of components running in kernel mode that interfaces between the subsystems in user mode and the HAL (hardware abstraction layer).

expand   The Windows command that extracts files from compressed distribution files, which are often used to distribute files for software installation.

expansion card   A circuit board inserted into a slot on the motherboard to enhance the capability of the computer.

expert system   Software that uses a database of known facts and rules to simulate a human expert's reasoning and decision-making processes.

ExpressCard   A PCMCIA standard for laptop I/O cards that uses the PCI Express and USB 2.0 data transfer standards. Two types of ExpressCards are ExpressCard/34 (34mm wide) and ExpressCard/54 (54mm wide). ExpressCards have been replaced by USB ports on today's laptops.

ExpressCard/34   A type of ExpressCard that is 34mm wide. An ExpressCard/34 can fit into an ExpressCard/54 slot.

ExpressCard/54   A type of ExpressCard that is 54mm wide.

ext3   The Linux file system that was the first to support journaling, which is a technique that tracks and stores changes to the hard drive and helps prevent file system corruption.

ext4   The current Linux file system, which replaced the ext3 file system. Stands for "fourth extended file system."

extended partition   On an MBR hard drive, the only partition on the drive that can contain more than one logical drive. In Windows, a hard drive can have only a single extended partition. *Compare with* primary partition.

extender   A device that amplifies and retransmits a wireless signal to a wider coverage area and retains the original network name.

extension magnet brush   A long-handled brush made of nylon fibers that are charged with static electricity to pick up stray toner inside a laser printer.

external enclosure   A housing designed to store hard drives external from the computer.

external SATA (eSATA)   A standard for external drives based on SATA that uses a special external shielded SATA cable up to 2 meters long.

F connector   A connector used with an RG-6 coaxial cable and is used for connections to a TV and has a single copper wire.

factory default   To restore a mobile device or other computer to its state at the time of purchase. The operating system is reinstalled and all user data and settings are lost.

fanless CPU cooler   A processor cooler that instead of using fans, uses heat pipes that contain a small amount of liquid that becomes vapor when heated, and the vapor draws the heat away from the processor toward the fins on the cooler. There the heat can be blown away by case fans. *Also called* passive CPU cooler.

Fast Ethernet   *See* 100BaseT.

Fast Startup   A Windows 8 feature to speed up startup by performing a partial hibernation at shutdown. At shutdown, Windows saves the drivers and kernel state in the Windows hibernate file, hiberfil.sys, and then reads from this file on the next cold boot.

FAT (file allocation table)   A table on a hard drive, USB flash drive, or floppy disk used by the FAT file system that tracks the clusters used to contain a file.

fat client   *See* thick client.

fault tolerance   The degree to which a system can tolerate failures. Adding redundant components, such as disk mirroring or disk duplexing, is a way to build in fault tolerance.

Favorites tray   On Android devices, the area above the Action bar that contains up to seven apps or groups of apps. These apps stay put as you move from home screen to home screen.

ferrite clamp   A clamp installed on a network cable to protect against electrical interference.

fiber optic   As applied to Internet access technologies, a dedicated, leased line that uses fiber-optic cable from the Internet service provider (ISP) to a residence or place of business.

fiber-optic cable   Cable that transmits signals as pulses of light over glass or plastic strands inside protected tubing.

field replaceable unit (FRU) A component in a computer or device that can be replaced with a new component without sending the computer or device back to the manufacturer. Examples: power supply, DIMM, motherboard, hard disk drive.

file allocation unit *See* cluster.

file association The association between a data file and an application to open the file that is determined by the file extension.

file attributes The properties assigned to a file. Examples of file attributes are read-only and hidden status.

File Explorer The Windows 8 utility used to view and manage files and folders.

file extension A portion of the name of a file that indicates how the file is organized or formatted, the type of content in the file, and what program uses the file. In command lines, the file extension follows the file name and is separated from it by a period, for example, Msd.exe, where exe is the file extension.

File History In Windows 8, the utility that can schedule and maintain backups of data. It can also create a system image for backward compatibility with Windows 7.

file name The first part of the name assigned to a file, which does not include the file extension. In Windows, a file name can be up to 255 characters.

file recovery software Third-party software that can help recover deleted and corrupted files.

file server A computer dedicated to storing and serving up data files and folders.

file system The overall structure that an OS uses to name, store, and organize files on a disk. Examples of file systems are NTFS and FAT32. Windows is always installed on a volume that uses the NTFS file system.

Finder An app embedded in Mac OS X that functions similar to File Explorer in Windows; use it to find and access files and applications in OS X.

firewall Hardware and/or software that blocks unwanted traffic initiated from the Internet into a private network and can restrict Internet access for local computers behind the firewall.

FireWire 400 A data transmission standard used by computers and peripherals (for example, a video camera) that transmits at 400 Mbps. *Also called* 1394a.

FireWire 800 A data transmission standard used by computers and peripherals (for example, a video camera) that transmits at 800 Mbps. *Also called* 1394b.

FireWire port A port used for high-speed multimedia devices such as camcorders. *Also called* an IEEE 1394 port.

firmware Software that is permanently stored in a chip. The BIOS on a motherboard is an example of firmware.

fitness monitor A wearable computer device that can measure heart rate, count pool laps or miles jogged or biked, and a host of other activities.

fixboot A Windows 7/Vista command that repairs the boot sector of the system partition.

fixmbr A Windows 7/Vista command to repair the MBR (Master Boot Record).

flashing BIOS The process of upgrading or refreshing the programming stored on a firmware chip.

flat-panel monitor *See* LCD (liquid crystal display) monitor.

flip-chip land grid array (FCLGA) A type of socket used by processors that has blunt protruding pins on the socket that connect with lands or pads on the bottom of the processor. The chips in the processor package are flipped over so that the top of the chip makes contact with the socket.

flip-chip pin grid array (FCPGA) A type of socket used by processors that has holes aligned in rows to receive pins on the bottom of the processor. The chips in the processor are flipped over so that the top of the chip makes contact with the socket.

floppy disk drive (FDD) A drive that can hold either a 5½ inch or 3¼ inch floppy disk. *Also called* floppy drive.

floppy drive *See* floppy disk drive (FDD).

fluorescent backlighting *See* Cold Cathode Fluorescent Lamp (CCFL).

folder *See* subdirectory.

Folder Options applet Accessed through Control Panel, manages how files and folders are displayed in File Explorer or Windows Explorer.

force quit In OS X, to abruptly end an app without allowing the app to go through its close process.

force stop To abruptly end an app without allowing the app to go through its close process.

format The Windows command to prepare a hard drive volume, logical drive, or USB flash drive for use by placing tracks and sectors on its surface to

G

store information (for example, format d:). This process erases all data on the device.

formatting   *See* format.

form factor   A set of specifications on the size, shape, and configuration of a computer hardware component such as a case, power supply, or motherboard.

fragmented file   A file that has been written to different portions of the disk so that it is not in contiguous clusters.

front panel connector   A group of wires running from the front or top of the computer case to the motherboard.

front panel header   A group of pins on a motherboard that connect to wires that are connected to the front panel of the computer case.

Front Side Bus (FSB)   *See* system bus.

FTP (File Transfer Protocol)   A TCP/IP protocol and application that uses the Internet to transfer files between two computers.

FTP server   A server using the FTP or Secure FTP protocol that downloads or uploads files to remote computers.

full duplex   Communication that happens in two directions at the same time.

fully qualified domain name (FQDN)   Identifies a computer and the network to which it belongs and includes the computer name and domain name. For example, *jsmith.amazon.com*. Sometimes loosely referred to as a domain name.

fuser assembly   A component in laser printing that uses heat and pressure to fuse the toner to paper.

gadget   A mini-app that appears on the Windows 7 desktop or Vista sidebar.

gateway   Any device or computer that network traffic can use to leave one network and go to a different network.

geotracking   A mobile device routinely reports its position to Apple, Google, or Microsoft at least twice a day, which makes it possible for these companies to track your device's whereabouts.

gestures   In OS X, finger movements on a touch screen or the trackpad of a Mac computer.

ghost cursor   A trail on the screen left behind when you move the mouse.

Gigabit Ethernet   A version of Ethernet that supports rates of data transfer up to 1 gigabit per second.

gigahertz (GHz)   One thousand MHz, or one billion cycles per second. *Also see* hertz and megahertz.

global account   An account that is used at the domain level, created by an administrator, and stored in the SAM (security accounts manager) database on a Windows domain controller. *Also called* domain account or network ID. *Compare with* local account.

global address   *See* global unicast address.

global unicast address   In TCP/IP version 6, an IP address that can be routed on the Internet. *Also called* global address.

Globally Unique Identifier Partition Table (GUID or GPT)   One of two methods used to organize partitions on a hard drive. A GPT partitioning system installed on a hard drive can support 128 partitions and is recommended for drives larger than 2 TB. *Compare with* Master Boot Record (MBR).

Gmail   An email service provided by Google at *mail.google.com*.

Google account   A user account, which is a valid email address, that is registered on the Google Play website (*play.google.com*) and is used to download content to an Android device.

Google Play   The official source for Android apps, also called the Android marketplace, at *play.google.com*.

gpresult   The Windows command to find out group policies that are currently applied to a system for the computer or user.

GPS (Global Positioning System)   A receiver that uses the system of 24 or more satellites orbiting the Earth. The receiver locates four or more of these satellites, and from these four locations, calculates its own position in a process called triangulation.

gpupdate   The Windows command to refresh local group policies as well as group policies set in Active Directory on a Windows domain.

graphical user interface (GUI)   An interface that uses graphics as compared with a command-driven interface.

graphics processing unit (GPU)   A processor that manipulates graphic data to form the images on a monitor screen. A GPU can be embedded on a video card, on the motherboard, or integrated within the processor.

graphics tablet   An input device that can use a stylus to hand draw. It works like a pencil on the tablet and uses a USB port.

grayware   A program that is potentially harmful or potentially unwanted.

grep   A Linux and OS X command to search for and display a specific pattern of characters in a file or in multiple files.

ground bracelet   *See* ESD strap.

ground mat   *See* ESD mat.

Group Policy   A console (gpedit.msc) available only in Windows professional and business editions that is used to control what users can do and how the system can be used.

GRUB (GRand Unified Bootloader)   The current Linux boot loader, which can handle dual boots with another OS installed on the system. *Also see* LILO (LInux boot LOader).

GSM (Global System for Mobile Communications)   An open standard for cellular networks and cell phones that uses digital communication of data and is accepted and used worldwide.

Guests group   A type of user group in Windows. User accounts that belong to this group have limited rights to the system and are given a temporary profile that is deleted after the user logs off.

gyroscope   A device that contains a disc that is free to move and can respond to gravity as the device is moved.

HAL (hardware abstraction layer)   The low-level part of Windows, written specifically for each CPU technology, so that only the HAL must change when platform components change.

half duplex   Communication between two devices whereby transmission takes place in only one direction at a time.

Handoff   A technique of devices and computers made by Apple that lets you start a task on one device, such as an iPad, then pick up that task on another device, such as a Mac desktop or laptop.

hard boot   Restart the computer by turning off the power or by pressing the Reset button. *Also called* a cold boot.

hard disk drive (HDD)   *See* hard drive.

hard drive   The main secondary storage device of a computer. Two technologies are currently used by hard drives: magnetic and solid state. *Also called* hard disk drive (HDD).

hard-link migration   A method used by USMT (User State Migration Tool) that does not copy user files and settings when the source computer and destination computer are the same.

hard reset   (1) For Android devices, a factory reset, which erases all data and settings and restores the device to its original factory default state. (2) For iOS devices, a forced restart similar to a full shutdown followed by a full clean boot of the device.

hardware address   *See* MAC (Media Access Control) address.

hardware-assisted virtualization (HAV)   A feature of a processor whereby it can provide enhanced support for hypervisor software to run virtual machines on a system. The feature must be enabled in UEFI/BIOS setup.

hardware print server   A device that can connect to a USB, Bluetooth, or serial-port printer to connect the printer to the network as a network printer.

hardware RAID   One of two ways to implement RAID. Hardware RAID is more reliable and better performing than software RAID, and is implemented using UEFI/BIOS on the motherboard or a RAID controller card.

HD15 port   *See* VGA (Video Graphics Array) port.

HDMI (High Definition Multimedia Interface) port   A digital audio and video port currently used on televisions and other home theater equipment and is often used to connect a computer to home theater equipment.

HDMI connector   A connector that transmits both digital video and audio and is used on most computers and televisions.

HDMI mini connector   A smaller type of HDMI connector used for connecting some devices such as a smart phone to a computer. *Also called* mini-HDMI connector.

heat sink   A piece of metal, with cooling fins, that can be attached to or mounted on an integrated chip package (such as the CPU) to dissipate heat.

help   The Windows command to get help about another command.

hertz (Hz)   Unit of measurement for frequency, calculated in terms of vibrations, or cycles per second. For example, for 16-bit stereo sound, a frequency of 44,000 Hz is used. *Also see* megahertz and gigahertz.

hibernation   A power-saving state that saves all work to the hard drive and powers down the system.

G

hidden share In Windows, a folder whose folder name ends with a $ symbol. When you share the folder, it does not appear in the File Explorer or Windows Explorer window of remote computers on the network.

high-level formatting A process performed by the Windows Format program (for example, FORMAT C:/S), the Windows installation program, or the Disk Management utility. The process creates the boot record, file system, and root directory on a hard drive volume or logical drive, a floppy disk, or a USB flash drive. *Also called* formatting, OS formatting, or operating system formatting. *Compare with* low-level formatting.

high-touch using a standard image A strategy to install Windows that uses a standard image for the installation. A technician must perform the installation on the local computer. *Also see* standard image.

high-touch with retail media A strategy to install Windows where all the work is done by a technician sitting at the computer using Windows setup files. The technician also installs drivers and applications after the Windows installation is finished.

HKEY_CLASSES_ROOT (HKCR) A Windows registry key that stores information to determine which application is opened when the user double-clicks a file.

HKEY_CURRENT_CONFIG (HKCC) A Windows registry key that contains information about the hardware configuration that is used by the computer at startup.

HKEY_CURRENT_USER (HKCU) A Windows registry key that contains data about the current user. The key is built when a user signs in using data kept in the HKEY_USERS key and data kept in the Ntuser.dat file of the current user.

HKEY_LOCAL_MACHINE (HKLM) An important Windows registry key that contains hardware, software, and security data. The key is built using data taken from the SAM hive, the Security hive, the Software hive, and the System hive and from data collected at startup about the hardware.

HKEY_USERS (HKU) A Windows registry key that contains data about all users and is taken from the Default hive.

homegroup In Windows, a type of peer-to-peer network where each computer shares files, folders, libraries, and printers with other computers in the homegroup. Access to the homegroup is secured using a homegroup password.

Home Theater PC (HTPC) A PC that is designed to play and possibly record music, photos, movies, and video on a television or extra-large monitor screen.

host bus *See* system bus.

host name A name that identifies a computer, printer, or other device on a network, which can be used instead of the computer's IP address to address the computer on the network. The host name together with the domain name is called the fully qualified domain name. *Also called* computer name.

Hosts file A file in the C:\Windows\System32\ drivers\etc folder that contains computer names and their associated IP addresses on the local network. The file has no file extension.

hot-plugging Plugging in a device while the computer is turned on. The computer will sense the device and configure it without rebooting. In addition, the device can be unplugged without an OS error. *Also called* hot-swapping.

hotspot A small area that offers connectivity to a wireless network, such as a Wi-Fi network.

hot-swappable The ability to plug or unplug devices without first powering down the system. USB devices are hot-swappable.

hot-swapping *See* hot-plugging.

HTPC case A case used to accommodate a home theater PC and must be small enough to fit on a shelf in an entertainment center.

HTTP (Hypertext Transfer Protocol) The TCP/IP protocol used for the World Wide Web and used by web browsers and web servers to communicate.

HTTPS (HTTP secure) The HTTP protocol working with a security protocol such as Secure Sockets Layer (SSL) or Transport Layer Security (TLS), which is better than SSL, to create a secured socket that includes data encryption.

hub A network device or box that provides a central location to connect cables and distributes incoming data packets to all other devices connected to it. *Compare with* switch.

hybrid cloud A combination of public, private, and community clouds used by the same organization. For example, a company might store data in a private cloud, but use a public cloud email service.

hybrid hard drive (H-HDD)   A hard drive that uses both magnetic and solid-state drive (SSD) technologies. The bulk of storage uses the magnetic component, and a storage buffer on the drive is made of an SSD component. Windows ReadyDrive supports hybrid hard drives.

Hyper-Threading   The Intel technology that allows each logical processor within the processor package to handle an individual thread in parallel with other threads being handled by other processors within the package.

Hyper Transport   The AMD technology that allows each logical processor within the processor package to handle an individual thread in parallel with other threads being handled by other processors within the package.

hypervisor   Software that creates and manages virtual machines on a server or on a local computer. *Also called* virtual machine manager (VMM).

IaaS (Infrastructure as a Service)   A cloud computing service that provides only the hardware, which can include servers, storage devices, and networks.

iCloud   A website by Apple (*www.icloud.com*) used to sync content on Apple devices in order to provide a backup of the content.

iCloud Backup   A feature of an iPhone, iPad, or iPod touch whereby the device's content is backed up to the cloud at *icloud.com*.

iCloud Drive   Storage space at *icloud.com* that can be synced with files stored on any Apple mobile device or any personal computer, including an OS X or Windows computer.

IDE (Integrated Drive Electronics or Integrated Device Electronics)   A hard drive whose disk controller is integrated into the drive, eliminating the need for a controller cable and thus increasing speed, as well as reducing price.

IEEE 1394 port   *See* FireWire port.

IEEE 802.11ac   The latest Wi-Fi standard that supports up to 7 Gbps (actual speeds are currently about 1300 Mbps) and uses 5.0-GHz radio frequency and beamforming.

IEEE 802.11n   A Wi-Fi standard that supports up to 600 Mbps and uses 5.0-GHz or 2.4-GHz radio frequency and supports MIMO.

ifconfig (interface configuration)   A Linux and OS X command similar to the Windows ipconfig command that displays details about network interfaces and can enable and disable an interface. When affecting the interface, the command requires root privileges.

image deployment   Installing a standard image on a computer.

imaging drum   An electrically charged rotating drum found in laser printers.

IMAP4 (Internet Message Access Protocol, version 4)   A protocol used by an email server and client that allows the client to manage email stored on the server without downloading the email. *Compare with* POP3.

IMEI (International Mobile Equipment Identity)   A unique number that identifies a mobile phone or tablet device worldwide. The number can usually be found imprinted on the device or reported in the About menu of the OS.

impact paper   Paper used by impact printers and comes as a box of fanfold paper or in rolls (used with receipt printers).

impact printer   A type of printer that creates a printed page by using a mechanism that touches or hits the paper.

IMSI (International Mobile Subscriber Identity)   A unique number that identifies a cellular subscription for a device or subscriber, along with its home country and mobile network. Some carriers store the number on a SIM card installed in the device.

Infrared (IR)   An outdated wireless technology that has been mostly replaced by Bluetooth to connect personal computing devices.

infrastructure mode   Wi-Fi devices connect to a Wi-Fi access point, such as a SOHO router, which is responsible for securing and managing the wireless network.

inherited permissions   Permissions assigned by Windows that are attained from a parent object.

initialization files   Text files that keep hardware and software configuration information, user preferences, and application settings and are used by the OS when first loaded and when needed by hardware, applications, and users.

ink cartridge   A cartridge in an inkjet printer that holds the different colors of ink for the printer.

inkjet printer   A type of ink dispersion printer that uses cartridges of ink. The ink is heated to a boiling point and then ejected onto the paper through tiny nozzles.

G

in-place upgrade A Windows installation that is launched from the Windows desktop. The installation carries forward user settings and installed applications from the old OS to the new one. A Windows OS is already in place before the installation begins.

In-Plane Switching (IPS) A class of LCD monitor that offers truer color images and better viewing angles, but is expensive and has slower response times.

interface In TCP/IP version 6, a node's attachment to a link. The attachment can be a physical attachment (for example, when using a network adapter) or a logical attachment (for example, when using a tunneling protocol). Each interface is assigned an IP address.

interface ID In TCP/IP version 6, the last 64 bits or 4 blocks of an IP address that identify the interface.

internal components The main components installed in a computer case.

Internet Options A dialog box used to manage Internet Explorer settings.

Internet Protocol version 4 (IPv4) A group of TCP/IP standards that uses IP addresses that have 32 bits.

Internet Protocol version 6 (IPv6) A group of TCP/IP standards that uses IP addresses that have 128 bits.

Internet service provider (ISP) A commercial group that provides Internet access for a monthly fee; Charter, Earthlink, and Windstream are large ISPs.

Internet telephone *See* Voice over Internet Protocol (VoIP).

intranet Any private network that uses TCP/IP protocols. A large enterprise might support an intranet that is made up of several local networks.

intrusion detection system (IDS) Software that can run on a UTM (Unified Threat Management) appliance, router, server, or workstation to monitor all network traffic and create alerts when suspicious activity happens.

intrusion prevention system (IPS) Software that can run on a UTM (Unified Threat Management) appliance, router, server, or workstation to monitor all network traffic, create alerts, and prevent the threatening traffic from burrowing into the system.

inverter An electrical device that converts DC to AC.

iOS The operating system owned and developed by Apple and used for its various mobile devices.

I/O shield A plate installed on the rear of a computer case that provides holes for I/O ports coming off the motherboard.

iPad A handheld tablet developed by Apple.

IP address A 32-bit or 128-bit address used to uniquely identify a device or interface on a network that uses TCP/IP protocols. Generally, the first numbers identify the network; the last numbers identify a host. An example of a 32-bit IP address is 206.96.103.114. An example of a 128-bit IP address is 2001:0000:B80::D3:9C5A:CC.

ipconfig (IP configuration) A Windows command that displays TCP/IP configuration information and can refresh TCP/IP assignments to a connection, including its IP address.

iPhone A smart phone developed by Apple.

iPod touch A multimedia recorder and player developed by Apple.

ISATAP In TCP/IP version 6, a tunneling protocol that has been developed for IPv6 packets to travel over an IPv4 network and stands for Intra-Site Automatic Tunnel Addressing Protocol.

ISDN (Integrated Services Digital Network) A broadband telephone line that can carry data at about five times the speed of regular telephone lines. Two channels (telephone numbers) share a single pair of wires. ISDN has been replaced by DSL.

ISO file *See* ISO image.

ISO image A file format that has an .iso file extension and holds an image of all the data, including the file system that is stored on an optical disc. ISO stands for International Organization for Standardization. *Also called* disc image or ISO file.

iTunes Store Apple website *itunes.apple.com* where apps, music, TV shows, movies, books, podcasts, and iTunes U content can be purchased and downloaded to Apple devices.

iTunes U Content at the iTunes Store website (*itunes.apple.com*) that contains lectures and even complete courses from many schools, colleges, and universities.

ITX *See* Mini-ITX.

iwconfig   A Linux and OS X command similar to ifconfig, but applies only to wireless networks. Use it to display information about a wireless interface and configure a wireless adapter.

jailbreaking   A process to break through the restrictions that only allow apps to an iOS device to be downloaded from the iTunes Store. Gives the user root or administrator privileges to the operating system and the entire file system and complete access to all commands and features. Note that jailbreaking voids any manufacturer warranty on the device, violates the End User License Agreement (EULA) with Apple, and might violate BYOD (Bring Your Own Device) policies in an enterprise environment.

joule   A measure of work or energy. One joule of energy produces one watt of power for one second.

jumper   Two small posts or metal pins that stick up side by side on the motherboard or other device and are used to hold configuration information. The jumper is considered closed if a cover is over the wires and open if the cover is missing.

kernel   The portion of an OS that is responsible for interacting with the hardware.

kernel mode   A Windows "privileged" processing mode that has access to hardware components.

kernel panic   A Linux or OS X error from which it cannot recover, similar to a blue screen of death in Windows.

keyboard backlight   A feature on some keyboards where the keys light up on the keyboard.

Keychain   In OS X, a built-in password manager utility.

Key-enrollment Key (KEK)   *See* Key-exchange Key (KEK).

Key-exchange Key (KEK)   A Secure Boot database that holds digital signatures provided by OS manufacturers.

key fob   A device, such as a type of smart card, that can fit conveniently on a key chain.

keylogger   A type of spyware that tracks your keystrokes, including passwords, chat room sessions, email messages, documents, online purchases, and anything else you type on your computer. Text is logged to a text file and transmitted over the Internet without your knowledge.

keystone RJ-45 jack   A jack that is used in an RJ-45 wall jack.

KVM (Keyboard, Video, and Mouse) switch   A switch that allows you to use one keyboard, mouse, and monitor for multiple computers. Some KVM switches also include sound ports so that speakers and a microphone can be shared among multiple computers.

LAN (local area network)   A network bound by routers that usually covers only a small area, such as one building.

land grid array (LGA)   A socket that has blunt protruding pins in uniform rows on the socket that connect with lands or pads on the bottom of the processor. *Compare with* pin grid array (PGA).

laptop   A portable computer that is designed for travel and mobility. Laptops use the same technology as desktop computers, with modifications for conserving voltage, taking up less space, and operating while on the move. *Also called* a notebook.

laser printer   A type of printer that uses a laser beam to control how toner is placed on the page and then uses heat to fuse the toner to the page.

Last Known Good Configuration   In Windows 7/Vista, registry settings and device drivers that were in effect when the computer last booted successfully. These settings are saved and can be restored during the startup process to recover from errors during the last boot. Windows 8 does not save the Last Known Good Configuration.

latency   Delays in network transmissions resulting in slower network performance. Latency is measured by the round-trip time it takes for a data packet to travel from source to destination and back to source.

launcher   The Android graphical user interface (GUI) that includes multiple home screens, and supports windows, panes, and 3D graphics.

Launchpad   In OS X, the screen that shows all apps installed on the computer, similar to the Windows 8 Start screen.

LC (local connector) connector   A fiber-optic cable connector that can be used with either single-mode or multimode fiber-optic cables and is easily terminated and smaller than an SC connector.

LCD (liquid crystal display) monitor   A monitor that uses LCD technology. LCD produces an image using a liquid crystal material made of large, easily polarized molecules. *Also called* flat-panel monitor.

G

LED (light-emitting diode) A technology used in an LCD monitor that uses less mercury than earlier technologies.

Level 1 cache (L1 cache) Memory on the processor die used as a cache to improve processor performance.

Level 2 cache (L2 cache) Memory in the processor package but not on the processor die. The memory is used as a cache or buffer to improve processor performance. *Also see* Level 1 cache (L1 cache).

Level 3 cache (L3 cache) Cache memory further from the processor core than Level 2 cache but still in the processor package.

library In Windows 8/7, a collection of one or more folders that can be stored on different local drives or on the network.

Lightning port The connector used on newer Apple iPhones, iPods, and iPads for power and communication.

Lightweight Directory Access Protocol (LDAP) A protocol used by various client applications when the application needs to query a database.

LILO (LInux boot LOader) The outdated Linux boot loader that could handle a dual boot and has been replaced by GRUB.

line-of-sight connectivity A type of connection used by satellites that requires no obstruction from mountains, trees, and tall buildings from the satellite dish to the satellite.

line speed *See* bandwidth.

link (local link) In TCP/IP version 6, a local area network or wide area network bounded by routers. *Also called* local link.

link-local address *See* link-local unicast address.

link-local unicast address In TCP/IP version 6, an IP address used for communicating among nodes in the same link and is not allowed on the Internet. *Also called* local address *and* link-local address.

Linux An OS based on UNIX that was created by Linus Torvalds of Finland. Basic versions of this OS are open source, and all the underlying programming instructions are freely distributed.

lite-touch, high-volume deployment A strategy that uses a deployment server on the network to serve up a Windows installation after a technician starts the process at the local computer.

lithium ion Currently the most popular battery type for laptop computers that is more efficient

than earlier types. Sometimes abbreviated as "Li-Ion" battery.

live CD In Linux, a CD, DVD, or flash drive that can boot up a live version of Linux, complete with Internet access and all the tools you normally have available in a hard drive installation of Linux, but without installing the OS on the hard drive.

live sign in Sign in to Windows 8 using a Microsoft account.

live tiles On the Windows 8 Start screen, some apps use live tiles, which offer continuous real-time updates.

loadstate A command used by the User State Migration Tool (USMT) to copy user settings and data temporarily stored at a safe location to a new computer. *Also see* scanstate.

local account A Windows user account that applies only to the local computer and cannot be used to access resources from other computers on the network. *Compare with* global account.

local area network (LAN) A network bound by routers or other gateway devices.

local address *See* link-local unicast address.

local bus *See* system bus.

local link *See* link.

local printer A printer connected to a computer by way of a port on the computer. *Compare with* network printer.

Local Security Policy A Windows Administrative Tools snap-in in Control Panel that can manage the group of policies in the Local Computer Policy, Computer Configuration, Windows Settings, Security Settings group of Group Policy.

local share Folders on a computer that are shared with others on the network by using a folder's Properties box. Local shares are used with a workgroup and not with a domain.

local snapshot In OS X, the temporary backups that Time Machine creates when the Mac is not connected to the backup media. When the media is later available, local snapshots are copied to the media.

Local Users and Groups For business and professional editions of Windows, a Windows utility console (lusrmgr.msc) that can be used to manage user accounts and user groups.

location data Data that a device can routinely report to a website, which can be used to locate the device on a map.

location independence A function of cloud computing whereby customers generally are not aware of where the physical devices providing cloud services are located geographically.

logical drive On an MBR hard drive, a portion or all of a hard drive extended partition that is treated by the operating system as though it were a physical drive or volume. Each logical drive is assigned a drive letter, such as drive F, and contains a file system. *Compare with* volume.

logical topology The logical way computers connect on a network.

login item In OS X, programs that are automatically launched after a user logs in. Login items are managed in the Users & Groups utility in System Preferences.

LoJack A technology by Absolute Software used to track the whereabouts of a laptop computer and, if the computer is stolen, lock down access to the computer or erase data on it. The technology is embedded in the UEFI/BIOS of many laptops.

Long Term Evolution (LTE) The latest standard used to transmit both voice and digital data over cellular networks and is expected to eventually replace CDMA and GSM.

loopback address An IP address that indicates your own computer and is used to test TCP/IP configuration on the computer.

loopback plug A device used to test a port in a computer or other device to make sure the port is working and might also test the throughput or speed of the port.

low-level formatting A process (usually performed at the factory) that electronically creates the hard drive tracks and sectors, and tests for bad spots on the disk surface. *Compare with* high-level formatting.

LPT (Line Printer Terminal) Assignments of system resources that are made to a parallel port and that are used to manage a print job. Two possible LPT configurations are referred to as LPT1: and LPT2:.

LPT port *See* parallel port.

MAC (Media Access Control) address A 48-bit (6-byte) hardware address unique to each network interface card (NIC) or onboard network controller that is assigned by the manufacturer at the factory and embedded on the device. The address is often printed on the adapter as hexadecimal numbers. An example is 00 00 0C 08 2F 35. *Also called* a physical address, an adapter address, or a hardware address.

MAC address filtering A technique used by a router or wireless access point to allow access to a private network to only certain computers or devices identified by their MAC addresses.

magnetic hard drive One of two technologies used by hard drives where data is stored as magnetic spots on disks that rotate at a high speed. *Compare with* solid-state drive (SSD).

main board *See* motherboard.

malicious software Any unwanted program that is transmitted to a computer without the user's knowledge and that is designed to do varying degrees of damage to data and software. Types of infestations include viruses, Trojan horses, worms, adware, spyware, keyloggers, browser hijackers, dialers, and downloaders. *Also called* malware or computer infestation.

malware *See* malicious software.

malware definition Information about malware that allows anti-malware software to detect and define malware. *Also called* a malware signature.

malware encyclopedia Lists of malware, including symptoms and solutions, often maintained by manufacturers of anti-malware and made available on their websites.

malware signature *See* malware definition.

MAN (metropolitan area network) A type of network that covers a large city or campus.

man-in-the-middle attack An attack that pretends to be a legitimate website, network, FTP site, or person in a chat session in order to obtain private information.

mantrap A physical security technique of using two doors on either end of a small entryway where the first door must close before the second door can open. A separate form of identification might be required for each door, such as a badge for the first door and a fingerprint scan for the second door. In addition, a security guard might monitor people as they come and go.

mapping The client computer creates and saves a shortcut, called a network drive, to a folder or drive shared by a remote computer on the network. The network drive has a drive letter associated with it, which points to the network share.

G

Master Boot Record (MBR)   One of two methods used to organize the partition tables on a hard drive. On an MBR hard drive, the first sector on the drive is called the MBR and contains the partition table and a program BIOS uses to boot an OS from the drive. *Compare with* Globally Unique Identifier Partition Table (GUID or GPT).

master file table (MFT)   The database used by the NTFS file system to track the contents of a volume or logical drive.

Material Safety Data Sheet (MSDS)   A document that explains how to properly handle substances such as chemical solvents; it includes information such as physical data, toxicity, health effects, first aid, storage, disposal, and spill procedures.

md (make directory)   The Windows command to create a directory.

measured service   When a cloud computing vendor offers services that are metered for billing purposes or to ensure transparency between vendors and customers.

megahertz (MHz)   One million Hz, or one million cycles per second. *Also see* hertz and gigahertz.

memory bank   The memory a processor addresses at one time. Today's desktop and laptop processors use a memory bank that is 64 bits wide.

memory bus   *See* system bus.

Memory Diagnostics   A Windows utility (mdsched.exe) used to test memory.

Metro User Interface (Metro UI)   *See* modern interface.

Micro-A connector   A USB connector that has five pins and is smaller than the Mini-B connector. It is used on digital cameras, cell phones, and other small electronic devices.

microATX (MATX)   A smaller version of the ATX form factor. MicroATX addresses some new technologies that were developed after the original introduction of ATX.

Micro-B connector   A USB connector that has five pins and has a smaller height than the Mini-B connector. It is used on digital cameras, cell phones, and other small electronic devices.

microprocessor   *See* central processing unit (CPU).

Microsoft account   For Windows 8 and above, an email address and password that allows access to several types of online accounts, including Microsoft OneDrive, Facebook, LinkedIn, Twitter, Skype, Outlook, and others.

Microsoft Assessment and Planning (MAP) Toolkit   Software that can be used by a system administrator from a network location to query hundreds of computers in a single scan to determine if a computer qualifies for a Windows upgrade.

Microsoft Exchange   A server application that can handle email, contacts, and calendars and is a popular application used by large corporations for employee email, contacts, and calendars.

Microsoft Management Console (MMC)   A Windows utility to build customized consoles. These consoles can be saved to a file with an .msc file extension.

Microsoft Store   The official source for Windows apps at *microsoftstore.com*.

microUSB   A smaller version of the regular USB connector.

MIDI (musical instrument digital interface)   A set of standards that are used to represent music in digital form. A MIDI port is a 5-pin DIN port that looks like a keyboard port, only larger.

MIMO   *See* multiple input/multiple output (MIMO).

Mini-B connector   A USB connector that has five pins and is often used to connect small electronic devices, such as a digital camera, to a computer.

Mini-DIN-6 connector   A 6-pin variation of the S-Video port and looks like a PS/2 connector used by a keyboard or mouse.

Mini DisplayPort   A smaller version of DisplayPort that is used on laptops or other mobile devices.

mini-HDMI connector   *See* HDMI mini connector.

Mini-ITX   A smaller version of the microATX form factor. *Also called* ITX.

Mini PCI   The PCI industry standard for desktop computer expansion cards, applied to a much smaller form factor for laptop expansion cards.

Mini PCI Express (Mini PCIe)   A standard used for laptop internal expansion slots that follows the PCI Express standards applied to laptops.

minicartridge   A tape drive cartridge that is only 3¼ x 2½ x 3/5 inches. It is small enough to allow two drives to fit into a standard 5-inch drive bay of a PC case.

miniUSB   A smaller version of the regular USB connector and is smaller than microUSB.

Miracast   A wireless display-mirroring technology that requires a Miracast-capable screen or dongle in order to mirror a smart phone's display to a TV, a wireless monitor, or a wireless projector.

mirrored volume   The term used by Windows for the RAID 1 level that duplicates data on one drive to another drive and is used for fault tolerance. *Also see* RAID 1.

Mission Control   In OS X, a utility and screen that gives an overview of all open windows and thumbnails of the Dashboard and desktops.

mobile hotspot   Created by a mobile device so that other devices or computers can connect by Wi-Fi to the device and on to the Internet.

mobile payment service   An app that allows you to use your smart phone or other mobile device to pay for merchandise or services at a retail checkout counter.

modem port   A port used to connect dial-up phone lines to computers.

modern interface   An interface that presents the Start screen to the user. *Also called* Windows 8 interface, *formerly called* Metro User Interface or Metro UI.

Molex connector   A 4-pin power connector used to provide power to a PATA hard drive or optical drive.

motherboard   The main board in the computer, *also called* the system board. The CPU, ROM chips, DIMMs, RIMMs, and interface cards are plugged into the motherboard.

motion controller   An input device that senses the motion of your fingers and hands. *Also called* motion sensor.

motion sensor   *See* motion controller.

mount point   A folder that is used as a shortcut to space on another volume, which effectively increases the size of the folder to the size of the other volume. *Also see* mounted drive.

mounted drive   A volume that can be accessed by way of a folder on another volume so that the folder has more available space. *Also see* mount point.

mstsc (Microsoft Terminal Services Client)   A Windows command that allows you to start Remote Desktop Connection to remote in to your host computer using Remote Desktop.

MT-RJ (mechanical transfer registered jack) connector   A type of connector used by fiber-optic cables and can be used with either single-mode or multimode fiber-optic cables and is more difficult to connect than the smaller LC connector.

multiboot   *See* dual boot.

multicast address   In TCP/IP version 6, an IP address used when packets are delivered to a group of nodes on a network.

multicasting   In TCP/IP version 6, one host sends messages to multiple hosts, such as when the host transmits a video conference over the Internet.

multicore processing   A processor technology whereby the processor housing contains two or more processor cores that operate at the same frequency but independently of each other.

multifactor authentication (MFA)   To use more than one method to authenticate access to a computer, network, or other resource.

MultiMediaCard (MMC)   A compact storage card that looks like an SD card, but the technology is different and they are not interchangeable. Generally, SD cards are faster than MMC cards.

multimeter   A device used to measure the various attributes of an electrical circuit. The most common measurements are voltage, current, and resistance.

multimonitor taskbar   The Windows 8 option to extend the desktop taskbar across multiple monitors. Use the taskbar properties box to adjust the taskbar.

multiple desktops   A feature of Mission Control in OS X, where several desktop screens, each with its own collection of open windows, are available to the user.

multiple input/multiple output (MIMO)   A feature of the IEEE 802.11n/ac standards for wireless networking whereby two or more antennas are used at both ends of transmissions to improve performance.

multiple monitor misalignment   When the display is staggered across multiple monitors, making the display difficult to read. Fix the problem by adjusting the display in the Windows Screen Resolution window.

multiple monitor orientation   When the display does not accurately represent the relative positions of multiple monitors. Use the Windows Screen Resolution window to move the display for each monitor so they are oriented correctly.

multiplier   The factor by which the bus speed or frequency is multiplied to get the CPU clock speed.

multiprocessing   Two processing units installed within a single processor and first used by the Pentium processor.

multiprocessor platform   A system that contains more than one processor. The motherboard has more than one processor socket and the processors must be rated to work in this multiprocessor environment.

G

multitouch A touch screen on a computer or mobile device that can handle a two-finger pinch.

mutual authentication To authenticate in both directions at the same time, as both entities confirm the identity of the other.

name resolution The process of associating a character-based name with an IP address.

NAND flash memory The type of memory used in solid-state drives (SSD). NAND stands for "Not AND" and refers to the logic used when storing a 1 or 0 in the grid of rows and columns on the memory chip.

NAT (Network Address Translation) A technique that substitutes the public IP address of the router for the private IP address of computer on a private network when these computers need to communicate on the Internet. *See also* Destination Network Address Translation (DNAT).

native resolution The actual (and fixed) number of pixels built into an LCD monitor. For the clearest display, always set the resolution to the native resolution.

navigation pane In File Explorer, Windows Explorer, or the Computer window, the pane on the left side of the window where devices, drives, and folders are listed. Double-click an item to drill down into the item.

nbtstat (NetBIOS over TCP/IP Statistics) A Windows TCP/IP command that is used to display statistics about the NetBT protocol.

Near Field Communication (NFC) A wireless technology that establishes a communication link between two NFC devices (for example, two smart phones or a smart phone and an NFC tag) that are within 4 inches of each other.

neighbors In TCP/IP version 6, two or more nodes on the same link.

net localgroup A Windows TCP/IP command that adds, displays, or modifies local user groups.

net use A Windows TCP/IP command that connects or disconnects a computer from a shared resource or can display information about connections.

net user A Windows TCP/IP command used to manage user accounts.

NetBIOS A legacy suite of protocols used by Windows before TCP/IP.

NetBIOS over TCP/IP A feature of Server Message Block (SMB) protocols that allows legacy NetBIOS applications to communicate on a TCP/IP network.

netbook A low-end, inexpensive laptop with a small 9- or 10-inch screen and no optical drive that is generally used for web browsing, email, and word processing by users on the go.

NetBoot A technology that allows a Mac to boot from the network and then install OS X on the machine from a clone DMG file stored on the server.

netdom (network domain) A Windows TCP/IP command that allows administrators to manage Active Directory domains and trust relationships for Windows Server from the command prompt on the server or remotely from a Windows 8/7 workstation.

netstat (network statistics) A Windows TCP/IP command that gives statistics about TCP/IP and network activity and includes several parameters.

network adapter *See* network interface card (NIC).

Network and Sharing Center The primary Windows utility used to manage network connections.

Network Attached Storage (NAS) A device that provides multiple bays for hard drives and an Ethernet port to connect to the network. The device is likely to support RAID.

network drive map Mounting a drive to a computer, such as drive E:, that is actually hard drive space on another host computer on the network.

Network File System (NFS) A Windows component that is a distributed file system used to manage shared files on a network.

network ID *See* global account.

network interface card (NIC) An expansion card that plugs into a computer's motherboard and provides a port on the back of the card to connect a computer to a network. *Also called* a network adapter.

network multimeter A multifunctional tool that can test network connections, cables, ports, and network adapters.

Network Places Wizard *See* User Accounts.

network port   A port used by a network cable to connect to the wired network. *Also called* an Ethernet port or RJ-45 port.

network printer   A printer that any user on the network can access, through its own network card and connection to the network, through a connection to a stand-alone print server, or through a connection to a computer as a local printer, which is shared on the network.

network share   One computer (the client) on the network appears to have a hard drive, such as drive E:, that is actually hard drive space on another host computer (the server). *Also see* mapping.

next-generation firewall (NGFW)   A firewall that combines firewall software with anti-malware software and other software that protects resources on a network.

node   Any device that connects to the network, such as a computer, printer, or router.

non compliant system   A system that violates security best practices, such as out-of-date anti-malware software or no anti-malware software installed.

nonvolatile RAM (NVRAM)   Flash memory on the motherboard that UEFI firmware uses to store device drivers and information about Secure Boot. Contents of NVRAM are not lost when the system is powered down.

North Bridge   That portion of the chipset hub that connects faster I/O buses (for example, the video bus) to the system bus. *Compare with* South Bridge.

notebook   *See* laptop.

Notepad   A Windows text editing program.

notification area   An area to the right of the Windows taskbar that holds the icons for running services; these services include the volume control and network connectivity. *Also called* the system tray or systray.

notifications   Alerts and related information about apps and social media sent to mobile devices.

nslookup (namespace lookup)   A TCP/IP command that lets you read information from the Internet namespace by requesting information about domain name resolutions from the DNS server's zone data.

NTFS permissions   A Windows method to share a folder or file over a network and can apply to local users and network users. The folder or file must be on an NTFS volume. *Compare with* share permissions.

octet   In TCP/IP version 4, each of the four numbers that are separated by periods and make up a 32-bit IP address. One octet is 8 bits.

Offline Files   A Windows utility that allows users to work with files in the folder when the computer is not connected to the corporate network. When the computer is later connected, Windows syncs up the offline files and folders with those on the network.

ohm (Ω)   The standard unit of measurement for electrical resistance. Resistors are rated in ohms.

OLED (organic light-emitting diode) monitor   A type of monitor that uses a thin LED layer or film between two grids of electrodes and does not use backlighting.

onboard NIC   A network port embedded on the motherboard.

onboard port   Ports that are directly on the motherboard, such as a built-in keyboard port or onboard network port.

on-demand   A service that is available to users at any time. On-demand cloud computing means the service is always available.

OneDrive   Microsoft cloud service that allows users with a Microsoft account to store, sync, and share files with other people and devices.

Open Database Connectivity (ODBC)   A technology that allows a client computer to create a data source so that the client can interface with a database stored on a remote (host) computer on the network. *Also see* data source.

open source   Source code for an operating system or other software whereby the source code is available for free and anyone can modify and redistribute the source code.

operating system (OS)   Software that controls a computer. An OS controls how system resources are used and provides a user interface, a way of managing hardware and software, and ways to work with files.

optical connector   A connector used with a fiber-optic cable.

G

option ROM   A Secure Boot driver required as the computer first boots, which is digitally signed and identified in the signature database.

Original Equipment Manufacturer (OEM) license   A software license that only manufacturers or builders of personal computers can purchase to be installed only on a computer intended for sale.

OS X   The latest version of the proprietary operating system only available for Macintosh computers by Apple Inc. (*apple.com*). OS X was originally based on UNIX.

OSI Model   A model for understanding and developing computer-to-computer communication, it divides networking functions among seven layers: Physical, Data Link, Network, Transport, Session, Presentation, and Application.

overclocking   Running a processor at a higher frequency than is recommended by the manufacturer, which can result in an unstable system, but is a popular thing to do when a computer is used for gaming.

PaaS (Platform as a Service)   A cloud computing service that provides the hardware and the operating system and is responsible for updating and maintaining both.

packet   A message sent over a network as a unit that contains the data and information at the beginning that identifies the type of data, where it came from, and where it's going. Also called data packet or datagram.

pagefile.sys   The Windows swap file that is used to hold the virtual memory that is used to enhance physical memory installed in a system.

pairing   The process of two Bluetooth devices establishing connectivity.

PAN (personal area network)   A small network consisting of personal devices at close range; the devices can include smart phones, PDAs, and laptop computers.

parallel ATA (PATA)   An older IDE cabling method that uses a 40-pin flat or round data cable or an 80-conductor cable and a 40-pin IDE connector. *Also see* serial ATA.

parallel port   An outdated female 25-pin port on a computer that transmitted data in parallel, 8 bits at a time, and was usually used with a printer. Parallel ports have been replaced by USB ports. *Also called* an LPT1 port, LPT2 port, and LPT port.

parity   An older error-checking scheme used with SIMMs in which a ninth, or "parity," bit is added. The value of the parity bit is set to either 0 or 1 to provide an even number of 1s for even parity and an odd number of 1s for odd parity.

parity error   An error that occurs in parity error checking when the number of 1s in the byte is not in agreement with the expected number.

partition   A division of a hard drive that can hold a volume. MBR drives can support up to four partitions on one hard drive. In Windows, GPT drives can have up to 128 partitions.

partition table   A table that contains information about each partition on the drive. For MBR drives, the partition table is contained in the Master Boot Record. For GPT drives, the partition table is stored in the GPT header and a backup of the table is stored at the end of the drive.

passive CPU cooler   *See* fanless CPU cooler.

patch   A minor update to software that corrects an error, adds a feature, or addresses security issues. *Also called* an update. *Compare with* service pack.

patch cable   *See* straight-through cable.

patch panel   A device that provides multiple network ports for cables that converge in one location such as an electrical closet or server room.

path   A drive and list of directories pointing to a file such as C:\Windows\System32.

PC Card   A card that uses a PC Card slot on a laptop, and provides a port for peripheral devices or adds memory to the laptop. A PC Card is about the size of a credit card, but thicker.

PCI (Peripheral Component Interconnect)   A bus common to personal computers that uses a 32-bit wide or a 64-bit data path. Several variations of PCI exist. On desktop systems, one or more notches on a PCI slot keep the wrong PCI cards from being inserted in the PCI slot.

PCI Express (PCIe)   The latest evolution of PCI, which is not backward compatible with earlier PCI slots and cards. PCIe slots come in several sizes, including PCIe x1, PCIe x4, PCIe x8, and PCIe x16.

PCIe 6/8-pin connector A power cord connector used by high-end video cards using PCIe x16 slots to provide extra voltage to the card and can accommodate a 6-hole or 8-hole port.

PCI-X The second evolution of PCI, which is backward compatible with conventional PCI slots and cards, except 5-V PCI cards. PCI-X is focused on the server market.

PCL (Printer Control Language) A printer language developed by Hewlett-Packard that communicates to a printer how to print a page.

PCMCIA card A card used with older laptops that was one or more variations of a PC Card to add memory to a laptop or provide ports for peripheral devices. For example, modem cards, network cards for wired or wireless network, sound cards, SCSI host adapters, FireWire controllers, USB controllers, flash memory adapter, TV tuner, and hard disks.

peer-to-peer (P2P) As applied to networking, a network of computers that are all equals, or peers. Each computer has the same amount of authority, and each can act as a server to the other computers.

Performance Monitor A Microsoft Management Console snap-in that can track activity by hardware and software to measure performance.

permission propagation When Windows passes permissions from parent objects to child objects.

permissions Varying degrees of access assigned to a folder or file and given to a user account or user group. Access can include full control, write, delete, or read-only.

personal assistant *See* virtual assistant.

personal license A license to use software that gives the right to install one instance of the software.

phablet A mobile device that has the same capabilities of a smart phone or tablet and is smaller than a tablet and larger than a smart phone.

phishing Sending an email message with the intent of getting the user to reveal private information that can be used for identity theft. *Also see* spear phishing and spoofing.

physical address *See* MAC (Media Access Control) address.

physical topology The physical arrangement of connections between computers.

pickup roller A part in a printer that pushes forward a sheet of paper from the paper tray.

ping A TCP/IP command used to troubleshoot network connections. It verifies that the host can communicate with another host on the network. Stands for Packet InterNet Groper.

pin grid array (PGA) A socket that has holes aligned in uniform rows around the socket to receive the pins on the bottom of the processor. *Compare with* land grid array (LGA).

pinning To make a frequently used application more accessible, add its icon to the taskbar on the desktop.

pixel A small spot on a fine horizontal scan line. Pixels are illuminated to create an image on the monitor.

pixel pitch The distance between adjacent pixels on the screen.

plasma monitor A type of monitor that provides high contrast with better color than LCD monitors. They work by discharging xenon and neon plasma on flat glass and don't contain mercury.

platform The hardware, operating system, runtime libraries, and modules on which an application runs.

Platform Key (PK) A digital signature belonging to the motherboard or computer manufacturer. The PK authorizes turning on or off Secure Boot and updating the KEK database.

plenum The area between floors of a building.

PoE injector A device that adds power to an Ethernet cable so the cable can provide power to a device.

POP or POP3 (Post Office Protocol, version 3) The protocol that an email server and client use when the client requests the downloading of email messages. The most recent version is POP version 3. *Compare with* IMAP4.

port (1) As applied to services running on a computer, a number assigned to a process on a computer so that the process can be found by TCP/IP. *Also called* a port address or port number. (2) A physical connector, usually at the back of a computer, that allows a cable from a peripheral device, such as a printer, mouse, or modem, to be attached.

G

port address *See* port.

port filtering To open or close certain ports so they can or cannot be used. A firewall uses port filtering to protect a network from unwanted communication.

port forwarding A technique that allows a computer on the Internet to reach a computer on a private network using a certain port when the private network is protected by NAT and a firewall that controls the use of ports. *Also called* port mapping.

port mapping *See* port forwarding.

port number *See* port.

port triggering When a firewall opens a port because a computer behind the firewall initiates communication on another port.

POST (power-on self test) A self-diagnostic program used to perform a simple test of the CPU, RAM, and various I/O devices. The POST is performed by startup UEFI/BIOS when the computer is first turned on.

POST card A test card installed in a slot on the motherboard or plugged in to a USB port that is used to help discover and report computer errors and conflicts that occur when a computer is first turned on and before the operating system is launched. *Also called* POST diagnostic card.

POST diagnostic card *See* POST card.

PostScript A printer language developed by Adobe Systems that tells a printer how to print a page.

Power Options applet Accessed through Control Panel, manages power settings to conserve power.

Power over Ethernet (PoE) A feature that might be available on high-end wired network adapters that allows power to be transmitted over Ethernet cable to remote devices.

power supply A box inside the computer case that receives power and converts it to provide power to the motherboard and other installed devices. Power supplies provide 3.3-, 5-, and 12-V DC. *Also called* a power supply unit (PSU).

power supply tester A device that can test the output of each power cord coming from a power supply.

power supply unit (PSU) *See* power supply.

Power Users group A type of user account group. Accounts assigned to this group can read from and write to parts of the system other than their own user profile folders, install applications, and perform limited administrative tasks.

powerline networking A technique to allow Ethernet transmissions over power lines. A powerline adapter is plugged into the electrical circuit(s) at both ends and the adapters connect to the Ethernet network. Because the transmissions are not contained, encryption is required for security. *Also called* Ethernet over Power (EoP).

Preboot eXecution Environment (PXE) Programming contained in the UEFI/BIOS code on the motherboard used to start up the computer and search for a server on the network to provide a bootable operating system. *Also called* Pre-Execution Environment (PXE).

Pre-Execution Environment (PXE) *See* Preboot eXecution Environment (PXE).

presentation virtualization Using this virtualization, a remote application running on a server is controlled by a local computer.

primary partition A hard disk partition that can be used to boot the system. An MBR drive can have up to three primary partitions. In Windows, a GPT drive can have up to 128 primary partitions. *Compare with* extended partition.

principle of least privilege An approach where computer users are classified and the rights assigned are the minimum rights required to do their job.

print head The part in an inkjet or impact printer that moves across the paper, creating one line of the image with each pass.

Print Management A utility located in the Administrative Tools group in Windows 8/7/Vista professional and business editions that allows you to monitor and manage printer queues for all printers on the network.

print server Hardware or software that manages the print jobs sent to one or more printers on a network.

print spooler A queue for print jobs.

printer maintenance kit A kit purchased from a printer manufacturer that contains the parts, tools, and instructions needed to perform routine printer maintenance.

printer self-test page   A test page that prints by using controls at the printer. The page allows you to eliminate a printer as a problem and usually prints tests, graphics, and information about the printer such as the printer resolution and how much memory is installed.

printui   The Windows Printer User Interface command used by administrators to manage printers on the local and remote computers.

privacy filter   A device that fits over a monitor screen to prevent other people from viewing the monitor from a wide angle.

private cloud   Services on the Internet that an organization provides on its own servers or established virtually for a single organization's private use.

private IP address   In TCP/IP version 4, an IP address that is used on a private network that is isolated from the Internet. *Compare with* public IP address.

PRL (Preferred Roaming List)   A list of preferred service providers or radio frequencies your carrier wants a mobile device to use and is stored on a Removable User Identity Module (R-UIM) card installed in the device.

process   A program that is running under the authority of the shell, together with the system resources assigned to it.

processor   *See* central processing unit (CPU).

processor frequency   The speed at which the processor operates internally. Usually expressed in GHz.

processor thermal trip error   A problem when the processor overheats and the system restarts.

product activation   The process that Microsoft uses to prevent software piracy. For example, once Windows 8 is activated for a particular computer, it cannot be legally installed on another computer.

Product Release Instructions (PRI)   Information published by the manufacturer of an operating system that describes what to expect from a published update to the OS.

Programs and Features   A window within Control Panel that lists the programs installed on a computer, where you can uninstall, change, or repair programs.

projector   Used to shine a light that projects a transparent image onto a large screen and is often used in classrooms or with other large groups.

protocol   A set of rules and standards that two entities use for communication. For example, TCP/IP is a suite or group of protocols that define many types of communication on a TCP/IP network.

proxy server   A computer that intercepts requests that a client (for example, a browser) makes of a server (for example, a web server) and can serve up the request from a cache it maintains to improve performance or can filter requests to secure a large network.

PS/2 port   A round 6-pin port used by a keyboard or mouse.

public cloud   Cloud computing services provided over the Internet to the general public. Google or Yahoo! email services are examples of public cloud deployment.

public IP address   In TCP/IP version 4, an IP address available to the Internet. *Compare with* private IP address.

pull automation   A Windows installation that requires the local user to start the process. *Compare with* push automation.

punchdown tool   A tool used to punch individual wires from a network cable into their slots to terminate the cable.

push automation   An installation where a server automatically pushes the installation to a computer when a user is not likely to be sitting at the computer. *Compare with* pull automation.

PVC (polyvinyl chloride)   The product used to cover Ethernet cables that is not safe to be used in a plenum because it gives off toxic fumes when burned.

quad channels   Technology used by a motherboard and DIMMs that allows the memory controller to access four DIMMS at the same time. DDR3 and DDR4 DIMMs can use quad channels.

Quality of Service (QoS)   A feature used by Windows and network hardware devices to improve network performance for an application that is not getting the best network performance. VoIP (Voice over IP) requires a high QoS.

quarantined computer   A computer that is suspected of infection and is not allowed to use the network, is put on a different network

G

dedicated to quarantined computers, or is allowed to access only certain network resources.

quick format   A format procedure, used to format a hard drive volume or other drive, that doesn't scan the volume or drive for bad sectors; use it only when a drive has been previously formatted and is in healthy condition.

Quick Launch menu   The menu that appears when the Windows Start button is right-clicked or the user presses Win+X.

QuickPath Interconnect (QPI)   The technology used first by the Intel X58 chipset for communication between the chipset and the processor using 16 serial lanes similar to that used by PCI Express. Replaced the 64-bit wide Front Side Bus used by previous chipsets.

radio frequency (RF)   The frequency of waves generated by a radio signal, which are electromagnetic frequencies above audio and below light. For example, Wi-Fi 802.11n transmits using a radio frequency of 5 GHz and 2.4 GHz.

RAID (redundant array of inexpensive disks or redundant array of independent disks)   Several methods of configuring multiple hard drives to store data to increase logical volume size and improve performance, or to ensure that if one hard drive fails, the data is still available from another hard drive.

RAID 0   Using space from two or more physical disks to increase the disk space available for a single volume. Performance improves because data is written evenly across all disks. Windows calls RAID 0 a striped volume. *Also called* striping or striped volume.

RAID 1   A type of drive imaging that duplicates data on one drive to another drive and is used for fault tolerance. Windows calls RAID 1 a mirrored volume. *Also called* mirrored volume.

RAID 1+0   *See* RAID 10.

RAID 10   A combination of RAID 1 and RAID 0 that requires at least four disks to work as an array of drives and provides the best redundancy and performance.

RAID 5   A technique that stripes data across three or more drives and uses parity checking, so that if one drive fails, the other drives can re-create the data stored on the failed drive. RAID 5 drives

increase performance and provide fault tolerance. Windows calls these drives RAID-5 volumes.

RAID-5 volume   The term used by Windows for RAID 5. *See* RAID 5.

RAM (random access memory)   Memory modules on the motherboard containing microchips used to temporarily hold data and programs while the CPU processes both. Information in RAM is lost when the computer is turned off.

ransomware   Malware that holds your computer system hostage with encryption techniques until you pay money or a time period expires when the encrypted content is destroyed.

rapid elasticity   A cloud computing service that is capable of scaling up or down as a customer's need level changes.

RAS Latency   A method of measuring access timing to memory, which is the number of clock cycles required to write or read a row of data off a memory module. RAS stands for Row Access Strobe. *Compare with* CAS Latency.

raw data   Data sent to a printer without any formatting or processing.

RCA connector   A connector used with composite and component cables that is round and has a single pin in the center.

rd (remove directory)   The Windows command to delete a directory (folder) or group of directories (folders).

ReadyBoost   A Windows utility that uses a flash drive or secure digital (SD) memory card to boost hard drive performance.

ReadyDrive   The Windows technology that supports a hybrid hard drive.

read/write head   A sealed, magnetic coil device that moves across the surface of a disk in a magnetic hard disk drive (HDD) either reading data from or writing data to the disk.

recover   The Windows command that can recover a file when part of the file is corrupted.

recovery drive   A Windows 8 bootable USB flash drive that can be used to recover the system when startup fails and can be created using the Recovery applet in Control Panel.

recovery image   A backup of the Windows volume.

recovery partition   A partition on a hard drive that contains a recovery utility and installation files.

Recovery System In OS X, a lean operating system that boots from a hidden volume on the OS X startup disk and is used to troubleshoot OS X when startup errors occur.

rectifier An electrical device that converts AC to DC. A computer power supply contains a rectifier.

Recycle Bin In Windows, location on the hard drive where deleted files are stored.

refresh A Windows 8 technique to recover from a corrupted Windows installation and can recover using a custom refresh image, a recovery partition, or the Windows setup DVD. Depending on the health of the system, user settings, data, and Windows 8 apps might be restored from backup near the end of the refresh operation.

refresh rate As applied to monitors, the number of times in one second the monitor can fill the screen with lines from top to bottom. *Also called* vertical scan rate.

registry A database that Windows uses to store hardware and software configuration information, user preferences, and setup information.

Registry Editor The Windows utility (regedit.exe) used to edit the Windows registry.

Regsvr32 A utility that is used to register component services used by an installed application.

Reliability and Performance Monitor A Vista utility (perfmon.msc) that collects, records, and displays events, called Data Collector Sets, that can help track the performance and reliability of Windows.

Reliability Monitor A Windows 8/7 utility that provides information about problems and errors that happen over time.

Remote Admin share Gives an administrator access to the Windows folder on a remote computer in a Windows domain.

remote application An application that is installed and executed on a server and is presented to a user working at a client computer.

Remote Assistance A Windows tool that allows a technician to remote in to a user's computer while the user remains signed, retains control of the session, and can see the screen. This is helpful when a technician is troubleshooting problems on a computer.

remote backup application A cloud backup service on the Internet that backs up data to the cloud and is often used for laptops, tablets, and smart phones.

Remote Desktop Connection (RDC) A Windows tool that gives a user access to a Windows desktop from anywhere on the Internet.

Remote Desktop Protocol (RDP) The Windows protocol used by Remote Desktop and Remote Assistance utilities to connect to and control a remote computer.

Remote Disc A feature of OS X that gives other computers on the network access to the Mac's optical drive.

remote network installation An automated installation where no user intervention is required.

remote printing Printing from a computer or mobile device to a printer that is not connected directly to the computer or device.

remote wipe Remotely erases all contacts, email, photos, and other data from a device to protect your privacy.

ren (rename) The Windows command to rename a file or group of files.

repair installation A reinstallation of Windows using the recovery utility and installation files stored on the recovery partition.

repeater A device that amplifies and retransmits a wireless signal to a wider coverage area and uses a new network name for the rebroadcast.

reset Restore a Window 8 installation to factory state or to the state after a clean install of Windows. The hard drive is formatted and all user data and settings are lost.

resiliency In Windows 8 Storage Spaces, the term refers to the degree the configuration can resist or recover from drive failure.

Resilient File System (ReFS) A file system that offers excellent fault tolerance and compatibility with virtualization and data redundancy in a RAID system.

resolution The number of pixels on a monitor screen that are addressable by software (example: 1024 x 768 pixels).

Resource Monitor A Windows tool that monitors the performance of the processor, memory, hard drive, and network.

G

resource pooling Cloud computing services to multiple customers that are hosted on shared physical resources and dynamically allocated to meet customer demand.

response time The time it takes to build one frame on a monitor screen.

restore point A snapshot of the Windows system, usually made before installation of new hardware or applications. Restore points are created by the System Protection utility.

REt (Resolution Enhancement technology) The term used by Hewlett-Packard to describe the way a laser printer varies the size of the dots used to create an image. This technology partly accounts for the sharp, clear image created by a laser printer.

retinal scanning As part of the authentication process, some systems use biometric data by scanning the blood vessels on the back of the eye and is considered the most reliable of all biometric data scanning.

reverse lookup To find the host name when you know a computer's IP address. The nslookup command can perform a reverse lookup.

revoked signature database (dbx) A Secure Boot database that is a blacklist of signatures for software that has been revoked and no longer trusted.

RFID badge A badge worn by an employee and used to gain entrance into a locked area of a building. A Radio Frequency Identification token transmits authentication to the system when the token gets in range of a query device.

RG-59 coaxial cable An older and thinner coaxial cable once used for cable TV.

RG-6 coaxial cable A coaxial cable used for cable TV, which replaced the older and thinner RG-59 coaxial cable.

RGB port *See* composite video port.

RIMM An older type of memory module developed by Rambus, Inc.

riser card A card that plugs into a motherboard and allows for expansion cards to be mounted parallel to the motherboard. Expansion cards are plugged into slots on the riser card.

RJ-11 *See* RJ-11 jack.

RJ-11 jack A phone line connection or port found on modems, telephones, and house phone outlets.

RJ-45 A port that looks like a large phone jack and is used by twisted-pair cable to connect to a wired network adapter or other hardware device. RJ stands for registered jack. *Also called* Ethernet port.

robocopy (robust file copy) A Windows command that is similar to and more powerful than the xcopy command, used to copy files and folders.

root account In Linux and OS X, the account that gives the user access to all the functions of the OS; the principal user account.

root certificate The original digital certificate issued by a Certification Authority.

root directory The main directory, at the top of the top-down hierarchical structure of subdirectories, created when a hard drive or disk is first formatted. In Linux, it's indicated by a forward slash. In Windows, it's indicated by a backward slash.

rooting The process of obtaining root or administrator privileges to an Android device, which then gives you complete access to the entire file system and all commands and features. Note that rooting may void any manufacturer warranty on the device and might violate BYOD (Bring Your Own Device) policies in an enterprise environment.

rootkit A type of malicious software that loads itself before the OS boot is complete and can hijack internal Windows components so that it masks information Windows provides to user-mode utilities such as File Explorer or Task Manager.

router A device that manages traffic between two or more networks and can help find the best path for traffic to get from one network to another.

RSA tokens A type of smart card that contains authentication information.

S1 state On the UEFI/BIOS power screen, one of the five S states used by ACPI power-saving mode to indicate different levels of power-savings functions. In the S1 state, the hard drive and monitor are turned off and everything else runs normally.

S2 state On the UEFI/BIOS power screen, one of the five S states used by ACPI power-saving mode to indicate different levels of power-savings functions. In S2 state, the hard drive and monitor are turned off and everything else runs normally. In addition, the processor is also turned off.

S3 state On the UEFI/BIOS power screen, one of the five S states used by ACPI power-saving mode to indicate different levels of power-savings functions. In S3 state, everything is shut down except RAM and enough of the system to respond to a wake-up. S3 is sleep mode.

S4 state On the UEFI/BIOS power screen, one of the five S states used by ACPI power-saving mode to indicate different levels of power-savings functions. In S4 state, everything in RAM is copied to a file on the hard drive and the system is shut down. When the system is turned on, the file is used to restore the system to its state before shut down. S4 is hibernation.

S5 state On the UEFI/BIOS power screen, one of the five S states used by ACPI power-saving mode to indicate different levels of power-savings functions. S5 state is the power-off state after a normal shutdown.

SaaS (Software as a Service) A cloud computing service whereby the service is responsible for the hardware, the operating systems, and the applications installed.

Safe Mode The technique of launching Windows with a minimum configuration, eliminating third-party software, and reducing Windows startup to only essential processes. The technique can sometimes launch Windows when a normal Windows startup is corrupted.

safety goggles Eye goggles worn while working in an unsafe environment such as a factory where fragments, chips, or other particles might injure eyes.

sag *See* brownout.

SATA power connector A 15-pin flat power connector that provides power to SATA drives.

SC (subscriber connector or standard connector) connector A type of snap-in connector used by fiber-optic cables and can be used with either single-mode or multimode fiber-optic cables. It is not used with the fastest fiber-optic networking.

scanstate A command used by the User State Migration Tool (USMT) to copy user settings and data from an old computer to a safe location such as a server or removable media. *Also see* loadstate.

screen orientation The layout or orientation of the screen that is either portrait or landscape.

screen resolution The number of dots or pixels on the monitor screen expressed as two numbers such as 1680 x 1050.

Screen Sharing In OS X, a utility to remotely view and control a Mac and is similar to Remote Assistance in Windows.

SCSI (Small Computer System Interface) An interface between a host adapter and the CPU that can daisy-chain as many as 7 or 15 devices on a single bus.

SDK (Software Development Kit) A group of tools that developers use to write apps. For example, Android Studio is a free SDK that is released as open source.

SDRAM II *See* Double Data Rate SDRAM.

secondary click In OS X, right-click the mouse or tap the lower-right corner of the trackpad on a Mac laptop.

secondary logon Using administrator privileges to perform an operation when you are not logged on with an account that has these privileges.

sector On a hard disk drive or SSD, the smallest unit of bytes addressable by the operating system and UEFI/BIOS. On hard disk drives, one sector usually equals 512 bytes; SSD drives might use larger sectors.

Secure Boot A UEFI feature that prevents a system from booting up with drivers or an OS that are not digitally signed and trusted by the motherboard or computer manufacturer.

Secure Digital (SD) card A type of memory card used in digital cameras, tablets, cell phones, MP3 players, digital camcorders, and other portable devices. The three standards used by SD cards are 1.x (regular SD), 2.x (SD High Capacity or SDHC), and 3.x (SD eXtended Capacity or SDXC).

Secure FTP (SFTP) A TCP/IP protocol used to transfer files from an FTP server to an FTP client using encryption.

Secure Shell (SSH) A protocol that is used to pass login information to a remote computer and control that computer over a network using encryption.

Security Center A Vista utility where you can confirm Windows Firewall, Windows Update, anti-malware settings, including that of Windows Defender, and other security settings.

G

security token A smart card or other device that is one factor in multifactor authentication or can serve as a replacement for a password.

self-grounding A method to safeguard against ESD that involves touching the computer case or power supply before touching a component in the computer case.

separate pad *See* separation pad.

separation pad A printer part that keeps more than one sheet of paper from moving forward.

sequential access A method of data access used by tape drives, whereby data is written or read sequentially from the beginning to the end of the tape or until the desired data is found.

serial ATA (SATA) An ATAPI interface standard for hard drives, optical drives, and other drives that uses a narrower and more reliable cable than the 80-conductor cable and is easier to configure than PATA systems. *Also see* parallel ATA.

serial port A male 9-pin or 25-pin port on a computer system used by slower I/O devices such as a mouse or modem. Data travels serially, one bit at a time, through the port. Serial ports are sometimes configured as COM1, COM2, COM3, or COM4. *Also called* DB9 port.

Server Message Block (SMB) A protocol used by Windows to share files and printers on a network.

Service Set Identifier (SSID) The name of a wireless access point and wireless network.

server-side virtualization Using this virtualization, a server provides a virtual desktop or application for users on multiple client machines.

service A program that runs in the background to support or serve Windows or an application.

service pack A collection of several patches or updates that is installed as a single update to an OS or application. *Compare with* patch.

Services console A console used by Windows to stop, start, and manage background services used by Windows and applications.

set-top box A device that makes a regular TV function as a smart TV.

setup UEFI/BIOS Used to change motherboard settings. For example, you can use it to enable or disable a device on the motherboard, change the date and time that is later passed to the OS, and select the order of boot devices for startup UEFI/BIOS to search when looking for an operating system to load.

shadow copy A copy of open files made so that open files are included in a backup.

share permissions A method to share a folder (not individual files) to remote users on the network, including assigning varying degrees of access to specific user accounts and user groups. Does not apply to local users of a computer and can be used on an NTFS or FAT volume. *Compare with* NTFS permissions.

sheet battery A secondary battery that fits on the bottom of a laptop to provide additional battery charge.

shell The portion of an OS that relates to the user and to applications.

shell prompt In Linux and OS X, the command prompt in the terminal.

shielded twisted-pair (STP) cable A cable that is made of one or more twisted pairs of wires and is surrounded by a metal shield.

Short Message Service (SMS) A technology that allows users to send a test message using a cell phone.

shoulder surfing As you work, other people secretly peek at your monitor screen to gain valuable information.

shutdown The Windows command to shut down the local computer or a remote computer.

sidebar Located on the right side of the Vista desktop and displays Vista gadgets.

side-by-side apps In Windows 8, an application or page can be snapped to the left or right side of the screen so a second page can share the screen.

signature database (db) A Secure Boot database that holds a list of digital signatures of approved operating systems, applications, and drivers that can be loaded by UEFI.

SIM (Subscriber Identity Module) card A small flash memory card that contains all the information a device needs to connect to a GSM or LTE cellular network, including a password and other authentication information needed to access the network, encryption standards used, and the services that a subscription includes.

SIMM (single inline memory module) An outdated miniature circuit board used to hold RAM. SIMMs held 8, 16, 32, or 64 MB on a single module. SIMMs have been replaced by DIMMs.

Simple Network Management Protocol (SNMP) A TCP/IP protocol used to monitor network traffic.

simple volume A type of volume used on a single hard drive. *Compare with* dynamic volume.

single channel The memory controller on a motherboard that can access only one DIMM at a time. *Compare with* dual channels and triple channels.

single-sided A DIMM that has memory chips installed on one side of the module.

single sign-on (SSO) An account that accesses multiple, independent resources, systems, or applications after signing in one time to one account. An example is a Microsoft account.

site license A license that allows a company to install multiple copies of software, or to allow multiple employees to execute the software from a file server. *Also called* enterprise license.

slack Wasted space on a hard drive caused by not using all available space at the end of a cluster.

sleep mode A power-saving state for a computer used to save power when not using the computer. *Also called* suspend mode. *Also see* S3 state.

sleep timer The number of minutes of inactivity before a computer goes into a power-saving state such as sleep mode.

small form factor (SFF) A motherboard used in low-end computers and home theater systems. Often used with an Intel Atom processor and sometimes purchased as a motherboard-processor combo unit.

S.M.A.R.T. (Self-Monitoring Analysis and Reporting Technology) A system BIOS and hard drive feature that monitors hard drive performance, disk spin-up time, temperature, distance between the head and the disk, and other mechanical activities of the drive in order to predict when the drive is likely to fail.

smart camera A digital camera that has embedded computing power to make decisions about the content of the photos or videos it records, including transmitting alerts over a wired or wireless network when it records certain content. *Also called* a vision sensor.

smart card Any small device that contains authentication information that can be keyed into a sign-in window or read by a reader to authenticate a user on a network.

smart card reader A device that can read a smart card used to authenticate a person onto a network.

smart phone A cell phone that includes abilities to send text messages, text messages with photos, videos, or other multimedia content, surf the web, manage email, play games, take photos and videos, and download and use apps.

smart TV A television that has the ability to run apps, store data, and connect to the Internet.

SMB2 *See* CIFS (Common Internet File System).

S/MIME (Secure/Multipurpose Internet Mail Extensions) A protocol that encrypts an outgoing email message and includes a digital signature and is more secure than SMTP, which does not use encryption.

SMTP (Simple Mail Transfer Protocol) A TCP/IP protocol used by email clients to send email messages to an email server and on to the recipient's email server. *Also see* POP and IMAP.

SMTP AUTH (SMTP Authentication) An improved version of SMTP and used to authenticate a user to an email server when the email client first tries to connect to the email server to send email. The protocol is based on the Simple Authentication and Security Layer (SASL) protocol.

snap-in A Windows utility that can be installed in a console window by Microsoft Management Console.

social engineering The practice of tricking people into giving out private information or allowing unsafe programs into the network or computer.

socket An established connection between a client and a server, such as the connection between a browser and web server.

SO-DIMM (small outline DIMM) A type of memory module used in laptop computers that uses DIMM technology. A DDR3 SO-DIMM has 204 pins. A DDR2 or DDR SO-DIMM has 200 pins. Older, outdated SO-DIMMs can have 72 pins or 144 pins.

soft boot To restart a computer without turning off the power, for example, in Windows 8, press Win+X, point to Shut down or sign out, and click Restart. *Also called* warm boot.

soft reset (1) For Android, to forcefully reboot the device (full shut down and cold boot) by pressing and holding the power button. (2) For iOS, to put the device in hibernation and not clear memory by pressing the Wake/sleep button.

G

Software Explorer A Vista tool used to control startup programs.

software piracy The act of making unauthorized copies of original software, which violates the Federal Copyright Act of 1976.

software RAID Using Windows to implement RAID. The setup is done using the Disk Management utility.

solid-state device (SSD) An electronic device with no moving parts. A storage device that uses memory chips to store data instead of spinning disks (such as those used by magnetic hard drives and CD drives). Examples of solid-state devices are USB flash drives, flash memory cards, and solid-state disks used as hard drives. Also called solid-state disk (SSD) or solid-state drive (SSD). *Compare with* magnetic hard drive.

solid-state drive (SSD) A hard drive that has no moving parts. *Also see* solid-state device (SSD).

Sound applet Accessed through Control Panel, used to select a default speaker and microphone and adjust how Windows handles sounds.

sound card An expansion card with sound ports.

sound port *See* audio port.

South Bridge That portion of the chipset hub that connects slower I/O buses (for example, a PCI bus) to the system bus. *Compare with* North Bridge.

Space In OS X, one desktop screen is called a Space. Multiple desktops or Spaces can be open and available to users.

spacer *See* standoff.

spanning A configuration of two hard drives that hold a single Windows volume to increase the size of a volume. Sometimes called JBOD (just a bunch of disks).

S/PDIF (Sony/Phillips Digital InterFace) sound port A port that connects to an external home theater audio system, providing digital audio output and the best signal quality.

spear phishing A form of phishing where an email message appears to come from a company you already do business with. *See also* phishing.

spoofing A phishing technique where you are tricked into clicking a link in an email message, which takes you to an official-looking website where you are asked to enter your user ID and password to enter the site. *See also* phishing.

spooling Placing print jobs in a print queue so that an application can be released from the printing process before printing is completed. Spooling is an acronym for simultaneous peripheral operations online.

Spotlight In OS X, the search app that can be configured to search the local computer, Wikipedia, iTunes, the Maps app, the web, and more.

spyware Malicious software that installs itself on your computer or mobile device to spy on you. It collects personal information about you that it transmits over the Internet to web-hosting sites that intend to use your personal data for harm.

staggered pin grid array (SPGA) A type of socket used by processors that has pins staggered over the socket in order to squeeze more pins into a small space.

standard account The Windows user account type that can use software and hardware and make some system changes, but cannot make changes that affect the security of the system or other users. *Compare with* administrator account.

standard image An image that includes Windows, drivers, and applications that are standard to all the computers that might use the image.

standoff Round plastic or metal pegs that separate the motherboard from the case, so that components on the back of the motherboard do not touch the case. *Also called* spacer.

Start screen Introduced in Windows 8, the Start screen contains tiles that represent lean apps, which use few system resources and are designed for social media, social networking, and the novice end user.

startup disk In OS X, the entire volume on which OS X is installed.

startup items In OS X, programs that automatically launch at startup. Apple discourages the use of startup items, which are stored in two directories: /Library/StartupItems and /System/Library/ StartupItems. Normally, both directories are empty.

startup repair A Windows utility that restores many of the Windows files needed for a successful boot.

startup UEFI/BIOS Part of UEFI or BIOS firmware on the motherboard that is responsible for controlling the computer when it is first turned on. Startup UEFI/BIOS gives control over to the OS once the OS is loaded.

static electricity   *See* electrostatic discharge (ESD).

static IP address   A permanent IP address that is manually assigned to a computer.

static RAM (SRAM)   RAM chips that retain information without the need for refreshing, as long as the computer's power is on. They are more expensive than traditional DRAM.

ST (straight tip) connector   A type of connector used by fiber-optic cables and can be used with either single-mode or multimode fiber-optic cables. The connector does not support full-dupex transmissions and is not used on the fastest fiber-optic systems.

stop error   *See* blue screen of death (BSOD).

storage card   An adapter card used to manage hardware RAID rather than using the firmware on the motherboard.

Storage Spaces   A Windows 8 utility that can create a storage pool using any number of internal or external backup drives. The utility is expected to replace Windows software RAID.

straight-through cable   An Ethernet cable used to connect a computer to a switch or other network device. *Also called* a patch cable.

striped volume   The term used by Windows for RAID 0. A type of dynamic volume used for two or more hard drives that writes to the disks evenly rather than filling up allotted space on one and then moving on to the next. *Compare with* spanned volume. *Also see* RAID 0.

striping   *See* RAID 0.

strong password   A password that is not easy to guess.

stylus   A device that is included with a graphics tablet that works like a pencil on the tablet.

su   A Linux and OS X command to open a new terminal shell for a different user account. Stands for "substitute user."

subdirectory   A directory or folder contained in another directory or folder. *Also called* a child directory or folder.

subnet   A group of local networks when several networks are tied together in a subsystem of the larger intranet. In TCP/IP version 6, one or more links that have the same 16 bits in the subnet ID of the IP address. *See* subnet ID.

subnet ID   In TCP/IP version 6, the last block (16 bits) in the 64-bit prefix of an IP address. The subnet is identified using some or all of these 16 bits.

subnet mask   In TCP/IP version 4, 32 bits that include a series of 1s followed by 0s. For example, 11111111.11111111.11110000.0000 0000, which can be written as 255.255.240.0. The 1s identify the network portion of an IP address, and the 0s identify the host portion of an IP address. The subnet mask tells Windows if a remote computer is on the same or different network.

subscription model   A method of licensing software with a paid annual subscription where the software is installed on your local computer. For example, Office 365 uses a subscription model.

sudo   A Linux and OS X command to execute another command as a superuser when logged in as a normal user with an account that has the right to use root commands. Stands for "substitute user to do the command."

superuser   Refers to a Linux or Mac OS X user who is logged in to the root account.

surge supressor   A device designed to protect against voltage spikes by blocking or grounding excessive voltage.

suspend mode   *See* sleep mode.

S-Video port   A 4-pin or 7-pin round video port that sends two signals over the cable, one for color and the other for brightness, and is used by some high-end TVs and video equipment.

switch   A device used to connect nodes on a network in a star network topology. When it receives a packet, it uses its table of MAC addresses to decide where to send the packet.

synchronous DRAM (SDRAM)   The first DIMM to run synchronized with the system clock that has two notches, and uses 168 pins.

system board   *See* motherboard.

system bus   The bus between the CPU and memory on the motherboard. The bus frequency in documentation is called the system speed, such as 400 MHz. *Also called* the memory bus, Front Side Bus, local bus, or host bus.

system clock   A line on a bus that is dedicated to timing the activities of components connected to it. The system clock provides a continuous pulse that other devices use to time themselves.

System Configuration   A Windows utility (msconfig.exe) that can identify what processes are launched at startup and can temporarily disable a process from loading.

G

System File Checker (SFC)   A Windows utility that verifies and, if necessary, refreshes a Windows system file, replacing it with one kept in a cache of current system files.

system image   The backup of the entire Windows 8/7 volume and can also include backups of other volumes. The backup is made using the Windows 8 File History or Windows 7 Backup and Restore utility.

System Information   A Windows tool (msinfo32. exe) that provides details about a system, including installed hardware and software, the current system configuration, and currently running programs.

system partition   The partition of the hard drive that contains the boot loader or boot manager program and the specific files required to start the Windows launch.

System Preferences   In OS X, a utility to customize the OS X interface and is available on the Apple menu.

System Protection   A Windows utility that automatically backs up system files and stores them in restore points on the hard drive at regular intervals and just before you install software or hardware.

system repair disc   A disc you can create using Windows 7 that can be used to launch Windows RE. The disc is not available in Windows 8.

System Restore   A Windows utility used to restore the system to a restore point.

system state data   In Windows, files that are necessary for a successful load of the operating system.

system tray   *See* notification area.

system UEFI/BIOS   UEFI (Unified Extensible Firmware Interface) or BIOS (basic input/output system) firmware on the motherboard that is used to control essential devices before the OS is loaded.

System window   A window that displays brief and important information about installed hardware and software and gives access to important Windows tools needed to support the system.

systray   *See* notification area.

T568A   Standards for wiring twisted-pair network cabling and RJ-45 connectors and have the green pair connected to pins 1 and 2 and the orange pair connected to pins 3 and 6.

T568B   Standards for wiring twisted-pair network cabling and RJ-45 connectors and have the orange pair using pins 1 and 2 and the green pair connected to pins 3 and 6.

tablet   A computing device with a touch screen that is larger than a smart phone and has functions similar to a smart phone.

tailgating   When someone who is unauthorized follows an employee through a secured entrance to a room or building.

Task Manager   A Windows utility (taskmgr.exe) that lets you view the applications and processes running on your computer as well as information about process and memory performance, network activity, and user activity.

Task Scheduler   A Windows tool that can set a task or program to launch at a future time, including at startup.

taskbar   A bar normally located at the bottom of the Windows desktop, displaying information about open programs and providing quick access to others.

taskkill   A Windows command that uses the process PID to kill a process.

tasklist   A Windows command that returns the process identifier (PID), which is a number that identifies each running process.

TCP (Transmission Control Protocol)   The protocol in the TCP/IP suite of protocols that works at the OSI Transport layer and establishes a session or connection between parties and guarantees packet delivery.

TCP/IP (Transmission Control Protocol/Internet Protocol)   The group or suite of protocols used for almost all networks, including the Internet. Fundamentally, TCP is responsible for error-checking transmissions, and IP is responsible for routing.

technical documentation   The technical reference manuals, included with software packages and hardware, that provide directions for installation, usage, and troubleshooting. The information extends beyond that given in user manuals.

Telnet   A TCP/IP protocol used by the Telnet client/ server applications to allow an administrator or other user to control a computer remotely.

Teredo   In TCP/IP version 6, a tunneling protocol to transmit TCP/IPv6 packets over a TCP/IPv4 network, named after the Teredo worm that bores holes in wood. Teredo IP addresses begin with 2001, and the prefix is written as 2001::/32.

terminal In Linux and OS X, the command-line interface.

tether To connect a mobile device with a cellular connection to the Internet to a computer so that the computer can access the Internet by way of the mobile device.

thermal compound A creamlike substance that is placed between the bottom of the cooler heat sink and the top of the processor to eliminate air pockets and to help to draw heat off the processor.

thermal paper Special coated paper used by thermal printers.

thermal printer A type of line printer that uses wax-based ink, which is heated by heat pins that melt the ink onto paper.

thermal transfer printer A type of thermal printer that uses a ribbon that contains wax-based ink. The heating element melts the ribbon onto special thermal paper so that it stays glued to the paper as the feeder assembly moves the paper through the printer.

thick client A regular desktop computer or laptop that is sometimes used as a client by a virtualization server. *Also called* fat client.

thin client A computer that has an operating system, but has little computing power and might only need to support a browser used to communicate with a virtualization server.

thin provisioning A technique used by Storage Spaces in Windows whereby virtual storage free space can be configured as if it has more virtual storage than the physical storage allotted to it. When the virtual storage free space is close to depletion, the administrator is prompted to install more physical storage.

third-party driver Drivers that are not included in UEFI/BIOS or Windows and must come from the manufacturer.

thread Each process that the processor is aware of; a single task that is part of a longer task or request from a program.

Thunderbolt port A port that transmits both video and data on the same port and cable. The port is shaped the same as the DisplayPort and is compatible with DisplayPort devices.

ticket An entry in a call-tracking system made by whoever receives a call for help and used to track and document actions taken. The ticket stays open until the issue is resolved.

Time Machine In OS X, a built-in backup utility that can be configured to automatically back up user-created data, applications, and system files onto an external hard drive attached either directly to the computer or through the local network.

TKIP (Temporal Key Integrity Protocol) A type of encryption protocol used by WPA to secure a wireless Wi-Fi network. *Also see* WPA (Wi-Fi Protected Access).

tone probe A two-part kit that is used to find cables in the walls of a building. *Also called* a toner probe.

toner probe *See* tone probe.

toner vacuum A vacuum cleaner designed to pick up toner used in laser printers and does not allow it to touch any conductive surface.

touch pad A common pointing device on a laptop computer.

touch screen An input device that uses a monitor or LCD panel as a backdrop for user options. Touch screens can be embedded in a monitor or LCD panel or installed as an add-on device over the monitor screen.

tower case The largest type of personal computer case. Tower cases stand vertically and can be as high as two feet tall. They have more drive bays and are a good choice for computer users who anticipate making significant upgrades.

TPM (Trusted Platform Module) A chip on a motherboard that holds an encryption key required at startup to access encrypted data on the hard drive. Windows BitLocker Encryption can use the TPM chip.

trace A wire on a circuit board that connects two components or devices.

tracert (trace route) A TCP/IP command that enables you to resolve a connectivity problem when attempting to reach a destination host such as a website.

track One of many concentric circles on the surface of a hard disk drive.

tractor feed A continuous feed within an impact printer that feeds fanfold paper through the

G

printer rather than individual sheets, making them useful for logging ongoing events or data.

transfer belt   A laser printer component that completes the transferring step in the printer.

transfer roller   A soft, black roller in a laser printer that puts a positive charge on the paper. The charge pulls the toner from the drum onto the paper.

transformer   An electrical device that changes the ratio of current to voltage. A computer power supply is basically a transformer and a rectifier.

trip hazard   Loose cables or cords in a traffic area where people can trip over them.

triple channels   When the memory controller accesses three DIMMs at the same time. DDR3 DIMMs support triple channeling.

Trojan   A type of malware that tricks you into downloading and/or opening it by substituting itself for a legitimate program.

TV tuner card   An adapter card that receives a TV signal and displays TV on the computer screen.

Twisted Nematic (TN)   A class of LCD monitor that has fast response times to keep fast-moving images crisper, but monitors are brighter, consume more power, and have limited viewing angles.

twisted-pair cabling   Cabling, such as a network cable, that uses pairs of wires twisted together to reduce crosstalk.

Type 1 hypervisor   Software to manage virtual machines that is installed before any operating system is installed.

Type 2 hypervisor   Software to manage virtual machines that is installed as an application in an operating system.

UDF (Universal Disk Format)   A file system for optical media used by all DVD discs and some CD-R and CD-RW discs. *Also see* CDFS (Compact Disc File System).

UDP (User Datagram Protocol)   A connectionless TCP/IP protocol that works at the OSI Transport layer and does not require a connection to send a packet or guarantee that the packet arrives at its destination. The protocol is commonly used for broadcasting to multiple nodes on a network or the Internet. *Compare with* TCP (Transmission Control Protocol).

UEFI CSM (Compatibility Support Module) mode   Legacy BIOS in UEFI firmware.

ultra-thin client   *See* zero client.

unattended installation   A Windows installation that is done by storing the answers to installation questions in a text file or script that Windows calls an answer file so that the answers do not have to be typed in during the installation.

unicast address   Using TCP/IP version 6, an IP address assigned to a single node on a network.

UEFI (Unified Extensible Firmware Interface)   An interface between firmware on the motherboard and the operating system that improves on legacy BIOS processes for booting, handing over the boot to the OS, and loading device drivers and applications before the OS loads. UEFI also manages motherboard settings and secures the boot to ensure that no rogue operating system hijacks the system.

Unified Threat Management (UTM)   A computer, security appliance, network appliance, or Internet appliance that stands between the Internet and a private network and runs firewall, anti-malware, and other software to protect the network.

uninterruptible power supply (UPS)   A device that raises the voltage when it drops during brownouts.

unique local address (ULA)   In TCP/IP version 6, an address used to identify a specific site within a large organization. It can work on multiple links within the same organization. The address is a hybrid between a global unicast address that works on the Internet and a link-local unicast address that works on only one link.

Universal Plug and Play (UPnP)   An unsecure method a router can use to allow unfiltered communication between nodes on a private network. Hackers sometimes are able to exploit UPnP, so use with caution.

unshielded twisted-pair (UTP) cable   The most popular cabling method for local networks and is the least expensive and is commonly used on LANs. The cable is made of twisted pairs of wires and is not surrounded by shielding.

Upgrade Advisor   *See* Upgrade Assistant.

Upgrade Assistant   Software used to find out if a system can be upgraded to Windows 8.1.

update   *See* patch.

upgrade path   A qualifying OS required by Microsoft in order to perform an in-place upgrade.

USB 3.0 B-Male connector A USB connector used by SuperSpeed USB 3.0 devices such as printers or scanners.

USB 3.0 Micro-B connector A small USB connector used by SuperSpeed USB 3.0 devices. The connectors are not compatible with regular Micro-B connectors.

USB (Universal Serial Bus) port A type of port designed to make installation and configuration of I/O devices easy, providing room for as many as 127 devices daisy-chained together.

USB optical drive An external optical drive that connects to a computer via a USB port.

USB to Bluetooth adapter A device that plugs into a USB port on a computer to connect to Bluetooth devices.

USB to RJ-45 dongle An adapter that plugs into a USB port and provides an RJ-45 port for a network cable to connect to a wired network.

USB to Wi-Fi dongle An adapter that plugs into a USB port and provides wireless connectivity to a Wi-Fi network.

User Account Control (UAC) dialog box A Windows security feature that displays a dialog box when an event requiring administrative privileges is about to happen.

User Accounts A Windows utility (netplwiz.exe) that can be used to change the way Windows sign-in works and to manage user accounts, including changing passwords and changing the group membership of an account. *Also called* Network Places Wizard.

user mode In Windows, a mode that provides an interface between an application and the OS, and only has access to hardware resources through the code running in kernel mode.

user profile A collection of files and settings about a user account that enables the user's personal data, desktop settings, and other operating parameters to be retained from one session to another.

user profile namespace The group of folders and subfolders in the C:\Users folder that belong to a specific user account and contain the user profile.

User State Migration Tool (USMT) A Windows utility that helps you migrate user files and preferences from one computer to another to help a user make a smooth transition from one computer to another.

Users group A type of Windows user account group. An account in this group is a standard user account, which does not have as many rights as an administrator account.

usmtutils A command used by the User State Migration Tool (USMT) that provides encryption options and hard-link management.

vendor-specific software *See* closed source.

vertical scan rate *See* refresh rate.

VGA (Video Graphics Adapter) port A 15-pin analog video port popular for many years. *Also called* DB15 port, DE15 port, or HD15 port.

VGA mode Standard VGA settings, which include a resolution of 640 x 480.

vi editor A Linux and OS X text editor that works in command mode (to enter commands) or in insert mode (to edit text).

video capture card An adapter card that captures video input and saves it to a file on the hard drive.

video memory Memory used by the video controller. The memory might be contained on a video card or be part of system memory. When part of system memory, the memory is dedicated by Windows to video.

virtual assistant A mobile device app that responds to a user's voice commands with a personable, conversational interaction to perform tasks and retrieve information. *Also called* a personal assistant.

Virtual Desktop Infrastructure (VDI) A presentation of a virtual desktop made to a client computer by a server that is serving up a virtual machine.

virtual machine (VM) Software that simulates the hardware of a physical computer, creating one or more logical machines within one physical machine.

virtual machine manager (VMM) *See* hypervisor.

virtual memory A method whereby the OS uses the hard drive as though it were RAM. *Also see* pagefile.sys.

virtual printing Printing to a file rather than directly to a printer.

virtual private network (VPN) A security technique that uses encrypted data packets between a private network and a computer somewhere on the Internet.

virtualization When one physical machine hosts multiple activities that are normally done on multiple machines.

G

virtualization server A computer that serves up virtual machines to multiple client computers and provides a virtual desktop for users on these client machines.

virtual XP mode The term used by CompTIA for Windows XP mode. *See* Windows XP mode.

virus A program that often has an incubation period, is infectious, and is intended to cause damage. A virus program might destroy data and programs.

vision sensor *See* smart camera.

Voice over LTE (VoLTE) A technology used on cellular networks for LTE to support voice communication.

VoIP (Voice over Internet Protocol) A TCP/IP protocol and an application that provides voice communication over a TCP/IP network. *Also called* Internet telephone.

volt (V) A measure of potential difference or electrical force in an electrical circuit. A computer ATX power supply usually provides five separate voltages: 112 V, 212 V, 15 V, 25 V, and 13.3 V.

volume A primary partition that has been assigned a drive letter and can be formatted with a file system such as NTFS. *Compare with* logical drive.

wait state A clock tick in which nothing happens, used to ensure that the microprocessor isn't getting ahead of slower components. A 0-wait state is preferable to a 1-wait state. Too many wait states can slow down a system.

Wake-on-LAN Configuring a computer so that it will respond to network activity when the computer is in a sleep state.

WAN (wide area network) A network or group of networks that span a large geographical area.

warm boot *See* soft boot.

watt (W) The unit of electricity used to measure power. A typical computer may use a power supply that provides 500 W.

wearable technology device A device, such as a smart watch, wristband, arm band, eyeglasses, headset, or clothing, that can perform computing tasks, including making phone calls, sending text messages, recording and transmitting data, and checking email.

wear leveling A technique used on a solid-state drive (SSD) that ensures the logical block addressing does not always address the same physical blocks in order to distribute write operations more evenly across the device.

WEP (Wired Equivalent Privacy) An encryption protocol used to secure transmissions on a Wi-Fi wireless network; however, it is no longer considered secure because the key used for encryption is static (it doesn't change).

Wi-Fi (Wireless Fidelity) The common name for standards for a local wireless network as defined by IEEE 802.11. *Also see* 802.11 a/b/g/n/ac.

Wi-Fi analyzer Hardware and/or software that monitors a Wi-Fi network to detect devices not authorized to use the network, identify attempts to hack transmissions, or detect performance and security vulnerabilities.

Wi-Fi calling On mobile devices, voice calls that use VoIP over a Wi-Fi connection to the Internet.

Wi-Fi Protected Setup (WPS) A method to make it easier for users to connect their computers to a secured wireless network when a hard-to-remember SSID and security key are used, and is considered a security risk that should be used with caution.

wildcard An * or ? character used in a command line that represents a character or group of characters in a file name or extension.

Windows 7 Windows 7 editions include Windows 7 Starter, Windows 7 Home Basic, Windows 7 Home Premium, Windows 7 Professional, Windows 7 Enterprise, and Windows 7 Ultimate. Each edition comes at a different price with different features and capabilities.

Windows 8.1 A free update or release of the Windows 8 operating system. The edition of choice for a laptop or desktop computer used in a home or small office. This edition supports homegroups, but it doesn't support joining a domain or BitLocker Encryption.

Windows 8.1 Enterprise A Windows 8 edition that allows for volume licensing in a large, corporate environment.

Windows 8.1 Pro for Students A version of Windows 8 that includes all the same features as Windows 8 Pro, but at a lower price, available only to students, faculty, and staff at eligible institutions.

Windows 8.1 Professional (Windows 8.1 Pro) A version of Windows 8 that includes additional features at a higher price. Windows 8.1 Pro supports homegroups, joining a domain, BitLocker, Client Hyper-V, Remote Desktop, and Group Policy.

Windows Assessment and Deployment Kit (ADK) The Windows ADK for Windows 8 contains a group of tools used to deploy Windows 8 in a large organization and contains the User State Migration Tool (USMT).

Windows Automated Installation Kit (AIK) The Windows AIK for Windows 7 contains a group of tools used to deploy Windows 7 in a large organization and contains the User State Migration Tool (USMT).

Windows Boot Loader One of two programs that manage the loading of Windows 8/7/Vista. The program file (winload.exe or winload.efi) is stored in C:\ Windows\System32, and it loads and starts essential Windows processes.

Windows Boot Manager (BootMgr) The Windows program that manages the initial startup of Windows. For a BIOS system, the program is bootmgr; for a UEFI system, the program is bootmgfw.efi. The program file is stored in the root of the system partition.

Windows Defender Anti-malware software embedded in Windows 8 that can detect, prevent, and clean up a system infected with viruses and other malware. Antispyware utility included in Windows 8/7/Vista.

Windows Easy Transfer A Windows tool used to transfer Windows 8/7/Vista user data and preferences to the Windows 8/7/Vista installation on another computer.

Windows Experience Index A Windows 7/Vista feature that gives a summary index designed to measure the overall performance of a system on a scale from 1.0 to 7.9.

Windows Explorer The Windows 7/Vista utility used to view and manage files and folders.

Windows Firewall A personal firewall that protects a computer from intrusion and is automatically configured when you set your network location in the Network and Sharing Center.

Windows Phone (WP) An operating system by Microsoft (*microsoft.com*) that is based on Windows and is used on various smart phones (not on tablets).

Windows pinwheel A Windows graphic that indicates the system is waiting for a response from a program or device.

Windows PowerShell A command-line interface (CLI) that processes objects, called cmdlets, which are prebuilt programs built on the .NET Framework, rather than processing text in a command line.

Windows Preinstallation Environment (Windows PE) A minimum operating system used to start the Windows installation.

Windows Pro Pack An upgrade available to Windows 8 that adds the functionality of Windows 8.1 Pro to the more basic edition.

Windows Recovery Environment (Windows RE) A lean operating system installed on the Windows 8/7/Vista setup DVD and also on the Windows 8/7 volume that can be used to troubleshoot problems when Windows refuses to start.

Windows RT A Windows 8 edition that is a lighter version, designed for tablets, netbooks, and other mobile devices.

Windows Store Access to purchase and download apps that use the Windows 8 interface.

Windows Vista Windows Vista editions include Windows Vista Starter, Windows Vista Home Basic, Windows Vista Home Premium, Windows Vista Business, Windows Vista Enterprise, and Windows Vista Ultimate. Each edition comes at a different price with different features and capabilities.

Windows XP Mode A Windows XP environment installed in Windows 8/7 that can be used to support older applications. *Also called* virtual XP mode.

Windows.old folder When using an unformatted hard drive for a clean installation, this folder is created to store the previous operating system settings and user profiles.

wireless access point (WAP) A wireless device that is used to create and manage a wireless network.

wireless LAN (WLAN) A type of LAN that does not use wires or cables to create connections, but instead transmits data over radio or infrared waves.

wireless locator A tool that can locate a Wi-Fi hotspot and tell you the strength of the RF signal.

wireless wide area network (WWAN) A wireless broadband network for computers and mobile devices that uses cellular towers for communication. *Also called* a cellular network.

wire stripper A tool used when terminating a cable. The tool cuts away the plastic jacket or coating around the wires in a cable so that a connector can be installed on the end of the cable.

G

workgroup   In Windows, a logical group of computers and users in which administration, resources, and security are distributed throughout the network, without centralized management or security.

worm   An infestation designed to copy itself repeatedly to memory, on drive space, or on a network, until little memory, disk space, or network bandwidth remains.

WPA (Wi-Fi Protected Access)   A data encryption method for wireless networks that use the TKIP (Temporal Key Integrity Protocol) encryption method and the encryption keys are changed at set intervals while the wireless LAN is in use. WPA is stronger than WEP.

WPA2 (Wi-Fi Protected Access 2)   A data encryption standard compliant with the IEEE 802.11i standard that uses the AES (Advanced Encryption Standard) protocol. WPA2 is currently the strongest wireless encryption standard.

x86 processor   An older processor that first used the number 86 in the model number and processes 32 bits at a time.

x86-64 bit processor   Hybrid processors that can process 32 bits or 64 bits.

XaaS (Anything as a Service or Everything as a Service)   An open-ended cloud computing service that can provide any combination of functions depending on a customer's exact needs.

xcopy   A Windows command more powerful than the copy command that is used to copy files and folders.

xD-Picture Card   A type of flash memory device that has a compact design and currently holds up to 8 GB of data.

XPS Document Writer   A Windows feature that creates a file with an .xps file extension. The file is similar to a .pdf file and can be viewed, edited, printed, faxed, emailed, or posted on websites.

zero client   A client computer that does not have an operating system and merely provides an interface between the user and the server. *Also called* dumb terminal.

zero-day attack   When a hacker discovers and exploits a security hole in software before the developer of the software can develop and provide a protective patch to close the hole.

zero-fill utility   A hard drive utility that fills every sector on the drive with zeroes.

zero insertion force (ZIF) socket   A socket that uses a small lever to apply even force when you install the processor into the socket.

zero-touch, high-volume deployment   An installation strategy that does not require the user to start the process. Instead a server pushes the installation to a computer when a user is not likely to be sitting at it.

ZIF connector   A ZIF (zero insertion force) connector uses a lever or latch to prevent force from being used on a sensitive connection.

zombie   A computer that has been hacked, and the hacker is using the computer to run repetitive software in the background without the knowledge of its user. *Also see* botnet.